HOME IMPROVEMENT BOOK

The Family Handyman

HOME IMPROVEMENT BOOK

By the Editors of *The Family Handyman* Magazine

CHARLES SCRIBNER'S SONS   New York

Printed in the United States of America
Library of Congress Catalog Card Number 72-1211
SBN   684-12910-8 (cloth)

CONTENTS

vi

INTRODUCTION

For the home owner, quality of living is no mere theme phrase. It has real expression in home improvement, that is, making the home more comfortable, more convenient, more spacious, or just more attractive. Hardly a home is complete and perfect when purchased, whatever wonderful attributes it may have. And new ideas and wonderful new materials keep coming along, offering many more advantages and benefits.

Yours may be an old home, built with spacious rooms and plenty of them for your needs, large hallways, perhaps an enormous porch. But much can be done to make even such a home more livable and enjoyable—while preserving its finer qualities.

Why put up with a drab kitchen, not so much old-fashioned perhaps as archaic and inefficient? You'll want to make it more pleasant and carefree, with labor-saving appliances, a joy to all members of the family.

Particularly interested in expansion and efficiency ideas are owners of the so-called "postwar" homes, those built a decade or two after World War II, when, because of soaring materials prices and labor shortages, many homes were built with minimum dimensions. For example, kitchens were so tiny that they could not receive appliances such as a dishwasher, or a combination refrigerator-freezer which make so great a contribution to good living. But even in those situations, expert planning goes far to solve these problems.

As the first years of home ownership pass, the family begins to realize that some change or addition would make for greater comfort, such as finishing a basement playroom, or building a back yard patio. An urgent need in many homes is for more bedrooms to accommodate a growing family.

Home improvements aren't all major and costly projects. Some are quite simple and can be done by the home owner with only nominal outlay. Their benefit lies in the added convenience, the solution perhaps to the need for more storage space. Just as with the major improvements, ingenious solutions have developed through the efforts of others confronting the same problems, and the answers finally arrived in print in *Family Handyman* magazine for others to benefit also.

This book is an effort of many people to bring you the ideas, together with the practical how-to details, to help you make your home a happy, comfortable place for your family.

ACKNOWLEDGMENTS

While it is impractical to acknowledge individually all who contributed in some measure to this work, mention must be made of the combined efforts of Ralph Treves, contributing editor, who assembled and revised the material into the form in which it is seen here, and Morton Waters, Editor of FAMILY HANDYMAN Magazine, under whose supervision this volume was prepared. Thanks also to the staff of FAMILY HANDYMAN, without whose skills and dedication the magazine could not exist, including Arnold Romney, Managing Editor; Franc L. Roggeri, Executive Art Director; Victor Closi, Art Director; and Burt Murphy, contributing editor. Our thanks also to the hundreds of writers, photographers and artists whose work was published in the magazine and is seen here in revised form.

Arnold E. Abramson, Publisher
The FAMILY HANDYMAN Magazine

January, 1973

Chapter 1
A KITCHEN YOU'LL LOVE TO LIVE IN

One of the top priorities for your home improvement program is the rejuvenation of the kitchen, bringing it right up to par in efficiency and handsome appearance for family living. Naturally it needs to be tailored to a home owner's special requirements, so that the work will be easier and take less time to accomplish. Just as important, since so much time is spent there, the kitchen must be attractive and even luxuriously appointed, to make it as pleasant as a room can be. And because the kitchen also is the main family center with constant traffic by every member of the household it must be both spacious and comfortable.

Whatever the shortcomings of your present kitchen, many improvements can be achieved with the bright new ideas presented in the following pages, all of which make interesting projects for the family handyman.

SPREADING OUT

How often have you realized that the old kitchen just wasn't designed for *you*, nor was any effort made to provide for the things you feel are essential now? But there's no reason why you have to be bound by an inefficient floor arrangement, or even by the extreme space limitations imposed by some thoughtless builder. A little creative imagination can work wonders at overcoming a seemingly insoluble problem. For example, you've desperately wanted a dishwasher, but never could figure how to get one into the available space. Well, a new tabletop stove and a wall oven (or above-the-stove oven) can provide the answer.

How? The wall oven, for example, is recessed into the back of a closet. A floor cabinet then goes under the tabletop stove, utilizing the space of the former oven, and the space vacated by the floor cabinet allows for fitting in a dishwasher.

This is but one example of "finding" space. The standard floor arrangements of even a decade ago are out of date now, replaced by more effective planning that makes the most of the available space while enhancing the efficiency of the work areas, like free-standing island cabinets with handy storage shelves underneath, and dual-purpose folding snack bars that save the work of setting the dining room table during the day, and pass-throughs that save steps when serving meals.

Best results in remodeling are usually obtained the simplest way—by rearranging all cabinets around the walls. In more than one problem situation, changing the swing of a door so that it opens outward instead of inward has made all the difference. A bit more complicated, but even more effective, may be the relocating of a doorway a few feet one way or the other—perhaps adding four or more feet of valuable wall space to the kitchen area. Shifting a doorway leading to the dining room or a hall is a project that most handymen can handle satisfactorily.

WHAT IT TAKES

Complete remodeling of a kitchen is not a task to be undertaken lightly, nor is it one that can be done in a weekend, even under the best of circumstances. But it *can* be done, giving you a sparkling new and efficient kitchen well worth the cost, the

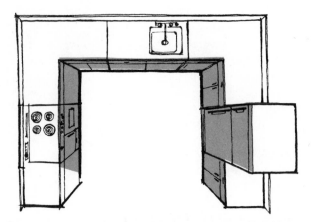

Floor plan of U-shaped kitchen arranges all cabinets around the three wall areas. The traffic pattern always will be diagonal from the two wings of the room toward the center area.

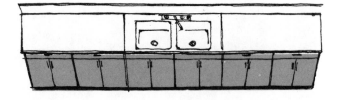

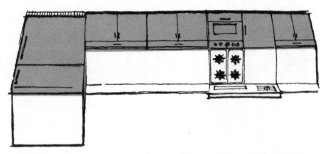

Corridor plan involves crisscrossing to reach facilities on both sides. Some homemakers prefer sink and stove on same wall, others favor sink and refrigerator together as closely as possible. An effort should be made in planning to divide the two lines of cabinets and equipment as equally as possible.

effort, and the temporary mess that will inevitably result as the work progresses.

There are several ways to go about the project to make things easier. Much will depend, for example, on whether any part of the original kitchen arrangement is to be changed, or any basic structural alterations are required, like closing off a door. Sometimes this work cannot be started until some of the cabinets have been taken down out of the way. Another factor will be whether you plan to build all the cabinets yourself, which certainly can be done if you have a modest workshop with a few power tools. The project no doubt will go much quicker—and smoother—if you intend to purchase ready-made cabinets and sink tops, and just do the installation and finishing touches yourself. Another possibility is to tackle the work in stages, completing one section before starting on the next, so that there is minimum disturbance of the kitchen facilities and the least possible disruption of household activities.

The kitchens shown in the illustrations were designed with duplication by the average home owner in mind. What's more, if portions of the design provide answers to your special problems, other sections of the plans described on the following pages can be adapted to an existing kitchen without complete remodeling. Just take advantage of the details that serve your purpose.

INSTANT RENOVATING

Perhaps you feel that the kitchen is annoyingly drab, that the most urgent thing right now is to perk it up, to give it a face lift without going to the expense and mess of an extensive remodeling. There's an answer to that, too, in an innovative concept that lets you keep your present serviceable cabinets, but gives them an entirely new, attractive, up-to-date appearance. Thus, you get a sparkling fresh kitchen without even having to empty the shelves, all in jiffy time, and at a nominal cost for the whole project.

You have a choice of two approaches. The first and simplest one is to reface your present cabinets —doors, drawer fronts, and the exposed cabinet stiles and rails—with either real wood veneer or plastic sheeting in natural wood grain or solid colors. The second method is to create an entirely new styling, using new doors and drawer fronts of hardwood plywood, thus forming a new cabinet surface,

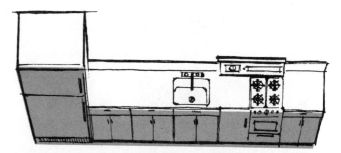

One-wall plan forms straight line across, in which the sequence of equipment should be followed as closely as windows, doors, and plumbing lines permit. The chief deficiency in this arrangement is the limited amount of working counter space. The plan is compact and workable otherwise.

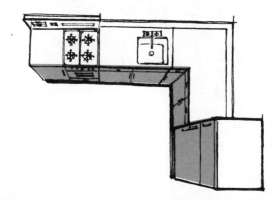

The most common layout is the L-shape which has some of the merits of the U-kitchen. Placement of the utilities is often set by the window location and limited wall space.

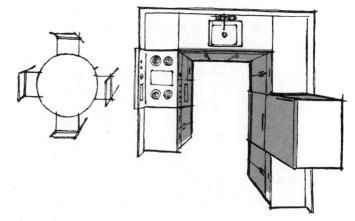

A popular arrangement in contemporary design is a modified U-arrangement with one segment serving as a free-moving island cabinet. This island can double as a snack bar when dining space is limited, a desirable feature.

If your cabinets are serviceable but your kitchen could use a face-lifting rejuvenation, the quickest and easiest way— without the mess and expense of a complete remodeling—is simply to redesign the cabinet doors. Note that all the door and drawer fronts in the illustration are flush, forming a continuous, smooth, and clean surface. The ornamental molding trim is the final decorative treat.

4

all parts flush, any exposed sides of the cabinets covered with matching wood veneer, and finished with interesting decorative molding trim.

With either method, metal cabinets also can be given the more pleasing appearance of wood, either by laminating the veneer or plastic directly to the old metal door, or by replacing the door and drawer fronts with new ones of ¾" plywood.

NEW CABINET FACING

The first step is to remove all wood cabinet doors by unscrewing the hinges. Remove any crown molding at the top of the cabinets, and take off all doorknobs and other hardware. Metal doors need not be taken down if they have square edges, as the veneer can be applied to these doors just as they are.

Many wood doors are of the bullnose overlap type; that is, they have rabbet cuts all around so that the doors fit into the cabinet opening to half their thickness, the other half overlapping the cabinet stiles and cross members, and the exposed edges are rounded. Wood veneer will bend sufficiently to follow this curve, but only when the bend is with the grain. You cannot bend the veneer against the grain to conform. This requires that the overlap lip at the top and bottom of the doors be sawn off, leaving a full ¾" plywood edge.

The veneer is laminated onto the face of the door, the grain runs vertically and covers the rounded ends. Narrow ¾" strips of the veneer are cemented to the squared top and bottom door edges. If you want a still better-looking result, laminate the veneer to the inside surface of the doors also. The hinge positions and clearances have not been affected, and the doors can be replaced as before.

The technique of laminating both veneers and plastic sheeting with contact cement is described in specific detail later in this chapter. See page 22. A word of caution: some contact cements are flammable. Use only small amounts at a time, extinguish any pilot lights in the kitchen, and avoid smoking.

The same veneer is cut to cover the cabinet stiles and cross members, also laminated with contact cement. Since most cabinets are joined together, only the fronts are seen. However, on the end cabinets, one side is exposed, which should be surfaced with the same veneer. Finish the veneer with stain and shellac or lacquer. Replace the ceiling crown molding as before.

Treat yourself to good quality doorknobs and

magnetic catches and, voilà! the kitchen looks brand-new.

Picking the Veneer

Real hardwood veneer, ⅟₂₈" thick, is available in many interesting and even exotic woods, and will assure a professional looking result. The veneers are available from crafts supply firms, such as Constantine's and the Craftsman Wood Service,* in sheets approximately 8' long, and 8" to 12" wide. Prices for birch, maple, cherry, and other woods start at about 15 cents a square foot, with selected qualities running between 24 and 35 cents. The veneer is cut very easily with a thin hand saw that has tiny teeth. You will also need a metal straightedge at least 4' long. Veneering is a simple and interesting technique that you will quickly master and use for various other projects also.

For the restyling project, one or two panels of ¾" plywood will be needed, with hardwood veneer "good both sides." This project requires the use of a bench saw, as the new doors and stiles must be accurately cut. The idea of this design is that all the cabinet doors, drawer fronts, and door stiles will be flush, forming a smooth, continuous surface throughout, as seen in the photographs.

In addition to your choice of cabinet hardware, which has come a long, long way from the standardized knobs of a few years ago, a dramatic touch is added with molding trim and a decorative medallion on each of the doors.

For surface finishing, this project also offers a remarkable advantage in that all the plywood and veneer sections can be prefinished before they are attached to the cabinets. Thus the finishing can be done with a spray gun for the lacquer coating in the workshop or the garage, in order not to contaminate the house with the fine spray.

Another suggestion: if you're not prepared to do the finishing yourself, and want a fine professional job, just take the precut and partly assembled door parts to a commercial furniture sprayer, get the entire job done at the lowest possible cost since the pieces will be small, easily laid out in a spray booth, and all done at one time.

Making the New Doors

Remember that all parts of the cabinet fronts will butt together, edge to edge and end to end,

A. Constantine & Son, Inc. 2050 Eastchester Road, New York, N.Y. 10461.
Craftsman Wood Service Company, 2729 South Mary Street, Chicago, Illinois 60608.

Remove doors from the cabinets by detaching the hinges. For metal doors, drill out the hinge rivets. Doors will be replaced with square-cut plywood.

Stile is attached to the cabinet face, together with its door, all in one operation. In this cabinet, two doors and their stiles together will cover the entire face of the cabinet.

New doors are made of hardwood veneer plywood, or plywood with plastic laminated surface. The doors are easily made as they are straight runs without shaped edge.

An exposed side of a cabinet is surfaced with matching veneer or plastic. This may be applied before or after the door stile is attached.

Door and its stile are fitted together, hinges mounted before the stile is nailed up on the cabinet. Edges of the doors are trimmed with matching veneer strips.

Drawers receive new front panels that are flush with the adjoining cabinet doors. Holes are drilled for the new drawer pulls.

Decorative trim molding in matching finishes is attached with ⅝″ brads, which are countersunk. Molding should cover any nailheads of the door stiles.

Medallions for door centers are nailed on in uniform positions, which can be assured with use of a template. There are many styles to choose from.

For a finishing touch, nailheads are easily concealed with a filler stick in matching color.

forming a flush and continuous surface. Thus the doors no longer just cover and slightly overlap the cabinet opening, but extend from the bottom of the cabinet (or above the toe space in base cabinets) upward to the top, or to butt against the lower edge of a drawer front, which in turn will just clear the overhang of the counter top.

Doors and their stiles are joined together with hinges, before being attached to the cabinets. This is done more easily on a workbench than on the cabinet itself as the hinge holes can be centered correctly to assure smooth swinging of the doors.

The stiles are attached to the cabinet, using both glue and a row of finishing nails. The nailheads will be covered later with the decorative molding. Before attaching the doors, cover the end grain either with strips of the veneer or by smoothing on a sealer. Another end grain finishing material consists of plastic T-Strips, in a neutral tan color. Narrow grooves are cut into the plywood all around, the strips mitered, and T-flanges tapped into the grooves.

Where the vertical stile will be exposed on an end cabinet, do not trim the exposed edge, as this will be covered by veneering the entire cabinet side with contact cement. Before applying the veneer, be sure to wash down the cabinet thoroughly with a detergent to remove any grease and dirt.

Building Up the Drawer Fronts

The drawers will present special problems. With wood drawers, you may saw off the projecting lips at the sides and bottom of the drawer fronts and attach a section of the ¾″ plywood to continue the flush design. This may result in thick drawer front, which can be overcome by leaving the original drawer front as is, and attaching plywood of sufficient cross section, probably ¼″ or ⅜″, to match the door thickness. Then insert wood strips all around to square the edges of the new front.

Metal drawers are handled differently. Take out the drawer and make two cuts along the sides with a hack saw, then work the front back and forth until it snaps off. Cut the new ¾″ plywood facing, to correct flush dimensions, then make two filler blocks ½″ or ¾″ thickness, which are attached to the drawer sides with screws through the metal, for securing the new front to the drawer.

Another location that will need attention is the strip just below the sink counter, usually of perfor-

Cut off overlap lips on wood drawers to make the front edges flush with the sides.

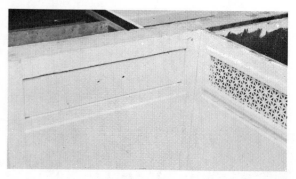

Drawers should go in all the way so that the original front edge is flush with cabinet sides. If necessary, change position of drawer stops.

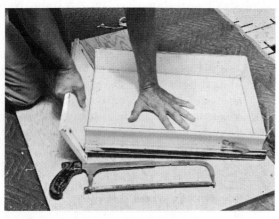

On metal drawers, use hack saw to remove the front panels, making the two cuts shown. Bend the front back and forth until it snaps.

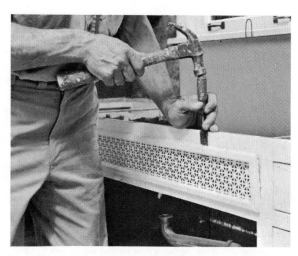

Old metal panels in sink and range fronts are removed with chisel. Leave surface flush and clean up well.

Cut filler blocks from ½" or ¾" stock and fasten to the sides of the drawer, to hold the new front panel.

ated metal. Remove the strip and replace with a section of the ¾" plywood to fill the area. If ventilation is desired at this point, drill a number of ¼" holes in a neat arrangement.

Aside from the wood finishing stage, which may be handled as described earlier, either in the home workshop or by a commercial furniture finisher, the final stages include applying the molding and decorative medallions and doorknobs, which also can be done before attaching the door stiles.

Here's an easy way to make sure the rectangular molding design is done uniformly: cut a piece of ¼" plywood to the outline that the molding will take, use it as a template for aligning and holding the molding strips. Wall cabinets are somewhat longer, and the pattern may change slightly; if so, simply use a separate template for them.

If the cabinet doors are of uniform width, the same system can be used for locating the doorknob holes: cut a strip of 1/4" plywood the width of the door, mark and drill the correct hole positions for the screws, and drill through these template holes.

PLANNING YOUR DREAM KITCHEN

Before starting a major remodeling or rejuvenation project, work out the best possible floor plan, discarding perhaps dozens of variations before you find the best arrangement. No matter what your final plan is like, the details listed below should be taken into consideration.

The three main factors that determine the usefulness of a kitchen are: (1) the amount of storage cabinet space; (2) the amount of working counter space; and (3) the location of the equipment in relation to each other and to the general plan of the room. There are additional, secondary details, such as traffic flow and position of work areas in relation to natural light. While you can, and certainly will, provide ample lighting fixtures, there's no point in wasting the pleasures and advantages of being able to glance outside. So try to locate your main work counters at or near the windows.

Top priority, for most housekeepers, goes to storage space, so plan to line all wall areas with cabinets along the floor and on the walls, but allow sufficient space for your appliances, such as the dishwasher and refrigerator. Also, aim to allot part of the space for a breakfast room or snack counter. This space should be arranged in such a way that it can be set off from the rest of the kitchen—by an ornamental divider or some other means.

Dimensions of Cabinets

A good arrangement that makes the most of the available space and serves the best of all possible worlds is an island type floor cabinet, perhaps only 12" or 18" deep, with drawers for tableware and other storage, while the top is used as a serving counter. This cabinet makes an excellent divider to set off a breakfast nook.

Standard base cabinets are 24" deep, providing ample storage space, and this dimension also matches the required depth for installation of a tabletop range or dishwasher. Refrigerators vary somewhat in depth, and most types also call for at least a 6" clear space at the rear for ventilation of the compressor coils, but you will find that most models will fit the standard 24" depth module. The base cabinets vary in width, generally from 2' to 6', depending on their purpose. All are provided with toe spaces 3" deep, 3⅝" high.

Wall-hung cabinets should be no more than 12" deep, so that they do not overshadow the countertop workspaces underneath. Allow a space of 15" to 17" between the counter top height and the lower edge of these wall cabinets—the unfilled wall area at the rear of the counters will be covered later with splashboards to match the counter tops, or with easy-to-clean decorative materials such as ceramic tiles.

Height of the upper cabinets is a matter of personal preference. Where there is a soffit (see page 12) overhead, the cabinet can reach to the very top, and continue on that same level around the room even if there remains an open space above some of the wall cabinets. The idea is that, in some instances, cabinets reaching to the ceiling line all around the room may give an overbearing aspect. A good rule to follow is to keep the top of the cabinets no more than 7' above the floor. Thus the highest shelf is within easy reach, at about 6', from a small stool or ladder.

If it is possible, include in your plan one or preferably two floor-to-ceiling cabinets—one for use as a pantry to store canned goods and similar items; the other to use as a broom closet, and for cleaning supplies. If there is room for but one such cabinet, it can be partitioned and compartmented to serve both purposes.

Get Appliance Dimensions

Before you start on the working drawings, it's wise to decide definitely on any new appliances or fixtures that will be included in the modernization, and either make the purchase or obtain the specific dimensions from the dealer.

It would be annoying obviously, after all your cabinets are built, to find the space allotted to the dishwasher is just an inch too narrow, or that the counter recess has been cut just a fraction too large for the drop-in sink. Be certain that you get an installation and operating manual for every one of your major appliances.

Drawing the Floor Plans.

Use graph paper, ruled in $\frac{1}{4}''$ uniform squares, to draw floor plans that will provide an accurate visualization of the project details. A scale of 1″ to the foot usually works out best, and can be done if your graph sheets are large enough—that is, equal in inch size to the dimensions of your kitchen in feet. Graph sheets are available at stationery supply stores in sizes of 10″ x 14″, and 12″ x 18″. If your room is larger than these sizes, then scale the floor $\frac{1}{2}''$ to the foot. Count off the number of squares necessary to show the space occupied by each cabinet or other installation. Show also the location of doors and windows, and indicate traffic patterns.

Another effective way to work out the floor plan is to make small cutouts, using thin cardboard of contrasting colors, each made to the proportionate size, so these can be moved around in various positions on an accurately drawn open floor plan until you have achieved the desired result, afterward pasting the cutouts into place.

Working out the floor plan on a separate paper frees you from the "fixation" that has been established by the present arrangement of your kitchen

TYPICAL CABINETS

Kitchen cabinets remain basically standard regardless of the many variations in door design, arrangement, floor layout, and surface finishes.

These are the usual types:

Wall cabinets, with sliding or hinged doors, generally 24″ wide but varying in width to fit available spaces. Corner cabinets may have revolving shelves.

Base cabinets: standard base cabinets, usually 36″ wide, having two drawers at the top, double doors with shelves below. Variations include sink and tabletop stove cabinets, usually 48″ to 60″ wide. Corner cabinets have revolving shelves.

Full-height cabinets: standard dimensions for wall oven 24″ wide, with drawer below and shelf space above the oven. Similar cabinets of varying width are built for pantry purposes.

Island cabinets are variations of base cabinets, as are L-shaped and round-end cabinets.

Planned for convenience, a remodeled kitchen in limited floor area incorporates all the required cabinets, work surfaces, appliances, and those special features that provide step-saving efficiency and reduce needless effort.

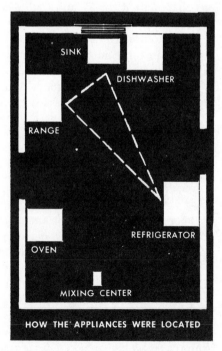

This sketch of the floor plan before renovation indicates the locations of the various appliances, in relation to the work areas and storage cabinets.

This is a highly practical arrangement, conserving space and providing the maximum of utility, which brings the range, sink, and L-shaped work counter in close proximity.

Dual purpose peninsula counter is handy work surface, also serves as serving counter when children show up for snacks after school.

fixtures. In this way you can maneuver them around to squeeze in a floor cabinet or dishwasher where there was none before, or maybe find room for a snack table. Also, you can see at a glance the possible benefits of making basic changes in the room's structural arrangements—closing off a window, shifting an entrance door just a few feet, or turning the position of a radiator. There's usually no reason why these things cannot be done, and since they are not major projects they may be well worth the effort.

Don't accept the first plan that looks practical. Juggle the parts around, and keep at it with new arrangements. You'll be astonished to find how many possibilities exist.

Links to Utility Lines

Also remember that you will have the flexibility of custom-made cabinets and are not restricted to just standard module sizes. You can fit a somewhat shorter cabinet in one direction if it allows a better placement of appliances on the adjacent wall. One thing that cannot be disregarded is the location of your basic utility lines: the water inlets and the plumbing waste line. These can, of course, be shifted if there would be substantial benefit, but the cost might be high.

The present electric wiring need not be of too much concern in deciding the appliance locations. With the kitchen remodeling you will no doubt want to update your electrical service, install at least one heavy duty appliance circuit, and add some convenience receptacles at the counter tops. In any event, some electrical wiring changes will most likely be necessary, and in that case it will not take much more money to locate new service boxes for the relocated stove, refrigerator, and other major appliances. Moving gas lines for the stove and wall oven will not be a significant factor either.

How Much Will It Cost?

Before you spend a cent, you can get a pretty accurate figure of what the cost will be. Of course, the cost will depend on how much remodeling you want to do—whether to have entirely new cabinets or just pretty up the ones you have with veneer facings on the doors; whether to rearrange the cabinet positions and thus require outside electrical and plumbing work, all adding to the expense, or to keep the sink and stove where they are now;

whether to get new floor covering, modern lighting fixtures, additional electric receptacles, attractive new counter tops, or additional appliances.

To a large extent, cost will depend on how much of the work you will be doing yourself, since the labor cost and contractor's profit in kitchen remodeling account for one-half or more of the total outlay for a contracted job, where factory-made cabinets are supplied. If you will be building the cabinets yourself, and making the needed utility connections, the savings will be even greater as only the cost of the raw materials will be involved.

After you decide what you want, use the plans you have prepared to compile a list of materials, making certain that you've included all the items such as doorknobs, hinges, adhesive for the counter-top plastic laminate, flexible gas hose for the stove, etc. Using this list, get quotations for the quantities needed from your local lumber dealer, hardware store, or mail order catalogs. When you know the prices and have computed the total outlay, you may want to trim your sails a bit, perhaps cutting a corner here or there.

STANDARD KITCHEN DIMENSIONS
AND MODULE SIZES

floor cabinets	24″ deep; 30″ wide; 36″ high (including the counter top)
wall cabinets	12″ deep; 15″ to 17″ clearance above counter tops; height variable
dishwashers	24″ deep; 35″ high; 30″ wide
tabletop range	24″ deep (total space of counter to drop-in type; others fill full 24″ depth); width up to 30″
sink bowl	single: 18″ x 22″ double: 18″ x 29″ or 32″

Structural Changes

Any structural alterations of the kitchen area should be completed before the final planning of cabinet sizes, as unanticipated changes may become necessary. These alterations include change of size of door openings, shifting of door locations, enlarging or reducing a window, making an opening into an adjoining closet for installing an appliance or wall oven, putting up a soffit or ceiling beams. Usually these jobs will require removal of some

of the cabinets in that particular area. Another important hint: any electrical work that is required should be done at the time the old cabinets are removed, so that the wiring cables can be drawn up through the walls. Don't worry if you don't yet know the exact locations for the receptacles or appliance connections. After the electrical wiring is roughed in, the final locations can be determined. Ceiling lamps can be installed early in the project.

The Cabinet Work

While decorative details such as the window valances can be done quite well by a skilled home owner with ordinary hand tools, building the cabinets requires a precision that can be obtained only with a good bench saw. Additional power tools will be helpful, such as a router, electric drill, and sander. A power saw will pay for itself in both the time saved and the avoidance of waste material. What kind of saw is best? A table saw of adequate size and quality is most versatile, lasts indefinitely, and will be used for many additional projects. A radial saw is a fine asset to any shop, may be easier for the novice to use, can rip large panels, but may present minor problems in handling materials when it comes to cross-cutting parts for the 24″ standard cabinet width. The ideal equipment would include both types of saws. This would involve a considerable investment but would make a really efficient workshop setup. In addition you would need a handy sabre saw for trimming, fitting, and cutting irregular surfaces.

Making the counters and backsplashes requires large sections of plywood and plastic surfacing material, often cut into an L shape and with rounded ends. Laminating the plastic is an interesting technique, but if you are not equipped to do this counter laminating, you can buy stock lengths at reasonable prices, already cut for the sink bowl, or including the sink bowl and rim if the complete unit is desired. Special sizes can be ordered from local custom shops specializing in such laminated counters.

Framing a Soffit

A soffit is a boxlike enclosure along a wall at ceiling level, used to enclose plumbing pipes and other utility installations. In older homes with very high ceilings, a soffit may be built to lower the ceiling, at least in part, along the walls. If you have a soffit at one wall, you may want to build another on the opposite or adjoining wall to equalize them. Another reason for having a soffit is to enclose the space between the top of your wall cabinets and the ceiling, for cleanliness and better appearance. The soffit is invariably finished—with paint, wallpaper, or vinyl-coated wall covering—in a light color to contrast with the kitchen cabinets.

The soffit is framed with 2-by-3's as shown in the sketch. A 2-by-3 plate is nailed to the ceiling joists, 11½" from the wall, and a similar plate is nailed to the wall an inch or two above the height of the wall cabinets. The framing assembly is put together, securely nailed, before being raised into place and secured by toenailing the short pieces of 2-by-3's to the top and wall plates. The framing is enclosed with pieces of gypsum board, which can be painted or covered with wallpaper. When the wall cabinets are hung, the gap remaining between the top of the cabinets and the soffit will be hidden by a cove molding.

Cabinet Details

There are three basic kitchen cabinets: the floor cabinet; the wall cabinet; and the floor-to-ceiling cabinet. Although there are many variations in styling, features, and other details, the fundamental construction of each type remains standard—the use of wide sections of ¾" plywood for enclosing the back and sides, and for the shelves.

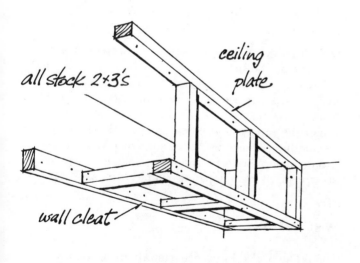

Soffit is framed out with 2-by-3 stock, starting with cleats nailed to the wall and the ceiling. Preassembled boxlike sections are attached to these cleats. Cover with plasterboard, taping the joints for final finishing.

Floor cabinets (sometimes called base cabinets) all have toe spaces at exposed front areas. These cabinets vary as to purpose; they may have drawers, or shelves, or a combination of both. Corner cabinets may have lazy Susan revolving shelves. Width of the cabinets ranges from 24" to about 6'. One is specially planned to receive the sink, another for a tabletop range if there is to be one. Some cabinets may be planned for L-shaped installation. In nearly every case, a base cabinet will have a specially built counter top.

Wall cabinets are shallow, nearly always limited to shelves only. Floor-to-ceiling cabinets are usually so bulky that they cannot be carried in but must be assembled right in the room. At ceiling height, they will require full length of the plywood panel, and a cabinet 24" deep will use a full panel just for the two sides, with another panel required for the back and the doors.

Remember, do not "squeeze" the floor dimensions when planning the cabinet sizes. Allow ample clearance, up to an extra inch between cabinets. This space will be filled in when you fit the front stiles for the cabinet doors.

Building a Base Cabinet

Details of a typical base cabinet are shown in the sketch. This corner cabinet contains sink bowl, has swing-out shelves, an open back for access to the plumbing lines, and ample space underneath for the sink trap and storage of cleaning materials.

The cabinet is built essentially of ¾" plywood, preferably with a hardwood veneer such as birch if the plywood is to remain unsurfaced, or a lower-priced fir plywood if plastic sheeting will be laminated to the raw surface. While use of the ¾" plywood is recommended throughout to give the cabinet solidity, some savings in cost and weight are obtained with the use of ¼" plywood for the backing panels, as shown in the sketch.

The panels may be joined by simple nailing, through the sides into the bottom and through the bottom panel into vertical dividers. However, a more rigid and professional result will be assured if the joints are mortised—that is, shallow grooves are cut with a set of dadoing blades on the power saw so that the panel sections are set in and glued.

At exposed cabinet sides, the end pieces are not mortised, but rather set into L-shaped rabbet cuts, half the thickness of the panel. The supporting strips at the bottom, 3⅝" high, set back 3" from

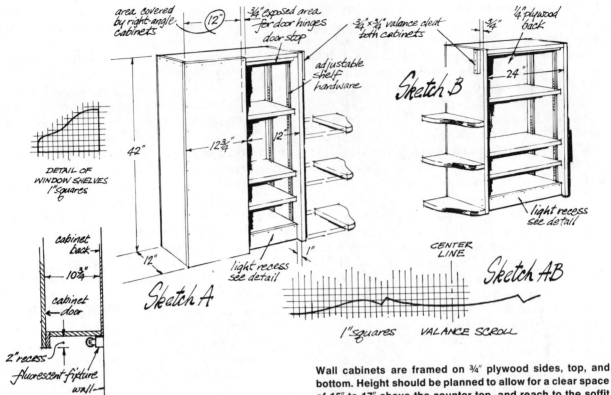

area covered by right-angle cabinets

(12")

¾" exposed area for door hinges door stop

¾" × ¾" valance cleat both cabinets

Sketch B

¼" plywood back

¾"

24"

DETAIL OF WINDOW SHELVES 1" squares

42"

12¾"

12"

adjustable shelf hardware

light recess see detail

cabinet back

10¾"

cabinet door

2" recess

fluorescent fixture

wall

DETAIL UNDER-CABINET LIGHT RECESS

12"

light recess see detail

1"

Sketch A

CENTER LINE

Sketch AB

1" squares   VALANCE SCROLL

Wall cabinets are framed on ¾" plywood sides, top, and bottom. Height should be planned to allow for a clear space of 15" to 17" above the counter top, and reach to the soffit or a predetermined top level all around the room. Recess for light fixture is provided at bottom of each cabinet. Note that sketch showing details of undercabinet light recess has 2" clearance to allow for installation of fluorescent strip at the back wall.

the front for the toe space, can be of solid 1″ lumber, or you can use up waste strips of the ¾″ plywood panel for this purpose.

A variation of the corner cabinet is also shown, having one section containing a row of drawers instead of being reserved for the sink bowl. The one special detail about both these cabinets is the extra provision for mounting hinges for the swing-out shelf door. This allows the door to be set in full-size into the opening, resulting in more clearance for the shelves. Wherever drawers are used, metal slides are recommended for smooth performance.

Details of the swing-out shelves are shown in a separate sketch. The shelves are rounded at one corner with a sabre saw, on the arc of a circle with a 12″ radius measured on the piece that forms the door. Concealed ¾″-by-¾″ cleats, glued and screwed to the door, support the shelves, which are edged

with 2″-wide aluminum strips to prevent stored objects from falling.

Drawers are always difficult to make because so many parts are needed, each precisely cut and fitted. However, the use of metal drawer slides simplifies the process and when properly done assures a smoothly performing drawer of which you can be proud. Complete instructions on making the drawers are given in a separate chapter, on page 418.

Wall Cabinets

Boxlike wall cabinets vary mostly in the door design. These cabinets are usually 12″ deep, 42″ high. The cabinets are built of ¾″ plywood for the sides, top, and bottom, with ¼″ plywood backing. Shelves may be permanently set into dado grooves,

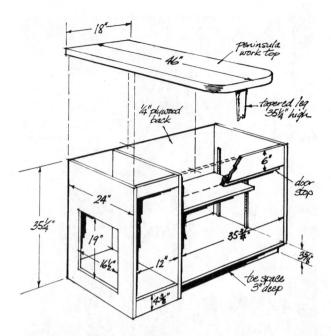

Base cabinet height overall, including the 1½" thick counter top, usually is 36". This height may be varied to the convenience of the owner. Sides of cabinets are of ¾" plywood, with shelves of same stock set into dado grooves if possible. Back panel is ¼" plywood. All base cabinets have 3"-deep toe space at front. Sketch shows details of stove cabinet with peninsula counter over corner section.

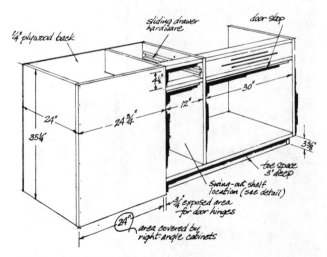

Sink cabinet with swing-out shelf section and drawers. Width of cabinet is variable according to type and size of sink bowl. Back panel leaves open space for plumbing connections.

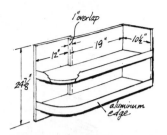

Sketch shows details of swing-out shelf construction. Note the 1" overlap for hinging to the extended portion of the corner cabinet.

a method recommended unless adjustable shelves are desired, in which case include adjustable shelf support strips on each side.

The sketches show several arrangements of the basic wall cabinet, including a corner area to be joined by cabinets at a right angle, and a cabinet covering a wall obstruction. Be sure to attach the back panel very securely, to help hold the box together. A shallow space is provided at the bottom of these cabinets for a concealed lighting fixture.

Floor-to-Ceiling Cabinet

Full-length cabinets, about 8' tall and reaching nearly to the ceiling or, rather, to the soffit, are required for a wall oven. The cabinet will be 24" wide and 24" deep. In the sketch shown, the oven is located at eye level, leaving space above for storage and a drawer underneath. Despite its size, this cabinet is probably the easiest to build, but assembly must be done in the kitchen as it would be impossible to move it in when assembled. Rip a 4'-by-8' panel in half, the long way, to get two pieces, each 2'-by-8', for the sides. Make the toe-space cut at one corner of each side. The back does not receive a full panel, since there must be access to the plumbing and electrical lines. Also an opening must be left for ventilation. It is sufficient to enclose the back only at the upper shelves and the bottom drawer.

Attach the metal drawer slides at the bottom on each side, then raise the sides and join them with 1-by-3 stretchers, front and back. At the front, place two stretchers across the bottom, into the toe space, then one across the very top of the cabinet. A stretcher is placed at front and back in a position to support a shelf that holds the oven. You must

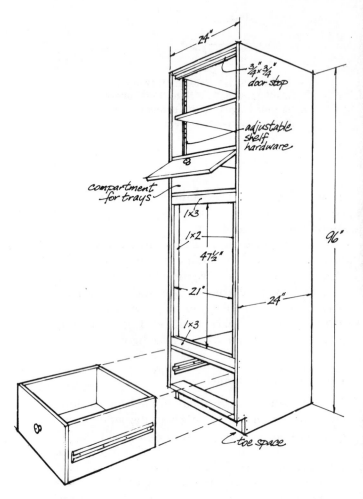

Wall oven is admired for its convenience and as a space saver, often solving the problem of providing room for a dishwasher.

Wall oven cabinet is assembled right in the kitchen from precut sections. These consist of the sides, which are obtained by ripping in half, the long way, a 4'-by-8' panel of ¾" plywood, giving you two pieces, each 2'-by-8'. The sides are first cut back at the bottom corner for the standard toe space, 3" deep, 3⅝" high. The oven slides in on a ¾" plywood shelf which is supported by 1-by-3 stretchers securely attached across the front and back at the proper position so that the oven controls will be at eye level. The cabinet is left open in back of the oven, but ¼" or ¾" plywood backing is placed at the drawer and upper shelves level. When shifted into its position, make sure that the cabinet stands plumb, otherwise put shims under the base.

Full-length cabinet has adjustable shelf brackets to take maximum advantage of the available space for assortment of silverware and glass items, all of varying heights.

decide that height yourself, based on the level at which you want the oven controls. When you have that level, leave 47½" (check that distance with the size of your oven, as more or less space may be needed, depending on make and model) then put in the supports for the upper shelf. Attach adjustable shelf strips into the upper section before putting on the back panel. After the unit is assembled, shift it partly into position, but do not attach it until the plumbing and electrical connections have been made and the oven installed.

Additional tall cabinets, though not of quite such huge size, should be built if there is space for them, to be used for storage of canned foods and cleaning supplies.

Cabinet Doors

The appearance of the cabinets goes far to set the style of the kitchen. All you see of the cabinets is the doors, so it is the door that carries the main

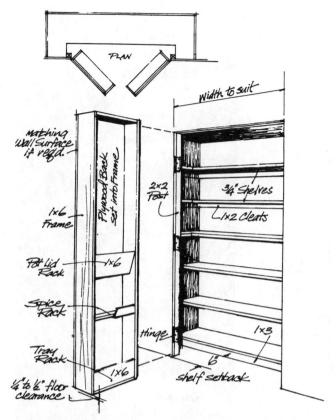

Cleverly contrived storage section owes its unique quality to the depth of the double doors. The back wall shelves are standard ¾" shelving stock on 1-by-2 cleats. The doors also are easy enough to assemble, being merely boxes of 1-by-6 lumber, fitted with pot lid racks and provisions for other supplies. The main element is that the hinges are mounted at the outside, rather than the inside edge of these doors, as shown. Three hinges on each are necessary.

Kitchen tidiness is a goal sought by every housewife, and in this room there obviously must be "a place for everything." The cabinet shown utilizes simple bins as well as shelves, built right into the doors for convenient storage of awkwardly shaped items.

decorative weight of the room. It is obvious, then, that whatever attention you give to making the doors particularly attractive will be well worthwhile.

Modern power tools make fine door cabinetry possible, in addition to precise fit and effective detail. One especially useful and versatile power tool is the router, ideal for shaping the edges of cabinet work, and for many other workshop tasks.

The style in cabinet doors that has become almost standard has a bullnose-shaped overlap on all four sides. The exterior overlay is equal to half the thickness of the door stock; the interior side of the door is recessed into the cabinet opening. The advantages are that the exposed surface does not show

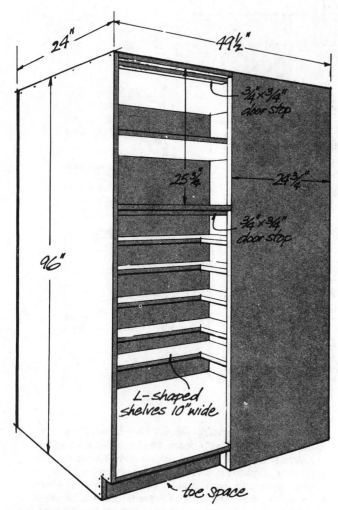

24"

49½"

3/4" x 3/4"
door stop

25¾"   24¾"

3/4" x 3/4"
door stop

96"

L-shaped
shelves 10" wide

~ toe space

Details of large storage pantry, or similar purpose cabinet, with L-shaped shelves allowing entrance to reach all positions. The 24″ depth makes possible storage of large articles that are difficult to place elsewhere.

the full ¾″ bulk of the door, but instead appears neat and trim with its smoothly rounded edge, while the cabinet opening is adequately covered against entry of dust and dirt. These doors are made by cutting the plywood ¾″ oversize in four width and length dimensions, then shaping the edge all around with a router bit, and finally making rabbet cuts on the underside to half the thickness of the stock.

The novel and particularly attractive cabinet doors seen in the illustrations are made by cutting the arched design in ¼″ plywood, then shaping the inside edge and gluing the ¼″ plywood onto a

¾″-thick door frame. The arched design produces a three-dimensional profiled effect that sets an elegant tone for the entire kitchen. Many variations of this design are possible for individualized styling.

Making Kitchen Counter Tops

Kitchen counter tops are made separately as a complete unit, then installed atop the base cabinet. The counter top consists of a ¾″ plywood core, built up underneath with ¾″ wood strips for reinforcement and extra thickness at the front edge. It is surfaced with a melamine plastic sheeting which is laminated to the plywood with contact cement.

Usually the counter top is fitted with a backsplash of the same plastic, and the exposed front and side edges are "self-edged" with strips of the same plastic material. Additionally, the counter tops may join corner cabinets in an L-shaped arrangement, for example, or cutouts may be required for attaching a sink bowl or recessing a tabletop stove. Whatever the requirement, the laminating technique remains the same.

Complete plastic-laminated sink counters, stove counters, and other kitchen counters can be ordered to exact shape and specifications from local shops specializing in this work. Stock sizes also are available, often with the sink bowl already installed, and it is possible that you will find just what you need, or can cut them to fit. But the selection of colors and finishes in the plastic, and the complexity of some installations, in addition to the money savings, make it worthwhile to produce your own. And the saying "When you've made one, you can just as easily make a dozen," applies here. It's just a matter of getting the technique down pat, and having the right equipment to work with—from then on the progress is almost routine.

HEAT-MOLDED COUNTERS

You have no doubt seen some counters made all in one piece, including the front edge and the backsplash, which are gracefully curved. These counters are made in huge heat-forming presses, and are laminated to wood blocks of corresponding shapes. This process is beyond the capacity of any home workshhop. If you wish to have the molded type, rather than to make your own as described on page 20, these counters can be purchased from supply houses or from Sears, Roebuck. The Sears counters come in stock sections, ranging from 2′ to

Novel design of cabinet doors consists of cathedral-like arched contours, combined with laminated wood overlay for attractive two-dimensional effect.

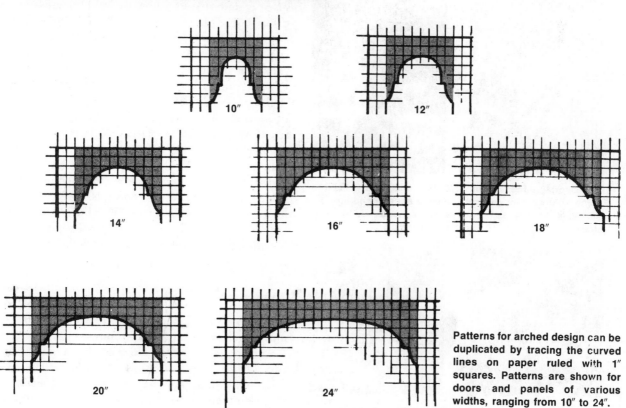

10″

12″

14″

16″

18″

20″

24″

Patterns for arched design can be duplicated by tracing the curved lines on paper ruled with 1″ squares. Patterns are shown for doors and panels of various widths, ranging from 10″ to 24″.

Make the overlay from ¼" veneered plywood, cut to same size as basic door panel. Lay out the pattern, make the inside cuts with a sabre saw, using the saw guide at straight sides. Then continue with the project as shown at right.

When cutting the curved section, clamp a piece of waste ¾" stock underneath and cut through both pieces. Leave the backup piece as a guide for the router bit when shaping the curved section. A similar guide strip is clamped on for routing the straight sections.

Thin overlay panel is laminated with contact cement or glued to the ¾" door stock.

Cross section of cabinet door is seen in photograph, with shaped edge and thicker stock.

Edge grain of plywood is trimmed all around with thin wood tape, applied with contact cement.

Completed door shows cutaway design of overlay plywood. Prepunched holes for the hinge screws assure correct hanging and smooth operation of the hinges.

12' in length, and can be cut down to size with a hand saw. There also is a corner section which is used to make an L-shaped counter. Straight sections are joined where necessary by tightening Lock-Joint bolts underneath to form continuous units. The price is $4.65 per linear foot for 2' long sections, slightly higher for the longer counters, while a corner unit somewhat larger than 2' square is priced at $32, plus shipping charges. A choice of four colors is offered. Matching sections with sink cutouts also are available, in various lengths from 66" to 96". Also, there is a counter with a solid maple cutting-board top which would make a splendid addition to your new kitchen.

MATERIALS FOR MAKING THE COUNTER TOP

For making your own counters, first find the dimensions. If you're replacing an old counter that has been satisfactory, just repeat the same size and shape. But an entirely new counter will require careful figuring. Don't forget to allow for the overhang at the front, usually 1", and don't have the counter go all the way to the back wall—an open space is desirable and will not show because of the backsplash. Thus, while the base cabinet is 24" deep, and half a standard plywood panel is 24" wide, the open space allowed at the back wall will give you enough plywood for the front overhang.

The counter core can be of ¾" flakeboard as well as plywood. Flakeboard often is preferred because there is less chance of warping, and the absence of grain and surface defects eliminates any distortion of the surface plastic. Standard size of these panels is 4'-by-8', but sizes up to 4'-by-10', and 4'-by-12', now are available at many lumberyards.

The plastic also comes in standard 4' widths, and in various lengths up to 12'. There are many brands, the best known and most popular being Formica. Colors and patterns change annually, and can be selected from sample chips at your dealer.

CUTTING THE CORE PANELS

Here are some important instructions for the various stages of building the counter top.

Saw your plywood or flakeboard core panels into two 2'-wide lengths. The panels can be cut accurately on a table saw, but you may need assistance in guiding and supporting the huge panel through the blade. Part of the answer lies with the quality of the bench saw you have. If it's a heavy floor model, with a good-size table that allows setting the

A new plastic-surfaced counter adds a dash of color to the kitchen, often replacing a water-logged linoleum top. In place of the old-fashioned metal molding, the new cabinets are edged with strips of the same plastic for a neater, more practical result.

fence to 24″ center, the cutting will go smoother and more accurately than on a saw of inadequate size and power.

The large panels can be cut to size with a portable circular saw, when used in conjunction with a straightedge board, as a saw guide, clamped securely to the work. The panel must be supported off the floor at a number of points for this purpose —and not just on a pair of sawhorses, since the panel will buckle and drop when the cut is completed. When clamping the straightedge, which should be a full inch or more thick and at least 3″ wide so it will stay true, make sure to figure the width of the saw shoe which will ride against the guide, adding this width to the width of the guide

strips. Make a tiny cut first and remeasure, to be sure that you have it right before continuing.

CUTTING THE PLASTIC SHEETING

There are some important details to watch when cutting the plastic sheeting. The panel must be placed so that the saw teeth enter through the plastic-coated surface, or the face of the panel. Thus, with a table saw or radial saw, the plastic is set face up, since the blade teeth bite in from the top. But with a portable circular saw, the teeth turn upward from below, so the panel should be face down. The same is true of a sabre saw blade, which cuts on the up-stroke. The reason: the plastic would chip off, rather than cut, if the blade came through from the back of the panel. And with close measurement, a sizable chip off the edge could well spoil the panel for your project.

Another detail is that the plastic is not cut to the exact size of the panel to which it will be cemented, but from ¼″ to ½″ extra allowed. This waste stock will be trimmed off later, perfectly smooth, with a router bit, or with a file.

When counter edges are to receive trim of the same plastic, the narrow strip is cemented on first, the edges then trimmed smooth with the router. The top panel is then put on, and this time the excess is bevel-trimmed against the front edge.

Remember when cutting the plastic that the extremely hard and brittle melamine is tough on saw blades, even the carbide-tipped ones. Use an old, fine-tooth blade, or buy a cheap one for that purpose. Also, be sure to wear goggles when sawing this plastic, as the tiny chips really fly and can cause devastating damage.

The standard thickness for a laminated counter top is 1½″. Since the core material is only ¾″ thick, you build it up with strips of ¾″ stock along the edges, plus a few crosspieces at points where they will rest against the tops of the cabinet partitions, distributing the support. The pieces used for this purpose may be waste strips from your panel. Attach these strips with glue and screws to the underside of the ¾″ panel, making sure that the screws do not penetrate through the top surface.

Laminating the Plastic Surface

The plastic is bonded to the core stock with contact cement. There are two types of this cement: one is an acetone-type solvent which is highly flammable and has a strong odor. The other is a water-base type which is free of these disadvantages, but you must be sure that the cement has not been subjected to freezing. Laminating should be done at temperatures above 65 degrees, and only after the parts to be bonded have been kept in the same room for a sufficient time to equalize their temperature. The cement must be well mixed, not by shaking the can, but by stirring it thoroughly.

For the laminating you will need some sort of trowel (a small piece of hardboard will do) to spread the cement, and a slip-sheet of heavy kraft paper as long and wide as the counter top. A sheet of wrapping paper will be suitable although you may have difficulty obtaining paper 24″ wide. If necessary, paste two or more pieces of the paper to-

gether to form one continuous sheet.

Before applying the cement, wipe both the plywood and plastic to remove any dust and splinters or other debris sticking to the surface. Place both materials—the plywood and the plastic—on sawhorses or other support, making sure that you have the correct surfaces, those that will be bonded together, facing up. Start with either one, applying the cement. Pour a quantity of the cement on the plywood and spread it around to completely cover every spot, right up to the edges—this can be checked visually as you go. Then do the same on the plastic backing. The cement application goes quickly, taking just a few minutes.

It won't matter if there's any spot that has a bit too much cement, but make sure that there's no spot uncovered. When this is done, let the cement dry. This usually takes twenty to thirty minutes depending on the room temperature. Test for dryness by pressing a small piece of the kraft paper on the surface, then pulling it off. The paper should stick slightly, but none of the cement should come away with it.

With contact cement, as the name implies, the parts are bonded immediately on contact, and it would be impossible to shift the plastic panel around to align the edges properly. The slip-sheet method has been developed to overcome this. Place the paper over the plywood, then put on the plastic panel—the paper acts as a barrier to prevent bonding. Shift the plastic until the edges are all in alignment with the core. Now place your knee over the center to hold the plastic in position while you raise one end of the plastic, and with the other hand fold back the paper underneath as far as you can. Then let the plastic drop slowly down into place, and press down on it, rubbing your hand over the surface so that the end becomes firmly bonded. Now lift up the opposite end, reach under and carefully pull out the folded end of the kraft paper. As you do this, press down on the plastic until the entire paper has been removed. To complete the lamination, go over the plastic with a block of wood and a mallet or hammer, tapping down every part of the surface. This will ensure that every part has become firmly bonded.

Applying Edge Strips

As mentioned previously, the plastic edging is put on first, before the top is laminated. Cement is spread over the edge most conveniently with a

Prepare the counter core by first cutting ¾" plywood panel to correct size, then building up the edge all around with added strips of ¾" stock. Add reinforcing pieces where they will fit across the tops of supporting cabinets.

Slip-sheet technique involves use of kraft paper separation between the plastic and core until the edges can be lined up. Then one end of panel is lifted, the paper folded back, and plastic allowed to become bonded to the panel. Then rest of paper is pulled out.

Plastic sheeting is cut to slightly oversize dimensions. For laminating, apply contact cement to back of plastic sheet and surface of the core stock. Use a brush, trowel, piece of hardboard to spread the cement so every part is covered.

Allow cement to dry for 20 to 30 minutes, until a piece of kraft paper pressed to it will come away without sticking.

To assure good bonding, go over entire top with wood block and hammer, tapping every inch of the surface.

A KITCHEN YOU'LL LOVE TO LIVE IN

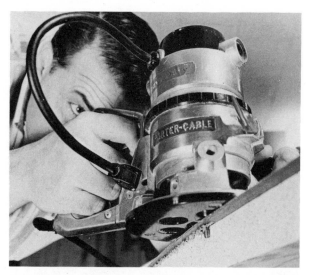

Excess plastic is trimmed along edge with router bit. Use straight bit at edges that will be joined or overlapped, bevel cutter for free edge.

brush. Because the edge consists of end grain and there will be a certain amount of absorption, it is a good idea to double up on the cement application—waiting until the first coat has become dry before applying a second heavy coat.

The edging will be only 1¾" to 2" wide, and can be handled without a slip-sheet, as the fingers can guide the plastic into place and there is plenty of leverage to make slight corrections.

After the cement has dried, as proved by the test previously described, start the strip square at one end, pressing it down tightly. Hold the hand over the strip so that the bottom counter edge and the strip edge are even, and press down on the strip as the hand moves along until the strip is completely in place. The excess overlap at the top edge is trimmed off with a router. A special carbide-tipped veneer trimmer, such as the Stanley 82 917 kit, does the job best. Use the straight cutter bit on the edging. Later, when the top plastic edge is trimmed for a bevel cut, there will be a neat, uniform bevel that shows as a straight dark line. One value of this bevel is that it helps prevent lifting or chipping of the plastic edge.

Edge trimming with the router is a snap, once you get the hang of it. Just set the depth so that the cutter is level with the edge of the laminate. The trimmer guide rides along the edge of the core material, while the fast-spinning cutter trims the laminate flush. There is one thing to watch for if you are using a plywood core: if there is a hole in

the edge from open knots, the cutter pilot can drop out of line and cause a deep notch in the plastic. If you see any holes, fill them with wood putty, or bypass them freehand, and trim the laminate excess there with a file. The straight cutter is used for all edges that will butt up against another piece of laminate; all exposed edges are trimmed with the bevel cutter.

MAKING THE BACKSPLASH

The backsplash is simply a double thickness of the core material, of the same length as the counter, and several inches high, faced with the same plastic material. It is attached along the back end of the counter with screws through the bottom, reinforced with metal mending plates at the back.

The backsplash joint must be drawn up tight, otherwise water on the counter may seep underneath. To assure a satisfactory joint, use a series of clamps with an intervening thick board to apply pressure uniformly along the entire length of the backsplash while the screws are being driven in from below. Also, it's a good idea to use washers under the screwheads so there will be no "give" as the screws sink deeper into the plywood core.

L-SHAPED COUNTERS

Making an L-shaped counter is not as tricky as it would appear. The core sections (that is, the two legs of the L) are cut separately to the required length, keeping in mind the distance occupied by the corner. Thus, one leg will be measured from

Backsplash is butted on top of counter, attached with screws through the bottom. Apply clamp pressure and drill pilot holes in bottom stock to assure tight joint all along.

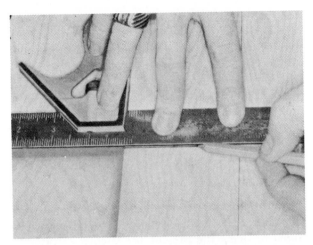

For joining panels to form L-shaped counters, special fasteners are inserted into bored holes underneath. Align panels and draw lines across for locating the locking bolts.

Use drilling guide to locate holes bored into the cross section and also part way through depth of stock.

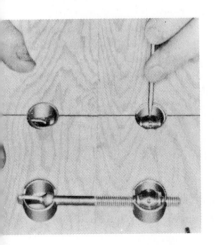

Special pins are used for tightening fasteners that draw up the butted edges of the panels.

the corner outward, but the second leg will be measured 24″ from that corner, the distance occupied by the first leg. It is surprising how many times even experienced shopworkers overlook that detail. The two parts are then joined together with a special hardware item, Lock-Joint bolts, by drawing up the nuts to tighten the bolts. Details on this procedure are shown by the illustrations on page 25.

If the L is not too large, the plastic top may be cut to shape so that it will cover in one piece without a seam. However, with a larger L you should make a single tight seam if the two sections are laminated separately and then joined.

Rounded ends of cabinets present another problem, but only with the self-edging trim. The plastic has limited resiliency, and cannot take a sharp radius bend without cracking. If you have a special problem, try soaking the narrow banding strip in hot water to obtain a slight additional flexibility of the backing material.

ATTACHING THE SINK BOWL

The sink bowl is completely installed before the counter panel is set into place. You will need a special Houdaille rim for mounting the sink; make

Sink counters are fully laminated first, then the sink opening is cut with a saw. Obtain sink rim and mark the cutout with a grease pencil, drill starting holes for sabre saw blade at corners. Slight chipping of plastic along edges will be covered by the rim flange, or the opening may be cut face down.

Sink rim is attached first, then bowl is dropped into a bed of mastic sealer, and locked in with corner clips.

sure that you get the right size to fit. Locate the position of the bowl (take into consideration the location of the water pipes and waste line), and use the rim as a guide for the cutout, which is done with a sabre saw.

Place the rim on the top of the plastic and outline it with a grease pencil, then drill a hole at one corner for starting the sabre saw blade. Most new type sinks have the water lines coming up through holes at the back ledge of the sink bowl itself, but some types may require drilling the holes into the backsplash. If these are needed, use the old sink as a template for locating the holes.

Before fitting the rim in place, spread the calking compound along the open edges of the counter core, then apply a bed of the compound into which the sink flanges are pressed, and finally draw up on the attachment clips for the bowl.

INSTALLING THE NEW COUNTERS

If your measurements have been correct, the new counters simply slip into place, ready to be attached with a few small right-angle brackets. Put these anywhere that is convenient, where you can reach the underside of the cabinet through a drawer or shelf section, to place one or more of the brackets. These will not bear any weight or strain, but are there simply to prevent any side movement of the counter.

One important detail that requires attention, however, is that the counter must be so set that it is pitched from all sides toward the sink. In that way any water spillage will not accumulate, but will drain off into the sink. After the counter is set into place, use a bubble level to determine the direc-

tion of the pitch. Wherever necessary, place pieces of wood underneath as shims, between the counter-reinforcing strips and the tops of the supporting cabinets, to raise or lower the counter as necessary. The sink part, because of both the cutout of the plywood and the weight of the sink bowl, will naturally tend to sag a bit lower than the rest, and that takes care of the runoff problem if the outer edges of the counter have been shimmed up.

One-Armed Faucet

In any popularity contest of the wonderful new materials, ideas, and appliances that have done so much to make the present-day kitchen so pleasant and efficient, the prize winners surely would include the one-arm faucet. This handsome and efficient device is rapidly becoming a standard item in any kitchen modernization.

Housewives appreciate the smooth and easy operation of the faucet, even when both hands are occupied, simply by pushing the single lever rather than turning faucet handles. Adjusting the water temperature is easier too: just push the lever a little farther to right or left. The secondary benefit is also important: there'll never be any drip-drip-drip, nor will washers ever have to be changed, or washer seats replaced. The one-armed faucet works smoothly and efficiently and is trouble-free. And it's good-looking, too.

Switching from the old-fashioned sink fixtures to the new-style faucet usually is quite simple. The faucet fits neatly into the back-flange openings of all new sink bowls, as shown in the photographs. In most cases, only a minimum of plumbing work is required.

The installation steps will vary somewhat, depending on whether your water lines are of pipe or tubing. Here's a valuable reminder: if your water lines do not have shutoff cocks at the sink, this is a good time to install a set, while the water supply is shut down. The cost is nominal for a complete two-valve set, and it's a good idea to have these valves at every plumbing fixture so that repairs can be made without shutting off the water main.

Although it is usually possible merely to shift the water lines from the old faucet to the new one, some obstructions may prevent this. The faucet installation shown started with required cutting of the water lines. This was done quickly with a tubing cutter, a few inches above the shutoff valves. The new one-arm faucet fits into openings in the

One-arm kitchen faucet combines the benefits of greater convenience and total freedom from maintenance, as there are no washers to be changed.

Original supply lines come through cabinet floor straight up to old faucet. Shutoff cocks eliminate closing main water valve while switching the faucets.

Water lines are cut close to the shut-off valves with a rotating tubing cutter. Make sure to ream inside of tubing after cutting. In most situations, flexible tube connections make the cutting unnecessary.

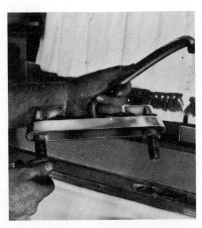

Old faucet, with individual hot-and-cold handles, is removed after the water line tubing is disconnected.

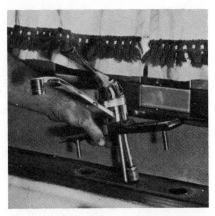

Single handle replacement faucet fits into the sink bowl flange holes. The holes are spaced either 6″ or 8″ apart, on centers.

Original tube fitting was found in satisfactory condition, and was used for the new connection.

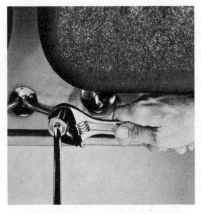

Draw up the fitting hand-tight, then pull up a bit more with a wrench — no need to put on too much pressure or you could twist the tubing.

Join sections with a short piece of tubing, sweat-soldered to two elbow fittings, forming an offset joint and avoiding excess bending to bypass an obstruction.

An island cabinet for your kitchen can save you many steps, provides an excellent working surface and a handy storage for frequently needed articles, including a row of spices on the narrow shelf, and an array of pots and pans.

MATERIALS LIST

(All dimensions, stated in inches, are approximate)

A.   1 pc., 24 x 48 x ¾"
B.   3 pcs., 20½ x 44½ x ¾"
C.   2 pcs., 1½ x 1½ x 44½" (1 pc. not shown)
D.   2 pcs., 1½ x 1½ x 17½" (1 pc. not shown)
E.   random width boards, 31¾ x ¾"
EE. random width boards, 35¼ x ¾"
F.   2 pcs., 11 x 20½ x ¾"
G.   1 pc., 7½ x 20½ x ¾"
H.   2 pcs., 3½ x ¾ x 44½" (1 pc. not shown)
I.   3 pcs., 3½ x ¾ x 19" (1 pc. not shown)
J.   2 pcs., 2 x ¾ x 31¾"
K.   1 pc., 2 x ¾ x 29¾"
L.   1 pc., 2 x ¾ x 42"
M.   4 pcs., 1 x 1½ x 20½"
N.   4 pcs., 1 x ⅞ x 20½"
O.   5 pcs., ¾ x ¾ x 20" (1 pc. not shown)
P.   Formica top, 24 x 48"
Q.   stainless steel edging
R.   1 pc., 6 x 48 x ¾"
S.   12 feet of 1" brass pipe
T.   edge molding
U.   4 pcs., 5½ x 20⅛ x ⅜" (2 pcs. not shown)
V.   2 pcs., 5½ x 19 x ⅜" (1 pc. not shown)
W.   2 pcs., 6 x ¾ x 20" (1 pc. not shown)
X.   random width boards, 22¾ x 20 x ¾"
Y.   2 pcs., 20 x 10⅞ x ¼"
Z.   ⁵⁄₃₂" wire bent to hooks
ZZ. 4 pcs., 20½ x 18⅝ x ¼"
UU. 4 sides, 11 x 20⅛ x ⅜"
VV. 2 backs, 11 x 20 x ⅜"
WW. 2 fronts, 11½ x ¾ x 20"

Cutaway sketch shows the construction details of the island cabinet, containing three slant-front drawers, a shelf section with door, a Formica-laminated counter, and a pipe frame holding a spice shelf and hooks for pots and pans. Note that the baseboards are set back fore and aft for toe spaces.

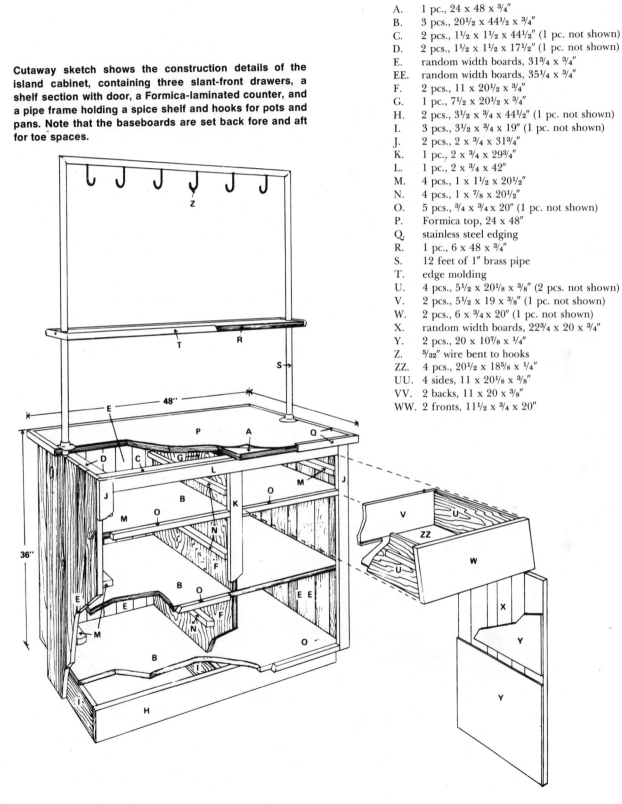

back of the sink flange, and is fastened from below with large nuts and washers. The new water lines no longer go separately to each side, but rather both feed into the middle of the faucet.

A professional plumbing tip may be mentioned here: the water remaining in the short tubing stubs above the shutoff valves should be blown out; otherwise when soldering the new connection later with a propane torch, the water could turn into steam. The easiest way to remove standing water is to blow it out with a drinking straw.

Since the fittings were found to be in good condition the old water-line tubing was connected to the new faucet. The cut ends then were rejoined with a pair of elbow fittings to provide an offset, which was deemed preferable to bending the tubing sharply as would otherwise be required. Detailed information on sweat soldering of the tubing is on page 27.

An Island Cabinet

A free-standing base cabinet can become the key to a happy kitchen, functioning as the halfway link between the various counters, the stove, and the refrigerator. This island cabinet saves steps by serving as a handy work surface within reach of everything for meal preparation, adding its own convenient storage facilities for cutlery, spices, and other fixings, and even the necessary pots and pans.

The design, most attractive in its simplicity yet highly utilitarian, emphasizes the rustic look of random-size pine boards, but the cabinet may be built also of the most advanced materials to match any kitchen styling, while retaining its common-sense values. In this one cabinet, besides the spacious 24"-by-48" Formica-covered working counter, there are four handy drawers and a double-shelf section at the bottom, large enough to hold all your mixing bowls, while at fingertip reach there is a long shelf of spices, with a row of gleaming pots and pans directly above.

The counter, at a good working height of 36", is planned to be used from both sides so you don't always have to walk around to the front. However, the drawers and storage shelves can be used only from one side.

The list of materials is supplied for duplicating the cabinet in its original form. However, you can easily substitute where necessary if the appearance of the cabinet is to match your present kitchen.

The pipework frame holding the pots and pans is easier to make than it looks. Use brass or black iron pipe, buying a 12' length threaded at both ends. Cut the pipe with a hack saw into three sections, each 4' long, but make the cuts at a 45-degree angle so that the pipe can be welded or brazed together at two joints. The side lengths must be uniform. Brass screw flanges turned onto the threaded ends serve to attach and support this pipe structure. The pot holders are simple hooks of 1/4" soft rod, bent into shape and welded or brazed into a series of uniformly spaced holes along the top. The narrow spice shelf, which has molding strips along both sides to keep the spice bottles from falling off, is secured with either a pair of pipe clamp brackets or with screws through holes drilled in the pipe. Brass pipe can be polished for that ship-shape look many homeowners like.

The laminated Formica top is banded all around with a stainless steel molding, made for this purpose, and available at larger hardware stores. Notch the wide flange of the molding to permit bending it around the corners, but plan the bends so that the joining seam will fall midway at one of the sides. Attach the molding with tiny brads driven into the flange and plywood underneath.

No Pass-Through? Just Make One

There's nothing so effective in eliminating needless steps as a pass-through between the kitchen and dining room. You can make one in your home easily, turning a blank wall into a functional utility. Combining the pass-through with wall cabinets above and below the wall opening will provide even greater convenience. The cabinet top acts as a buffet, holding coffee setups and dessert until ready; the drawers and spaces underneath can contain the tableware and linens, and the upper cabinets can hold your service pieces and accessories.

At mealtime, food servings are placed on the dining room side through the opening and, after the meal, the dishes can be passed through to the kitchen. With the addition of stools, the pass-through shelf on the dining room side can be used for children's snacks, or even for their meal servings when an adult gathering crowds the dining table.

The hinged doors permit closing the pass-through during meal preparation and kitchen clean-up times, or when there's company visiting.

Making the opening is quite simple if it is to be in a partition wall, but if it involves a load-bearing wall, a support replacement must be supplied, as explained later, for the weight-bearing studs that will be cut. The width of the opening desired will determine the number of studs to be cut.

To make the opening in the wall, start by outlining the area of the pass-through. Break a hole in the plaster to help locate the stud positions, then nail boards horizontally across the top and bottom distances. These temporary boards will help prevent excessive breaking of the plasterboard. Use the boards as guides for a plasterboard saw so that the opening is squared off with neat edges.

The sides of the opening will end at stud position, so you need cut only those studs that are between these ends. But if two or more studs are cut away, there may be a sag or shift in the bearing structure of the house. To avoid this, break out some plaster at the center stud above the top of the pass-through and firmly clamp a length of 2-by-4 to that stud. Set up an auto jack on a wide plank, then fit a length of 2-by-4 between the jack and the piece of 2-by-4 that is clamped to the wall stud. Jack up that 2-by-4 just enough to exert a slight pressure on the clamped 2-by-4—the purpose is to temporarily support the weight when that stud is cut away.

With a hand saw or sabre saw, cut the studs, at top and bottom of your pass-through line, straight across.

Cut and fit a long 2-by-4 across the tops of the short or cripple studs, to form the lower frame of the opening. Then cut a pair of 2-by-6 beams to form the header across the top, supporting the original weight-bearing studs. But before putting up this heavy double beam, cut two 2-by-4's so they will fit tightly between the lower beam and the header. These 2-by-4's, which are nailed to the end studs, will help hold the header while it is toe-nailed in place, completing the basic frame. The jack can now be removed.

The counter is ¾″ plywood with a laminated

Convenient wall opening saves steps between kitchen and dining room, permits the hostess to remain seated and relaxed with her dinner guests as food servings and coffee setups are easily reached.

Opening is cut in wall for kitchen-dining room pass-through. Center stud of load-bearing wall is temporarily supported with auto jack until double 2-by-6 header is set in place. The header is supported by double 2-by-4's at the sides. Inside frame is faced with 1-by-5 board. Shelf is 16″ wide, surfaced with Formica plastic.

A KITCHEN YOU'LL LOVE TO LIVE IN

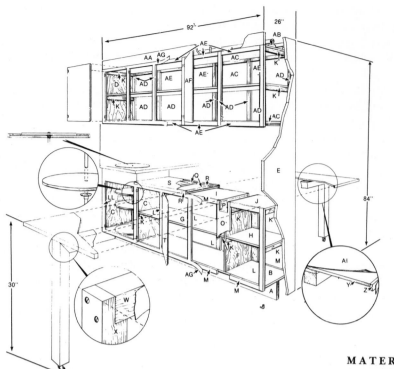

Sketch shows assembly of pass-through cabinet, containing slide-out breakfast nook table and lazy Susan shelves inside end unit. Cabinet is built of ¾" plywood having hardwood veneer facing on one side. The table leg assembly is of 4-by-4 stock, with plastic sheeting laminated to the table top. The letters refer to parts in List of Materials. Parts sizes will be different if overall dimensions vary from those given. The table may be made longer if more than two people are to be seated at it.

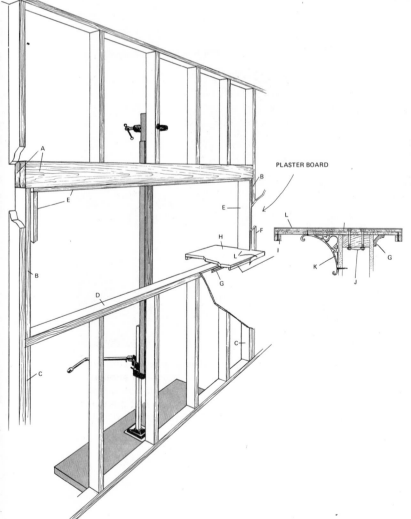

MATERIALS LIST

A. One base, 90½ x 4 x 1″
B. One piece, 90⅜ x 22 x ¾″
C. Two pieces, each: 30 x 22 x ¾″
D. One piece, 30 x 22 x ¾″
E. One piece, 80 x 24 x ¾″
EE. Angle irons (number and size variable)
F. One piece, 23 x 22 x ¾″
G. One piece, 46⅞ x 22 x ¾″
H. One piece, 22 x 15½ x ¾″
I. One piece, 46 x 22 x ¼″
J. One piece, 22 x 14¼ x ¼″
K. Eighteen pieces, each: 18 x 2 x 1″ (eight not shown)
L. Six pieces, each: 25 x 2 x 1″ (two not shown)
LL. Four pieces, each: 30 x 2 x 1″ (two not shown)
M. Eight pieces, each: 12 x 2 x 1″ (three not shown)
N. Eight pieces, each: 14 x 2 x 1″ (not shown)
O. Two pieces, each: 25 x 6 x 1″
P. Three pieces, each: 24 x 4 x ¼″ (one not shown)
Q. Three pieces, each: 24 x 2 x 1″ (one not shown)
R. Two pieces, each: 32 x 2 x 1″
S. One piece, 32 x 26 x ¼″
T. Four doors, each: 23¾ x 14¼ x ¾″ (three not shown)
U. Four doors, each: 23¾ x 12¼ x ¾″ (not shown)
V. One door, 24¼ x 23¾ x ¾″ (not shown)
W. One piece, 64 x 4 x 4″
X. Two pieces, each: 26 x 4 x 4″
Y. One piece, 66 x 33¼ x 1″
Z. Two pieces, each: 66 x 2 x 1″ (one not shown)
AA. Two pieces, each: 91¼ x 5 x 1″ (one not shown)
AB. One fluorescent lamp fixture, 72″
AC. Three pieces, each: 90½ x 24 x ¾″
AD. Twelve pieces, each: 25 x 2 x 1″ (one not shown)
AE. Twenty pieces, each: 16 x 2 x 1″ (nine not shown)
AF. Ten doors, each: 21½ x 16¼ x ¾″ (nine not shown)
AG. Plywood veneer tape, 1200 x 2½″
AH. Plywood veneer tape, 90 x 26″
AI. Plastic laminate, 66 x 33¼″
AJ. Plastic laminate, 135 x 2″
AK. Plastic laminate, 400 x 4″

plastic surface. The counter shelf is secured in place with ¼″ countersunk lag screws through the plywood into the supporting 2-by-4 horizontal beam, before the plastic surfacing is laminated with contact cement as previously described in this chapter.

The amount of damaged plasterboard that remains exposed can be patched by troweling on plaster where necessary, or covering the edges with a frame of attractive wood molding.

An even more useful type of pass-through is this wall divider cabinet which was designed to include a sliding table. This table can be used as an additional working surface in a kitchen with limited space, and converted instantly into a convenient breakfast nook. The smartly styled cabinet in itself increases working efficiency by its special features, such as the lazy Susan shelves which give access to stored items from both sides of the wall.

Note that the table rolls out on either side of the cabinet—for use in the kitchen or in the dining room, as needed, on the same pair of casters, one leg on each side of the cabinet.

The cabinet is built with hardwood veneer plywood over a frame constructed of 1-by-2 stock, while the sliding table is supported on a leg assembly made up of 4-by-4 stock, as shown in the sketch. All exposed plywood edges are dressed with bands of veneer tape to match the basic plywood. These tapes are applied with contact cement, brushed over the edge grain, even though the tapes usually come with a cement coating. The table top is surfaced with plastic laminate, which is also used to cover the table leg stretcher.

The sizes of the wall unit shown in the sketch are those of the cabinet in the photograph. While arbitrary overall dimensions might have been given, they would have affected the resulting list of materials. The dimensions may be altered to a different length or height, as necessary for your particular space and room characteristics, but retain the dimensions of at least the slide-out table and the counter height.

Indirect lighting of both the kitchen and breakfast nook areas is provided by recessed fluorescent lamps, installed at the top of the cabinet.

Great Ideas for Storage Space

Long ago, the only place where food supplies and utensils were kept in the kitchen was the pantry—except for those pots and kettles that were always kept in the open. Modern progress has found space where none existed before, not only in outer space, but right in the kitchen where you'd least expect it or, at least, where it had been overlooked. Here are some typical storage ideas that are so efficient you might be able to adapt them to fit your own home.

KITCHEN ORGANIZER

A kitchen organizer incorporates several smart ideas. The sliding doors serve as small bulletin boards for reminder memos. One is finished with blackboard paint that accepts chalk writing; the other has a cork facing to hold thumb tacks, or a panel of sheet steel for magnetic memo holders.

The spacious top shelf holds all the cookbooks you're likely to own, while the four small drawers at the bottom section can be used for filing recipe cards, small utensils, bills, and so on. The section at the lower left is for the telephone. In this instance, an optional panel holds a wall-mounted type of phone, but if yours is the standard desk type, leave the space open to hold the phone on a corner shelf.

The cabinet is made of ¾″ plywood stock, jointed in rabbet recesses at the corners, with shelves set into shallow dado grooves at the sides. The boxlike section at the bottom may be assembled complete with half-lap center joints, and inserted into the cabinet as a single unit. The shelves behind the sliding doors may be used for keeping telephone directories handy, or may be divided by vertical partitions arranged so that there is easy access when a single door is opened at each side. The cabinet, hung directly on a wall, does not require a back panel.

AN EXTRA STORAGE RACK

Here's how you can make something useful out of nothing—a handy and attractive storage rack formed out of the hollow space inside a partition wall. Only a few pieces of lumber and some plasterboard are needed, which you may already have on hand from a previous project, or which will cost just a few dollars to purchase.

The project consists of cutting away a section of the plasterboard on the kitchen side of the partition, removing one of the studs, then fitting in a neat, new panel at the back, trimming the raw edges of the plaster, and inserting shelves on adjustable metal standards. The work will necessarily cause a bit of mess with broken plaster and plaster dust, but a quick vaccuming will restore all to neat order again.

Spice cupboard is located in what would otherwise be wasted space, a shallow area above the oven.

Sliding drawer hardware has opened what some grateful homemakers could well call a new era of smooth efficiency. The metal slides carry considerable weight, are smooth as silk, and never balk or bind. Seen in photograph are large storage drawer in wall oven cabinet, and a pair of sliding trays that hold an array of utensils in the most convenient manner.

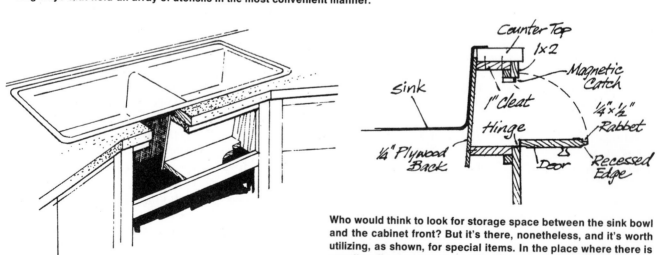

Who would think to look for storage space between the sink bowl and the cabinet front? But it's there, nonetheless, and it's worth utilizing, as shown, for special items. In the place where there is usually a fixed and useless strip of perforated metal, a drop-front door is hinged, providing access to the shallow space in front of the sink bowl. Sketch shows details of the enclosure.

Wall-mounted cabinet serves as a kitchen organizer because it has so many special purpose segments, each designed for a particular use. Hung directly on wall cleats, the cabinet does not need a back panel.

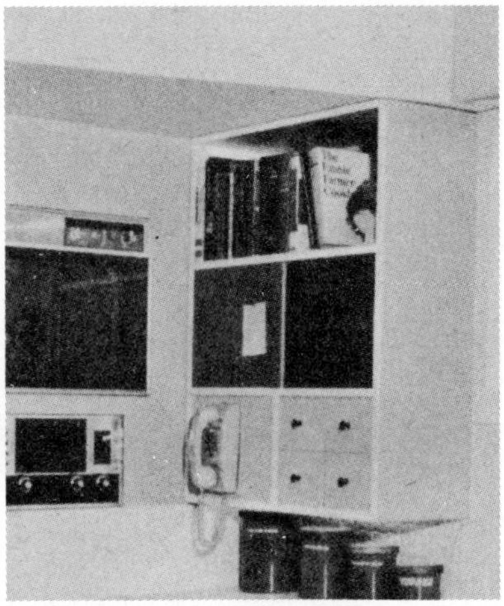

MATERIALS LIST

2 pcs. 33 x 10 x ¾″ sides
2 pcs. 23½ x 10 x ¾″ top and bottom
2 pcs. 23½ x 9 x ¾″ two center shelves
2 pcs. 12½ x 10½ x ⅛″ hardboard doors
2 pcs. 10½ x 10 x ¾″ vertical shelf dividers
1 pc. 10¾ x 10 x ¾″ horizontal drawer separator
1 pc. 10⅞ x 10 x ½″ optional phone panel
1 x ¾″ sliding door track
2 pcs. 1 x ¾″ cleats

Drawers
4 pcs. 5 x 4⅝ x ½″ fronts
8 pcs. 8 x 4⅝ x ½″ sides
4 pcs. 4½ x 4⅛ x ½″ backs
4 pcs. 7 x 4 x ½″ bottoms

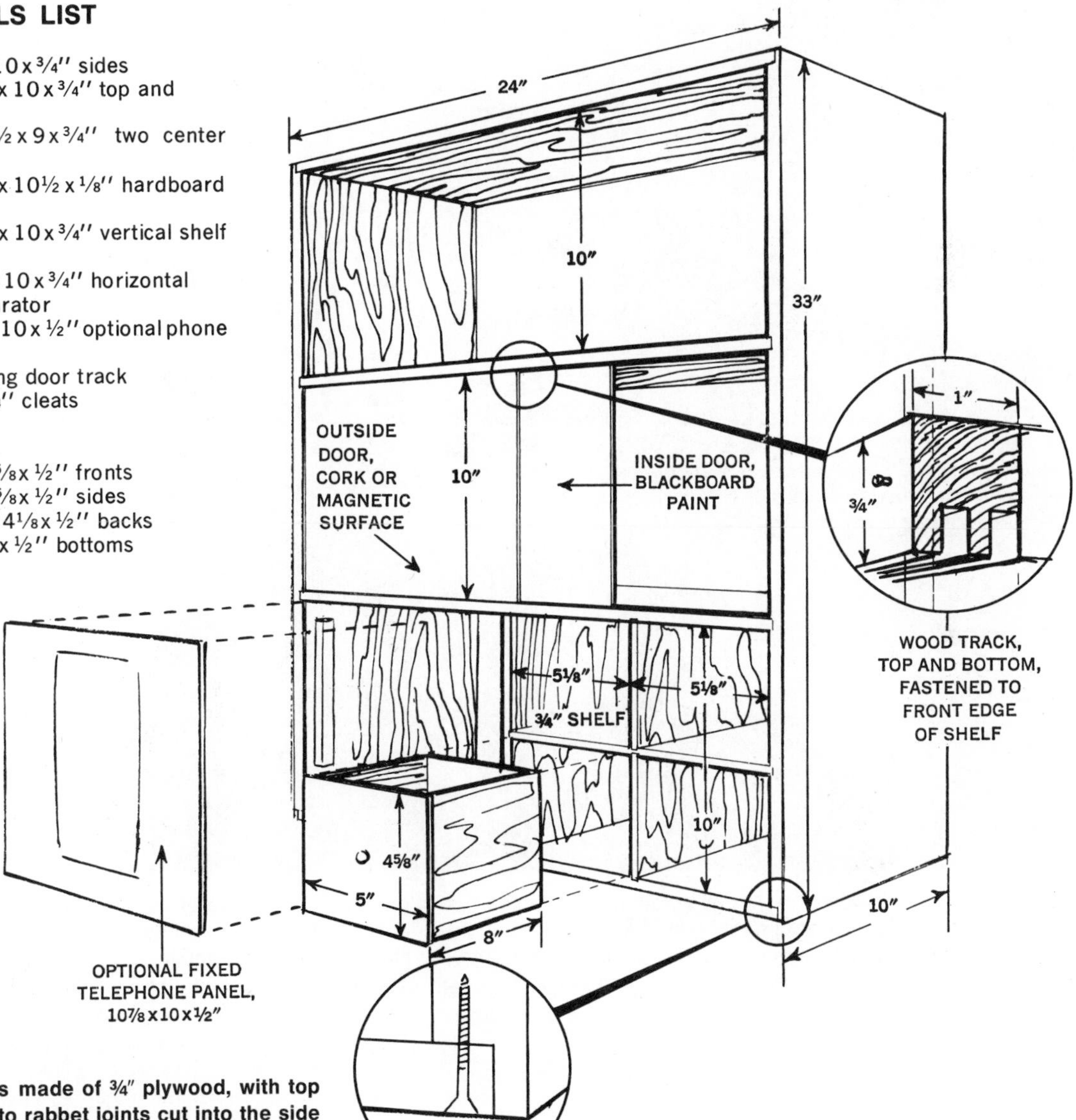

24″
10″
33″
1″
¾″
OUTSIDE DOOR, CORK OR MAGNETIC SURFACE
10″
INSIDE DOOR, BLACKBOARD PAINT
WOOD TRACK, TOP AND BOTTOM, FASTENED TO FRONT EDGE OF SHELF
5⅛″
5⅛″
¾″ SHELF
10″
4⅝″
5″
8″
10″
OPTIONAL FIXED TELEPHONE PANEL, 10⅞ x 10 x ½″

Wall hung cabinet is made of ¾″ plywood, with top and bottom fitted into rabbet joints cut into the side members. The two intermediate shelves are held in dado grooves, while the thin doors slide in double wood or aluminum tracks. Cabinet is hung with iron angles directly on wall cleats.

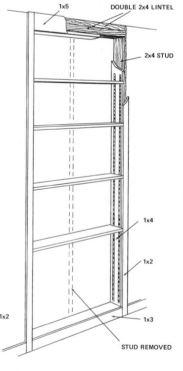

Space where none existed before is obtained by opening a section of the kitchen partition wall. Sketch shows how opening is framed after removal of one stud at center, and breaking out of plasterboard to form the opening. Double 2-by-4's serve as lintel, toenailed to remaining studs. Inside area is finished with 4″-wide stock, on which adjustable shelf standards are attached.

36

Start by breaking a hole in the plaster wall to locate the stud positions. Clear away enough plaster to reach the middle stud, which can be cut at any two or more places with a sabre saw and broken out as high as you can reach. Now you want to cut the plaster neatly along the inside edges of the remaining studs to form the opening.

The quickest way to cut the plaster is with a resin-bonded cutoff disk in a portable circular saw, using the edge of the studs as a straightedge. Another effective way is to nail strips of scrap lumber on the wall directly over those studs, and break out the plaster with a hammer—the top boards will prevent the breaks from going too far. A keyhole saw will cut the plaster more neatly and evenly.

To replace the center stud, make a lintel of a doubled 2-by-4, toenailed up into the side studs, then trim the plaster along the line of that lintel.

The final stages are to cover the inside wall with a clean new piece of gypsum board, then frame the opening with ½" stock, covering the inside studs and also placing 3"- or 4"-wide strips along the outside edges. If much of the plaster has been damaged at the top, where the center stud has been removed, simply place a wider board there, filling the space between the opening and the ceiling.

Adjustable shelf brackets, two on each side, are fastened to the uprights, and shelves of ¾" or 1" stock are cut to fit. The woodwork may be stained or enameled to match your present wall cabinets, or left in the natural wood color with two or three protective coats of shellac.

SPACE INSIDE THE WALL

The spaces inside your walls may be shallow, but they are highly suitable for storage of canned goods, glass jars, and other supplies. If you don't have an ample pantry, here's a way you can utilize the otherwise wasted recesses *inside* a wall. It won't matter, either, whether it's a load-bearing wall, since the studs alone are the supporting members. The wallboard that will be cut away is just covering, and the spaces otherwise serve no purpose in an interior wall.

The cabinets shown in the illustrations were purposely built high on the wall so that the doors would clear the heads of persons seated at the kitchen table below. But you can have these recessed cabinets reach all the way from floor to ceiling if you wish—just make sure to use sliding panels at the lower sections. The sketches show all necessary construction details of the cabinets, including both the hinged and sliding doors.

The complete cabinet takes the place of an old-time pantry, holds as many as 60 cans, or a variety of glass jars and supplies of other food items. The cabinets are practical and easy to reach since the stored items are all in front and solidly supported on short shelves.

The four sections shown here will hold 50 to 60 cans. One advantage of the shallow shelves is that the cans are all up front. There's no reaching, and you can tell at a glance just how much of each kind you have on hand.

Control of food dating is easier, too: make all withdrawals from the lower cabinets, replace with cans from the upper cabinets, and store newest purchases in the top cabinets.

A glance at the sketches will show that the conversion of wall recesses into shallow storage cabinets involves cutting away of the facing plasterboard, framing the opening with thin wood stock, covering the back part of the cabinet with a panel material, fitting in the shelves, and installing the doors.

The only difficulty that may be encountered is if you find plumbing, heating, or electrical lines within the selected area. So before starting, check in the basement and on the floor above for pipes, ducts, cables, or radiators.

You may not be able to find anything and still come across one or another obstruction later. You can still proceed, either by skipping that one sec-

Think you've run out of available space? Now put the recesses in your walls to work, as an auxiliary and very handy pantry. Cabinets are shallow, but practical.

tion and using those on both sides or by framing out the obstruction so that you can use the area with shorter shelves, while proceeding with the others as full-width cabinets. If there are electric cables, either armored BX or conduit, it's all right to notch the shelves to clear them. Just be careful about driving nails nearby.

The first step is to locate a wall stud, and drop a plumb line to mark the full cutout. Do this at both sides of each stud, since you want to cut the plasterboard without damaging the studs in any way. The cutting may be done with a sabre saw, using a hardened hack-saw-type blade, or with a keyhole type saw. Best for this purpose is the Stanley Wallboard Saw No. 39-206, designed especially for plasterboard cutting. Drill holes at the corners of the marked area for starting the saw blade. Cover the floor with a painter's drop cloth to catch the plaster dust and pieces of the plasterboard.

You won't be able to cut away the pieces of plaster that will remain nailed to the face of each stud. The plaster can be removed with a chisel and a nail puller, or just left where it is, to be covered later with the vertical strips that will trim the outside of each cabinet.

Locate wall studs, mark outline for opening wall by removing sections of the plasterboard. Cutting is best done with special wallboard saw, hardened to stand up against plaster. Then, as shown below, attach 1-by-1 cleats to side of the wall studs with nails and glue. Cut Marlite plastic-coated hardboard into pieces to cover back wall of the openings. Apply adhesive with notched spreader.

One 4'-by-8' panel of Marlite plastic-coated hard-board, plus a small quantity of ⅜" and ¾" ply-wood, and some 1"-by-1" scraps, will suffice to complete the row of cabinets illustrated. The Marlite can be cut with a bench saw, circular saw, sabre saw, or fine-tooth hand saw. When using a saw that cuts on the up-stroke, such as the portable saw, cut the panel with the finished surface face down.

After the wall opening is completed, start the fittings as shown in the sketch. Cut a number of 1-by-1 cleats, about 3½" long, drive in 6d finishing nails until the points just come through. Then, using glue as well as the nails, fasten the cleats to the side of each exposed stud, so that the top of the cleat is flush with the lower edge of the wall open-ing.

Next cut the Marlite into panels that will fit into the openings. Make the panels a little longer so that the top edges will be covered with the in-side framing members. The panels are cemented into place, using a special adhesive applied to the backs with a notched spreader. Slip these panels into place, press firmly against the back wall, and rest the bottom edge on the stud cleats.

The bottom shelf is next, supported by the cleats, followed by a Marlite strip across the top. The side panels, each about 5¼" high, are in-stalled in matching pairs, simultaneously with the shelves that they support. Two panels are glued in, the shelf set in place resting on the panel edges, then the next pair of panels and another shelf. Fi-nally, the front of the opening is trimmed all around with 2"-wide strips. First the end facings go on, top to bottom; then strips the entire length hor-izontally across the cabinets, top and bottom, and finally facings over the intermediate studs.

Door construction is kept as basic as possible. The hinged doors are composed by laminating a Marlite facing to a piece of ⅜" plywood that just fits the cabinet opening, but the Marlite surface overlaps ⅜" on all sides. For a neater appearance, shape the Marlite edges as shown. The doors are hung with offset hinges made for ⅜" overlap.

The sliding door is even simpler, consisting merely of ¼" Marlite panels, sliding in top and bottom aluminum tracks. When using the sliding doors, omit the facing trim at intermediate studs, and use the cabinets in pairs, so that the door of one cabinet when opened will slide across over the front of the matching cabinet.

The screws holding the aluminum track must be deeply counterset so that the screwheads won't

Slip Marlite pieces into openings, press firmly against the back wall, and rest bottom edges on the stud cleats. Glassy smooth Marlite surface makes for easier cleaning, colors add brightness.

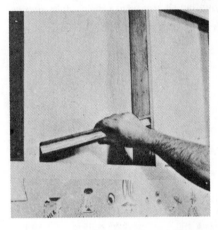

Bottom shelf is inserted, with glue for bonding to the supporting cleats and the back panel.

Shelves are inserted above each pair of side panels, which are glued to the studs. If you wish, provide some clearance for removal of the middle shelves so the back panel may be washed periodically.

Strips of 2"-wide stock frame out the entire opening, trim the rough-cut plasterboard edges, and also cover the front edges of the studs.

Doors are attractive with their Marlite facing, which also provides a slight overlap all around to keep cabinet interior free of dust.

block movement of the door panels. To install a door, raise the panel high into the upper track, then ease it down so the lower edge fits into the bottom track. And that's it!

Lighting the Kitchen

Good lighting is as important as any other detail in creating the qualities that make up the modern kitchen. Just as so many new materials and improved devices make the kitchens more pleasant and efficient, so also have there been considerable advances in lighting equipment, not only in the types of fixtures but also in a whole new concept of complete illumination, achieved by luminous ceilings, which cover every part of the room uniformly,

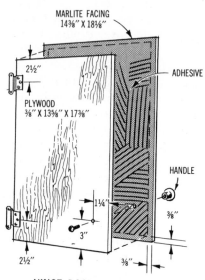

MARLITE FACING
14⅜″ X 18⅛″

2½″

PLYWOOD
⅜″ X 13⅝″ X 17⅜″

ADHESIVE

HANDLE

1¼″

3″

2½″

⅜″

⅜″

HINGE DOOR DETAIL

Hinged door overlaps surface ⅜″ all around. This is accomplished by laminating a Marlite facing to the ⅜″ plywood door insert which is sized to fit opening. The Marlite, with rounded edges, is ⅜″ larger than the backing panel on all sides.

MATERIALS LIST

(Panel parts numbered in order of installation)

Part	Description	Dimensions	Quantity
1	rear panels	14¼″ × 19″	4
2	bottom shelves	3⅞″ × 14⅜″	4
3	side panels	3⅞″ × 5½″	8
4	side panels	3⅞″ × 5½″	8
5	side panels	3⅞″ × 5⅝″	8
6	top panels	3⅞″ × 14⅜″	4
7	end facings	3¾″ × 21⅝″	2
8	top and bottom facings	2″ × 62″	2
9	divider facings	2″ × 17⅝″	3
10	doors	14½″ × 18⅛″	4
	¾″ plywood bottom shelves	3⅜″ × 14⅜″	4
	⅜″ plywood shelves	3½″ × 14⅜″	8
	⅜″ plywood doors	13¾″ × 17⅜″	4
	1 × 1 cleats	3⅝″	8

Hardware: 4 door pulls; 4 magnetic latches; 4 pairs ⅜″ offset hinges; nails; waterproof adhesive.

Note: Dimensions above apply only when studs are spaced exactly 16″ o.c., are full 1⅝″ × 3⅝″ actual dimension, and wall is ½″ gypsum wallboard or other ½″ material. Any deviation, such as studs dressed undersize or inaccurately spaced, or wall thickness greater than ½″ can be compensated by cutting individual parts to fit as cabinets are assembled. Differences in dimensions will be slight, so basic cutting diagram can be followed to get all required material from one 4′ × 8′ Marlite panel.

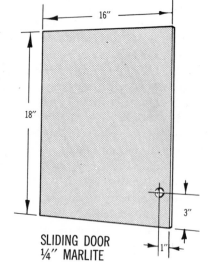

16″

18″

3″

1″

SLIDING DOOR
¼″ MARLITE

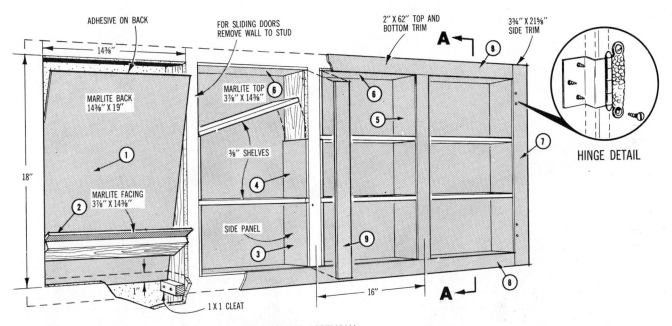

ADHESIVE ON BACK

FOR SLIDING DOORS
REMOVE WALL TO STUD

2" X 62" TOP AND
BOTTOM TRIM

3¾" X 21⅝"
SIDE TRIM

A

⑧

14⅜"

MARLITE BACK
14⅜" X 19"

MARLITE TOP
3⅞" X 14⅜" ⑥

⑥

18"

①

⑤

⑦

HINGE DETAIL

⅜" SHELVES

MARLITE FACING
3⅞" X 14⅜"

②

④

SIDE PANEL

③

⑨

1"

1 X 1 CLEAT

⑧

16"

A

CABINET ASSEMBLY

Cutaway sketch shows construction of the wall recess cabinets. Parts are numbered in the sequence of their installation. Circled blowup shows details of offset hinge. Precise dimensions are not given as there usually is some variation in stud thickness and spacings, which will affect slightly the sizes of the cabinet parts. The quantity of each part needed will depend on the number of individual cabinet sections to be constructed.

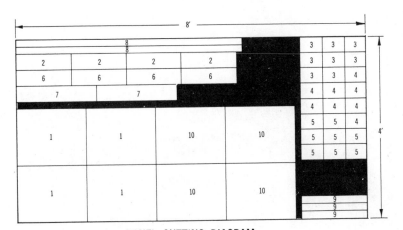

8'

				8		
				8		
2	2	2	2	3	3	3
6	6	6	6	3	3	3
7		7		3	3	4
				4	4	4
				4	4	4
1	1	10	10	5	5	4
				5	5	5
				5	5	5
1	1	10	10			
				9		
				9		
				9		

4'

PANEL CUTTING DIAGRAM

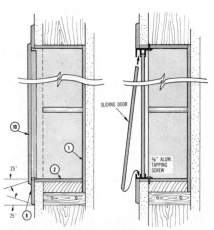

⑩

SLIDING DOOR

①

②

⑤⁄₃₂" ALUM.
TAPPING
SCREW

25°

25° ⑧

HINGED DOOR
SECTION A-A

SLIDING DOOR SECTION

Cross section shows how hinged door partly overlaps the opening. The curve of the Marlite edges is given for guidance, but any radius curve will achieve the result of reducing the visible thickness. The sliding door is wider than the wall opening, since it covers the center stud at that position. Facing trim of that stud is omitted for door clearance.

The newest word in kitchen lighting is the luminescent ceiling, comprising box-like areas that are fully illuminated, providing a diffused but non-reflective brightness in the kitchen.

without glaring hot spots and without shadows. All this adds up to brighter, better kitchens, the kind you love to live in, the kind you enjoy working in, and having the family gather in.

The latest word in ceilings is the illuminated variety with built-in box beams, truly an attractive feature in remodeling plans. If the old ceiling is in disrepair, don't bother patching and painting—with doubtful results—since the new beam ceiling completely covers the old.

Complete layout flexibility is permitted by the modular panels which fit between ceiling channels. Light fixtures can be located above work areas, a breakfast bar, or wherever desired, and a translucent plastic diffuser is placed in the channels to transmit the light.

The idea is particularly useful for the older home with very high ceilings, since the new ceiling can be set at any desired height. Even with conventional ceilings, there is a loss of only a couple of inches for the panels. The depth of the box beams does not visually detract from the ceiling height.

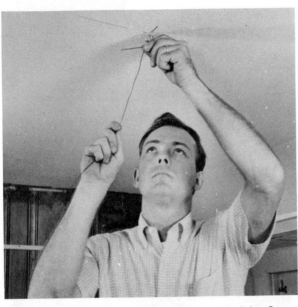

Nail molding around the room at desired height. Screw steel eyelets into joists on 4' centers, and attach lengths of no. 12 steel wire to support the beams.

Box beams are prefinished, wood-grained sheet steel, which are cut to length with hack saw. The ends rest on the wall molding; wires from ceiling eyelets add support.

Four-foot across tees are installed between the main runners at 24" intervals. Special end tabs on tees fit into slots in flange of beams. Bend tabs to lock them in place.

With beams and tees in place, ceiling panels are laid into the grid. When the panel is tilted slightly, it fits through opening and comes to rest on the grid flanges.

Close-up views of suspended ceiling system in other installations show alternate pattern of light diffusers. As they have the same dimensions as the normal ceiling panels, they can be interchanged freely and relocated.

Chapter 2
MORE SPACE FOR GROWING KIDS

Of all the household-variety problems befalling large families, none are as immediate or ponderous as what to do about more space. In a disenchanted sort of way, home owners see their once spacious ranch literally closing in on them, particularly where children are concerned. Gangly little girls take on ladylike ways, pouting for a room all their own, Saturday's hero demands quiet for study (as well as immunity against curious little brothers), and the youngest ones, of course, require some semblance of room order, despite their riotous living.

In doing something about it, images of dollar signs needn't delay or change the basic course. Renovations are nice, additions even nicer, but these visions shouldn't becloud the key elements in the space struggle—primarily simple but smart built-ins, dividers, and convertibles. Thus previously cramped quarters are magically transformed into attractive, orderly, and livable rooms for work, play, or sleep. The budget is kept to a sensible level through do-it-yourself, the kids take a proud attitude in their special accommodations, and mothers are given a lift in housekeeping chores when there is a place for everything.

The place to start is on one or more of the following pages of simple projects. Study the basic ideas, feeling free to condense or expand the plans, for the construction and materials will literally fit any mold. Remember, too, that any of the wall-type built-ins can be used as free-standing units (back-to-back for twice as much inner space), thus serving as dividers or separators.

ROOM DIVIDER

You'll have to go a long way to find a room divider as ingenious as this one—a substantial unit housing six drawers on each side of the louvered partition, a desk or dressing table in each section, all surfaced with attractive and carefree Formica

laminate. The single beds are identical in construction, but very different in styling.

Length of the divider will be determined, in any room, by the door position, allowing ample clearance for passage to both sides. The unit is built largely of ¾" plywood, of which all exposed surfaces will be covered with the plastic sheeting. Framing consists of 2-by-3 and 1-by-2 stock, as shown, while the base contains a 1-by-4 kickboard along its length. The bureau top and two desk tops are ¾" plywood panels. The desks are supported on wall cleats. The boy's desk also has a lathe-turned leg representing a sentry on guard—the contours are shown in the drawing which can be copied on 1" square graph paper, for duplication either in a lathe, or by profile cutout from a piece of 1-by-6 stock.

The louvers are 1"-by-10" boards, each panel fitted with a short dowel at the center, top, and bot-

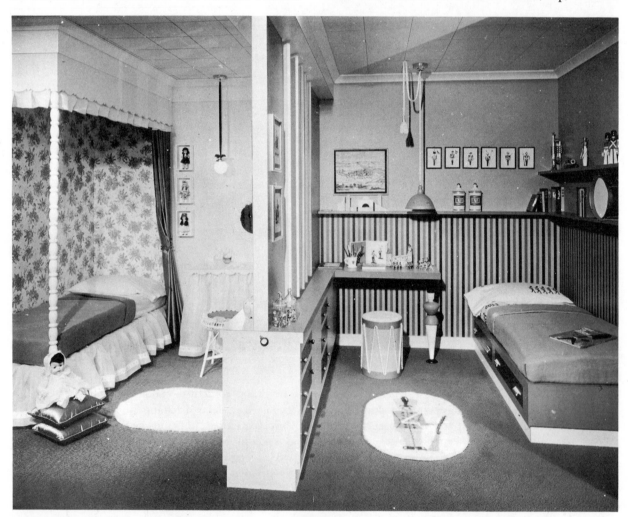

This ingenious room divider creates the privacy your youngsters require—and, as a bonus, each child gets a desk and twelve new drawers to take care of storage problems.

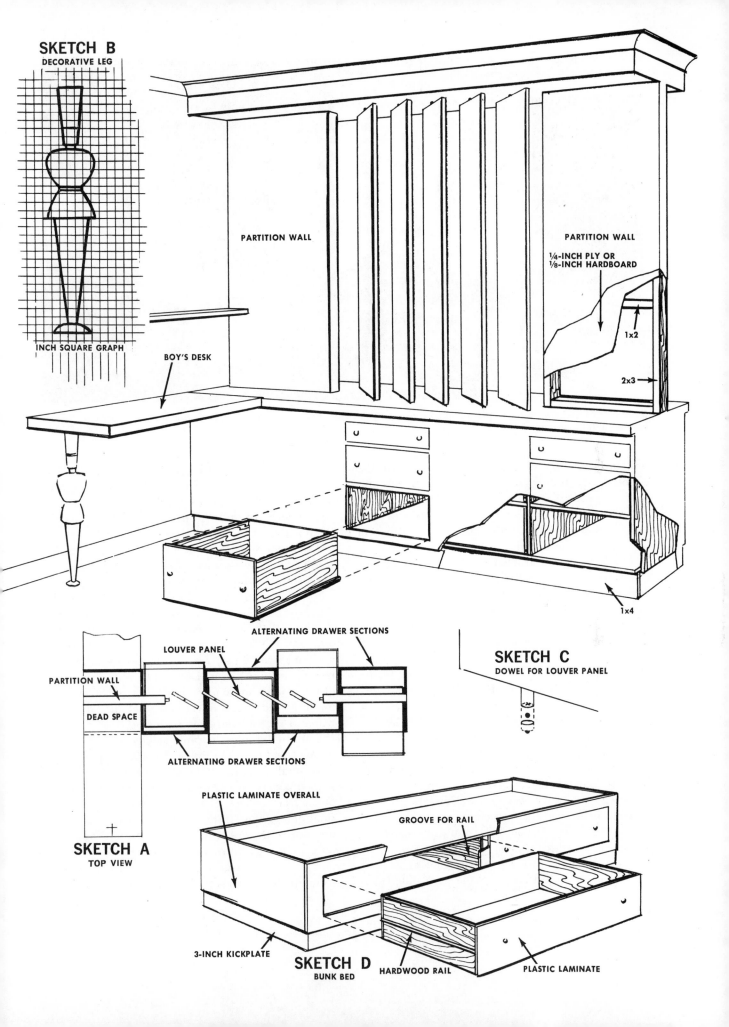

SKETCH B
DECORATIVE LEG

INCH SQUARE GRAPH

PARTITION WALL

PARTITION WALL

¼-INCH PLY OR
⅛-INCH HARDBOARD

1x2

2x3

BOY'S DESK

1x4

ALTERNATING DRAWER SECTIONS

LOUVER PANEL

SKETCH C
DOWEL FOR LOUVER PANEL

PARTITION WALL

DEAD SPACE

ALTERNATING DRAWER SECTIONS

SKETCH A
TOP VIEW

PLASTIC LAMINATE OVERALL

GROOVE FOR RAIL

3-INCH KICKPLATE

SKETCH D
BUNK BED

HARDWOOD RAIL

PLASTIC LAMINATE

Built-in beds that pull up out of the way give your youngsters plenty of play area when beds are not in use. Just look at all that storage space!

tom, for pivoting in corresponding holes in the counter top and overhead. The top dowels are longer to permit installation by first lifting the louver higher to clear the counter, then allowing the bottom dowel to drop into place. For information on applying the Formica laminate, see Chapter 1.

The beds are constructed of ¾" plywood sections like open boxes raised on 1-by-3 baseboards. Provide cutouts for the drawer openings, using ¾" dividers grooved for the drawer rails, and to give added support to the ¾" panel that will rest on cleats all around to hold the mattress.

ROOM FOR TWO

Do you have to shoehorn a teen-ager and a younger child into the same room? Here's a solution that not only provides both children a measure of privacy but also assures them of maximum space to pursue their individual interests. This is achieved by folding beds and considerable storage space to help keep the area clear.

The room divider doubles as a hideaway for two full-size beds, which do not need fixed supports because of the novel suspension arrangement.

The entire project can be made from pine. As is

usual in projects of this type, the fixed portions of it should be built first, with movable portions such as the bed (S,T) and its supports (R) being built last. There are bullet-stop catches (AE) embedded in the edge of piece S that serve as a bed stop.

Most pieces of the project can be joined together using simple butt joints, nails, and glue. One of the exceptions to this is the bookcase portion, most of whose shelves (L) are dadoed into the uprights (E). The overhead storage cabinets located in the upper portions of the room divider open from either side and use a different type of joint. Both its center and end boards (M) are notched in the middle to receive the crosspieces (L,PP). The center piece (H) of the storage space underneath the beds is notched on either side of its lower end to fit into the space between the two horizontal pieces (G).

Start by building a frame against the wall using items B and C in the list of materials as part of the horizontal framing elements at top and bottom with pieces A and D forming the vertical elements of the frame. Pieces E and F are then used to cover the frame. Before installing the piece (E) that forms one side of the bookcase, it is a good idea to cut dadoes in it to receive the horizontal members (L).

Two of the uprights (F) are anchored to the floor using angle irons (W). Additional anchoring is obtained by securing Q to ceiling joists with screws and attaching PP to it.

BUNK BED COMBO

Here's another project that will take care of the needs of two young boys in one room. This easy-to-make bunk bed has a platform that pulls out on which you can install a good-sized train-track layout. And if your boys' room already has sufficient space for a train track, why then, you could use the platform as a movable storage shelf or as an additional bed if your family grows larger and you find that you need more space.

The partition behind the bed is an effective room divider to separate the sleep and play areas from the study areas. The framework of the partition is made up of 2-by-2's and is anchored to the wall on the left side with 4" lag screws driven through piece C. Left side of the partition is covered with painted plywood (KK) and the remain-

der (LL) with veneer plywood or woodgrain hardboard. The reverse side of the partition is covered with plywood (Y) that goes all the way to the floor.

As can be seen from the diagram, this project is relatively easy to build. There are, however, a few construction details that should be pointed out.

Piece A should be anchored firmly to the floor with screws. Detail 2 shows the way pieces A, F, C, and G are joined together to form a strong corner. As can be seen from detail 3, Piece D has been deliberately installed a bit higher than piece LL and KK. Piece OO, a ½" plywood sheet (not shown) fits on the exposed end of the bunk. Detail 1 shows one-half of the pattern that fits on the wall which can be made of ⅛" hardboard.

Note that the blocks (Q) above the casters are cut to fit. The thickness of these blocks depends on the total height of the casters. The combined thickness of the blocks and height of casters should allow ¼" clearance off the floor for the front of the rolling shelf (T).

The little rope ladder and the open barrel are

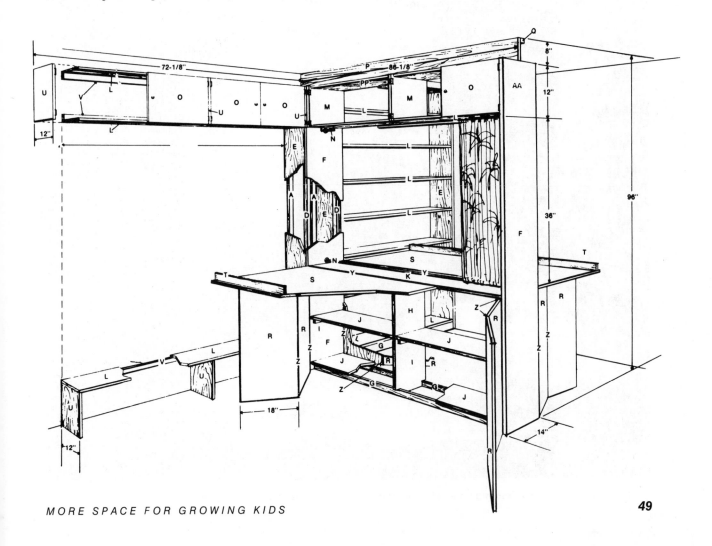

play devices that simulate a ship's ladder or rigging going up to a crow's nest. You may wish to add these to the project.

The finishing of the project is up to your own discretion but, as you can see, the method used in the photo does come off quite nicely.

BUILT-IN BUNK BEDS

Here's an attractive project for the home owner who likes built-in bunk beds. They are easy to make and have a neat, clean, uncluttered look about them. The dimensions given are for a mattress and box spring 6′ long and 3′ wide. Different sizes will require a few changes in the measurements.

Basically, the bunk beds consist of a framework, a shell, and a storage drawer. The framework is made up of two parallel frames of 2-by-3's, one above the other (A), connected to each other by short lengths (G) of 2-by-3 lumber. The crossbars of the upper and lower frames are connected to the longer members with half-lap joints. In the upper frame, midway between the central and end crossbars, there are additional supports (D). These are 1-by-3's (one each side of the central cross-bar) dadoed into the sidebars (B) of the frame. They provide the extra support that prevents the dust cover (E) from sagging. The dust cover, a ⅛″ sheet of tempered hardboard, keeps dust from accumulating under the bed or getting into the storage drawer. The frames should be made 1″ larger on all four sides than the box spring and mattress to allow room to tuck in blankets and covers.

The shell is made of ¾″ plywood and is nailed and glued to the framework. The two ends (K) are each plywood pieces nailed to spacers (P) on the

Give your two "seafarers" room galore with this nautical arrangement. The project provides ample area for sleep, study, and play.

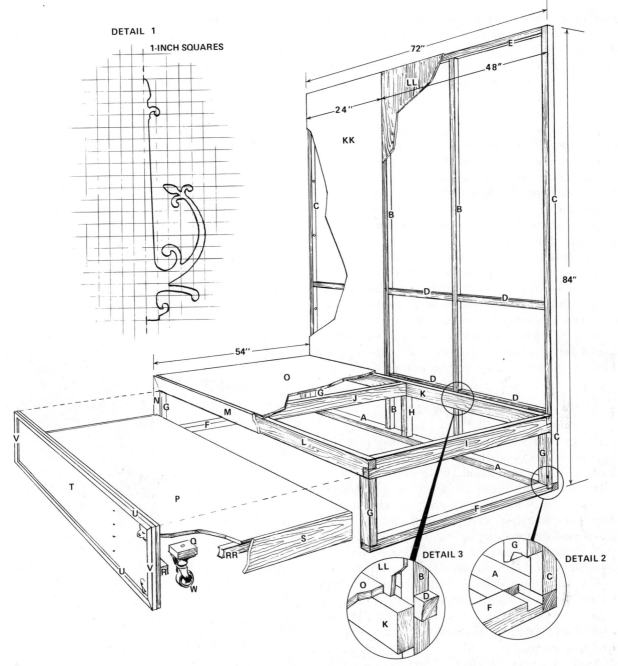

DETAIL 1
1-INCH SQUARES

72"
48"
24"
84"
54"

LL
KK
E
C
B
D
N G
V
T
P
U
Q
RR
S
R
W
M
F
L
O
G
J
A
B
H
K
I
G
D

DETAIL 3
DETAIL 2

MATERIALS LIST

A. One piece, 72 x 1½ x 1½"
B. Two pieces, each: 81 x 1½ x 1½"
C. Two pieces, each: 82½ x 1½ x 1½" (one not shown)
D. Six pieces, each: 22 x 1½ x 1½"
E. One piece, 69 x 1½ x 1½"
F. Two pieces, each: 54 x 2½ x 1½"
G. Four pieces, each: 11¾ x 2½ x 1½"
H. One piece, 11 x 2½ x 1½"
I. Two pieces, each: 54 x 3½ x 1½" (one not shown)

J. One piece, 50¼ x 3½ x 1½"
K. One piece, 69 x 3½ x 1½"
KK. One piece, 68 x 24 x ¼"
L. One piece, 72 x 3½ x 1½"
LL. One piece, 68 x 42 x ¼"
M. One piece, 72 x 4 x ¾"
N. Two pieces, each: 16 x 2½ x ¾" (one not shown)
O. One piece, 72 x 54 x ½"
OO. One piece, 54 x 16 x ½" (not shown)
P. One piece, 67 x 51½ x ¾"
Q. Four pieces, each: 48½ x 3½ x 1½" (three not shown; cut to fit)

R. One piece, each: 67 x 1½ x 1½" (one not shown)
RR. Two pieces, each: 50 x 1½ 1½" (one not shown)
S. Two pieces, each: 51½ x 5½ x ¾"
T. One piece, 68½ x 12 x ¾"
U. Two pieces, each: 68½ x 1 x ½"
V. Two pieces, each: 12 x 1 x ½"
W. Four plate swivel casters (1½" diameter wheel; three not shown)
X. Two pieces, each: 20 x 10 x ⅛ (shown in Detail 1 only)
Y. One piece, 84 x 72 x ¼"

MORE SPACE FOR GROWING KIDS

ends of the framework as shown in the corner detail. The upper parts of the ends are attached to the back (Q) and to the corner posts in front with angle irons. The back is a single sheet of ⅜" plywood and functions mainly as a dust cover.

The shell has two drawer fronts, one of which (the left) is a dummy, and one long piece (I) which forms the upper part. The upper part is nailed and glued along its lower edge to the frame and is attached to the corner posts (C) with angle irons. The ends of this piece should be driven through the corner posts into these glued ends. To make the rest of the front flush with the upper part, 1-by-2 material is nailed to the spaces (F) around and beneath the drawer fronts.

The drawer sides and back are made of ½" plywood and are rabbeted together. The bottom is ¼" plywood and fits into a groove ½" from the bottom of the sides. The front is made of ¾" plywood and is rabbeted all around its inner edges to overlap the front by ⅜". The outer edges of both drawer fronts are slightly rounded. The bottom edge of the back is notched to ride on the drawer guide (J).

BUNKHOUSE WALL

If they can't have a room of their own, give the youngsters a wall of their own—that is, a bunkhouse wall done in natural knotty pine.

Using 1"-by-12" knotty pine shelving, you'll have a handy dimension to work with for the hinged doors, dropleaf desk, wall paneling, and the edge-glued platforms making up the two bunks.

The two end components of cabinetry serve as the framework for the dropleaf bunk beds between.

The base for the bunk bed consists of three boards, doweled and edge-glued. Upon this platform is an inner frame of ¾"-by-4" strips, set on edge. This framework serves as an inset for a foam rubber mattress.

Detail A shows the specifics for anchoring the supporting chain to the bed's platform—the device being a length of strap steel, shaped in the profile shown. Note that the mattress framework is slotted to accept the bracket, and that the base is screwed to the platform in four places—two from above, one from below and one from the side.

Note that the bed, when folded into the wall, appears to have an inlaid effect. Actually, the mattress framework is secured to the bed's platform with screws from the outside, the screw heads being concealed by the molding all around. For a finishing touch, the outside band is painted a bright color.

The space under the folding bunks wisely is put to use for three separate storage boxes, the center one in a fixed position with a bottom-hinged door. The two boxes on either side are removable with lift-up lids, serving for storage as well as for seating.

Dimensions are not given in the sketch, as they will vary according to your available space and other factors.

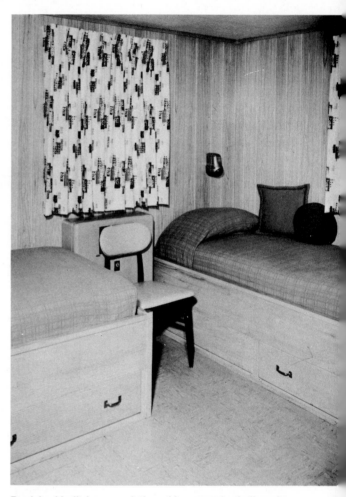

Bunk bed built-ins, consisting of framework, shell, and a storage drawer, give room a neat, uncluttered look.

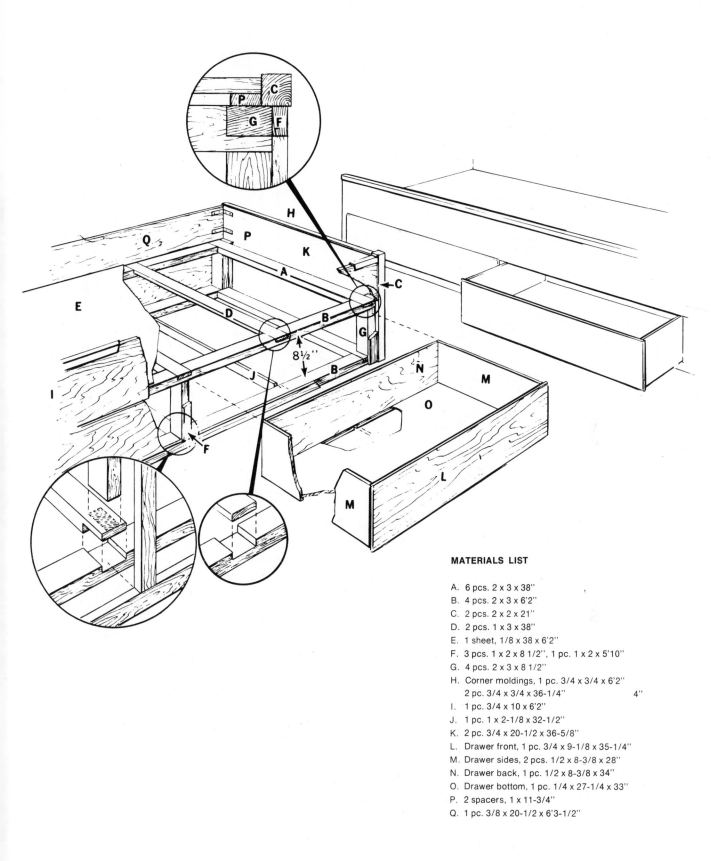

MATERIALS LIST

A. 6 pcs. 2 x 3 x 38"
B. 4 pcs. 2 x 3 x 6'2"
C. 2 pcs. 2 x 2 x 21"
D. 2 pcs. 1 x 3 x 38"
E. 1 sheet, 1/8 x 38 x 6'2"
F. 3 pcs. 1 x 2 x 8 1/2", 1 pc. 1 x 2 x 5'10"
G. 4 pcs. 2 x 3 x 8 1/2"
H. Corner moldings, 1 pc. 3/4 x 3/4 x 6'2"
   2 pc. 3/4 x 3/4 x 36-1/4"   4"
I. 1 pc. 3/4 x 10 x 6'2"
J. 1 pc. 1 x 2-1/8 x 32-1/2"
K. 2 pc. 3/4 x 20-1/2 x 36-5/8"
L. Drawer front, 1 pc. 3/4 x 9-1/8 x 35-1/4"
M. Drawer sides, 2 pcs. 1/2 x 8-3/8 x 28"
N. Drawer back, 1 pc. 1/2 x 8-3/8 x 34"
O. Drawer bottom, 1 pc. 1/4 x 27-1/4 x 33"
P. 2 spacers, 1 x 11-3/4"
Q. 1 pc. 3/8 x 20-1/2 x 6'3-1/2"

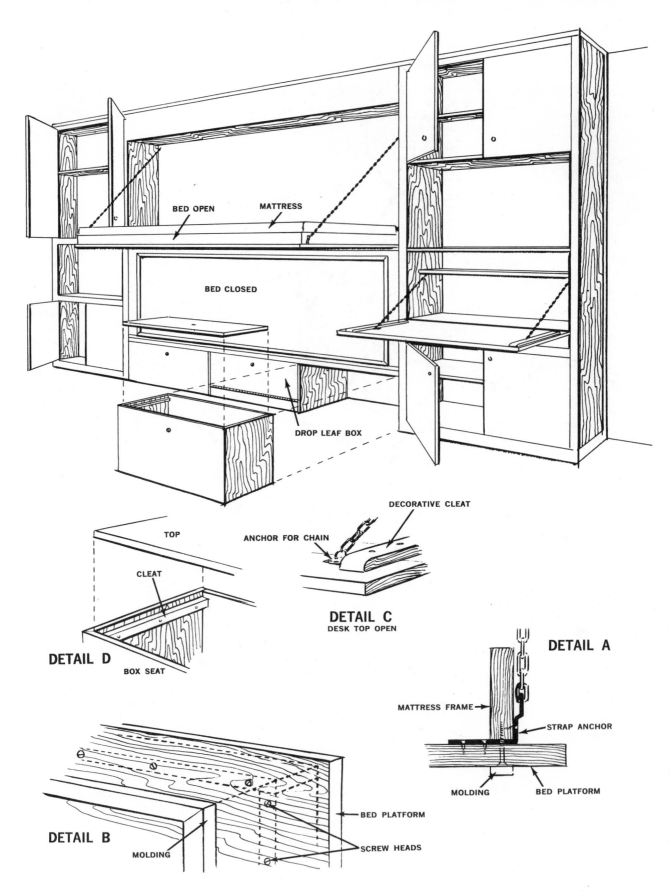

BED OPEN

MATTRESS

BED CLOSED

DROP LEAF BOX

DECORATIVE CLEAT

ANCHOR FOR CHAIN

DETAIL C
DESK TOP OPEN

TOP

CLEAT

DETAIL D

BOX SEAT

DETAIL A

MATTRESS FRAME →

STRAP ANCHOR

MOLDING   BED PLATFORM

BED PLATFORM

DETAIL B

MOLDING

SCREW HEADS

Dropleaf bunk beds solve the problem of a limited amount of space in a bedroom for two active youngsters. Note the inlaid effect created by the bed that is folded up.

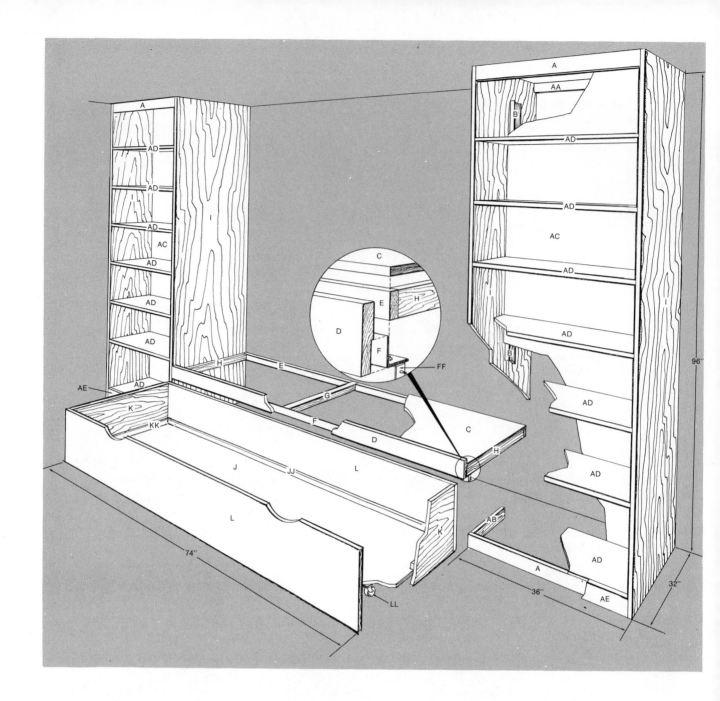

MATERIALS LIST

BED

A. Four pieces, each: 34½ x 4 x 1″
AA. Two pieces, each: 34½ x 2 x 2″
AB. Four pieces, each: 31 x 3 x 1″
AC. Two pieces, each: 96 x 34 x ¼″
AD. Fourteen pieces, each: 34½ x 12 x 1″
AE. Two pieces, each: 34½ x 5 x 1″
B. Four pieces, each: 96 x 2 x 1″
C. One piece, 74 x 31 x ½″
D. One piece, 74 x 4 x 1″
E. One piece, 74 x 2 x 1″

F. One steel angle iron, 74 x 2 x 2″
FF. Two angle irons, each: 2 x 2 x 1″
G. One piece, 30¾ x 2 x 2″
H. Two pieces, each: 29¾ x 2 x 1″
I. Four pieces, each: 96 x 32 x ¾″
J. One piece, 72½ x 30½ x ¾″
JJ. Two pieces, each: 72½ x 2 x 1″
K. Two pieces, each: 30½ x 14 x ¾″
KK. Two pieces, each: 28½ x 2 x 1″
L. Two pieces, each: 74 x 14 x ¾″
LL. Four casters with 1½″ soft rubber tires

GIRL'S ROOM

This built-in bunk, storage drawer, shelves, and desk arrangement for a girl's room makes an attractive and practical combination.

The two bookshelves are made of ¾" plywood with shelves that are glued and nailed through the sides. To avoid making the shelves too deep, cleats (B) are nailed to the inner surfaces of the sides. The ¼" plywood that forms the back of the shelves is nailed to these cleats as well as the back of each shelf. A 1-by-4 facing (A) provides additional reinforcement at the top in front.

The ½" plywood sheet (C) that supports the 4" thick foam mattress of the bunk bed rests on cleats (E,H) which are nailed to the studs of the back wall and to the inner sides of the bookshelves (I). A brace (G) half-lapped to the side cleats (E) helps prevent any possible sagging of the plywood sheet (C) which is nailed and glued to the cleats.

To strengthen the front edge of the bed on which an adult might sit, the 1-by-4 facing (D) is reinforced by a steel angle iron which runs along the full length of the facing on the inner side and is screwed to it. A pair of 2" angle irons supports the ends of the long angle iron (F) and are screwed to the sides of the bookshelves (I) and bolted to F as shown in the detail.

The bunk bed should provide a 1" space all around the mattress to permit the tucking in of blankets and sheets without cramping the fingers. The storage drawer may be used as a second bed if you have two children in this room. The second bed is simply a large box made of ¾" plywood and is glued and nailed with butt joints.

The ¾" plywood sheet (J) that supports the mattress in this drawer bed is attached to the sides (L) and ends (K) with nails and glue. The exact position of this plywood sheet inside the box depends on the thickness of the mattress, which should come no higher than ½" below the top of the drawer.

Four casters with 1½" soft rubber tires attached to the bottom of the plywood sheet (J) will permit the bed to be moved in and out with the greatest of ease. If the bottom of the plywood sheet is too high for the casters, use wooden blocks glued to the underside of the sheet to make up the difference. The caster wheels should protrude at least ¼" below the bottom edges of the sides.

The girl's desk seen at the left in front of the window, is modernistic and unusual, yet eminently practical, the open left side permits a child to

MATERIALS LIST

DESK

A. One piece, 36 x 18 x 1"
B. One piece, 34 x 2 x 2"
C. One piece, 36 x 3 x 1"
D. One piece, 17 x 3 x 1"
E. Three pieces, each:
   17 x 12 x 1"
EE. One piece, 17 x 12 x 1"
F. Four pieces, each:
   17³⁄₁₆ x 5³⁄₁₆ x ½"
G. Two pieces, each:
   11⅞ x 5³⁄₁₆ x ½"
H. Two pieces, each:
   14 x 4¹⁵⁄₁₆ x ¾"
I. Two pieces, each:
   16¹⁵⁄₁₆ x 12 x ¼"

J. Two drawers, each:
   one front,
      14 x 2¹⁵⁄₁₆ x ¾";
   two sides,
      17³⁄₁₆ x 2³⁄₁₆ x ½";
   one back,
      11⅞ x 2³⁄₁₆ x ½";
   one bottom,
      16¹⁵⁄₁₆ x 12 x ¼"
K. Two pieces, each:
   17 x 2 x 1"
L. Two pieces, each:
   25 x 17 x 1"
M. Two pieces, each:
   17 x 3 x 1"
N. One piece, 14 x 4 x 1"

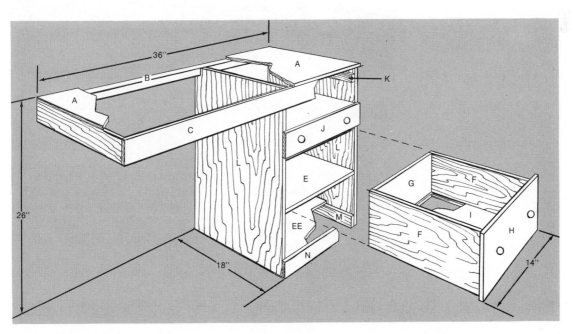

57

swing her legs in or out under the desk with ease and comfort.

The desk top (A) is nailed to a cleat (B) which is fastened to the wall with screws and is also nailed to the apron supports D and C. The butt-joint outer corners (B-D, C-D) are reinforced on the insides with 2″ angle irons. The wall cleat (B) and front apron (C) are nailed and glued to the sides of (L) of the drawer cabinet. The shelves on which the drawers slide (E) are fastened in place with finishing nails driven through the sides (L). However, the bottom shelf (EE) rests on two side cleats (M) as well as one in the back against the wall.

Note that the drawer fronts (H,J) overlap the edges of the sides (L) and that their ends are flush with the sides.

The drawers are very simply made of ½″ plywood (F,F,G) with glued and nailed butt joints. The drawer fronts (H,J) are made of ¾″ lumber and, like the sides and back (G) are grooved to receive the ¼″ plywood bottom (I).

The decorative aspects depend on your own taste. In this particular case the back wall above the bunk beds and foot and head walls were covered with Cannon Mills "Rhapsody" sheets and the window curtains are made of the same material. The foam-rubber mattresses on both beds are covered with towels of a harmonizing pattern. Use a good grade of semigloss interior enamel for the desk, beds and shelves applied with brush or spray.

TWIN DESKS

If you've got two boys in a room you'll find this project a very satisfying way of providing ample storage space for their clothing, toys, and athletic equipment as well as splendid desks for schoolwork.

The desk tops (C) consist of the two halves of a standard, hollow, birch veneer door cut down its length with a saw. Each half was laid on top of a pair of cabinets (B and H,D,) as shown in the drawing. The desk tops are fastened to the cabinets by screws driven through the undersides of the cabinet tops into the framework of the hollow door (C).

You may find it necessary to insert wood blocks between the veneered sheets of the door halves along the edges that touch the wall in order to

A built-in bunk bed, storage shelves, and a modernistic desk make this a delightful hideaway for a young girl.

Plenty of storage space and a more beautiful room are just two of the benefits your children will derive from this attractive twin desks arrangement.

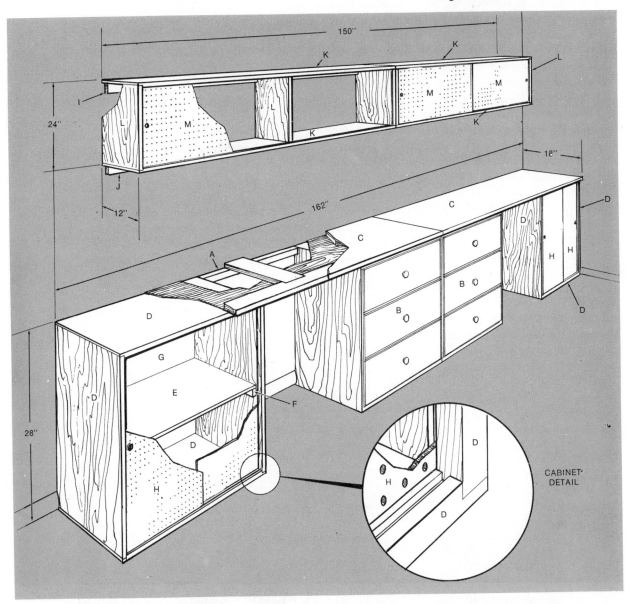

CABINET DETAIL

MATERIALS LIST

A. Two pieces, each: 79 x 2 x 1″ (one not shown)
B. Two chests of drawers, each: 28 x 28 x 18″
C. One standard hollow birch veneer door, 81 x 36 x 1″
D. Eight pieces, each: 28 x 18 x 1″ (one not shown)
E. Two pieces, each: 26 x 16 x ¾″ (one not shown)
F. Four pieces, each: 16 x 2 x 1″ (three not shown)
G. Two pieces, each: 28 x 28 x ⅛″ (one not shown)

H. Four pieces, each: 26 x 15 x ⅛″
I. Two pieces, each: 73 x 2 x 1″ (one not shown)
J. Two pieces, each: 75 x 2 x 1″ (one not shown)
K. Four pieces, each: 75 x 12 x 1″
L. Six pieces, each: 24 x 12 x 1″
M. Four pieces, each: 38½ x 22 x ⅛″ (one not shown)

MORE SPACE FOR GROWING KIDS

stiffen the surface at these points because there is no framing. If you find this necessary, fasten the blocks in place with glue and clamps instead of nails to avoid marring the surface of the top.

The two center cabinets (B) are unfinished furniture purchased from mail-order houses and stores which specialize in unfinished furniture. The overhang of the tops of these two cabinets were cut flush with the sides and fronts. Both cabinets are screwed to each other through the two sides that butt together.

The cabinets at the far ends are made of ¾" plywood with the tops and bottoms rabbeted to the sides and fastened with nails and glue. The sliding doors (H) of these cabinets are made of tempered, perforated hardboard and slide in grooves (cabinet detail) cut into the tops, bottoms, and sides. The doors must be slipped into their grooves when the cabinet is assembled.

The two wall cabinets, like the two end cabinets below them, have no backs and are assembled with rabbet joints and fastened with nails and glue. Both wall cabinets are nailed to cleats (I,J) which are screwed to wall studs. The upper cleat (I) is inside the cabinets. The center partition (L) is nailed through the top and bottom. Both sliding doors

(M) are made of perforated hardboard and slide in tracks as shown in the cabinet detail.

BUILT-IN DESK-BENCH

Frank Lloyd Wright, who was often called the dean of American architects, felt that built-ins were hard to beat for efficient space usage, convenience, and beauty.

This desk-bench combination creates a well-organized work-study center for children and teen-agers. It is particularly well suited to attic areas—although it can be just as useful in almost any part of the house. Simple butt joints, nails, and glue are used almost exclusively throughout for joining with the sole exception of the baseboard moldings, which require miter joints. Most of the stock used is ¾" plywood except for the drawers and frames (A-C-D-F) which are 1" stock. The cross-hatched area of the baseboard is a warm-air register, which, of course, need not be included in your own construction.

The desk—essentially a series of side pieces held together with frames—should be built first. You will end up with a much sturdier piece of work if

An attic area is turned into a teenager's "private pad" by building in this desk-bench combination.

you cut, glue, nail, and clamp all the frames in one operation and let them set a day or so before using them. Later, join them to their individual plywood sides and partitions with glue and screws. The method of construction is side, frame, side, frame, and so on starting with the enclosure (F, M), one side of which is attached to the wall, until the last one you construct is the largest bay of drawers (A, G). Mark off the dimensions of the drawer sides, adding $\frac{1}{16}$" clearance to ensure correct spacing and easy sliding.

Before attaching the front of the enclosure (M), cut out the area for the door (N). The door overlaps its opening $\frac{3}{8}$" on all except the hinge side. Leave the top off and the drawers out in order to give the glued drawer bays plenty of air circulation to dry. Drawer construction is relatively straightforward—no dadoes or rabbeting are used. The drawer runners are actually $\frac{1}{4}$" projections of the bottom, which is nailed and glued to the sides, front, and back. Before installing the drawers, the runners should be waxed on their bottoms and edges to facilitate sliding.

Construction of the bench should take only a short time once the wood is cut. Under the bottom of the bench at the back edge (not shown) is a 2-

MATERIALS LIST

A. Four frames, each: one front, $18\frac{7}{8}$ x 2 x 2"; two sides, 18 x 2 x 2"; one back, $14\frac{7}{8}$ x 2 x 2"

B. One frame base: one front $18\frac{7}{8}$ x 5 x 1"; two sides, each 18 x 2 x 2"; one back, $14\frac{7}{8}$ x 2 x 2"

C. Two frames, each: one front, $24\frac{1}{4}$ x 2 x 2"; two sides, 18 x 2 x 2"; one back, $20\frac{1}{4}$ x 2 x 2"

D. Eight frames, each: one front, $14\frac{1}{4}$ x 2 x 2"; two sides, 18 x 2 x 2"; one back, $10\frac{1}{4}$ x 2 x 2"

E. Two frame bases, each: one front, $14\frac{1}{4}$ x 5 x 1"; two sides, each: 18 x 2 x 2"; one back, $10\frac{1}{4}$ x 2 x 2"

F. Three frames, each: one front, $13\frac{7}{8}$ x 2 x 2"; two sides, $19\frac{1}{4}$ x 2 x 2"; one back, $9\frac{7}{8}$ x 2 x 2"

G. Six sides, each: $28\frac{1}{2}$ x 20 x $\frac{3}{4}$"

H. One drawer, one front, $19\frac{1}{2}$ x $3\frac{13}{16}$ x $\frac{1}{2}$"; two sides, $18\frac{1}{2}$ x $2\frac{13}{16}$ x $\frac{1}{2}$"; one back, $17\frac{3}{4}$ x $2\frac{13}{16}$ x $\frac{1}{2}$"; one bottom, 19 x $18\frac{1}{4}$ x $\frac{1}{4}$"

I. Three drawers each: one front, $19\frac{1}{2}$ x $4\frac{13}{16}$ x $\frac{1}{2}$"; two sides, $18\frac{1}{2}$ x $3\frac{13}{16}$ x $\frac{1}{2}$"; one back, $17\frac{3}{4}$ x $3\frac{13}{16}$ x $\frac{1}{2}$"; one bottom, 19 x $18\frac{1}{4}$ x $\frac{1}{4}$"

J. One drawer: one front, $24\frac{7}{8}$ x $3\frac{13}{16}$ x $\frac{1}{2}$"; two sides, $18\frac{1}{2}$ x $2\frac{13}{16}$ x $\frac{1}{2}$"; one back, $23\frac{1}{8}$ x $2\frac{13}{16}$ x $\frac{1}{2}$"; one bottom, $23\frac{5}{8}$ x 19 x $\frac{1}{4}$"

K. Two drawers, each: one front, $14\frac{7}{8}$ x $3\frac{13}{16}$ x $\frac{1}{2}$"; two sides, $18\frac{1}{2}$ x $2\frac{13}{16}$ x $\frac{1}{2}$"; one back, $13\frac{1}{8}$ x $2\frac{13}{16}$ x $\frac{1}{2}$"; one bottom, 19 x $13\frac{5}{8}$ x $\frac{1}{4}$"

L. Six drawers, each: one front, $14\frac{7}{8}$ x $4\frac{13}{16}$ x $\frac{1}{2}$"; two sides, $18\frac{1}{2}$ x $3\frac{13}{16}$ x $\frac{1}{2}$"; one back, $13\frac{1}{8}$ x $3\frac{13}{16}$ x $\frac{1}{2}$"; one bottom, 19 x $13\frac{5}{8}$ x $\frac{1}{4}$"

M. One enclosure front, $28\frac{1}{2}$ x $14\frac{5}{8}$ x $\frac{3}{4}$"

N. One door, $12\frac{1}{4}$ x $9\frac{1}{4}$ x $\frac{1}{2}$"

O. One piece, $82\frac{1}{2}$ x 4 x 2"

P. One piece, $82\frac{1}{2}$ x 4 x 1"

Q. One piece, $82\frac{1}{2}$ x 13 x $\frac{3}{4}$"

R. One piece, $82\frac{1}{2}$ x $17\frac{1}{4}$ x $\frac{3}{4}$"

S. Two pieces, each: 18 x $16\frac{1}{4}$ x $\frac{3}{4}$"

T. One piece, 84 x 18 x $\frac{3}{4}$"

U. Three pieces, each: $17\frac{1}{4}$ x $11\frac{1}{2}$ x $\frac{3}{4}$"

V. Desk top, 20 x 20 x $\frac{3}{4}$"

W. Plastic laminate, 90 x 20 x $\frac{1}{16}$"

X. Baseboard molding, $155\frac{1}{8}$"

Y. One cushion, 84 x 18 x 3"

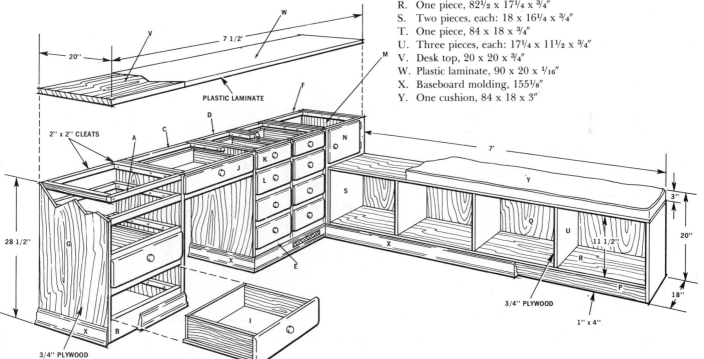

by-4 which extends the entire length of the bench and is included for additional stability. The bench side (S) at the extreme left end is attached to the lower front of the enclosure (M) with glue and countersunk screws. Following this, the front 1-by-4 (P) and the extreme right side of the bench (S) are joined using nails and glue. The next operation is to install the bottom of the bench (R). The three partitions (U) are attached to the top (T) using nails, glue, and countersunk 2″ angle iron braces—leaving the other, unattached ends of the partitions sticking up in the air temporarily. When the glue on this partition-top unit is dry, the entire unit is turned over, glued to the bottom (R), and the joints are reinforced with 2″ angles and screws.

In this particular project it is necessary to raise the cushion (Y) on top of the bench before you can use the door (N) to the enclosure (M). There are two alternate solutions to this problem. The first and most obvious one is simply to make a false door to the enclosure or to do away entirely with any sort of opening. Of course, you could also cut and install hinges on the part of the top of the desk directly over the enclosure and thus have storage room for long objects.

After the glue in the desk is dry, attach the top (V) with glue and nails. Cut and attach the base-board molding. Finally, attach the plastic laminate (W) with contact cement. See separate instructions on laminating the plastic in Chapter 1.

RECLINING HEADREST

Here's a one-day project that can be built by any-one, tailored to fit every child's room. All you need is a piece of 1″-by-12″ shelving lumber, a few pieces of 1-by-2 wall cleat, and some hinges to make the reclining headrest detailed in the sketch.

The shelf, which may do double duty as a desk, extends the entire length of the wall. It should be placed at table height of 30″ if you intend it to be used that way. The shelf rests on 1-by-2 cleats, one at each end, and others placed along the back wall. Cleats are nailed into wall studs.

The swinging leaves of the headrest are attached to the wall with small butt hinges and cleats.

The entire unit can be painted to suit the decor or may be covered with Formica plastic laminate.

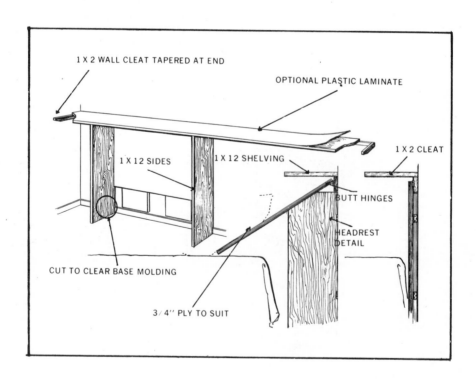

1 X 2 WALL CLEAT TAPERED AT END

OPTIONAL PLASTIC LAMINATE

1 X 12 SIDES

1 X 12 SHELVING

1 X 2 CLEAT

BUTT HINGES

HEADREST DETAIL

CUT TO CLEAR BASE MOLDING

3/4″ PLY TO SUIT

This combination wall shelf and reclining head rest can be built in one day. The shelf extends the entire length of the wall, and can double as a desk.

THE L-SHAPED DESK

What better stimulus for studying could you provide a youngster than this efficient and attractive corner desk? Commodious drawers and cabinet space are right at hand, the L-shaped counter provides the most effective work surface, and the seating area is most comfortable.

Construction of this unit is not quite as simple as it appears: each side of the desk top is cut at an angle so the drawer fronts and cabinet doors are also angled to run parallel to the front edge (see detail A). The drawers and shelves are of irregular shape, as in details B and C. But the plan can be modified with straight lines if you wish, and then the drawers and doors also will lose their angles.

The top is cut from one sheet of ¾" plywood to which Formica, or a similar material, is laminated.

The two cabinets are built first and their interiors finished. Drawer slides are fitted to one, and cleats or shelf tracks to the other. Doors and drawers can be built later.

The top is cut from a 4'-by-8' sheet. The corner cleats at the point of the L are nailed to wall studs and the entire unit is then put in place. Any type of door hardware can be used. Edge trim is attached last.

The drawers require careful construction. Stock is ½" throughout. The front edges of the sides have to be carefully cut and fitted in a compound miter, as they not only slope outward from top to bottom, but are also angled along the front edges to permit the face to fit flush. Detail drawings B and C will help you cut them accurately.

See the instructions in Chapter 1 on laminating plastic sheeting.

An L-shaped desk turns previously wasted space into a well-organized work-study center for any child. The drawers at the end of the short arm will hold all of the child's school supplies, and the large cabinet has adjustable shelves for storing books, clothing, toys or sports equipment.

MATERIALS LIST

Drawer Cabinet
2 pcs. 16½ x 13½ x ¾"
top and bottom
1 pc. 15 x 28½ x ¾"
outside upright
1 pc. 16½ x 28½ x ¾"
inside upright

Storage Cabinet
2 pcs. 16½ x 52½ x ¾"
top and bottom
1 pc. 12 x 28½ x ¾"
outside upright
1 pc. 16½ x 28½ x ¾"
shelf
2 pcs. 26¼ x 27¾ x ¾"
doors

Drawers
see detail drawings B and
C for dimensions.
use ½" stock throughout.

Top
1 sheet 4 x 8-feet ¾"
fir plywood

Miscellaneous
drawer slides
1 x 2" wall cleats
½ x 1½" face trim

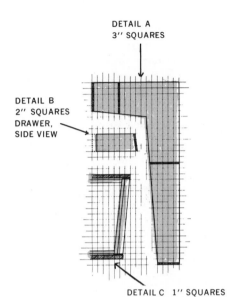

DETAIL A
3" SQUARES

DETAIL B
2" SQUARES
DRAWER,
SIDE VIEW

DETAIL C 1" SQUARES
DRAWER FRONT, TOP VIEW

1 x 2 CLEATS NAILED TO STUDS

PLASTIC LAMINATE OVER ¾" FIR PLY

½ x 1½" TRIM

15"

30" 15"

16½"

16½"

¾" SHELVES
AND DOORS

12"

CUT OUT FOR
BASEBOARD

OPTIONAL KICK SPACE, 1 x 2 FRAME

DRAWERS, ½" STOCK

1 x 2" FRAME

54"

SEE DETAILS B AND C FOR DRAWER DIMENSIONS

DOOR, 26¼" WIDE X 27¾" HIGH X ¾"

WALL TO WALL . . . AND THEN SOME

Another and more elaborate arrangement of an L-shaped desk includes a sweep of low cabinets along two walls of a child's room. There are a plenitude of dresser drawers in various sizes, commodious enclosed shelving, and a desk with almost unlimited top space. With it all, the combined unit does not detract a bit from the size of the room, as the upper walls are open to view.

The long right-angle counter is surfaced with white plastic laminate, including the self-edge. While the top is of ¾″ plywood, the framing to which the plywood is glued forms a deeper, thicker edge.

The sketches show the various segments of the unit, the parts that are used, and the assembly of the sections. Overall dimensions are omitted so that the design can be adapted to any available space or room situation. The 30″ desk height is standard, but can be adjusted for the comfort of the individual—some may prefer a 28″ or 29″ height, and the difference of even 1″ in desk height often is important.

The two plywood sections forming the L are joined at the corner with special fasteners, called Lock-Tite, which are placed into drilled holes and tightened to pull the plywood edges together.

A more elaborate design for the L-shaped desk includes cabinets along both walls, various sizes of dresser drawers, and a spacious desk top.

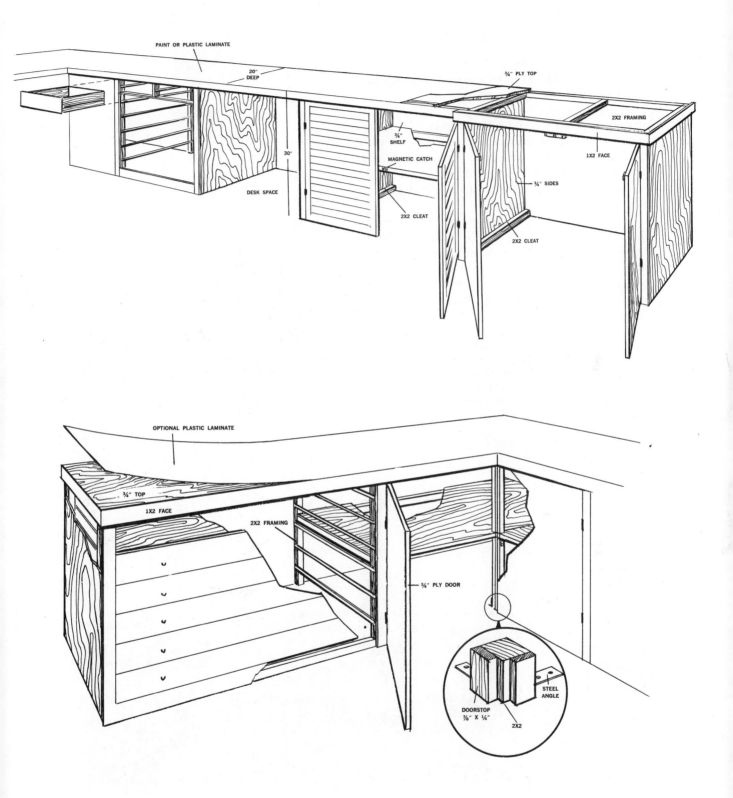

PAINT OR PLASTIC LAMINATE

20" DEEP

¾" PLY TOP

2X2 FRAMING

1X2 FACE

¾" SHELF

¾" SIDES

MAGNETIC CATCH

30"

DESK SPACE

2X2 CLEAT

2X2 CLEAT

OPTIONAL PLASTIC LAMINATE

¾" TOP

1X2 FACE

2X2 FRAMING

¾" PLY DOOR

STEEL ANGLE

DOORSTOP ⅞" X ¼"

2X2

MORE SPACE FOR GROWING KIDS

BUILT-IN BEDROOM DRESSER

Some things naturally go into drawers, some must hang on closet rods, others fit best on shelves. A combination of these facilities makes what can be called a storage wall. The one shown here is an excellent example, in which a wall niche is utilized for the best of all possible arrangements for bedroom storage needs.

The very large drawers are just right for bed linen, extra blankets, and similar items. The lower drawers are used by the young room occupant for clothing articles and accessories. Though extremely wide, the drawers move smoothly on metal slides with nylon bearings, and have inside divider partitions to better organize their contents.

The sketch shows the basic construction details. The closet is framed with 2-by-3 uprights, covered with gypsum board. The cabinet is built as a unit and moved into place against the wall, tied in with picture frame molding over the front edges. The shelves are held by pairs of adjustable brackets.

This spacious, versatile storage wall is built so that it can be reproduced entirely or in sections. The combination of drawers, shelves, and closet rods makes the wall a must for organization-minded families.

³⁄₄″ PLY SHELVES AND SIDES

ADJUSTABLE SHELF HARDWARE

PICTURE
FRAME
MOLDING

1X2 FACING

SLIDING DRAWER HARDWARE

1-BY-3 FRAME

SHELF CLEAT

MINIMUM USABLE
DEPTH 18″

2X3 STUDS

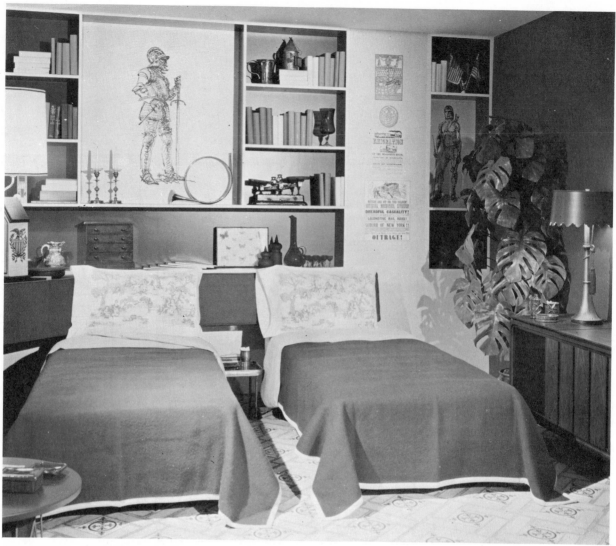

Do your guests make do by sleeping on a sofa or cot? Why not give your guests a room of their own by adopting this attractive alternative to your sleeping problem.

DEN CONVERTS TO BEDROOM

The recreation room or den is often utilized for overnight guests, or as a combination bedroom for a member of the family. Usually, this purpose is performed by a sofa or a pair of cots, either arrangement requiring considerable effort for setting up when needed, aside from the problems of storing the folded cots.

As shown in the photograph and drawings, there is an alternative that is far better in appearance, comfort, and practical application. A pair of beds, twin or three-quarter size, appears to be part of an attractive built-in L-shaped seating arrangement. The beds may be either ready-made units with

their legs shortened to standard couch height, or constructed from a pair of flush-type doors, mounted on wooden legs and covered with a foam-rubber pad two or three inches thick. The key to the arrangement is the built-in bolsters. Without them, the beds would be too deep for comfortable seating, but the bolsters are extended from the wall by the 12″ depth of the wall shelves, giving sufficient back support for seating comfort.

The bed legs may be fitted with smooth metal glides, or with small-wheel casters. In everyday use, the beds are pushed back all the way to the wall, under the bolsters and the wall-mounted shelves, and appear to be part of a modern built-in wall

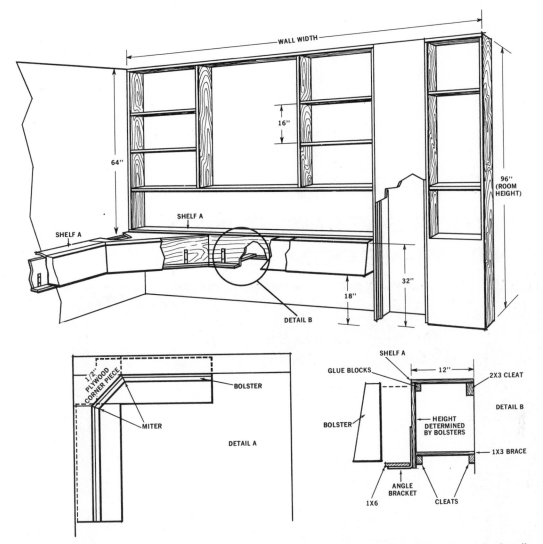

Details of right-angle construction holding the bed bolsters, made of 1″ stock supported by 2-by-2 or 2-by-3 wall cleats. Floor-to ceiling shelf unit may be made of ¾″ plywood or 1-by-10 shelving boards.

unit. When needed for guests, the beds are easily rolled or pulled out away from the wall into any desired position.

A cross section of the built-in wall unit is shown in detail B of the drawing with construction details. It will be necessary to make or obtain the bolsters first so that you can determine the dimensions of the built-in sections.

A 1″-by-12″ shelf, supported at one edge by a 2-by-3 cleat, is joined with a vertical board which is attached along the front edge of this shelf, butted to the underside and reinforced with glue blocks at the back. Another 1″ board, ¾″ narrower than the top shelf, is placed between the lower section of

this vertical member and the wall, supported on a 1-by-3 brace, as shown, forming a box shape.

What remains is to attach right-angle iron brackets along the face of the vertical member to support the bolster. The brackets are spanned along the top by a running board which is just narrower than the bottom width of the bolsters which it will support.

The two lengths of wall shelves may meet directly in the corner or, better still, converge at a corner section into which the ends of the side bolsters are angled.

Above the beds are wall shelves which make an attractive addition to the room and emphasize the built-in character of the seating arrangement.

MORE SPACE FOR GROWING KIDS

Chapter 3

TURN YOUR BASEMENT INTO A FAMILY FUN ROOM

Basement finishing is one of the most rewarding projects a home owner can undertake. This is the quickest, cheapest, easiest way to expand the home living space. What you will have is not only a new recreation room that possibly will be the largest room in the home, and the easiest one to keep tidy, but will provide additional facilities that are essential to the growing family. With proper planning, you can make use of every inch of the basement space to include a workshop, laundry room, large storage closets, a cedar closet, children's study areas, a darkroom, even a separate home office, if desired, which can be insulated against noise.

With housing space in such short supply, it is sometimes incomprehensible that these valuable possibilities for home expansion would be so widely neglected. The only logical explanation is that there still is a remnant of the old-fashioned prejudice against the basement as living quarters. This attitude no doubt originated in the old days of

A nautical family, obviously, thought up the styling of this room, and it does look ship-shape. A few imaginative decorative touches, including an anchor on the wall, compass points on the floor, and the imposing ship's figurehead, set the tone for sailing in all seasons.

grimy coal bins, dim lighting, dusty concrete floors, and drab, damp walls.

All that has been completely changed, of course, by our modern automatic heating systems, brilliant fluorescent lighting, dust-sealing floor tiles and mastic, vapor barrier insulation, attractive wall paneling, and other technological achievements.

A beneficial byproduct of the rec room project will be to transform the basement from a cluttered depository of discarded junk, which constitutes a fire hazard, into an attractive and useful room easy to keep clean and orderly.

Why is it quickest? The space is already there—all that is needed is to make it habitable and partitioned off into areas for the various purposes. This means framing out the walls for paneling, putting down floor tiles over the raw concrete, covering the ceiling beams with tiles, and installing lighting fixtures. The room will be usable almost from the start—as soon as floor tiling and paneling are finished. No waiting to file plans, no construction delays. You can proceed at your own pace, but the basement will be in use at the same time.

Why is it cheapest? Again, because the space is

This is how it looked before. The horrible example of a junk-cluttered cellar forcefully emphasizes an extra benefit of basement finishing, removing an unnecessary fire hazard. Instead of a useless pile of discards, the project produces a spacious room for family activities.

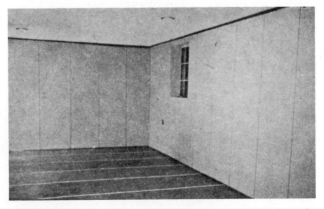

Now it's a room, with basic finishing completed and ready for the built-in units, and boasting a delightful window that had been all but covered up by accumulated discards.

Another seafaring family designed this recreation room to look like a ship's cabin, including typical built-ins and nautical decorations. Is that a belaying pin on the T-shaped desk?

A room at ground level has sliding glass doors opening onto a back yard patio. Basement rooms not so fortunately situated can have the "outside" effect by including a wall of patterned glass or translucent plastic that diffuses the lighting at the back to simulate a large open window.

Open fireplace with brickwork covering almost an entire wall imparts a manor house luxury to the basement. The fireplace permits indoor barbecues during inclement weather.

already there, fully enclosed, just waiting for the finishing touches. The work can be done at the lowest possible cost, for the following reasons: (1) you can do every bit of the finishing project yourself, except perhaps the electrical installation; (2) this project need not take up any of your regular working time. It can be done piecemeal, whenever you have the chance and the inclination to move ahead; (3) the materials may be of the most inexpensive kind since no structural changes are involved, only decorative finishing. Of course, you will want to make the playroom as attractive as possible, and it certainly won't be worthwhile to stint, but *you* set the amount you want to spend, and it can stay there.

In most areas of the country, building costs run approximately $15 to $20 a square foot. A 12′ x 15′ extension built onto your home to give you a moderate-size den or recreation room would most likely cost $3,500. That amount could be reduced if you do your own finishing work, but most of the job will require a contractor for the excavation, foundation, wall framing, siding, windows, door, floor, roof, heating and electrical work, and that's not counting the architect's fee, inside wall finishing, and other details.

The basement project can be done for as little as one-tenth that amount. The walls, floor, and ceiling are all there, including the heating in most cases, and the electrical system is nearby, requiring just additional circuits for outlets and lighting, which can be wired easily because there's no snaking of the wires behind walls. What is needed, then, is mostly "finishing," which is really just covering the floor, the walls, the ceiling—and you can do all that as cheaply as you wish, since no structural materials are involved. Equally important, perhaps, is that you wind up not with a single, modest 12′ x 15′ room, but really spacious quarters, using almost every bit of the basement space, except the furnace room, for your family needs.

Why is it easiest? No structural changes are involved in finishing the basement for a playroom and other facilities unless there are certain obstacles that must be overcome. The work divides into several specific stages: floor tiling, framing and paneling the walls, finishing the ceiling, installing better electric lighting. Each of these requires a certain amount of knowledge and ability, certainly, to do the job correctly. Any home owner who has had any experience at all with tile laying and carpentry should have no difficulty in following the detailed instructions for these phases of the work.

Anyone who hasn't yet developed the various

Games, anyone? Activity unlimited for every generation of this family, with chess table, archery range, table tennis. Built-in storage benches covered with foam cushions line the walls. False windows with concealed lighting display photomurals of rustic scenes. Everything, including the knotty pine paneling is kept in light, bright tones.

Simple does it. Spaciousness is the key theme of this concept, including a couple of built-in units to keep the floor area clear and adaptable to changing purposes. Dark floor and wall colors are modified by shaded "high hat" ceiling spotlights, resulting in an intimate, discotheque effect.

BEFORE: Does this scene look familiar? If so, then your home needs a basement rejuvenation too. Let's face it—many a fine home has allowed its basement to get like this. No wonder the young lady on the stairs looks discouraged! But not for long, because the rubbish room was soon to be converted into a rumpus room.

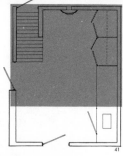

THE PLAN: Room is completely partioned off, including a brick curtain wall 2′ from furnace flue. Stair location is retained, but rebuilt with more sturdy risers and treads. One wall is devoted to storage wardrobes and built-in cabinets, with shallow shelving on opposite wall.

Massive closets were assembled before installation. Idea for door shelving was borrowed from the design of the family refrigerator. Shelving inside closet is ¾″ plywood with edge-grain veneer trim. Doors are made of ½″ plywood. The fireplace is a prefabricated unit, mounted on a wall and connected with its own flue to the outside.

THE RESULT: Suspended fireplace on brick curtain wall accents the modern styling. Heat also is provided through register cut into existing duct, as seen in ceiling above door. Rebuilt open staircase provides safer footing, actually lends decorative value to the room.

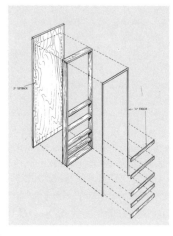

Door-mounted shelving, of either ½″ or ¾″ plywood, is useful for keeping small items easily accessible. Limit the depth to 3″ or so, to avoid both excessive weight and impediment to closet access.

skills needed around the house would do well to pick up this ability. This basement-finishing project is an excellent way to gain the experience; you set the pace for the work, and you have the benefit of the step-by-step instructions in this book.

Your family room should be a room for all the family—a place where youngsters and teenagers will be pleased to gather and engage in the many and varied interests of their generation, but a place, also, where parents can entertain informally or pursue their hobbies, where grandparents can relax, watch TV, play family games, or listen to the hi-fi. In short, a real family room for the older folks as well as the youngsters.

The arrangement and style of the room should reflect the family's particular interests, and provide the maximum facilities for individual activities. The

latter need not require unlimited space; rather, proper planning and a little imagination can make each small area serve several purposes.

Start by collecting pictures of various basement rooms clipped from magazines. These will be invaluable in supplying ideas that you will want to incorporate in your basic plan. At the same time, make a list of the things you want to include. Ultimately, some of the items will have to be eliminated in favor of more important objectives, or because they will not fit into the overall plan.

The photographs on these pages show many types of completed basement family rooms. You certainly can have a similar room for your own home, by lifting some of the ideas presented here and combining them with others you have seen either in visits to other homes or illustrated in magazines.

DIVIDER CONQUERS
BASEMENT CLUTTER

Many walls have two sides, but this one is definitely two-faced. That doesn't imply any falseness or undependability; on the contrary, this wall is most serious and honest about its purposes. In any finished basement, on all counts, a divider wall like this certainly would be the star feature, making the entire project a huge success.

Where it faces the beautifully finished recreation room, this divider wall is as neat and functional as anyone would want, comprising a lovely upholstered lounger and also containing a storage bin large enough for any of your outsize articles like a table-tennis table.

On its other side, the divider closes off a well-equipped workshop, and even acts as the backup wall of a workbench, for which it holds an array of hand tools.

Thus, the wall resolves a number of the basic problems that usually arise with a finished basement: how to keep it neat and clean with minimum effort, how to provide pleasant lounging space for social gatherings, how to keep the workshop activities and mess clear of the recreation area, and what to do about storage of large articles that otherwise tend to encumber the play area and limit its usefulness.

The divider wall, built in the shape of an alcove, did not come about as a whim, but represents a carefully developed plan to overcome certain problems and to provide maximum practical benefits. The open end of the wall is sharply angled toward the back, thus allowing an easy right-hand turn into the workship for handling large plywood panels, since the corridor also serves the laundry room. Without this angled modification of the plans, it would be necessary to locate the wall 4' farther into the recreation room, thus making a critical reduction in the length of that room.

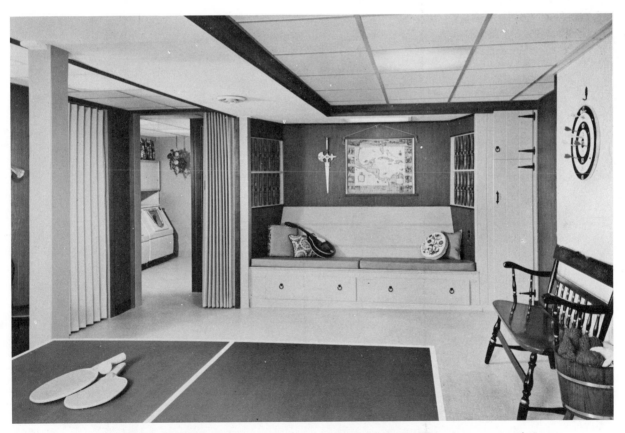

Good planning solves most of the difficulties encountered in basement finishing. This alcove seat and storage closet are part of a divider wall which has a workshop on the other side. Cutting the open end of the wall at an angle provides easy access to the workshop and saves 4' of space for the recreation room.

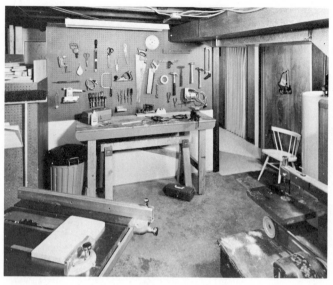

Storage bin to right of the alcove lounge accommodates bulky table tennis table and bridge tables. Space at top is entered from the other side of the wall, to store lumber and other workshop materials.

At the other side there is a workshop, its noise and dust closed off from the rec room by the well-built wall, which also has perforated hardboard panel to hold workbench tools.

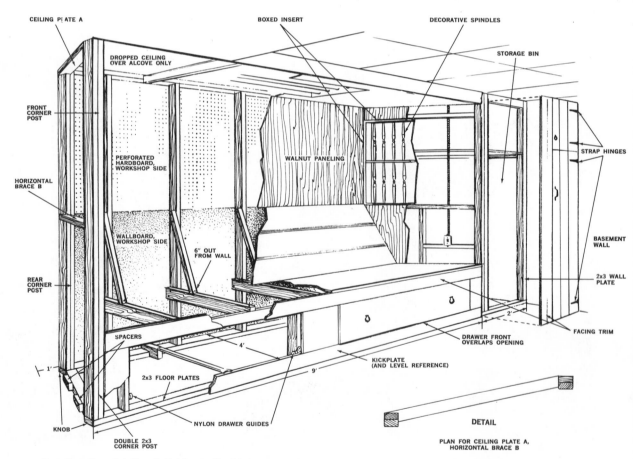

CEILING PLATE A

BOXED INSERT

DECORATIVE SPINDLES

DROPPED CEILING OVER ALCOVE ONLY

STORAGE BIN

FRONT CORNER POST

PERFORATED HARDBOARD, WORKSHOP SIDE

WALNUT PANELING

STRAP HINGES

HORIZONTAL BRACE B

WALLBOARD, WORKSHOP SIDE

6" OUT FROM WALL

BASEMENT WALL

REAR CORNER POST

2x3 WALL PLATE

SPACERS

2'

FACING TRIM

1'

DRAWER FRONT OVERLAPS OPENING

4'

2x3 FLOOR PLATES

KICKPLATE (AND LEVEL REFERENCE)

9'

DETAIL

KNOB

NYLON DRAWER GUIDES

PLAN FOR CEILING PLATE A, HORIZONTAL BRACE B

DOUBLE 2x3 CORNER POST

Construction details of divider wall with lounger alcove and storage bins, shown in sketch. Open end at left is cut back at sharp angle, from total 11' length to 9', so that workshop access is not impeded. The pitch of the back braces is exaggerated in the sketch in order to show detail.

Alcove Design

The alcove section is 9' wide, with an additional storage bin, 2' wide, at the end. This storage unit serves both rooms: on the rec room side, the lower portion is used for storing the bulky table-tennis table, which is regulation 5' wide, in two parts, and there's enough additional space for a folding card table. A shelf divides the storage bin above the height of the table-tennis table. Thus, on the workshop side, there is an opening at the top into the same storage bin so that lumber and other supplies can be kept there, high off the floor.

Construction Stages

The recreation room side is finished with Gold Bond paneling, in Heritage walnut; the workshop side has ½" gypsum wallboard plus perforated hardboard for tool hangers. In starting construction of the wall, plumb lines are dropped from the joists, providing reference points for snapping chalk lines on the concrete floor. Floor plates of 2-by-3 stock are then secured to the deck with masonry anchors, extending the entire distance to the foundation wall. Ceiling plates are installed, both over the floor plates, and turning across the end.

Two 2-by-3 studs are set between the floor and ceiling plates, and attached to the concrete wall, and double 2-by-3 corner posts set up on the opposite end of the wall, reinforced with a horizontal brace, as shown in the sketch.

Framing for the seat allows a 48" distance from front edge to rear of the wall. The seat rails hold angled braces that support the back panel of the seat—this can be set at any incline to meet your own preference. The wall panels are put up then, followed by the back and bottom panels, for the seat support. The other stages of the work are shown in the photographs.

The end studs and their top and bottom plates are squared off, using spacers nailed to the bottom plate, and a full-length panel put up to enclose the end. The storage bin has two separate doors, cut from the same plywood panel with planked grooves, and hung with black iron strap hinges.

With walnut paneling in place, cut and fit the seat and its backing. Molding and face trim are added later to the seat edge for a neater finished look.

Framing for seat, the back braces are set about 6" out from the wall. Test first to be sure that this slant provides the desired seating comfort.

Install wall panels on the upper half of the alcove's back wall and the lower half of the sides, including strips above the inserts.

Drawers are large and rugged, butt-jointed with overlapping fronts. Nylon slides and metal rails assure smooth and easy operation, even with considerable weight in the drawer.

Decorative insert is a simple box frame with prefabricated spindles set into pre-drilled holes. All you do is slip it into the wall opening.

IT'S A CIRCUS!

Delightful is the word that describes this unique basement recreation room which, like its prototype, is sure to find favor with "children of all ages." The single feature that contributes most to the three-ring air is the gracefully draped cotton canvas ceiling, in red and white striped panels, for an entrancing effect.

The canvas has its utilitarian side as well, permitting ready access to wiring, plumbing, and heating facilities. These need not be boxed in or covered as with normally finished rooms. Just paint everything a dull flat black and you'll be surprised how invisible the jungle of wood, wire, and pipe becomes. When further hidden by the canvas panels, the background all but disappears.

Cotton canvas has another inherent advantage. When it becomes soiled, it need only be popped into a washing machine (cold water only). Large pieces can be hosed down or sent out to the dry cleaner's. An easily installed system of rods supports the cloth on the ceiling, and permits control of the amount of drape.

Other touches throughout the room add their bit to the circus atmosphere. Colorful canvas panels are laced between bright brass poles to form walls that can be moved readily. The poles, available in most department stores, are held in place by the pressure of an internal spring.

Let the bright colors and magical effect of canvas transform your cellar space into an exciting basement recreation room which will be the talk of the neighborhood. Unique built-ins add to the decorative style and provide functional values that will make the room useful to all members of the family.

Three built-ins add their share to the room's at-
tractiveness. An old-fashioned steam calliope, without which no circus was ever complete, disguises a
hi-fi system. The calliope is represented by a combination of cutout plywood and paper tubing. In another wall recess, a television set is built in, giving
life to one special corner. On one wall is a wooden
elephant; drop it down and it becomes a table.

Other clever ideas contribute to the overall effect.
Cellar windows are magically transformed into
miniature menageries by the addition of a few dowels and some stuffed toy animals. Support columns
can be disguised, too. One here is dressed up so
that it becomes a giraffe. Another is a home for a
make-believe serpent.

Even the lighting fixtures have been carefully
chosen. Their bubble shapes suggest balloons, and
their reds and blues add to the illusion.

A photograph of that fearsome "wild man of Borneo" is in reality a prosaic switchbox, containing
the fuses for the house wiring. Clever use of paint
makes the miraculous transformation.

The large space in this basement is wasted as a repository
for a few items that could just as well be stored in the
garage. The basement is dry, has a high ceiling, easy
access stairway from the upper floor—a perfect combination for a perfect rec room. The open area is unobstructed.

As dramatic and exciting as a three-ring circus, this colorful basement recreation room has a tent-like canvas
top and panel walls, with lighting fixtures to accentuate the total effect.

TURN YOUR BASEMENT INTO A FAMILY FUN ROOM

Wall panels are made of canvas stretched across brass poles and held with laced cord. A ceiling plate is required, of 1-by-6 board, attached at a convenient height to the ceiling joists, with 2-by-2 spacers. Continue as shown below.

Tent canvas, of lightest available weight, is held up with brass curtain rods. Rod locations are first located and marked, strips of canvas tested to find the correct length for the desired drape.

The retainer poles are brass, held in place by internal springs pressing against the ceiling plate. The canvas is held up with wood strips, ¾″ x ¾″, put through a hem at the top, and nailed directly to the ceiling plate.

Canvas strips run from one short side of the room to the other. The ceiling strips should be neatly hemmed, with open ends for inserting the supporting brass rods.

Venetian blind cord is laced through eyelets in canvas and around the poles, to hold the panels taut. Instead of the spring-loaded brass poles, 2-by-2 stock or clothespole dowels may be used.

Ends of the canvas strips are tacked to 1-by-6 plates which are installed behind a facing strip made of ¾″ lathing. The ceiling area beyond the drapes should be painted flat black to disguise any pipes or wiring seen through canvas gaps.

Under the Big Top

Brightly colored canvas walls and ceiling create a real circuslike atmosphere in our recreation room. Although the same material is used for both, each requires different handling and preparation.

The walls are created from floor-to-joist strips of solid colored canvas. Use a scheme of alternating pastels, but limit yourself to no more than three or four basic shades.

Working with canvas suggests needle and thread as a useful tool, and that is correct. Some sewing will have to be done, so here's the opportunity to make this a family project. For best results all canvas edges should be neatly hemmed, a job that can be done quickly on the family sewing machine, using a heavy needle and thread. Once the hemming is out of the way, the distaff side of the family can assist even further by eyeletting the wall strips with two-piece brass eyelets, a hammer, and the eyelet-forming tool that you can purchase at most notion shops. Progress then becomes rapid and easy.

As shown in the photo series, the process is as follows: A plate of 1-by-6 stock is placed horizontally at a convenient distance below the joists (make it as high as possible) and fastened to steel angle brackets. It is also braced by 2-by-2 blocking nailed to the overhead joists.

How-to-build techniques appear on the following pages. Take them one step at a time and you'll be ready to put on your own private circus before you can snap your ringmaster's whip.

Supported by Poles

For the poles that support the canvas panels, choose the brass variety with built-in spring tension, available at department stores. Later, if you decide to change the room layout, it is simply done. The poles are taken away just as easily as they are installed.

For economy's sake, however, wood dowels, or even lengths of 2-by-2 lumber may replace the poles. If dowels are used, drill holes in the top plate to receive them, and install a bottom plate as well, with matching holes to retain the dowels. Or, with the 2-by-2's, nail the top ends to the ceiling plate, and toenail the bottoms.

Once their poles are positioned, the panels go up in a jiffy. A brace of ¾" x ¾" stock is at each panel top, held in place by wrapping the end of the panel around it and stapling or nailing through

the canvas to the wood. Nail through the brace into the top plate with 1½" brads. Now lace the panels to the poles with Venetian blind cords. No brace should be necessary at the bottom of the panels but it can be added if needed.

The distance between poles will depend on your taste and the widths in which you can buy the canvas. As a standard of comparison, 30" is adequate.

The ceiling "tent" is attached by a completely different system, no lacing being used. The graceful drape is the result of using strips of canvas longer than the span they are to cover. To determine the proper length, take Venetian blind cord or other heavy string. Drape it from point to point across the ceiling, attaching it at points of contact with thumbtacks into the joists. When you have the desired number of drapes, and each falls properly, you can then note the contact points, remove the string and measure it. Its length will give you the exact amount of canvas you'll need for each strip. For the ceiling, use the very lightest weight canvas you can obtain.

Ceiling strips should be hemmed neatly also. Simple brass rods, attached by conventional hardware, will suffice for supporting the circus roof, and will permit easy removal when washing is needed.

Ready Access to Utilities

One of the most attractive aspects of this circus basement is the fact that you always have access to utility lines that run between or along the basement ceiling joists. Getting to them is easy: just remove the canvas panels. But since there are gaps between the ceiling strips, you will want to hide what's overhead. Paint the entire structure—joists, subfloor, pipes, ducts, wiring—flat black. With small gaps between canvas strips, the overhead fades away into nothingness. It will amaze you!

The Calliope Plays Again

The site recommended for a hi-fi system is under an existing staircase, a space often wasted. Construction details appear in the accompanying sketches. Framing is simple, since you need concern yourself only with enough strength to support the equipment.

The sliding drawer should be made to whatever dimensions will fit your phonograph, with the drawer slides being fastened to the sides of the 2-

The facade of a steam calliope hides a modern audio system, built on a cabinet under the otherwise wasted staircase space. The colorful calliope of former days produced sounds through whistles rather than finely tuned organ reeds.

Framing of the audio support rack, and placement of the 2-by-4 uprights, floor plate, and incline attached to the stair stringer, are detailed. Record player drawer goes on the top shelf, while the lower shelf holds your amplifier-tuner.

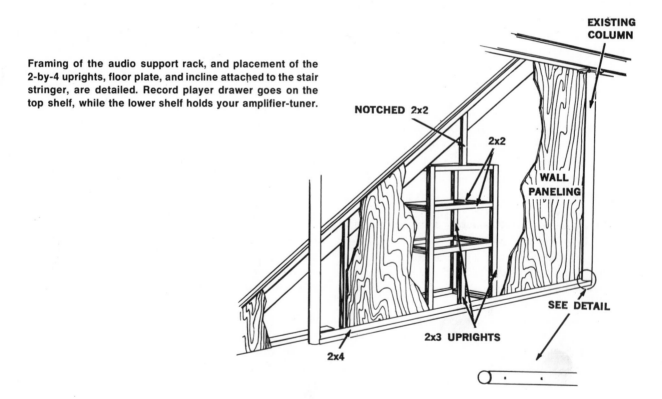

HOME IMPROVEMENT BOOK

Plywood cutouts representing the calliope wagon are fastened over the wall paneling, with cutouts for record player drawer and amplifier controls. Access to back of set, for servicing, may be through the door built to enclose the understair space.

by-3 framing uprights. The amplifier and tuner, if you have one, can be located below, with controls accessible through an opening in the calliope. The size of this opening should also be made to suit your equipment.

The construction sequence is (1) the framing; (2) the calliope silhouette; (3) temporary positioning of the cutout on the framing; (4) transferring the opening height to the framing for location of the shelf, making allowance for the height of the amplifier; (5) installing shelf; (6) paneling the wall; (7) attaching the calliope to the paneling.

Let your imagination run riot in painting the calliope. Practice drawing various shapes on scrap paper until you find a combination that pleases you, then use it on the wood. Carry out the canvas color scheme on the calliope, using mostly white with red as the major second color. Additional accents matching other room colors may be applied wherever appropriate. Don't be afraid to experiment. You can always repaint if you don't like the results.

High-gloss enamels should be used for their wearing qualities and washability. Apply an enamel undercoater to the raw plywood before attempting finish coats.

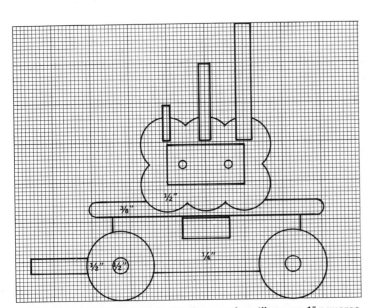

Silhouette can be copied by tracing graph outlines on 1″ squares. Parts are cut from ¼″ plywood, with some duplicated parts doubled to obtain greater thickness, as shown. Cross bar, however, is of ⅜″ stock for variety.

The calliope's "organ pipes" are lengths of cardboard mailing tubes, of different diameters, sliced in half lengthwise and glued in place, after being painted. The ornate curlicues are marked out with a pencil-compass and a drafting instrument called a French curve, which is a plastic device similar to a protractor.

Here Come the Animals

An elephant, made of several pieces of plywood of varying thicknesses, becomes a two-way feature of the circus basement. On the wall, folded flat—it's a charming decoration. Flip the retaining hook out of the way, let the trunk leg swing free, attach the wire hook hidden behind it, and you've got a sturdy table.

The main piece of the table, forming its surface when lowered, is cut from ¾" plywood to the silhouette shown in the ½" square graph. Squared off, it measures 48" wide and 36½" long. Next, cut the round head (omitting the ears) and the trunk-like bottom, as well as the tusks, from ¾" plywood and attach it to the first piece with glue and nails. Clamp and let dry before going on to the next step.

To bring the tusks out against the head, cut another layer, following the diagram silhouette, from ¼" stock. Attach this with glue and brads also.

The ears are last. Use ½" stock here, shaping the crescents carefully to fit snugly against the ¾" head. Glue and tack to the back piece.

Draw the eyebrow outline on the face as shown in the graph. Then, with a very sharp chisel, working with small cuts, take off the top layer of ply-

Converted into a play table, supported by its trunk, the elephant is lowered by releasing a wall hook. Another long hook, recessed into the back of the elephant's face, secures the supporting trunk leg, when table is open.

This wall elephant presents an amusing aspect, playing its part to the circus crowd, as many an elephant has done before. But this one has a dual role, as you shall see.

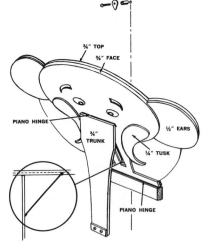

Details of the table components are shown in sketch. Tabletop is attached with piano hinge to 2-by-4 plate bolted to the wall. The retainer hook is recessed into the back of the face. Insert circle shows hook holding trunk leg support.

wood to form the eyebrow recess. You can, if you choose, paint on eyebrows later, instead of chopping them out.

Fill all edges that may have been chipped in sawing, then sand edges and surfaces smooth.

The table is hinged to, and supported by, a 20" piece of 2-by-4 lag-bolted to the wall studs, or right into the concrete. The table is quite heavy, requiring most of a sheet of ¾" plywood, so the support must be well fastened. Attach a length of piano hinge with flathead screws to the 2-by-4 wall

cleat and the edge of the table, while supporting the table temporarily on blocks.

With the hinge properly aligned, lower the table to a horizontal position, checking with a level, then measure its height above the floor. That will give you the exact length of the trunk leg, which can now be cut from ¾" ply. Attach it to the face of the elephant with another piece of piano hinge, as seen in the construction drawing.

A long hook and eye holds the trunk secure when the table is lowered. It is recessed into the el-

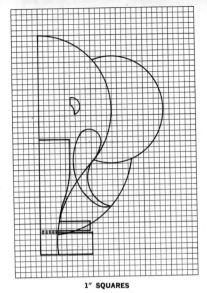

Parts of elephant face outlined on graph for tracing on 1″ squares. When one part is traced, cut out cardboard and turn it over to obtain exact duplicate of other half, for cutting with jig or sabre saw.

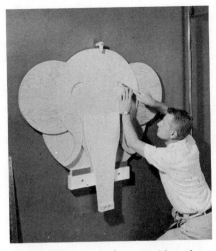

The assembled table parts hinged on wall plate. Note type of retainer hook at top, which is turned sideways to release the table. Eyebrows may be recessed into the face with a sharp chisel.

Use different colors for the trunk, face, ears, and tusks. Before applying the finish coats, brush on primer coat to seal the plywood grain. For the eyes, use large washers or similar round objects with open centers.

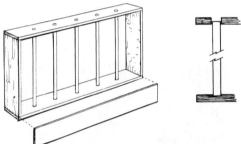

Windows are turned to advantage by making each a miniature wild animal cage. Titan the Tiger (the lettering is a press-on variety you can get at art stores) is locked in behind a simple 1-by-4 frame set into the window opening. The bars are black-painted ¾″ dowels set in the frame. Drill holes for them through the top piece, but make only shallow blind holes below. The dowel length is ¼″ more than the distance from the bottom of the blind hole to the underside of the window frame.

ephant face, where it remains hidden while the table is folded. An eye is screwed into the back of the leg for the hook to grab. Make the recess in the face to fit your hardware, using a sharp chisel, and provide enough depth or length so that the eye also fits into the recess, otherwise the leg won't fold away flat.

A small block at the bottom of the leg has two holes drilled in it, to simulate nostrils. Attach it with glue, or omit it if you like.

If you'd prefer another animal for your model instead of the elephant, try your hand at designing one of your own. It's not at all difficult if you use the technique shown here.

The top of the table may be finished with enamel, or for a really sturdy, low-maintenance surface, cover it with one of the plastic laminates. If you paint, be sure to prime all surfaces first with undercoater—a technique that is always advisable with plywood.

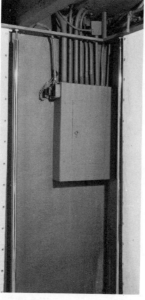

FAMILY ROOM ACTIVITY CORNER

An activity corner gives you "the most for the least." The "most" is the extent to which the corner will be used by everyone in the family, youngsters and grownups alike, because it is so inviting and convenient. The "least" is the amount of disturbance and mess that normally results from such playtime or hobby participation, since everything is kept in one place instead of being strewn over every inch of floor and table space; also the counter shown here is so easily tidied when things quiet down again. And having the spacious drawers right at hand, under the counter top, encourages even the junior set to clear the decks.

The imaginative setup illustrated, built as part of a basement family room project, is based on a large L-shaped counter. One side is 18″ deep, with drawers underneath and a pair of wall-hung cabinets above. Light, supplied by fluorescent lamps mounted under the cabinets, is diffused by frosted glass. The other side of the L counter is only 10″ deep, and comprises part of a bookcase wall, as well as serving as the top of a floor cabinet.

Covered with smooth, stainproof melamine plastic laminate, the counter very likely will become the most popular spot in the house, serving as a snack counter for your social gatherings, attracting the young student who will appreciate the well-lighted and spacious work area for studying, and being used for hobby work, for sewing, and many other chores.

Making the Counter

The counter is made of ¾″ plywood in two sections, joined at right angles to form the L-shape, using special internal fasteners. The counter edges are given extra thickness by attaching scrap lengths of the plywood, forming a total 1½″ skirting all around. The outside corner is gently rounded.

The entire counter is surfaced with Formica plastic laminate, first along the edge, then the top, as described in detail in Chapter 1. The counter, mounted on the wall at a 36″ height for use with the tall "soda-fountain" stools, is supported at the rear on a 1-by-2 wall cleat, and also has a supporting prop at the front edge consisting of 1″ black iron pipe, threaded into a flange which is attached with screws to the underside of the counter.

The under-counter drawers are 16″ wide, 3″ high, and about as deep as the counter itself since the drawers are almost flush with the front edge.

Here's a chance to put your artistic talents to work. Disguise basement columns with a giraffe head, making it from papier-mâché, or from whatever other materials you can dream up. Other columns in this basement are decorated with rope serpents, twisted around and glued to the columns. The giraffe, with its long neck, is ideal, but you can stretch any animal or simply hang other circus ingredients on the column. If you have two columns, run a tightrope between them, letting a troupe of toy monkeys hang from it by their hands.

Danger! Ingenuity at work! What was once a run-of-the-mill switchbox becomes with the application of imagination and paint a "wild man from Borneo." The conduits become the wild man's hair, while the rest of his body is shaped from hardboard or plywood. Paint does the rest.

Activity corner for family room has long L-shaped counter in inviting colors, convenient drawers and cabinets for materials, ample lighting. The L-shaped counter is surfaced with almost indestructible Formica, which makes tidying up a breeze.

TURN YOUR BASEMENT INTO A FAMILY FUN ROOM

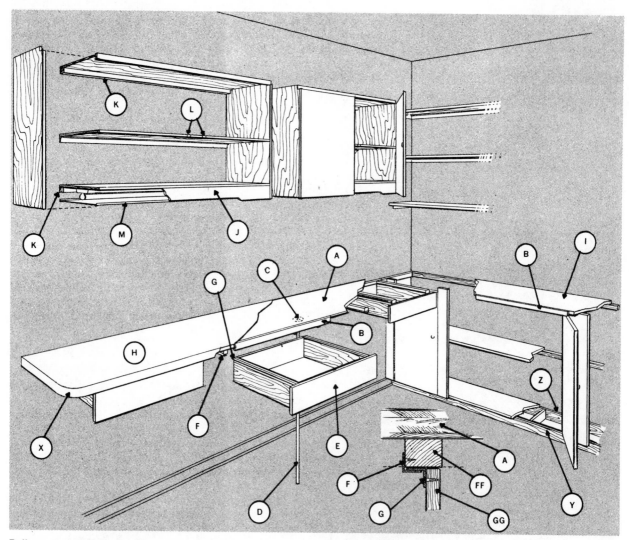

Pull-apart sketch shows construction details of activity counter and its satellite cabinets overhead and at side. The letters designate the following parts:

A—L-shaped counter
B—Counter skirting
C—Pipe flange
D—1″ supporting pipe
E—Drawer fronts
F—Upper drawer runners
G—Lower drawer runners
H—Formica plastic laminate
I—Narrow side of counter

J—Front of light box
K—Wall cleats
L—Door catches
M—Diffuser glass support
X—Rounded counter end
Y—Toe plate
Z—Wall cleat
FF—Counter cleats
GG—Drawer sides

90

The sides are ½″ solid stock, the back and bottom are of ¼″ plywood. The fronts, of ¾″ material, are long enough to overlap each side by 1½″, with about 3″ spacing between each of the drawers.

Drawer runners are cut from ½″ aluminum angle strips. The upper runners are attached to cleats nailed to the underside of the counter, the lower runners fastened flush with the top edges of the drawer sides, with ⅜″ screws through pre-drilled holes.

The Base Cabinet

The cabinet under the bookshelves is 9″ deep, of a height so that the countertop just rests on it without sag or strain. Shelves inside are approximately 8″ deep, supported on a cleat extending the full width of the cabinet and attached directly to the wall. In addition, nails are driven into the middle shelf through the plywood front, while the bottom shelf is fastened to the top of the shoe plate. The toe or kick plate is 3″ high, and recessed about 2″ or 3″. The toe plates usually are painted black.

Piano hinges are used for the doors, but the door at one end under the counter cannot be opened fully because of obstruction by one of the drawers.

Wall Cabinets

Like the base cabinet, those on the wall above the counter are made of ¾″ plywood, and have no backs. The recommended dimensions are 24″ high, 30″ wide, and 12″ deep. All parts are jointed with glue and finishing nails. Pivot hinges like those on TV cabinets are used for the doors, installed on the top and bottom edges, and are almost invisible.

A fluorescent light strip, attached to the underside of each cabinet, is shaded in a box 4″ high. Plastic or glass diffuser material is supported by a frame made of the same ½″ aluminum angle strip used for the drawer runners. Note that the front of the light box, 4½″ high, has a section ½″ deep cut along the bottom edge, affording a finger grip to open the doors, since the doors have no handles. The doors are held with magnetic catches.

KEEP YOUR BASEMENT DRY

The biggest single drawback to utilizing the basement for your family purposes is *water,* and the problem is so important that unless it is solved it may rule out finishing the basement altogether. But considering the value of the space that is going to waste, in addition to the discomfort dampness causes, it pays to make every possible effort to correct the condition.

Water conditions may be manifested as dampness resulting from persistent condensation, minor wall leaks and seepage, underfloor springs or high water table, or occasional flooding during rainstorms. There are many causes of water problems, and these trouble spots are often so difficult to trace that some detective work may be called upon to locate the direct cause or source.

In every home, certain measures for protection against water entry are essential. These include (1) surface drainage away from the house walls, particularly where the soil does not readily absorb the water flow; (2) proper pitch of adjacent patios and other paved surfaces; (3) splash pans under roof downspouts, to prevent pooling of rainwater against the foundation wall; (4) waterproofing outside foundation wall, and drain tile at wall footings; (5) dry well, of adequate size; (6) all siding in perfect condition, carefully calked, to prevent water entry that may find its way down to the basement; and (7) windows fully closed during rains.

When these conditions are met, most basement water problems can be generally attributed to one of the following: condensation, leakage, seepage, and flooding. Of course, you must diagnose the cause correctly before deciding on the remedy. Leaks can usually be spotted at their source, although some leaks are extremely puzzling, as water can trickle over an irregular course once it comes through the wall.

Persistent condensation is one of the most annoying home deficiencies. If allowed to go unchecked, it creates an unpleasant damp odor, makes the entire cellar excessively chilly all year, and promotes destructive mildew. Some leaks can be cured quite easily, and there are effective solutions even to high water table seepage. Storm flooding and sewer backup are more difficult to control, but don't give up hope—some of the suggestions given here may correct your particular condition, and most cases can be kept under control by conservative measures.

Condensation

If the cause of dampness is condensation on the basement walls, no amount of coatings, repairs, paints, or magic formulas will stop it. It isn't a question of keeping the water out; it is there in the form of water vapor, and you would be astonished to learn how much water there may be floating around in the air with you. If you were to plug in an electric dehumidifier this fact would be brought home with considerable impact. In a matter of a few hours, the receiving tank would be full of water, perhaps three or four gallons, pulled right out of the air. This appliance is an excellent aid in combating dampness odors, but in itself cannot do the entire job.

First, a brief explanation about the cause of condensation: water evaporates into the air, as everyone knows. Warm air holds more vapor than cold air. The warm water-laden air moves constantly toward colder surfaces, where the vapor condenses in the form of moisture. From this simple statement, you can draw two conclusions: the walls of the basement are colder than the other house walls because of contact with the earth; covering these walls with panels thus creates a warmer interior wall surface that inhibits condensation, although a vapor

barrier is needed behind these panels to prevent moisture becoming locked within the wall air space, continuing to cause a dampness odor.

The other conclusion is that the house humidity (volume of vapor in the air) can be reduced by an exhaust fan, moving the humid air outside.

So a program to eliminate basement dampness would involve the following: (1) panel the foundation walls, with or without insulation, but include a vapor barrier directly under the paneling to prevent condensation on the exterior masonry walls; (2) reduce the humidity level in the house by better ventilation, perhaps with a small exhaust fan. Check also to make sure that there are adequate vent louvers in the attic, and that they are unobstructed; (3) use an electric dehumidifier to reduce the water content of the air in the basement; (4) rip up old wood flooring if there is reason to suspect moisture condensation on the basement floor (replace with vinyl-asbestos tiles which have a warmer touch); (5) wrap all exposed water lines with insu-

Possible trouble spots shown by the letters A: generally damp surface indicates seepage or condensation; B: leakage through nonmoving cracks; C: leakage through moving cracks; D: active (pressure) leaks; E: trouble at floor-wall joint; F: floor-slab problems; G: requires exterior drainage of surface water.

lating tape to end moisture beading and dripping.

A simple test to determine the presence of condensation is to tape a piece of bright tin (a cover cut from a can) in direct contact with the damp surface, and leave it there for twenty-four hours. Beads of moisture on the outside of the patch show condensation. If the tin is wet on the back, this may be an indication of moisture seepage through the wall.

Flooding

Storm flooding is indeed a profound problem that usually can be solved only by a large-scale public works such as huge drainage sumps or installation of storm sewers. Where the condition is more moderate, some success has been achieved by individual action in erecting earthen barrier walls around vulnerable parts of the foundation, and by installing culverts to divert water flow.

Basements with high water tables that are subject

Asphalt coating over interior foundation wall helps to assure a dry basement. Waterproofing material is spread with a roller or brush, deeply covering every part of surface.

to damp spots on the floor and occasional underground water seepage, can obtain complete relief from this condition by installing an automatic sump pump. This requires a covered sump excavation about 2′ square, 2′ or 3′ deep, into which the water will collect and be pumped out as soon as it reaches a predetermined level that starts the pump.

For city homes subject to sewer backflow during heavy rains, a check valve in the sewer line is usually effective.

Seepage

Selection of the most satisfactory solution to your seepage problem depends mainly on how wet the walls are. Whichever waterproof coating you choose, apply it thoroughly—water denied entrance one place will seek another. Your best bet is to do the whole basement, first attending to any leaks or cracks tht may be present. When your plans include application of an interior surfacing material, an asphaltic or bituminous waterproof coating will help to ensure a dry wall.

Waterproof Cement

If you have an uneven concrete block wall, or one that is very damp most of the time, the safest measure is to apply a thick coat of waterproof cement and cover this with cement paint. Add a waterproofing chemical to water, and use this to make a mortar of 1 part cement 2½ parts sand. Trowel the coat ¼″ thick, dampening the wall first if necessary. If the wall is "running" water, relieve pressure by chipping weep holes at the base. (These are filled in after all repairs are completed.) When the mortar sets, apply not more than two coats of cement paint.

Many manufacturers package companion products for the home handyman—quick-setting hydraulic patching compound, a thick pore-filling base coat, and cement paint. Base coats are purchased dry and require mixing with water. Follow the manufacturer's directions carefully on the amount of material to use per yard for a satisfactory job. After prime-coating any repair areas with base coat and allowing it to set, dampen the walls. Apply a heavy application of base coating from the floor up, three or four block courses (heaviest water pressure is there after it rains). A scrubbing brush or other coarse-fibered brush is suggested for working the material well into the concrete surface. When the coating has set, apply cement paint.

After patching wall to stop leaks, apply prepared sealer first to lower portions, then coat entire wall. Use stiff cement brush.

PORTLAND CEMENT PAINT

Most cement paints can be applied over cinder or concrete block, poured concrete, stone, stucco, and unglazed brick. They are ideally used over the heavier base coaters for interior waterproofing or over a previous cement paint coat, but they cannot be used over any other type of paint.

If the walls are dry when you are ready to paint, dampen them, but if considerable water pressure is present, relieve that condition first (weep holes again). Let the paint coat damp-cure thoroughly before subjecting it to water pressure again.

LATEX PAINTS

When there is only periodic seepage and you are able to paint while the walls are dry, latex cement paints may be your solution. These may also be used if the surface has previously been painted with cement paint that is in good shape and not chalking. New concrete should be washed down with a 5 per cent solution of trisodium phosphate before you begin painting.

Leakage

Wherever you see evidence of water penetration, something needs fixing. Any cracks or crevices that aren't wet when you look are apt to be wet after the next good rain. Defects should be repaired whether they leak or not.

NONMOVING CRACKS

This is the so-called "common crack" and is simplest to repair, but it is usually neglected until it finally becomes troublesome—then you have to apply more extreme methods. You can safely afford to ignore only the tiniest hairline cracks, and then only if you use a pore-filling coat over the entire wall. There are several methods for patching nonmoving cracks.

SAND-CEMENT PATCHING MORTAR

Undercut the crack with a cold chisel, then brush clear of loose particles. Wet down and fill solid with a patching mortar, 1 part cement to 2½ parts sand. Certain chemicals are available which, when included in the mortar mix, prevent it from shrinking as it sets. Wet down and then scrub in grout for the best bond. Immediately fill and pack solid with a stiff mortar made with a nonshrink additive. Careful proportioning of additive and water is essential—be sure to follow manufacturer's instructions exactly.

For repairing wide cracks, use cold chisel to first chip off small particles at opening, allowing crack to be packed tightly with sand-cement mortar.

Large moving crack is packed with a joint sealer, using a hot iron, such as brick pointing tool, to force in the compound.

LATEX CEMENT PATCHING COMPOUND

The latex cement products are easiest to use but most expensive. You simply mix latex liquid with prepared powder to produce a mixture that can be troweled to a feather edge. The mix requires no preliminary wetting of the area. Once set, latex cement forms a waterproof bond, but it's only as strong as the surface to which it is bonded. If that is dust or loose cement, the bond doesn't break— the loose surface just comes off with the patch.

MOVING CRACKS

Moving cracks are the result of some sort of movement, and most causes of movement are recurrent. You'll only have repeated patching jobs if you use nonmoving methods in attempting to seal moving cracks. Proper solutions include bridging the crack (fine for small ones) with a flexible surface patch that will give with the movement, or filling it (the better choice for large ones) with a mastic joint sealer that will maintain a bond although it is pushed and pulled by the movement of the joint.

BRIDGING

A fiberglass fabric, specifically sold for that purpose, is used to bridge the crack. Clean the crack

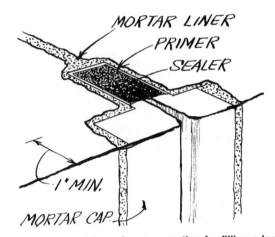

Proper steps are shown in cross section for filling a large moving crack. Mortar liner is packed deeply into the slot and allowed to dry, followed by the joint sealer filling the rest of the T stem, and finally the slotted mortar cap.

and a portion of the wall at least as wide as the membrane will be. Then apply a generous coating of patching compound with a brush and immediately place a piece of the fabric, cut to size, over the crack. Brush another coat of the compound over the membrane. A final coat may be applied the following day.

FILLING.

For a large moving crack, the filling method is preferred. First chip out the crack to a T-shaped slot, leaving the sides rough. Apply a mortar liner, using a quickset compound, to form a neater slot; when that is completely dry, apply primer and allow that to dry. Next use a hot iron (heat a bar or a cold chisel with your propane torch) to pack the joint sealer in place, filling almost the full depth of the T-stem. Finally, apply a mortar cap.

WET AND FLOWING LEAKS

If seeping water is present in a crack or an area to be patched, use a hydraulic setting mortar. You can purchase quickset additives to be used with ordinary mortar, but the pre-mixed compounds are easier to use. They just require the addition of water. Shape it quickly into a plug, shove it into the hole that's leaking, and hold it in place until it sets—a minute or so with most types. When filling cracks with this material, start at the top and work down.

Where water is actually flowing into your basement in streams, more work is needed. Chip away all defective concrete, keeping in mind that a deep narrow slot is easier to seal than a flat, shallow area.

Enlarge the worst leaks and cut weep holes near the bottom of the walls. Water under pressure goes the easiest way—give it an easy out. Into the largest leaks insert lengths of hose or tubing, held in place with quickset mortar if necessary, to relieve pressure on areas of lesser leakage. Plug the leaks with a quickset compound. Let stand at least overnight. When thoroughly dry, apply the coating, still letting the flood of water run free. When this has cured, return with more quicksetting plugs. Pull the bleeder hoses and force the plugs into the holes, holding them rigidly in place the minute or so it takes them to set.

CRACKS AT FLOOR-WALL JOINT

A frequent trouble spot is the floor-wall joint, resulting from water pressure beneath the floor slab that tends to lift it up, like floating a boat. Perimeter cracks are often the result. The first thing to do

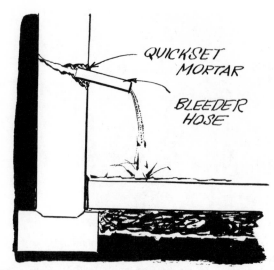

Bleeder hose inserted into large pressure leak carries away excess water while patching with quick-setting mortar.

is relieve the pressure. Use a sump pump if necessary, or direct surface water and rainwater away from your house foundation. After you relieve this situation, fix the joint, using moving crack methods.

You can bridge it with a flexible surface sealer and fabric. Paint on the sealing compound and embed the fabric membrane, forming a base cove as you go. Apply a second coat of the compound, carrying it out onto the floor and up the wall. If the crack is large and wet, filling it is the better method. Enlarge it to 1½" to 2" deep, fill with hot tar or tar and sand. If it is large but dry, repair with a mastic seal, coving the mortar cap to suit the joint location.

If a crack leaks periodically and you can wait for a long dry spell, use an epoxy resin compound to form the flexible seal. Just pour it into the cleaned-out crack.

Methods used for masonry walls are generally effective for filling similar cracks in floor slabs. Chip out cracks, put tape down in the bottom, run in epoxy crack filler, filling the crack to overflowing. Let floor repairs stand as long as possible, preferably for a year or more, before applying any concrete floor coating.

No coating we know of designed to protect masonry walls from seepage has good enough abrasion resistance to do the same job successfully on a floor. Portland cement paints will not take foot traffic. Paints, notably rubber-base paints and some of the newer latex-based masonry products, have the requisite wear qualities but will not be enough to prevent seepage.

Epoxy resin forms seal at floor-wall joint.

Latex liquid poured against outside foundation wall plugs hairline cracks by following the course of water leaks.

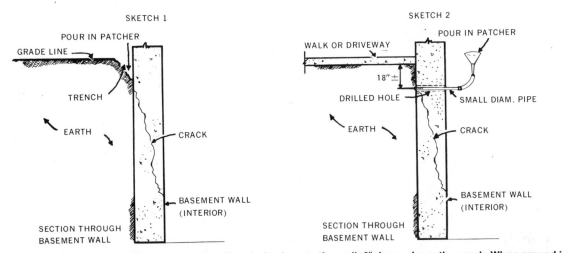

SKETCH 1

POUR IN PATCHER

GRADE LINE

TRENCH

EARTH

CRACK

BASEMENT WALL (INTERIOR)

SECTION THROUGH BASEMENT WALL

SKETCH 2

POUR IN PATCHER

WALK OR DRIVEWAY

18" ±

DRILLED HOLE

SMALL DIAM. PIPE

EARTH

CRACK

BASEMENT WALL (INTERIOR)

SECTION THROUGH BASEMENT WALL

When ground is accessible, pour the liquid into hole close to the wall, 6″ deep, above the crack. When ground is covered over, liquid may be poured from inside of basement through tube in a drilled hole.

TURN YOUR BASEMENT INTO A FAMILY FUN ROOM

HOW TO WARM UP YOUR BASEMENT

During the bitter winter days, when you need the space most, the basement is apt to be just too cold for comfort. The furnace is functioning well, and the upstairs is cozy, But downstairs—brrrr.

Insulation will minimize temperature swing, but won't keep in heat that isn't there. The same is true of weatherstripping and storm sash. Even putting in a wood floor may make it comfortable underfoot, but does nothing to raise the temperature.

Some basements can be made more livable with salvaged heat. There are devices to do this. One device substitutes for a section of pipe, between furnace and chimney, a fan that forces room air through this unit, where it is warmed. Another system makes use of snap-on fins to increase the radiating surface of hot water or steam pipes as they pass through the basement area. Both these salvage systems have one drawback—you have to take the heat where you find it, which just possibly will not be in the part of your basement where it is most needed.

The way to add warmth is to install a heater. Your present heating equipment may be oversized enough to supply an additional radiator or two, but the only way to be sure it has that capability is to have your local heating contractor check it out. A heating system is a *system,* and tinkering in the basement can easily upset the works.

Where you can supply a suitable flue, an oil- or gas-fired space heater is another possibility. So is a real fireplace. But finding an unused existing flue or installing an approved new one, won't be easy. Forget about dual use of an existing flue—it's too easy to produce dangerous smoke and draft disturbances. One alternative, where you have a wall above grade, is to use a through-wall heater. Your local fuel supplier will be glad to suggest units that would be suitable.

Installation of heater starts with fastening brackets to wall within 18″ of either end of the unit.

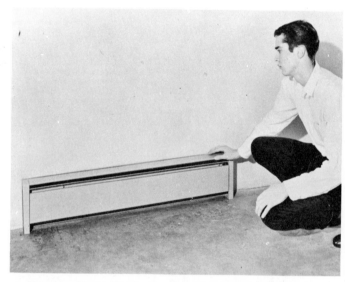

Heater is then attached to the brackets. Wiring should be planned before the heater location is selected.

Heater is thermostat-controlled, operates like conventional hot water heaters but has self-contained fluid.

HOME IMPROVEMENT BOOK

Facts On Space Heaters

All factors considered, supplementary electric heating is probably the most economical choice in the long run. You need no flue, it is clean, easy to operate and to control. When you compare on a total-cost basis (equipment, installation, and operating costs), electric heat is more practical than you might think.

Electric heaters, regardless of type, work on the same principles. There are radiant types (heat waves hit you and make you warm); natural convection types (warm air rises and cool air falls; air drawn in cool at the bottom of the heater is warmed and flows out the top); and there are forced convection types with a fan to blow air over the heating elements and aim it where you want it.

A built-in heater may necessitate additional electric service installation if you don't have an adequate system to carry the load—the same as you'd need for a dryer or an electric range.

Spot heating can be supplied by portable electric units that require only an outlet to plug them into. Fan-forced portables are usually more satisfactory than radiant types, but neither is very effective for larger areas unless used in groups, nor are they especially good looking. Where utility is the key word, however, they often fill the bill, but may blow the fuses.

Electric Fireplace

False fireplaces are at the other end of the appearance range. Designed to make an attractive focal center, such units incorporate either a radiant or a forced air circulation heater. Installation consists simply of hanging the fireplace on the wall and plugging in the heater. No flue is needed because there is no flame with electric heaters.

The best solution, of course, is built-in heaters. Installing them is simple for anyone with a practi-

The only thing false about this fireplace is that it is not woodburning, but contains an electric heater. It not only supplies that supplementary warmth so important at certain times, but also serves as a decorative focal point for the room.

TURN YOUR BASEMENT INTO A FAMILY FUN ROOM

cal knowledge of electrical wiring, but building codes in some cities forbid owner installation and you'll have to pay for professional wiring. Whether or not you actually do the electrical work you should understand the procedure well enough to know at which point you can do what.

The easiest time to install built-in heating is while finishing a basement room. First plan with your electrical contractor on the type of units, how many, and where they will go. With the basement dry and treated to stay that way, install furring or framing. Then the wiring can be roughed in and the insulation installed. Depending on the heater design, this is often the time to finish the walls, too. The heater is then fastened in place and the electrical connections made. Thermostat wiring is similar to that required for a light switch. If your base-

ment is already finished, surface mounted heaters may be your best choice.

In addition to direct radiant and forced circulation units, there are some which provide the advantages of hydronic heat without plumbing. In these, an antifreeze solution is hermetically sealed inside copper tubing. The electric element heats and causes the liquid to circulate to the finned area, where heat is distributed by air circulation.

There's news, too, in *overhead* electric heating. Resistor-coated gypsum panels can be nailed up and finished like other ceiling panels; they are joined together with special electrode clips. Another new product—radiant heating ceiling panels, one of the best-looking systems and most easily installed—is wired as easily as a lighting fixture.

A permanent source of supplementary heating is this baseboard radiation system, available in many sizes.

Ceiling heater panels are wired similarly to any electric fixture, and installation is designed particularly for do-it-yourselfers. The packing box is used as the template to locate fastening points for the panels.

Resistor-coated gypsum panels on ceiling are joined with special electrode clips, which look the same as standard panels, but provide comfortable overhead heating.

PLUMBING TASKS

The home owner who knows his way around the plumbing system and how to handle the necessary tools, has the advantage of being able to make improvements around the house quickly and at a minimum cost. The savings obviously will be substantial for the do-it-yourselfer who can connect the water and soil lines for a new laundry sink, a bathroom in the finished attic, who can install a sink in a darkroom or a wet bar in the recreation room.

Other occasions when his knowledge of plumbing will be needed will be when installing a new dishwasher for a kitchen-remodeling project, setting up a shower head outside for those using the swimming pool, or putting in a convenient hose faucet in the driveway for washing the car.

Many home owners develop a keen interest in plumbing work and take pride in being able to make these improvements in addition to doing all repairs at considerable savings.

Plumbing tools are not expensive and very few are needed, so the total investment is minimal compared to the benefits. The assortment required will depend on the type of plumbing system in your home. If you have pipe, and the local ordinances require that all new installations also be of pipe, you will need the following: a pipe vise (or a notched insert for use with a large bench vise); a pair of Stillson pipe wrenches, one 8″ and one 12″ size; a hack saw or pipe cutter, and a reamer. A threading die is used rarely, and this tool can be rented for the day whenever needed.

For homes with copper tubing systems, a tubing cutter and reamer combination, propane torch, and set of bending springs constitute the basic tools.

When you want to tap a water branch off a pipe, to connect a sink, for example, the water pipe must be cut and a section inserted. The best way to start

An important detail in plumbing technique is to support the remaining part with a second wrench when applying pressure on any pipe.

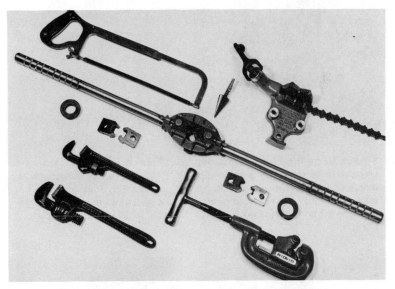

Typical assortment of tools used for pipe work includes Stillson pipe wrenches, hack saw, reamer, chain clamp, pipe cutter. The threader and dies are used infrequently and may be rented.

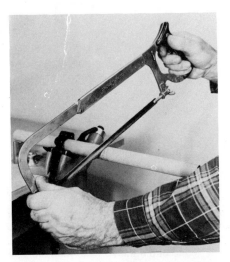

Pipe is cut with hack saw or rotary pipe cutter. When using hack saw, hold front with one hand, applying downward pressure on forward stroke.

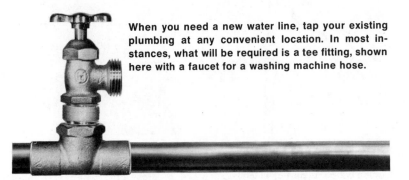

When you need a new water line, tap your existing plumbing at any convenient location. In most instances, what will be required is a tee fitting, shown here with a faucet for a washing machine hose.

101

is to make up a complete insert in advance, consisting of a T-fitting, two nipples, and a union. In this way, the measurement can be marked off precisely for the pipe cutting. Remember to allow for the distance that the old pipe will run into the new fitting, which is five or six threads or about ¾". This is for only one end of the insert, since the other end, which contains the union coupling, already has the two parts of the union turned on both sides of the joint, which will meet flush.

A union has three parts, two of which are turned onto the ends of the pipes that are to be joined; the other is a large collar nut with internal threads that pulls and locks the other two parts together.

The purpose of the union is to make possible the disassembly of threaded piping without having to saw through any of the pipe to remove a section or make an insert. Once the union collar is opened and the pipe is free at one end, it is possible to turn the pipe out of its fitting at the other end of the run. Most plumbers spot several unions at strategic places in pipe assemblies for this reason.

Pipe threads should be coated with plumber's compound and wound with strands of lampwick cord to obtain positive joint seal. A more advanced way is with Hercules Tape Dope, a thin plastic tape made of duPont Teflon that lubricates and seals the threads.

Section to be inserted into existing water line is made up beforehand, including the new faucet, to get accurate measurement and avoid putting strain on the lines. Continue as shown at right.

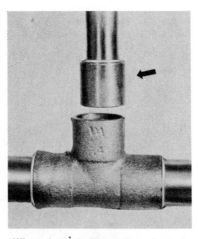

When branch line taken from tee fitting is of smaller diameter, a reducing bushing does the trick. These reducers and other adapters are available in all sizes.

When you tap a line for a faucet, use a tee with threaded opening. Reinforce the tubing while you tighten the faucet into the threads.

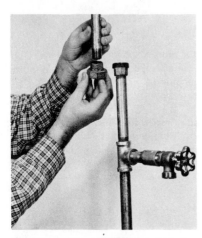

New assembly, inserted into line, will be connected to original pipe with union coupling, part of which is being threaded on opposing pipe.

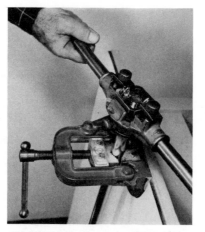

Special vise holds pipe while threads are cut with steel dies. Watch outside of dies, stop when first full-depth thread is seen.

Plastic tape is faster, cleaner, more efficient than plumber's compound for lubricating and sealing pipe joints. One and a half turns around the pipe are sufficient.

Copper tubing is a salvation to home owners in localities that permit its use for water and drain lines. Not only is the copper lighter, cheaper, and more flexible, it needs no threading and is easily joined by soldering in special fittings right at the installation. When the water line meets obstructions, or must go up into the walls, the tubing can be simply bent as required. With pipe, by contrast, fittings must be threaded on at every bend or turn in the line.

Copper tubing is cut with a simple rotary cutter which leaves the ends square to seat perfectly into the fittings. There are dozens of types of fittings, to meet every possible situation, including adapters to permit use of tubing together with brass pipe in the same system, and to use various size tubing at different fixtures.

The big deal with tubing is the sweat-soldering technique that can make a permanent joint in minutes. The essential step in sweat soldering is cleaning, which means getting right down to the bright copper metal. The tube ending, and the inside of the fitting, are polished with emery cloth, then coated with solder paste. The tube is pushed into the fitting so that it is firmly seated and heat is applied with a propane torch. When sufficiently heated, the flame is removed and the solder placed at the joint.

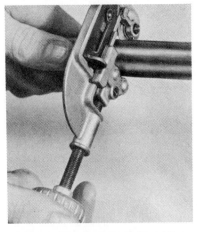

Copper tubing is cut quickly with an inexpensive wheeled cutter. Cutting wheel is moved into the tube by turns of the knurled knob.

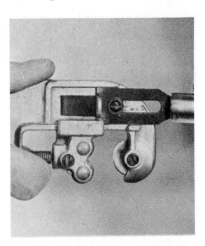

Reamer blade, which is a part of the cutter, is used to remove inside burrs formed when tubing is cut.

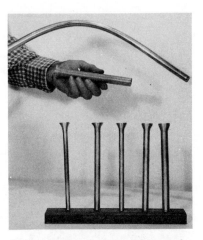

Coil springs permit the tubing to be bent without kinking. Springs of various diameters are shown in the rack.

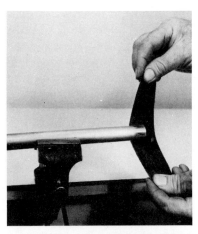

First step in sweat-soldering is to sand and polish both the tubing and the inside of the fitting, down to the bright metal. Coat with soldering paste.

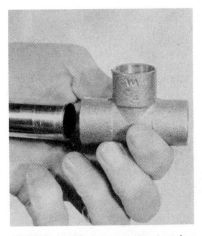

Tubing must have square cut end, so it can be pushed deeply into the fitting and properly seated.

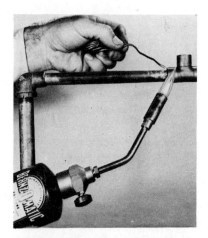

Heating is done with propane torch. Move flame over entire fitting to get even heating, along the flanges. Do not put flame on the solder.

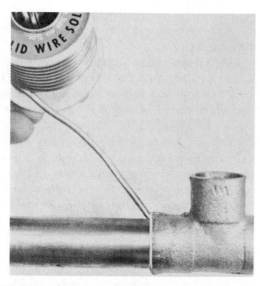

Remove flame and touch solder to the fitting. If heat is adequate, solder will melt and flow into the flange.

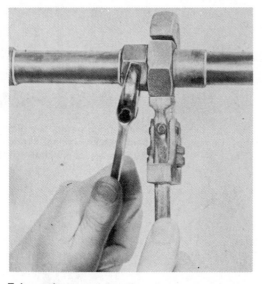

Tube ends are put together, then a ring nut that fits against flange on one side is tightened on the threads of the opposite side, pulling both ends tightly together.

A union joins two cut ends of existing line together, or allows a new insert into the line. Here are shown both flange ends of the union, soldered to the tubing.

If the heat is sufficient, the solder will melt and run into the joint. Do not play the flame on the solder itself—that will simply burn it up. It won't matter in what position the solder is applied—above or even underneath the fitting—since the molten solder is drawn in by capillary action.

As soon as the solder has run in, use a cloth to "wipe" the joint, removing the excess paste and smoothing the surface solder for a trim appearance.

Cutting in on a Line

Here are the actual steps for cutting into a copper tubing line, specifically in this case to put in a T-fitting and faucet for a washing machine hose. The procedure is the same as for other tubing connections.

Begin by shutting off the water supply and, if possible, draining the line, leaving faucets open in other parts of the house. Mark the existing line for the T-fitting you want to insert, and cut the line at this point, using a tubing cutter. Make a second cut about a foot away and remove the section, but don't discard it.

Fit the T on one end of the old section, then take the 1' cut-away piece and shorten it to go into the remaining space between the T and the union.

The important thing is to determine how much to cut away, since the tubing must go into two flanges—that of the T at one end, and the union at the other—it is necessary to allow just enough length, plus the distance between the outside surfaces of the two fittings. This can be done by measuring the depth, but if the existing line has some free play, it will move either way enough to make up for any discrepancy in the measurement.

The sweat soldering is done as described earlier. First one side of the union is soldered on an open end of the line, then the other part soldered to the take-up piece. This insert piece is soldered to one side of the T-fitting and the T soldered to the other open end of the line. The take-up piece should just fit in at the union, which is then drawn up tight by turning the collar nut.

BUILD A WALK-IN CLOSET
UNDER THE STAIRS

The under-stairs area in the basement, when properly enclosed, can be transformed into what every homemaker appreciates—an attractive and convenient walk-in closet, with easy access to neatly hung garment bags and spacious storage shelves.

The enclosure is made with paneling, either ¼" hardwood veneered plywood or knotty pine boards, to match the rest of the basement finishing—and in fact this staircase wall itself becomes part of the basement finishing project.

Every part of the under-stairs area is utilized. The walk-in area, which is of full height, includes not only rods for a number of garment bags but also a drawer cabinet or open steel shelving. Where the stair stringers slope downward, and overhead clearance decreases, two shelves can be installed that are quite deep and suitable for off-the-floor storage of luggage and other large items.

Far inside this area, the sharp slope prevents access from inside the enclosure, but this very useful, deep storage space need not be wasted. Instead, a hatch is provided in the covering panel wall, effectively providing access to this area from the side.

Materials required for the project are 2-by-4 framing members, ¼" veneered plywood panels, preferably prefinished, a 24" louver door, or a pair of 12" doors, and the various hardware items, including some masonry anchors. For the inside installations, there will be the 1½" diameter clothing rods, steel shelving of your choice, and some 1" x 12" shelving lumber.

Construction procedures vary somewhat according to position and type of stairs; some are free-standing, away from any wall, others may be alongside and attached to a wall. The type of landing above also will affect the arrangement. Most stairways will extend for a 6' length, extending from top to bottom treads, as measured in floor distance. There usually is an additional space of 3' below the upper landing, making a minimum of 9' for the closet enclosure. This often is extended a few feet more to an end wall, below some first-floor installation. In any event, try to allot a total exterior length of 12' for this closet.

Enclosing the Treads

If your basement stairs have only treads but no risers (the vertical boards between the treads) the

Understairs area, typically cluttered with assorted odds and ends, seen before start of project to convert the space into a practical closet for garment storage.

Completed paneling not only encloses the understairs closet, but serves also as a finished wall for the basement playroom project. Bifold louver doors are at extreme left.

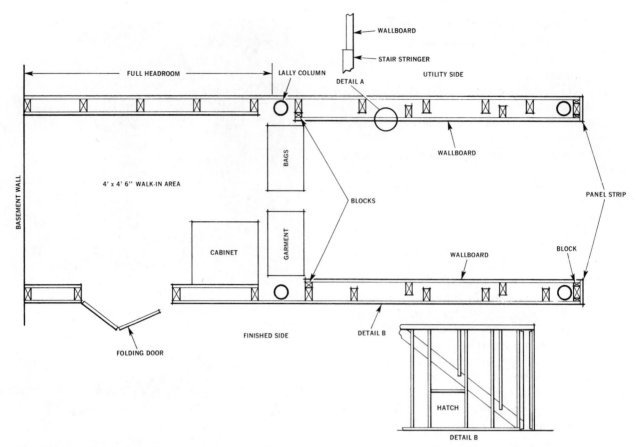

Plan for enclosing area under basement stairs includes spacious walk-in closet, and section under stringers to be utilized with shelving and hatchway.

first necessary step is to cover the back of the stair-case, to seal out the dust that inevitably results from use of the stairs. The preferred way would be to install risers, cut from 1½″ stock, to fit behind each of the treads, nailed in through the stringers from the sides, and into the back edge of the treads. A simpler method would be merely to cover the entire bottom of the stairs with one plywood panel, ½″ or ¾″ thickness, fitted to the underside of the stair stringers and securely nailed in place.

In the project shown, the wall paneling was placed to enclose the entire staircase, but this may be modified so that the stair section is left partly open for better lighting and increased visibility in the playroom.

The actual closet framing starts with attaching a length of 2-by-4 across the ceiling joists, either directly against the stairs or some inches away. In the project shown in the photograph, there was a ceiling beam which served this purpose, so no top plate was necessary.

Framing the Closet

Plumb lines dropped from the ceiling plate (or present beam) will show the location for placing a floor plate directly below. This plate should be fastened to the concrete floor with several masonry anchors. An additional plate is turned at the end toward the wall, first framing out the 24″ wide opening for the bifold louver doors; then the other uprights are spaced 16″ apart.

The plywood paneling is put up directly over the wall studs, starting at one side of the door frame, as less than a full-width panel may be needed at the other end. In one panel, at the position of the lower stair treads, a hatch opening is cut into the panel, and the piece attached with flexible strap hinges on the inside, for access to the shallow space there. The panels are secured to the studs with finishing nails, the heads counterset, and the holes puttied with matching filler. Nails in grooves of the plywood do not need puttying.

The louver doors are hung in the wall opening, the frame then trimmed with standard molding.

Interior Finishing

The closet interior should be made as bright and pleasant looking as possible. That means, first, good lighting, so be sure to install an overhead lamp, controlled by a wall switch. Second in importance is tiling the floor, with as light and bright a color as you can obtain: white or light yellow would be best. Thirdly, do not leave the 2-by-4 wall framing exposed inside. Put up inexpensive gypsum panels over the frame, with molding trim at all edges. This not only improves the appearance but also helps to seal out dust from the closet.

STEEL BASEMENT DOORS
REPLACE WOOD COVERS

A separate basement entrance from the back yard is a boon to the home owner. If you have such an entrance now, here is information on better protecting your basement against the weather, making it safer from intruders, neater, and more convenient. For those who would like to have such an entrance, details are supplied on how to go about it.

The short flight of steps and unencumbered entryway make it easy to bring large plywood pan-

Hatch opening, almost invisible in the finished panels, is framed around the inside. This gives access to space at lower end of the staircase.

els and lumber into the basement—a particular advantage when you're finishing the playroom and building other projects. Children can enter and leave by this door from the back yard, rather than tracking through the upstairs rooms—something every homemaker will appreciate. Lawn chairs and other outdoor items can be taken in more easily through the convenient basement door.

An ideal replacement for a typical wooden hatchway that has seen better days, and is at best a constant source of annoyance, is a lifetime steel basement door that is weathertight, attractive, and easy to use. Known as the Bilco door, it comes in stock units that replace the old wood doors. Installation usually requires some masonry work. This may be limited to just laying bricks at the part in front of the steps, and some mortaring of the outside joint at the bottom for water protection. In some instances, a concrete base is laid all around the stair opening to which the door housing flange is bolted.

Pool Cabanas

A valuable additional benefit, not always realized when the doors are installed, is as an adjunct to the swimming pool. The dressing room cabanas can be set up right inside the basement, which are then easily reached by the bathers through the door directly from the back yard, where an outside shower can be set up most easily adjacent to the driveway or basement entrance.

Framing involved placement of floor plate and raising of 2-by-4 studs. House beam served as top stud plate. Note cross piece in framing for an access hatch to reach lower storage section.

Opening For New Stairway

In homes not equipped with this convenience, it is not very difficult or expensive to cut through the average basement wall, build concrete stairs, and put in a door hatch. The work requires cutting an opening in the foundation wall, which is done with a pneumatic hammer and takes an experienced contractor about half an hour for a cement block wall, and a little less than an hour for a poured concrete wall.

The rest follows a method developed by the Bilco Company and requires excavating an area for the stairwell, lining this area with cement blocks on both sides, and either forming the stairs of Portland cement, or attaching steel stringers which have supporting slots for the treads. A concrete curbing is formed around the outside of the well, and to this the steel hatch doors are bolted.

The many advantages of an outdoor entry to the basement are often offset by the disreputable appearance and poor condition of old-fashioned wood hatch covers. A modern prefab steel unit, attractive, easy to use, and weathertight, can be installed quickly by the family handyman at modest cost, for permanent carefree service.

First step is to remove and discard the old rotting door and all house trim around the hatchway. A crowbar makes short shrift of the job. Continue as at right.

Stairwell completely cleared. Part of beam extending from house into the stairwell area also has been cut away to square the opening.

Any damaged parts of the house siding are now patched. Side panel of new steel hatch is tried in to check the level.

Prefabricated parts are easily assembled. All necessary fasteners are supplied. Set the hatch closely against the house siding.

Use spirit level to position the assembled hatchway, propping where necessary to overcome uneven grading. If frame is twisted, doors will not function properly.

If area is unpaved, excavate section in front of the steps, also under the steel framing for brick foundation. This work can be done beforehand, providing a ready-made base.

Foundation laid with brick, to height somewhat above grade. The frame, attached to house with lag screws through predrilled holes, supports the hatch frame during masonry work.

After foundation is completed, check that frame is square. This can be done by measuring the diagonals from corner to corner—when exactly equal, the frame is square.

Final touchup is made by applying mortar to cover the bricks, also to form a cove where the hatch fits on the foundation, so that rain water will drain away.

Wall joints are waterproofed with bead of nonhardening calking compound. Where there are large gaps between hatch flange and siding, fill first with scraps of wood or steel wool to support the calking compound.

Replace the house trim that had been removed. Final step is to hang the doors on the hatchway. Holes are predrilled so doors are easily fitted.

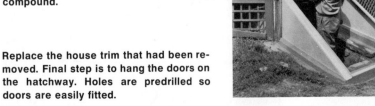

BASIC PARTITION FRAMING

Since none of the basement partitions will be load-bearing, 2-by-3 lumber can be used for the framing in most cases.

For economy, the studs may be placed on 24″ centers rather than the 16″ centers normally used. Utility grade lumber is fine for framing purposes. At the lumberyard, select pieces as straight as possible for use as plates and studs. (Plates are the horizontal 2-by-4's attached to the floor and ceiling.)

Select a straight piece of lumber for the plate and secure it to the floor—use helix screw nails on a concrete floor, 12d common nails on a wood floor. Extend the plate across those sections where doors will be located, but do not put nails in these sections, as they will be cut out later.

Select another straight piece of 2-by-4 for the top plate and lay it alongside the sole plate. The location of studs should be marked simultaneously on both plates.

If your partition begins at a wall that will be furred (as will be the case with many basement walls), allow for the width of the furring strip (usually ¾″) before marking the position of the first stud. Place a framing square across both plates and carefully make a pencil line. Mark an **X** on each plate on the side of the line where the stud is to be located.

Locating the Studs

Studs are spaced 16″ or 24″ apart, on centers. The reason is that this provides a modular basis for putting up the wall panels, which are standard 48″ width. Studs 16″ or 24″ apart always provide a full nailing surface for the panel edges, with intermediary supporting surfaces.

The stud positions can be marked off directly on your floor and ceiling plates. The best way to determine the correct locations of the studs is to cut a spacer strip of scrap wood. This should be 16″ long, less the thickness of your stud lumber. Thus, the spacer is short by two halves, or half the thickness of two studs. In arithmetical formula, the actual thickness of a 2-by-3 usually is 1½″. Subtracting 1½″ from 16″ leaves 14½″, the length of your spacer. To prove the arithmetic: the distance between the studs will be 14½″, and the centers of the two adjoining studs will add ¾″ on each side or 1½″, making a total spacing of 16″ on center. This method can be used to work out all your wall framing setups.

There's one vital detail, however, over which many mistakes occur. The first stud against a wall will be fully covered with the wall panel, not just to its center—so this stud is measured from its far edge to locate the second stud. In practice, the spacing for the second stud must subtract an additional ¾″ (or whatever is the actual half of the stud dimension) leaving just 13¾″. Mark the lines for both sides of this stud and continue with the full 14½″ spacer, marking off the rest of the studs.

A quick and efficient way to put up a partition is to prefabricate the framing, then erect it for nailing into position. As shown in the sketches, the studs are set in proper position (for 16″ centers) and nailed through the top and base plates. This eliminates the difficult toenailing and assures a more accurate alignment of the studs.

The frame need not be built the entire length of the partition wall, if that would require an extremely heavy and unwieldy structure. Rather, make it in two or more parts, which can be joined together when the frames are put up. But be careful when doing this to retain the correct continuity

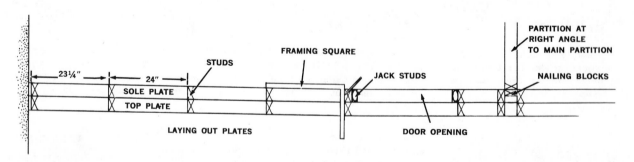

Partition framed with door opening, studs at 24″ spacing on centers. Top and bottom plates are set side by side and marked for positioning the studs, allowing for wall panel to cover the first stud completely, then panel edges reach to centers of all other studs for nailing.

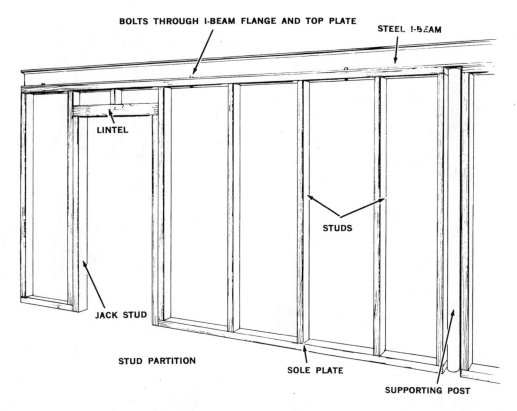

BOLTS THROUGH I-BEAM FLANGE AND TOP PLATE

STEEL I-BEAM

LINTEL

STUDS

JACK STUD

STUD PARTITION

SOLE PLATE

SUPPORTING POST

Sole plate is secured to the floor while the top plate is attached to ceiling joists, or as in this case, to the steel I-beam. Methods of bypassing a lally column or other obstruction, and framing of the door opening, are shown.

of stud spacing—that is, do not measure from the outside stud of the second frame but from the center of the last stud of the previous frame. Always keep in mind that the wall is designed for modular spacing of 4'-wide panels.

When measuring for the frame, allow sufficient clearance at the top to swing the frame upright from the floor. Test the maximum height with a length of 2-by-4 to be sure you have it right; otherwise the frame may have to be disassembled and cut down for as little as a half-inch just to clear the ceiling joists.

Snap a chalk line across the ceiling to get a straight line for the partition. After raising the frame, shim the top or bottom with strips of wood to take up the slack, then secure the top and bottom plates to the floor and the ceiling joists with nails or masonry anchors, as needed. If the partition goes out from a side wall, nail the end stud solidly to that wall, all with the objective of a sturdy, vibration-free wall.

The next step is to prepare the partition framing as a base for the wall panels. While the plywood or gypsum panels can be put directly over the studs, the most approved method is to place furring strips horizontally across the studs. The prime benefit is that this enables you to shim the furring strips into perfect alignment—something that can't be done as precisely with the 2-by-4 studs.

Furring may be 1-by-2 or 1-by-3 strips. But many walls are higher than the 8' length of the panels. The way to handle this is with a baseboard, perhaps 4" high, covering 1" or 2" of the bottom panel edges.

First nail on a strip of 1-by-4 furring (or two continuous 1-by-2 strips) along the bottom, then continue with the horizontal furring about 18" apart to the top, placing a nail or two at every intersection with the studs.

Use a long straightedge board to check the furring as you go to see that they are all even—that is, in alignment. Any sections that bow inward should

TURN YOUR BASEMENT INTO A FAMILY FUN ROOM

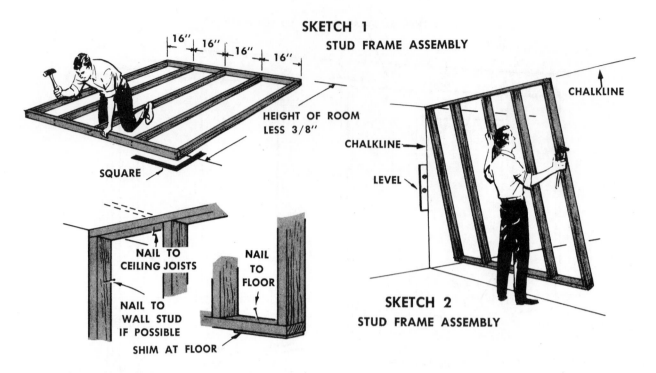

SKETCH 1
STUD FRAME ASSEMBLY

16" 16" 16" 16"

HEIGHT OF ROOM
LESS 3/8"

SQUARE

CHALKLINE

CHALKLINE

LEVEL

SKETCH 2
STUD FRAME ASSEMBLY

NAIL TO
CEILING JOISTS

NAIL
TO
FLOOR

NAIL TO
WALL STUD
IF POSSIBLE

SHIM AT FLOOR

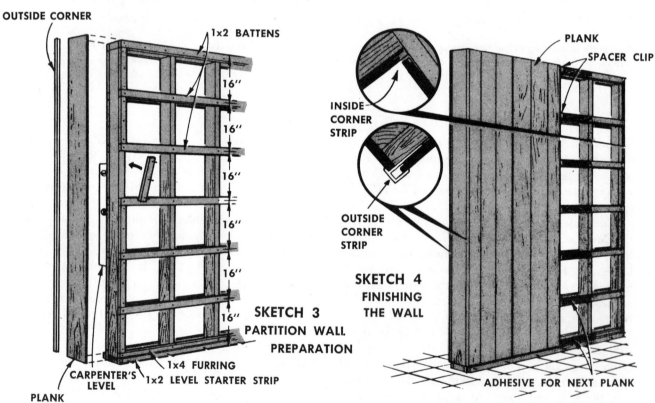

OUTSIDE CORNER

1x2 BATTENS

16"

16"

16"

16"

16"

16"

SKETCH 3
PARTITION WALL
PREPARATION

1x4 FURRING

CARPENTER'S
LEVEL

1x2 LEVEL STARTER STRIP

PLANK

PLANK

SPACER CLIP

INSIDE
CORNER
STRIP

OUTSIDE
CORNER
STRIP

SKETCH 4
FINISHING
THE WALL

ADHESIVE FOR NEXT PLANK

Prefabricated partition frame is assembled on the floor, with studs nailed through the top and bottom plates. Use trysquare for truing up the frame assembly. Frame is ⅜" shorter than ceiling height to allow clearance. Chalk line across the ceiling assures straight aligning of partition sections.

be backed up with thin plywood shims as needed, then nailed through. If the furring bows *outward* at any point, because the stud may be somewhat warped there, the easiest correction is to plane down the stud sufficiently for the furring to clear without distortion, or replace the stud.

Finally, temporarily nail a 1-by-2 starter strip over the bottom furring, making sure that this is level. The wall panels will rest on this strip for plumb alignment. Later, the strip will be removed and the space covered with the base molding.

LAUNDRY BUILT-IN

Where to locate the laundry? The most sensible and economical place is where the water is—or at least the soil line. Most likely, that's the most cramped space of all; but obviously it's easier to adapt the laundry to the available space rather than to move the utilities.

While you're at it, there's a chance that you can solve some additional problems, particularly the important one of a means for sorting laundry items for separate washes—dyed fabrics, synthetics, woolens, and the heavier (and dirtier) youngsters' togs. This is taken care of in the illustrated plan by four storage bins, although additional ones can be provided if required.

A sink with plastic counter top, and a group of wall cabinets, provide the rest of the facilities. Remember that the sink also will be invaluable as an adjunct of the playroom, for preparing and serving light refreshments, and for convenient clean-up without carrying things upstairs to the kitchen.

Good lighting, bright colors, a resilient waterproof floor covering are requisites that can make doing the laundry a pleasure instead of a chore.

Here's another example of two-for-one planning that fits a practical laundry arrangement into a playroom corner. When washday chores are over, mangle rolls under shelf at left, and drapes cover the entire laundry area.

The whole wide playroom is a pleasant laundry with the washing machine, hamper, and dryer lined against the wall under a window. The mangle is conveniently mounted inside a sturdy floor cabinet.

Instant transformation to hide laundry requires only closing the bifold louver doors, swinging the mangle back into the cabinet, which now becomes a serving bar.

114

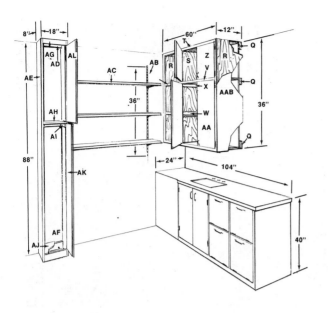

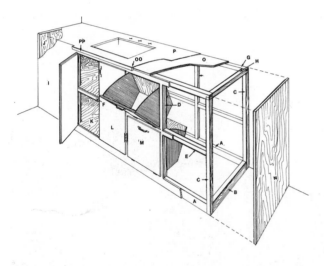

Bottom Cabinet

A. Two pieces, 101 x 4 x 2″

B. Two pieces, 21 x 4 x 2″

C. Four pieces, 38 x 2 x 2″

D. Eight pieces, 35 x 2 x 2″

E. Four pieces, 21 x 2 x 2″

F. Four pieces, 14 x 2 x 2″

G. Two pieces, 104 x 2 x 2″

H. Two pieces, 24 x 2 x 2″

I. One piece, 24 x 40 x 1/4″

J. Four pieces, 24 x 16 x 3/4″

K. Two pieces, 30 1/2 x 24 x 3/4″

L. Two doors, flush, each: 34 x 14 x 1/2″

M. Four bins, each: one front, 21 x 16 1/2 x 1/2″; two sides, 16 x 15 x 1/4″; one back, 18 7/8 x 11 x 1/4″; one bottom, 19 7/8 x 8 1/2 x 1/4″

N. One side, 40 x 24 x 3/4″

O. One piece, 104 x 25 x 3/4″

OO. One piece, 16 x 2 x 1″

P. Plastic laminate, 104 x 25″

PP. Plastic laminate, 16 x 2″

Wall Cabinet

Q. Three cross rails, each: 58 1/2 x 4 x 3/4″

QQ. One piece, 58 x 36 x 3/4″

R. Two sides, each: 36 x 12 x 3/4″

S. One center piece, 34 x 10 3/4 x 3/4″

T. Two pieces, each: 58 1/2 x 12 x 3/4″

U. Two pieces, each: 18 x 10 3/4 x 3/4″

V. One piece, 36 3/4 x 10 3/4 x 3/4″

W. One piece, 36 3/4 x 9 1/4 x 3/4″

X. Six cleats, each: 9 x 1 x 3/4″

Y. Two door stops, each: 1 x 3/4 x 3/4″

Z. Two doors, each: 18 7/16 x 10 15/16 x 3/4″

AA. Two doors, each: 21 15/16 x 18 7/16 x 3/4″

AB. Plastic laminate, 36 x 12″ 1/16″

Shelves

AAB. Two standards, each: 36″

AC. Three pieces each: 48 x 8 x 1″

Utility Cabinet

AD. Three cross rails, each: 18 x 4 x 3/4″

AE. Two sides, each: 88 x 8 x 3/4″

AF. One piece, 16 x 4 x 3/4″

AG. One piece, 16 x 2 x 3/4″

AH. One piece, 16 x 8 x 3/4″

AI. Two cleats, each: 7 x 2 x 3/4″

AJ. One piece, 16 x 7 x 3/4″

AK. One flush door (1/2-inch lip), 33 x 16 1/2 x 1″

AL. One flush door (1/2-inch lip), 48 x 16 1/2 x 1″

The sink counter is built on a frame of 2-by-2 stock, fitted into glued half-lap joints at corners, dado joints at inside assemblies. The completed frame is attached to the wall studs with nails or screws, reinforced with angle brackets attached to the floor.

The clothes bins are made of 1/4″ plywood, except the fronts, which are of 1/2″ stock. The sides are curved on the top for a 15 1/2″ radius from the hinge, which is at the front edge. The back and bottom pieces are glued to 1/2″-by-1/2″ gluing blocks in the bins, while the front is rabbetted back half its thickness for attaching the side pieces with finishing nails.

Detailed instructions for making the counter top with laminated plastic surfacing, and for attaching the sink bowl, are given in the chapter on kitchen remodeling.

Organize your laundry room for more efficiency with this easy-to-build arrangement.

HIDEAWAY LAUNDRY ROOM

It's one thing to cover up laundry equipment when using the area for other purposes, but it's a great advance when the laundry room can be as glamorous as a movie star's studio trailer and the equipment still be inconspicuous when not in use.

The quality of this latter arrangement is apparent in the illustration, which shows the laundry equipment neatly arranged into a straight wall recess, completely enclosed by folding doors that slide across on their track. When the laundry is idle, an attractive wall of panel doors is seen, each with inserts of translucent fiberglass laminated with colorful natural leaves, sprays of grasses, and butterflies.

The folding doors shown are suspended from a single overhead track which guides the nylon pivot rollers. The full-length door panels, available as stock lumberyard items, are linked with three hinges on each. The plastic panels, which are easily cut to size, are held with quarter-round molding trim.

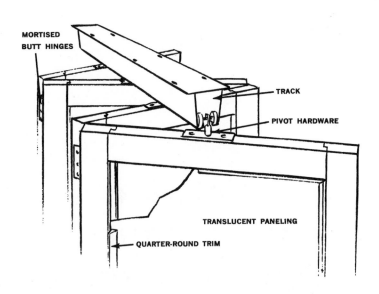

Compact laundry, built into wall recess, has all necessary equipment conveniently arranged in a row, with diffused lighting from soffit. Sketch shows how triple panel doors on each side move in single overhead track.

117

Chapter 4

BETTER BATHROOMS

Gleaming tiles and mirrors and softly diffused lighting comprise one aspect of the modern bathroom. Color and design add individuality. More basic, perhaps, is that the bathroom must be practical, its construction and furnishings easily maintained, resistant to moisture, and trouble-free.

For many families, the top home improvement priority is that of modernizing an antiquated bathroom; others have the long-hoped-for objective of obtaining one or even two additional bathrooms in the home.

The contents of this chapter will be helpful to home owners who need a guide for improving the family's bathroom: restoring damaged or inadequate walls, putting in a separate shower, installing the latest style lavatory faucets, providing more storage space for linens and other necessary bathroom supplies, and much more.

FACE LIFT FOR A DRAB BATHROOM

Owners of older homes, thinking of going the remodeling route, often tend to delay bathroom proj-

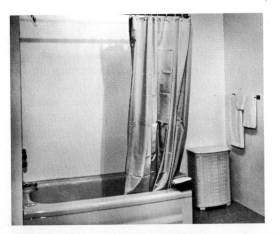

Before installing closet, bathroom has no storage space for linens, toiletries, and other bathroom supplies.

By the addition of a closet, wasted space is put to use and the bathroom's appearance is dramatically altered.

ects because of the complexity of the job, or the large costs involved.

Neither of these need concern you any longer for the project shown here is quickly finished, easily done, and costs surprisingly little. True, it isn't re-modeling in the fullest sense, but you will have changed the bathroom dramatically while adding a useful storage closet.

Some preparation of the walls is advisable before starting work. Their surfaces should be clean, dry,

and reasonably smooth if the covering panels are to bond well. If the wall was painted with a high gloss enamel, go over it with coarse sandpaper to break the film, before washing. Be sure to scrape away all loose paint chips and cracked plaster. Follow with patching plaster to fill all cracks.

For the first step, build the stud frame that will separate the closet from the tub. The partition should be at least as wide as the bathtub.

To gain maximum storage area, construct the

Studding is turned sideways to make a 2-inch wall. Note the spacer between tub and studs. Continue as below.

Cut gypsum to size and nail in place over frame. Cover front header panel and strips alongside door opening.

Build identical framework for other side. Use rustproof nails throughout. Header framing fits prenotched studding.

Closet interior is lined with perforated hardboard for easy shelf adjustment. Mount rear panel on wall cleats.

studding from 2-by-4's turned to make a 2″ wall rather than the conventional 4″ thickness, using rustproof nails throughout because of the moisture ever present in bathrooms. The framing for each side may be preassembled and nailed in position as a unit or built in place. In either case, notch the front studs beforehand, to accept the framing for the header panel that is above the door opening.

A small sheet of gypsum wallboard must be placed between the foot of the tub and the studding. Without this spacer, the partition would intrude into the space above the tub.

From this point onward, the project rapidly takes shape. Partition and header are covered with gypsum board panels, the framework at the sides of the door opening being covered with scraps.

Perforated hardboard lines the inside of the closet. It carries the fixtures which support the shelves and other stored objects. Mount the rear panel on cleats; the space thus provided behind the panel allows the hanger fixtures to seat properly.

The decorative doors are both practical and attractive, the grillework consisting of stamped-out hardboard panels. Doors can be purchased already made up or you can make them yourself.

PLASTIC-COATED PANELING

For the tub enclosure, the rustproof retainer moldings are nailed into place in each corner and at both ends. Use a level when setting the moldings for they must be parallel to one another. The tile-like paneling, a melamine plastic-finished hardboard, comes with the moldings, adhesive, trowel, etc., as a kit. The paneling is supplied in two pieces, one for the rear wall of the enclosure, while

Nail mouldings supplied with the kit to both corners and outside edges. Mouldings are grooved for panels.

Shelf arrangement can be changed at any time due to use of adjustable shelf supports.

Apply adhesive to panel back with notched trowel. Spread liberally but not excessively.

Measure recessed area around the tub so that prefinished wall panels can be cut to correct dimensions.

Bow the panel enough to allow it to fit in the moulding grooves, then snap panel into place and press against wall.

Side panels must be cut to fit. Use a fine-toothed saw and cut with finished side up. Mouldings hide cut edges.

the other must be cut into two pieces for the sides.

Check the measurements across the back of the tub to make sure the single panel will fit properly. Trim to size if necessary, using a fine-toothed saw, cutting the panel with the finished side up.

Apply adhesive to the panel back with the trowel, then, bowing the panel slightly, insert the ends in the grooves of the molding. Let it snap in place, then press the board against the wall, giving the adhesive a chance to take hold. One side panel is mounted the same way, The other must be cut out to pass faucets and spigot if they are on the wall above the tub.

Remove faucet handles and spigot after temporarily shutting off the water supply, then make a cardboard template, laying out the holes in their proper position. Test-fit the template, then transfer

After removing faucets and spigot, make cardboard template and transfer the hole locations to the remaining panel.

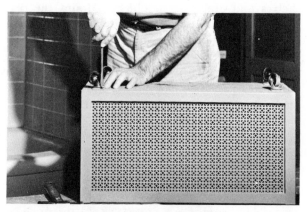
Rolling laundry bin is a box on wheels. Make it from ½" plywood, attaching swiveling casters at corners.

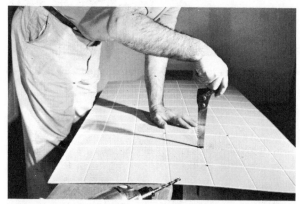
Start holes with drill, then cut with a keyhole or sabre saw. When cutting, press only on the downstrokes.

By covering one side of the box with the same hardboard used on the doors, design motif is carried out.

the hole locations to the remaining piece of paneling. The holes may be cut with a keyhole saw or sabre saw after starting them with a drill. Apply adhesive to the back of the panel and put in position. Replace faucets and spigot.

If you've done a neat, workmanlike job, and the tub was level, no further work should be necessary. Calk any gaps between panel and tub.

The interior arrangement of the storage closet is flexible, due to the manner in which shelves are hung. The choice is up to you, but we have suggested one useful idea in the photographs. A box that rolls on casters makes a convenient laundry bin. It can be built from five pieces of ½" plywood nailed together, or one face can be covered with grillework hardboard that matches the framed closet doors.

The final step before painting is to hang a valance that unifies the whole project. Use either tempered hardboard or ¼" plywood here, but if the latter is your choice, paint both sides for better moisture resistance. The valance covers the header panel of the closet and extends to the far side of the tub. Note that you will not be able to hang a valance if closet depth is greater than that of the tub. The valance is fastened to the end of the tub enclosure, to the header panel above the closet, and to a small ceiling cleat.

Use enamel in finishing all woodwork, priming well first. Match or provide contrast with existing bathroom colors, as taste dictates. A color accent can be achieved by painting the grillework doors with a bright, contrasting pastel shade.

Renovation gives young homeowners a glamorous bathroom with the advantages of modern fixtures, including the plastic-topped vanity cabinet. Walls are warm-hued Marlite in natural walnut.

BETTER BATHROOMS

UPDATING AN OLD BATHROOM

The bathroom in this seventy-five-year-old-house had certainly outlived its usefulness, as is evident in the photograph that was taken before the young home owners decided to undertake a complete remodeling. It was, indeed, time for a change! But the couple's budget had definite limits and they could proceed with the project only if costs could be kept to a minimum and if they could do most of the work themselves.

They started by ripping out almost everything in the room—ancient tub, sink, bowl, and all. They went shopping for the materials needed to do the job, and the secret of their success lay in the intelligent selection of harmonizing components from the attractive bathroom fixtures available today. They chose a cabinet-type vanity sink with oval bowl and preformed plastic top, an enameled pressed steel tub with glass door shower stall, and added some glamorous touches with accessories, including an illuminated wall cabinet, satin chrome towel bars, and soap holders.

For the finishing touches, wall paneling of Mar-

Old-style tub in 75-year-old house just had to go, so a complete renovation was undertaken. Existing water and drain lines made it easy to install the new fixtures. Wall in shower area above tub is lined with ceramic tile for a pleasant contrast to the wood-grain paneling. Glass shower doors ride in chrome tracks.

lite plastic-coated hardboard was chosen because the couple wanted natural wood color and graining. They also chose Wearathon plastic fiber carpet by Armstrong—which has a foam-rubber backing—for its warmth, resiliency underfoot, and interesting antique avocado color.

The young couple installed all the new fixtures themselves by using the existing water lines and drain connections. They also did every part of the room renovation, including putting up the wall paneling, painting the ceiling, and laying the poly-propylene carpet.

Removal of old bowl fixture starts with dis-connecting the water supply line at bot-tom of tank, then the connecting elbow to tank is removed.

The old tank is held in place by lag screws, one at each upper side. Support the tank from below while loosening the screws.

Taking off the bowl requires unscrewing of the floor bolts. Lift the old fixture straight up to clear the drain.

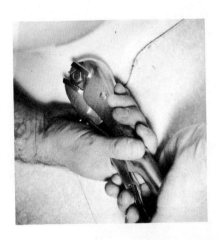

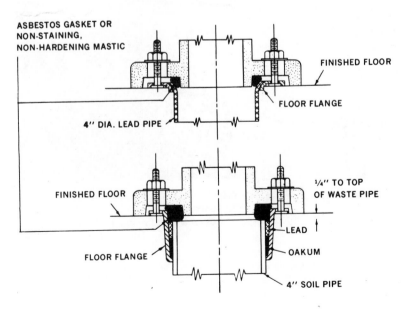

ASBESTOS GASKET OR NON-STAINING, NON-HARDENING MASTIC

FINISHED FLOOR

FLOOR FLANGE

4″ DIA. LEAD PIPE

FINISHED FLOOR

¼″ TO TOP OF WASTE PIPE

LEAD

FLOOR FLANGE

OAKUM

4″ SOIL PIPE

Installing new bowl is aided by viewing these cross-section draw-ings, which show the two most common types of floor connec-tions—a flared 4-inch lead pipe or straight 4-inch soil pipe. Place new bolts upright in the flange slots, then the wax ring or gasket on the bottom of the outlet horn. Set the bowl over the flange, guid-ing the bolts through the holes in the china base. Place washers over bolts and tighten snugly, but don't overtighten as that may crack the base. Some installations require application of waterproof-ing compound.

The renovation required about seventy-five working hours, and the couple figured that they saved at least $600. When it was all finished, they felt the gratification of having planned and carried through a project of their own. But what was even more important, they decided, was the experience and skill they had gained in the course of the work, and the feeling that they could tackle other projects and maintenance repairs with confidence.

New wall alongside tub provided for a much-needed linen closet. Framing was erected after the tub was positioned and the drain connected.

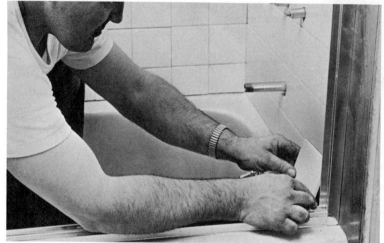

Ceramic tile is applied on tub side of partition wall, and over entire shower enclosure. The title is laid in over mastic troweled on the gypsum wallboard backing.

Walnut finished hardboard paneling hides the scars left after removal of old bathroom fixtures and wall linoleum. The same paneling was used for surfacing the closet doors.

Bathtub fixtures come same size as the wall tile, so they just fit into space of a tile, as with this combination hand grab and soap holder.

TILE YOUR TROUBLES AWAY!

The first step to partial floor reconstruction is to clear away all of the old asphalt tiles, tapping or prying with a chisel the undamaged, more tenacious pieces. The subflooring usually reveals that the top ply or layer of the plywood subfloor nearest the tub has separated.

The separated portions of plywood are easily pulled all the way off. Areas not yet separated but thought to be seriously dampened are also stripped away, using a broad-bladed chisel at a depth equal to the other stripped areas. This done, the overall surface of the plywood is dried; the areas near the tub should be specially treated with the heat from a couple of photoflood lamps (standard heat lamps or sun lamps may also be used).

Next, the uneven subfloor has to be leveled. And here, ⅛″ tempered hardboard does the trick, being the approximate equivalent in thickness to the torn

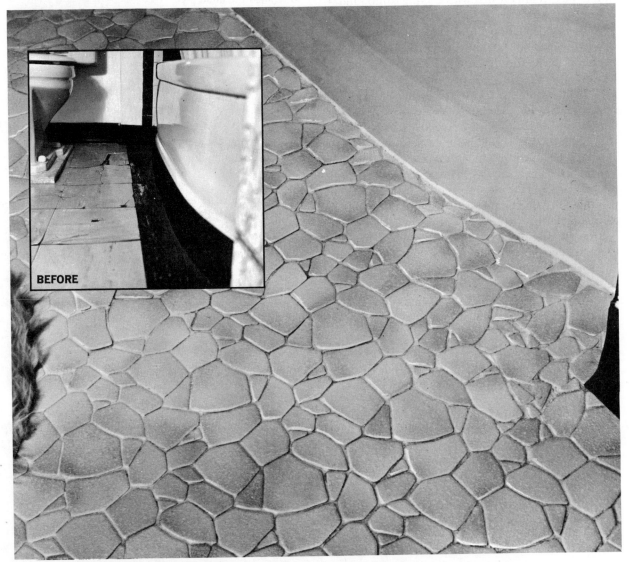

BEFORE

Ceramic tiles transform a tired old bathroom floor, correcting a moisture condition which previously had caused deterioration of the plywood floor base. New tiles add attractive color and texture.

top ply. Because the ripped areas are more or less square, it is a simple task to trim patches to fit, fastening them with linoleum paste.

In order to produce a uniform level overall, a new subsurface of ¼″ hardboard is cemented (linoleum paste again) and nailed to the patched subfloor, allowing ⅛″ at the joints for expansion. The perimeter of the bath-tub and the wall near the sink should be carefully sealed with calking compound—before and after the ¼″ hardboard is laid.

With the subflooring now reinforced and sealed at critical points, sections or squares of gauze-backed ceramic tiles (random-shaped round and elliptical tiles were used in this project) are laid out for fit on the dry floor. TEC-7 white latex emulsion-type cement, formulated especially for use on hardboard, is spread with a notched trowel. As the tiles are positioned on the mastic, a small roller will be useful in leveling the surface.

Irregular edges, such as the base line of the bathroom bowl, are the slowest going, since individual tiles have to be chipped with nippers in order to get an exact fit.

After the tiles have set for a full day, a white tile grout is mixed with water to a buttery consistency and spread over the surface with a rubber squeegee. It should be worked back and forth to be sure all joints are filled with the stuff, then set for twenty minutes before excess is wiped away with a sponge and cheesecloth.

Later on, a thin film may persist on the surface, especially noticeable if your tiles are one of the darker colors. Just sponge mop the floor a couple of times, using clear, cold water, and you won't find a trace of the stuff anywhere.

To complete the job, a sealer should be sprayed (aerosol spray can) along the grout lines to inhibit soiling. Then the wall joints along the tub and sink will be calked again.

A chisel was required to remove all the old tiles and the separated layer of the plywood underbase.

Thin hardboard is used to replace the lifted plywood layer, equalizing the surface with remaining plywood floor.

Hardboard patch is cemented down, then additionally fastened with closely spaced nails to assure tight fit, no squeaking.

The entire floor is next covered with an underlayment of ¼″ hardboard panels, in 4-by-4 size, thoroughly nailed.

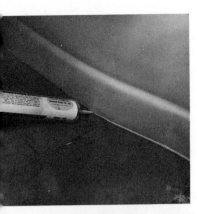

All joints at wall and the bathtub are caulked as safeguard against further water penetration.

Where necessary to fit tiles at walls and other obstructions, nippers are used to chip and shape the tiles to size.

Special mastic for hardboard surfaces is applied with notched steel trowel for the layer of ceramic tiles.

Grout, a fine white cement, is mixed with water to a cream consistency, then spread over the tiles with a squeegee.

Floor area around the bowl is confined but must be given the mastic application right up to the wall joints.

After the grout has set for about half an hour, wipe the surface with a sponge or damp cloth to remove excess on surface.

Ceramic tile, with their net backing, are laid in sheets onto the mastic in the planned order so they fit.

BUILT-IN WEIGHT WATCHER

The current trend to multiple-bathroom homes has had a recessive effect on the size of these bathrooms—they're considerably smaller, so much so that there's hardly a bit of extra space for such necessary items as a floor scale. Fortunately, the problem has prompted a solution. In this case, it's a pull-down platform on which the scale is mounted.

The hinged platform is part of a frame that is recessed into the wall, so that the scale is completely concealed and out of the way when the spring-loaded platform is raised. Not only is a floor impediment eliminated, but the scale housing is an attractive addition to any bathroom, with a chrome molding all around and a surface panel that can be finished to match the rest of the bathroom walls.

Installation involves making an opening in the wall, about 10¾″ wide and 18¼″ high, from the floor up. This is easily done if the wall is plaster or gypsum board, as the opening can be cut with a keyhole saw. Just select a spot between two wall studs. It won't be necessary to cut away any stud. Any slight irregularity in the cutting will be covered by the inch-wide metal flange. The panel box is just deep enough so that it can fit into the hollow wall space, and is secured with four chrome screws driven into the nearby studs.

A ceramic tile wall presents more difficulty, but the job can be managed neatly without causing any damage to the rest of the wall. The professional approach would be to use a portable circular saw fitted with a special masonry or diamond grit

Concealed in wall, scale is quickly accessible for use by dropping its platform. The chrome handle is covered with rubber where it rests on the floor. The attractive and efficient unit is installed into hollow space of wall by cutting an opening in the wall panel or tiles.

blade, which can be purchased for just a few dollars. The saw will make a clean cut through the tiles along the lines that you mark, just as it would cut through brick and other masonry or clay materials. Cutting to only 1/8" depth will be sufficient, as the tiles then can be cleaved with a chisel after the "inside" tiles have been removed from the area.

The more elemental method of making the opening is to first remove the tiles, make any necessary cuts separately, then re-cement the tiles in place. This requires first the removal of one inside tile, which is done after chipping out the grout all around, then tapping the tile with the back of the hammer handle to loosen it so it can be pried out. The remaining tiles in the marked area then can be removed one by one.

Plan the installation so that only one vertical and horizontal row of tiles need be cut. For cutting, score the surface glaze of the tile with a sharp awl or a glass cutter, place the tile over a large nail or spike that is centered exactly under the score line, then step on both sides of the tile. It should cleave nicely along the line.

If the scored line is nearly in the center of the tile it is possible that you'll have to break only half the number of tiles needed. Save the remainder for possible replacements.

The rest of the opening is simple, done with a keyhole saw in the same manner the plain plaster wall was done. The scale frame then is fitted into place so that the flanges cover the edges all around. The unit shown is one of the Hall Mack specialized bathroom accessories, and comes complete with a standard full-size scale.

Opening of required size is marked on the wall between studs, so that no stud need be cut. Use china marking pencil for drawing lines on glazed tiles. Follow at right.

The first step is to remove an inside tile. Start by chipping out the grout all around, then tap with hammer handle to loosen, and pry out.

A masonry blade in portable circular saw set to 1/8" cutting depth scores the tile along the guide line. No need to cut deeper, since the tiles can be cleaved with a chisel.

Once scored, the chisel completes the break. Jagged edges of the wall opening will be covered by the inch-wide flange of the scale unit.

Once the tiles are out, it's a simple matter to break or cut the exposed wall backing, flush with the edges of the tiles that have been trimmed to needed size.

The scale housing is fastened into the wall recess with four screws. Thereafter, you just grab the handle and pull the scale down to the floor when you want to use it.

CERAMIC TILE "KNOW-HOW"

Vast changes have taken place in ceramic tiles—the materials, the tiles themselves, and the installation techniques—all made possible by recent technological advances. Times were when we'd look at our ceramic-tiled baths with their fine, even rows of glazed squares, and wonder at the intricacy of it all, but never dare to do a thing like that ourselves. It was obviously the handiwork of professional craftsmen who required years of experience, special tools, and materials available only to their trade.

True enough then, of course, but its quite a different matter today for the do-it-yourself home owner. Formerly the tile-setter worked with cement mortar, meticulously building up a uniform base into which the tiles were laid and leveled. Now there are special mastics for every type of wall, spread on easily with a trowel, and the tiles almost zip into place. The tiles themselves now have special aligning lugs that assure just the right amount of separation and help keep them in straight and level rows.

An equally important innovation was applying the tiles directly on gypsum wallboard—eliminating the mortar base. Now, just see that the wall panel is plumb, snap a level line across it, and the tiles go on straight and true, in even rows that match the professional tile-setter's efforts.

Ceramic tile gives bathroom walls a gleamingly solid appearance. Tiles are colorful, waterproof, maintenance free, and easily cleaned. The type used here is designed to eliminate the need for specially shaped trim pieces, even when used on shower stall sill.

Before tiling, bathroom has monotonous enameled walls, old-fashioned appearance, and water-logged woodwork.

New Tiles Easier to Cut

What is more, the new tiles are somewhat thinner in cross section, so they can be "cut" more easily. While the tile-setter uses a cutting fixture that speeds this task, the do-it-yourselfer can do almost as well by scoring and snapping his tiles. (You've spotted the two references: the tiles are not cut but are cleaved by snapping them along a scored line.)

All this sounds quite simple, and it is, to a marked degree. But there are still many details of the installation that require careful attention and also some familiarity with the technique. The job must be laid out correctly, as explained in the following paragraphs, and good tile-setting calls for patient workmanship.

Certainly the amateur will not completely outshine the old pro who spent years at an apprenticeship and can turn out intricate designs, square up uneven walls, and otherwise do an exemplary job. But the home owner need not feel his work is in any way inferior. For the purpose intended, a do-it-yourself installation that is carefully worked out can match the very best standards.

Preparing the Walls

A new wall of gypsum panels, or plaster that is smooth and plumb, is in a ready condition. Old walls should be carefully washed down to remove any grease or dirt, all dents and cracks repaired, any wallpaper removed, and surfaces sanded smooth. If the wall is in damaged condition and has a number of defects, a good solution is to put up a new surface of ⅜"-thick gypsum panels, applied with adhesive to the original wall. The purpose is to get a smooth and plumb base for the tiles, including all areas that will be tiled—such as under and around windows, inside the shower stall, and around the bathtub alcove. Of course, all moldings, fixtures, and wood trim must be removed before starting the installation.

Purchase the tiles all in one lot, at the same place, to be sure that they are uniform in color and size. You'll probably find it better to stick to a standard brand of American-made tiles than to take a chance with an unknown quality from a questionable source, which may have many variations in color, sizes, and quality of the glaze. You can com-

Tile will break more easily if placed over a large nail along the scribed line, and pressure applied to both sides.

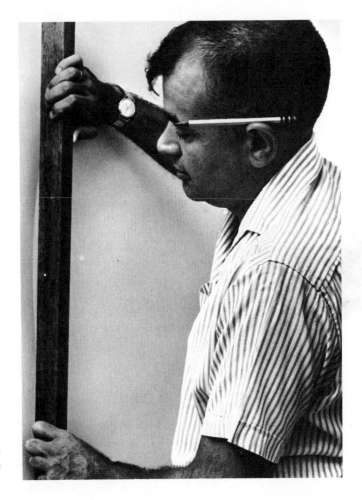

Surface to be tiled must be flat, clean, and dry. Use straightedge board to find any low spots or bulges on wall, correct any defects with plaster until wall is leveled.

Cracks and holes are repaired with plaster, then sanded smooth. Any irregularity will result in tiles being out of alignment.

Start by drawing a level baseline on which to begin the tile installation. Adjust this line so that tiles at top will be of adequate size.

pute the quantity of tiles needed for the job when you know the total area of wall to be covered and the dimensions of the tiles themselves. If in doubt, you can rely on the dealer's figures, and possibly get a commitment from him allowing the return of any excess full cartons.

Steps in Tiling

The tiling procedure consists of troweling on the mastic adhesive, then affixing the tiles one by one in the proper order and, finally, grouting the tile joints with a special fine white cement. There are capping tiles and other special types, even right-angle inside and outside corner tiles, but these are really not necessary and just add flourishes to what can be a simple and perfectly acceptable job.

The worst pitfall you face in a tiling project is planning the position of the tile. The object is to avoid cutting and fitting entirely, or to reduce it to an absolute minimum. Plan the layout so that you never have to fill corners or edges with strips of tile so narrow that they are difficult to handle. Do this by measuring the work area and planning before you begin.

To work out perfectly, the width and height of the area would have to be exact multiples of 4" since each tile measures 4"-by-4". But this is almost too much to expect, so it's best to solve the problem before you literally work yourself into a corner.

In a typical case, we'll say the width of the work area is 96½". If you start with a whole tile, and continue, you'll set 24 tiles. But when you reach the other end, you'll finish with a ½" gap. You can

Determine the dimensions of area to be tiled, so that fitting will work out easily. Tiles here are 4"-by-4". Adjust the rows to use whole tiles if possible, otherwise balance starting and ending rows so they won't be too narrow.

A special adhesive mastic is spread with trowel over no more than 4 square feet of area at a time. Be sure that mastic covers entire surface so that it will be waterproof. Continue as shown at right.

Applying tile, place them on wall and slide them along until they butt together squarely. Some of the adhesive is drawn between the tiles, sealing the spaces against moisture.

Clean the face of freshly set tile with solvent before the mastic hardens. Use a soft cloth to wipe surface, but be careful not to shift the tiles, as mastic has not yet become set.

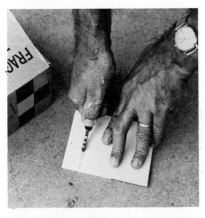

Some tiles must be cut for every installation. Place tile on a flat surface, hold another tile along cutting line as a guide, and score the glazed surface with a glass cutter.

After scoring, lay the tile on a piece of straightedge board and apply pressure so that the tile will snap along the scoring.

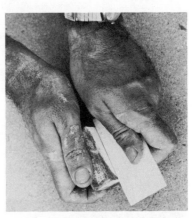

Any roughness along the edges can be quickly removed with a sharpening stone drawn across the edge with firm strokes.

When tiles must be fitted around pipes or faucet stems, irregular shapes can be made with a pair of nippers, chipping out tiny pieces at a time.

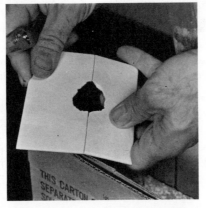

Where necessary to bypass a pipe, a good method usually is to cut the tile in two, chip a semicircular opening, then cement the two halves around the pipe.

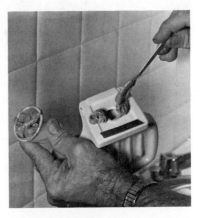

A variety of accessory fixtures, such as this soap holder, is available for attachment to ceramic tile wall with epoxy adhesive. Double faced tape holds fixture in place until the epoxy sets hard.

see how much easier it is to start with a tile cut to a width of 2″, set 23 full pieces, and come out with a 2½″ space at the end. A like adjustment should be made in up-and-down positioning, too.

When fitting is necessary, these thin tiles are much easier to cut. The glazed face is first scored with a glass-cutter guided along a straightedge, and the break is made by snapping the tile smartly against a piece of board, as shown in the photos.

Curved cuts are necessary when tile is to be fitted around a pipe. This is easy, too, with the special nippers you can get when you buy the tile. Just take little bites at a time until the hole is made.

The step-by-step photographs will guide you in the actual installation, including placement of the specialty bathroom fixtures, some of which are made with backing the same size and shape of the tiles and are to be installed in place of a tile.

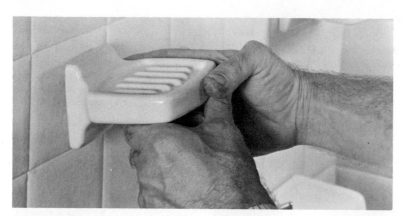

The taped, epoxied fixture is pressed into position on the face of the tile. Once firm contact has been made, do not attempt to shift the fixture until adhesive sets.

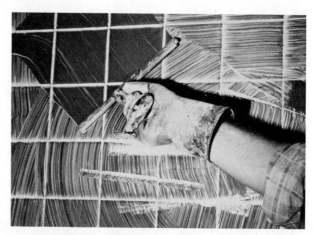

When grouting is necessary, mix the fine white cement into a workable consistency, spread over the tiles with a sponge, working the grout deeply into the line spaces.

Remove the surface grout, after it has set for about half an hour, with a conventional window squeegee. Rubber gloves protect the hands from chemicals in the cement.

A dry film remaining on the tile surface indicates that the grout has fully set. Rake the joints with a striking tool such as a toothbrush handle or ice cream stick, then wipe surface with a damp sponge.

136

Chapter 5

HOW TO CREATE STORAGE SPACE

If any single subject is universally interesting to home owners, it is *storage space* or, perhaps more to the point, lack of it. The vast majority of handymen home owners find their families need more places in which to store the things they wear, or use, or read; things that clutter up the home if not put away.

Here are ideas on how to find and use space in places you just never thought about, based on the supposition that you have already used the obvious sites and are now casting about for more room.

Some of these ideas are for very special conditions; others have much broader application, but all are intended to suggest ways to look at your home from a new perspective.

You will be able to see it as never before—and perhaps one of the things you see will be a brand-new built-in in a place you've always ignored.

STAIR LANDING CABINETS

Good taste in design and simplicity of contruction are the hallmarks of this two-piece project that creates attractive storage space on a stairway landing. Despite its large capacity, it takes little room, and—circumstances permitting—could be made even larger by extensions on either or both sides in an L- or U-shaped configuration.

The bookshelf half is built as a frame with mitered corners, but butt joints are equally acceptable. The sides are dadoed for the shelves which, in turn, are given blind dadoes for the vertical dividers.

An alternate method, without dadoes, would be to build the outer frame first, then glue and butt-nail shelves through the sides. The uprights between the intermediate shelves are then glued and nailed from above and below. Lastly, the remaining uprights could be nailed through top and bottom shelves and toenailed at the intermediate points. Either method applies to both cabinets, the only difference between them is that piano-hinged drop-down doors are fitted to the lower unit.

Where they reach adjoining walls, fasten the units by nailing through sides into wall studs. When they must be supported by the wall on which they hang, cleats nailed to wall studs will carry the bulk of the load, and L-brackets at the tops will finish the job.

This beautiful stair landing cabinet creates a maximum of storage space in what would otherwise be wasted room.

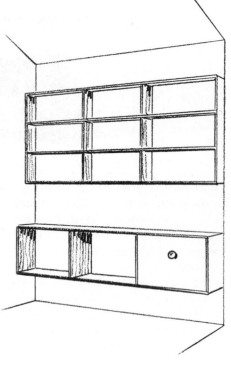

MATERIALS LIST

Bookshelves
2 sides 30 x 7″
4 shelves 48 x 7″
6 uprights 9 x 7″

Cabinet
2 sides 11½ x 9″
2 uprights 10 x 9″
top and bottom 48 x 9″
3 doors 10 x 15″

OVERHEAD CRAWL SPACE

Have you been overlooking overhead space? Look up and you may be pleasantly surprised. The accompanying sketch indicates a means of providing access to an attic or garage loft, by a folding stairway, sold by most lumberyards as a ready-to-install unit. Installation varies slightly from one to another; you will receive instructions with yours. Most require only fitting into an opening that you create by cutting one overhead joist, then framing.

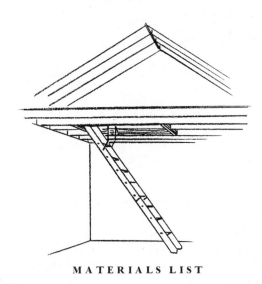

MATERIALS LIST

Folding stairway (available at most large lumberyards)
½" plywood flooring

For framing members, use the same stock as the joists, spiking them in place.

Flooring of some sort has to be installed over the joists. The lowest priced grade of ½" plywood is adequate. No attempt should be made to use this space without flooring.

This idea is applicable also where joists are covered by a ceiling. You must first remove the covering in the area where the stairway is to be installed, of course.

GARAGE CEILING

Good use can be obtained from the top of your garage for storage of bulky items such as ladders, out of season storm windows or screens, lumber, and even fishing rods and skis.

In the upper drawing, an extension ladder is supported at each end by two pairs of heavy steel angle brackets screwed together into a U. One side of the U is fastened to the joist, the other is the support for the ladder. You slide the ladder between the brackets. Surprisingly heavy loads can be carried in this manner.

The lower drawing differs in that the support comes from a piece of 2-by-3 stock placed between a pair of ordinary shelf brackets. Screws through the ends of the brackets hold the 2-by-3 in place. The

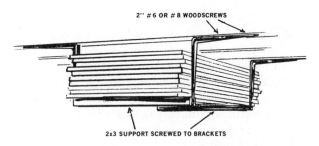

MATERIALS LIST

Top Sketch	Bottom Sketch
4 or more pairs heavy angle brackets	2 or more pairs steel shelf brackets
2" no. 6 or no. 8 wood screws and washers	2 lengths 2 x 3 to suit
	2" no. 6 or no. 8 wood screws and washers

result is a sort of open shelf whose width is determined by the length of the 2-by-3's. Similarly, the size of the bracket will decide the depth of the space.

Load-carrying capacity can be increased by adding sets of brackets at intermediate points.

BATHROOM WALL RECESS

In every wall lies hidden space, waiting only to be tapped. Here is one basic idea which has innumerable variations and adaptations. In this instance, it's a clothes hamper built into a bathroom wall, but with the addition of some shelves and a

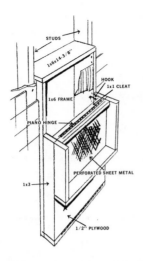

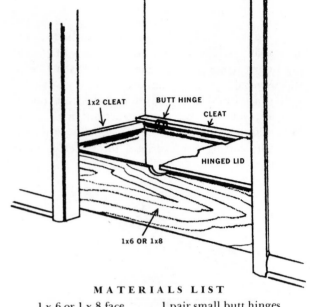

MATERIALS LIST

1 x 6 inner wall frame	1 sheet perforated metal
1 x 3 outer frame	½" plywood face
2 lengths piano hinge	hook-and-eye
1 x 1 cleat	

MATERIALS LIST

1 x 6 or 1 x 8 face	1 pair small butt hinges
1 x 2 cleat, size to fit	1 lid, any ¼" or ½"
closet	stock

full-length hinged door it's an ideal kitchen closet for canned goods. In your workshop, it's useful for small tools and hardware.

Wall studs must be located first. Drill a small hole in the wall near the floor and probe through it with a stiff wire until you locate the studs. Then cut back along the stud edge to the desired height. Trim edges neatly.

In the opening, build a frame of 1-by-6 stock, nailing it to the sides of the studs. Another frame, made of 1-by-3 hinged at the bottom and about 12" below the top, is a double door that also drops down to let soiled clothing be tossed inside and when the hamper is to be emptied a hook-and-eye latch allows the entire front to open.

A piece of perforated sheet metal is inserted in the top door for ventilation. Finish woodwork and metal with two coats of a good enamel. If difficulty is encountered in filling gaps between wall and hamper, nail trim molding around sides and top before painting.

CLOSET FLOOR

Bring order to the floor of your closet by building this hinged-top box in which can be placed out-of-season bedding, footwear, rain boots, or just the clutter that accumulates in clothes closets.

You'll want to use as much of the closet floor as possible, but the presence of the door frame will interfere. The face of the box, then, should be placed

as far forward as possible, butting against the inside edges of the frame.

Cut a piece of 1-by-6 or 1-by-8 stock wide enough to reach from one side of the closet to the other. Stand it on edge against the inside of the doorway, then mark the side walls at the ends of this board. Nail small vertical cleats at these points, making them just as long as the board is high. Since you won't be able to nail to the cleats, glue the board instead. When the glue has dried, you can continue with the rest of the job. Nail two 1-by-2 cleats along the sides. Nail another 1-by-2 across the back of the closet with its top edge higher than the other cleats by the thickness of the lid.

Attach small butt hinges to the lid and the back cleat. Cut a half-moon finger hole in the facing board. Paint with a tough gloss enamel to match the closet interior.

UNDERSEAT AREA

Kitchens that have been equipped with built-in bench type seats hold a storage bonus for the space-conscious home owner. The interior framework of the seat often encloses a large area that is usually ignored.

By simply removing the cushion and opening the top, space is immediately available. But this is just a take-it-as-you-find-it measure, which can be improved on in the manner shown, to produce a feature that is most useful in smaller kitchens.

By partitioning off one end of the bench a niche is created which is perfect for handy storage of a toaster. It can be made even more useful by devising a swing-out platform, allowing use of the toaster without removal.

To determine whether your bench is suitable for this use, remove the cushion and the board on

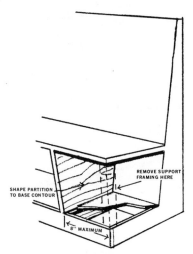

MATERIALS LIST

¾″ plywood partition, size to fit bench cross section
2   1 x 2 cleats

which it rests. Examination of the interior framework will quickly tell you whether or not you can do it. Caution: don't attempt this project if the cushion is a part of permanent upholstery, unless you are ready to do a reupholstering job too.

The partition wall at the end of the niche is ¾″ lumber shaped to the contour of the base, nailed to cleats at the top and bottom.

ISLAND COUNTER

Admittedly it is a specialized condition, but common to the increasingly popular island kitchen counter plan, that is, space often wasted behind drawers. It's easy to find out if unused cubic inches are hiding in your island counter.

Remove a drawer, measure its depth, then compare with the full depth of the island, the difference in dimensions telling the tale of waste space. On finding enough to warrant going ahead, the counter back must be opened up and the recessed area framed in.

When a small recess is to be created, access to the interior for framing is easiest through the front of the cabinet, but if the entire back is to be rebuilt,

it's best to remove it, place the interior framing, then reface as necessary.

The planter should be waterproofed, most easily accomplished by lining the interior with a thorough coating of fibreglass resin applied to glass cloth stapled temporarily in place. Be sure the

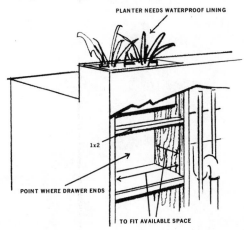

wood is completely protected from water, or rot may get a foothold.

Finish the exposed surfaces of all new woodwork to match the rest of the counter.

BUILD A DRESSING ROOM

Here's real luxury—a dressing room of your own. Or, if your wife won't let you get away with it, you can make twin *His* and *Her* sections.

Although the entire project can be easily duplicated in your workshop, there's a shortcut that can literally make it something you can do in less than a weekend.

The speedy secret is to start with a chest of drawers you can buy, or you may already have a suitable one that can be refinished.

The photograph shows one of a pair of twin units built on a long wall in a narrow lavatory, but you might want to consider placing it on a bedroom wall instead.

The size of the chest sets the overall dimensions of the unit. Fur out walls with 1-by-2 strips, then attach hardboard with screws or nails. Build the double semi-shelves atop the chest before placing it against the wall. You'll want to remove the drawers to gain access to the underside of the top, in order to fasten the shelf uprights.

All dimensions are decided by the size of the chest used. It is suggested, however, that the local lumberyard be checked before construction begins to determine availability and size of the bifold doors which enclose the unit.

His and her dressing rooms are easily built, starting with refinished cabinets. The cabinet size sets the dimensions for the units.

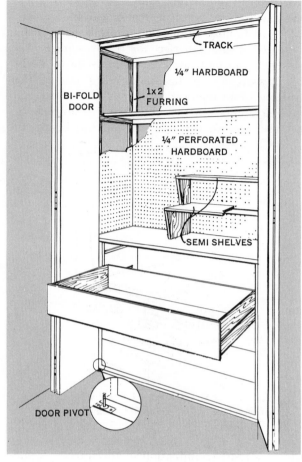

MATERIALS LIST

(All dimensions to suit)
1 pc. chest of drawers
1 pc. overhead shelf
1 x 2 furring strip
2 pcs. semi-shelves

4 shelf uprights
Perforated and solid
hardboard
1 pair bifold doors with
hardware and track

FLOATING BOOKWALL IN HALLWAY

The walls of halls and passageways offer an ideal solution to the problem of storing large numbers of books. Install sectional bookwalls like the one shown, which can be assembled at an approximate cost of $75 per 8′ section.

Each section of the bookwall is custom-sized to your individual book collection, and one or more reading racks can be provided for dictionaries, atlases, and magazines.

The bookwall consists of the number of sections, each 24″ to 30″ wide, built of ¾″ birch veneer plywood whose grain and natural color go nicely with most home decoration.

All pieces are cut from 4′-by-8′ panels. One panel, used for the sides and vertical members, is cut to 4′-by-6′—the remaining 2′ piece is used for the racks.

Ripping for Uprights

The 6′ section and the remaining 4′ by 8′ panels are cut into 12″ widths, providing four strips per panel. If your panels are birch veneer plywood, use birch veneer tape to cover all exposed edges.

The open-backed self-supporting frame consists of as many sections, approximately 24″ wide, as are needed to fill the wall space. Each section should be no wider than 30″ to ensure no-sag shelves.

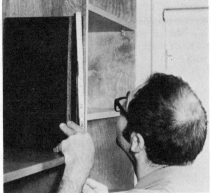

Organize books into groups by height, and space the shelves to accommodate the maximum height for each group.

To insure warp-free shelves, use a level and try-square when you mark the holes for the shelf clips.

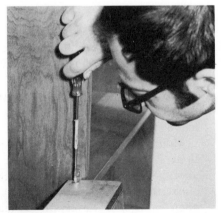

Two shelf clips, screwed into the reading rack's underside, provide complete support.

Floating bookcases are custom-sized to fit your particular collection. Sectional construction allows you to determine the size of bookwall unit.

143

The reading rack supports the heaviest dictionary when it is rotated so the back rests against the wall.

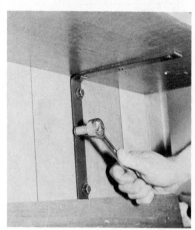

Heavy corner braces spaced 16" on centers, secure frame to the wall. Use lag screws ⁵⁄₁₆"-by-2½".

Fitting the Parts

The end pieces are fitted to the top and bottom using ¼" deep rabbet cuts on both pieces. The interior verticals are set into ¼" deep dado cuts. White glue and two 2" No. 8 screws at all joints ensure a rigid frame. The screws are countersunk flathead, filled with wood putty or plastic wood.

Mount the frame on the wall before sizing the shelves and reading racks. For a floating appearance, position the bottom shelf about 12" (or more) above the floor. The frame is held to the wall with angle irons spaced every 16" to match the studs in the wall. Use three ⁵⁄₁₆"-by-2½" lag screws into the studs and ½" No. 10 flatheads between the braces (angles) and the frame.

Varied Shelf Clearances

No matter how you arrange the final shelf layout, for an integrated appearance the top shelf should run level across all sections.

Other shelves can be spaced to accommodate books grouped by specific height. Good general heights are 18" for large books, 8" for small books.

Each shelf is individually supported by four shelf clips or brackets—the type that plugs in ³⁄₁₆" or ¼" holes. To ensure rock-steady shelves that won't warp or tilt, use a level and try square rather than a ruler to position the holes for the shelf clips.

The racks are mounted waist high and are self-supporting on two shelf clips, which are screwed to the bottom edge of the rack. Insert two clips in the vertical members, hold the rack upward from the bottom and then attach the clips with ½" No. 6 flat-head screws. When the rack is swung up and backward the top of it will rest against the wall, providing a firm support without need for screw supports.

Selecting the Finish

Just about any final finish can be applied to the bookwall. A professional furniture grade appearance is obtained by using a stain such as Weldwood Colortone, followed by two coats of flat satin polyurethane varnish, with a light sanding between coats. For a silk-smooth final finish use a tack-rag between sandings to remove all traces of "dust."

Since the back of the frame is the wall itself, the bookwall can be blended into virtually any decorating scheme by simply decorating the wall area inside the frame. By removing the shelves and rotating the racks down the entire back wall is exposed, and you can decorate the wall with paint.

BOX ON BOX

It has often been noted that the best ideas are the simplest. This one must take top rating for being simple, practical, and very handsome either in the bright solid colors that enchant a child or in the more formal finishes for a family room or the living room.

The basic unit is, simply, a cubelike box, having a door on one of its sides. The boxes are arranged by stacking some right on the floor, with others supported by shelf brackets fitted into regular metal standards on the wall. While all the cubes are hollow, their interiors may be varied with sepa-

Cubistic? Just simple boxes that provide a maximum of easy storage space and contribute a decorative value to a child's room. Blackboard paint on doors permits scribbling without damage, divider panels at rear enclose a projection screen.

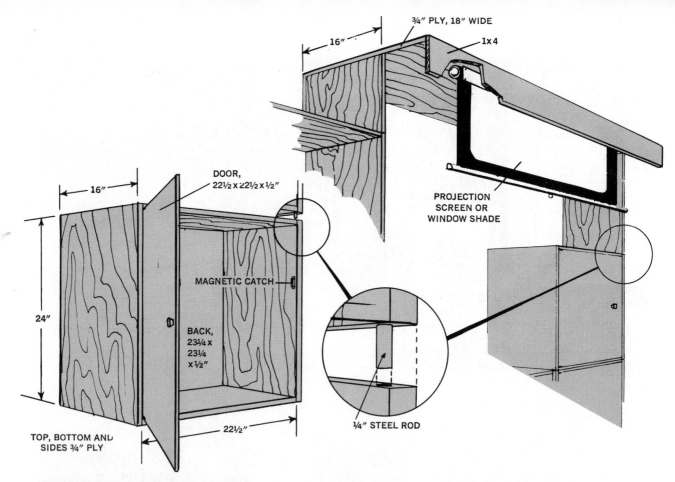

3/4" PLY, 18" WIDE

16"

1x4

PROJECTION SCREEN OR WINDOW SHADE

DOOR, 22½ x 22½ x ½"

16"

MAGNETIC CATCH

24"

BACK, 23¼ x 23¼ x ½"

¼" STEEL ROD

TOP, BOTTOM AND SIDES ¾" PLY

22½"

Boxes of ¾" plywood have backs of thinner plywood fitting into rabbets all around. Doors are of ½" plywood. Stacked boxes are interlocked with ¼" steel dowels. The projection screen is mounted between side panels.

rator partitions or shelves for specific purposes.

Extending the value of the setup, the space between two groupings of the boxes may be utilized for a pull-down projection screen (a plain white window shade will serve the purpose admirably).

Blackboard paint on a couple of the cube doors will enable the tots to scribble to their hearts' content. Other cubes may be finished with high gloss enamel in bright colors.

MATERIALS LIST

Per cube	Projection screen frame (exact sizes to suit your own layout)
2 pcs. 16 x 22½ x ¾" ply top and bottom	
2 pcs. 16 x 24 x ¾" ply sides	1 pc. ¾" ply, 18" wide
1 pc. 22½ x 22½ x ½" ply door	1 pc. 1 x 4 fascia board
1 pc. 23¼ x 23¼ x ½" ply	2 pcs. ¾" ply, 16" wide
	1 screen or window shade
	4 pcs. ¼" steel rod, 2" long

GIVING A CLOSET A CEDAR LINING

Be bold. Strip your closets to the bare walls and start all over. Only this time, organize. And make it luxurious with a cedar lining that fights moths.

In this working model, the closet is 7½' long, 3' deep—more than enough space for some really imaginative designing. After first removing all the old moldings, brackets, and hooks, prepare to install the cedar lining on the three walls, floor to ceiling. Cedar comes in prepackaged strips of assorted lengths, 4" wide, each bundle yielding about 32 square feet of coverage. The boards are tongued and grooved so the pieces lock together effortlessly.

In the case of a dry wall base, simply attach the boards directly with 6d finishing nails. You don't have to worry about hitting studs or wonder whether you'll have snug joints where two board ends butt (these are tongued and grooved too).

If you are working with a plaster wall, install furring strips along the full length of the closet. Then

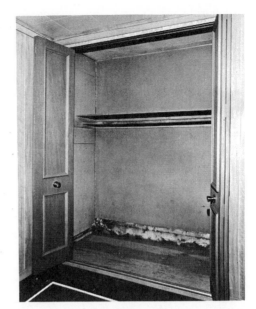

Before renovation, closet is typical with clothes pole and single, limited-use shelf.

Reorganized closet makes best use of space and provides convenience facilities with lower clothes rod at one side, doubled rod at the other for suits and slacks. Multiple shelves are handier. Cedar lining helps protect garments.

Tongue-and-groove aromatic cedar strips interlock on all edges for tight seal. A lining of builder's paper helps keep out dust.

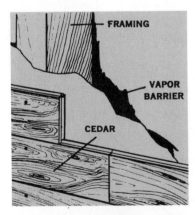

It's a good idea to line the closet with a vapor-sealing membrane, or insulation blankets with the vapor barrier facing inside the closet (always toward the warmer side) so that the possibility of dampness or mildew will be minimized. If necessary, keep a bag of copper sulphate crystals to absorb excess moisture in the closet.

Cedar strips can be nailed or glued to an existing wall. Joints of the strips need not fall on the studs, as they interlock with the tongue-and-groove. Start the strips at the bottom of the wall, and work upward.

147

nail hardboard sheets to the furring skinning-over the three wall surfaces. Apply adhesive to the backs of the cedar boards, driving a nail at the tongue of each board length to assure the best bond.

More cedar lumber is used for the shelves and dividers, the most convenient stock being 1-by-6's, using only half the closet's depth (18″) for the shelf network—or the equivalent of three boards in union. Referring to the sketch, 1-by-6's also are used for wall cleats and cross members for the units of three 1-by-6's.

Whatever arrangement you choose, install the long top shelf first, then the tallest upright. Follow this with the shorter of the two long shelves, then the shorter upright and all the little shelves. These little shelves are secured with thin cleats and nails.

Solid, bifold doors lend an air of elegance, a feeling of roominess.

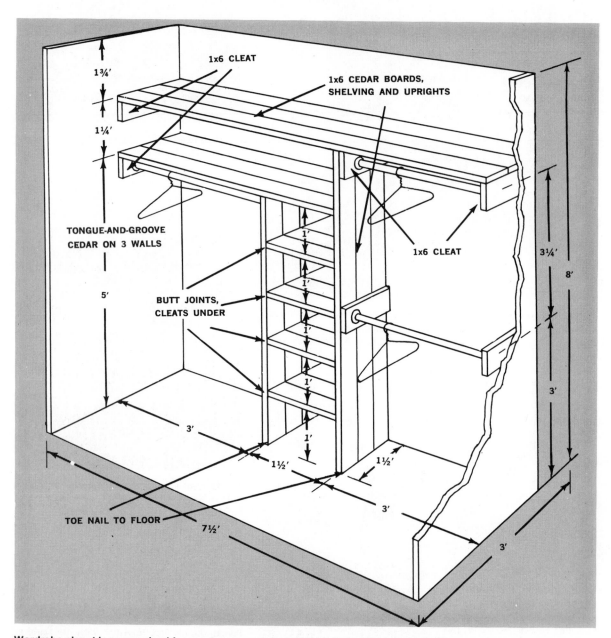

Wardrobe closet is reorganized for greater convenience and maximum storage value. Shelves are cedar boards, joined together to desired width. Note lower clothes rod at one side allowing for extra shelf above.

CEDAR CLOSET—ROOM DIVIDER

This cavernous closet, lined with moth-repelling red cedar, is perfect for storage of out-of-season clothing and other things that need long-term protection. Installed in the basement, it also makes a good room divider.

If you'll look at the cut-away drawing, you'll note that it is partitioned into storage cubicles, with access doors on both sides. Here, the two large cubicles on the right are for hanging items; one at the left is for shelf storage, the other for bulk. But you can vary the arrangement to suit your own needs. By moving the partitions that run lengthwise you can vary the depth of the cubicles.

The closet is 7½′ long, 7′ high and 4′ wide. The main construction material is plywood. Because of its structural strength, minimum framing is sufficient—a base of 2-by-4's laid flat, 2-by-4 uprights at the corners, a pair of 2-by-4 headers and a pair of 2-by-6's as middle upright members.

Note the shims under the base. They provide ventilation and keep the unit off the floor out of harm's way in the event of basement flooding.

All surfaces inside the closet are lined with aromatic red cedar—walls, ceiling, floor, even doors. Humans find the aroma of the wood pleasant, but it paralyzes moths at the larva stage and they starve to death. The cedar wood should not be sealed in any way—any kind of finish would inhibit the scent, destroying its effectiveness.

Conveniently, red cedar is available in strips tongue-and-grooved at the sides and ends. It's just a matter of tapping them together, fastening with nails or panel adhesive, If you'd like, you can apply them to the doors vertically for design variation.

The strips should meet snugly throughout. If you are concerned about accurate fit in the corners, just cut the pieces as well as you can, and finish the corners with cedar molding. This will hide the ends that do not butt snugly and make for a good seal.

Huge cedar closet offers perfect solution for household items requiring long-term storage.

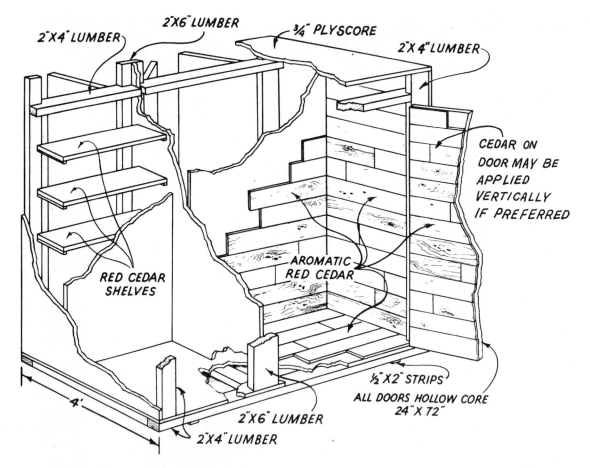

2"X4" LUMBER

2"X6" LUMBER

3/4" PLYSCORE

2"X4" LUMBER

CEDAR ON DOOR MAY BE APPLIED VERTICALLY IF PREFERRED

RED CEDAR SHELVES

AROMATIC RED CEDAR

1/2" X2" STRIPS

ALL DOORS HOLLOW CORE 24" X 72"

4'

2"X6" LUMBER

2"X4" LUMBER

MATERIALS LIST

6 hollow core doors 2/0 x 7/0
8 pieces 2 x 4 x 7 No. 1 construction lumber—corner uprights, headers
4 pieces 2 x 4 x 8 No. 1 construction lumber—base

4 pieces 2 x 2 x 7 No. 1 construction lumber—filler between top and joists
2 pieces 2 x 6 x 7 No. 1 construction lumber—middle upright members
5 panels 4 x 8 x 3/4 ply-

wood, sides, etc.
2 panels 4 x 8 x 5/8 C. D. plyscore
For the top and bottom
8 bundles 4" aromatic red cedar
2 1 1/4" aluminum poles
2 shelf supports for use

with poles
2 pr. pole sockets
6 pr. 3 1/2" brass butt hinges
6 magnetic catches
6 brass knobs
1 panel 4 x 8 x 1/4" hardboard
1 cartridge adhesive

AN ALCOVE GOES TO WORK

An empty alcove is easily converted into a practical pantry or storage closet. While the extra storage is the most important part, the variety of decorative possibilities is bound to intrigue the housewife. The perforated door panel material is extremely attractive and lends itself to a variety of schemes.

It is also quite economical. There are, for example, no back or sides to build, the walls of the alcove being used instead. The closet and all the doors are framed in 1-by-2 stock. The smaller door frames have miter or half-lap joints. The large doors have miter joints at the top and butt joints at

the bottom and in the middle, fastened with glue and corrugated fasteners. All door frame sections have a groove on the inner edge which receives the 1/8" perforated hardboard. The groove should be 1/2" deep. The dimensions of the panels are 1/16" less on all four sides than required for exact fit to allow for expansion of the hardboard. The dividing bar between the upper and lower fillers is made of 1-by-4 stock.

The shelves are of 3/4" plywood, supported by 1-by-2 cleats. The cleats on the walls are fastened with 2 1/2" nails driven into the studs. Both sides of the shelves are grooved to permit the insertion of 1/8" hardboard divider partitions.

150

A wasted alcove was converted into this convenient storage closet for linens, cleaning utensils, and odds and ends.

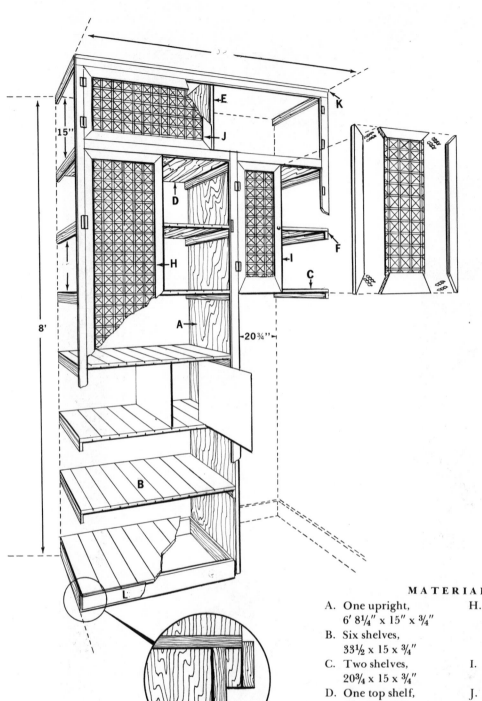

15"

8'

20¾''

A
B
C
D
E
F
H
I
J
K
L

SIDE VIEW

MATERIALS LIST

A. One upright,
   6' 8¼" x 15" x ¾"

B. Six shelves,
   33½ x 15 x ¾"

C. Two shelves,
   20¾ x 15 x ¾"

D. One top shelf,
   55 x 15 x ¾"

E. One partition,
   15 x 15 x ¾"

F. Seventeen cleats,
   1 x 2 x 15"

G. Kick frame, 2 pcs.
   4 x 33½ x ¾"
   2 pcs. 4 x 13½ x ¾"

H. Door fillers (upper)
   38 x 12⅝ x ⅛" (2)
   (lower) 31 x 12⅝ x
   ⅛" (2)

I. Door fillers,
   7⅛ x 21⅝ x ⅛" (2)

J. Door fillers,
   9⅛ x 23⅜ x ⅛" (2)

K. 55 ft. of ¾" quarter
   round molding

L. One pc. 33½ x 2½ x
   ¾"

door framing, 54 ft. of
1 x 2"

closet trim, 28½ ft. of
1 x 2"

DINING ROOM CABINET

Designed to augment the dining room storage space for serving plates and the larger utensils such as a chafing dish, this ceiling-height wall cabinet can be built using only hand tools.

All major parts of the 6' long unit are cut from 1"-by-12" pine boards. There are four vertical members, faced with 1-by-2 strips, and the top board under the ceiling. The interior shelves are supported on wood cleats which are fastened in uniform positions to the uprights before they are installed, while the shelves at the open center section rest on the lugs of adjustable standards.

The louver doors may be purchased ready made in appropriate sizes. The lower doors are cut from ¾" plywood. The doors are then hinged to the 1-by-2 facing strips.

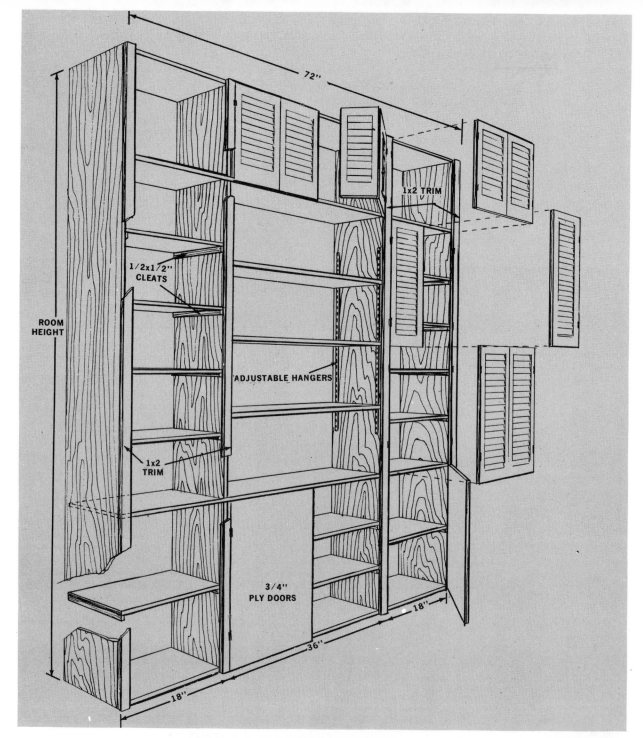

ROOM HEIGHT

72"

1/2x1/2" CLEATS

1x2 TRIM

ADJUSTABLE HANGERS

1x2 TRIM

3/4" PLY DOORS

18"

36"

18"

MATERIALS LIST

1 x 12 stock:
4 uprights, 92" (or room height)
4 main horizontal shelves, 72"
10 shelves, 18"
5 shelves, 36"
24 feet, ½ x ½" cleats
31 feet of 1 x 2 trim

(quantity will vary with room height)
4 lower doors, ¾" ply, size to suit
8 pairs of louvered doors, size to suit
2 pairs adjustable shelf brackets and hangers, knobs, hinges, etc.

THE WELL-ORGANIZED CLOSET

Closets are for hiding things, and they generally look it, jammed with clothing and shoes on the floor and all sorts of items on the shelves. What makes this project interesting is not only that it is so well organized with a place for everything but also because it includes a vanity table (shelf) and a chest of drawers—two pieces of furniture that would ordinarily be taking up space in the room. The removal of these two pieces can make even a small room look spacious.

This triple closet is 9' long, 16" deep. The compartments are separated by ¾" plywood partitions (A) that are fastened to cleats at the ceiling and floor. The top shelves in each compartment rest on cleats attached to the sides. The slanting shelves (C) in the left and center compartments also rest on cleats and are made of ¾" plywood. To prevent the clothes from sliding off the slanting shelves, strips of transparent plastic are screwed to the shelf edges.

The Peg-Board sheets (B) at the back and sides of the first compartment are screwed to a frame (F) of 1-by-2's nailed to the walls.

The vanity table in the center is simply a ¾" piece of plywood that rests on cleats and measures 16"-by-36". The boxes at the back of the vanity for cosmetics, earrings, and other trinkets are 4" deep.

Organization is the theme of this triple dresser. The arrangement includes a handy vanity table and a huge chest of drawers.

The ¼" groove in the top of the box drawer section is 2" away from the wall and holds the bottom edge of the mirror. (See mirror detail G.)

The drawer runners (E) are of special interest because of their ingenious construction. They are made of aluminum angle with ¾" legs screwed to 1-by-2 cleats on the underside of the vanity shelf. The aluminum runners on the drawer are flush with the top of the sides. Screws used to fasten the runners to the drawers should be No. 8, flathead, sheet metal type, ⅜" long and spaced 2" apart. Holes in the runners should be beveled to permit the flathead screws to be driven flush. The runners should be waxed or lubricated with silicone spray for easy operation.

The drawer under the vanity shelf has ½" plywood sides and back, a ¼" plywood bottom and a ¾" front which should overlap the side by two inches on each side.

The folding doors are hung from an aluminum track. Each compartment has a pair of 2-panel doors which cover the compartment when closed.

The chest of drawers is a ready-made unfinished pine unit, painted white.

MATERIALS LIST

A. Two partitions,
   8' x 16" x ¾"
B. Two pieces of Peg-Board, 24 x 16 x ⅛"
   One pc. of Peg-Board,
   24 x 36 x ⅛"
C. Four slanting shelves,
   36 x 10 x ¾"
D. Four pcs. plastic,
   36 x 2 x ⅛"
E. Four pcs. aluminum angle, 14 x ¾ x ¾"
F. Peg-Board framing,
   2 pcs. 36 x 2 x 1"
   6 pcs. 24 x 2 x 1"
   4 pcs. 16 x 2 x 1"
G. Mirror, 36 x 24¼"
H. Three top shelves,
   36 x 12 x ¾"
I. Three pcs. 8' x 3" x 1"
J. Two sides,
   14 x 3 x ½"
   One back,
   22 x 3 x ½"
   One front,
   26 x 3 x ¾"
   One bottom,
   22 x 14 x ¼"
K. One vanity shelf,
   36 x 16 x ¾"
   18 ft. of 1 x 2" for cleats
L. Two pcs. 36 x 4 x ½"
   Two end pcs. 4 x 3 x ½"
   Three boxes to fit
M. Six pairs 2-panel folding doors sized to cover compartments
N. Optional fluorescent light

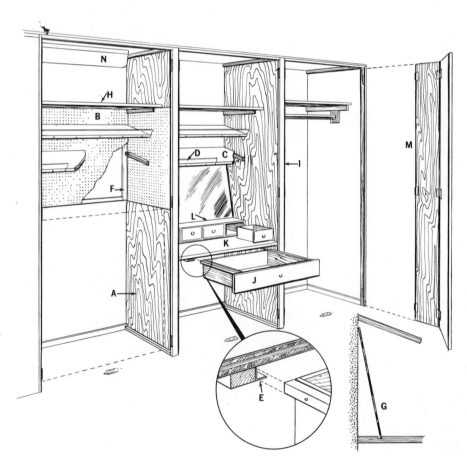

BINS FOLLOW STAIRS

With storage bins like these, you don't have to become a squirrel when you want to store or remove an item from under your basement stairs. Just grip the handle on the particular unit and pull. Rails and casters let it slide out easily like a drawer, and it's just as easy to close.

The methods and materials for building the closet and bin are essentially the same. The main members—back, front, sides—are made of ½" plywood butt-jointed together; the bottom, ½" plywood, is dadoed into the sides for extra strength. Triangular cleats were also glued to some strategic corners on the sides, as you can see in the photos. Shelves drop in on one-inch cleats.

The rails used on these units act as guides and supports, with nonswivel casters attached to 2-by-3's fastened to the underside of the bottom helping out. The bin has three rails, one along the top and one near the bottom on each long side. The broom closet uses two, one on each side along the top.

Like drawer rails, you make a grooved section that is attached to the side, and a corresponding part rides the groove. Meeting parts are sanded and slicked with tallow or an appropriate product.

The units are faced with material to match the surrounding wall area. Handles are fastened securely with bolts that go through the facing and front material.

Exterior of closet reveals only the pull handles of the sliding storage bins, which slide completely out of the way.

Handy storage bins, shaped to the angle of the basement stairs, slide out of the stair enclosure wall for easy access to the stored items on the shelves. Bin moves back and forth on casters, is kept in line by wood guide rails.

Underside view shows type of plate caster used for bins.

Similar understair storage bin is used as broom closet. Units are fitted with large pull handles for drawer-like action. Non-swivel casters and waxed guide rails help assure smooth movement.

157

STORAGE TRAIN RIDES THE JOISTS

The attic crawl space can provide lots of valuable storage space, and you don't have to lay a floor to use it with this idea.

This system works somewhat like freight trains on rails. Small plywood platforms on ball-bearing casters or skate wheels ride on the attic joists. Each platform has wooden guides that run along the sides of the joists and keep it from derailing. To store things, you load up a platform from a ladder at the attic access hole and push it toward the eaves. Want to remove the stored items? Just pull on a rope you attached to the first platform and it comes forward.

A handy platform size is 24″ x 36″. Scrap pieces can be used in any length, but the 24″ width should be kept standard, based on 16″ joist spacing. For platforms handling heavy loads, use ¾″ plywood and ball-bearing casters.

STORAGE TRAIN RIDES THE JOISTS

Plywood platform piled high with cartons for storage rides atop the floor joists as it is pushed far into the eaves. The rope is used to retrieve the platform when needed. An advance on this system would be a pulley mounted far under the eaves so that a double strand of rope can be used to pull the platform in either direction.

Platform is shown with 1-by-2 guides mounted underneath that keep the unit from sliding off the joists. Casters or skate wheels may be used for traction.

SPORTS CABINET

Sportsmen know the importance of preventing unauthorized use of their weapons and realize that a safe place for them is a necessity. The cabinet shown here not only stores guns safely, under lock and key, but provides a lot of other useful space.

In addition to the locking gun rack, there is ample space for ammunition storage in the small drawer immediately below the guns.

The storage door is also a very good idea—it provides space in which to hang several fishing rods, and has shelves below for associated paraphernalia.

The bottom shelves are more than adequate for a large accumulation of hunting accessories, and many other bulkier items such as tackle boxes, creels, and boots.

Our project is a free-standing cabinet, but the same arrangement could be built into a conventional closet. However, dimensions and materials

A safe place for guns and ammunition is provided by this sports cabinet. Note the storage space for bulky items under the locking gun rack.

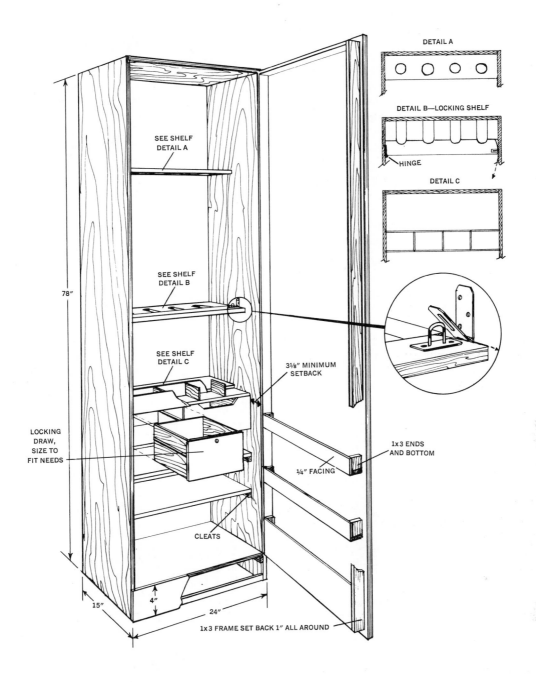

DETAIL A

DETAIL B—LOCKING SHELF

HINGE

DETAIL C

SEE SHELF
DETAIL A

SEE SHELF
DETAIL B

SEE SHELF
DETAIL C

3⅛" MINIMUM
SETBACK

1x3 ENDS
AND BOTTOM

¼" FACING

LOCKING
DRAW,
SIZE TO
FIT NEEDS

CLEATS

78"

15"

4"

24"

1x3 FRAME SET BACK 1" ALL AROUND

are given for constructing an independent unit. None of the dimensions are critical. You'll want to be most careful about the frame on the door. Its exterior dimensions must be at least fractionally less than the inside measurements of the width and height of the cabinet proper. The gun racks must be custom fitted to make sure your weapons will fit properly.

Except for a few pieces, ¾" plywood is used throughout. Our model cabinet is finished in gloss enamel on a spackled undercoater.

MATERIALS LIST

2 pcs. 78 x 15 x ¾" sides
1 pc. 23½ x 15 x ¾" top
1 pc. 14¾ x 22½ x ¾" bottom shelf
2 pcs. 22½ x 11⅞ x ¾" storage shelves
1 pc. 24 x 4 x ¼" kick-plate

1 pc. 74 x 24 x ¾" door
21 feet of 1 x 3 for door frame and pockets
Assorted small pieces for gun holders, drawers, shelf facings, etc.

HOW TO CREATE STORAGE SPACE

IDEAS GALORE!

You'll have to study these photographs closely to spot all the ingenious ideas that are built into the furniture of this girl's room. The desk is far more than appears at first glance—all three sections look like rows of drawers, an effect that was deliberately chosen for the sake of unifying the design. But the left side is the back of a rolling chair that is just the right height for its user, and the space beneath the chair seat has doors on both sides for convenient book storage. The center section really has drawers, but even here there's a bit of legerdemain, because instead of the six shallow drawers you think you see, there are only three deep ones.

The remaining section at the right is really a door to an open cabinet with a single shelf inside for storing large objects.

The desk top, covered with smooth and easy-to-clean Formica, extends the full width of the three compartments below, with an overhang of several inches at each end.

Dimensions are given in the sketch as a guide, but these will have to be adjusted when duplicating these units to conform to the available space and your individual requirements.

Visual illusions make their contribution to the unique effect of this combination unit, designed for a small girl's room. A drawer section turns out to be the back of a chair; there are just three deep drawers at the center, not the six that the knobs would lead you to suppose, and the right side is the door of a shelf cabinet!

160

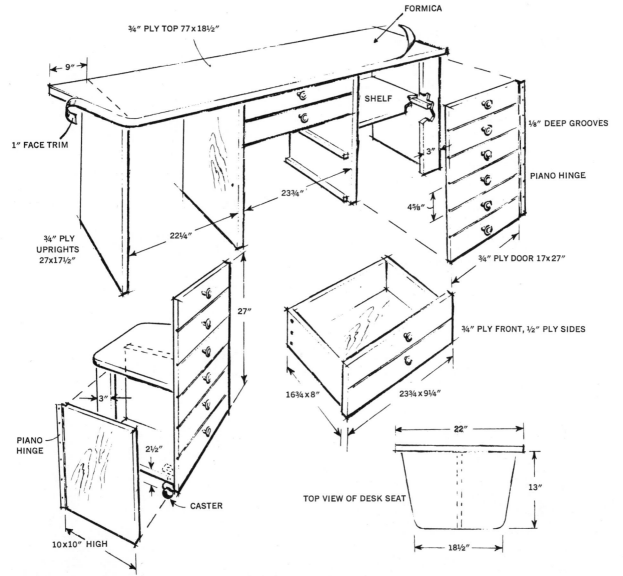

FORMICA

¾" PLY TOP 77 x 18½"

9"

SHELF

⅛" DEEP GROOVES

1" FACE TRIM

PIANO HINGE

3"

¾" PLY
UPRIGHTS
27x17½"

23¾"

4⅝"

22¼"

¾" PLY DOOR 17x27"

27"

¾" PLY FRONT, ½" PLY SIDES

PIANO
HINGE

3"

16¾ x 8"

23¾ x 9¼"

2½"

22"

13"

CASTER

TOP VIEW OF DESK SEAT

18½"

10x10" HIGH

Sketch—Sketch shows construction and assembly details sufficiently to be followed by the home do-it-yourselfer. The basic unit has four vertical supports, with drawer rails fastened inside the center portion before assembly to the top, which is surfaced with white Formica and has a self-edge of the same material. The roll-out seat, drawers, and cabinet door are made separately to complete the project, as shown.

MATERIALS LIST

4 pcs. 27 x 17½ x ¾"
uprights
1 pcs. 77 x 18½ x ¾"
top
1 pc. Formica, same size
as top (optional)
1 pc. 27 x 17 x ¾"
storage door
1 pc. 20 x 14 x ¾"
storage shelf
Drawer and shelf cleats
as needed

Chair
1 pc. 27 x 22¼ x ¾"
back
1 pc. 20 x 13 x ¾" seat
2 pcs. 10 x 10 x ¾" side
doors

1 pc. 12 x 9¼ x ¾"
interior divider
1 pc. 18 x 10 x ¾" front
2 pcs. 10 x 3 x ¾" side
uprights
1 pc. 18½ x 12¼ x ¾"
bottom
4 swivel ball casters

Drawers
3 pcs. 23¾ x 9¼ x ¾"
fronts
6 pcs. 16¾ x 8 x ½"
sides
3 pcs. 22¼ x 8 x ½"
backs
3 pcs. 23¼ x 16¾ x ¼"
bottoms

WALL-TO-WALL BUILT-IN

Floor-to-ceiling, and wall-to-wall, this built-in unit has many practical functions in addition to a decidedly decorative value. One end houses a complete audio entertainment center, comprising the TV, a complete audio system, and convenient record album racks below. At the other end are bookcases with glass doors and a pair of filing cabinet drawers on smooth-functioning extension slides.

Tying the unit together is the long center desk counter under the window, with a row of handy drawers below, and double-door storage compartments overhead. The radiator under the window is faced with a framed panel of perforated metal. Nice finishing touches are the louver doors and the scroll-cut valance over the desk.

Bare wall before installation of the wall unit shows how such space is totally wasted without a planned installation.

Wall-to-wall built-in unit serves many purposes in the most effective manner. The desk counter is spacious, the record player and TV set are enclosed by the louver doors, and the bookshelves at right have glass doors, a sensible revival of past practices.

Construction Details

The detailed sketch clearly shows the construction details. The basic material, ¾" hardwood veneered plywood, is used for the vertical supports, counter, shelves, and drawer fronts.

There are three floor-to-ceiling panels, of which one is attached to the end wall. The other two are used for framing the audio section which, when positioned, supports one end of the desk counter, which also is completely assembled before installation. These two plywood panels should be grooved to receive the shelves, and also cut back in front at the bottom corners for recessing the baseboard.

A fourth upright member is installed, resting on the desk counter, to enclose the book shelves and also to serve as a support for the row of top compartments. The single-drawer filing cabinet does not rest on the floor, but rather is suspended under the counter and attached also to the end upright.

The valance, shaped with a sabre saw, follows the traditional scroll pattern, while the radiator cover is a removable panel with center cutout covered with the metal grille. The plywood doors are all set in flush, the faces trimmed with a narrow bead molding set in rectangular arrangement. The louver doors are stock lumberyard items available in a wide range of sizes and trimmed down to fit the opening.

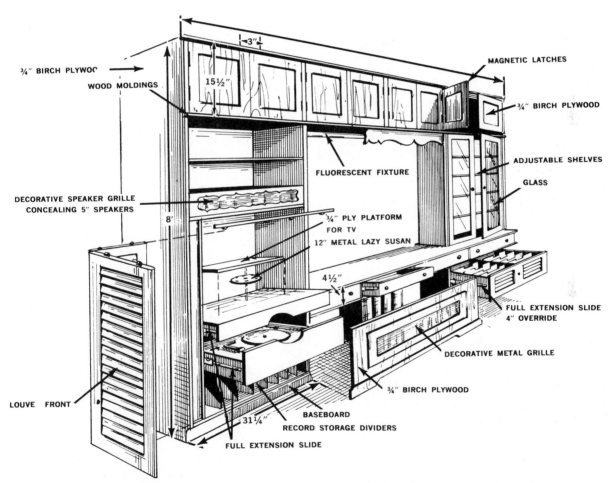

Built-in unit stretches almost 12 feet along the wall. The three basic supporting members are full-length pieces ripped from 4-by-8 hardwood veneer plywood panels. The audio section, desk counter, and filing cabinet are assembled separately, then joined and the other parts added. The desk counter, which contains four shallow drawers, is surfaced with Formica plastic laminate. Louver doors are standard stock items, trimmed to fit.

HOW TO CREATE STORAGE SPACE

163

The TV set and record player are mounted on pull-out platforms, supported by metal drawer slides for safety and easy gliding action. Both units plug into wall receptacles at the back, thus avoiding need for the electric cords trailing along the floor. Light for the desk is supplied by long fluorescent tubes overhead, shielded by the long valance.

Entertainment department deserves applause. TV set on pull-out platform has swivel mount so it can be turned in any direction for viewing. Underneath are the record player, and a record album rack below.

HIS AND HER'S BUILT-IN WARDROBE

Need more wardrobe and drawer space? Build this closet that contains fourteen drawers and four separate clothes hanging sections. Save on floor space as well—make use of the space normally used by bureau drawers.

While there is no particular way to start this project, it is suggested that you begin by securing the cross rail (L) to the wall studs and the drawer section supports (B) to the floor. A few construction details, however, should be pointed out.

At the top of the closet, the piece across the front (P) is end-lapped with the side piece (O). Pieces between the drawers (G) are dadoed into the uprights (F). The drawer sides (I) are dadoed into the upright frame (C) and fit into grooves on the sides of

the drawers. The drawers have ¼" rabbets in their fronts, backs, and sides to receive the bottoms. No drawer stops are necessary as a ½" overlap on the top of the drawers effectively serves this purpose.

One of the many nice things about this closet is that it can be quickly hidden by the sliding doors (Y), each of which comes in two sections to make it easy to reach inside without having to open the door completely.

MATERIALS LIST

A. Three pieces, each: 21 x 4 x 2"
AA. Two ¼-round moldings, each: 21" (one not shown)
B. Four pieces, each: 20 x 2 x 2" (one not shown)
C. Four pieces, each: 56 x 2 x 2" (three not shown)
D. Eight pieces, each: 21 x 2 x 2" (seven not shown)
E. Two pieces, each: 20 x 4 x 2"
F. Four pieces, each: 57 x 2 x 1"
G. Fourteen pieces, each: 21 x 2 x 1"
H. Four pieces, each: 57 x 2 x 2" (two not shown)
I. Twenty-eight pieces, each: 20 x 1 x 1" (eighteen not shown)
J. Ten drawers, each: one front, 19⅞ x 4½ x ¾"; two sides, 22⅛ x 4 x ½"; one back, 20⅜ x 4 x ½"; one bottom, 21⅛ x 20⅜ x ¼"
K. Four drawers, each: one front, 19⅞ x 10½ x ¾"; two sides, 22⅛ x 10 x ½"; one back, 20⅞ x 10 x ½"; one bottom, 21⅛ x 20⅜ x ¼" (one not shown)
L. One piece, 143¾ x 4 x 2"

M. Five pieces, each: 80 x 24 x ¾" (one not shown)
MM. One piece, 80 x 21 x ¾"
N. Three pieces, each: 74 x 4 x 2" (one not shown)
O. Two pieces, each: 23 x 4 x 3"
P. One piece, 147¾ x 6 x 2"
Q. Eight pieces, each: 20 x 6 x 1" (three not shown)
R. Two pieces, each: 24 x 1½ (dia.)" (one not shown)
S. Two pieces, each: 23¼ x 1½ (dia.)"
T. Two pieces, each: 24 x 20 x 1"
U. Two pieces, each: 23¼ x 20 x 1"
V. Two pieces, each: 73⅞ x 6 x 1"
W. Two pieces, each: 74 x 4 x 1"
X. One piece, 74 x 5 x 1"
Y. Two folding doors, each: 73⅞ x 74" (one not shown)
Z. Two moldings, each: 73⅞"
BB. Two mirrors, each: 21 x 19"
CC. Two ¼-round moldings, each: 22" (not shown)
DD. Two ¼-round moldings, each: 20" (not shown)
EE. Two fluorescent lamps, each: 21" (not shown)

Hideaway built-in wardrobe occupies the full length of a wall, contains four separate clothing racks and individual bureaus with seven drawers in each. The entire unit is enclosed in a long sweep of the accordion doors.

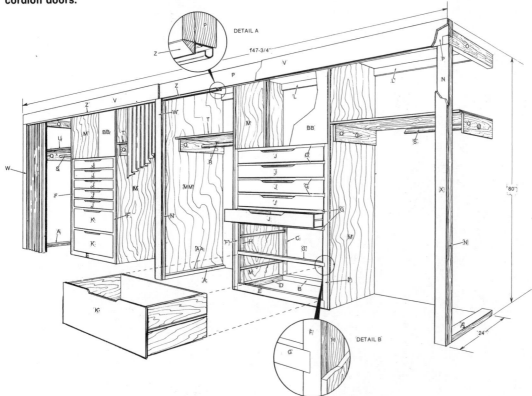

Sketch shows arrangement of wardrobe components, and the assembly details. The door tracks are neatly trimmed with a cove molding. Drawers move on 1″-by-1″ slides.

PLENTY OF CLOSET SPACE

Fortunate is the young miss who possesses such an attractive room. This original modular design has four separate sections. Three parts, enclosed with easy-action folding doors, are for clothing. The fourth consists of open shelves for toys, dolls, books, games, or whatever holds the occupant's interest at the moment. The modular design permits flexibility of arrangement to suit individual needs. Principal construction material is ¾" gum or birch plywood, which is painted. The drawer section is built separately and installed at a convenient height. The doors are hung in pairs from overhead tracks with nylon gliders.

Living can be quite complex these days, even for the very young miss seen here surveying the orderly arrangement of her clothing and possessions in storage unit designed by her mother and built by her father.

Closeup shows drawer cleat construction, using wood strips. Metal slides can be used instead. Despite appearance, there are only three drawers, each having double rows of knobs.

Head-on view of bedroom storage wall assembly with doors open shows the flexibility of arrangement, with open shelving at right to receive articles of bulky shapes and sizes.

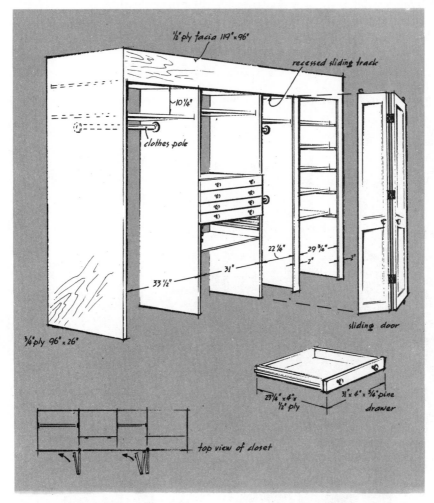

General construction details show divider panels and door positions. Dimensions can of course be adjusted to the situation and personal requirements.

A STORAGE BONANZA

This project is rich in design, offering at least three basic components, two of which accommodate average needs. The third component, of course, is the built-in desk to the right in the photograph, a design for utilizing the wall recess. While you probably will not have an identical situation, it could still be built out from a conventional wall.

Beginning with the ceiling height book-and-display shelves, far left in the photograph, use ¾" plywood, the shelves edge-trimmed and the overall frame trimmed in a convenient molding. Note sketch A for details of notched shelf and molding.

The lounger is built to window-sill height, accommodating six drawers and a foam rubber pallet. Also using ¾" plywood for the basic framework of two sides, two center uprights, and pallet platform, our model uses ¾" by 2¾" trim for drawer openings as well as front and back trim. Sketch B shows the pallet platform butting against one side, and the placement of both vertical and horizontal trim. Two and three-quarter-inch trim has been specified for average use only, based on side-mounting, slid-

ing track hardware; depending on manufacture, each slide may require up to one-inch accommodation space. Drawer faces overlap trim when closed.

If you prefer to use regular hardwood runners and guides for drawer slides, reduce the face trim accordingly.

The recessed built-in is actually a natural situation for a partially self-supporting unit, the shelves and shelf uprights in the recess serving as an ideal anchor. From this unit, the dresser and desk are built outward, the dresser having its base support partially in the recess and the desk being cleated on the left to the wall and on the right to the dresser.

The desk is a simple box-like treatment using ½" stock with a ¾" top, drawers being boxlike also, sliding into the openings. The dresser is built in the same manner as the window wall unit, except that drawer faces meet flush when closed, eliminating the need for horizontal trim between drawers. The dresser top extends back into the recess as well as to the far left, serving as the uppermost shelf over the desk.

If you wish, of course, you can extend the dresser to floor level, adding another drawer.

The addition of a book case, locker-lounger, and desk increased the efficiency and the beauty of this room.

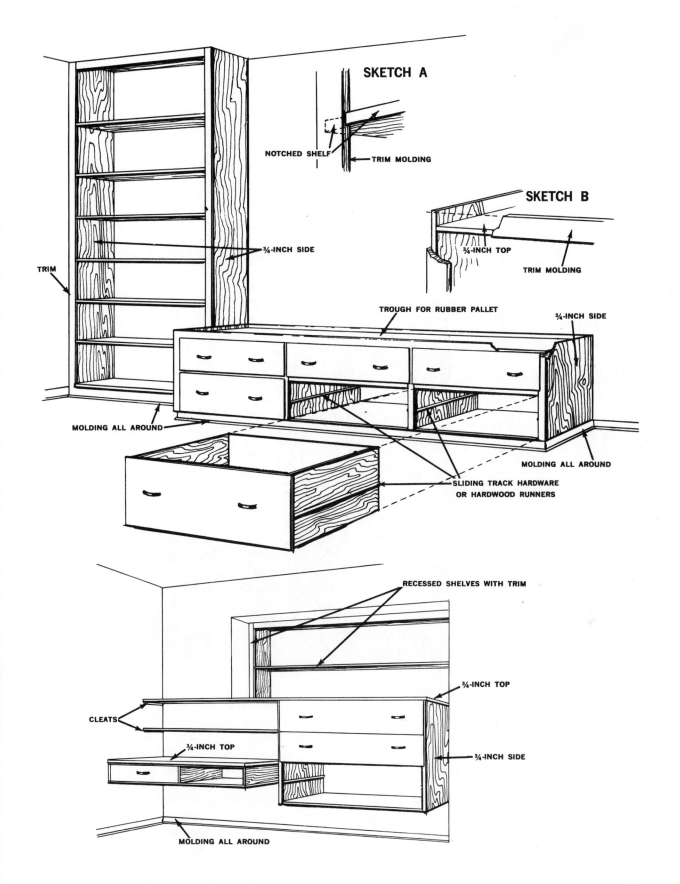

SKETCH A

NOTCHED SHELF

TRIM MOLDING

SKETCH B

¾-INCH TOP

TRIM MOLDING

TRIM

¾-INCH SIDE

TROUGH FOR RUBBER PALLET

¾-INCH SIDE

MOLDING ALL AROUND

MOLDING ALL AROUND

SLIDING TRACK HARDWARE
OR HARDWOOD RUNNERS

RECESSED SHELVES WITH TRIM

¾-INCH TOP

CLEATS

¾-INCH TOP

¾-INCH SIDE

MOLDING ALL AROUND

HOW TO CREATE STORAGE SPACE

169

Chapter 6
HOW TO RELIEVE THE SPACE PINCH

Everyone knows that buying a house has become more and more costly in recent years. The old rule of thumb, spend no more than 25 per cent of annual family income for housing, is often impossible to observe. Actually, costs have risen so far beyond this point that many families have been forced out of the housing market.

The reasons why houses are so expensive these days are well-known. Everything that goes into them—land, building materials, and labor—is up sharply. And the money that you borrow with

which to buy the house costs a great deal more than it did. Then there are the less visible items—taxes, insurance, utilities—all of which have risen to a greater or lesser extent.

To some degree, everyone is affected by this, but we are concerned here with families who already have a home and now require a larger one. Sadly, this is all too common, because if you are like so many others, your present home is probably not much bigger than the size you actually needed when you bought it, unless you were unusually farsighted. What matters most is that your house is too small and the family is feeling the pinch of too little space.

The question is, of course, what can be done about it? What options do you have? Should you stay or move? Unless there are pressing personal reasons which dictate a move, or your house is literally impossible to enlarge, you most likely are far better off electing to stay where you are.

One major determining factor is whether local zoning laws and building ordinances permit an addition to the house within the limitations of the plot. You can quickly learn this from your local building officials or from a contractor. If the regulations appear to forbid an extension, it is nevertheless often possible to obtain special permission in the form of a variance from the building regulations by applying to your local zoning board or other competent authority. Should you attempt this, it's advisable to retain an attorney who is familiar with these matters. All is not lost, however, if the effort is not fully successful.

You may still be able to enlarge your house by building *up*, instead of out. Building up may be as simple as expanding a small attic, or as complex as adding a second story to the house. Here again, building regulations may dictate what you can or cannot do.

Once you've made your decision to expand, visit several home improvement contractors to get ideas as to the type of expansion that will best suit your needs, and remain within your budget. Many contractors can offer helpful suggestions. Some even have files of photographs of jobs they've done.

CHOOSING A CONTRACTOR

Nothing is more important to the ultimate success of your project than selecting a contractor who will build it properly. But finding and choosing one is a process full of pitfalls. Your best chance of avoiding a mistake lies in personal recommendation by someone you know and trust. If this is not possible, your local bank, Chamber of Commerce or Better Business Bureau may give you the names of some reliable firms. Ask for bids from at least three contractors, preferably local firms willing to give you the names of four or five customers for whom they have recently done similar work. Later, after you've received the bids, you should visit these customers and judge the work quality for yourself. But equally important is what they tell you of their experience and their satisfaction with the job.

If you are an expert on construction, you will have no difficulty comparing one contractor's bid with another. But if you are an average home owner, you may not be able to decide which bid represents the greatest value. It is at this point that grade or quality of materials becomes a factor.

The ideal way in which to compare proposals is by furnishing the bidder with a complete list of specifications and a set of blueprints. Usually, this is only possible if you have retained an architect to design the addition.

Fortunately, however, you are a do-it-yourselfer who is ready to undertake a large part of the work. This is important here, because the largest cost differentials occur when you are contracting for a finished addition. If you do all the interior work yourself, you will want a bid only for the shell—completed outside, but rough carpentry inside. You will then have the option of buying your own paneling or wallboard, floor covering, ceiling, lighting, and so on. It is on these materials that you can be most confused in trying to compare one bid with another, unless you have that detailed specification list. Wood paneling, for example, can be bought as cheaply as three or four dollars per 4′ x 8′ sheet—or thirty times as much if you have exotic tastes. Odd lots of asphalt tile can be found for only a few cents each—or you may want to spend two dollars or more for the finest quality heavy gauge vinyl.

BUILDING A SHELL

For a shell, the builder will almost certainly use construction grade 2-by-4's for walls, ⅜″ or ½″ plywood sheathing, plus whatever exterior finish you specify—clapboard, cedar shingles, hardboard, aluminum, etc. In relative terms the amounts by which bids will vary should not be as much as when interior finishing materials are included, so there is less chance that you will be misled. Should one of the contractors' bids be far in excess of the others, you can be reasonably sure something is wrong. It works the other way too; be suspicious of a bid that is outstandingly low. Somewhere, somehow, that builder is planning on some shortcuts you won't know about until it's too late.

Insist that the contractors submit their bids in

writing, specifying the grade of all materials to be used, and pay special attention to proposed stud spacing; thickness of concrete slab, if any; use of reinforcing in the slab; depth and thickness of footings; type and weight of roofing; termite proofing by use of pressure-treated lumber or other approved method. Many of these items are controlled by local building ordinances, but they should nevertheless be specified in the bid.

GETTING ESTIMATES

On this job, three contractors located in the same suburb were asked to bid. Each was asked for a price on a completely finished room, as well as a shell. Specifications were given to the contractors for the shell only. One never returned a bid, and was not heard from again. It's interesting to note that the two shell bids received were only $100 apart, but there was a difference of $450 for the finished room, which seemed to be attributable to the use of cheaper grades of materials by the lower bidder. The job was given to the higher bidder because his references checked out far better, and he had been doing business locally for twenty-one years, a most important factor.

No matter how trustworthy you believe your contractor to be, take certain precautions in making an agreement. Get it all down in the contract. First, there's that schedule of payments. In no event should you pay the contractor in advance—even in part. Your agreement should spell out at what points in the construction you will be called on to pay. If your contractor hires subcontractors to do part of the work, and he fails to pay them, they can obtain a mechanic's lien on your house. In plain language, without protection you may have to pay twice: once to the contractor, and again to the subcontractor if he has been left holding the bag. The best protection you can have is to insist that the contractor give you copies of receipted bills from all subcontractors and suppliers involved. If he will not, you can ask him to sign a waiver stating that he has paid for all such obligations. Finally, never pay in cash. If you do not have a checking account, get a bank check.

It should be clear at this point why it is advisable to have an attorney approve the contract *before you sign it*. Don't be carried away by your desire to have the job started. You'll have lots of time for regrets later if you do.

FINANCING YOUR PROJECT

While ideas are being gathered and plans being made, the question of paying for the project should also be examined. If you're one of the majority, you'll borrow the money from an outside source, unless rich Aunt Matilda will lend it to you interest free. Sources are many. If your credit standing is reasonably good you should have no difficulty qualifying for a home improvement loan of up to several thousand dollars. These may vary from one part of the country to another—and there may be a type of loan available in one section that can't be found elsewhere.

It is important for you to know that, as with any other commodity, you can shop for money. There are not only many ways to borrow, but you will often find differences in the cost of similar loans from one bank to another.

One New York State savings bank offers home improvement loans up to $5,000 for up to five years, with payments at the rate of $110.14 per month, including life insurance coverage. Interestingly enough, another savings bank in the same city offers $5,000 for five years at a monthly payment of $111.11 without the life insurance feature. That's what we mean about shopping for the best buy. You need not have an account at a particular institution to apply there for a loan.

FHA Loans

Most banks also handle Federal Housing Administration Title 1 loans. These usually cost a little less, and are available for longer periods of repayment. You can borrow $5,000 and repay it at the rate of $104.61 per month for sixty months, but there is no life insurance feature. However, your FHA loan can be for as long as seven years, in which case your monthly payment would be $80.51.

There is yet another kind of FHA loan: the 203K Home Improvement Mortgage Loan. Where the others are generally restricted to $5,000 or less, this one begins at $5,000 and goes up to $12,000. You borrow the money for ten, fifteen, or twenty years. It is quite similar to obtaining a mortgage on a house—except that this is a *second* mortgage. There are closing fees which range from $200 to $300 to cover title searches, etc. To qualify for a 203K loan, you must have detailed plans prepared by a professional, complete lists of materials and costs. In short, everything you would need if you were financing a new house. An advantage of this type of loan is that the construction must be inspected and approved by FHA before the contractor gets his money, pretty good assurance that you're getting a job up to standards. 203K loans are limited to major home improvements. The others can pay for such things as swimming pools and air conditioning in addition to conventional construction; 203K will not. A ten year, $5,000 loan would be repaid at $64.02 per month.

Bankbook Loan

Probably the cheapest of all bank loans is the type known as a *passbook loan*. Here you are borrowing from a bank where you have a savings account. The repayment period is usually limited to three years. Your own bank account, which you put up as security, nevertheless continues to draw normal interest.

Policy Loans

Here is another method of borrowing money at low rates.

Life insurance policies (except term) have a stated cash surrender value. If you read the fine print in yours, you'll discover that you may borrow up to 95 per cent of that amount at a fixed rate, also appearing in the policy—usually 5 per cent or 6 per cent simple interest—and repay it at your convenience. If you are a former serviceman, you may have a policy issued by National Service Life Insurance. If so, the interest rate is only 4 per cent.

HOW THIS PROJECT WAS PLANNED

The house shown in the accompanying photos was enlarged to create a den—a place where office

This spacious den was built onto a home to provide additional living space needed by the family. Opening at left leads to other rooms in house, which are at a level about three feet lower than the new den.

work could be done at home, space for hobby activities, and privacy away from normal family activity.

The house is of the type known as a front-to-back split level with an attached one-car garage. When it was erected fifteen years ago, the builder had obtained a zoning variance because his plans called for a house wider than would fit the prescribed minimum side yard width. It was believed, therefore, that any effort to obtain a new variance for further encroachment would be doomed.

In viewing the house from the street on which it faces, the structure appears to be one-story tall, with windows somewhat higher than normal. From the rear, the house seems to be a conventional two-story building. On closer inspection, however, one notes that the first floor windows are nearer the ground than would be expected. Indoors, the rooms in the front half of the house are about 3' above grade. Moving toward the rear, you may descend a short flight of steps to the family room level which is about 3' below grade.

The left side of the house, to which the 12' wide garage is attached, extends about 17' beyond the back of the garage. Enclosing the L formed by this 17' wall and the 12' back wall of the garage would produce a room of approximately those dimensions without exceeding the building boundaries. Since only two walls and a roof would be needed, construction would cost less. Another major economy was achieved by deciding that the floor of the new

AFTER—The new roofline is sloped to clear an existing window on house wall above the den. The exterior of the addition is finished to conform to the rest of the house walls.

HOME IMPROVEMENT BOOK

room would be at grade level, saving the cost of excavating to the floor of the family room, an item on which the contractor quoted $800 more. There would have to be a short stairway no matter which level was chosen, since doors both to the garage and the family room would be included and they were at different levels.

ROOM ADDITION TEST PROJECT

An economical and successful project for building an additional room onto a home is presented here, completely detailed from start to finish. Designed and carried through by the staff of *Family Handyman* Magazine to work out the best combination of do-it-yourself and outside contractors' services, the project proved a practical base for scheduling and dovetailing the various stages of construction. Observations in the course of this project provided guidelines for determining which portions of the work might be beyond the skills or physical capabilities of the average home owner, so would best be let out to trades people, and which parts could be satisfactorily done by those home owners who have some manual skills or are ready to learn by doing.

The problems that arose, some of which were fully anticipated but others that were unexpected, are also detailed here. While these problems were specific for this particular project because of its location and special circumstances, they are quite typical and very likely will be similar to those encountered in other room construction jobs. The measures taken to overcome them will no doubt be helpful to those undertaking similar construction.

The text and illustrations also include details concerning the work done by contractors. The purpose is in part to assist those home owners who undertake to do the entire construction work but, in addition, in showing the details of these phases of the project, the reader who plans to have the work done by contractors may be helped. A familiarity with the steps involved will enable him to negotiate knowledgeably and to check on the progress of the work.

Three Jobs for Contractors.

Three major parts of the project were let to contractors. These were for: (1) masonry work, which involved placing the footings and pouring the concrete slab; (2) carpentry work, which included framing the room (walls, roof, windows, doors; and (3) electrical installations, which in this case went far beyond merely the wiring for lights and receptacles in the new room. Rather, because a larger service was decided on to provide for both the electric heaters and air conditioning equipment in the new room, a new 200-ampere service panel was installed.

While the circumstances may have been exceptional in this particular case, it is reasonable to expect that in many homes that add on a room, the house electric service might well be updated at this time to provide both for the circuits needed for the new room and for the additional appliances and equipment that most likely will be utilized when the electric service is available.

First Step Taken.

With plans and contracts concluded and starting dates confirmed, a necessary task was to dig out the foundation plantings at the site, which were to be preserved for replacement around the new structure. The plants, carefully taken with their root balls, were temporarily heeled in at a remote part of the ground so they would not be damaged in the course of the work.

Removing these plantings was the first step in building the addition. Be certain to preserve your plants and shrubbery by removing them with their roots intact and temporarily heeling them away from the construction site.

Pouring the Footing and Slab.

Construction starts with the masonry work. In one day two experienced masons dug the perimeter trench for the foundation footing, leveled the site and placed the required wood forms, poured the ready-mixed concrete and finished the concrete smooth and level.

POURING THE SLAB

Siding on garage wall is broken away, providing access to top of concrete footing for coordinating the new foundation. Garage wall forms one side of addition.

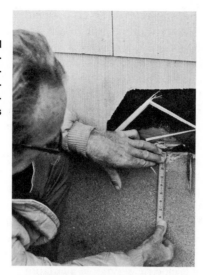

Taut string between stakes guides worker digging trench for footing. Some of excavated earth was used for leveling the site.

Footings around perimeter of slab must be deep enough to penetrate the frost line. A depth of 3 feet is required in northern sections of the country.

Trenching completed, forms are set and leveled to show height to which the concrete will be poured. The form board is aligned with side wall of the garage.

Footing dimensions vary in different localities and are usually determined by local building codes. In construction of this type—a single-story frame addition—a footing 8″ thick is usually standard specification, while the depth must be below the frost line. In the northern part of the country this would be at least three feet below ground level.

Preparation of the base for the concrete slab varies according to the soil factors that may be present. When any grading is done to level the site, at least a few days should be allowed for the earth to settle before further work is done. Drainage also is important, but here, too, much will depend on the type of soil. You must determine whether it is sandy soil, which rapidly absorbs water, or clay, which does not—and also the pitch of the ground. In most cases,

a topping of gravel over a sand base is advisable to assure adequate drainage.

The ready-mixed concrete must be moved *fast*. Usually it is impossible for the heavy trucks to back all the way up to the pouring site, so sufficient manpower must be available to move the concrete in wheelbarrows to the work area. In this case, the two workers were able to trundle the concrete from the curb to the pouring in rapid time.

The footing trenches were filled first, then the concrete was wheeled into the slab section, spread evenly at once with a rake. As the forms began to fill, one mason used a long 2-by-4 to "strike" the surface level with the tops of the form. When the forms were completely filled, the concrete was left to set for a while, then a trowel about 3′ wide at the

Plywood form is built to be placed at stairs area, which must be kept clear of concrete.

Wheelbarrows bring in concrete from ready-mix truck at curb. Footing trenches are filled first, then the slab is poured.

Concrete is first spread evenly with a rake to the approximate level, indicated by the wood forms.

Work moves quickly and soon the trenches are full. Masons are expert at handling the huge wheelbarrows with their heavy load.

Stairway form is set into place and leveled with main form boards. An entry to house from new room will be opened at this point.

Long 2-by-4 used to "strike" the concrete acts as a crude trowel to bring the slab to approximate level surface. The strike is long enough to rest on the form boards as it is drawn over the wet concrete.

Long-handled trowel, several feet wide, is used to smooth the fresh concrete mixture in this next finishing stage.

Long bolts, hooked at one end, are inserted into the concrete to provide anchorage for the wood plates that will be put down.

First stage of the project is completed. The slab is sprinkled several times a day for a few days to assure proper curing of the concrete. Wood forms, which had been coated with crude oil, will then be broken away from the footing.

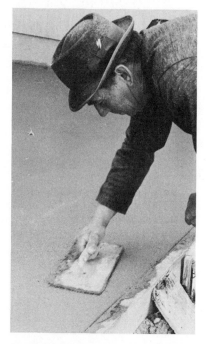

Entire slab is then hand-troweled as mason rests on wide board placed over the partially set concrete.

Bolt is set into the concrete, plumbed with a level. Bolts are spaced at uniform distances.

end of a long handle, was carefully wielded back and forth to smooth the surface. Finally, crouching on heavy boards resting on the wet surface, and starting at the farthest corner, the mason finished the surface with a hand trowel. Anchor bolts to hold the sill were then set into the concrete at uniform distances and trued up with a level.

For three days following, the slab was sprinkled lightly several times each day to promote better curing of the concrete. The concrete surface then had a smooth, almost polished appearance.

In this project there was one unusual detail that required special attention. The room being built would not be on a level with other rooms in the house, necessitating an interior access stairway. Provision for this stairway was made before pouring the slab by enclosing the area with a plywood form, carefully reinforced, to keep the concrete from entering the area.

Electrical Installation

A novel and interesting arrangement of the electrical wiring developed as a result of the room addition project. A new meter and service panel (fuse box) were installed, providing for heavier 200-ampere service. To keep costs down, the original panel box and some of the circuits were left as they were —shifting them to the new panel would have involved considerable rewiring in various parts of the house. It was then decided to transfer only those appliance circuits that were in constant use, thus eliminating a possible overload condition, while the circuits that remained would be supplied by a line drawn from 60-ampere breakers in the new box. Thus, what developed was, in fact, a secondary circuit box supplied from the main feeder box, which contained the house service lines. This arrangement is helpful in any situation where problems arise in wiring for heavier electric service.

ELECTRICITY

Electric service lines will be drawn overhead to a tall mast (really a large-diameter vertical conduit) that is securely fastened to the house wall. Here a saddle clamp is placed around the mast and joined to a bracket on the wall.

Heavy feeder wires from the circuit panel box indoors are brought into the meter box. Later the service wires are connected into this box from the overhead mast.

Fully wired meter box, showing cables from service entrance and those feeding the circuit panel. The bare center wire is the neutral or ground.

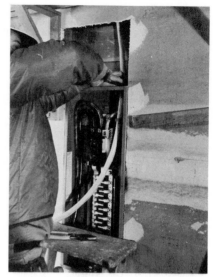

Meter is simply plugged into the box. This is the task of the electric company. A metal cover slips over the round meter.

Circuit-breaker panel box is being installed into wall opening. Feeder cable is seen entering box through bottom.

A heavy cable is run from the new panel to the original fuse box where it will supply a number of existing circuits that remain undisturbed. Other circuits are then "pulled" from the new panel.

Framing the Walls

Carpentry work begins with laying the sill plates over 10″ wide strips of copper sheeting that serve as a protective shield against termites. The sill plates, consisting of doubled 2-by-4's, are anchored by the hooked bolts which had been embedded into the concrete around the edge of the slab, as mentioned previously. The copper, punched to fit over the anchor bolts, is placed so that it overhangs the slab about 4″. After the wall sheathing and siding are installed, this excess width is bent upward underneath to enclose the sill plates.

The plates are carefully squared up at the corners, then nailed together and locked in with the anchor bolt nuts, establishing the base for the wall framing. This goes up with amazing speed once the preliminaries have been completed. In the test project, a half-hour was spent on preparatory cutting and assembling, and only about ten minutes more to raise and nail in the sections.

WALL FRAMING

Plate is laid on slab to locate holes for anchor bolts. Dark thin strip is copper sheet that protects against termites.

Copper termite shield is placed along outer perimeter of slab over anchor bolts. Sheet overhangs the edge by about 4 inches.

Double 2-by-4 plate, with holes drilled for anchor bolts, lies over copper shield. Large nuts will hold the plates in place.

Wall framing is assembled on the floor. Studs are 16 inches on centers. Double 2-by-4 plate at left is at the top of the wall.

Prefabbed section is pushed erect. The large opening is for a window. Edge of termite shield is folded up against sill.

Double 2-by-6 header reinforces structure above window opening. Note also the construction of corner post in foreground.

The secret of speedy construction lies in prefabricating the frame on the ground, then lifting it into position and nailing it in place. First the top plate is formed by spiking together two 2-by-4's. The necessary studs are all cut to uniform size, with double 2-by-4's for the corner posts. The plate is nailed to the studs and post, then the section is raised and plumbed into position, and all that remains is to toenail each stud to the sill plate. In forming the wall frame, studs are omitted from areas where windows or doors will be placed; these areas are framed in later with cripple studs and headers.

Where windows will be located, pairs of 2-by-6 are nailed between studs above the window openings for headers, and a 2-by-4 set across underneath, supported by several short studs reaching to the floor for sill support. All these parts are leveled and plumbed carefully to keep the opening square.

Short studs at more or less regular spacing are placed beneath horizontal 2-by-4's and toenailed top and bottom.

Roofing Timbers

Spaced 16″ apart on centers, 2″-by-12″ beams are used for the rafters, with one rafter nailed directly to the house wall. These rafters must be angle-cut at the end to match the slope of the garage roof to which they will be fitted. In this particular project, windows in the house wall just above the garage roof presented a difficulty. They were at a level where the new rafters would normally have been inserted into the wall in order to obtain the slope required for the new roof.

It was decided, in the interest of economy and speed, to have a flat roof which does not require so great a pitch. The roll roofing material which

First rafter, a 2-by-12, is brought up to roof to find cutting angle for end. It must match the slope of the garage roof. Continue as shown below.

Rafter end is nailed to garage roof. Old overhang beneath new rafter will be covered later by ceiling in the new room.

One cut is made at angle determined in previous step. Same cut also removes waste piece at the end.

Notched ends of rafters are spiked to the top plate. Spacing between them is the standard 16 inches, center to center.

The opposite end of the rafter has to be notched out, as here, to fit over top plate, and extend beyond for the overhang.

Shingles are broken out to provide flush nailing surface for rafter. Roof had to pass underneath window seen here.

182

Rafter along outer edge of roof is reinforced by nailing in short fitted 2-by-4 pieces placed above each full length stud.

This view shows how rafters are spiked to garage roof. The member at the left is nailed to the wall of the house as well.

With rafters in place, roofing begins with exterior grade plywood sheathing. Use thickness dictated by building code.

would then be used has a shorter useful life than shingles, but the cost of reroofing is not so great.

The roof deck is sheathed with exterior grade plywood, of sufficient thickness to withstand the local snow loads as dictated in the building code. Double $3/4''$ roof decking is preferable to avoid possible sagging, which would cause standing puddles of water after a rain.

Sheathing and Door Framing

Large sheathing panels applied over the studs enclose the room area in short order. One detail is worthy of mention: instead of precutting the panels to the required size, they are simply nailed onto the studs, each panel butting against the next. Those ends that overhang a stud are simply sliced off with a portable circular saw having the blade set to the correct depth equal to the thickness of the sheathing material. Thus, the panels can be cut at the center of a stud so that a larger piece of the sheathing can be nailed on.

Many types of material are used for sheathing. Formerly, all sheathing consisted of tongue-and-groove lumber, and this is still widely used because of the dimensional support that is given to the structure, in addition to the weather-sealing qualities. Modern architectural concepts and construction practices favor the use of large composition sheathing panels, usually with protective coatings, for their insulating values.

Building paper goes over the sheathing, dropped in long strips from the roof. Each strip overlaps the next by about 6", and is held with heavy staples. Where application of the siding is to be delayed for a day or two, long batten strips are nailed temporarily to hold the paper against the wind.

Matching the Shingles

The exterior wall of any room addition should be finished with the same materials as the rest of the house so that the new wing blends with and becomes part of the overall structure. But even with use of the same siding, there may be some difference in appearance between the new and old material due to the weathering process. This is not an important factor, of course, when the siding is to be painted, such as when clapboard is used, as the paint soon will lose its "newness" and blend well with the original walls unless there has been a very long gap in the painting periods. Vinyl-coated aluminum siding also presents no "matching" diffi-

Exterior grade plywood is nailed to structural members. Excess lengths are trimmed after nailing, saving fitting. Continue as below.

Metal bead is nailed at outside corner of new walls. This strip seats corner and provides a guideline for shingles.

With sheathing completed on walls and roof, next operation is to cover wall with building paper. Staple hammer is best tool.

First course of shingles must be carefully leveled to assure horizontal shadow lines. Lower edge overlaps concrete slab.

Some shingles must be stripped away where new wall meets old. New shingles will interlace with old ones at joint.

Double sash fits into prepared opening, is leveled, shimmed and nailed in. Awning type windows were used for this project.

184

culty, since the original installation may well have kept its fresh appearance for the years that it has been exposed since installation. The same is true of cedar shingles which can be stained for a fairly close match.

Prefinished materials, such as the asbestos shingles used for the exterior walls of the described project, would show a distinct variation in color shade due to weathering. In this case, however, a supply of new shingles was fortunately obtained of the same color that matched the faded ones on the house wall.

The shingle installation is a routine procedure; each shingle is attached with special nails through predrilled holes. One detail of the installation demonstrates the time-saving techniques developed by professional craftsmen. Instead of cutting and fitting individual asbestos shingles to fit the sloped roof line, the installer simply nails up full-size shingles, then attaches the wood trim over the end course at the proper angle. It is a quick and easy matter, then, to break off the excess ends of the shingles with a hammer, obtaining a neat edge line.

The exterior door and all windows are set into the prepared openings before the shingle siding is nailed in around them. Final stages of the enclosure are fitting and nailing up the soffit, fascia, and trim boards. Finally, aluminum gutter and downspouts are set into position, properly pitched and reinforced.

Insulating

The inadequate attention given to insulation when constructing a room addition is often regretted afterward by the home owner and his family, since heating a slab-based room may present difficulties. Full-thick 6″ insulation batts between roof rafters, and 4″ batts in the side walls, carefully fitted at all obstructions, should give satisfactory results. In the project described here, these specifications were followed, particularly since expensive electric heating would be used.

Insulation always is installed with the vapor barrier facing inside the room. In this case, the vapor barrier is a built-in layer of aluminum foil which has the additional quality of a reflective surface. The insulation may be obtained in continuous rolls cut to required lengths so that a single segment stretches across the full length of the rafter. With batts of 8′ lengths, however, each batt must be carefully "jointed" into the next, which is at best a

HOW TO RELIEVE THE SPACE PINCH

Shingling proceeds to roof line. Part of old trim is cut off. New length will be fitted to it and run along the new wall.

Final course of shingles is nailed in place with top edge well above the roof line. This is trimmed flush in the next step.

Much fitting time is saved by nailing trim over last shingle course, then breaking off excess with a hammer.

Soffit is nailed to bottom of rafter ends, followed by fascia and trim boards, finally the aluminum gutter and downspout.

messy job. With the roll there also is likely to be less waste, since the correct lengths are cut as needed. The batts are gently pressed into the open space between the joists, the folded edges of vapor barrier material serving as a means for stapling the batts to the studs or joists. Keep in mind, though, that the insulation, light and fluffy as it might be, has a tendency to sag down at the center and requires adequate support. This usually is provided to some extent by the furring strips nailed up for the ceiling tiles.

Plywood Paneling

Plywood paneling is most effective when applied over a wallboard backing, such as gypsum board or similar solid material. This not only increases the insulating value, but also makes the plywood firmer, less subject to vibration or buckling. In addition, the wallboard backing permits application by the advanced adhesive method which many find superior to nailing.

After being conditioned to the room's atmosphere for a week or more, during which time the gypsum board can be installed, the panels can be matched for grain and color to achieve the most pleasing effect. Number the panels in sequence so you'll know where each belongs.

One or two of the panels are then fitted into corners. This step is necessary because the walls and ceiling or floor are never as square as the plywood. The panel must fit neatly into the corner, with the vertical edge held plumb. Don't try to "make it" by tipping the panel just a bit.

Also, the panel should be raised to actual installation height if there is to be a base molding. The best way is to hold a carpenter's spirit level against the near edge of the panel, while the far edge is moved into the wall corner—gently, not forced. Then, using the level, align the panel edge plumb. It may be possible then to move the panel in closer to the wall. The panel is now held in its plumb position, either supported by a second person, or blocked up underneath. Using a compass and scribe, follow the contours of the wall so that they are transferred to the panel. Now examine the edge and determine how much planing is necessary to make the panel conform to the wall contours and bring the edge up flush, with the panel always plumb. You will have to do the same thing with the opposite corner when you come to it.

That is the first part. The ceiling also will have to be contoured to fit in a similar way, unless you intend to put up a ceiling cove molding, which will cover any irregularities in the fit.

Fastening may be done by nailing, or by the adhesive method as explained in detail in Chapter 7. Adhesive is more expensive. It costs about $1.50 a tube and you may need a tube for every three panels or so, which comes to much more than finishing nails, but eliminates the tedious work of countersinking the nails and produces a better-looking result, even when the nailheads are covered with matched color in crayon. For a 12′ x 16′ room, the adhesive for paneling all the walls would cost less than $7.

But before fastening the panels, there is much to be done, such as cutting the openings for electric switches and receptacles, for wall fixtures, and around windows and doors. It will surprise you how many jobs there are to cope with. These cuts must be made with extreme care as any error in spacing a hole, or cutting it just a bit too large, can spoil an expensive panel. It is suggested that you first make small test holes, then, after checking the accuracy of the location and double-checking the dimensions of the cut, proceed with the final cutting. This method may be slow, but it can save you some disappointing mistakes.

Trim moldings complete the paneling job. These include corners, coves, baseboards, shoes, and clamshells around windows and doors. Many panel manufacturers produce prefinished molding to blend with or match their panels.

INSULATING AND PANELING

Applying fiberglass insulation is the easiest part of the entire project. Insulation blankets are stapled into each stud space.

Gypsum wallboard provides a good base for plywood paneling, although it is not absolutely necessary. Nail to studs.

Walls are not always plumb, as here. Butt first panel into corner. Trace profile with compass then cut to fit.

Use panel adhesive for easiest results. Apply bead all around edge, and two beads vertically, spacing them evenly.

After placing fitted panel on adhesive and tacking at top, use block and tap with hammer to adhere firmly.

Panels must be carefully fitted around all openings if you want to retain a smooth continuous look.

Ceiling System

The ceiling style for the room addition project is the suspended type, designed on a 2' module—that is, each opening in the grid is 24" square—permitting a wide choice of ceiling blocks, and utilizing fluorescent lamps flush with the ceiling surface for maximum lighting. A total of eight fixtures, each with a pair of 20-watt fluorescent lamps, are placed in groups of four. A useful feature of this system, which is an Armstrong Cork Company product, is that the lights are easily relocated should you find the arrangement unsuitable. So it is advisable to leave extra length on the supply lines for this purpose. Detailed information on the installation of the suspended lighting system will be found in the chapter on modern kitchen improvements.

CEILING STYLE

Snap leveled chalk line around wall at desired ceiling line. Make sure the fourth line meets the first one. Then continue as shown below.

Main runners, which carry most of the load, must be supported every few feet. Use heavy wire and tie to the roof.

System consists of main runners plus assorted 4 and 2 foot pieces which lock into each other, as is shown here.

Installation starts with angle brackets nailed to wall on the guide line you snapped in the previously described step.

Nearly completed gridwork shows one lighting fixture in place and several of the supporting wire ties for runners.

Lighting fixtures complete with reflectors, slide onto channels. Note extra wire coil to permit moving later.

Carpeting in Tiles

Carpeting, the tough indoor-outdoor type, won the decision for the room floor covering for a number of reasons. Chief among them were the toughness of the carpeting to withstand the comings and goings to the back yard, and the fact that the carpet is available in self-adhesive do-it-yourself squares, which can be put down at a considerable saving in total cost. Installation is similar to that of other floor tiles.

The center point of the room is located, then shifted as needed so that narrow strips will not fall at the wall edges in any direction. Then two guidelines are snapped with chalk at right angles to each other, each parallel to a wall, whereupon the tile laying can begin. Start where the guidelines cross, then follow along the lines, filling in as you go to widen the area of coverage.

The tiles are self-adhesive—the smoother the flooring material, the better they stick. There is no problem getting them to hold on concrete, but a few drops of water sprinkled on the back of each prior to positioning resulted in a major improvement. There is one precaution to take: while the face of the tile does not appear to have a grain, each tile has an arrow marked on the back. Lay the tiles with all the arrows pointing the same way. Done properly, the finished job should look like a single piece of fitted carpet.

FLOORING
Measure both dimensions of room and find center point, adjusting it to avoid narrow strips around edges.

Start tiles at center, laying into L-shape, then fill in behind the L until you have reached the edge of the area.

At edge, place whole tile against wall with adhesive side up. Be sure it fits snugly and doesn't move around.

Take another whole tile, and lay over empty floor space, on top of the tile mentioned in the previous photo.

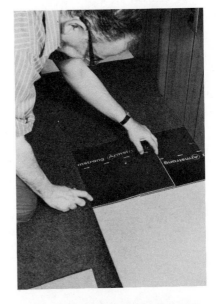

With tailor's chalk or marking crayon, draw line on bottom tile. The line will be a cutting guide for your knife.

Utility knife and steel straight-edge are good for quick accurate cuts. We got best results with this method.

Strip cut in previous steps is now ready to be put down. It should fit perfectly. A little practice can be a big help.

Moisten back of whole tile with a few drops of water sprinkled on, then place in position against other tiles.

Force edges flat with thumb, running thumb along seam. Properly laid, you cannot see seams between tiles.

CONVERTING A PORCH

There it was—a screened open porch built onto the back of the house, with three low framed walls, a concrete slab floor, and a good roof with finished ceiling inside. There were two doors—a screen door on the outside, a jalousie door leading into the house—and several electric outlets.

The objective was to obtain an all-weather family room by converting the open porch at the lowest possible cost, salvaging and using as much of the existing material as possible.

What was done: with all screens discarded, framing to enclose the remaining wall areas was put up. The same awning-type windows as the rest of the house were selected and fitted into the wall framing. The screen door was discarded, and the jalousie door shifted to take its place in the same open-

ing, which was of the right size. Then the exterior was covered with additional 1-by-6 wood siding, fitted at the wall joints to tie in with the existing wall section. Scrap pieces of siding were used to make the inside window sills.

With the room now fully enclosed, inside work went forward rapidly. First, a few additional electric outlets and ceiling lights were roughed in, then the wall framing was packed with insulation batts. The walls were then paneled with plywood, and the floor was covered with a deep pile rug, completing the basic conversion.

This house is in Florida, so heating and floor insulation required no attention. In northern areas, it is advisable to build a wood floor over 2-by-6 sleepers and provide underfloor insulation. Heating may be provided by electric zone heaters, or radiators connected to the house system.

Extra room, urgently needed by growing family, was obtained by converting an open porch quickly at minimum cost. The only expense was for materials: siding, windows, insulation, and wall panels.

The screened porch which was converted, retaining the original framing and roof. Additional siding was added to completely enclose the walls.

Cozy and comfortable on rug, family enjoys the additional living space provided by converting the porch into a usable room.

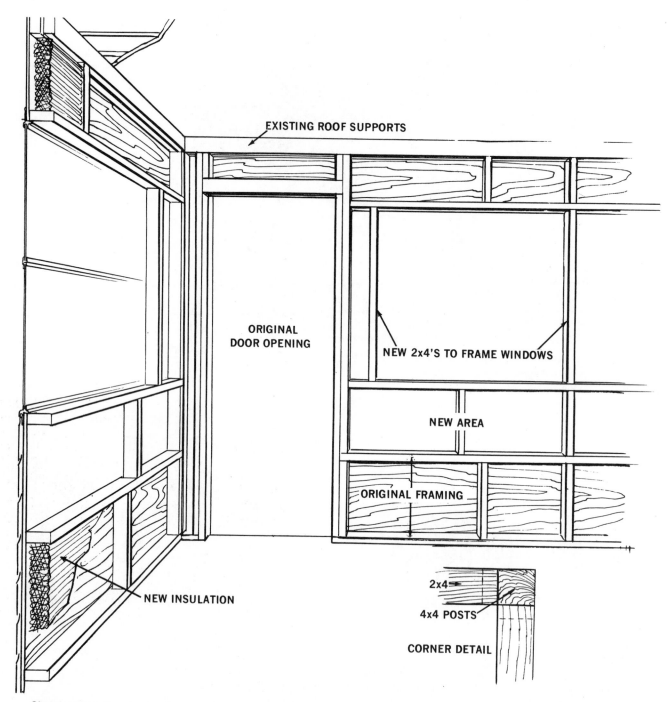

EXISTING ROOF SUPPORTS

ORIGINAL
DOOR OPENING

NEW 2x4'S TO FRAME WINDOWS

NEW AREA

ORIGINAL FRAMING

NEW INSULATION

2x4

4x4 POSTS

CORNER DETAIL

Sketch shows the simple steps required to complete the framing for porch enclosure. Windows are set at same levels as those in rest of the house. Original 4-by-4 roof posts and lower framing were retained and extended, windows fitted in, walls packed with insulation and finished with plywood paneling. Floor could be built up with 2-by-6 sleepers, by modifying the original door frame for full clearance.

New wall framing consists of 2-by-4s, except the vertical members between the windows, which are 4-by-4s to assure a necessary stability for window function. Windows must be squared up carefully when installed.

New siding is same type as original section along the bottom area of porch. The clapboards are notched to fit neatly around the new window frames.

Corner view shows how new framing was tied into the original corner roof posts, and supports placed under the horizontal headers.

Completed wall with awning windows makes a handsome extension on the house. Old and new sections of siding are indistinguishable.

AN ATTIC "PAD"

Though they may have comfortable bedrooms in spacious homes, teen-age boys often prefer private "digs" of their own, even the seeming isolation of the attic. The finished room shown here was designed to comply with such a preference while making the attic retreat attractive, function, and individual as well as secluded.

The two rooms occupying the entire attic space are intended to serve two young brothers, providing them with a quiet haven for school work in addition to recreational and entertainment facilities and a modest gym for exercise and workouts.

Two essential details are good lighting and soundproofing. In addition to the standard table and desk lamps, there are a half-dozen recessed ceiling lights and an additional built-in lamp above each of the beds.

Soundproofing and ease of maintenance are im-

Low closet with louver doors is cleverly designed, as the sloping rear wall which conforms to the rafters allows ample clearance for hanging suits on the clothes pole.

A "pad" all their own is evidently enjoyed by young brothers, who make good use of the gym equipment to keep in trim. Thick foam floor mat helps assure quiet.

Two sides of room are identical. Each bed is located next to a dormer window. Reading lamp is built-in over bed, shielded by perforated hardboard strip.

portant elements of the plan, which involve particular attention to materials and finishing details. The floor is heavily insulated and the walls have double panels of gypsum board. One layer is securely nailed to both knee walls and the ceiling collar beams, then an additional panel layer is cemented to the walls while sound-absorbing acoustical tiles are cemented to the ceiling. Floor rugs, and a thick mat at the gym corner, help control unwanted vibrations.

Homework-hobby corner doesn't look much like the grim attic before it was given the finishing treatment. Acoustical ceiling tiles help create the quiet environment for studying.

The attic as it was—a vast space unused for many years, yet adaptable into excellent living quarters.

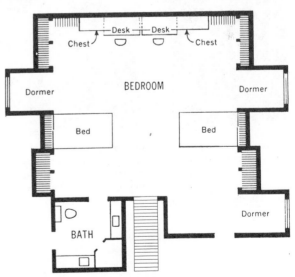

Open floor plan makes most use of the available space, and keeps cost down by avoidance of partitions.

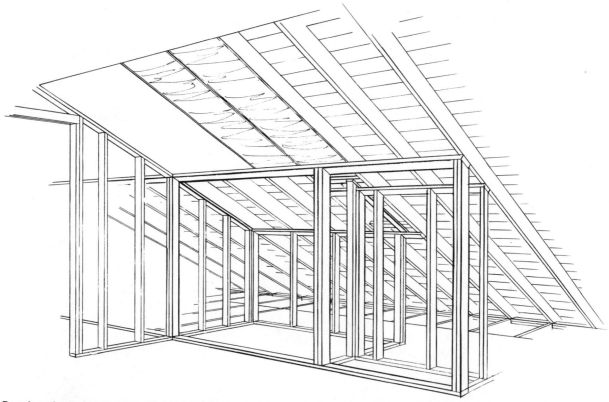

Drawing shows how knee-walls and small closets were framed with 9-by-4's. Headers were nailed across the rafters, and studs with ends shaped to fit were nailed in to form the frame.

Insulation blankets are fitted between the rafters and the ceiling collar beams. Adequate rating of insulation is essential.

First step in the final finishing is nailing of gypsum backing panels to the framing members, covering the walls and ceiling.

Finish panels of vinyl-coated gypsum are applied with adhesive over the backing panels, eliminating need for nailing.

Ceiling receives acoustical tiles, stapled to the back panels. Openings are left for ceiling lamps.

Chapter 7
PANELS AND WALL COVERINGS

Few improvement projects around the home produce as rapid and effective a result as does wall paneling. Whatever the reason—whether it is appreciation of the wood graining, or its color, or the warmth and natural feel of the wood—the essential explanation for the popularity of wall paneling is that it creates a more attractive and relaxing atmosphere. Whether just one wall or all the walls are covered, the paneling brings a new character to a living room, a basement playroom, a den, recreation room, bedroom—any room, in fact.

But there are even more practical reasons for favoring this project. An important one is that paneling may well be the only practical solution to a damaged or defective wall that has become an eyesore, perhaps because the gypsum panels were installed incorrectly and are showing signs of popping away from their retainer nails. Another sound inducement for wood paneling is its insulation value, particularly in rooms difficult to heat properly, which face prevailing winds. A third reason is the shortage of experienced plasterers, with the result that it's so much simpler and even cheaper to panel a room than to go through the difficulties of having cracked or damaged walls redone properly. And last, but not least, the paneled wall needs little or no attention, and its durability is permanent.

FAVORITE WOODS AVAILABLE

For a while it looked like the much-beloved American walnut would no longer be available for home use because the limited supply was being gobbled up for fine executive offices and similar exclusive purposes. There was a time also, when ex-

perts foresaw very high prices or the complete disappearance from the market of rare African mahogany, teak, Brazilian rosewood, and similar beautiful and exotic woods. What really happened was a rejuvenation, which luckily came about at the time when home owners were developing a keener interest in wall paneling than ever before in modern history. At that same period, both technology and industry came to the rescue with creditable solutions. It was plywood, of course, that stretched out the supply in the best possible way.

Then came factory-finished panels, which were made possible largely by the development of contact cements. New installation methods were devel-

Paneled walls are more popular each year as homeowners increasingly appreciate the decorative qualities of wood colors and the infinite variety of the natural grain.

oped that eliminated face nailing. Another contribution was the constant improvement in both quality and design of plastic-coated hardboards, finished in wood grainings so realistic that only a cabinetmaker would know the difference.

TECHNOLOGICAL ADVANCES

One big advantage of prefinished paneling is that it is ready for use as soon as it is installed. No painting, no staining, no varnishing, or even waxing is required, yet the panels will have as tough and smooth a finish as any you could obtain with any amount of time and effort. Once the wall is prepared, installation is speedy. The large 4' wide panels go up quickly to cover a lot of surface.

Another happy development was the combining of plastic with hardboard. At first there were just a few solid colors, then a few textures, like leather. Ultimately, surfaces were developed that have all the characteristics of the natural wood color and graining. Offered in an extensive range of color variations and rare woods, they retain the original advantages of the hardboard material, having marproof, easily cleaned surfaces, freedom from rotting, fire resistance, and impermeability to insects.

The various natural woods and finishes available include everything from the light blond birch and maple, the medium tones of oak, ash, knotty pine, and sycamore, to the deeper shades of mahogany, walnut, chestnut, cherry, and teak.

Most fine paneling comes stained and tinted to accent the natural grain and pattern of the wood. Some are finished with clear coatings, others have grain fillers to minimize any defects and achieve a more uniform appearance. Some are lacquered, others finished with synthetic resin, plastic sealer, or just varnish. Any of these would give good service: the critical factors are whether the plywood has been properly sanded and sealed before finishing, and if the final coat has been buffed and given a protective coat of wax. A panel that has a fuzzy, uneven look, and a surface that is less than perfectly smooth, is definitely competitive-grade merchandise that should be accepted only if price is the prime consideration in the selection.

WHAT IS HARDWOOD PANELING?

Basically, the panel is plywood, nearly always ¼" thick, with a hardwood veneer facing. What makes

Random widths of the grooves in maple wall panels provide an additional facet for decorative glow of a recreation room or den.

the paneling so attractive is the rich variety of the grain, no panel being exactly like another because of the natural differences in grain configurations. There are many domestic and foreign species, most of them the familiar pine or birch, walnut and maple, but there are countless other varieties and some exotic woods from every part of the world.

Most panels come in standard 4' x 8' size, although 10' lengths are also available. Many have vertical grooves, usually V-shaped to simulate planks, or U-shaped with darker staining in the grooves for accent. Grooves may be spaced at random, or uniformly 4" or 8" apart. One purpose of the grooves is to permit nailing without going into the face of the panel, and for that reason there is a groove every 16", even in random-grooved panels, to conform to the wall stud positions.

Nails driven into the grooves are easily concealed with a putty stick of matching color. Although the adhesive method of installation without nails now eliminates the need for grooving, there is a continued preference for grooved panels because of their pleasing appearance.

How Much Does It Cost?

Prices range widely from about 20 cents a foot or $6 a panel (32 square feet) for Philippine mahogany, to over $100 a panel for selected Brazilian rosewood. Most home owners can readily find what they want in panels priced at from $8 to $15. A single wall, 12' long, would require three full panels, at a cost of $25 to $45 for the panels, while a complete room, say a dining room 12'-by-12' with two doors, would require eleven panels for as little as $100. The additional items required, which are 1-by-2 furring strips and the adhesive, would come to an additional $30 or $40.

Hardboard panels with a printed or embossed grain cost somewhat less. These are excellent, durable materials that in the better qualities offer a greater choice of finishes. Some home owners may regard them as a compromise, and feel that they lack the warmth of real wood panels. However, there are many advantages, one of which is the range of novel finishes that can give an unusual decorative effect to any room.

Moldings Make the Job Better

An important contribution to the attractive snug appearance of wall paneling is the assortment of special moldings. These cover a wavy ceiling line, the jointing of panels at inside and outside room corners, or the fit under windows and around doors. Thus, moldings eliminate much of the tedious and difficult planning to fit the panels precisely, and assure a neat and attractive installation. Your dealer has a variety of moldings in factory-finished hardwood to match your panels, or neutral tones that will harmonize with them.

If the matching moldings are not available, you can use stains, some of them specially formulated by the manufacturers for the purpose of matching molding to panels. But be sure to obtain completely unfinished moldings for this, not any that have been

waxed or varnished and therefore will not accept the color stains. Some manufacturers of high quality prefinished hardboard paneling have developed aluminum moldings with veneer facings that match their panels. The metal moldings are less bulky than most wooden ones and permit a neater, smoother installation.

HOW TO PANEL A ROOM

Wall panels can be put up over the present wall, or can be used to form the finished wall in a newly built room addition. In either case, the panels are applied to horizontal and vertical furring strips of 1-by-2 or 1-by-3 lumber, shimmed out to be perfectly plumb.

Although most paneling is still put up by nailing, new adhesives have practically eliminated the need for face nailing of the panels—except along the top, where these nails will be covered with the

Adhesive system has revolutionized panel installation. The adhesive cartridge fits into regular calking gun. Single cartridge contains sufficient adhesive for installation of six full size 4-by-8 panels.

cove molding. The adhesives are sold in cartridge form, so you can use them in an ordinary half-barrel calking gun. Aside from the absence of nailheads, a great advantage of the adhesive method is that it speeds the installation time to almost half of what it would normally take to nail the panels.

Gluing the Panels

The adhesive technique is simple enough: apply the adhesive with the calking gun onto the furring surfaces that the panel will contact. Place the panel on the wall and slide it into position, butting against the next panel. Then drive three or four nails partway in along the top edge to act as a "hinge"—the panel is then pulled out at the bottom and propped away from the wall until the adhesive becomes tacky. This takes less than ten minutes, after which you let the panel swing back into position against the wall.

Tap the surface sharply with a padded wood block and hammer to bond the panel securely and permanently, then drive the top nails all the way in and counterset the heads. No additional nailing will be required.

That is the essence of the paneling procedure, but there are many details of each step that require careful attention to assure a satisfactory result. First, obtain your panels early and unwrap their cartons to allow them to adjust for at least two days to the humidity conditions of your home. Lay the panels flat with spacer strips (the furring strips will do fine for this) between them, to allow air to circulate freely. Take precautions to protect the finished surface. This conditioning will avoid problems with expansion and contraction after the panels are installed.

Installation Over Old Wall

Next comes preparation of the wall. Remove all electric fixtures and trim, including the ceiling crown molding and the base shoe molding, but leave the original baseboard. (The new panels may go over the present baseboard face, and a new baseboard can be placed later if desired.)

Although panels may be cemented to present walls that are in good condition, furring strips should be used. They permit making adjustments for any uneven parts of the wall, and also provide an air space at the back which will help prevent moisture absorption from an exterior wall. The furring strips are usually 1-by-2 lumber, which may be of rough commercial quality, but straight and true stock nonetheless. Do not use warped or twisted material. If you have some ¾" plywood stock not otherwise needed, it would be perfect for the furring when cut to 2"-wide strips.

Drop a plumb line at various points along the wall to see if there is any point where the wall

Not only the panels, but also the furring strips, may be affixed with the adhesive method. Here adhesive is shown applied directly to a concrete foundation wall, on which the furring strips will be placed. Adhesive may be used on any type of wall.

bulges outward. If so, place the first horizontal strip on the farthest-out position, nailing the strip firmly through the plaster or gypsum board along the entire strip, using enough nails to assure good fastening. See that at least a few of the nails have been driven into the wall studs.

Furring out the Wall

The rest of the horizontal furring is spaced 16" apart, plus one each at the very top and bottom. Each strip should be plumb with the others. The easiest way to do this is to nail up all the strips lightly; that is, driving the nails in only partway. See if there are any low spots behind the furring, or use a straightedge against the strips to see if any are out of alignment. Those that are can be adjusted by placing pieces of thin wood, or even cardboard, as shims at the back until the furring is fully braced so that when the nails are driven in tightly, the strips remain straight and true.

If the furring is not in true alignment, the thin panels will be distorted into a wavy surface.

Vertical strips are nailed between all the horizontals, starting at the first panel position and spaced 48" apart, to provide support along the panel edges. It may be better to put up these vertical members only as you reach each position with a new panel, to be sure that the verticals are correctly placed. Make sure that these verticals also are plumb and level with the others.

On masonry walls, such as in basements when finishing a playroom, furring is essential as a nailing surface. The furring can be attached directly to the concrete wall, but a preferred method is to erect wall studs and nail the furring over these studs—locating the panels so that the vertical furring will also fall on the stud positions. Direct nailing or gluing of the panels to the studs, instead of to furring strips, is not advisable as there is considerable movement and variation in the 2-by-4 studs, and greater difficulty in adjusting any unevenness.

Preparing the Panels

Some preparation will be required on most panels before they can be put up. Cutouts must be made to clear electric switches and receptacles, or to bypass other obstructions. In regard to the receptacles, if furring strips are used over an existing wall, the panels will extend out about 1" more than previously (the thickness of the furring plus the panel plywood). The receptacle wiring allows a certain amount of leeway, but possibly not sufficient for this situation. One way is to substitute longer retainer screws on the receptacle so it can be pulled farther out of the box to meet the panel surface, where it will be covered with a standard plate. But this leaves the connecting wires pulled out of the metal box and exposed behind the panel, which is a violation. The correct way would be to loosen the box itself, bring it out from the wall another ¾", and refasten it to the stud. This is a most difficult process.

A better solution is to use flanged outlet plates, which leave the outlet deeply recessed. Another acceptable solution is to surround the electric box with small pieces of the furring all around, then pull the receptacle outward sufficiently so that it can be gripped by the cover plate screws, resulting in a flush and normal installation.

Horizontal furring strips, 1"-by-2" lumber, are placed 16" apart. Vertical strips are located 48" apart, but arranged so that there is a strip at each edge of a panel. Here the adhesive is being applied in intermittent beads, 3" long.

Each panel is carefully prepared beforehand. Note cutout for clearance of an electric receptacle. Panels here reach to the floor, but shorter panels may be placed on 4" or 6" baseboards to get full reach to high ceiling.

Fitting the Panels

When sawing a prefinished panel, do the cutting so that the ragged edge comes out at the back, rather than the face side. This means that if you're using a hand saw, a radial saw, or a bench saw, you will do the cutting with the prefinished face up. If using a portable circular saw or sabre saw, do the cutting with the finished face down. When using a hand saw, select one with a crosscut blade for a smoother cut. These restraints need not prevail in certain circumstances where it is preferable to cut through the face in order to follow template or guide markings, and where the cut edges will be covered later—an example is an electric receptacle opening, which can be cut most conveniently from the front with a sabre saw, but where the uneven opening will be fully covered and overlapped by the receptacle plate.

Cutouts must be correctly located, by careful measurement; otherwise entire panel can be spoiled. Here the location of a wall switch is measured from both the adjoining panel and the baseboard. Remove covers from electrical devices to obtain accurate dimensions.

When cutting with a handsaw, panel may be face up, since the saw teeth enter from the top. When using a portable circular saw, however, place panel face down since the blade cuts from bottom up.

Measurements are transferred with aid of a trisquare directly onto the panel, and the outline is carefully drawn for making the cutout.

Saber saw with fine tooth blade makes the cutout. Panel can be cut from the front in this case, as the cutout edges will be covered by the switchplate. In other situations, saber saw cuts should be made with the panel face down so ragged edge of cut will be at back.

Walls usually are out of plumb, especially the wall corners. For a neat fit into the corner, unless you are using an inside corner molding, scribe the panel edge to conform to the wall contour, then plane edge to fit.

After panel is fitted over the adhesive and shifted to correct position, it is held in place with a few finishing nails driven halfway into the top.

Bottom of panel is pulled away from wall and held with a spacer stick until the adhesive dries. Drying time usually is 8 to 10 minutes.

After adhesive dries, spacer stick is removed and panel pressed against wall, where it adheres on contact. A padded block of wood is tapped with hammer along all the furrings to assure a good bond.

A home with unusually high ceilings may pose a problem, as standard 8' panels would be too short. For example, if your ceiling is 8½' but the baseboard is only 4" high, leaving a 2" gap, this may necessitate purchasing 10' panels (some companies make 9' panels but they are not always available), resulting in extra cost and considerable waste. You might overcome the problem by planning to use a higher baseboard, 6" wide instead of 4", thus making the 8' panel length sufficient. Remember that the original baseboard is "lost" because it will be covered by the new paneling; thus a new baseboard will be needed and that can be of the greater height. Another possibility is to use the standard 4" baseboard, but with a wider base shoe molding, perhaps 1½". When combined with a crown molding at the ceiling, the panel will reach.

The Adhesive System

The new wallboard adhesives method offers the advantages of contact cement but without its disadvantages. Instead of bonding immediately on contact, the panels can be moved around sufficiently to get them into correct position, then the panel is partly pulled from the wall until the adhesive sets.

Nails are placed along the top to serve as a hinge, keeping the panel in true alignment so that when the panel is dropped back against the wall, it is correctly positioned, and the adhesive then bonds on contact.

The adhesive most widely used comes in a tube with a plastic nozzle. The tube will fit any calking gun and comes out of the nozzle as a bead of heavy paste. If the wall is smooth and plumb, the adhesive can be applied to the back of the panel, all around the edges in intermittent beads about 3" long and spaced 3" apart, also around all open cutouts that are made to clear electric switches and receptacles. Additional beads of the adhesive should be placed horizontally across the back, every 16" or so. The panel is then pressed against the wall and moved as needed for adjustment, then three or four finishing nails are driven partway through the panel near the top edge.

The panel is pulled back from the wall at the bottom, held with a spacer stick, while the top nails serve as a hinge. After some eight or ten minutes, the panel is pressed back on the wall and the nails driven in all the way. A padded wood block is tapped with a mallet or hammer on the face of the panel to assure good adhesion with the wall. This

is essentially the system used also with furring strips, except that the adhesive is applied on the furring rather than on back of the panels. Keep in mind that the adhesive is flammable, so take all necessary fire precautions.

Nailed Panels

If you prefer to nail your panels, use 3d or 4d finishing nails, countersinking the heads sufficiently so that the holes can be filled with a putty stick. Place the nails into the panel grooves; the nailheads will be invisible, and in any event that is where the nails are most likely to meet the furring strips. On furring, space the nails 18" apart in the grooves. Edge nailing also falls on the groove, since half the groove will appear at each edge of the panel. As the grooves are generally finished with dark coloring, use a putty stick of similar color to fill the nail holes and eliminate imperfections.

Molding trim completes the paneling. Baseboard in matching wood color is applied with finishing nails. Crown moldings are fitted with coping saw.

Completed installation of plastic-coated hardboard in pecan wood with random-width plank effect shows how natural-looking and warm the paneling makes the room. This paneling has certain valuable advantages over the natural veneered plywood. The extremely hard coating resists damage, is long-lasting, retains original appearance.

Like prefinished plywood, Marlite coated panels are also installed with adhesive on a framework of furring strips. The plastic-coated panels are somewhat more flexible than 1/4" plywood.

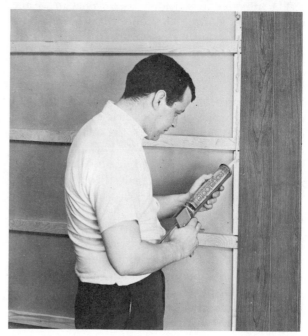

Moldings Make the Difference

Moldings are attached with finishing nails, except for certain aluminum types which are attached with clips. Where moldings meet at a corner, the ends should be carefully mitered for a neat joint.

The panels usually are raggedly uneven at the ceiling line, except where each panel has been carefully scribed and planed to fit precisely into its space. However, a narrow crown or cove molding not only provides a neat tie from ceiling to wall, but also serves to mask all such irregularities.

Various shapes and types of molding are available, often in the same wood as the panels, to make a professional quality installation. Shown here are, left to right, base, stool, casing, crown cove, stop, base shoe, mullion, inside and outside corners.

Slight gaps where panels meet at corners are inevitable, even with the best of craftsmen. Corner molding fills the spaces, while shoe moldings atop the baseboards cover bottom panel edges.

Hardwood cove molding, finished at the factory to blend with the panels, is installed at the ceiling with finishing nails. For combining two lengths, use a scarf joint as shown. At corners, use a coping saw to miter the molding into a neat joint.

Hardboard panels are neatly installed, either by nailing or adhesive method, as here. Tapping with mallet assures permanent bond to wall.

PANELS AND WALL COVERINGS

SIMULATED WINDOW—LIGHT
BUT NO DRAFTS

Many a drab *interior* wall would be improved immeasurably—and instantly—with a window of its own. And that's not as wild an idea as it seems. Like many other things, we use the best available imitation when the real thing isn't to be had, and in this case a fake window can do the job pretty well. While you're at it, you can pick exactly the kind of window you've always wanted, as wide as the available space allows, anywhere from 3' to 8' would be quite suitable.

What is proposed here is to build a backlighted enclosure with patterned or frosted glass, or a rigid grade of translucent plastic sheeting, to simulate the appearance of a full-length window. What's more, this is a window that provides radiant diffused brightness all evening, as well as in the daytime. A pair of shallow shelves at staggered heights for books or art objects adds effectively to the dramatic scheme.

A frame for the window is made of 1"-by-8" stock, as shown. Nail a ceiling-high length into the corner wall, making sure that it is set plumb, and nail identical lengths to the floor and to the ceiling joists. A full-length 1-by-2 cleat is attached to the wall at the far side, and another piece of the 1" x 8" is set up there, nailed to the floor and ceiling plates, and also to the supporting cleat.

Insert vertical section dividers, or 1-by-2 stock, uniformly spaced to receive the width of the glass or plastic material that you will use. Before putting in these uprights, nail quarter-round molding on both sides of each upright (only on the inside of the end ones) to hold the translucent material or glass. Locate these strips so that when the glass is in place, another molding strip at the front will be flush with the front edge of the upright.

Fasten these uprights into position by toenailing top and bottom.

Paint the wall white inside the frame and also the interior sides of the window framing, to provide maximum light reflection. Next, install two 30-watt fluorescent fixtures (each 36" long) on each side of the frame, wiring them to a switch located conveniently in the room. Attach full-length shelf support brackets to the outside face of the uprights and the end pieces.

Quarter-round molding strips are nailed to the top and bottom plates, between each of the uprights, and equally inside the end pieces, matching the molding positions on the uprights. The pat-terned glass panels then can be set into place and held with additional quarter-round moldings at the front. The moldings may be nailed in at the center panels, but should be attached with screws at the ends to permit access to the fluorescent fixtures for servicing when necessary.

Shelves of 1"-by-6" stock are set on the brackets, and located where they will suit your needs on the support strips. Paint the window frame and shelves to match the room colors.

A LOW COST WALL TREATMENT

A bare expanse of wall can be transformed in a couple of hours, and at minimal cost, into an eye-catching background. The entire idea is amazingly simple and easy to accomplish, because all it involves is tacking up common lattice strips to create a paneled effect, as shown in the photograph.

The lattice strips, of ponderosa pine, are usually $1\frac{3}{8}$" or $1\frac{5}{8}$" wide, and about $\frac{3}{8}$" thick. They range in price from 3 to 5 cents per foot, depending on the finish and the locality. Thus each strip on an 8' high wall will cost only between 25 cents and 40 cents, and if spaced uniformly a foot apart on a 12' wide wall, the total cost for the strips will be less than $5.

Effects from subtle to bold may be achieved. When painted the same color as the wall, the strips blend with your decor and are obvious only for the shadows they cast. But when the strips are painted a contrasting color, a strong pattern effect is obtainable.

When a finish different from that of the wall is desired, the face and edges of the lattice should be prefinished before attaching. It's a good idea first to sand the strips smooth for a better finish and to avoid splintering, which will expose the raw wood.

The actual fastening is done with either glue or counterset nails. If a mastic adhesive is used, put in a few nails partway to hold until the adhesive sets, then withdraw the nails and touch up the spots.

The wood lattice strips provide an excellent base for hanging groupings of pictures or posters that are changed frequently.

A WALL OF SPOOLS

Man's history is to a great extent the story of how he made use of the materials at hand, wherever he was. Here is an example of how the

Appealing in its simplicity, this wall of prefinished lattice strips produces an effect of paneling, although the entire cost was barely $5 for the materials.

younger generation utilized otherwise discarded materials to serve a useful purpose. The idea came about because a family was confronted with the necessity of dividing a large playroom to set off a separate bedroom for a youngster. The objective was to build a divider wall that would provide privacy, yet be easily removed when the entire playroom was needed. But there was a problem! Since the playroom had only one window, the wall had to be of a type that would let light through, allow ample air circulation, and obtain its heating from another part of the playroom.

The youngster came up with a solution when his art class at school distributed some cardboard thread cones which were obtained from a local garment factory. A telephone call revealed that these cones were available free in almost unlimited quantity. Each cone measured 6¾" long, tapered from ½" diameter at the top to 2⅝" at the bottom. Gluing the bottoms together in pairs produced interestingly shaped spools of 13½" length, with tapered ends. Six such pairs strung together measured 6' 9", the perfect height for a divider partition.

The spools were painted in two colors while held on a ¼" dowel, then strung on a clothesline. To assure closer meshing and provide greater stability, alternate rows were topped with half spools, or single cones, inside which sawed-off cone tops were glued. All the rows were hung on a long rail attached just below the ceiling, the clothesline threaded through holes drilled as far apart as the diameter of the cones.

The result—a unique divider wall obtained at minimum cost, and with it the growth of character that comes with effectively solving a difficult problem in a sensible way, using available resources.

Temporary partition made of cardboard spools divides portion of family room for a youngster's bedroom. Begin by following painting instructions at right.

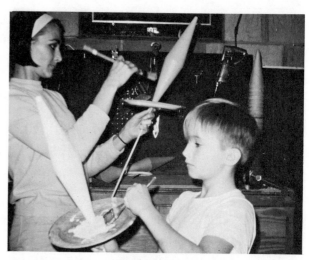

Cardboard spools, obtained free from local factory, are held on a ¼" dowel while they are painted in two contrasting colors for decorative effect.

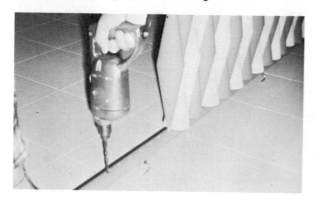

Wood rail attached just below ceiling is drilled at distance equal to diameter of the spools for hanging the rows so that they mesh together.

Spools are strung on clothes line to form rows that would mesh together into a curtain-like wall allowing air, heat and light in room, while providing a measure of privacy.

WOOD BEAMS

As a quick and simple way to give a room a dramatic and attractive appearance, simulated ceiling beams are hard to fault. There are various types. Some are made of thin hardboard with wood-grained vinyl coating, which is formed into a U-shape. Others are lumber but also hollow, with the difference that they are scored and burned with a torch to obtain a rough-hewn texture.

The latest and most sensational contribution to the art of false ceiling beams is foam plastic. It defies identification of its real substance because it looks and even feels like wood, with the natural graining, knotholes, wormholes, and marks, and all the rest.

However you want it—Old English style, Spanish hacienda, or plain rustic—you can put up the

The "before" picture of same room looks drab by comparison, although the only change made was the installation of several ceiling beams.

The word is "fantastic" for ceiling beams that look exactly like the genuine adze-hewn article, but are actually made of urethane plastic. The beams are accurate replicas with natural graining, knotholes, even wormholes.

ceiling beams you want for your home in just a few hours, at a small fraction of the cost and weight of solid wood beams.

Ceiling beams are excellent for concealing major cracks and other deterioration of plaster ceilings, including wallboard panels that show signs of popping or sagging. The beams can be so placed that they serve also to reinforce such ceilings, and one type permits an adequate repair by nailing up furring strips right into the joists, with the U-shaped beam covering the strips completely.

This foam plastic is not the fluffy, squishy kind. It is tough, lightweight Styron material that comes in lengths from 8′ to 18′, and in various thicknesses and widths to give you a full choice. Some are solid, others conveniently channeled so you can run concealed wire through them. While primarily designed for installation on a ceiling, the beams can also be used on walls, perhaps as a rugged type of shelving, or as vertical columns at entrance doors.

The plastic bears a variety of wood finishes—oak, mahogany, maple, and birch, for example. You can also get ceiling beams in neutral tones for finishing with your own varnish or straining. The beams are cut with a hand saw and applied to the ceiling with beads of special adhesive. Just press into place and set up a couple of braces to hold until the adhesive dries. And your manor house now has ceiling beams.

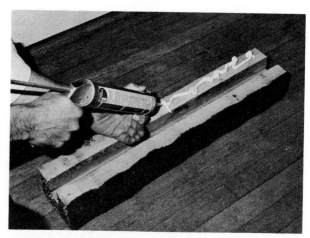

Adhesive from calking gun cartridge is applied along the underside of the beam in a continuous bead. The adhesive is colorless when dry, so excess won't show.

The plastic strip is cut to length with a hand saw, or even just a knife. Take accurate measurement with an extension rule—beware of cutting it just a bit too short.

Beams are pressed up against the ceiling, can be shifted to correct position so they are parallel. Use long boards or 2-by-4s as braces, padded at end, to hold beams until adhesive sets.

Beams come flat, with two grooves in which a bead of resorcinol glue is laid before the hardboard is folded up along the grooves. Hardboard is first cut to required length with a saw, taking care not to damage the vinyl coating.

U-shaped channel is formed by simply folding the hardboard up along the two grooves. For attaching at end wall, one side of channel is sawed off, so beam can be nailed at both top and bottom onto two supporting plates.

Ceiling plate, of 1″ lumber and width equal to the open side of the U channel, is nailed directly across the ceiling to support the vinyl-coated beam. Try to find a joist for at least a few of the plate nails.

Vinyl-coated hardboard strips in various wood finishes, make realistic-looking ceiling beams that are light in weight, easy to install, very handsome. Hollow channel is nailed up to ceiling plate.

An equally effective type consists of a hardboard covered with vinyl in realistic wood-grain finishes. Although their appearance imparts the very nature of solid old world ceiling beams, these are very lightweight and exceptionally easy to install.

The material comes in long flat strips, having two grooves. After cutting to required length, a bead of white resorcinol glue is run into each of the grooves and the hardboard then is folded along the grooves into a U-channel.

The beams are installed on the ceiling with small finishing nails through the sides into plates of 1″ board. These ceiling plates of the same width as the open end of the U-channel are attached to the

ceiling either with nails or Molly anchors. Be sure to leave space gaps between each end of the ceiling plates and the wall surface that they meet.

Before installing the beams, make a scale drawing of the arrangement you like, with accurate measurements of the distances. Run the beams across the narrower width of the room, parallel to each other and with separations at suitable distances depending on the height of the ceiling and length of the room. The beams also can be crisscrossed by simply running the furring strips at right angles and fitting the beams into the spaces. For close fitting of these joints, strip back the vinyl coating, cut back the hardboard slightly, and pull the vinyl over the joint with enough tension for a smooth fit.

WALL COVERING FACTS

The job of picking out a wallpaper for one or more rooms of your house used to be a simple matter. At your local dealer's you'd thumb through the five or six books on display—or go through the few patterns of paper he had in stock—until you found one that was acceptable. The process didn't take long because there wasn't much to pick from.

Nowadays it's not that simple. Besides offering a tremendous variety of designs in all price ranges, most dealers also have wallpapers that are not made of paper at all. Many are made of vinyl, metallic foil, burlap, fabric, cork, and other eye-catching materials. In fact, so many are "paperless" that most manufacturers now refer to them no longer as wallpapers, but as wall coverings.

But while selecting a wall covering has become more difficult because of the great variety, the do-it-yourselfer will find ample compensation in the fact that hanging, or applying, these coverings is much easier than ever before. Another important detail is that, while the coverings are more expensive than the old-fashioned paper type, they have much more style, and are also considerably more attractive and durable.

There are a few highly specialized, expensive wall coverings that are indeed tricky to hang and should be put up only by experienced paperhangers. Most of the materials, however, have been de-

Bold mural brings vision of great outdoors into the home. This one, by Sanitas, is called Whispering.

Another set of murals shows the range of variety that can be encompassed in the decorating scheme, adding color and fluid motion for contrast.

It's *WILD*, but fascinating. The filigree effect adds depth and excitement to the kitchen, which often suffers from a drab background. This pattern is called Saracen.

signed with the do-it-yourselfer in mind. For example, most medium-priced coverings are pretrimmed at the factory, saving you a difficult job of cutting off the selvages from each strip.

In addition, an increasingly large number of wall coverings are also available prepasted—that is, with the paste already applied on the back. No mixing of the paste, no swabbing with the brush, no mess. All you have to do is wet the strip to make it ready for hanging. And even this has been simplified by a special waterbox, which is placed on the floor next to the wall and in which the rolled-up strip soaks for less than a minute. (See page 224.)

Additionally, the wall coverings are now printed on stock that is exceptionally resistant to tearing even when sopping wet, so they can be handled with assurance. Some have plastic coatings that make them more resistant to staining, and there are the textile-backed products, like Sanitas, which will not show any cracks in the wall, but so effectively reinforce the wall, that they actually help retard further cracking of the plaster.

What is more, when the time comes to redecorate the room, the Sanitas can be removed in a jiffy without soaking or using a steamer—simply by loosening a corner and pulling it off, leaving the wall smooth and clean. Or if you decide to paint, go right ahead, right over the old Sanitas, which offers a perfect, smooth base without any preparation.

Wallpapers Still Plentiful

The widest selection is still in standard wallpapers, available in patterns to fit every decorative scheme. Some papers come with textured or embossed finishes that resemble various materials such as leather, cork, burlap, wood, brick, or grasscloth. Most of the papers are made with a plastic coating to make them more washable, or you can pick an uncoated paper and spray on a liquid after the paper is on the wall to give the same protection.

Vinyls and Other Plastics

Vinyl-coated and fabric-backed wall coverings have made the greatest strides as a result of both home owner demand for more durable products that would lower maintenance requirements and growing preference of style-conscious women for wall coverings that will withstand attacks by crayons, greasy fingers, and other soiling hazards around the home.

These vinyls are so graphically adaptable they also can be textured to resemble wood paneling, hand-woven grasscloth, burlap, and other decorator materials. For dressing up a bathroom or powder room, there are nontarnishing metallic or foil-backed materials. Flocks and velour-type materials or vinyl are completely washable, making them practicable for any room in the house.

Bricks and Stones

Another type of plastic wall covering that has become quite popular is a molded vinyl material which comes in three-dimensional semirigid panels, rather than in strips or rolls. Sold in sheets that are molded to resemble brick, fieldstone, rock, mosaic tile, and many other similar materials, these plastic panels have the adhesive already applied to the back. You can put them up on any reasonably smooth wall simply by peeling off the paper backing and pressing them into place. They can be cut to size and shape where necessary with scissors. The sheets come in various sizes, depending on the patterns from 12"-by-12" to 12"-by-24", and are available in a variety of colors. When installed, they create a realistic three-dimensional textured wall which is permanent and almost stainproof. They are particularly useful for refurbishing a damaged or cracked wall which otherwise would require the expensive services of a plasterer.

Panels of scribed tiles (4 tiles comprising one design element) are self-sticking and easily applied.

Mosaic tiles come adhered to flexible backing which contains the adhesive for quick installation. A line of tiles may be trimmed off the panel, or for close fit if necessary, the tiles can be cut to required size with nippers.

You can add variety and interest to your entrance by using boldstriped patterns, such as this one, both as ceiling and dado decoration to highlight an entire area in a striking manner.

Wallpaper Roll Requirements

A single standard roll is 24″ wide, 18′ long, and covers 36 square feet. A double roll equals two single rolls in coverage area.

Size of Room in Feet	Ceiling Height 8′ to 9′	For Covering the Ceiling
	Single Rolls	Single Rolls
8 x 12	10	3
10 x 12 or 8 x 14	11	4
9 x 12	11	5
9 x 14	12	5
9 x 16	13	5
10 x 14 or 12 x 12	12	5
10 x 16 or 14 x 14	14	7
12 x 18 or 14 x 16	15	7
14 x 18 or 16 x 16	16	8
16 x 18	17	8
16 x 20	18	10

Hanging Wall Coverings

Redecorating doesn't have to be a big deal. Any do-it-yourselfer can become an expert paperhanger just by trying—learning by doing. It's really fun and provides much satisfaction at seeing the room take on a new appearance under your hands.

Many recent improvements make the decorating project much easier than it ever was before—so you can do it quicker, with less fuss and mess, and obtain a lovely result at a considerable saving in cost. And the new coverings offer so many advantages in durability and low maintenance that they actually pay for themselves as time goes by. They are more beautiful, with better and cleaner colors, more creative patterns. They are also more practical, with plastic finishes that are almost stainproof and can be scrubbed over and over again without damage.

The strips go up quickly and cover an amazing amount of surface in a short time. Several improvements speed the application even more. Most wall coverings now come with trimmed edges, eliminating the difficult and painstaking selvage trimming that required special long tables and cutting guides, and sometimes resulted in spoiled material.

While stressing the advances that have made room decorating easier and which help to assure a satisfactory final result, there is no intention here to oversimplify the process. Certain details need careful attention if you are to achieve the kind of job you would expect from a professional paperhanger.

First is preparation of the wall. If the room now has wallpaper, make a careful inspection to be sure that the surface is smooth, the paper is down tight everywhere, and that there are no signs through the paper of deep wall cracks. Loose corners of the paper can be pasted back again. Pencil markings and stains won't matter, but if the paper is streaked with grease, which often occurs in rooms near the kitchen, then the walls should be carefully washed down with a detergent type of wall cleaner. Torn or uneven wallpaper should be completely removed. After attending to these details and making necessary adjustments, the new wall covering may be applied, usually right over the present walls.

But if the walls presently are painted, they will require sizing before a wall covering can be applied. The sizing is simply a wash coat of glue brushed over the paint.

Spackling the Wall

The next question is the condition of the wall. Are there any cracks, dents, gouges, or other damage to the plaster? These must be repaired by spackling, as any blemish of the basic wall will show up as an imperfection of the new wall covering. While the covering will cover up cracks that develop later, as has been mentioned, any existing cracks will provide an imperfect base for the new covering.

The following instructions are to be regarded as general, and do not necessarily apply to all types of wall coverings. Always follow the manufacturer's instructions, particularly with the adhesive, as some coatings prevent rapid drying of the paste and thus subject them to mildewing unless an antimildew preparation is included. Most prepasted wall coverings come with specific instructions packed with each roll, and every retailer can supply you with printed hanging instructions.

This is a brilliant example of using wallcovering for everything in the room. Notice contrast with uncovered door panels, cocktail table, and planter stand.

PANELS AND WALL COVERINGS

219

Scrubbable and moisture-proof qualities of some coated wall coverings make them suitable for use in bathroom, even at shower level.

Flock made with acrylic fiber bonded to vinyl acrylic base is now really washable for the first time.

Strong backings and substrates permit easy stripping of old wallcoverings, without messy steaming or scraping.

Prepasted papers remain moist for several minutes, permitting aligning of strips or even shifting of paper around to correct mistakes.

How Many Rolls?

The chart on page 218 will help you determine the number of single or double rolls that you will need, but first you must have the dimensions of the walls to be covered. There are certain ways to measure—even that process isn't entirely simple.

For example, a room is 10' wide by 15' long, with a 9' ceiling height and two doors and one window. First you add up the number of "running" feet along the walls, and multiply by the height of the wall. Thus, the 10' x 15' room will add up to 50 linear feet of walls. Multiplied by the 9' height gets 450 square feet of wall surface.

What about the doors and window? They won't be papered, to be sure; but what about the inevitable waste in matching the pattern? The rule is generally to deduct one single roll for every two windows or two doors. In this room there are two doors and one window, but deduct just one roll, as it is more advisable to overestimate and have a bit left over than to run short on the job. The excess can be used for other purposes, or saved for possible repairs if a part of the wall becomes damaged through some cause, such as moving of furniture.

No matter how wide the material is, every *single* roll covers 36 square feet, but it also comes in two- or three-roll bolts. The larger rolls give you an advantage by cutting down the waste, since you might often find that the last length in a single is just a bit too short to provide a full strip, when the pattern is matched, and is therefore wasted.

First find the number of single rolls needed—in this case, 36 square feet into 450 total equals 13 single rolls. Deduct the one roll for the doors, add a couple for matching, and you have 14 single rolls, or 7 double rolls. Simple! Or isn't it? A tip on buying: compare the print numbers on all the rolls to make sure they are not only of the same pattern but also are of the identical print run. Most stores, incidentally, will take back extra rolls, so don't be fearful of overordering.

Preparing the Walls

Before you hang new wall coverings it is well to consider whether other work in the room is necessary, because that is the right time to do it. Painting the ceiling, for instance, is much easier when you don't have to worry about brushing the paint perfectly at the cove molding around the walls. Any irregularity will be squared away with the new wall covering. If your ceiling is in good condition, however, just a quick wash with a sponge will be sufficient preparation.

Painting of woodwork also should be done ahead of the new wall covering, for obvious reasons. Door trim, ceiling cove and base shoe moldings, window frames, all should be painted or washed down as a preliminary step. Once the new wall covering is in place, such painting of the woodwork will become doubly difficult.

Next comes the wall inspection and preparation. First check the old wallpaper to see that is down good and tight, firmly pasted with no bubbles or ragged seams. Any loose edges or ends can be repasted easily, using regular wheat paste, or any white library paste, if the repairs are very small.

Removing Old Paper

If the old wallpaper is in poor condition, or there are many layers that begin to show signs of sagging on the wall, or the surface is uneven, don't think that the new wall covering will make everything nice and smooth again. On the contrary, all the defects of the basic wall will show up to spoil your new application.

The solution? Remove all the old paper, down to the original plaster. This is not such a difficult job, and will be well worthwhile as it is the best way of getting a perfect, like-new wall again. Old paper is removed most easily by steaming, using an electrically heated steamer with a special pad that takes off large strips at a time. Some coated papers may not respond as well to the steaming; these will require some scraping to break through the coated surface so the steam can penetrate to the adhesive.

Another problem sometimes encountered is that the original paper was applied with overlap seams, thus creating bulge lines at each panel. You can be sure that these bulges will make their presence known right through the new wall covering, so you would do well to correct this deficiency by taking down the old paper completely. Another possibility is sanding off the overlap paper, but that's a tough job at best.

Now you're down to the base wall. The smoother you get it, the better your decorating job will be. First correct any cracks in the plaster by widening the cracks as much as possible, using an old-fashioned beer can opener (one with a long handle will be easier to work) to form a deep groove.

Pack in plaster mix, not completely full. When the plaster has set, finish with spackling plaster for a smooth surface. If there seems to be a bit too much plaster, wipe the surface with a damp sponge to remove the excess before it sets.

Any other holes, dents, or scratches can be filled and smoothed with a quick stroke of a broad plastering knife. Go over the wall carefully to find any spots that need attention. Finally, with a piece of sandpaper on a wood block, give the wall a once-over rubdown to clean off any stubble. Any considerable area of fresh plaster should be given a coat of glue sizing. It would be a good idea to size all the walls; it takes just a few minutes to brush on the thin sticky liquid.

Tools You Need

For wall-covering applications, in addition to scissors and sponges, you will need a plumb line and chalk, a wallboard knife with razor blade, a stepladder or stool of adequate height, a 12″ smoothing brush, a yardstick or folding 6′ rule, a wide-blade putty knife, a large pan for paste, a paste brush and seam roller, a screwdriver to remove receptacle plates, a water bucket, and a table

Chalked plumb line will give you a true vertical starting point, so the strips will go up straight. Best start is alongside an entrance doorway, or along wall corner allowing a 1″ turn.

to work on, the longer the better, but a minimum of 6′ will be necessary.

Many wallpaper dealers rent paperhanging tables and other supplies at a low daily charge. Most of the items needed are usually sold in low-cost kits, which are worth buying if you intend to do more than one room.

Before starting, remove the covers from all electric receptacles, drop any wall fixtures that would be in the way, and clear away as much furniture as you can. It won't be necessary to cover the floor or rugs, but it's a good idea to pile crumpled newspapers along all the exposed areas near walls to absorb any water that drips down.

Locating the First Strip

Start at the right of the door leading into the room and measure to a point one inch less than the width of the wall-covering strip. Tack a chalked plumb line (or any weighted cord) from the ceiling at this point, letting it hang freely, then hold the string taut at the baseboard and snap the string against the wall. If your strips are 24″ wide, the resulting vertical chalk line, your starting point, will be 23″ from the edge of the door frame.

Your first strip will be aligned with this position, the right-hand edge of the strip even with the

Tools used for the usual installation include a water bucket, 12″ smoothing brush, plumb line, wallboard knife with razor blade, scissors, yardstick, paste brush, seam roller and straight edge. A rubber squeegee will also be useful for smoothing out wrinkles and bubbles.

chalked line. This will assure that the first strip is straight or, rather, plumb.

What happens to the left side of the first strip? The lower portion is folded up 1″ against the door frame, while the upper section is brushed flat, covering the wall an inch beyond the edge of the door frame.

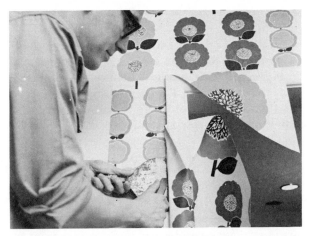

At doors and window frames, cut a 45-degree angle from the corner, so that material can be folded over and onto the edge of the frame. Trim excess part of strip with razor blade or scissors.

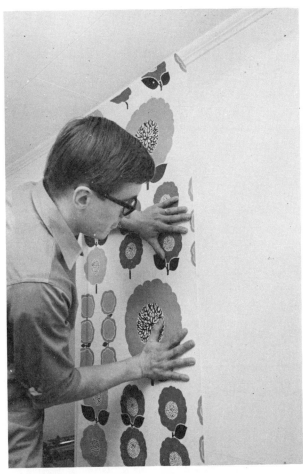

Strip is carried around the corner, extending about 1″, which will be overlapped by succeeding strip. Cut off excess. This part of the strip may be used to start the new wall, but get a plumbed line after every corner.

Right side of the first strip is positioned along the chalk line. The material is then smoothed and trimmed top and bottom.

Closeup view of cornering shows the turn bringing no more than 1″ of material around the corner. Part of this overlap will be covered by the new strip on the side wall, and the slight bulge will be hardly visible because of the corner contour.

Plumbing the Corners

When you come to an inside or outside corner, fold the strip around it and slice it down so that only about 1″ continues to wrap around the corner to the next wall. As the walls are not perfectly straight, snap another plumb line 23″ away to make certain that the first strip on the new wall is vertical. This new strip will overlap the previous 1" extension around the corner, which should be feather-edged by sanding to reduce the bulk that may show through. The new strip may be used for the continuation at the corner, if the plumb line is set to the correct distance.

Cutting the Strips

Unroll about 6' of the material, pattern side up, pulling it gently but firmly over the edge of the table to remove the curl. Measure and cut your first strip to the necessary length, plus an extra 3" or 4" at both top and bottom. For the next strip, you may need more than this extra allowance for matching if the pattern is very large, so before hanging the first strip see how the patterns match up and cut the next strip. After that, the strips will run the same for the rest of the room, but it still is advisable to cut them one at a time, as needed.

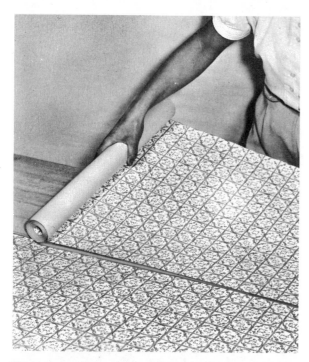

Most new wallcoverings come with pre-trimmed edges, ready to hang. When cutting your wall strips, be sure to match the topmost pattern with the previous strip before measuring off the required length. Leave several extra inches top and bottom.

Applying the Paste

The paste, as described previously, is mixed with cold or warm water to a workable consistency—not too thin, but also not too thick. The package nearly always indicates the recommended quantity of water that should be used. Stir sufficiently to be sure that all lumps are dissolved. If there's any doubt, put the paste through a cheesecloth strainer. The paste is applied with a brush. Special paste brushes are best as they never drop bristles and are easier to use.

Place the wall covering face down on the table and spread the paste over the top third of the strip.

After cutting strip to length, put paste on top third, then fold it over on itself, and cover the rest, which also is folded same way so it can be carried to the wall.

Fold this section over in half, paste to paste, without creasing the fold, to keep it from drying while you apply paste to the remaining two-thirds. Fold this section onto itself in the same way. Carry the folded strip to the wall to start hanging.

Prepasted Wall Coverings

Each strip is soaked separately for less than a minute in a waterbox. Place waterbox against the wall where you are working (the waterboxes are available from your dealer free or for a nominal charge) and half fill it with warm water. A newspaper underneath the box will enable you to slide it easily along to the location of the next strip.

Prepasted wallcovering eliminates much of the mess and bother formerly required. The strips are cut and rolled in a water box at the wall position. After half a minute, lift end of strip up to the ceiling, and press against the wall, leaving a few inches excess at the top.

Butt the edges of the strips together, moving the material with the fingers as necessary to align the pattern sections perfectly.

Roll up the cut strips, making certain the pasted side is out, and put it into the water. Then grasp the top of the strip and slowly unroll it from the water-box while you step up the ladder. Look to see that all the paste is wet.

Press the top of the strip against the wall, allowing a few inches to overlap onto the ceiling. Keeping the right edge against the plumbed line, smooth the wallcovering with a damp sponge or wallpaper brush, removing all wrinkles and bubbles. Unfold the bottom two-thirds section and allow it to drop. With the palm of both hands, smooth and press the covering upward against the corners to counteract slippage caused by the weight. Check the alignment, moving the material with palm or fingers as necessary to straighten the right edge. With the scissors, make a diagonal cut at the top of the door frame so that the material can be folded flat against the wall above the door, and folded up against the door frame below. Trim the line at ceiling and baseboard with the razor blade, using the wide putty knife blade as a guide.

The next strip will be pretty much the same except for two very important details. One is that the strip must be started at the top in such a position that the pattern parts match. The second detail is that of butting the two strips together neatly and tightly, so there is no open space between the edges, nor any overlap.

Cutting Around Obstructions

Wall receptacles, switches, and most other items involve no difficulties. Merely allow the strip to cover the entire area, then when it is smoothed out, use a razor blade to cut away enough material to clear the openings. But be sure not to trim too generously, as the wall plates, when replaced, should overlap the trimmed edges.

Wall fixtures present a different problem. If it is not convenient to disconnect the wiring and remove the complete lamp so that the wall covering can cover the fixture box, there are two possible methods. One is to cut the strip its entire length, measured so that each half will pass along a side of the fixture box, with cutouts made to pass around it. A more professional approach is to leave the strip intact at the top part, but sliced below the fixture down to the floor. Thus there will be no seam on the wall above, and an easily managed single seam below.

Repairs to damaged section of strippable wallcoverings can be easily done by matching, double cutting and applying new piece.

Same section of wall, with repair completed by inserting an irregularly-shaped piece to replace one that was stripped out.

Match pattern of next strip to the first, then butt both edges tightly together, without bulges or skips.

Matching the Pattern

As each strip goes up, the first concern is to see that the pattern is precisely matched with the next one—even a slight variation will become exaggerated farther along so that the wall will look tilted! As the strip is smoothed out, it tends to slide down slightly over the paste, so keep returning to the matching indices to correct any changes.

You may find that the patterns match neatly at one level, but are a bit off farther down. This may be due to stretching of the material under the weight. If so, use the palms of your hands, one on each strip, smoothing and working the material in the direction necessary to butt both sides of the pattern together.

Each strip is trimmed after it is smoothed in place. The excess is cut off by first gently creasing the wall covering with the fingers or a putty knife to follow the contour of the ceiling molding and base molding shoe at the bottom, then slicing off the excess with the razor blade or cutting with scissors along the creased marking. Smooth the strip down again, and with a sponge wipe off all surface adhesive from ceiling, baseboards, and the wall covering itself.

Handling Flock Material

The same basic methods are used for applying flocks as for other wall coverings, but extra care is necessary in some instances. Note whether your material is made of acrylic or rayon flocking. Acrylic flocks are stainproof and crush-resistant, while the rayons are not. Be sure to follow the manufacturer's directions in applying flocks.

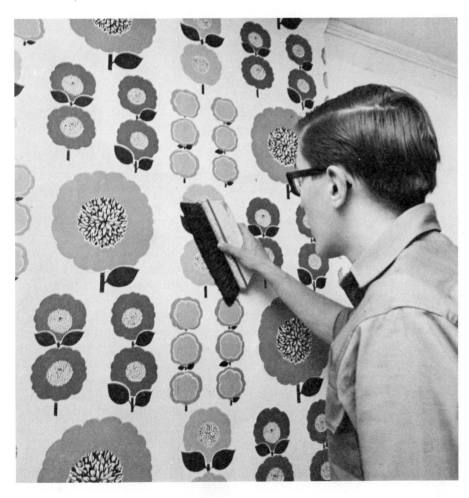

Starting at the middle of the strip, work towards the edges to eliminate bubbles and smooth the material before the paste dries. Use smoothing brush or damp sponge.

With a damp sponge, smooth the surface to remove air bubbles and assure good adhesion.

Another effective way of smoothing out wrinkles and eliminating the air bubbles is with a rubber squeegee, the kind used generally for window washing.

MAKE YOUR OWN BRICK WALL

Do you like the three-dimensional quality of natural brick walls? It's an ideal surface for certain rooms—in the den, at the living room fireplace, in the entry hall, or as an emphasis wall in any social room. Not only can you make your own brick wall but also the "bricks" to make the wall—and they will cost about 2 cents a piece.

The "bricks" are made of plaster, poured into shallow plastic forms that are available in two brick styles: Roman and Decorator. The procedure is simple as can be: you mix the plaster of Paris with water to the proper consistency, and pour it into the forms. The plaster hardens in just about five minutes, when the brick tiles can be removed and a new batch poured. The tiles are about ¼" thick.

The wall to be covered needs no special preparation other than to level out any surface irregulari-

ties such as large bumps or depressions with plaster. Any good mastic tile adhesive can be used to apply the tiles to the concrete or plaster wall. For dry-wall applications, you can use the dry-wall joint compound, which is cheaper.

A horizontal guideline should be drawn at each new course to keep the tiles approximately straight. Use a spirit level to find the first line, then repeat by measuring or use a piece of hardboard as a spacer. Weighted lines dropped from the ceiling molding will help keep the vertical joints in alignment. The entire wall may be painted after the tiles are put up, or the mortar joints touched up with the lighter color to accentuate the brickwork.

If you object to the limitations imposed by the plaster-molded tiles, there is another possibility. Factory-made bricks in several different colors and styles capture the appearance and the "feel" of real brick with subtle texture, shape, size, and the usual irregularities of this noble material.

Plaster of paris brick tiles, molded quickly in plastic forms, can give any wall the popular three-dimensional appearance of natural brick.

Add 7 parts of plaster of paris to 1 part water, to obtain the desired consistency.

Pour the mixture immediately into the plastic molds. Tap molds gently to settle the mix, disperse bubbles.

Plaster hardens in about 5 minutes. Remove the brick tile by flexing the plastic mold, pour another batch.

Tiles are cut if necessary, with a coping saw, as here, or with hacksaw. They also can be scored with knife point and snapped.

Wall to receive tiles should be reasonably smooth. Fill in all large recesses, chisel down bumps.

Horizontal guide, obtained with level, is drawn with pencil or snapped with chalked line.

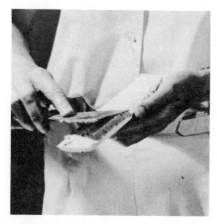

Brick is applied to wall with any standard tile adhesive or mastic. Butter the back of tile with putty knife.

Press tiles into place. Weighted string helps keep the vertical joints in alignment.

Chapter 8

PATIOS

Simple, yet attractive and functional, the concrete patio meets most requirements of family outdoor living. The smooth floor is excellent for dancing, particularly when surfaced with vinyl composition tiles described in this chapter.

A patio, sun deck, open porch, terrace—all are variations on the great theme of outdoor living. It's more apparent than ever that a good way to enjoy the sun and fresh air is in your own back yard. Travel is great fun, the seashore or mountains hold their seasonal joys, and camping is healthy and recreational as well as educational. But for everyday pleasure in the company of family and friends, or sometimes quietly alone, the back yard social center offers the most.

You'll even have pleasure planning and building

your preferred project. Would you like a terrace with an old-fashioned brick floor, a wood deck, or a sleek slate surface? Are you partial to a formal setting, or would you prefer an easygoing concrete expanse? Do you prefer to duck the direct sun rays and seek a shaded retreat?

On the following pages are presented many variations from which you can select the outdoor installation that best meets your wishes, or perhaps will stimulate you to work up your own design using the information provided here as a foundation. In no other home construction is there so wide a range of possibilities.

Whatever the design, the basic construction techniques and procedures as outlined here remain quite standard. Refer to them to aid your planning, and for the actual construction work.

One aspect of the planning should be emphasized at the start—make the terrace or porch as large as you can. One reason for being outdoors is the feeling of outdoor spaciousness, not a cramped postage-stamp-sized corner. It's true that the terrace can be enlarged later, but you might as well enjoy the benefits at once.

IT ALL BEGINS WITH CONCRETE

Concrete has an ancient and honorable history. Its good name is well deserved, for surely there isn't another material that lasts so long, is so readily available, easy to work and economical to use.

It makes a sturdy foundation for your house, so it is certainly capable of providing a base for your patio—actually, a basic patio is often no more than a concrete slab, as you will see in the diagram illustrating the various layers that go into it.

To prepare for the pouring, level the ground, breaking it up as necessary, then spread a bed of gravel or crushed rock for drainage to help protect against heaving. Following the dimensions of the layers given in the sketch, excavate as deeply as necessary. Keep in mind the desired height of the patio surface with relation to the ground around it, making adjustments in your plan as needed.

With the excavation made, leaving about 3″ of clearance for the forms all around, drive 2-by-2 stakes at least 18″ into the ground at each corner. Hammer a nail into the head of each stake, then stretch guide strings between them. Using a small line level hung from the string, adjust stake height to the proper level, but if the patio is to abut the house or another structure, it should be graded slightly to channel rain away from the house. Next, nail 2-by-4's on edge to the corner stakes, reinforcing the form later with two more stakes at each cor-

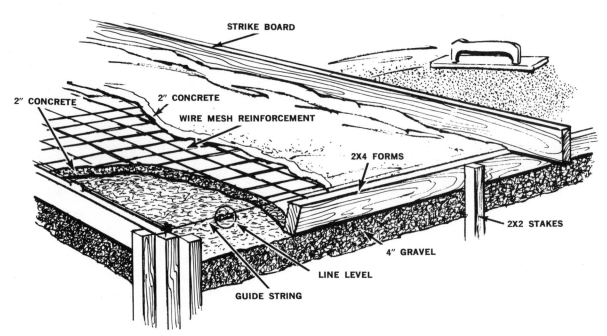

Gravel base for the concrete is important to assure rapid drainage. Set up form of braced 2-by-4 or 2-by-6 boards preferably oiled on the inside face to assure easy breakaway after concrete sets. Determine pitch of the form boards by stringing a level line from posts at each end, then raising the higher end for the proper pitch. After half of the depth has been filled with the concrete, put in the reinforcing metal mesh, then continue filling to the top of the form boards. The concrete is leveled immediately with a long and straight strike board, worked back and forth as it is moved along the top of the form board.

ner, plus others spaced 2' or 3' apart along the sides. You can use an alternate method along the sides, with 2-by-4 stakes at 4' intervals, and braces, as shown.

Depending on the amount of concrete you'll require (see chart for estimating), it may be wise to order ready-mixed concrete. If you're not in that much of a hurry and want to do it all yourself, you can rent a small mixer, or mix it in a mortar box.

The following mix is recommended for your patio:

1 part portland cement
2¼ part sand
3 parts gravel or crushed stone (1" maximum size)
⅔ part water (5 gallons per sack of cement).

The key to quality concrete is the proportion of water and cement. Maintain this relationship but if, after mixing the first batch, the concrete is too stiff, use less sand and aggregate. If too soupy, add sand and aggregate to reach the desired consistency.

Typical quantities of materials for making 1 cubic yard (enough to cover 81 square feet with 4" of concrete) are:

6¼ bags of portland cement
14 cubic feet of sand (1260 lbs.)
19 cubic feet of gravel or crushed stone (1900 lbs.)
31½ gallons of water

Ready for the Pour

The job will go much smoother and faster if you're ready. Check the forms carefully for adequate bracing, alignment, and tightness of joints. If you're purchasing ready-mix, be sure the truck can get as close as possible to the job. Have a couple of friends standing by for the arrival of the truck, to help with the work of spreading and striking off.

Once the concrete has filled the form, it should be struck (leveled) immediately with a straight-edged board, then let stand until the film of water on the top begins to disappear. At this time, smooth it quickly with a wood float, which is to be preferred for this purpose to a steel trowel, because it results in a relatively nonskid surface. However, if you do want a smooth finish, go over it again with a steel trowel after wood-floating, when the surface has become quite stiff. The less troweling, the more durable the finished job will be.

The final step in any concrete job is curing. It

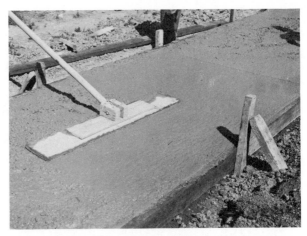

After pouring and leveling with a strike board, the surface is smoothed with wood float.

The perimeter of the slab is trimmed and finished with this edging tool, also making it easier to remove form.

should be kept moist by occasional sprinkling for above five days. In hot weather, keep the surface from drying too rapidly by covering with burlap, damp sand, or a waterproof covering. The slower it cures, the stronger the job.

Estimating the Materials

The table below gives the number of cubic yards of concrete in slabs of different thicknesses and areas. Multiply the slab length by its width to get the area in square feet. Then read quantity of concrete from the table for desired thickness.

TO MIX 1 CUBIC YARD OF CONCRETE

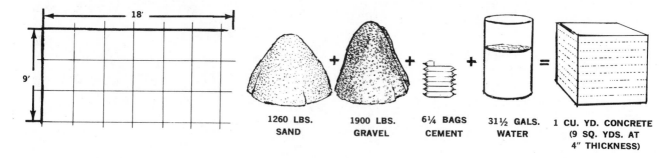

1260 LBS. SAND + 1900 LBS. GRAVEL + 6¼ BAGS CEMENT + 31½ GALS. WATER = 1 CU. YD. CONCRETE (9 SQ. YDS. AT 4″ THICKNESS)

EXAMPLE

The slab is 20′ x 30′ and 4″ thick. Find quantity of concrete needed.

Area = 20′ x 30′ = 600 sq. ft.

Since the table does not go as high as 600 sq. ft., use the concrete quantity for 300 sq. ft. and multiply it by 2.

Quantity for 300 sq. ft. = 3.7 cu. yd.

2 × 3.7 = 7.4 cu. yd.

CUBIC YARDS OF CONCRETE IN SLABS

Area in square feet (length X width)	Thickness in inches		
	4	5	6
50	0.62	0.77	0.93
100	1.2	1.5	1.9
200	2.5	3.1	3.7
300	3.7	4.6	5.6
400	5.0	6.2	7.4
500	6.2	7.7	9.3

CAST YOUR OWN TERRACE

A simple wooden form enables you to cast enough cement flagstones for a colorful terrace, a flagstone pathway, even the driveway. The colors are through and through, mixed right into the portland cement, not just on the surface. They may fade a bit, but so uniformly they will look even more natural and in harmony with the back yard setting. The flagstones are laid in mortar or, even simpler, on a sand base.

The casting process is done in a form made of wood, divided to obtain flags of various shapes, one inch thick. One advantage here is that you can ar-range the shapes so that the individual pieces fit neatly together, although in a random-appearing pattern. The form may be 2′ x 3′, or 3′ x 4′, but the smaller size will be much easier to handle when loaded, as it contains just half the square footage, and thus weighs half as much.

The stones need be only 1″ thick if they are to be laid in mortar on a concrete slab. For a sand base terrace, the stones should be at least 1½″ or, better still, 2″ thick. With the smaller form, you're casting enough to cover 6′ of area each time; if you're anxious to move the project faster, and want to get more stones done with each batch of concrete you mix, make two or even more casting forms.

As for stock, use ¾″ exterior grade plywood as the base, cut to the unit or section dimension. Then rip some 1″ boards into 1¾″ widths, for use as edge strips or lips around the four sides of the base. Rip some more 1″ boards into several beveled strips (see photos), ⅝″ wide at the base and ⅜″ wide at the top. These will be the pattern in the form.

Now comes the time to test your flair for design, outlining the pattern on the base that will deter-mine the shapes of the flagstones. Follow any ar-rangement you like, as long as all the sides are straight. This done, nail the edge strips to the base, cut the pattern strips to the various lengths, gluing and nailing them to the outlines you have made. Use wood filler to round the corners or joints wher-ever two pattern strips meet—and use more of it along the strips next to the base. Allow enough time for drying, then sand the edges and surfaces.

Finally, moisture-proof the form with three coats of spar varnish. An added precaution against mois-ture, which also speeds removal of the flagstones, is to brush used cooking fats or crankcase oil on the form before each casting operation.

In a couple of hours you can build a form for casting colorful concrete stones in irregular shapes to make your terrace of individual design, and at lowest cost.

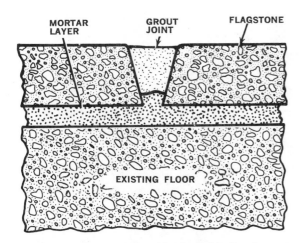

MORTAR LAYER   GROUT JOINT   FLAGSTONE

EXISTING FLOOR

Cross-section shows relationship of existing floor to mortar layer, the new cement flags and the grout-filled joint.

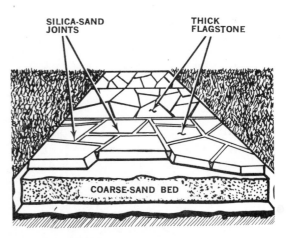

SILICA-SAND JOINTS   THICK FLAGSTONE

COARSE-SAND BED

Sketch shows installation of cement flags on bed of sand only, using silica sand in the joints instead of grout.

To make beveled pattern strips, tilt the table (or blade, of a radial unit) about 10 degrees, as shown.

Cut pattern strips to length, following marked outline on base board, nailing and gluing into place.

How to Color Flagstones

Of all the coloring materials—dry powders, penetrating stains, and masonry floor paints—the powders and stains are best because of their durability and color fastness. Powders, available in several decorator colors (or in three primaries for mixing your own hues), are simply added in a dry state to the dry cement mixture.

For bright, white flagstones, mix white cement with silica (white) sand. Light gray flagstones result when portland cement is mixed with silica sand, whereas portland cement mixed with brown sand produces a dark gray.

Stains are applied like paint, with a roller, on the individual flags, after they're cast.

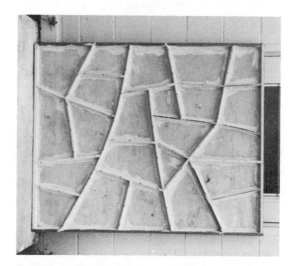

Typical random-design form produces 23 flags at a time; can be halved with temporary pattern strips.

Casting a Full Form

If, for example, eight forms are needed to surface your intended terrace, you can have as many as eight colors, using one color per form. The individual flagstones can be intermixed later, when you're ready to install them.

For best results, place the form on a level surface. Prepare a mix of 1 part portland cement, 2 parts sand, 3 parts fine gravel, and the recommended amount of coloring powder, adding water until you achieve a workable consistency. Shovel or pour about ½" of the mixture into the form (be sure to grease it in advance), place wire mesh cut to size in the flag molds, add more cement and strike level with the tops of the pattern strips and edge strips. If you need to raise the level slightly, sprinkle gravel into the mix.

Having poured cement mixture onto form, spread and strike it level with top edges of pattern strips.

236

When cement has set, invert the form, easing the face against a plywood sheet, or as here, an old door, lowering it to ground.

Rap the back of the form lightly with a hammer, dislodging flags, then carefully raise the emptied form.

Tamp or compact the mixture, eliminating bubbles and voids, by raising each corner of the form about 4″ and dropping it. Don't trowel the mixture smooth, as the pebbly surface (really, the undersurface of the stone) will assure a better bond when installed. Wait at least forty-eight hours for partial curing and shrinkage before removing the stones from the form.

To simplify removal, place an equivalent-sized sheet of ¾″ plywood (an old door was used in the photos) on top of the form, turning it gently onto its face. The form now inverted, insert thin wood strips under the four corners, tapping the form's back with a hammer, dislodging the flagstones. Carefully raise the emptied form.

Transfer the stones to a place where they can cure thoroughly, covering them with the burlap, canvas or plastic sheeting. See to it that everything stays moist for about four days.

Half-units, Partial Forms, Precast Openings

By temporarily altering or adding to the full unit or form, you can cast sections of flagstones to fit irregular shapes or accommodate protrusions.

For a partial section of flagstones, such as a 1-by-3 or 2-by-2 (within a 2-by-3 form) or a 2-by-4 or 3-by-3 (within a 3-by-4 form), nail temporary pattern strips where needed. Omit gluing and wood filler, as you'll want to remove these strips soon after the smaller section is cast.

You can also provide openings for obstructions by placing similarly shaped objects in the form. A can, for example, produces a circular opening for

poles, and can be notched to fit over pattern strips, as well. A strip of thin sheet metal, also notched, if necessary, can be bent to any contour.

Lay Stones on Sand Bed

By preparing a sand bed for flagstones, you can install a terrace directly on the ground. However, in choosing this method, the stones must be made at least 1½″ thick, compared to the form described earlier which produced inch-thick stones. This means that your pattern strips would have to be 1½″ also and that the edge strips would have to be increased to 2¼″ widths, ripped from 1″ boards.

As for the sand bed, excavate the site to a 5″ depth and level the surface. Spread 4″ of coarse sand in the excavation, wetting it first, then tamping the bed smooth. Now lay the stones—with their bottom edges abutted—and fill the joints with silica sand. Lightly spray, sweep clean when dry, and lightly spray again.

. . . or Cover Existing Surfaces

If your terrace consists of an existing cement patio, this surface will do very well as a base for your new flagstones.

First, thoroughly clean and repair the surface, removing dirt, dust, and grease. A mortar of 1 part masonry cement and 3 parts mortar sand is best for implanting the stones over the old work. Wet the surface, then spread a ½″ layer over an area slightly larger than one section of stones. Lay the full section but don't press the individual stones into the

Installing flags over existing concrete, first spread a full ½ inch layer of mortar, leveling it with board.

Lightly place the stones on the mortar, avoiding unnecessary pressure.

mortar—instead, use a striking board across the section to press the stones level. This done, about a ¼" of mortar should have squeezed into the spaces between the stones, this bead forming a dovetail joint that locks the stones securely in place.

After the remaining sections have been installed, wait about twelve hours before using the terrace.

. . . or Cover Newly Poured Slabs

Flagstones can be laid on newly poured concrete floors or patios without using a mortar layer. Just lay your stones as quickly as possible after striking the final course of the slab, following the same leveling technique described earlier.

Be sure to keep the slab and stones wet for a few days to assure adequate curing.

The final steps in either this example or the covering of an old surface include filling and finishing the joints between the flagstones. Briefly, grout is a soupy mortar which uses 1 part masonry cement and 2 parts mortar sand, and is poured into the joints and leveled.

But there's more to it than that with flagstones. Before pouring the joint grout (you can make a whiter grout than above with white cement and silica sand), lubricate the tops of the stones with used

With a straight-edged board, press the stones partially into the mortar.

238

cooking fats or oil. Use a paint roller for convenience, but keep the stuff out of the joints.

Now you can fill and finish the joints, striking the line level with the tops of the stones (the grout will shrink to a slight concave). Do not clean the stones at this time—rather, sprinkle the joints lightly, keeping them moist for a few days. Finally, you can clean everything—steel wool soap pads do nicely—flushing the stones several times with water.

Fill the joints with grout, then draw a putty knife along joints to level.

TERRACE IN THE ROUND

These stone terraces are so individual in design that even the materials are custom-made—by you. That doesn't mean the family's handyman need get into a sweat casting hundreds of the colorful patio blocks; you can buy them at very modest prices, in a variety of colors, at any local landscaping dealer or building material supply yard.

What makes these terraces so neat and trim is

that all irregular gaps in laying the stones are accurately filled by casting the required shapes right on the spot. The drawing here shows the procedure for building a terrace of any shape you desire. The models shown were made quite large, dominating the yard and deliberately reducing the lawn area, while providing extra places for beds of shrubs which require relatively little care.

Planning and Leveling

The first step is to lay out the shape you want. Dig a trench around the circumference. It need be no wider than the shovel blade, and about 12″ deep. Afterward, drive a number of stakes at random around the area, outside the trench. Prepare forms for the concrete edging, using 3/16″ or 1/4″ hardboard for long straight runs, and 1/8″ for curves. Stretch strong cord from stake to stake, leveling it at the edging height desired, with the help of a line level. Three inches above grade is good. Adjust the forms so that the top edges are even with the reference height. As this is being done, you will find some areas where the trench will need deepening, others where partial filling will be needed.

The thickness of the edging is optional. Two inches is the minimum, three is better and four is best. The diagram shows how the forms are made, with pieces of 1-by-2 wedged inside them to keep the hardboard steady against the stakes. Brush the hardboard with oil for easy removal later. Use any heavy lubricating oil—old crankcase drainings will do. Apply the oil thickly to the form's inside faces. Pour the concrete mix in strips no longer than 5′; less on curves. Wedge strips of oiled hardboard into the form at appropriate places to divide the pours. They are later removed and the gaps filled with tar, to provide expansion joints.

After pouring, level the top surface with a strike board to remove excess mix. Work the board back and forth. When the pour begins to harden—you can tell by water that floats to the surface—smooth it with a small trowel.

The area enclosed by the edging can now be excavated to the proper depth, taking grading into consideration. Dig 8″ lower than the top of the edging, and level roughly. Now put down a 3″ layer of gravel for drainage, followed by 3″ of fine clean builder's sand, which should be raked, leveled, and tamped down. If you've done everything correctly thus far, two inches will remain unfilled below the top of the edging. The patio blocks which form the finished surface measure 8″ x 16″ and are 2″ thick.

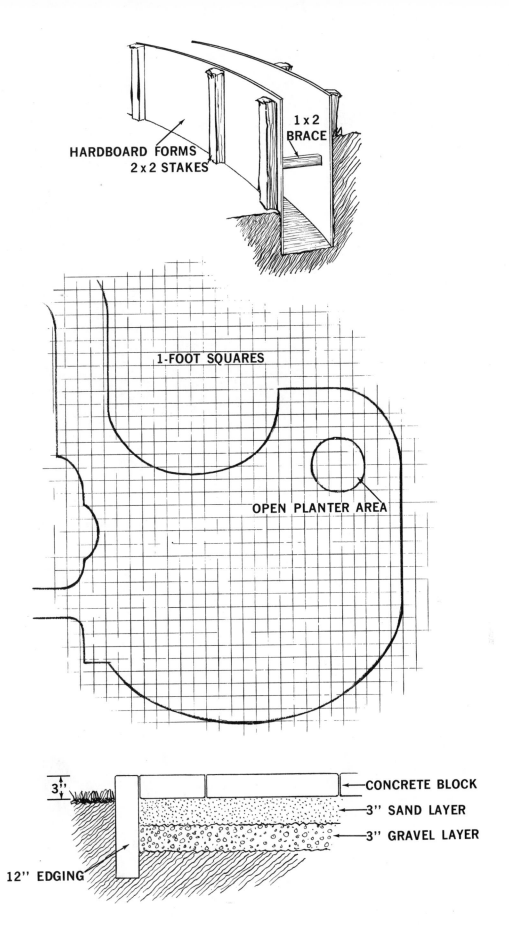

1 x 2
BRACE

HARDBOARD FORMS
2 x 2 STAKES

1-FOOT SQUARES

OPEN PLANTER AREA

3"

CONCRETE BLOCK

3" SAND LAYER

3" GRAVEL LAYER

12" EDGING

Laying the Blocks

Start laying the blocks at one side of the terrace area, butting them against the concrete. You will immediately see that gaps will occur, especially where the edging curves. Ignore these gaps for now. Butt the blocks against each other as tightly as possible, tapping each snugly against its neighbors with a hammer, making sure it is adequately supported by packed level sand.

Continue with the blocks until the patio surface has been completed except for the gaps mentioned before. These can be filled by making a series of small forms, right in place, and pouring concrete to fill. Make these small forms from pieces of ⅛″ hardboard. Brush on oil as before. Pour small quantities of mix carefully, avoiding splashes on the blocks. Use a small trowel to smooth the new pour when it begins to set. Later, pull out the form boards and fill the small remaining gaps with clean sand broomed into the cracks.

Build a frame using 2-by-2s notched as shown, to suit needs.

Frame can also be divided, for casting two blocks at once.

Place form on tarpaper and grease surfaces. Pour concrete.

Lay block on sand. Level by adding or removing fill as needed.

Trowel surface smooth and use edging tool; let dry an hour.

Spread liberal amount of sand on surface, filling all cracks.

Smooth sand bed and place blocks; spacing may vary to suit.

SAND FOR SMOOTH SAILING

Placing a layer of masonry blocks on a bed of sand is surely the easiest, quickest way to build a terrace. Like most shortcuts, however, it has minor drawbacks: it is not permanent and may require occasional, simple maintenance.

Construction is a four-step process. Excavate the area 4″ deep plus the thickness of the proposed surfacing material. Spread a 4″ layer of clean damp sand, rolling or tamping it firm and level. Next, place each block on the sand bed in the desired pattern, leveling it with those adjacent. Finally, when all are in place, sprinkle more sand on top and sweep it into the cracks until they are filled.

The choice of materials is wide. Use flagstone, brick, patio block, or cast your own, using the technique shown in the accompanying photos. Maintenance consists of occasionally replacing sand that may have washed away, causing a block or two to settle a bit.

WOOD DECKS POPULAR AGAIN

Though not as widely accepted as masonry, a wood deck is nevertheless often the most attractive terrace of all. Wood's easy workability offers the do-it-yourselfer the opportunity to undertake elaborate designs and to build in features such as benches and planters with, perhaps, less effort and better results than with concrete. In naturalistic settings, wood appears to be more at home than masonry, blending well with informal landscapes.

A deck is, basically, a wooden framework above ground level, on which flooring has been laid. Posts of 4-by-4 stock are the foundation. Plan to stud the deck area with posts on 4′ centers. Bolted to these are joists; 2-by-8 stock is sufficiently rigid to handle all normal loads, but 2-by-6's are also used with satisfactory results.

Flooring planks may be laid conventionally, diagonally, or checkerboard style—or in any combination. Numbers of attractive patterns can be

Like a floating deck, wood-floored patio offers an extra ration of luxury in outdoor living space, flexible enough to meet every demand from just relaxing to a midnight dance party.

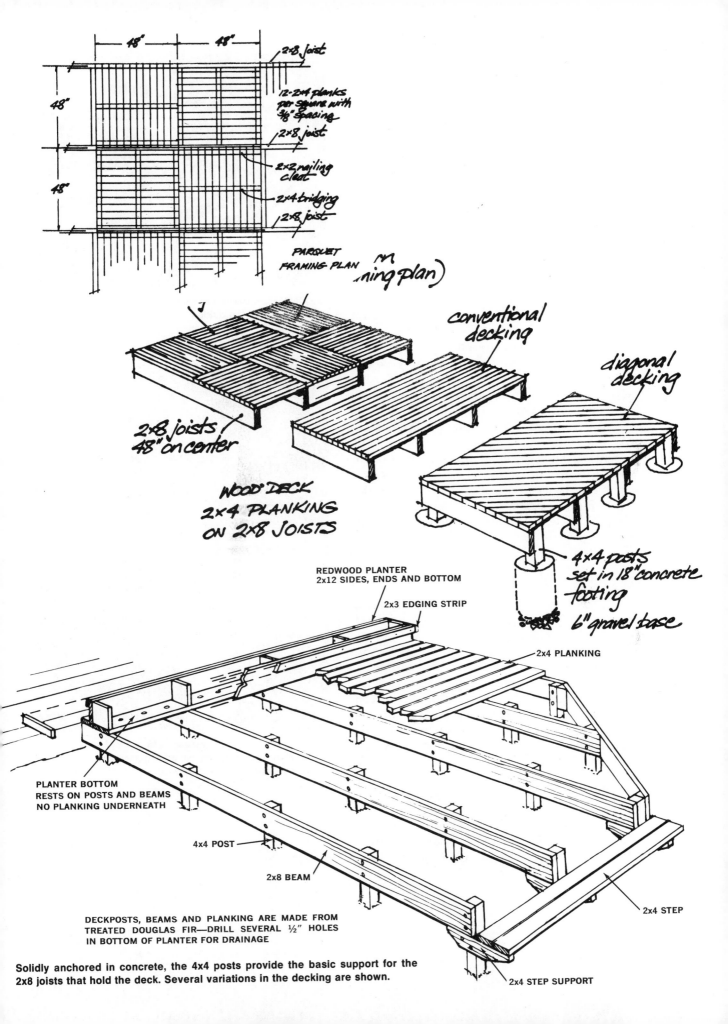

18" 18"

48"

2×8 joist

12-2×4 planks per square with 3/8" spacing

2×8 joist

2×2 nailing cleat

2×4 bridging

2×8 joist

48"

48"

PARQUET FRAMING PLAN (framing plan)

conventional decking

diagonal decking

2×8 joists 48" on center

WOOD DECK 2×4 PLANKING ON 2×8 JOISTS

4×4 posts set in 18" concrete footing

6" gravel base

REDWOOD PLANTER 2×12 SIDES, ENDS AND BOTTOM

2×3 EDGING STRIP

2x4 PLANKING

PLANTER BOTTOM RESTS ON POSTS AND BEAMS NO PLANKING UNDERNEATH

4x4 POST

2x8 BEAM

2x4 STEP

DECKPOSTS, BEAMS AND PLANKING ARE MADE FROM TREATED DOUGLAS FIR—DRILL SEVERAL ½" HOLES IN BOTTOM OF PLANTER FOR DRAINAGE

2x4 STEP SUPPORT

Solidly anchored in concrete, the 4x4 posts provide the basic support for the 2x8 joists that hold the deck. Several variations in the decking are shown.

created this way. The sketches will give you an idea of the appearance of the styles mentioned.

Redwood Preferred

All deck lumber should be carefully treated to retard rot and inhibit termites. The most resistant variety is redwood; it is, however, expensive. Cypress is also rot resistant and costs less than redwood. It is very good for the posts, but since it splinters easily, it isn't too well suited for decking. Make your choice here either pine or fir, if you are unwilling to pay for the more expensive redwood. All varieties should receive treatment with a preservative such as Penta, available at most lumberyards, and the buried portions of the posts should be given a liberal coat of asphalt roofing compound.

Begin building by outlining the area with posts and string, as you would a concrete terrace. Dig postholes 24″ deep and place a 6″ layer of gravel in each. Next, cut the posts to the roughly desired length, allowing a little extra for trimming. After the preservative treatment, set them into the holes, with temporary braces. Mix 1 part cement, 2½ parts sand, and 4 parts gravel, plus enough water to make a stiff but workable mix, and pour around the posts to fill the holes. Trowel the top of the concrete so that the surface slopes away from the post. When the concrete dries—allow a day for this—remove the temporary braces. Spread a layer of at least 3″ of clean sand over the ground below the deck to prevent grass or weeds from growing through the deck.

Beams Held with Bolts

Fasten each joist temporarily with nails, making sure it is level, then drill holes through the beam and post. Fasten at each post with heavy carriage bolts as shown in the sketch. Then cut off the tops of the posts flush with the top of the beam.

With all beams in place, paint or finish as desired. Cut and fit the 2-by-4 planks, but finish sides, ends, and bottoms before nailing in place. The top surface can, of course, be finished later. Now, nail 2-by-4 planks securely at each joist, using 10d nails. Space the planks ¼″ to ½″ apart. If it is necessary to use more than a single plank to span the deck, be sure to stagger the joints, so that adjacent planks do not end at the same beam.

When the terrain is such that one or more sides of the deck are high enough to make steps advisable, they can be constructed by the method shown in the sketch.

Massive wood-decked terrace is an extension of the house itself, serves as an outdoor living room.

Combination of wood planking with gravel beds and concrete lawn figures make exceedingly attractive settings. Textures contrast nicely, create an harmonious atmosphere.

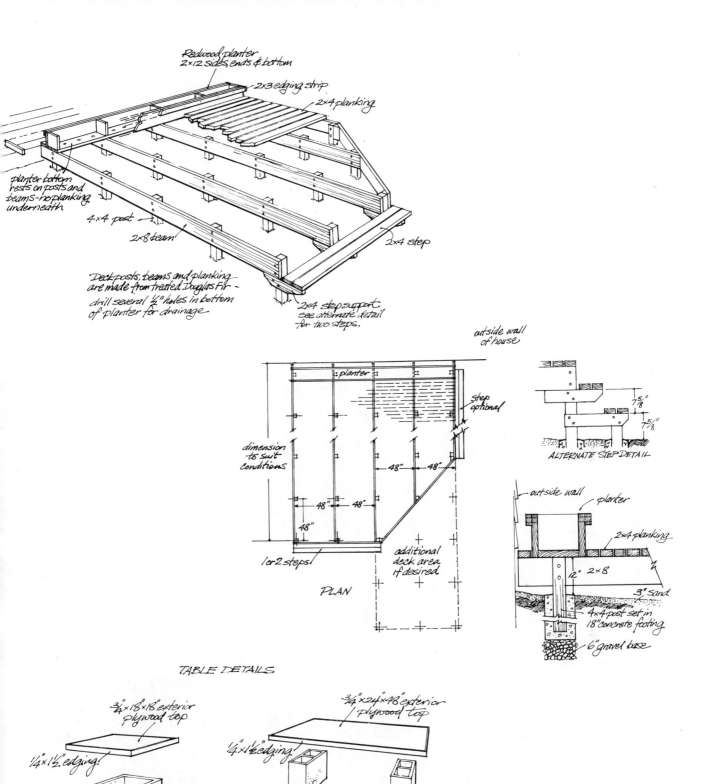

Redwood planter
2×12 sides, ends & bottom

2×3 edging strip

2×4 planking

planter bottom rests on posts and beams-no planking underneath

4×4 post

2×8 beam

2×4 step

Deck posts, beams and planking are made from treated Douglas Fir - drill several ½" holes in bottom of planter for drainage.

2×4 step support see alternate detail for two steps.

outside wall of house

step optional

ALTERNATE STEP DETAIL

7 5/8"

7 5/8"

dimension to suit conditions

48"   48"

48"   48"

48"

1 or 2 steps

additional deck area if desired

PLAN

outside wall

planter

2×4 planking

12"   2×8

3" sand

4×4 post set in 18" concrete footing

6" gravel base

TABLE DETAILS

3/4"×18"×18" exterior plywood top

1/4"×1½" edging

12"×12" flue tile

3/4"×24"×48" exterior plywood top

1/4"×1½" edging

8"×16" flue tiles

Sketch shows how easily extra tables can be assembled for the outdoor "room" from standard masonry forms such as flue tiles. Table tops may be cast of concrete with wire mesh reinforcement, or made of plywood as shown.

BACK YARD SUN DECK

With a pleasant sun deck such as this, which blends in nicely with your back yard plantings, you can get a panoramic view of your garden while enjoying the summer sun.

This deck or garden platform was one of a group of exhibits called "A Garden of Ideas" at Sterling Forest Gardens in Tuxedo, New York.

The platform is set on slightly sloping ground with the rear almost at grade level, and the front up a few steps. The platform is made up of four squares, but could vary depending on your particular needs.

The rough timbers which come in contact with the earth, such as F,G,H,I,J, should be soaked in creosote or Penta to resist decay and termite damage. These pieces could be Douglas fir or whatever wood your lumber dealer supplies in large timbers.

However, the platform at Sterling Forest is supported on pieces of used railroad ties. As shown in the photographs, the first steps (which simply lie on the ground) are also railroad ties. These first steps are optional and are therefore not shown in the drawing. The four sections making up the deck or platform are bolted together with zinc-plated ½″ x 3½″ bolts, nuts, and washers.

Step stringers (F,G) are held together with zinc-plated ½″ threaded steel rods (K1, K2). Corner pieces (H,I) are secured to the garden steps with zinc-plated ½″ x 3½″ lag bolts and washers, counterbored and plugged. Paint nuts, bolts, and washers with two coats of exterior grade flat black paint.

The deck in Sterling Forest was surrounded by a mulch of broken bark. However, you may prefer to have grass or other plantings in this area. Or for texture and contrast, you can use crushed bluestone or gravel.

Huge redwood platform serves as an observation deck midst garden scenery, but the structure blends into the surroundings rather than dominating them.

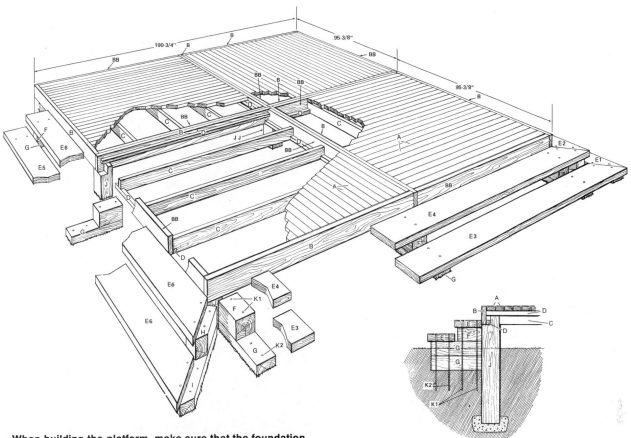

When building the platform, make sure that the foundation pieces (labeled G and J in the sketch) are perfectly level. Following placement of the foundation posts in 8"x16" puddles of concrete, proceed to the outer pieces such as the H, I and the various E items. Deck boards are $3/16$" apart, automatically positioned by a spacer strip of that thickness when the boards are nailed.

MATERIALS LIST

A. One hundred pieces, each: $92\frac{3}{8}$ x $3\frac{1}{2}$ x $1\frac{1}{2}$"

B. Eight pieces, each: $95\frac{3}{8}$ x $7\frac{1}{4}$ x $1\frac{1}{2}$"

BB. Eight pieces, each: $92\frac{3}{8}$ x $7\frac{1}{4}$ x $1\frac{1}{2}$"

C. Twelve pieces, each: $92\frac{3}{8}$ x $5\frac{1}{2}$ x $1\frac{1}{2}$"

D. Sixteen pieces, each: $92\frac{3}{8}$ x $1\frac{1}{2}$ x $1\frac{1}{2}$"

E1. One piece, 96 x $11\frac{1}{4}$ x $2\frac{1}{2}$"

E2. One piece, $84\frac{3}{4}$ x $11\frac{1}{4}$ x $2\frac{1}{2}$"

E3. One piece, $235\frac{3}{4}$ x $11\frac{1}{4}$ x $2\frac{1}{2}$"

E4. One piece, $213\frac{1}{2}$ x $11\frac{1}{4}$ x $2\frac{1}{2}$"

E5. One piece, $211\frac{3}{4}$ x $11\frac{1}{4}$ x $2\frac{1}{2}$"

E6. One piece, $200\frac{1}{2}$ x $11\frac{1}{4}$ x $2\frac{1}{2}$"

F. Six pieces, each: $10\frac{1}{2}$ x $7\frac{1}{4}$ x $5\frac{1}{2}$"

G. Twelve pieces, each: $22\frac{1}{2}$ x $7\frac{1}{4}$ x $5\frac{1}{2}$"

H. Two pieces, each: 14 x $7\frac{1}{4}$ x $5\frac{1}{2}$"

I. Four pieces, each: 30 x $7\frac{1}{4}$ x $5\frac{1}{2}$"

J. Eight pieces, each: 46 x $7\frac{1}{4}$ x $5\frac{1}{2}$"

JJ. One piece, $41\frac{3}{4}$ x $7\frac{1}{4}$ x $5\frac{1}{2}$"

K1. Twenty zinc-coated threaded steel rods, each: 27" x $\frac{1}{2}$" (diameter)

K2. Twenty zinc-coated threaded steel rods, each: 21" x $\frac{1}{2}$" (diameter)

PLAIN AND FANCY IDEAS
FOR CONCRETE

There are more ways to dress up a concrete slab than you can shake a trowel at. A few are shown here. Let these simple suggestions spark your own bright ideas. For example, instead of using tin cans for sharply defined circles, the bottom of a milk bottle will give a less obvious pattern. If a rectangular design holds more appeal, get a 5-gallon oil can from your local service station and use it. Vary the depth of the impressions from a mere touch to a strong push.

One ingenious method is to cut a silhouette from heavy, felted building paper or cardboard. The silhouette can be anything—a stylized outline of your house, a monogram, a date, a floral design. Press the cutout against the wet cement until it is implanted level with the surrounding surface. Let the mix set firm and remove the pattern before it dries completely, breaking it away piece by piece if it can't be withdrawn intact.

PLANTER WALL WITH BENCH

Having decided on the dimensions you want for the wall, dig a 6"-deep trench wide enough to accommodate a concrete block plus the brick being used as facing. Spread 2" of small stones for drainage, then pour a concrete mix to within an inch or two of the trench's surface. Install two courses of concrete block, which will be about 16" high. This done, be sure to drive some "whistles" in the joints (metal wedges with wood cores for nailing the seat planks to the wall) before they set.

Then lay the brick with mortar, following the key steps illustrated in the photos, finishing with a pointing tool.

Redwood boards are used here for the seating—a random-width design, in any pleasing combination, as long as the seat isn't more than 16" to 18" deep. The redwood crosspieces, equal to the depth of seat, should be secured to the whistles embedded in the blocks—and the planks secured to the crosspieces, the arrangement allowing an air space under the seat for drying after rains.

For the final step, clean out the grooves with an old brush before the cement hardens and can't be removed.

Irregularly-shaped flagstones can be simulated in concrete by outlining "stones" with a piece of pipe.

When the design has been completed, clean up the areas near the grooves with a trowel, restoring finish.

The leaf pattern, a most novel idea, is not always successful. Press leaves with trowel, using great care.

Geometric designs are the work of but a moment. Three sizes of cans, as shown, make interesting pattern.

An ordinary stiff-bristled broom, moved· in a curve or a swirl, will impart both texture and design to concrete.

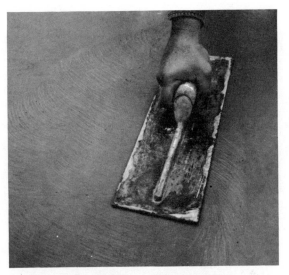

Surface of the concrete should be given a graceful look by using a finishing trowel in smooth strokes.

Similar to the idea in the previous photo, many finishes are obtained by changing tools. Here an aluminum float is used.

This is one of the best looking and most interesting forms of concrete patios. This smart looking wall doubles as a bench and as a retaining wall for a king-size planter.

Metal wedges with wood-cores are imbedded in mortar joints, allowing planks to be securely nailed.

Whenever more mortar is needed, prepare small batches (packaged Sakrete is convenient) as shown.

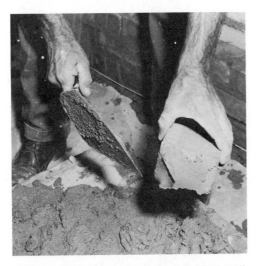

Constructing brick face on concrete block wall, butter ends and set in bed of furrowed mortar (photo right).

Tap the brick snugly in position, following the string guideline, producing a joint 3/8 to 1/2-inch thick.

Scrape away the excess with your trowel, producing a flush surface at the joints, and check guideline again.

After joints have set for about 15 minutes, smooth them with a pointing tool or use any rounded stick.

KEYS TO COLORING CONCRETE

Although concrete may be the handyman's best answer to many construction problems, to the color-conscious housewife its dull, gray appearance is enough to ruin any decorating scheme. Actually, there's no excuse for having a drab concrete surface since it's so easy to brighten it with color. You can add colors to existing concrete as well as freshly poured concrete, without affecting its strength or durability. In fact, the coloring material usually makes the surface a lot easier to maintain. The different coloring methods you can use and the proper procedures to follow are explained below.

Mixing

This method is used on new construction and involves mixing a dry coloring powder with the cement or concrete before it is poured. The key to success here is to mix the ingredients thoroughly and accurately before adding water. Mix the sand, cement, and coloring powder until the batch is perfectly uniform in color, then add the proper amount of water for the job. Always prepare a few samples beforehand, to determine the exact proportion of coloring powder needed to get the right shade. If you keep accurate track of the pigment used in the samples, you'll have the right formula for the shade you want.

You can save expense by coloring only the top 1" or 1½" of cement instead of the entire batch used for the job. However, this entails mixing and pouring two separate batches of cement. The first pour, or base, for the colored topping should be given a rough surface with a stiff broom. When the pour has partially set, place the colored topping and trowel it to a smooth finish. If the exposed edges are to be in color, you'll have to move the forms out 1" or more to place the colored topping there. The biggest advantage of this coloring method is that the color is built in from the start and can't wear off.

Dusting

The dusting technique is also used only on new construction, but it is much simpler and cheaper.

COLOR MIXING

Add dry color powder gradually to the cement mixture until the desired color has been attained, then make concrete batch as usual.

DUSTING

Sprinkle the coloring powder on fresh concrete surface, then.

... smooth with wood float and finish with the steel trowel.

STAINING

Scrub concrete surface with a detergent solution.

To obtain flagstone effect, brush on shellac lines.

Then paint the concrete surface with the staining chemical.

You merely sprinkle the coloring powder on top of the cement as soon as it has set up enough to support knee boards. The powder should be deposited evenly across the surface. Then it is worked in with a wood float and given a final light touch with a steel trowel. It's a procedure the handyman can easily master with a little practice. The only danger lies in too much steel troweling, which brings the lime to the surface. When the lime dries, it's opaque and the result is a mottled surface color. If the color is properly applied, the resulting surface will be dense, abrasion resistant, and more easily maintained than uncolored concrete.

Staining

This method is for use on old concrete surfaces or new concrete that has cured for at least six weeks. Just as stains do not hide spots and imperfections in wood, concrete stains will not obscure natural markings. The concrete surface must be clean and free of hardeners, waterproofing compounds, and paint. This is one job where cleanliness really shows up in the results. Use a good detergent to remove grease or oil and then rinse with plenty of water to remove all traces of the detergent. When the surface is dry, just brush on the stain in saturating coats. The more coats, the deeper the intensity of the color. The stain penetrates the surface of the concrete through chemical action.

For a flagstone effect, separate adjacent areas with broad lines of clear shellac before you apply the stain. On indoor surfaces, apply wax having the same shade as the stain to bring out the full depth of the color and to minimize upkeep.

Painting

Concrete is alkaline and, being porous, is likely to contain moisture. For this reason, not all of the paints on your dealer's shelves are suitable for applying color to concrete. The paint selected must be resistant to alkalis and its adhesion unimpaired by moisture. For floors, an added quality is necessary—resistance to abrasion.

Rubber-base paints, solvent-thinned masonry

PAINTING
First ingredient of portland cement paint is water.

Add powder according to directions on the label.

Mix paint until a consistency of thick cream is attained.

Apply with a scrub brush, dipped frequently for uniform color depth.

Keep surface damp for 24 hours to cure the paint.

paints, latex paints, and portland cement paints can be used successfully on concrete walls. Portland cement paint is the best solution for walls that are always subjected to moisture. If the surfaces are only slightly damp, most latex paints may be used. Rubber-base paints and solvent-thinned enamels that are formulated for greater wearability are preferred for use on floors. Never use portland cement paints on floors.

As with any painting project, the preparatory work is half the job. Paint won't stick to dirt, oil, grease, or dusty surfaces. Clean the concrete thoroughly before you start. On previously painted surfaces, if the paint is in good condition, get it clean. If it is loose or peeling, remove it by sanding. If portland cement paint is to be used, it must be applied to the bare concrete and not over other paints. The paint, usually sold in dry powder form, is mixed with water to a creamy consistency and then scrubbed into the porous surfaces of the concrete with a brush. The surface should be kept damp for two days while it cures.

Fillers Smooth the Concrete

With few exceptions, all types of paints may be used on floors as well as on walls. Some of the latex paints are sold as a dry powder and require mixing with water; others are sold ready-mixed. Some of the vinyl paints are formulated with a fibrous material that helps fill voids in the surface of the concrete. Since all of these paints vary so widely in their formulations, your best guide is to follow the recommendations on the product label.

Besides producing attractive colors, the proper paint can effectively waterproof interior and exterior concrete surfaces. It also simplifies cleaning on floors and walls, because dirt has less of a tendency to accumulate on a smooth, painted surface and it's easier to wash then bare concrete

SKYLIGHT FOR YOUR PATIO

A patio behind the house is a mighty pleasant place for outdoor living. But along about the middle of summer it may begin to lose some of its attraction when the sun gets very hot and you have to take refuge indoors to escape being broiled alive.

A fiberglass cover will shield you from excessive sunlight without darkening your patio. The carpentry is very simple and you can easily do the job in two weekends.

When choosing the fiberglass sheets be sure to get the kind recommended for patios and awnings. The reason this is important is that different colors transmit different amounts of sunlight and the more sunlight that gets through the fiberglass the more heat there will be under the patio cover. Fiberglass colors recommended for patio covers usually let less than 35 percent of sunlight come through. Manufacturers' literature indicates which colors are best for patios.

In addition to the fiberglass sheets, dealers also stock special wood moldings shaped to fit the corrugations of the fiberglass. All the specialized material and hardware as well as the lumber are shown in the list of materials which in this case is for a patio 16' wide and 20' long.

The first step is to install the front posts. These can be anchored to the concrete slab with 8" angle iron plates, using masonry anchors in the concrete and 16d nails in the posts. If there is no slab, use a concrete footing and the type of anchor shown in the patio drawing.

The next step is to place the 4-by-4 front header on the two posts and fasten them with nails and a steel T-strap, which should be placed on the insides of the posts and header so that it will not be seen from the front. (The T-strap in the patio drawing is shown in front only for clarity.) The bottom of the header should be not less than 7½" from the ground to allow for proper ventilation under the patio cover.

The 2-by-6 back header is then fastened to the house wall with ⅜" x 5" lag screws in every other stud. If the wall is made of stone or brick, drill

A patio skylight made of fiberglass will protect your family from the broiling summer sun without darkening your patio.

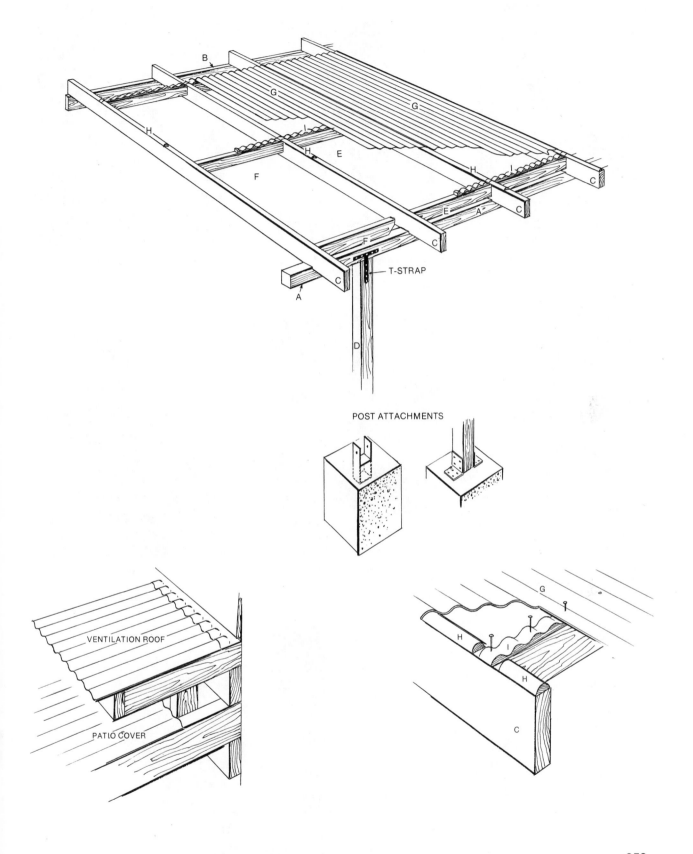

POST ATTACHMENTS

T-STRAP

VENTILATION ROOF

PATIO COVER

Front header post is securely anchored with steel bolts sunk into concrete slab.

Front header is mounted on 4x4 wood post and secured with a steel T-strap and bolts.

Rafters are notched to fit both headers. Photo shows rafter being fastened to front header.

Cross braces are toenailed to rafters. The braces must be flush with tops of the rafters.

Nail holes are pre-drilled using a ⁵/₃₂-inch bit to prevent hammer marks around the nails.

To waterproof overlapped joints, clear sealant is applied to the lower panel before lapping.

holes 32″ apart and use 5″ expansion bolts. The back header must be fastened at a height which will allow a drop of 1″ per foot of roof from back to front. If you live in a very heavy snow areas allow 3″ per foot.

Installing Rafters

The rafters are 2-by-6's that are toenailed to the front and back headers and are notched to fit both. It is important that the rafters be installed square with the headers so that the fiberglass sheets can later be nailed to them in the correct places.

Aluminum nails with water-sealing neoprene washers are nailed through crowns of ribs.

Note that the nine inside rafters are spaced 24″ on centers. However the outside rafters are only 22″ away from the next rafter.

Cross Bracing and Moldings

The cross braces *must* be flush with the tops of the rafters. The first line of braces should be 8″ away from the back header. This space is left open for ventilation and is not covered with fiberglass. If the eaves of the house do not overhang this space and you want more protection against rain, you can build a ventilation hood as shown in the drawing.

Maximum spacing between rows of cross braces should be about 32″. If all the recommended lumber sizes and spacing mentioned here are followed, your patio cover will be able to sustain loads of over 100 lbs. per square foot, which is sufficient to meet most building codes and withstand most snowloads and high winds.

With all cross braces in place, specially shaped wood moldings that fit the corrugations of the fiberglass sheets are nailed to the braces running continuously across the rafters. To make sure that the ridges and valleys of the moldings line up with each other from front to back, place a sheet of fiberglass over them. If they are properly lined up, the corrugated fiberglass sheet will fit over them snugly.

Wood filler strips are nailed to the rafter tops between the intersecting rows of configurated molding. The filler strips and moldings fill in the underside of each ridge or rib to permit firm nailing.

The completed framework should be painted or stained before the fiberglass panels are installed.

Installing the Panels

The panels are laid with their side edges curving down and are overlapped one rib. Lay the panels so that the prevailing wind will blow over rather than *under* the overlap. To waterproof the overlapped joints, apply a clear sealant (supplied by the manufacturer) to the lower panel before lapping.

Drill nail holes using a $\frac{5}{32}$″ bit to avoid hammer marks around the nail. Use the aluminum nails with a neoprene washer to prevent leaks. Nails should be driven into the crown of every third rib (ridge) of the panels over the cross braces and should be spaced 15″ apart along the rafters.

MATERIALS LIST

A. 1 piece 4 x 4 x 240″
B. 1 piece 2 x 6 x 240″
C. 11 pieces 2 x 6 x 194″
D. 3 pieces 4 x 4 x 90″
E. 40 pieces 2 x 4 x 22½″
F. 10 pieces 2 x 4 x 20⅞″
G. 20 fiberglass panels 8′ x 26″
H. 50 pieces 6′ filler strips
I. 24 pieces 6′ configurated moldings
post anchors, 3
aluminum nails, 4 boxes (100 each)
clear sealant, 3 cartridges

LIGHT AND SHADE

A variation on the patio roof just described is one that tries to give you the best of two possible situations: adequate shade from the strong summer sun yet providing sufficient light to brighten the rooms looking out on the patio.

This result is obtained by combining both translucent plastic and aluminum strips. The effect ren-

Just having a handsome terrace adjoining your home is not always enough. During the summer, the hot sun may make it uncomfortable in the extreme.

dered by this clever light-shade combination is quite pleasing to the eye.

Both materials are formed in the same structural shapes and are freely interchangeable as a result. Because of the inherent flexibility of this plan, the number of translucent strips can be varied according to individual needs, while additional variety is obtained from the range of colors in which the roof panels are made.

The addition of a roof provides shade while permitting light to pass through and complements the house well.

Canvas Patio Roof

A row of canvas strips, hanging from a framework of ordinary steel pipe, is regulated by ropes like a Venetian blind and controls the sunlight of an open patio. The canvas strips, 30″ wide and the length of the patio, are supported on a framework of ordinary pipe by a series of 1-by-1 wood strips. These wood strips, spaced 16″ apart, are attached to the canvas with small eye screws. Wire is stretched through the eye screws across the canvas. Thus, to open or close the canvas shades, just pull on one of the attached ropes

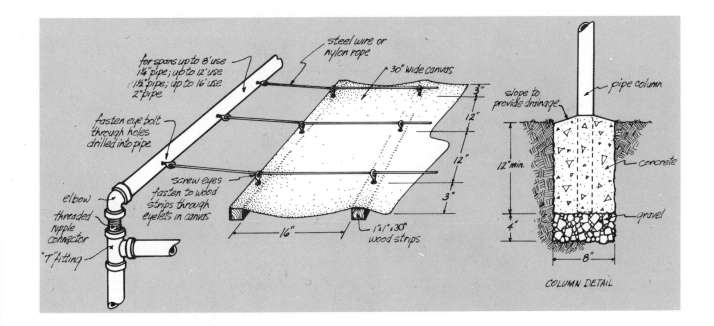

SANDBOX SUNROOF

The younger set will have a delightful play area out of the hot sun when the sandbox is fitted with a canopy. The fringe is optional, but beneficial.

Make the canopy frame of 1-by-3 wood strips, with a ½" or ¾" pipe at the center. A ¼" threaded rod, which is a standard hardware item, goes through the slotted upright, the canopy frame, and through the pipe, locked in place with bolts or thumb screws at each side. The sketch shows details of both sandbox and canopy construction. Select a colorful striped canvas for covering the canopy frame.

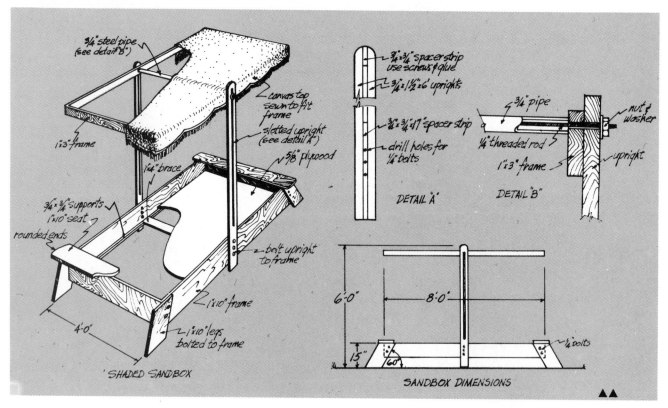

AN OUTDOOR FAMILY ROOM

An open terrace is great, but put on a roof and you increase its usefulness immeasurably, since you can enjoy it even when it rains. And screening assures ultimate, bugproof comfort.

The concrete slab gives you a good head start, particularly if it is large and abuts the house on at least one side. Construction should be sufficiently rugged so that all-weather sash can be substituted for the screen panels to make the room even more useful, through much of the year.

The structure consists of 4-by-4 supporting posts, a double 2-by-8 plate along the front to support the 2-by-8 rafters, which are either locked into the

house rafters or supported on a rear plate attached to the house wall. The sides are enclosed with siding nailed to 2-by-6 beams and short studs filling in the inclined area formed by the end rafters.

Start by putting up the 4-by-4 posts, located at the corners of the concrete slab and also in intermediary positions so that stock-size screen frames will fit into the spaces, or just space the posts uniformly if you will make your own screens. These posts are locked into position with a steel pin, ½" thick.

Outline your enclosure on the patio slab, then mark the exact positions of the posts, which must be in a straight line. Saw 5" lengths of ½" diameter steel rod. Find the exact center of each post by drawing diagonal lines across the corners (where

Multiply your summer pleasures and stretch the season by enclosing your open concrete terrace with a roof and screens.

View of enclosed patio showing door to yard and backwall of house. Translucent plastic roof allows ample light for room facing the enclosed patio.

the lines cross is the center) and drill a ½″ hole about 3″ deep. Drill the same ½″ holes of the center post positions into the concrete, also 3″ deep, with a star drill. Drive the steel dowel into the post, then set the posts erect, held up by the steel dowels into the concrete, and reinforced by 1-by-2 furring strips nailed across the posts.

Cut the 2-by-6's to length for the sides, nail them into pairs, and toenail these double 2-by-6's to the tops of the posts.

The front support member, consisting of a double 2-by-8, is notched back at the ends to overlap the side framing members, as shown in the sketch. The rafters may be supported at the rear on a 2-by-8 plate nailed to the house siding. In the installation illustrated, the overhang of the house roof is cut back, giving access to the rafters inside. Thus the patio rafters are aligned with and attached to the original house rafters, which are at a height that provides an adequate pitch for the new roof.

The new rafters are set on 24″ centers. If tied into the house rafters, which nearly always are 16″

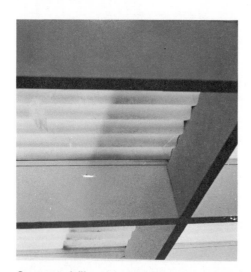

Corrugated fiberglass panels are overlapped and sealed at seams, flashed with similarly contoured moldings. Nails through predrilled holes are fitted with neoprene waterseal washers.

Open view of backyard garden is retained with screened wall, but area has feeling of spacious room. Outdoor dining is usually more pleasant in screened area.

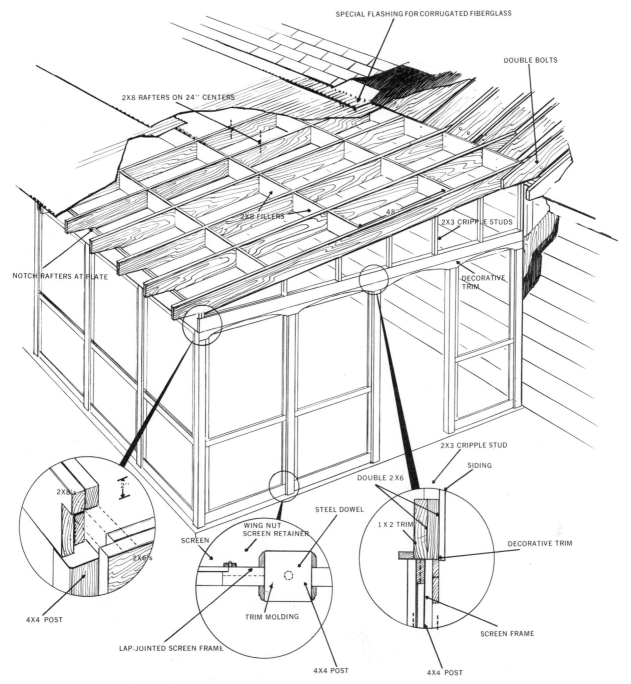

SPECIAL FLASHING FOR CORRUGATED FIBERGLASS

DOUBLE BOLTS

2X8 RAFTERS ON 24'' CENTERS

2X8 FILLERS

48''

2X3 CRIPPLE STUDS

NOTCH RAFTERS AT PLATE

DECORATIVE TRIM

2X3 CRIPPLE STUD

SIDING

DOUBLE 2 X 6

STEEL DOWEL

1 X 2 TRIM

DECORATIVE TRIM

WING NUT
SCREEN RETAINER

2X8's

SCREEN

2''

2X6's

TRIM MOLDING

SCREEN FRAME

4X4 POST

4X4 POST

LAP-JOINTED SCREEN FRAME

4X4 POST

4X4 POST

Framing of the roof supports is based on 4x4 posts, doweled into the concrete. Front and side plates are double 2x6s and 2x8s. Rafters shown here are bolted to house rafters, reached by cutting through roofing at overhang.

O.C., then only alternate rafters will join, others can rest on and be nailed to the house wall plate.

All rafters are beveled and notched as necessary to fit snugly on the front plates, and are either toe-nailed to the supporting plate at the house wall, or joined to the house rafters with bolts through drilled holes. Do not attempt to drive nails into the house rafters as the impact of hammering will shift them and may also damage the roofing. The rafters are reinforced with insert pieces of 2-by-8 nailed between them to form an egg-crate roof pattern which provides better support for plastic roofing panels.

The roof is covered with corrugated fiberglass panels, including special flashing which matches the contours of the panels. Installation of these panels is fully described in the section on skylights, page 261.

Siding and decorative trim are applied as shown in the diagram, following placement of the cripple studs which provide a nailing base for the siding between the side plates and the end rafters.

The screens are made up as removable panels, tightly fitted into the openings, with trim molding sealing the side joints, and the bottom fitted with a bevel molding to shed rain water. A bead of calking at top and bottom joints will be helpful, also, for insect-proofing.

OUTDOOR TILES FOR THE PATIO

Home owners with a concrete slab patio have another alternative to carpeting as a surface material, aside from expensive slate or flagstone jobs, or painting, which requires frequent renewal. The new flooring material is a vinyl composition tile in a fortified version that comes in 12″ squares, applied with a special weather-resistant adhesive.

The tile has a number of attributes: it is attractive, colorful, resilient, inexpensive, durable, easy to maintain, and has a smooth surface that will surely prompt dancing whenever you have a party.

Specifically designed for do-it-yourself installations, the tiles can be laid on any exterior concrete patio that is structurally sound and well drained. The tiles might be used also in semi-enclosed areas such as open porches, if the floor is concrete, but they are not recommended for use over wood.

A breakthrough in outdoor flooring material makes the once difficult job of resurfacing concrete patios a breeze. And the results are handsome, lasting and blend well with any outdoor decor.

Sweep and scrub concrete slab thoroughly, patch all cracks. Let dry, then apply neoprene primer evenly with roller on long handle, about 200 square feet to the gallon. Use brush to cover slab edges. Primer usually takes about two hours to dry. Then adhesive is applied.

Adhesive, laid on at the rate of 100 square feet to the gallon may be applied when primer is no longer tacky, with a heavier coat on rough spots to fill in or smooth. Adhesive is ready for the tile as soon as it no longer is tacky.

Job layout is like that for indoor tile. Bisect the slab with a chalkline and measure to parallel edges. Move chalkline if border tiles will be less than 6" wide. Bisect chalkline and again measure to edges, move line if needed as above. Start tiling at intersection of lines.

Before installing each tile, coat its bottom with adhesive at the rate of ½ pint per six tiles, using a 3" mohair roller. Let it dry 10-15 minutes. To save cleanup later, take care in applying adhesive—mainly, don't overload tiles—so the faces and edges are kept clean.

Quick, tenacious grip of adhesive makes it very difficult to slide tile into proper position once put down. Best method of positioning properly is to put down a corner of the tile, then one edge—check its position—and only then let it come into full contact.

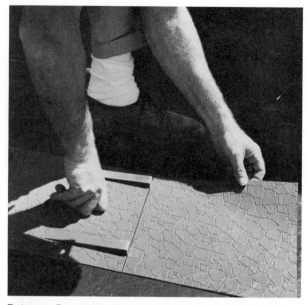

Between first, second, and all subsequent tiles, maintain $1/16''$ joints on all sides of tiles to allow for expansion and contraction caused by temperature changes; otherwise buckling is possible. Spacers, hooked on tile, insure their correct placement.

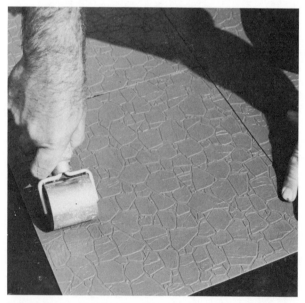

Roll each tile individually after it is in proper position, to insure strong bond. The entire bottom must be in full contact with the adhesive. Use the roller (which you can rent from flooring dealer) methodically, like you'd paint a wall.

Excess tile at edges of slab can be trimmed with sharp linoleum knife once it's in position, or pre-cut to necessary size with tin snips or heavy shears. Easiest method for fitting tile around odd shapes or obstructions is to pre-cut them.

If any of the adhesive spills on face or gets on edges of tile, let it dry. It can be removed easily with an eraser. Another method is to rub the affected area with a rag dipped in turpentine. The floor can be walked on right afterward.

Installation Step by Step

Installation is similar to that of indoor tiles, but first the slab must be scrubbed clean and any chips or cracks patched with cement. Then a neoprene primer is applied with a roller that is like a paint roller with a long handle.

A special adhesive is then rolled on the entire surface. The tiles are each given an extra coating of the adhesive on the back before being placed into position, then pressed down with a roller to assure a good bond. Installation is best done at a temperature range of 70 to 90 degrees.

The question you're asking is: "Can this tile take the onslaught of the weather?" Exhaustive laboratory and external exposure tests to every climatic condition have confirmed that it does not crack, bleach, or buckle under temperatures ranging from 150 degrees Fahrenheit down to 40 below zero. Just as importantly, the tests indicated the neoprene adhesive will hold the tile securely under the same conditions.

Maintenance is easy as the embossed surface of the tile resists scuff marks, dents, and chipping. All that is necessary to keep it clean and fresh looking is to sweep and hose it as necessary. Available colors are dark green, slate gray, beige, and terra cotta, to blend with your outdoor decor.

ENLARGING THE PATIO

Like so many other things, a small patio is nice to have, but a more spacious one is very much better. For one thing it permits placement of decorative outdoor furniture and other embellishments. When entertaining, there's room for dancing, com-

Attractive and useful patio extension shown here beautified the lawn area and, at the same time, created a place for outdoor entertaining.

Area alongside patio is excavated to depth of about 4 inches on two adjacent sides.

Frame of 1x4 redwood stock, 2 feet wide and 12 feet long, is built with dividers spaced 2 feet apart, for one side of patio.

The frame is carried into position at right angles to shorter frame. One end member is omitted from a frame so they do not double up where the frames meet into corner.

A carpenter's spirit level is used to check positioning of frame after it is blocked up flush with the patio surface.

Stakes are driven deeply into the ground on both inside and outside surfaces of frame to wedge it tightly against patio side.

Steel fasteners can be fired into the concrete with a rented powder-actuated "gun". In some localities, a license is necessary to operate this gun.

Sand is smoothed to proper 2-inch level with wood bar that just reaches two inches into the square.

The frame is fastened to the old slab with hardened concrete nails or cut nails, driven first through the wood.

The larger frame, 6 feet wide by 18 feet long, has interlocking grooves for eggcrate construction, with crosspieces 2 feet apart.

Concrete mix in one paper sack just fills one 2-foot square to the required 2-inch depth.

Concrete-sand and water are hoed to a thorough mixture in wheelbarrow.

Concrete is simply shoveled into the 2-foot frame squares. Each square can be done separately, or several at once.

Concrete is immediately leveled with a strike board so it is flush with the top of the wood form.

After partially setting, concrete is worked with a wooden trowel or float to make it even but slightly gainy for non-slip surface.

Once concrete is cured, any cement on top of the wood strips is removed with a cold chisel. Wood strips form interesting pattern in the patio surface.

fortable seating, space for the serving tables, a barbecue and, not least, no overflow onto the lawn that results in trampling of the grass.

An interesting and practical technique for expanding a ground-level concrete slab is shown in the accompanying photographs. The original size of the patio, 12'-by-16', is enlarged by adding a 2' wide strip along one side, and a 6' wide strip along an adjacent side. When the expansion is completed, the patio becomes a spacious square, 18'-by-18'.

In preparation for work, the turf on two adjacent sides of the patio is excavated to a depth of a little more than 4". Two frames are built of 1"-by-4" redwood stock—one frame is 2' wide and 12' long; the other is 6' wide and 18' long.

The frames are assembled with cross members nailed in 2' apart, thus forming an egg-crate pattern of 2' squares. The wider frame consists of four long boards, spaced 2' apart and also with the inserts forming 2' squares. For the patio size in this project, 18' square, a total of eight lengths of the 1-by-4 stock exactly takes care of the frame requirements, using the cut-off pieces from the shorter frames for the 2' cross members.

Actually, the 1" stock is available only in 8" widths, so only four boards are needed, ripped down the center to get the 1-by-4's.

The essential detail is linking the egg-crate frames to the original patio. They are set into the excavated area and blocked up so the top is flush with the patio concrete, then the frame is leveled (if the pitch of the patio is in the direction of the extension, the strip should be positioned to continue the slope; otherwise a water dam with pooling will result at that point). The frame is wedged tightly against the edge of the old concrete slab with stakes driven into the ground on the outside and inside of the frame.

In addition, the side of the frame is fastened to the slab with concrete nails. These can be most effectively driven with a rented powder-actuated "gun" that uses cartridges to fire steel fasteners into the concrete, but some local regulations restrict use of such equipment to persons who are specially licensed and have been trained in its use. Concrete or cut nails can do the job adequately although not as easily. A word of caution here, too: these nails are hardened to the point of being quite brittle and can snap apart if not driven straight in. In this case, however, the major part of the length will be in the wood of the frame so the nail is held firmly for the final two or three hammer blows that drive it into the concrete.

Prepared concrete mix (Sakrete) is most convenient for filling the form squares. A bag of the concrete-sand mixture makes enough to exactly fill a 2' square to a depth of 2". Sand is first distributed in the squares, spread evenly to a 2" depth with a board of that width having handles that rest atop the sides of the frame.

One advantage of the squares is that you can do as much concrete work at a time as you wish, completing just one or more square each time.

The concrete is mixed in a wheelbarrow, enough for one square at each mix. Shovel the concrete into the square and level with a straight board flush with the top edges. After the concrete has set for a while, work the top with a float or wooden trowel to make the concrete even but very slightly roughened for a safe non-slip surface. If you want a

Many homeowners would like to install a barbecue or charcoal grille in their backyards to enjoy outdoor living more. Here is such a project completely finished. Barbecue shown is a propane gas type.

The first step involves the area that will be the barbecue's concrete base. It is outlined with string which are tied to stakes.

More cement is added and mixture is pushed downward with long stick to make sure there are no open spaces under the cement.

A carpenter's level is used to assure that steel post is plumb.

Four pieces of 1x4 redwood are nailed together in the shape of a square. Wedges are used to securely seat frame.

Check the level of the frame after it is placed in area where turf has been removed to a depth of 4 inches.

Hole around the post is filled with cement to the top of sand. Copper line for propane gas is connected to the base of barbecue.

Poured cement is smoothed ith wooden float, leaving the surface a bit rough for non-skid safety.

Enough sand to provide a two-inch sand bed is poured into the frame and is smoothed with screed.

To install post, a hole about 12 inches in diameter is dug to depth suggested by barbecue manufacturer. A shovelful of cement is tossed in.

Smaller form for the base that will hold the propane gas tank is made in same manner. The cement is leveled with straight wooden board.

The finished base for the gas tank, hidden behind brick planter.

very smooth top, wait until the concrete has a water glaze on top, and work it with a finishing trowel.

After the concrete has cured, any cement remaining on the wood edges is chipped off with a cold chisel. The exposed 1-by-4 redwood remaining in the patio surface forms an interesting pattern of squares, and the wood is resistant to weathering.

For a similar expansion of a patio, the size of the frames must, of course, be dimensioned as required. Where the patio has curved sides, the frames may be shaped of plywood to conform.

BARBECUE ON A POST

Barbecue grilles mounted on a post are rapidly gaining popularity as their advantages become more widely known. The slender supporting post takes up minimum floor space while holding the grille securely at just the right height. There is no wheeling of the grille back and forth as is necessary with the standard models; there's no chance of a dangerous spillover with glowing coals and, best of all, a barbecue with ceramic brickettes fired by gas does away with messy charcoal. The gas may be drawn from the regular lines in your home that supply fuel for cooking and heating, or you can use propane gas from a small concealed tank. This type of barbecue grille has a swing-up cover, which is also very useful for keeping the grille clean.

If you are thinking of installing a grille on your patio, the simple method described below will be helpful. The best way to start is to outline with string and stakes the area you expect to cover with concrete for the barbecue's base, then build a form of that size of 1-by-4 redwood boards. Use galvanized or cement-coated nails to prevent rust, since the wood will remain embedded in the ground after the concrete is poured.

Remove turf to a depth of 4″ inside the outlined area and fit the redwood form into the excavation. Secure the form with foot-long stakes driven deeply into the earth so that the tops of the stakes are about an inch below the tops of the boards. Check to see that the form is precisely level, making any necessary adjustments, then attach the frame by driving nails through its sides into the stakes.

Lay in a 2″ bed of sand inside the square, spreading the sand uniformly with a board. Next comes installation of the post: dig a hole about 12″ in diameter to a depth recommended by the barbecue manufacturer. Mix a batch of cement using prepared cement mix. Put the post into the hole and toss a shovelful of cement around it. Use a long board to compact the cement in the hole and add more cement, then use a level to align the steel post so it is plumb, wedging it with stones as necessary. Fill the hole with more cement to the top.

If you have a gas-fueled model, make the gas line connections now, leading the copper tubing along the sand and through a hole in the side of the form. Outside the form, the tubing runs under the turf to the gas tank or other source connection. A propane gas tank should have its own concrete base made the same way with a wood form which will, of course, be much smaller than the barbecue base.

The barbecue form finally is filled with cement, leveled with a straight board moved across the top of the side boards, and smoothed with a wood float. After the concrete has hardened for twenty-four hours, you can set the grille on the post and connect the gas lines.

MAKING A PATIO BENCH

With simple lines, but exceedingly decorative nonetheless, the bench illustrated will be an important addition to your patio. Its construction, in itself, will provide a most interesting and instructive activity. The bench is built of six concrete blocks, the kind molded into special designs, plus three pieces of 2-by-6 redwood lumber about 8′ long, and a sack of mortar mix.

The bench can be placed on the lawn instead of the solid patio slab, but in that case you will have to prepare level concrete footings just a few inches deep on a sand base.

The bench is built by first forming the bases, each made by assembling three concrete blocks in the form of a T, as seen in the photographs. Allowing ½″ for mortar between the blocks, trace the outline of the blocks on the patio surface with a soft pencil. Locate a spot inside the outline where the mortar of all three blocks meet, and mark that spot.

Drill a hole in the patio surface at this spot about 1½″ deep with a ½″ carbide-tipped drill. Insert a ½″ diameter steel reinforcing rod in this hole. The rod should be about 1″ shorter than the top of the blocks.

Mix a small batch of the mortar and apply ½″ layer of mortar in the area of the T where the two blocks stand side by side. Set the first block in place, tapping it down into the mortar, and check-

Attractive garden bench has decorative concrete blocks for supports and three 18-foot planks of redwood.

Begin by tracing the outlines of concrete blocks on the surface of the patio with a soft pencil.

Drill a hole in the patio for a steel reinforcement rod using a half-inch carbide bit.

Mortar for two blocks is laid inside outline traced on patio. First block is set in place and plumbed with a carpenter's level.

Second block is loaded with mortar on the side where it will be in contact with the first one. Since only a small amount of motar is used on this job, it can be mixed most conveniently with trowel on a small wood platform.

Both blocks are now leveled. Note the position of steel rod.

Third block is set in place opposite other two in a T-shape. The rod is buried in mortar lines where all the blocks touch. They are then checked with a square. ·

The two T-shaped block supports are now ready for the plank seat.

Three redwood 2x6 planks are used for the seat. The planks are fastened together with two cleats near each end.

ing with a level to see that it is plumb. Add mortar to the side of the second block and set it in position against the first one. Then put the third block into position and check all three with a level and square. Repeat the operation with the other set of blocks, spaced about 4' apart on the inside measurement and in alignment with the first set, making certain that both sets of blocks are level with each other.

The redwood planks are held together with a pair of cleats at each end, the cleats set tightly against the two surfaces of the supporting blocks. It is advisable also to anchor the seat planks with epoxy cement—a spot of cement about the size of a half dollar will do the job.

The planks can be finished with stain and a clear exterior urethane varnish or a neutral exterior paint that blends with the concrete.

BACK YARD WATERFALL

One of the most delightful additions you can make to your back yard setting is a waterfall. This provides continual animation, and a glistening and refreshing backdrop for your leisure-hours viewing. The waterfall is easily and inexpensively made. The water is circulated with a pump and used over and over again, so there is no waste.

The materials you will need are a small circulating pump and some ¾" copper tubing, obtained at hardware stores, and some stone, sand, and cement. Half-inch pipe, galvanized or brass, can be used in place of the tubing.

After selecting the best location, start by outlining the shape of the waterfall and its pool with cord and stakes. Since the shape of the pool is irregular, the cord between the stakes can be simply laid

Waterfall project is started by outlining irregular shape of pool and steps with some cord simply placed on the ground.

Wrap cord around stakes. Place crossbar over two end stakes. Using carpenter's level, check the slope, if any, of the ground.

After turf has been removed and 2" of sand put in the bottom, drive stakes with pencil marks on them two inches above the surface of the sand.

When concrete is poured over the sand, the surface of the concrete should be even with pencil marks on the stakes.

Series of steps, each smaller than one below, are cut into sloping earth. Earth is tamped down hard and two inches of concrete is spread. Level is used to pitch the steps slightly lower at the front.

Flat stones, cemented over concrete steps, protrude about one inch beyond concrete slabs underneath. Sidewalls along steps are stones cemented in place with mortar. Sidewalls need only be two courses high.

Here second course of stones is being put down. Note pool needs sidewalls that are three courses high so walls around the pool and the steps are continuous.

Use trowel to remove excess mortar.

Recess mortar with stick or flat metal bar so that the effect of the stone is emphasized most.

The tower is used as a blind and shelter for the pump and its electric motor.

Cement coating on inside walls of the pool prevents leaking. Decorative gravel bed and outer stone wall are optional.

Smooth the interior cement wall of the pool with an ordinary curved trowel.

Use a trowel to pack in the cement between stones in each successive layer.

Opening in concrete pool floor has been left to expose copper pipe previously laid. Proper size grate is fitted over hole.

The completed stone garden pool and waterfall, which includes a decorative gravel bed, also has an outer stone wall.

out on the grass as a guide for excavating. A decorative pool of this type is quite shallow, holding just about 8″ of water at the deepest part. Whatever depth you choose, allow for a 2″ bed of sand and a 2″ concrete base over tamped earth of the excavated area.

Since the pool bottom may not be flat all over its area, drive stakes in the sand bed marked with a pencil 2″ above the sand as a guide for spreading the concrete surface. The stakes are removed as soon as they have served their purpose.

Before pouring the concrete, place the copper tubing in the sand and lead it back to the point at the base of the waterfall tower where you expect to locate the pump. You don't need to bury the tubing since the steps of the waterfall will conceal it. The end of the tubing protrudes into a circular recess or depression in the concrete bottom of the pool. Before pouring the concrete, make a circular collar out of sheet metal, preferably copper, and place it over the tubing, as illustrated. Notch the bottom of the collar so the tube can go through it. The diameter of this metal collar depends on the size of the round grate that will fit into a drain placed above it.

The waterfall is made up of a series of steps, each smaller than the one below, cut into the sloping earth. Suit your preference in designing the steps. The earth of the steps is tamped firmly and a 2″ layer of concrete is poured on them, contained by an oiled board along the front edge of the step until the concrete has set sufficiently. The steps should be pitched slightly to the front to facilitate movement of the water toward the pool.

The steps are paved with flat stones held in concrete and protruding an inch or so beyond the concrete edge. The exposed earth under the paved steps should be protected with small pieces of stone, in varied shapes and sizes, carefully fixed into concrete as a waterseal.

Low sidewalls now must be set up to contain the water flowing down to the pool. The sidewalls along the steps need be only two courses high. Around the pool, they will have to be three layers high because the pool is lower and the walls should be continuous. The mortar joining the sidewall stones should be "struck" so it is recessed—that is, a jointing tool compresses and forces the mortar deeply for a better appearance. The lower stones around the pool are completely surfaced with cement to prevent water leaks. This concrete surface can be painted to give it an interesting color, or tiles can be fitted into the surface.

The tower of the waterfall need not be very high. Some shelter should be provided for the pump and electric motor in the tower to protect the electrical connections from rain and weather.

The electrical cable to the pump should be buried in a shallow trench. Make sure cables and other electrical parts are the approved type for outdoor use, and that the entire electrical installation is properly grounded.

The pool will need enough water to start it up, and then will require the addition of a gallon or two from time to time to make up for evaporation. The drain at the circulating pump connecting tube will have to be cleaned out occasionally. The pool should be completely drained before each winter season (although it could continue to operate with the addition of an antifreeze solution).

Draining is easy when a piece of rubber tubing is attached to the outflow of the pump, allowing the water to be pumped out.

PLANTER AND GARDEN LIGHT

A brick planter that features an attractive garden lamp makes a dual contribution to any back yard view. The one illustrated on this interesting patio is quite easy to build for anyone with a bit of experience in bricklaying or masonry work; for those who haven't yet developed this capacity, the planter and lamp project is an excellent way to get started.

After deciding on the size of the planter, outline its rectangular shape on the lawn with strings and stakes. Use a line level on the strings, and make sure that the strings meet square at the corners. Excavate the outlined area to a depth necessary for the planter footing; this depth varies considerably depending on the local soil conditions, temperature range, and drainage at the site. Where the soil is sandy and drains well, and the winter temperatures are moderate, a depth of 4″ is sufficient. In areas of more severe winters, a 10″ depth allows for 3″ of gravel on the bottom, then 2″ of concrete and two courses of brick—all below the surface of the lawn.

In the center of this excavation, dig a hole about 12″ in diameter for the steel pipe which will be the lamppost. The hole should be about 18″ deep. Mix a batch of concrete from a sack of prepared concrete mix, throw a shovelful into the hole, and stand the lamppost in the hole. Wedge in some stones to get the post plumb, then pack the hole with concrete level with the sand.

From your house electric panel box, lay a

Brick planter with a garden light and bench is a decorative and practical addition to any patio.

Area to be covered by the planter is outlined with stakes and strings, and the soil is removed to a depth of four inches.

Wood frame is placed in excavation, a hole is dug within the area and the lamppost is inserted in hole.

Prepared mortar mix and water are then mixed in a wheelbarrow with a hoe.

Concrete is shoveled in around the post until the hole is about half full. Wet concrete is pressed down with a long stick to eliminate any air spaces.

The steel post is carefully plumbed with level, and wedged into position with small stones if necessary.

The hole is filled and leveled with trowel. Note the electric cable at right.

Narrow trench is dug for a waterproof electric cable for the garden light.

Sand is poured into wood frame to 2-inch depth and leveled with screed.

Bed of mortar is laid down on the sand and bricks are tapped into place.

Corners are built up first so that string can be placed for next course.

Mortar is laid on previous course in V-shaped layer with pointed trowel.

Completed course is checked with a level. Bricks are tapped down as needed with trowel handle.

To stagger the vertical joints, every other course begins at corners with the end of a brick from the adjacent wall.

All joints on the exterior sides of the walls are "struck" with a special metal finishing tool. Brickwork of planter now is completed.

Interior of planter is filled with earth and planted with a variety of flowers. Garden seat at the front is made of two 2-by-6 planks, fastened with epoxy glue or mastic cement.

grounded cable in a shallow trench to the planter base. This cable must be the approved type for underground in-soil installations, having a heavy waterproof vinyl jacket that resists soil acids. You can also plan to have an extra convenience receptacle located in the planter brickwork.

The soil inside the planter excavation now is tamped level, and bricklaying can start. The bricks are first sprinkled with a garden hose, enough to moisten but not soak them. The bricks are cemented with mortar, obtained as prepared dry mix in paper sacks such as Sakrete—but be sure you get the mortar mix and not some other type. Prepare the mixture with the correct amount of water as stated on the bag.

Put down a bed of mortar first, then butter one end of each brick that is placed in position with enough mortar to form a ½" joint. The horizontal line between each course also will have the ½" layer of mortar.

Bring the bricks into line with each other by tap-

ping them with the trowel handle; scoop up the squeezed-out mortar and work it in with the rest of your supply. Use a taut string as a guide for each course, and also check the plumb with a level. Professional masons usually build up two or three bricks at opposite corners, then insert a nail in the mortar at each corner and stretch a string across. Note, too, that every other course begins with the end of a brick from the adjacent side, so that the vertical joints will be staggered. Strike all the mortar joints with a metal finishing tool to depress and round them. Do the vertical joints first, then the horizontal.

On completing the brickwork, fill the planter interior with earth. The front can be made into a seat by placing a double row of 2-by-6 redwood planks, fastened to the brick with epoxy glue or mastic cement. The lamppost is fitted with an attractive globe. The control switch for the lamp may be at the house or located on the lamppost.

Chapter 9
THE GARDEN TOOLHOUSE—UPDATED

How easy it is to roll the lawnmower or wheelbarrow right into a toolhouse on the grounds! How pleasant it is to drive into the garage without first stopping to shift two or three pieces of gardening equipment out of the way! How efficient and practical to have all the small gardening tools together with the necessary supplies all in one handy place!

How to come by all this? Just put up a small toolhouse anywhere on the grounds. "Anywhere" is right, because a toolhouse, while intended as a down-to-earth practical storage place, can also be attractive enough to be part of your home setting.

No need to hide the potting shed somewhere behind the garage, or store your equipment in a disreputable outdoor cabinet. The toolhouse plans you will find here are practical indeed, but also were designed with an eye to the home environment. The toolhouse can come out into the sun at last.

GIVE GARDEN TOOLS A HOME

If you are the typical homeowner, you have spent many minutes searching for that elusive trowel or

Complete gardening center, located anywhere on your back lot, contains ample storage space for all your tools and equipment, together with a potting bench, all in an airy shed built on a flagstone or concrete base.

weeder or sprayer each time it was needed. Then, just as you reach the explosion point, you find it under a pile of odds and ends in the garage, or stuck into an overflowing toolbox down the cellar. You resolve to put it away carefully when you're through so that next time you won't have to play this exasperating game of hide-and-seek. But, more often than not, "next time" it happens again.

All of this frustration can be avoided if a specific area for the tool is set aside. There is no better way to accomplish this than to build a combination garden storage and work center in your yard, just like the one seen here.

It has capacity galore. Much of the interior wall space is covered with perforated hardboard from which all manner of tools and implements may be hung. There is ample shelf space as well; even more can be added for heavy or bulky objects that can't be hung conveniently. The doors haven't been neglected, either. Pockets here are good for small tools or flat objects, seed packets, and so forth. The pockets have been faced with perforated hardboard also, to supply a bonus in usable wall space.

One of the cubicles has been designed as a potting bench, with a work surface at a convenient height. The wall space above the bench is conve-

SKETCH A

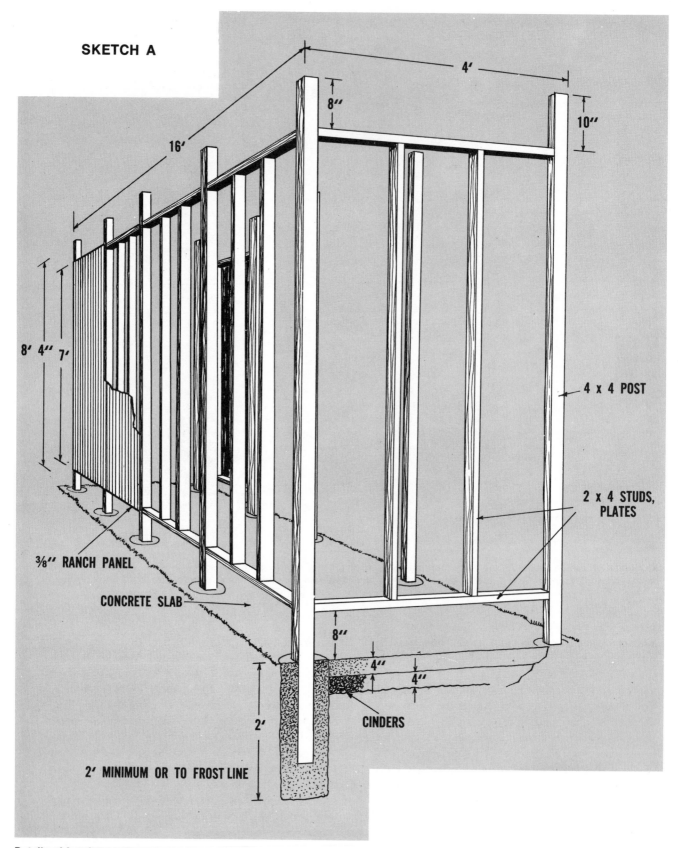

4'

8"

10"

16'

4 x 4 POST

8' 4" 7'

2 x 4 STUDS,
PLATES

3/8" RANCH PANEL

CONCRETE SLAB

8"

4"

4"

CINDERS

2'

2' MINIMUM OR TO FROST LINE

Details of framing posts and sub-core supports to keep the shed rigid in every kind of weather.

nient for a shelf or two and plenty of hooks to keep handy a supply of earthenware plant pots of varying sizes and the tools of transplanting.

What Do You Need?

Admittedly, some home owners are more actively interested in gardening than others. To the tried-and-true green thumber, the available space in this project may seem only a bare minimum, while to others, whose main interests lie elsewhere, it may be overly ambitious. These factors have been considered in the design. The entire structure is built on a module of 4', meaning that any 4' section can be eliminated or, for that matter, others can be added. Decide on a plan that will suit your special needs. Perhaps the potting bench area can be eliminated and the entire shed devoted to storage alone. Or one of the storage modules might be eliminated if the remaining units are enough.

Foundations: What's Underneath

The open, elevated plan permits the use of many materials for the floor. Flagstone, embedded in concrete, was our choice, but a more economical version might eliminate the flags, stopping at the slab. Brick laid loosely in sand would be a good choice, too, and in good drainage areas would provide a path for rainwater to seep into the ground—a condition which might be bothersome with a concrete slab unless it was properly pitched. Secondhand brick is often more attractive than new.

The concrete footings must be poured for each post as shown in detail in sketch A. Footings must extend below the frost line in your area, a depth easily learned by asking your local building department or a contractor. Treat the posts with a preservative such as Penta before pouring the concrete. If you are planning on a concrete slab it will be easiest for you to excavate for the slab and postholes to the proper depth, then carefully true up the posts with a level and temporarily brace them in the vertical position by nailing to lengths of 1-by-2 or 1-by-3. Be sure that the posts at the front are 2" longer than those at the rear wall. This will provide the proper slope for the roof. Footings can then be poured, allowed to set for a few hours and the slab poured on top. When it has cured for several days, work may proceed on the shed itself, which can be built in a single weekend.

From the Slab Up

Remove the braces that supported the posts and, following sketch A, begin framing. Nail the top and bottom 2-by-4 plates between posts, using a level at each step of the way. If the framing isn't square, you will have trouble later. Next, nail studs to plates, spacing them on 16" centers. When the framing is complete, the rear elevation may be covered with sheets of 4'-by-7' ⅜" Ranch Panel, Texture 1-11 plywood, which is a prefinished exterior-grade panel well suited to this use. Here and wherever else paneling is to be nailed to studs and posts, use 6d galvanized finishing nails. Perforated hardboard should be attached with aluminum, screw-threaded shank, needlepoint nails. All nails should be driven 4" O.C. on posts and 8" O.C. at intermediate members.

Referring now to sketch B, which is a view taken from the corner diagonally opposite the one in the foreground of sketch A, we can see additional steps in the construction. Interior surfaces are either perforated hardboard, such as Peg-Board, or Ranch Panel, Texture 1-11 again. Legs for the potting bench and the upright supporting the shelves may be cut from clear pine, 2-by-2 stock. The perimeter beams at the top may also be placed at this time, notching out posts as indicated in the sketch.

The Roof

The sloping roof is constructed of 2-by-4's laid on edge on perimeter beams and toenailed to them at the spacing shown in sketch C. Next, the front and rear fascia boards, also 2-by-4's, are nailed to beam ends. Lastly, the side fascia are nailed in place. This completes the roof framing and the actual roof covering may now be put down. The same ⅜" Texture 1-11 plywood is used here as for the wall paneling, but note carefully that it is nailed with the grooved side *down*. The backs of the panels, which are now the top sides exposed to the weather, are given a sealing coat of asphalt roofing compound. Refer to sketch D for roof details.

The Doors

The doors are easily constructed in this sequence. Nail together a frame of butted 2-by-4's measuring 40¼" by 7'. Cover one side of the frame with ⅜" Ranch Panel, trimmed flush with the frame edge. Nail on 4" centers with galvanized finishing nails. Inside corners of the frame can be reinforced with

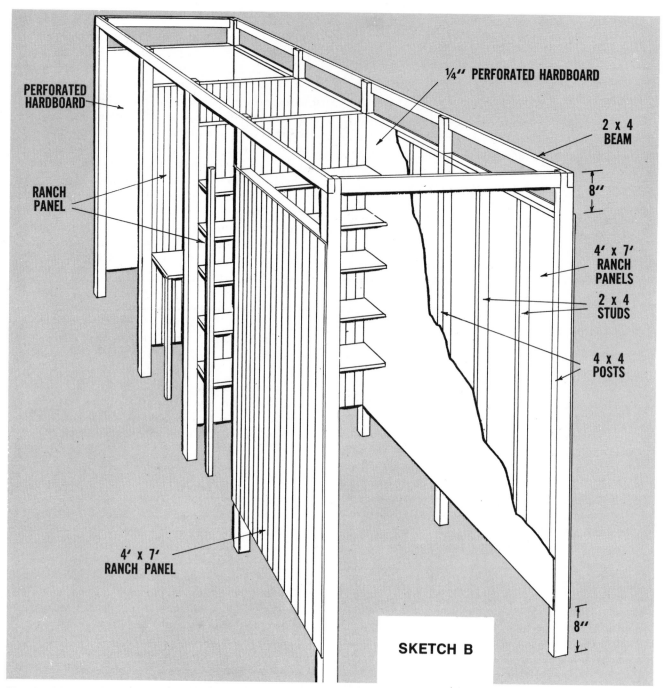

PERFORATED
HARDBOARD

RANCH
PANEL

4' x 7'
RANCH PANEL

¼" PERFORATED HARDBOARD

2 x 4
BEAM

8"

4' x 7'
RANCH
PANELS

2 x 4
STUDS

4 x 4
POSTS

8"

SKETCH B

Sketch indicates sizes and positions of the enclosing panels, together with storage shelving.

steel right-angle brackets screwed to each 2-by-4. Turn the frame over and, beginning at the bottom of the door, nail in 1-by-3 shelves and cleats as shown in the detail sketch E. Final step is the addition of the pockets, which are made by nailing strips of perforated hardboard to the shelves and

cleats. The finished door is heavy enough to require a minimum of three heavy-duty hinges. Use brass or plated hinges which will not rust from exposure. Door fastenings may be as simple as a hook-and-eye, or a locking-type hasp may be added.

All structural members and exposed paneling

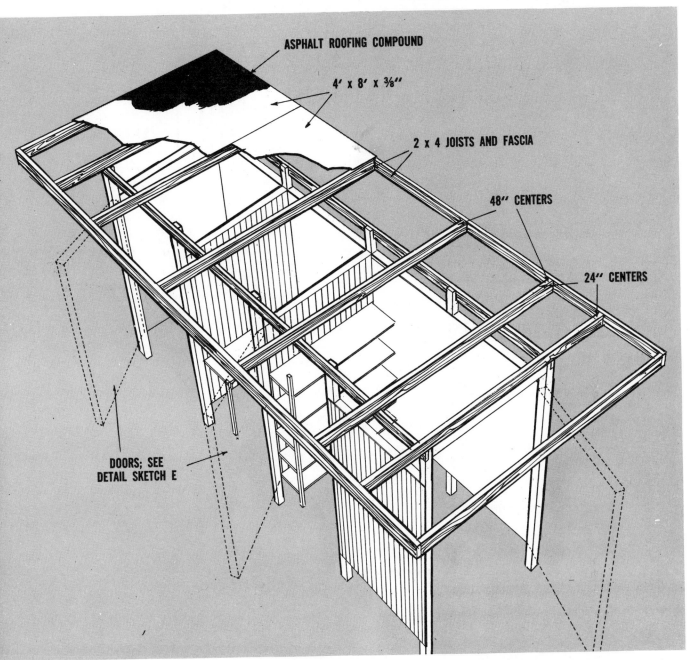

ASPHALT ROOFING COMPOUND

4' x 8' x 3/8"

2 x 4 JOISTS AND FASCIA

48" CENTERS

24" CENTERS

DOORS; SEE
DETAIL SKETCH E

Roof construction consists of 2-by-4s throughout, as shown, decked with 4-by-8 panels and topped with asphalt compound.

should, of course, be painted. Use a good grade of trim paint for posts, joists, and fascia, applying an undercoater first. The prefinished Ranch Panels need no further treatment but hardboard should be painted with a good grade of house paint, in a color to suit.

NEW LOOK IN GREENHOUSES

Sturdy, shatterproof, translucent fiberglass panels over an easy-to-build A-frame give you a greenhouse that is attractive as well as practical. The fiberglass panels are available in a wide range of col-

THE GARDEN TOOLHOUSE—UPDATED

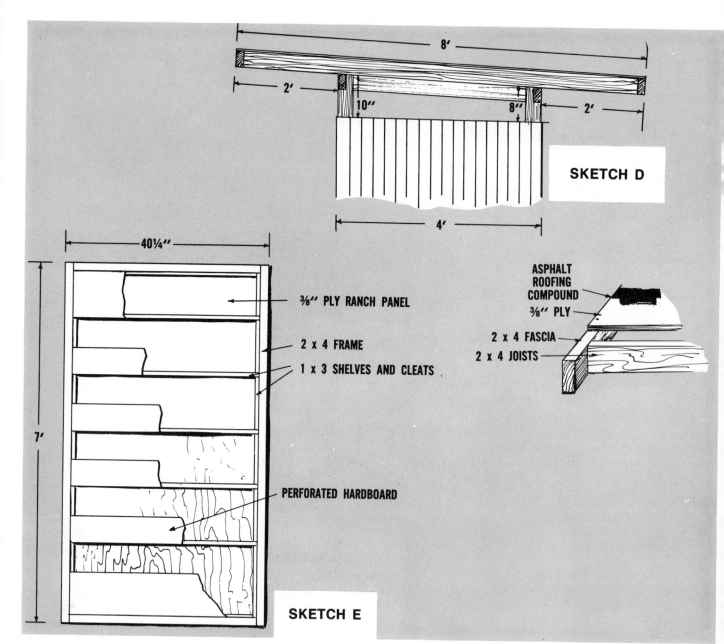

SKETCH D

³⁄₈" PLY RANCH PANEL

2 x 4 FRAME

1 x 3 SHELVES AND CLEATS

PERFORATED HARDBOARD

ASPHALT ROOFING COMPOUND

³⁄₈" PLY

2 x 4 FASCIA

2 x 4 JOISTS

SKETCH E

Door dimensions, including the built-on shelves, are adjusted for snug fit.

ors designed to admit glare-free daylight and diffuse it evenly over the growing area.

Begin building your greenhouse by laying out the dimensions on level ground. Dig two parallel trenches 10″ deep x 12″ wide for the footings. Cut eight 2-by-4 rafters to fit the ridge and the trench and treat the bottom ends of the rafters liberally with Penta solution as protection against decay.

Secure four rafters to one side of the 1-by-10 ridge with 10d nails and fasten bridging between the rafters. Then raise this section into place in the footing trench and support it temporarily with braces to the ground. Next, nail the remaining rafters to the other side of the ridge and fasten bridging between these rafters.

Complete the A-frame by nailing 2-by-4 and 2-

288

his attractive greenhouse is easy to build, using the A-frame principle, and the plastic walls eliminate the former problems that ere present with glass panes.

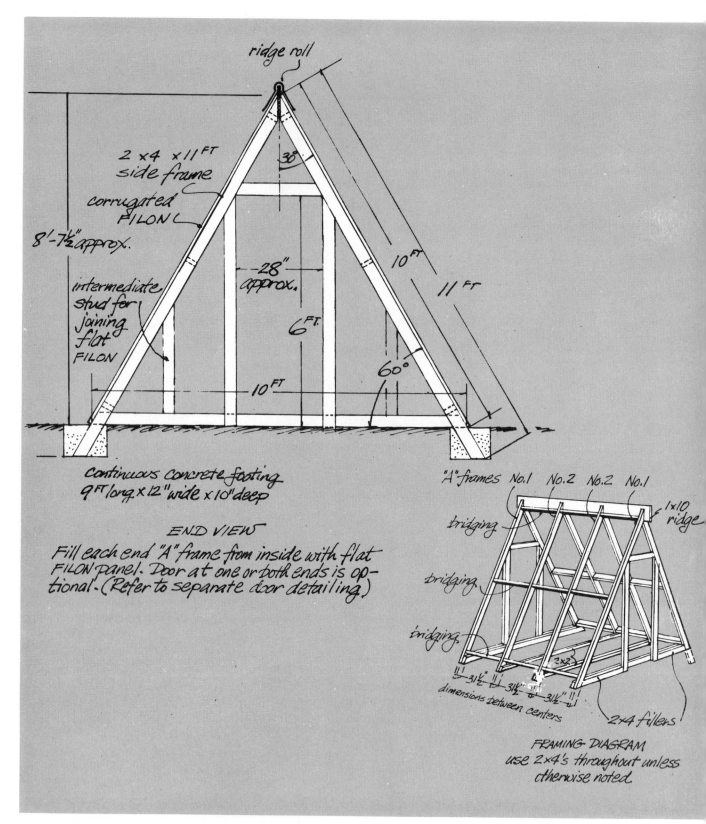

ridge roll

2 x 4 x 11^{FT}
side frame

corrugated
FILON

8'-7½" approx.

intermediate
stud for
joining
flat
FILON

35°

28"
approx.

6^{FT}

10^{FT}

11^{FT}

60°

10^{FT}

Continuous concrete footing
9^{FT} long x 12" wide x 10" deep

END VIEW

Fill each end "A" frame from inside with flat
FILON panel. Door at one or both ends is optional. (Refer to separate door detailing.)

"A" frames   No.1   No.2   No.2   No.1

1x10
ridge

bridging

bridging

bridging

2x2

3½" 3½" 3½"
dimensions between centers

2x4 fillers

FRAMING DIAGRAM
use 2x4's throughout unless
otherwise noted

Construction procedure is clearly indicated in the sketch which shows how A-frame rafters are embedded directly into the concrete footings. Rafters are spaced for standard corrugated plastic sheets.

Pre-assembled section of wall, consisting of four rafters nailed to the ridge board, is raised into position and supported temporarily by braces. Second wall helps support the first.

After frame has been completed and concrete footing has set, apply the corrugated plastic panels. Mastic is spread on overlap of panels for sealing. Use aluminum nails.

by-2 cross braces between opposite rafters as shown in the sketch. Plumb the structure and brace it temporarily, then pour a mixture of water, 1 part cement, 2½ parts sand, and 3 parts gravel into the trench around the rafters; allow it to set thoroughly before removing braces.

Nailing the Plastic

Your greenhouse may have doors at both ends or just at one end, as you prefer, but the framing will be the same in either case. Erect door frame studs and headers and intermediate studs, then nail the 2-by-4 fillers in place. Now begin installation of the corrugated fiberglass side panels, using 34"-wide panels with one corrugation overlap between panels. To ensure a watertight, weatherproof joint, apply nondrying mastic between panels before nailing. Aluminum nails are driven through the panels into the rafters at 12" intervals. After all the side panels are in place, cap the roof with corrugated aluminum ridge roll, specially made to fit the panel corrugations.

Flat fiberglass panels are used on the insides of the front and back of the greenhouse, with openings left for doors and vents. The panels are cut to fit with an ordinary saw. When the end panels are set in place, attach 1-by-2 cleats to the front and back cross braces to provide bottom nailing. The two vents are triangular pieces of flat paneling with 1-by-1 frames and a triangular wood block at the top. Attach the vents to the structure with continuous hinges or butt hinges.

The vents are held shut by bullet catches mounted in blocks on the rafters at each side. Insert a screw eye in the triangular block and use a dowel with a screw hook in one end as a pole to open and close the vents. The pole may be conveniently hung on the stud alongside the door when not in use. A light sash chain is installed to support the vent when open.

Making Doors

Construct the door to fit the dimensions of the opening. Strengthen the corners by rabbeting the top and bottom pieces into the sides and screwing triangular corner braces to the frame. Fasten a 1-by-2 vertical stiffener inside the frame and cover the inside of the door with flat paneling. Attach hinges and hang the door. A hasp on the door also serves as a handle.

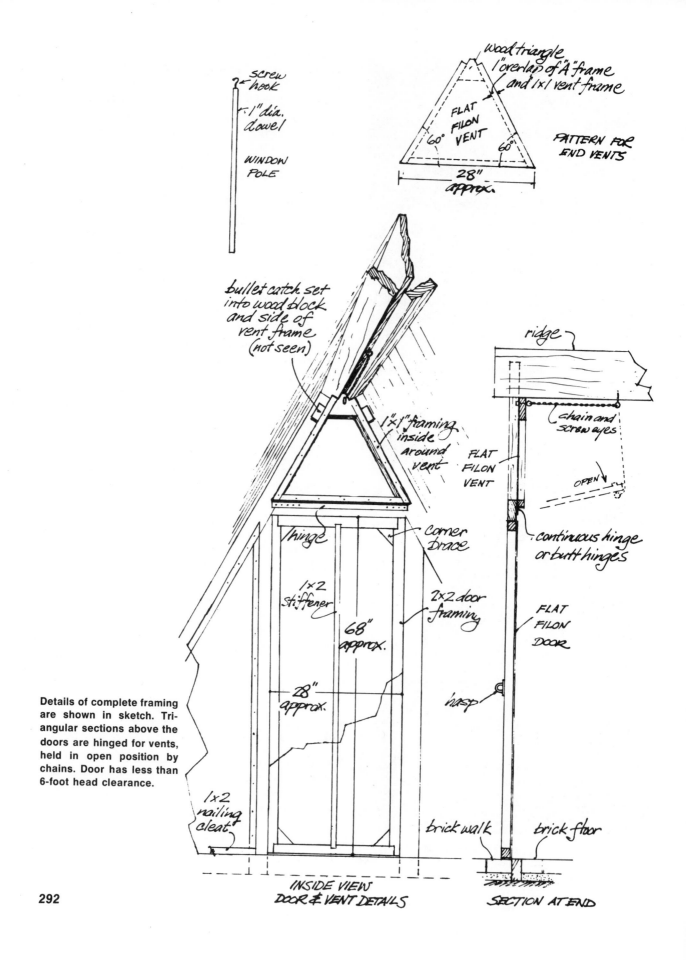

screw
hook

1" dia.
dowel

WINDOW
POLE

wood triangle
1" overlap of "A" frame
and 1x1 vent frame

FLAT
FILON
VENT

60°   60°

28"
approx.

PATTERN FOR
END VENTS

bullet catch set
into wood block
and side of
vent frame
(not seen)

ridge

chain and
screw eyes

OPEN

FLAT
FILON
VENT

1"x1" framing
inside
around
vent

hinge

corner
brace

continuous hinge
or butt hinges

1x2
stiffener

68"
approx.

2x2 door
framing

FLAT
FILON
DOOR

28"
approx.

hasp

**Details of complete framing
are shown in sketch. Tri-
angular sections above the
doors are hinged for vents,
held in open position by
chains. Door has less than
6-foot head clearance.**

1x2
nailing
cleat

brick walk   brick floor

INSIDE VIEW
DOOR & VENT DETAILS

SECTION AT END

292

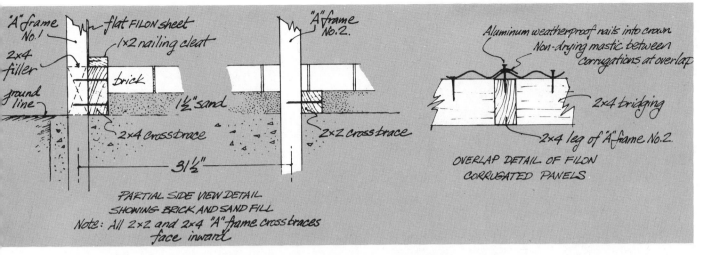

"A" frame No.1 — flat FILON sheet
1x2 nailing cleat
2x4 filler
brick
ground line
1½" sand
2x4 crossbrace
— 31½" —

"A" frame No.2.
2x2 crossbrace

Aluminum weatherproof nails into crown
Non-drying mastic between corrugations at overlap
2x4 bridging
2x4 leg of "A" frame No.2.

OVERLAP DETAIL OF FILON CORRUGATED PANELS

PARTIAL SIDE VIEW DETAIL SHOWING BRICK AND SAND FILL
Note: All 2x2 and 2x4 "A" frame crossbraces face inward.

Bricks are laid on sand for greenhouse floor, flush with height of the 2-by-2 cross braces.

Lay a row of bricks on edge under the bottom bridging along each side to keep sand from seeping out under the paneling. Spread 1½" of sand on the ground inside the greenhouse, leveling it with the tops of the 2-by-2 cross braces. Set bricks on the sand, then spread more sand lightly over the surface and sweep it into the joints between the bricks. This will provide a hard-working, easy-to-maintain floor. Prime all exposed wood and finish with two coats of exterior paint to match or harmonize with the colorful fiberglass.

STORE-ALL GARDEN PERGOLA

Equally adaptable to spacious grounds or a small back yard, this handsome structure is geared to the practicalities of life in the suburbs. It's designed to

A shaded bench for a relaxing chat after a spell of gardening is offered by the pergola which is designed partly on farm building principles.

THE GARDEN TOOLHOUSE—UPDATED

be a center of attraction as well as a center of activity. The storage space is more than ample for gardening tools, outdoor barbecue equipment, and other items, and the attractive slatted benches at the base of the unit are perfect for displaying colorful potted plants. A few seat cushions placed on these benches will quickly turn the structure into a barbecue shed. Although the building materials—plywood and framing lumber—have been used with a free hand to achieve an interesting, oriental

294

Footings are set into concrete, which is allowed to cure for at least three days before starting surface structure.

Posts go up first, then rafters, and the lower seat supports.

design, it is remarkably inexpensive to build.

The roof is an adaptation of a low-cost system originally worked out for farm structures. The plywood on the roof is lapped like giant shingles and left uncovered. The two front storage spaces under the roof are 4' wide and 2' deep. The rear two storage spaces are shallower, just 1' deep, so that you can reach smaller items easily. On the backs of all the doors there is a shelf arrangement which stiffens the panels and provides extra space for smaller knickknacks. All of the framing lumber used is 2-by-4 or 2-by-8, the plywood is all ⅜" thick exterior grade fir.

Building this pergola is an easy job, if the work is taken one step at a time. First, decide in which part of your yard you want the unit. Then, lay off locations for the five concrete footings, taking the dimensions from Fig. 1. The holes for the footings should be dug 18" deep or to frost-line depth, whichever is deeper. Simple scrap-lumber forms built inside the holes will make it easier to level off the tops of the footings. After pouring the footings, embed the steel U-shaped strap iron supports in the wet concrete. A strip of lumber laid across the forms can be used to align the metal supports accurately. When the concrete has thoroughly set up (three to four days), start on the framing, which consists of 2-by-4's bolted together as in Fig. 1.

Surfacing of the Ground Area

The area around the pergola may be filled with gravel if a neat, maintenance-free floor is desired. If this feature is to be included, the work should be performed before the pergola framing has progressed too far, otherwise the area beneath the storage cabinets will not be easily accessible.

The base framing for the storage cabinet section is a grillework of spaced 2-by-4's set on edge along a doubled 2-by-8 beam. This framework extends beyond the cabinet section on either side, forming shelves for potted plants. The ends of the 2-by-8 beams are cut in the decorative pattern shown in the detail sketch. However, they may be cut off square, if preferred.

After fastening the joists to the upright columns, tack a strip of scrap lumber across the joist ends to hold them in place while you toenail the 2-by-4 spacers between them. Next, nail spaced 2-by-4 slats across the joists and across the seating supports below. Join the cabinet ends, dividers, and top with resorcinol type waterproof glue and nails. Build in the shelving as shown in Fig. 3, supporting the front edges of these shelves on 1-by-4's. The double doors for the storage compartments are simply plywood panels framed with 1-by-4's. Hang the doors with strap hinges bolted to the cabinet ends and dividers, using 3 hinges per door, then attach suitable door catches or hasps.

The pergola is roofed with plywood panels lapped at the horizontal joints. Fasten the lower course in place first, nailing through into the joist, then nail on the second course to overlap the first by 4". The butt joints between panel ends are covered with battens. Leave approximately ⅛" space between panel ends, apply mastic roofing com-

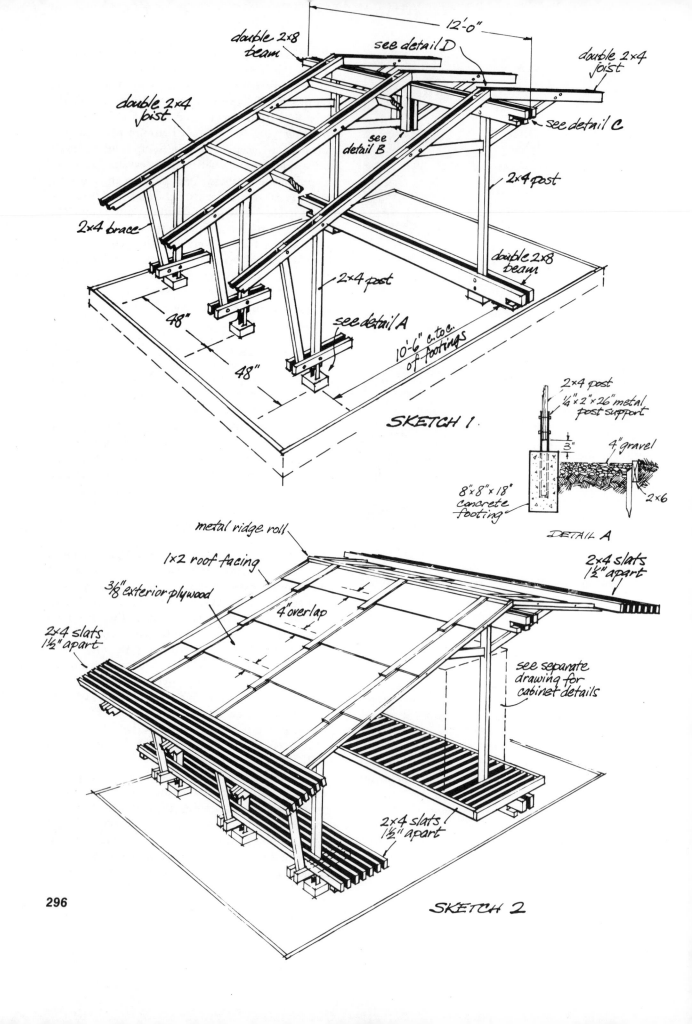

double 2×8 beam

see detail D

12'-0"

double 2×4 joist

double 2×4 joist

see detail C

see detail B

2×4 post

2×4 brace

double 2×8 beam

2×4 post

48"

see detail A

10'-6" c. to c. of footings

48"

SKETCH 1.

2×4 post

¼"×2"×26" metal post support

3"

4" gravel

8"×8"×18" concrete footing

2×6

DETAIL A

metal ridge roll

1×2 roof facing

3/8" exterior plywood

4" overlap

2×4 slats 1½" apart

2×4 slats 1½" apart

see separate drawing for cabinet details

2×4 slats 1½" apart

296

SKETCH 2

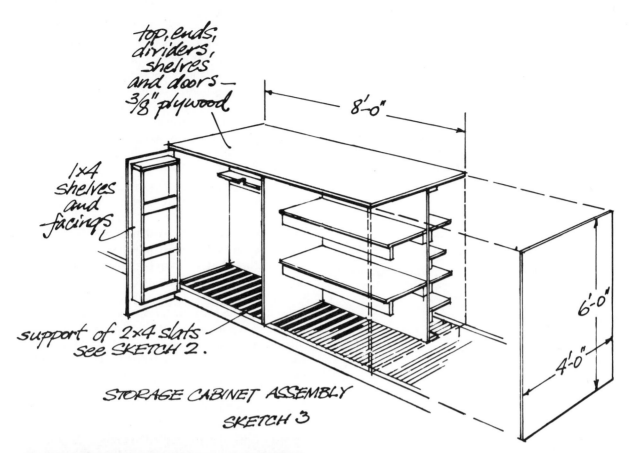

top, ends, dividers, shelves and doors — 3/8" plywood

1x4 shelves and facings

support of 2x4 slats see SKETCH 2.

8'-0"

6'-0"

4'-0"

STORAGE CABINET ASSEMBLY

SKETCH 3

Storage bins and closets are constructed after the framing is completed, followed by roofing panels.

pound to this joint and nail battens cut from 3/8" plywood over this, spacing the nails 4" apart. Use sheet aluminum ridge roll, which can be purchased at any building supply dealer, to cap the roof peak. Complete the roof with 1-by-2 trim strips nailed flat along the edges of the plywood, as shown in Fig. 2.

To protect the finished pergola from dampness and rotting, first apply a wood preservative solu-

tion, such as Penta, to all wood surfaces, then apply two coats of a good grade of exterior paint. An exterior sash and trim enamel may be used on the roof trim or framing members to introduce colorful accents. Daub the metal column supports and all bolt heads with an asphalt-asbestos roof cement to prevent rusting, and the structure is weatherproofed and ready for use.

MATERIALS LIST
Fir Plywood

Quan.	Size	Use
21 panels	3/8" x 4' x 8'	Shelves, cabinets, partitions, doors, roof

Lumber

Quan.	Size	Use
4	2" x 8" x 12'	Beams
6	2" x 4" x 16'	Joists
48	2" x 4" x 8'	Framing
12	1" x 4" x 10'	Shelf framing
6	1" x 2" x 10'	Facing, nailing strips

Hardware & Miscellaneous

Bolts, nails and other fastenings, as required.
Metal U-supports.
Hinges and hasps, as required.
Glue, non-drying mastic, concrete and finishing materials.

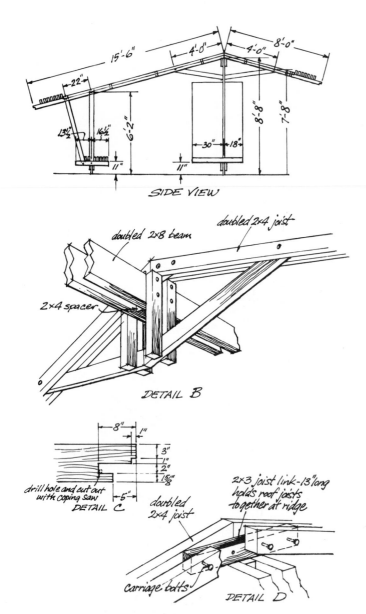

SIDE VIEW

doubled 2x8 beam

doubled 2x4 joist

2x4 spacer

DETAIL B

drill hole and cut out
with coping saw
DETAIL C

doubled
2x4 joist

2x3 joist link-13"long
holds roof joists
together at ridge

Carriage bolts

DETAIL D

TOOLHOUSE ON ALUMINUM FRAME

This garden storage shed is an important adjunct to the home. It provides a place where all sorts of bulky objects may be kept neatly and safely. This plan is based on garden requirements, but the interior may be altered to fit other ideas. A portion of the shed can, for example, solve the minor but annoying problem of where to store unsightly garbage cans. Or, with proper dimensioning, bicycles, sleds, baby carriages, snow blowers, and other bulky objects can be provided for.

While the utility of the structure is beyond question, this particular sample of the breed is of special interest to handymen because it introduces a construction method of combining extruded aluminum framing members with special matching corner fixtures that tie them together into a unitized structure. The openings in the framework are then filled with wood paneling of your choice which you fasten to the ribs of the framing members. Tied together by the panels, the entire structure becomes strong and rigid. Square corners are assured, too, by the fixtures at such joints. Appearance of the finished project is a big dividend, for the aluminum frame is revealed at each joint, providing a handsome setting that surrounds the wood panel like a picture frame. Oiled walnut or teak plywood used for building a desk, let us say, is especially beautiful against the satin finish of the metal.

The extrusions get their strength from their shape, basically an open square. The metal can be cut quickly with a fine toothed hacksaw; a table or radial arm saw will do even better when equipped with a blade designed for nonferrous metal cutting. It is inadvisable to use wood-cutting tools for this material, a fact that may surprise those who have already worked with the commonly available Reynolds Do-It-Yourself Aluminum line. The Reynolds product is quite soft in comparison.

Framing members are cut to length and ends are mitered if the builder is using the ribbed extrusions. Fixtures, with spring-locking clips, are then tapped into place at each end of the channel. When the framework is finished, wood panels are fitted and screwed to the ribs. More sophisticated construction is possible but it takes additional planning and work.

Shed Construction

As with any structure, one must start with a foundation. This shed was built on an existing concrete patio and a stud driver was used to implant anchor bolts to which the base framing members were fastened after cutting them to length and drilling to accommodate the bolts. If you have no concrete floor already available and one is to be poured, you can set anchor bolts in it at that time.

If a floor of gravel or other material is acceptable, the posts could be extended enough to be embedded in individual concrete footings, with the floor placed around them later. Footings should reach frost-line depth. Institutional-size food cans with tops and bottoms removed make convenient

A lean-to storage is the place to conveniently keep the lawn mower, bicycles, wheelbarrow, and other bulky items. This garden house is built by an unusual framing system.

Aluminum channel framework is bolted to concrete base and attached to the house wall at rear with lag screws. Ribbed extrusions are mitered at each end to fit.

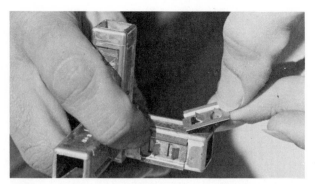

Fixtures fasten the extrusions rigidly together at the corners. Spring clips fit in recesses in each leg of the fixture.

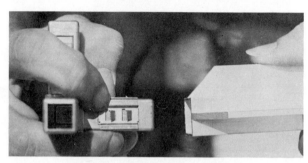

Note the mitered ribs, usually cut with a hacksaw. Channel slips over the fixture and clips. When driven home, the teeth on the clips prevent movement of the channel.

MATERIALS LIST

Aluminum Cutting List

6 Req.	72" long	ALE-16L Vertical
2 Req.	72" long	ALE-21L Vertical
2 Req.	11½" long	ALE-16L Vertical
2 Req.	5½" long	ALE-21L Vertical
2 Req.	5½" long	ALE-28L Vertical
2 Req.	28½" long	ALE-21L Bottom Horiz.
2 Req.	30" long	ALE-16L Door Header Jamb
1 Req.	14" long	ALE-21L Bottom Horiz.
2 Req.	7¾" long	ALE-21L Bottom Horiz.
2 Req.	28½" long	ALE-28L Top Horiz.
1 Req.	14" long	ALE-28L Top Horiz.
2 Req.	7¾" long	ALE-28L Top Horiz.

Plywood Cutting List

2 Req.	28½" x72" x ⅝"	Sides
2 Req.	28½" x 11½" x ⅝"	Top Sides
1 Req.	14" x 72" x ⅝"	Center Panel
2 Req.	7¾" x 72" x ⅝"	End Panel
1 Req.	29⅝" x 85" x ⅝"	Partition
1 Req.	36" x 96" x ⅝"	Roof
2 Req.	5½" x 38½" x ⅝"	Top Panel
1 Req.	5½" x 14" x ⅝"	Top Center Panel
4 Req.	15" x 72¾" x ¾"	Doors
2 Req.	16" x 47" x ⅝"	Shelves
2 Req.	12" x 47" x ⅝"	Shelves

forms in which to pour the concrete. Set the posts in the cans, making sure they are correctly spaced and are plumb as well. Stake them or tie them securely, then pour the mix into the forms. Let the concrete set for a few days before removing the braces. During this time keep the concrete damp with regular sprinkling to assure proper curing.

Insert corner fixtures in each open end of the base members, then erect the uprights. Finally, insert the horizontal members. The builder should carefully note that all framing members are ribbed —a fact that may not be seen due to the scale of the drawing. The ribs provide the surface to which wood panels are later fastened.

After cutting the panels to size, matching holes are drilled in the wood and through the aluminum ribs. The panels are attached with sheet metal

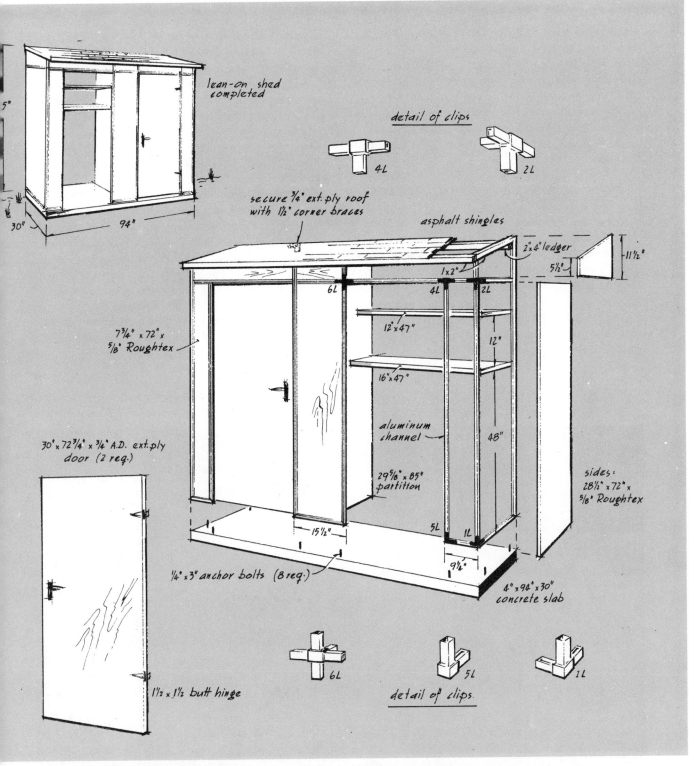

lean-on shed completed

5"

30"   94"

detail of clips

4L   2L

secure ¾" ext. ply roof
with 1½" corner braces

asphalt shingles

2 x 4" ledger

1 x 2"

11½"

5½"

6L   4L   2L

7¾" x 72" x
⅝" Roughtex

12" x 47"

12"

16" x 47"

aluminum
channel

48"

30" x 72¾" x ¾" A.D. ext. ply
door (2 req.)

29⅝" x 85"
partition

sides:
28½" x 72" x
⅝" Roughtex

15½"

5L   1L

¼" x 3" anchor bolts (8 req.)

9¼"

4" x 94" x 30"
concrete slab

1½ x 1½ butt hinge

6L   5L   1L

detail of clips.

Sketch of completed toolhouse reveals basic framework of aluminum channels, over which exterior grade
plywood is fitted into extrusion ribs. Dimensions shown are for example only, are to be modified as needed.

screws. Doors, hung as the final construction step, are ¾″ exterior plywood, grooved at the center to make them look like two narrow pairs. The illusion is enhanced by moldings which simulate the effect of paneling. The panels are painted differently from the surrounding surfaces to accent the idea even further.

The roof, placed before doors are hung, rests on a 1-by-2 and 2-by-4 frame, and is reinforced with angle brackets at back and front, as indicated on the sketch.

HOW TO WATER WITHOUT TEARS

Install an automatic underground sprinkler system and watch the dramatic change take place in your lawn. Day by day, almost visibly, the grass becomes greener, livelier, while weeds get crowded out and give up the battle. No more hour-long toil of watering the lawn—you'll be freed, once and for all, of the boring chore—and your neighbors will cheer the good news, too, as it assures a better landscape for all.

There are many types of sprinkler heads and line systems; all underground layouts use polyethylene plastic hose that is strong, flexible, and unaffected by freezing cold. The sprinkler heads, which normally remain flush with the ground to permit mowing the lawn, pop up when the water pressure is on, and deliver various spray patterns depending on the model, from full circle to controlled arc, and in squares, waves, and rectangles of various distances.

Installation of sprinklers for an average-size lawn can be completed in a day or a weekend. The budget-conscious, who may have thought of this convenience as "one of the last things" on the list of home improvements, are in for a pleasant surprise: a first-rate system that is particularly suited to do-it-yourself installation, involves only a modest outlay.

The cost will depend largely on the size of lawn to be covered, because that affects the number of sprinkler heads and fittings. Another cost factor is the automatic timer and the distribution controls that make the most of your available water pressure by alternating the timing of sprinklers in various

lawn sections. These are most ingenious and effective devices which make the lawn watering completely automatic, lifting the burden completely out of your hands. But the timer installation can be postponed if desired, for economy's sake, leaving the lawn chore one of merely opening and closing the faucet at desired times.

One very important detail that must not be overlooked is an antisiphon valve, or some type of vacuum-breaker, between the house water connection and the sprinkler system. The purpose is to prevent siphoning any water that stands in the plastic hose back into the house water system in the event of pressure drop. Most local plumbing codes require such a protective valve to prevent contamination, and you should make sure to put one in for your own protection, even if your sprinkler system is provided with drain fittings designed to empty any remaining water from the lines after the pressure stops. There always is the possibility that some of the tubing is not pitched on grade, so that water remains that may be siphoned back. There are various types of vacuum breakers, most of which are of simple but effective design, and cost very little.

A graph map of the grounds helps to lay out the sprinkler locations. First step in the installation is to drive marker stakes at these locations, then lay out the plastic hose along the path that will be followed, keeping the curves as gentle as possible to avoid reduction in nozzle pressure. Where necessary, however, elbow fittings can be placed into the lines.

A V-shaped slit for the pipe is cut into the earth with a flat-bladed spade, which avoids permanent damage to the lawn. This is done by working the spade down with the weight of a foot, then rocking it back and forth. The trench should be about 8" or 9" below grade. The pipe is laid in the trench, tamped down with a piece of 1-by-4 lumber, then the turf is closed, by the common method of stomping. With subsequent regular watering, the lawn will recover in a short period, sometimes less than a week, if the trenches are cut properly.

The actual cutting, fitting, and installation of the pipe and sprinkler heads are illustrated in the series of photographs.

Slit trenches for sprinkler pipe are cut with straight spade which is pressed in to the hilt, then rocked back and forth to open a vee-shaped cut.

With pipe in place, trench is closed by stomping edges together. Hardly a trace of the trench then can be seen.

Pipe is dropped into the trench, forced to the bottom with a length of 1-by-4 lumber. Don't worry about damaging the pipe; it's strong.

A tunnel has to be dug when pipe is to go below a walk. Remove sod and earth carefully so they can be replaced later.

Dig tunnel with spade from both ends. If tunnel is long, a steel pipe can be hammered through.

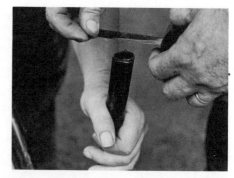

Before pushing pipe through tunnel, seal the open end with vinyl tape to prevent dirt and gravel from clogging.

Push pipe through the excavated tunnel to the other side of walk. Note depth of the excavation, about 6 inches.

Finished section before backfilling. Here plastic pipe goes through a piece of larger steel pipe which had been hammered through under concrete walk.

Digging is easier when the turf has been watered. This is done the old way—hosing down by hand.

At sprinkler heads with drain fittings that empty the water lines, dry wells are needed to absorb the excess water. Dig a hole 12 inches wide and the same deep. Fill with coarse gravel.

Wave sprinkler throws a fan of water over a large area in an adjustable rectangular pattern.

Tape covers the orifice of the wave sprinkler until it is installed, to keep dirt and sand from clogging it.

Another type of sprinkler head throws a moving stream of water. It can be set to sweep a complete circle or limited to a small arc.

Adjustment of sprinkler range is made with wrench after the cap is removed. Several tries may be needed to get it right.

Sprinkler head pops up when water pressure is applied. This one sprays in a fixed fan-like area.

To attach piping to sprinkler heads, slide a clamp onto the pipe, push pipe onto a head fitting from both sides.

Clamps are automotive type of stainless steel. Tighten with wrench or screwdriver.

Control box for the four sub-systems. White pegs in clock face turn system on as clock moves.

Controller box mounted indoors on wall. Fittings at bottom are for thin tubing that connects to the outdoor control valves.

Complex containing individual line connections is made up of tees joined with pipe nipples, and faucet adapter fitting.

Valve system in place, with faucet shutoff. Note the control tubes leading into the inside clock box.

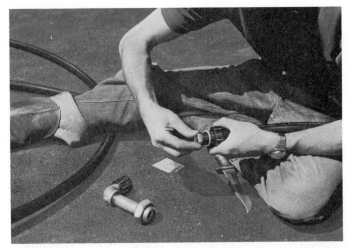

Some types of sprinkler pipe are connected with threaded fittings rather than band clamps. Nut is placed on hose, followed by O-ring, and then brass expander bushing is pressed into the pipe opening.

A water feeder line assembly which includes an antisiphon valve, required by some local plumbing codes. The assembly includes a faucet fitting to which the sprinkler lines are connected.

Tee fitting inserted into line by turning the nuts on both pipe ends on the tee threads. The bushing expands the pipe as the nut is tightened, for watertight seal.

Chapter 10
GOOD FENCES

A colorful, easy-to-build border fence that gives you just the right amount of privacy.

Some still think that a fence is a fence is a fence. Not so today's bright homemaker, who sees the multiple values of various fence designs and utilizes what she can as a picture frame for the house, a protective playpen for tots and a boundary line for older youngsters, a barrier for the swimming pool, a windbreak and privacy screen for tranquil afternoons on the lawn, a background for patio parties. The fence may even be a storage wall, a screen against the sun, or function as a garden toolshed as described later in this chapter.

Here is an array of fences—the designs and applications, together with the necessary "how-to" so you can go to it whenever you wish with assured results. One or more of them may be just what you've had in mind for a particular purpose; other fence ideas may prompt you to develop your own adaptation to improve the back yard scenery. With the basic details and techniques described herein, you can put those ideas into finished form at last, quickly and inexpensively.

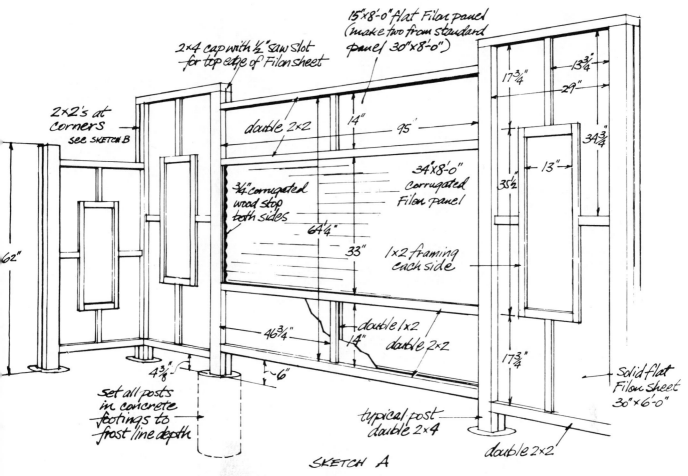

SKETCH A

Labels on Sketch A:

- 2×2's at corners see sketch B
- 62"
- 2×4 cap with ½" saw slot for top edge of Filon sheet
- 15"×8'-0" Flat Filon panel (make two from standard panel 30"×8'-0")
- double 2×2
- 14"
- 95'
- ¾" corrugated wood stop both sides
- 34"×8'-0" corrugated Filon panel
- 6¼"
- 33"
- 1×2 framing each side
- 17¾"
- 13¾"
- 29"
- 34¾"
- 13"
- 35½"
- 46¾"
- double 1×2
- 14"
- double 2×2
- 17¾"
- 4⅜"
- 6"
- set all posts in concrete footings to frost line depth
- typical post double 2×4
- double 2×2
- Solid flat Filon sheet 30"×6'-0"

A colorful border fence that stands on its good looks, provides just the right amount of privacy.

PLASTIC PANEL FENCE

Fencing in your back yard or patio for outdoor privacy can pose a ticklish problem—that is, if you don't wish to appear to be a recluse particularly unfriendly to your neighbors. The best way to overcome this impression and still have your privacy is to build a fence that both you and your neighbors will admire and consider an asset to the surrounding properties.

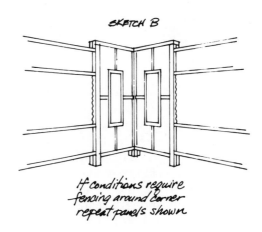

SKETCH B

If conditions require fencing around corner repeat panels shown

GOOD FENCES

Cut plastic sheet to size.

Paint lumber with Penta.   **Plumb posts.**   **Fill hole with concrete.**

Slip plastic into grooves.   **Toenail horizontal 2x4s.**   **Work upwards with panels.**

The fence shown here is designed to do just that. It consists of a series of translucent flat and corrugated plastic sheets set into a grooved supporting framework. Light passing through these plastic panels creates a soft, colorful glow that is bound to add a cheerful note to all of your outdoor activities.

All lumber used in the fence should be treated to prevent rotting by painting liberally with a wood preservative solution such as Penta. Begin the construction by setting all of the upright 2-by-4 posts into footings that extend to frost-line depth (about 24″ below the ground surface, in most areas). Each pair of 2-by-4's comprising a post should be spaced $\frac{1}{16}$″ apart with scrap pieces of plastic placed at the top and bottom, to allow space for the insertion of plastic panels, later. Check the post with a plumb line or level to make sure it is perfectly vertical and secure it in this position with a few rocks before you pour the concrete into the footing excavation.

After all of the posts are in place and the concrete has set (allow two to three days for curing), the horizontal 2-by-4 framing members may be nailed to the posts. Use a table saw to groove all of these 2-by-4's to a depth of ½", then toenail into place starting with the lowest member and inserting the plastic sheets as you proceed to the top (see photos). The corrugated plastic panels should be fitted into the saw grooves at the top and bottom, and secured at the ends with the special corrugated wood strips that are made for this purpose. The flat

plastic sheets are subdivided into smaller panel designs by toenailing 1-by-2 strips between the main members on both sides of the plastic sheet, as illustrated in sketch A.

The fence can be terminated with a smaller panel, or it may be continued around the corner with the same design repeated as shown in sketch B. You can paint the framing lumber before, or after, its final assembly. However, if the lumber is to be prepainted, do this before the grooves are cut, otherwise the paint may clog the grooves and make insertion of the plastic panels a difficult job.

Trim holds corrugated end.

The top sheet goes in last.

Place last of the 2x4s.

Proceed to next panel.

2x4 caps vertical panels.

Nail on dividing strips.

Woven fence erected in offset panels adds depth and interest to backyard garden. Fencing consists of plastic webbing woven into wire mesh, which is stretched tightly between the supporting posts.

WEAVE A PRIVACY FENCE

The sturdiness and durability of steel chain link fences were somewhat offset by their lack of esthetic appeal, until imaginative home owners found a way to overcome the objectionable metallic look by inserting strips of canvas webbing into the wire mesh. Here's another idea that combines many of the qualities in that kind of arrangement—this is a fence that you can build yourself with long-lasting vinyl strips woven into wire mesh held in attractive wood frames.

The fence can be built in sections consisting of double 2-by-4's for the posts, galvanized or vinyl-coated wire mesh ("hardware cloth" with mesh openings large enough to accept your vinyl webbing, which is usually 2" wide, and 2-by-4 cross members at the top). As the posts will be placed into the ground about 18", the 2-by-4's can be standard 8' lengths, leaving an open aboveground space. Decide on the width of your fence panels, which should be no more than 6'. You can, with the latter size as an example, make a 12' length of fence, or one of 4' multiples in this manner:

Lay out the hardware cloth on the ground and cut off a 12' length. Start weaving the vinyl strips in and out of the mesh, alternating the start of each course over or under the end wires. Each strip end is folded over the wire about ½" and fastened in place with a rivet.

Now the wire ends are placed between the double 2-by-4 post members, which are bolted tightly together to hold the wire. A slot cut partway into one of the 2-by-4's will make a neater job of attaching the wire links; the slotted surface is on the inside of the doubled 2-by-4 faces, thus the wire ends are neatly covered.

A center post is fastened in place, one 2-by-4 on each side of the woven fencing, the two parts drawn tightly together with machine bolts, then the end posts are put on in the same way, but the ends of the wire cloth are inserted into the ¼" slots before the bolts are tightened.

The critical part of the project is to spread the end posts for maximum spacing, on each side of the center post, using lengths of 2-by-4 as spacers. Do this by setting the spacers into the bottom opening at an angle, one end down to the level of the woven wire cloth, then tapping the other end with a small sledge until the wire cloth is stretched taut.

The fence section can now be raised so that the post ends drop into their prepared holes. After they

Using half-inch overlap, secure strip end with rivet; measure and cut length of strip.

Vinyl strip may be woven in any pattern. Shown here, an over-and-under design.

Two 2x4s make up end post; one is slotted as shown.

Bolt end post together and insert fence in slot; drive nails at midpoint of post.

Position center post at equal distance from end posts; nail and bolt the 2x4s together.

Wedge spacers between posts to assure tautness during installation; remove them later.

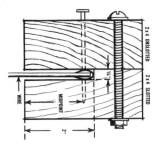

are aligned plumb and true, the posts are temporarily braced while the holes are backfilled and tamped. Better still, fill the holes with concrete to hold the posts more solidly. A 2-by-4 goes across the top, nailed to the ends of the side and center posts.

If the posts are redwood or cedar, they can receive a protective coating of special varnish after the fence is completed, but ordinary 2-by-4's should be fully painted before assembly.

FOR SHADE AND PRIVACY

Portability, practicality, personality, are the qualities that describe these privacy screens, designed for greater enjoyment of outdoor living.

The panel screens roll about on four swiveling casters. Caster size is determined largely by the surface where the screens are to be used. On smooth concrete, small casters will do, but larger ones will be needed for easy rolling on lawns. The base of the planter box should be cut from marine-grade plywood. Drainage holes are necessary to provide an outlet for water from plants or rainfall. Drill ¼" holes on 4" centers for this purpose.

Assemble the base first, then attach casters below. Apply a good grade of lubricating oil to them at once to prevent rust, or the screens will be difficult to move.

Build the upright frame last; attach it to the base. The back of each frame is covered with three strips of canvas, hemmed wide enough at both ends to pass the pipes that support the strips.

Before applying the canvas, paint all wood surfaces with exterior trim paint, using a color that will complement or contrast with the canvas.

To provide a steadying weight at the base, fill each planter box with a 1½" layer of gravel. Set potted plants into the base.

Three screens can be used together in a number of attractive designs. When set in a zigzag the broken line of the tops makes a pleasing composition, set off further by the canvas colors. In another arrangement, the screens are butted against one another to form a cozy nook.

This outdoor room divider is practical and easily moved. Build one or more —as many as you need. Vary the size to suit your own desires but keep the dimensions in proportion to those given in the sketch.

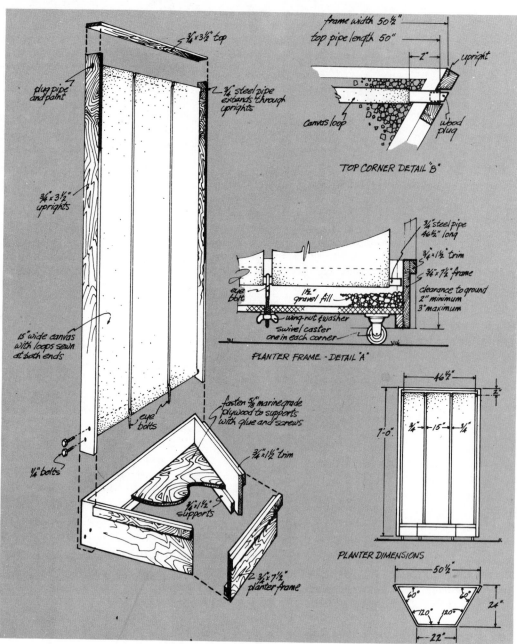

3/4 x 3 1/2" top

plug pipe and paint

3/4" steel pipe extends through uprights

3/4 x 3 1/2" uprights

15" wide canvas with loops sewn at both ends

eye bolts

1/4" bolts

frame width 50 1/2"
top pipe length 50"

2"

upright

canvas loop

wood plug

TOP CORNER DETAIL "B"

3/4" steel pipe 46 1/2" long

3/4 x 1 1/2" trim

3/4 x 7 1/2" frame

clearance to ground 2" minimum 3" maximum

eye bolt

1 1/2" gravel fill

wing nut & washer
swivel caster one in each corner

PLANTER FRAME - DETAIL "A"

fasten 5/8" marine grade plywood to supports with glue and screws

3/4 x 1 1/2" trim

3/4 x 1 1/2" supports

2 3/4 x 7 1/2" planter frame

46 1/2"

2"

7'-0"

3/4" — 15" — 3/4"

PLANTER DIMENSIONS

50 1/2"

60°   60°

120° 120°

24"

22"

FILIGREE PORTABLE WINDSCREEN

If you've ever wished the wind would stop blowing and let you enjoy your patio, join the club. There is something you can do to improve the situation, however. You don't need to completely enclose the patio either. Just build a set of portable windscreens and keep the weather outside.

These windscreens are made with individual lightweight panels of ¼" or 5/16" exterior plywood or ¼" tempered hardboard. The panels are drilled and bolted to standards of ¾" thin-wall conduit with three ¼" x 1½" screws. The standards are inserted into sockets driven into the ground at intervals around your patio. The sockets are also made of thin-wall conduit but are 18" long and 1" in diameter. Four sections of windscreen give you plenty of protection for reading the newspaper, sunbathing etc. Six sections should screen you and all the troops, too.

Comfortable relaxing out in the open is assisted by open-work panels that subdue the air currents.

Windscreen panels are cut from a sheet of ¼" plywood. Cutting was done with an electric jigsaw. Piece of plywood clamped to 4-by-8 sheet serves as straightedge guide for jigsaw which was also used to cut holes in panels.

The windscreen panels can be painted any color you like. Use a good grade of exterior paint that dries rapidly. A long-handled paint roller will make the finishing job much easier.

With portable windscreens you can move the protection around to where it's needed. In half a minute you can switch your windscreen to another side of the patio or porch.

The whole setup can be made in an afternoon. Finish bright or somber to suit your personality. If you like, you can cut holes out of the panels to lighten them and let a faint breeze through. A solid panel puts more stress on its tubing in a high wind than a perforated panel does. But don't leave them upright when strong winds are blowing.

During the off-season your set of portable windscreens can be stored in a few-inch-high area above the garage door. Disassembled, the screens take up even less space.

When selecting the material for windscreens, see what your building materials dealer has to offer. Look at medium density overlay exterior plywood

Sockets for the windscreen are made of one-inch thin-wall conduit, 18 inches long. They are driven into the ground with a heavy hammer and a block of wood to protect the top of the conduit. A carpenter's level is used to keep the socket straight as it is driven down.

With enough sockets around the perimeter of the patio, screens can be moved as the wind changes.

or any DFPA 303 textured exterior plywood siding. Don't, however, get materials that are intended for interior use only.

Finish your windscreen panels with stain or seal and paint them with exterior trim enamel.

FENCE INTO STORAGE WALL

Unless you are blessed with a toolshed or an oversize garage, the chances are good that you need a place in which to store your garden and outdoor equipment. Such labor savers as a power mower, lawn sweeper, snowthrower, and spreader, not to mention all the hand tools one tends to accumulate, unfortunately are bulky and get in the way. Then, too, if you are a garden enthusiast, you need space for potting, flats, fertilizers, and all the other supplies. Portable barbecues, ever more popular, are also large and demanding of storage space.

The storage arrangement shown here is notable for its versatility. It makes use of an existing fence as a sort of foundation. Each section of the structure can be made into a complete unit in itself, or you can build them in any combination you want.

Plan the interior arrangements in accordance with your special requirements. The combination illustrated will suit most needs, however.

Of special interest is the half-partition between the two sections at the left. This allows a lawn mower to be rolled in through the left side door. The lower part of the mower moves through the opening into the second closet, while the handle, which angles back toward the door, remains in the end section. The half-wall provides additional space for shelves, hooks, or other conveniences.

Each of the doors is constructed to provide rough shelf space for small garden implements, packaged insecticides and other chemicals, sprayers, and similar gardening requirements.

General Construction Details

Because the fence is utilized as the rear wall, our storage units match its height but can be made to any other dimension. Nor is there anything to prevent building the structure as a free-standing, completely independent unit.

Height is, therefore, a matter you must determine for yourself but it is suggested that it be kept to a minimum of 5½'. The cabinets are modular, each being 3' wide and 3' from front to back, but these dimensions need not be followed exactly.

The fence in the photo is made of 1-by-8 boards spaced approximately 1" apart, and the storage units match. This style of construction is not weatherproof and is therefore suited only to areas where winters are very mild. In other parts of the country, complete enclosure is desirable. There are several ways to accomplish this. In the case of our model, should you want to duplicate it exactly, the doors and all exterior faces can be lined with ⅛"

Storage of bulky garden equipment is solved with a storage shed built at an extension of an existing fence.

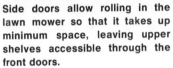

Side doors allow rolling in the lawn mower so that it takes up minimum space, leaving upper shelves accessible through the front doors.

This style of construction offers major advantages, since the spaces between the wallboards allow the shelves to be fitted at any level, changed with minimum fuss.

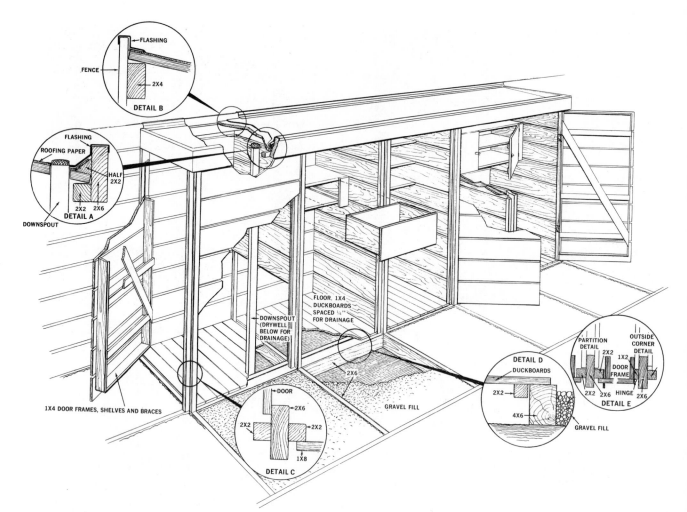

FLASHING

FENCE

2X4

DETAIL B

FLASHING

ROOFING PAPER

HALF 2X2

DOWNSPOUT

2X2 2X6

DETAIL A

FLOOR, 1X4 DUCKBOARDS SPACED ¼'' FOR DRAINAGE

DOWNSPOUT (DRYWELL BELOW FOR DRAINAGE)

2X6

GRAVEL FILL

1X4 DOOR FRAMES, SHELVES AND BRACES

DOOR

2X6

2X2

2X2

1X8

DETAIL C

DETAIL D DUCKBOARDS

2X2

4X6

GRAVEL FILL

PARTITION DETAIL

OUTSIDE CORNER DETAIL

2X2

1X2 DOOR FRAME

2X2 2X6 HINGE 2X6

DETAIL E

Sketch shows how fence is utilized as the back wall of the ''add on'' storage shed. Walls of the storage section should be same material as the fence.

tempered hardboard. Another solution, requiring less fitting and smaller amounts of material, would be to simply butt together all the face boards, omitting the spaces between them. The roof, on the other hand, is fully weatherproof and a drain has been provided to carry off rainfall (see detail A).

Before anything else, locate the place where the downspout will be located and prepare a drywell in the earth at this point large enough to handle the runoff. An old steel drum, punched full of holes and with its top and bottom sliced off, is most convenient. Dig a hole large enough to contain the drum, and deep enough so that the upper end of

the drum is at least one foot below grade. Fill with large rocks or very coarse gravel. Do not backfill until the downspout is in place.

For the structural members that come in contact with the earth, use lumber which has been pressure-treated to resist decay and termite damage. We used some of the western woods throughout. These include such varieties as Douglas fir, western red cedar, ponderosa pine, and many others.

To carry out the theme of the project, its finish should match that of the existing fence. Be sure to thoroughly seal the wood, using primers if the finish coats require them.

320

Interesting patterns in concrete blocks allow construction of attractive screenwalls that produce striking effects while screening the garden from passersby.

BUILDING A MASONRY SCREEN WALL

Concrete blocks have come a long way from their original plebeian appearance and purpose. They're available now in many shapes and patterns that can be put together for striking effects. One example is a decorative screen wall that assures utmost privacy, while allowing ample air movement and enhancing the architectural lines of the home.

You don't have to be a stonemason, but you must have some knowledge of masonry to put up an acceptable screen wall like the one illustrated, which consists of blocks in fleur-de-lis pattern.

The construction steps are clearly indicated by the illustrations, which show a wall being erected on an existing concrete slab. Instead of the slab, the wall may be built also on a concrete footing, placed into an excavated trench that extends below the frost line and provides a base that is twice the thickness of the wall—in other words, if the wall is made of 4″ blocks, the footing must be 8″ wide. Walls on concrete slabs are based on trim blocks recessed into the slab and set in mortar. Be sure your wall is plumb throughout, reinforced as shown with steel end posts, so that it is solid and secure, and never in danger of toppling.

To install wall braces, score slab ½″ deep with cold chisel or masonry saw. Break through and remove concrete within scored area with crowbar and sledgehammer.

Set bottom trim blocks and mortar them in place. Be sure they are absolutely level, or you will have trouble later on.

Next, set steel post in hole to proper depth. Plumb with level and tamp down gravel around base of the post.

The steel post, which is a conventional U-shaped channel, is later tied to horizontal reinforcing bars laid between courses. Fill the post hole with concrete, making sure post remains plumb.

End-cap blocks, U-shaped, add a nice finishing touch, although not essential. They also disguise any unevenness in the end row, if it should happen.

Reinforcing bar goes in the open area which is then filled with concrete to strengthen the wall.

With a level base and vertical end post to start you, the rest should be easy.

A taut, level string is the best guide you can use to position the concrete blocks properly.

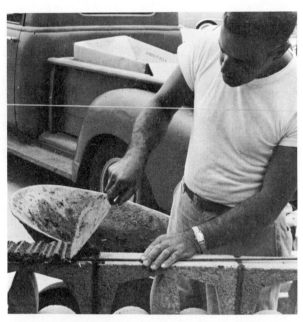

Horizontal reinforcing bar is laid atop course and mortared. Be sure wire ties to vertical steel post are attached to the horizontal bar before you trowel mortar over the rod.

Trim the top with same blocks used as a base. Check level constantly.

When mortar has set a bit, joints may be pointed. Clean away excess mortar with a wire brush.

Wheelbarrow is, of course, the most convenient place to mix mortar. A standard mix: 1 part Portland cement, 10% lime, and 2½ parts sand. Wet blocks before buttering.

Chapter 11

OUTDOOR GAMES FOR EVERYONE

Light from pole-mounted lamps permit night games, extending the possibilities for adult participation.

One way to enjoy sports is to sit in front of a television set and watch the players go through their paces. It's lots more fun, though, playing tennis, pitching horseshoes, swinging a golf club to sharpen your game, tossing a volleyball. The real nature of sports is in teaming up, striving to beat the opponent, aiming for top score—and joining in the laughter.

Having these sports facilities in your own back yard is the greatest incentive for continued participation. These games are sure to appeal to every mem-

ber of the family. And, as it has been said frequently the family that plays together stays together.

You don't need a huge estate to enjoy your own sports arena. Put up a basketball backboard on the peak above the garage door and you'll practice shooting the basket every chance you get. And if the area at the garage entrance is wide enough, you can make it into a half court to increase the fun.

Any 10′ strip of land, even the area between houses, can serve as a horseshoe court, but watch out for those wild pitches! Even less space is needed for a shuffleboard deck, but that requires a paved area—possibly part of the driveway will do (or you can put in a blacktop strip at very little cost).

Many of the games can be enjoyed after dark if good lighting is provided. Spot and floodlight fixtures can be mounted on trees or buildings, or poles erected for the purpose, but make certain the electrical components are all-weather construction, suitable for outdoor use.

HORSESHOES

Pitching horseshoes is a classic American game. We can imagine the early pioneers playing it as a welcome diversion from the hard toil of carving homes and farms from the harsh wilderness.

An official horeshoe court measures 10' wide by 50' long (40' for women's and boys' courts). Two feet in from each end is a 6' square pit. Excavate this area to a depth of 6½" to 7". Frame the pit with a square structure of 2-by-8's that have been treated with a preservative. The tops of the 2-by-8's are protected from near misses by ¼" strap iron, which also helps keep the frame in square.

With the frame in place (leveled and protruding 1" or less above grade), the area within is filled with potter's clay, or a mixture of clay and sand. The stake is a hardwood dowel or steel pipe, 36" long, driven into the exact center of the pit and protruding 10" above the top of the frame. The stake is slanted approximately 2" forward toward the opposite end of the court.

BASKETBALL

While a hard-surfaced court is desirable for basketball, many of the game's greats learned the fundamentals by shooting at a hoop hung on a tree in the middle of a field, or on the side of a barn or garage. Ideally, a concrete or asphalt playing surface should be provided (perhaps a widened driveway). But a level grassy area can also serve as a court (although dribbling becomes a bit more tricky). Overall court dimensions are quite flexible. Even some college gymnasiums have courts as small as 35'-by-60' (meaning 35'-by-30' for half-court games). So take advantage of as much—or as little—space as you have available.

Metal hoops and nets may be purchased at any sporting goods store today. An outdoor backboard can be cut from ¾" marine-grade plywood. This should be primed and painted before being hung. Make sure that the edges of the plywood are thoroughly protected by paint. Securely bolt the hoop to the backboard.

The backboard may be affixed to a garage or other building, or even to a tree if there are no long-hanging limbs to interfere with the arc of a long set shot. Or it may be mounted on a post (4-by-4 lumber or 1½" steel pipe) set into concrete.

If you are fortunate enough to have a hard-surfaced area for your court, you can make boundaries foul lines, keyholes, and so forth, with oil-base or varnish-base paint. Now all that is left is to sharpen that old eye.

An old-time American backyard game is pitching horseshoes. The dimensions given here are for an official court, but if space doesn't allow it, simply build a target area as described in the text and play your game from any convenient distance.

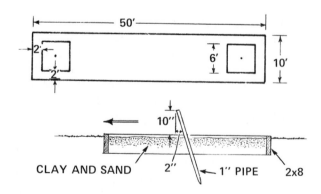

CLAY AND SAND   2"   1" PIPE   2x8

A basketball court may be concrete or asphalt, and the dimensions may be as small as 35 × 60 feet (or 35 × 30 for a half-court). For less formality, the backboard and basket may be constructed in any reasonably level open ground just for practice shots or general fun.

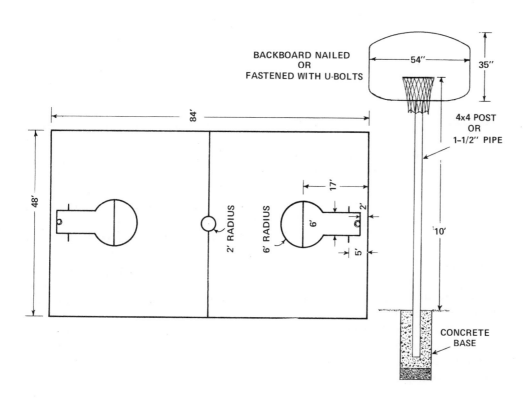

HANDBALL

Handball originated in Ireland in the tenth century and is still a favorite game on the Emerald Isle. It was introduced into the United States by Phil Casey, a handball star who emigrated to Brooklyn some time around 1882 and became world champion until his retirement from the sport in 1900. While the original game and many of the indoor games played today are of the four-wall variety, the one-wall version of this popular sport is most common for outdoor play.

Only the true devotee will build a regulation 16′ high wall of concrete or wood in his yard. But if you have a reasonably flat-walled, windowless structure available (the side of your stucco or concrete-block house or garage, for example), it may serve as your handball wall—even though you may have to sacrifice some of the height. Such a setup often combines well with a back yard basketball court.

The dimensions given in the drawing are for a regulation handball court, but these can, of course, be adapted to fit available space. Handball requires a hard-surfaced court, so you will need a concrete or asphalt playing surface. Often, a patio can serve as a part-time handball court. Such an area may also accommodate games such as shuffleboard.

Not many homeowners will go the the trouble of building a 16-foot high backstop for handball. If you do, be sure to provide adequate bracing, to prevent its being blown over by strong winds. It is suggested that several 4×4s be used for this.

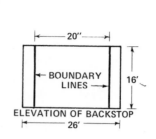

ELEVATION OF BACKSTOP

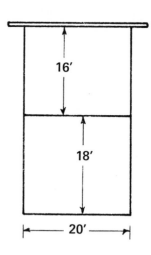

SHUFFLEBOARD

This game attained its peak of popularity during the era of leisurely and luxurious transoceanic steamer travel. The spacious decks of the mighty liners provided ideal playing "fields" for the game. A smooth concrete surface will serve the same purpose. If you have a reasonably level driveway, it will probably do.

If you are starting from scratch to build your shuffleboard court, select a well-drained, level site. Strip the area of all sod down to uniformly level ground—at least 9″ in depth. Fill the excavation with 4″ of cinders or gravel and tamp until firm. Over this base, pour 3″ of concrete and, as soon as it begins to set, cover this with reinforcing wire. Immediately pour a 2″ finish surface (1 part cement

to 2 parts sand) and smooth it to grade as carefully as possible.

Since a smooth surface with no expansion joints is desired, curing is most important. The new concrete should be kept continually wet for at least a week. After it has begun to cure, it may be covered with burlap, frequently wet down to retain moisture. When curing has been completed, the court should be allowed to dry for an additional week before the lines are painted on and play is begun.

You can use this time to make playing cues and disks of hardwood. One-inch dowels are used for cue handles. These are tapered at the end to fit into holes drilled into the ¾″ crescent-shaped heads, where they are glued in place. Both cues and disks should be finished with a good grade of varnish before use.

Shuffleboard is a delightful game that has its strongest appeal to young children and grandparents. A court may be laid out on an existing driveway, or may even be painted on a basement recreation room floor.

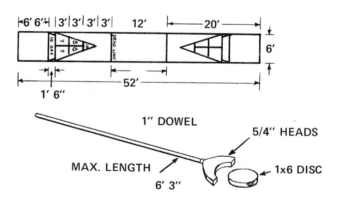

PUTTING GREEN

If you are a devotee of this grand old game of the Scots, why not build a practice green right in your own back yard? Main requirements are a smooth (but not necessarily level) stretch of ground —and a very green thumb.

Creeping bentgrass is generally recommended for a putting green. Cultivation and maintenance of this variety is quite difficult, but the reward— measured in strokes chopped off your golf score— may be well worth the effort of being your own greenskeeper.

For a cup, you can simply sink a 1-pound coffee can just below the level of the ground, after punching several holes into the bottom to allow drainage. Its dimensions are slightly under the regulation 4¼″ diameter x 6″ deep cup, but this will help you to sharpen your putting eye, and make you that much more of a terror on the full-sized golf course. The coffee-can cup should last a full season before rusting away, and it can easily be replaced when necessary.

Of course, if your golf game is such that you require a flag to help you zero in on your putt, you will need a more elaborate cup. Your local sporting goods store or pro shop should be able to supply you with one.

BADMINTON

Badminton is a descendant of the games of battledore and shuttlecock, which have been played in China, India, and other countries of the Far East for at least 2,000 years. It takes its modern name from Badminton, Gloucestershire, the country home of the Duke of Beaufort, where it was played by Victorian gentlemen and the more daring of their ladies.

A badminton court can be set up on any level lawn area without special preparation. Since only volley shots are played, there is no need for a fine, closely cropped turf. Rather, a hardy, rough-stock meadowgrass or meadow fescue is preferred to stand up to the hard pounding it will take from active players.

Net posts may simply be driven into the ground and braced with guy ropes attached to stakes in the ground. You may wish to make a more sturdy and permanent installation by implanting a galvanized-pipe socket in the ground into which the net posts can be placed. Diameter of the socket should be slightly larger than the net posts. The socket should be set at least 14″ into the ground. Use a posthole digger to excavate at least 16″ deep, then fill the bottom 2″ or 3″ of the hole with gravel to provide proper drainage.

Place the pipe, flush with grade, into the hole, and backfill around it. Or you may pour concrete around it to grade. Boundaries of your badminton court may be marked in the same way as for croquet, described in this section.

Now keep your eye on the birdie.

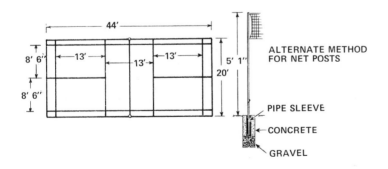

A badminton court may be set up on any reasonably sized area of level lawn with no special preparation. Beware of ground depressions which may catch a running player by surprise and cause a turned ankle. The detail shows one method for setting the net posts.

CROQUET

The popular lawn game croquet was played in late sixteenth-century France, whence it emigrated to England. It enjoyed its greatest popularity in the mid-Victorian era, when it was *the* summer social game.

A croquet ground is a level, well-rolled, closely cropped lawn. Boundaries are marked with a strong white cotton cord held in place by staples, or with a line of chalk, lime, or flour. Permanent corner markers of wood, metal pipe or concrete set flush with the ground will eliminate the need for remeasuring as these boundaries wear or fade.

Wickets and stakes are simply implanted into the earth, as shown in the drawing. If your family is completely devoted to the game, a more permanent installation may be made by embedding galvanized wire wickets and pipe stakes in concrete set 2″ below the surface of the ground. The concrete is then covered with sod. But think twice before making such an installation. Permanently planted, these items can be a hazard when the area is being used for some other purpose than playing the game, tripping up the unwary walker. Could be a sticky wicket!

To play croquet by the official rules, one requires a level area of close-cropped lawn. Wickets and stakes may be pushed into the earth and withdrawn at any time, or if you are an enthusiast, they can be placed in sod-covered cement permanently.

TENNIS

The most desirable location for a tennis court is an open, unshaded area with good natural drainage. When orienting the court, consider the direction of sunshine at time of greatest probable usage, and locate it, if possible, so that players will not have to face directly into the sun.

Drainage pitch of $\frac{1}{16}$″ per foot should be provided from center court to the end lines. Subsurface drainage may be necessary under impervious court surfaces if freeze-thaw damage is to be prevented.

On a grass playing surface, blue, fescue, or Bermuda varieties are recommended for most temperate areas of the country. A clay surface may be prepared by removing topsoil and leveling the subsoil, then filling with a sand-clay mixture. This is alternately sprayed and rolled until it is hard and smooth.

A concrete tennis court should include an expansion joint the full width of the court at the center (net) line. This can be filled with tar or felt material. It is not necessary to trowel the playing surface as smooth as for a concrete shuffleboard court, but the same curing process should be followed.

The net posts can be permanently installed or removable, as with badminton and volleyball net posts. Marking of court lines is also the same as for other games.

It is a good idea to provide a backstop of some sort at each end of the court, since a tennis ball gone awry can travel a considerable distance.

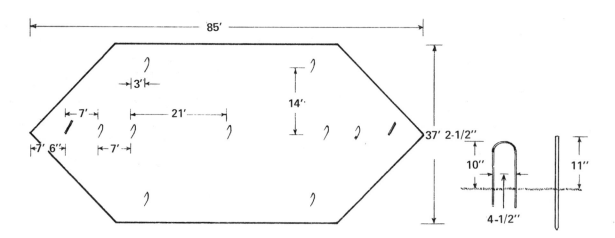

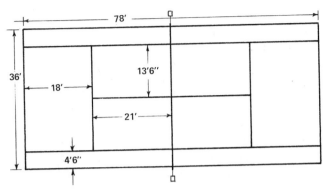

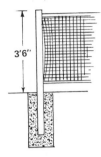

NIGHT GAMES

Today, when even golf courses are fully illuminated to allow round-the-clock play, there is no reason to call your games because of darkness. Lighting the outdoor play area is quite simple.

Buildings or trees provide excellent mounts for modern spot and flood lighting fixtures that will illuminate the court. Or telescoping poles may be purchased and installed, either permanently or in sleeves set into the ground (as with net posts) so that they can easily be removed.

Lights should be located at least 16' aboveground—20' where possible. They should be carefully aimed to cover the entire playing area, and to keep them from shining into players' eyes. Light coming from several directions reduces shadows and provides more uniform illumination. Three or more floods can be mounted in a single location, each aimed in a different direction, with overlapping areas of concentration to avoid dark spots. For example, poles can be placed a few feet outside the net posts of a badminton, tennis, or volleyball court, each holding three floodlamps to cover the entire court. It is wise to provide lighting beyond the ends of the court as well to facilitate the search for balls or birdies knocked out of bounds.

Now that your back yard sports arena is completed, don't sit back to rest—get out there and enjoy it.

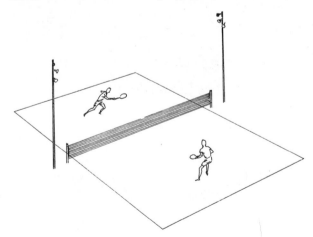

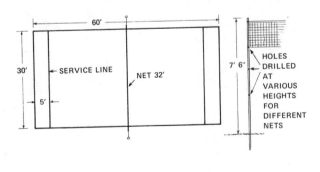

Many, if not all, of the games shown in this chapter can be enjoyed after dark if provision is made for good lighting. Arrange spotlights so that their beams overlap, lighting the playing area fully. Experiment with location to make sure they won't glare in your eyes.

Volleyball may be played on a concrete or blacktop court or on a level ground area. The posts may be set permanently or in similar fashion to that shown for badminton. Here too it is suggested that holes or depressions in the playing area should be leveled out.

BUILD YOUR OWN SKATING RINK

Put winter weather to work this season and provide fun and exercise for the family at the same time with this really simple back yard skating rink of 2-by-4 framing and polyethylene sheet film. Comes the first hard freeze, you'll be all set for hours of skimming and gliding—with the warmth of the house and hot refreshments only feet away.

The first step is to select a flat, level section of ground (if you are stuck with sloping ground, you can still make do by following the details in sketch C), laying out a practical rink size. One-piece sizes of plastic sheeting, such as VisQueen polyethylene film, are available up to 40'-by-100' if you want to go that large. Most rinks, however, run about 20'-by-50', 20'-by-40', or 20'-by-30'—all of which are ideal for cutting fancy figures and having fun.

Having roughed out the size, the next step is to take 2-by-4's and place them on edge around the rink's perimeter, the stock being as inexpensive as possible, as long as it is nearly straight. Butt join them at corners—and where two ends are butted in line, join them with a short length of 1-by-3 on the outside. When all the sides have been connected, drive stakes of scrap stock at intervals along the outside, also nailing them to the framework.

Now you can spread the polyethylene film over the rink enclosure, taking care to flatten and smooth it without puncturing the surface. To secure the film to the frame, place 1-by-2's or 1-by-3's or furring strips at the top, inside edge of the 2-by-4 frame; see sketches A and B. Serving as kickboards, they anchor the film firmly while also preventing rips or tears from skates. Excess film can be trimmed with a scissor at the top edge of the framework.

For $45 or less, depending on lumber grade, you can build your own skating rink in a matter of hours—using polyethylene sheet film, lengths of 2-by-4's and a pocketful of nails. As large or as small as your budget allows, you can also build around trees or other obstructions, thus transforming any yard into a winterland of fun for the family and friends.

Conventional square rink is typical of the layouts possible using polyethylene film and 2-by-4 stock.

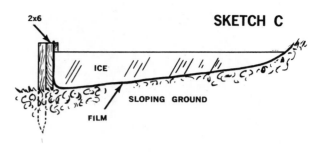

SKETCH C

ICE

SLOPING GROUND

FILM

SKETCH A

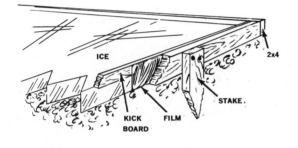

ICE

2x4

STAKE.

KICK BOARD

FILM

SKETCH B

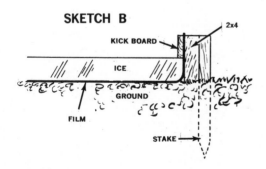

KICK BOARD

2x4

ICE

GROUND

FILM

STAKE

Finally, fill the rink with at least 3″ of water and wait for the first temperature dip.

It's essential, of course, to keep the framework at the same relative height. Where ground level varies, you may have to use 2-by-6's in combination with 2-by-4's or 2-by-6's only—as in the case of sloping ground. And wherever corners appear to need strengthening, as with 2-by-6's, use a triangular wooden plate, nailed into the top edges of the framework, for more stability.

If you want to dispense with the kickboard feature, bring the film under the frame, lap it over the outside, and secure it at the top with a thin strip of molding. Be sure, too, to use clear or translucent film, as opaque sheeting damages grass over long periods.

There's always the possibility that two or three neighbors may want to join you in a larger rink project, to be set up on adjoining properties or in a vacant lot, reducing costs through sharing expenses. If so, remember that any size rink may be built by simply connecting film sheets with pressure sensitive tape.

A TOWER OF FUN

Wait till the youngsters see this—a tower clubhouse more than 6′ off the ground, complete with trap door, a rope ladder they can pull up after them, and a parapet for protection against attack. All of which adds up to a tower of fun unlike anything the neighborhood has glimpsed yet.

From the practical point of view of the parent who would want to build it, the tower is a rock-steady construction with an 8′-by-8′ deck, a sturdy, bolted railing to keep everyone secure, and a pitched roof to keep everyone snug. It's built for years of wear and abuse, but is never an eyesore.

Building the tower presents no special problems,

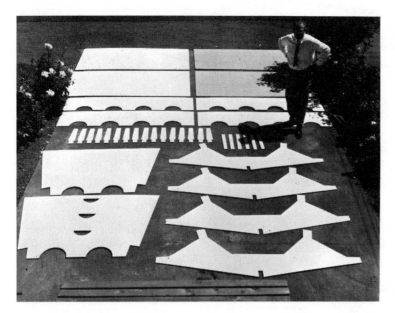

Shown here are the primary components of the play tower; all are cut from 4-by-8 plywood panels, exterior grade. The short pieces at the left are support posts for the railings; the pieces on the right are ladder steps.

despite what may at first seem the trick of getting everything up there. Following the order we describe, you'll stay out of trouble. So for a start, first consult the materials list.

You can see that 4-by-8 sheets of plywood are the heart of the project, some used whole or nearly whole and others for cutouts of structural components. Of the 12 sheets specified, 2 (with minor notching) serve as the floor, 2 whole sheets comprise the roof, 2 more sheets provide the 4 railings, 2 other sheets (with some waste) produce the 2 wall-stabilizers, and 4 sheets yield the 4 roof supports as well as the 16 rail posts. Quite a haul.

What remains are the four 4-by-4 legs, the 2-by-4 board lumber (primarily for the floor joists), and the 1-by-4's which are used for the roof trim. Scrap lumber (2-by-2's or 2-by-4's) in about 8' lengths is a must for bracing chores.

Assembling the A-frames

The idea behind assembly and erection of the structure is to make the modified A-frames first. Each A-frame consists of two 4-by-4 legs, two 2-by-4 joists (horizontal), and two roof supports with the two 2-by-4 spacers sandwiched between them. In order to assure the correct angle for assembling these parts on the ground, first temporarily tack the wall-stabilizer in place. After it has served as your guide, remove it. You'll be permanently installing the wall later.

With the two A-frames ready to go and the ends of the legs creosote-coated, prepare the post holes. Now you can set the frames in upright positions, using that scrap lumber to hold them securely—having double-checked everything with a level. Pour the cement footings and let set thoroughly.

In the next phase, install the floor framing or joists. Because 4 of the members are already in relative position, it's an easy job to frame the 4 sides, then the inner components. Be sure to allow for the trap door—you can, of course, provide for a second trap door opening on the opposite side, if you wish.

The floor goes on next. Follow the cuts described on the detail graph. Note that the slots, which are 16" deep, are 5" wide for the first 12", reducing to 4" wide for the last 4". When the two parts of the floor have been positioned and nailed, the slots hugging the 4-by-4 legs, fill in the space to the outside edge with the original but shortened (12") scrap. Having allowed the extra width in the basic cut, you now have a nailing edge in the joist below for a neat, flush patch.

This done, cut 16 holes in the deck for the rail posts. Place them near the outside edge, just inside the outer floor frame. A sabre saw will zip these up in no time. Then install the posts and the rails.

Wall Permanently Attached

The wall-stabilizers you used earlier as guides can now be permanently attached, using bolts.

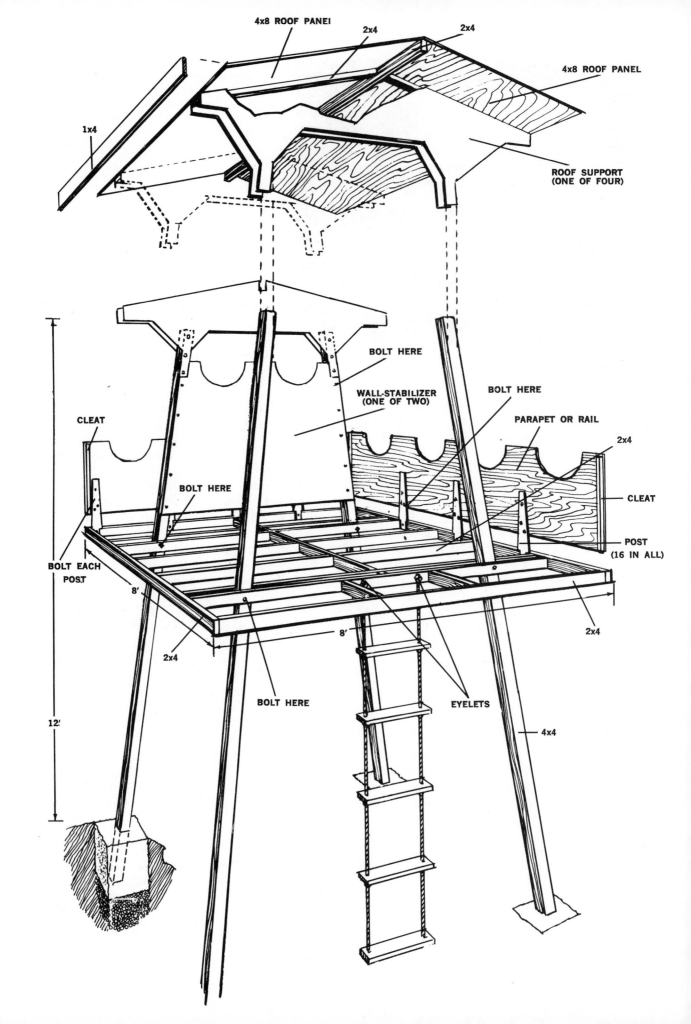

4x8 ROOF PANEL

2x4

2x4

4x8 ROOF PANEL

1x4

ROOF SUPPORT (ONE OF FOUR)

BOLT HERE

WALL-STABILIZER (ONE OF TWO)

BOLT HERE

PARAPET OR RAIL

2x4

CLEAT

BOLT HERE

CLEAT

BOLT EACH POST

POST (16 IN ALL)

8'

8'

2x4

2x4

BOLT HERE

EYELETS

4x4

12'

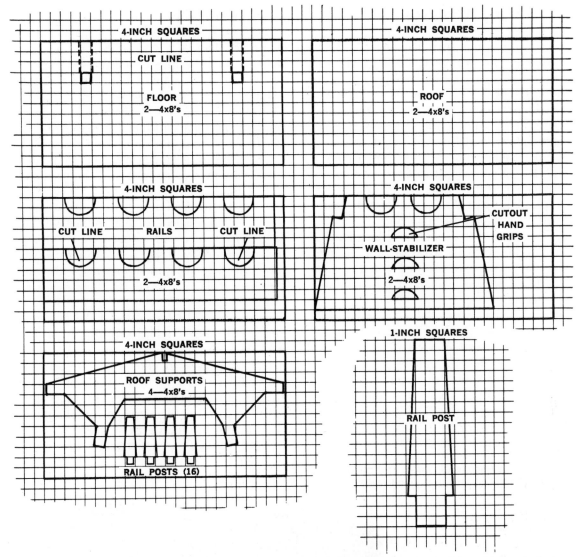

These six sketches detail the plywood requirements for the tower, including exact guidelines where cutouts and notches are made. Note that five of the sketches are graphed for 4-inch squares, the other one scaled to 1-inch squares.

MATERIALS LIST

2 4 x 8 sheets of ½" GPX High Density Non-Slip Overlaid Plywood (grid pressed into surface, for floor).

10 4 x 8 sheets of ⅜" GPX Medium Density Overlaid Plywood Siding (one side smooth for painting).

4 14-foot lengths of 4 x 4 redwood posts.

15 8-foot lengths of 2 x 4 fir.

4 8-foot lengths of 1 x 4 clear pine.

Nails and stove bolts.

Gravel and cement mix.

Roof coating.

Redwood paint and redwood stain.

Place the one with the ladder cutouts over the trap door, as this makes a convenient hand-up when ascending.

All that remains to be done is the roof—first, the roof spline, then the two 4-by-8's (their peak edges bevelled and over the spline), and finally, the 1-by-4 trim all around.

For the last piece of carpentry, make the trap door(s). Secure eyelets to the frame for the rope.

As for finishing, coat all the plywood with an acrylic redwood paint, and treat the redwood lumber with a redwood stain. This particular floor was not touched, as it is a nonslip type requiring no paint. The roof panels were treated with Butyl rubber roof coating.

SPACE AGE PLAYHOUSE

Have your youngsters been nagging you about that playhouse you promised them? Here's one that's not only easy to build but will be the envy of every kid in the neighborhood including those who already have playhouses. The house takes only a few days to build, requires almost no upkeep, and can take the abuse most children would give it.

A careful examination will show how closely it resembles that spindly-legged gadget that took the astronauts down to the moon. Add a coat-hanger antenna, pie-plate radar dish, and your kids' imagination will take off on a flight of fancy.

No playhouse, no matter how well constructed, is going to last forever. One word of caution, however: this playhouse is not too well suited to areas that have heavy winters, though it can withstand most weathering.

You'll need a level area of about 8 square feet, preferably in the back of your house, to build the playhouse whose overall dimensions are approximately 10' high by about 4' wide by about 6' long. Though most of the house can be built of pine, for the structural members that come in contact with the earth, use lumber that has been pressure-treated to resist decay and termite damage. Some of the western woods such as Douglas fir, western red

This modernistic play house will make your children the envy of the neighborhood. It is quickly and easily built, and only requires 8 square feet of space.

cedar, ponderosa pine, or similar woods are best.

The house lends itself easily to kids climbing on it. Rather than let it remain mobile, in which case it could possibly tip over, fix the six long legs (A) in concrete. No elaborate foundation is required—about 15" deep is sufficient. The vertical 2-by-2's (A,I,P) are on 24" centers. After wedging the 2-by-2 stock in the earth, fix them in place with enough concrete to furnish a 6" anchor on all sides of each piece. Allow at least two days for the concrete to cure before proceeding with final construction.

The frame should be completed before adding any other structural members, using countersunk screws. All pieces except those joined to B are secured with either butt or flat joints. Pieces joined to B are secured with lap joints. Build the two long pieces (B) first, tying them together with four cross members (C,D,F). Cross-brace these pieces temporarily to keep the frame square and set it in permanent footings. The four sides of the playhouse are built to the same specifications, that is, on 24" centers. About the most complicated cuts you'll have to make are in piece B, into which are fitted several pieces (E,F,G) as shown in the detail on the drawing. Bear in mind that these cuts must allow space not only for securing them to the upright pieces but also for cross members such as D and C.

After putting the frame together, but before add-

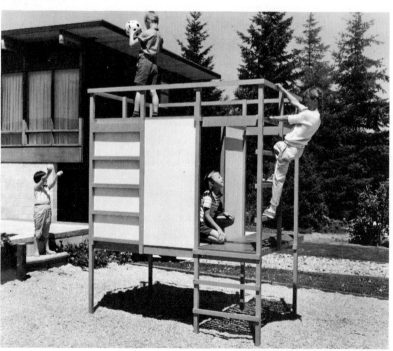

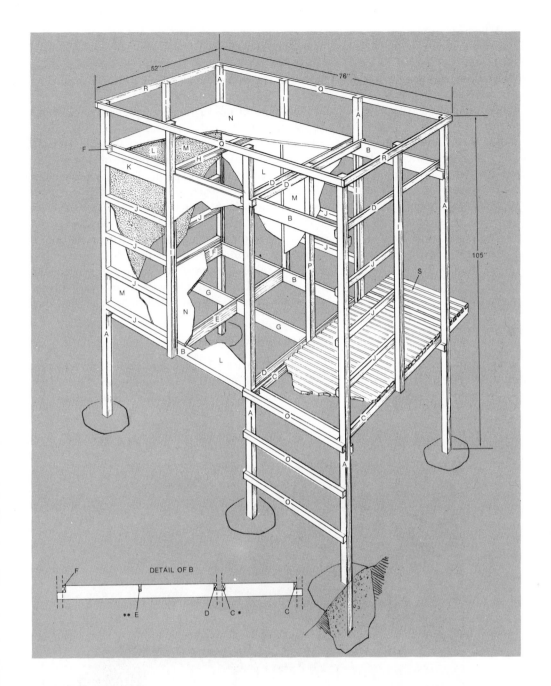

MATERIALS LIST

A. Six pieces, each:
120 x 2 x 2″

B. Four pieces, each:
74 x 4 x 1″

C. Two pieces, each:
60 x 2 x 1″

D. Four pieces, each:
50 x 2 x 1″

E. One piece,
46 x 4 x 1″

F. Two pieces, each:
50 x 4 x 1″

G. Two pieces, each:
22½ x 4 x 1″

H. One piece,
42 x 2 x 2″

I. Five pieces, each:
69 x 2 x 2″

J. Twelve pieces, each:
22 x 2 x 2″ (one not shown)

K. Three pieces, each:
22¼″ x 4 x 2″
(two not shown)

L. Three pieces, each:
53 x 23¾ x ⅛″
(one not shown)

M. Four pieces, each:
57 x 23 x ⅛″

N. Two pieces, each:
46 x 46 x ¾″

O. Three pieces, each:
26 x 2 x 1″

P. One piece,
57 x 2 x 2″

Q. Two pieces, each:
74 x 2 x 1″

R. Two pieces, each:
52 x 2 x 1″

S. Twenty-five pieces,
each: 22¼ x 22 x 1″
(some not shown)

ing the walls, roof, and flooring, be sure to seal thoroughly all wood surface with regular house paint. The walls, flooring, and roof consist of hardboard or any other material that withstands weathering. The hardboard is inserted in ½" slots in the vertical 2-by-2's and nailed or screwed from the inside. Roof and floor (N) are ¾" plywood nailed or screwed all around to B,C,D,E,F and G. A single 2-by-2 (H) is used under the roof to increase head room instead of crossed 1-by-4's (E,G,) such as are used under the floor. The reason for this is fairly obvious: it will bear more weight. It might also be a good idea to use the same construction for the roof as for the floor if you expect your kids to go climbing all over the roof, too. This means using some good stout ¾" plywood.

VINYL-LINER PREFAB POOLS

For many families the pool in the back yard has become the center of outdoor recreation. There are more than a million pools in the United States, 70 per cent of them residential. A key factor in this recreational explosion has been the prefabricated vinyl liner which has brought private swimming pools to the home owner's back yard for about the cost of a moderately priced car.

This type of pool consists of prefabricated, rigid supporting walls and a vinyl liner that fits snugly against these walls and a carefully shaped earth bottom. Because all the parts are prefabricated and assembled on the site, a capable do-it-yourselfer with the help of a few friends can install his own pool and save anywhere from $600 to $1,000. However, do-it-yourself installation may, in some cases, void the manufacturer's guarantee. Be sure, therefore, to discuss this point with the dealer. Both types of vinyl-liner pools—in-the-ground and aboveground—are described here along with their costs, advantages and disadvantages, and installation methods.

In-the-Ground Pools

The prefabricated vinyl-liner pool looks like any other conventional in-the-ground pool. The differences, however, are considerable. The prefab type

Who would believe you built it yourself! This beautiful above-the-ground pool can be in use within a week after construction starts.

costs around $2,000 less than a similar concrete pool and can usually be assembled in much less time. Prefab pools range in price from about $2,000 to about $5,000, or higher if installed by the dealer. Do-it-yourself prefabs are available at $1,000 and up depending on size and type. The panels that form the walls of the pool may be plywood, galvanized steel, or aluminum, with plywood costing less than steel, and aluminum at the highest level.

The particular pool shown here has galvanized steel panels. Dimensions of this pool are 18' x 32', with depths ranging from 3' to $8\frac{2}{3}'$.

With some help from family or neighbors, it should take as little as four days and not more than a week to install after excavation of the hole. The excavation work should be done by a contractor with a digging machine called a backhoe. Plenty of excavation contractors can be found in your local classified directory.

Before the backhoe work starts, outline the shape of the pool with stakes and powdered chalk or dry plaster. Excavation should start at the deepest end and should remove soil to the fullest dimensions of the excavation, as this will save you a great deal of shovel work later on.

This pre-fabricated kidney-shaped pool looks like a conventional concrete in-the-ground pool. There is one great difference though: The pre-fabricated pool costs at least $2,000 less than its concrete counterpart.

Pre-fabricated pools come in all sizes and shapes. However, the free-form pool is the most decorative, and it's very simple to install.

FRAME RESTS ON SAND

With the excavation finished, the steel supporting wall panels are set on a sand bed about 1½" thick around the edges of the hole. Since the panels are engineered for the proper arc of circle for this free-form pool and the bolt holes are predrilled, bolting these panels together is simple. All the panels are first bolted through their bottom holes, which establishes the proper free-form shape right from the beginning.

The upper edges of the steel panels are secured by special flanges that squeeze the panels together and form a support for the coping which goes on later.

Once the steel walls are erected, the soil in the excavation is graded and covered with a layer of sand which is then packed to fit the shape of the vinyl liner. A swivel type wooden template is used to shape the sand in the deep or hopper end of the pool. The swivel template is swung around, removing sand in some places and revealing spots in others that need to be packed with additional sand.

The shallow end of the pool is brought to its final saucer shape by using a bar that stretches across the pool on the panels and has weighted strings attached which mark the proper depths.

Plastic piping is then attached to the inlet and outlet of the pump and filtration unit. The cus-

Digging dimensions are 24" wider than pool perimeter to allow working room behind installed walls. Lay dimensions out with stakes and string; mark with lime.

Take depth readings during digging with transit level. Here, final check is made as backhoe slopes deep end. Homeowner sets up end walls between readings.

Following lime outline, excavator uses backhoe, most efficient tool, to dig hole. Meanwhile homeowner digs out and levels places where the A-frame wall supports rest.

After excavation, trim high spots, remove rocks from entire bottom of hole so that 3-inch sand base can be laid on evenly and the liner fits on tight and smooth.

INSTALL THE WALLS
Walls are prefabricated in sections for easy assembly. Just line up the side of the one you're installing with installed section side and bolt them together through pre-punched holes.

For strength, an A-frame support is bolted to panels at every joint, and staking rods anchor both walls and supports to ground.

To install coping, insert "T" bolts to its underside and fit them into matching holes on wall tops, then tighten.

Skimmer is inserted to pre-cut opening and screwed on.

Water recirculation fitting is also inserted in pre-cut opening and screwed on easily.

Sand is drenched, distributed on bottom of hole, raked to about 3" depth, then tamped or rolled smooth and hard.

For a better liner fit, a sand fillet is formed at angle where walls meet bottom with plastic pipe attached to 2-by-2.

INSTALL THE LINER
Liner is unrolled and let lie for 2-3 days prior to installation to make it more workable.

Begin installation by slipping two side corners of liner into coping, walk it open across pool and secure other two corners.

Liner can now be tugged or pulled into relative position without damage and its beaded edges worked into the slotted coping.

Rented vacuum cleaner is used to suck air from under liner and pull it into final position. Household vacuum can be used, but it's slower.

Pool can be filled by garden hose. As water rises, smooth wrinkles with soft bristle broom.

AND CONNECT THE PIPES
Polyethylene piping connects fittings with filter. Pipe is rugged, yet easily put in with knife and screwdriver.

Homeowner continues filling the pool with filter already operating. Water flows to and from filter for purification.

tom-tailored vinyl liner is set into the steel-paneled excavation and locked to the tops of the steel panels. Plastic piping connections are made from the filtration unit to the skimmer outlet (an opening a little below water level that sucks out debris), and to a main outlet at a lower level, as well as to a supply inlet at an opposite end of the pool. The connections where the pipes pass through the steel walls and liner are gasketed front and back to make them waterproof. The gaskets and pipes are part of the package as is the filtration unit. The liner may also be cut for an underwater light and its fittings, but this costs $200 to $300 and requires safe electrical connections to a grounded circuit.

Water Pressure Balanced

Water is let into the pool and its weight stretches the liner so that it fits snugly in the finished excavation. At this point, dirt is shoveled in to back-fill behind the steel walls, equalizing the water pressure and providing a balance that locks the paneling firmly in place.

With the water level at normal height, the final step is to complete the coping made of specially shaped concrete units. The coping has a groove underneath and fits over the panel tops and liner edge, locking the liner in place.

Your pool is now ready for use. There is one final matter that you have to consider. In many communities, local laws specify protective fences around pools. Many pool dealers can tell you the cost of a fence for your size of pool.

Excavation for in-ground pool is best done by contractor using machine called a backhoe.

Galvanized steel panels that form walls of free-form pool are fastened at the bottom with bolts.

Steel channels are bolted to fitting at top of panels that holds the panel flanges together.

Earth bottom of deep end is roughly shaped and then covered with damp sand firmly tamped.

The damp sand is smoothed to the right shape for the one-piece vinyl liner by a swivel template. As the template is rotated, it removes high spots or shows gaps that must be filled in for the proper slant.

Liner placed inside walls. Fitting with hole in front is for an optional underwater light.

Grooved concrete coping sections snapped on rubber strip anchors liner and completes job.

Above-the-ground Pools

Anybody traveling around the suburbs these days is bound to see a great many aboveground vinyl liner pools in back yards. The popularity of this pool is well deserved for it provides the home owner with a full-sized pool at a reasonable price.

Most aboveground pools are similar in construction and are basically wooden containers for a specially shaped vinyl liner. Usually they have plywood walls fastened to framing which supports a deck around the perimeter of the pool and strong wood braces from the bottom of the framing to the outer edge of the deck. A fence or railing goes completely around the pool deck—a necessary precaution since the deck may be five or six feet from the ground. In many instances the fence lends a decorative aspect to the pool.

Some pools are completely aboveground and require no excavation, but a majority have one end deeper than the other (about 7½') which has to be excavated. You can have the deep end dug for you by a contractor, but since there is not much excavation needed, the job can be done by hand.

The cost of an aboveground pool depends on its style, size, and whatever extras you want to add as accessories.

It should be noted that no two manufacturers build an aboveground pool in exactly the same way. Some parts of the pool described below are different from those of other aboveground types,

but the basic features are similar to other pools of its kind.

The entire pool package is delivered to your home and you are ready to start. The first thing to do is to drive stakes into the ground to show the exact outline of the pool. Next, you take the heavy steel channels on which the pool walls will rest and lay them on the ground. The channels are bolted and braced at the corners and you now have the rectangular outline of the pool on the ground. The channels are leveled with a carpenter's level. This may involve raising some parts of the channels on blocks or bricks.

Now the excavation for the deep end begins. In this case, the excavation is being done by hand. The hole is dug so that the four sides slant steeply toward a small flat bottom. A wood frame is nailed together as a template for the exact size of the bottom. When the hole has reached the right depth, the wood template is laid on the bottom. Four boards are placed together to form an upper template along the top edges of the excavation. A long board with a straight edge is laid on the upper and lower templates as a guide to show the proper slant for the walls of the hopper or deep end of the pool. The earth walls are roughly shaped to the right slant and a groove is cut in one corner for the plastic pipe which will go down to the main drain in the center of the bottom.

Prefabricated wooden "A" frames are placed in each corner of the steel channels on the ground.

The vinyl liner above-the-ground pool owes its popularity to its beauty, convenience, and low cost. Since one end of this pool is deeper than the other, some excavation will be required.

ABOVE THE GROUND POOLS
Galvanized steel channels which support walls of the pool are laid on the ground, bolted and braced at the corners and leveled. Then continue as shown at right.

Because excavation is required only for the hopper or deep end of pool, two men can do the digging by hand in a few hours.

A template or guide which outlines the flat part of the pool bottom is quickly nailed together on the site out of 1-by-4 lumber.

Bottom is dug out preparatory to placing template. Sides of the excavation are shaped so that they slant toward the bottom.

Long board that touches bottom template and boards around the top of hole serves as a guide to correct slant of hopper walls.

Narrow trench is cut into side of hopper for plastic piping which will connect main drain in pool bottom to the filter unit.

Prefab "A" frames are placed in steel channels on ground and are then temporarily braced.

Steel channels are put on top of "A" frames and are then fastened with bolts at the corners.

More "A" frames are then slipped between upper and lower channels at 4-foot intervals.

Pool walls are made of special metal-covered ⅜-inch plywood which is nailed to "A" frames.

Prefabricated wood deck sections are nailed to the "A" frames all around the pool perimeter.

More "A" frames and supporting beams for sun deck are placed in position on one side of pool.

Each frame is temporarily braced to hold it in place and intermediate frames are placed in the channels between those in the corners.

Steel channels similar to those on the ground are placed on top of the "A" frames and bolted together at the corners. Additional "A" frames are slipped between the channels so that each frame is 4′ from the next one.

A precut 2-by-4 midway between each pair of frames provides additional support for the plywood walls. These walls are made of a special type of ⅜″ plywood with aluminum foil on the inside (facing the pool) and metal sheeting with a baked enamel finish bonded to the outside. The plywood is nailed to the vertical edges of the "A" frames and to the 2-by-4's between them.

The prefabricated deck sections are placed over the frames and nailed into place. If a sun deck is desired, additional frames are placed in position, leveled and connected by long supporting beams to the frames already standing in the steel channels. A prefabricated sun deck is then nailed to the new frames and supporting beams so that it is flush with the narrower deck sections already in place.

The rail posts for the fence around the deck, all of them precut to the exact length, are placed between the two ends of each frame which protrude from under the decks and are bolted into place.

A special plastic edging called a liner lock strip is fastened with special nails to the inner edge of the deck all around the pool. When the pool liner is placed inside the walls, its upper edge will be anchored in the groove in this liner lock strip.

The pool bottom is covered now with a layer of builder's sand. (You will need to buy 3 to 5 cubic yards of sand for this purpose.) The sand is applied to both the shallow and the deep ends. A very fine mist of water sprayed on the sand makes it possible to shape it firmly to the desired contour. In the deep end, the long straight edge (which is just a 2-by-4) that lies on both the upper and lower templates permits you to shape the sand to the proper slant. The shaping and smoothing of the sand is done with a long trowel.

How do you get out of the hole without disrupting the sand? A board is placed on one of the slanted sides. With the aid of a helping hand from above and a long first step so that you can lock hands with the man above, you can easily walk up the board.

With the bottom now firmly shaped, the liner is placed inside and spread out on the bottom and up

A broad, prefabricated sun deck is placed flush with previosuly installed deck and nailed.

Plastic liner lock strip is nailed to deck edge. Vinyl liner will be anchored to this strip.

Layer of damp sand covers sides and bottom of excavation and is shaped to fit vinyl liner.

Vinyl liner covers walls and bottom of pool. Edges of the liner are anchored to lock strip.

A hole is cut through liner for main drain previously installed at the bottom of deep end.

Fence posts are bolted to deck edge and "A" frames. Dadoed 2-by-4 rail is nailed to post tops.

A white plastic channel is fitted over the top of the fence rail and is fastened into place with special white enameled nails.

the sides and the edges pressed into the groove of the liner lock strip. Weights are placed on the liner at the bottom of the walls to hold it in place against the walls until the pool is filled with water. At this point a hole is cut in the liner at the bottom of the hopper (deep end) for a previously placed main drain.

The top rail which is dadoed underneath to fit over the rail posts is nailed into place. A white plastic cover fits over the top of the rail and is fas-

tened to it with white-coated spiral nails driven through the sides of the plastic.

White corrugated fiberglass sheets are nailed to the rail posts leaving an opening for entry to the deck. Prefabricated steps that connect ground level with the deck are placed at this opening. An interesting feature of the steps is that they are pivoted at the deck end so that they can be swung off the ground and kept in a vertical position.

The pump and filter unit is placed under the

deck and connected with plastic pipes to the outlet and inlet openings of the pool. At this point you may want to install any accessories such as a diving board or stainless steel ladder. The plumbing connections between the filter and your house water supply can be handled by your plumber or you can make these connections yourself if your local building code permits it.

Because of its elevated position it is unlikely that any small child could climb up on the deck of an aboveground pool and fall into the water, provided that you are careful to keep the steps off the ground in a vertical position. This means that you won't have to buy a fence, which can be quite a saving. Nevertheless, check with your local building code just to make sure.

Finishing of the wooden parts can be either paint or stain and the colors are up to you.

White, corrugated fiberglass sheets are nailed to fence posts. Opening through fiberglass is cut for entry to deck from the stairs.

A stainless steel ladder is assembled with nuts and bolts on the sun deck preparatory to installation at the deep end of pool.

The pump and filter unit are concealed under the sun deck and connections are made with piping to inlets and outlets in the pool.

Chapter 12
AROUND THE HOUSE

Some home improvement projects are basic, requiring extensive alterations of the existing structure or considerable additions to it. Very often, however, some small modification makes all the difference, changing the entire character of the house, or enhancing its appearance, or helping to make the most effective use of the available home space.

One such project, described in detail in this chapter, on page 383 concerns changing a window.

This usually can be done entirely by the home owner at very modest total cost, and will do much to correct some deficiency of the original window while improving the appearance of the home. An alternative project would convert a row of massive windows into a sleek picture window at the back to both open the view of the garden and brighten the home interior with more sunlit rooms.

These and similar projects described here will

stimulate your thoughts, and perhaps prompt your action to undertake small but significant improvements, many of which can be completed in a weekend or two.

A DISTINCTIVE FRONT DOOR

Whatever the reason—indifference, the extra cost, or just plain insensitivity—builders of development homes don't put very much effort into getting some variation in the houses they mass produce. Lack of individuality is a prime objection to tract houses, each one a look-alike with its next door neighbors and every other house on the block.

But there's no necessity for residents to continue to accept this stamped-in-a-mold condition, when a new and more attractive appearance can be obtained at minimum cost.

The doorway is probably the easiest of all to make distinctly individual and more handsome,

too. With simple design applications, an ordinary-looking doorway can be transformed into an attractive architectural feature of your home.

A combination of moldings, latticework, shutters, and accessories like lamps, planters and statuary, sparked by a bit of color in an imaginative way, will give your home a new, different, and appealing appearance. Shown here are five decorator-inspired ideas that can be adapted to almost any home.

LOUVERS SPELL LUXURY

More popular than ever, louver doors are being used in many new ways for both decorative and practical purposes. They are inexpensive, come in a wide choice of styles with sizes to fit every situation, and are easily installed.

In addition to their obvious use on wardrobes and closets, louvers are excellent for cabinets, stor-

Lattice work between battens, made with 2″ × 2″ strips painted for contrast with the background color of the house, frames the doorway to produce the Oriental effect here. Shrubs trained to grow in interesting shapes set off the design gracefully. Suitable plantings are Scotch pine, firethorn, rock spray cotoneaster, or various juniper bushes.

Emphasize a door with a 1-inch color band and a 4-inch molding. Train an evergreen vine around the entrance and place dense round shrubs at both sides for contrast. Choose winter creeper, Baltic ivy or espaliered firethorn for the vine. Mugho pine, boxwood, Japanese holly or yew are good shrubs.

The delicate frosting of white ornamental grillwork against a grey house is set off by globe lights. The light colors contrast well with a base provided by dense, dark shrubs at both sides of the door. You can select upright yew, Mahonia, boxwood or bufordi holly. Any of these varieties will look well.

To carry out a Latin motif, paint the door a bright pastel shade if the house is white. Bars over the single door light and black wrought iron lamps add to the illusion. Heavy earthenware or masonry planters containing yucca plants carry out the theme.

356

A problem doorway between rooms becomes a decorative asset with the addition of a pair of folding louver doors. Close them for complete privacy, or fold them back against the wall.

age walls, room dividers, dressing room screens, window blinds, café doors in kitchens or pantries —any place, in fact, that benefits from dramatic good looks and the advantage of ventilation afforded by the air spaces between slats.

As outside window shutters, their gracefully slim lines need not be merely decorative for, when mounted on the proper hardware, they can be closed to serve as window blinds. Or, place a pair of narrow full-length doors at each side of your front entrance to give it an appearance of greater width. When painted a bright color, the louvers become an attractive accent, making your house look different and distinctive.

Inside the house, louvers fit every type of closet beautifully, providing ventilation to keep stored articles and the closet itself fresh-smelling and mildew-free, while blocking out dust. They are adaptable to every preference—slide them on a track; swing them on hinges; or use the special duofold type which narrows down the distance the folded door projects into the room. In this case, a pair of

This installation masks the entrance to a utility room in a basementless house. Instead of the ugly piping and furnace, only the attractive louvers appear. The shutters let air circulate.

A wide louver door with solid bottom section separates two rooms. The pine can be finished to match any style or decor.

You can't find a better use for louvers than on the door of a clothes closet. In addition to the textural interest they provide, the ventilation keeps the closet contents fresh.

narrow doors on each side of the opening folds together automatically as they open.

Café Doors Popular

Café-type "shorty" doors, hung on special hinges that permit them to swing in either direction, make a novel installation at kitchen, laundry, or pantry entrances. These doors are 24″ high, with a scroll-cut design top and bottom.

Another favorite application is for cabinet doors where their lightness and slim framing are an attractive asset. Ventilation is an advantage here, too. Use them on undersink cabinets, sewing boxes, air-conditioner enclosures, bathroom vanities, hampers, medicine chests and storage walls. They'll blend well with any decor—Early American, French Provincial, classic, traditional, or modern.

Louvers are also ideal for enclosing the furnace and water-heater area in a basementless house. When two children share a bedroom, give each a measure of privacy by strategic placement of a screen made of louver sections hinged together.

An always charming idea is the use of louvers as inside window blinds, with a pair of narrow doors either the full length of the window or in half-sizes which permit opening the top for full light and air, while keeping the lower part closed for privacy.

Louver panels come in so many sizes that you can find one to fit. Here the horizontal lines of the louvers used in a restricted area storage wall add the illusion of width.

Two-to-a-room can each have a measure of needed privacy when louver screens are used. Hinge them together at three points.

Outside the house, louvers hung on the proper hardware serve a dual purpose. When open, as here, their extra width and contrasting color adds distinction. Closed, they provide shade but admit air.

A gracious and charming entry to your home is the result of adding two full length panels, the same color as the door. They are fixed in position by nailing to the siding, make the entry appear wider.

Louver panels may be trimmed to precise requirements. Use a combination blade for smoothness.

When hinges require mortising, trace around the hinge on the edge of the panel to mark the area for chiseling.

Always use a sharp chisel—for this or any other job where one is required. Tap gently around line with a mallet.

Angling the chisel toward the work, remove waste a little at a time. Take care not to exceed the required depth.

Center a sharp awl in the holes and tap with mallet to start screws easily. Don't strip threads when tightening.

With hinge leaf in place on panel, prop it in position against frame; mark jamb. Use awl again to start holes.

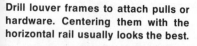

Drill louver frames to attach pulls or hardware. Centering them with the horizontal rail usually looks the best.

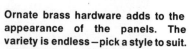

Ornate brass hardware adds to the appearance of the panels. The variety is endless—pick a style to suit.

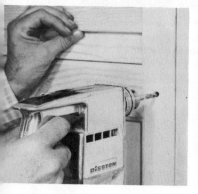

Types of Louvers

Style variations in louver doors are based on the panel concept—with or without crossrails. A one-slat panel means that the entire door is of slats set into a standard frame. Two-panel doors have a crossrail at center, with equal slats in top and bottom sections. You can also get two-panel doors with louvers in the upper section and solid paneling in the bottom. There are variations in the solid panels also, with standard cutouts such as fleur-de-lis, pine trees, crescents, and many others.

Louvered doors are either 1⅛″ or 1⅜″ thick, except on special order. Bottom rails, 4¾″ wide in the narrow doors and 8″ wide in full-length standard doors, may be cut down as much as 1″ for fitting. Many sizes are available, with 4″ graduations in height and 2″ in width. Stock sizes start at 15½″ high, and 12″ wide.

Quality louver doors and shutters are made of ponderosa pine, which has excellent weathering properties, straight grain and smooth surfaces for finishing. Those designed for exterior use are factory-treated with a water-repellent preservative. The doors can be varnished for outdoor use, or sprayed or brushed with paint. Indoors, of course, you can stain, paint, or wax as you see fit.

MAGIC FLUSH DOOR REJUVENATION

A few strips of wood molding will give your plain old doors a face-lift that will make them look like the latest thing in custom-made entrances.

Doors have come full cycle in the style parade. The once popular flush door has been relegated to inconspicuous areas, and the day of the decorator-styled paneled door is again with us.

Pictured here are several ways to transform your ugly-duckling flush doors. You don't need a magic wand—all it takes is a few feet of molding and a dash of imagination. Your local lumber dealer carries a large assortment of molding shapes and sizes from which to choose.

The variety of possible effects is limitless, but there are enough shown here to give you the idea and get you started. Even though the illustrations

Attractive, but not distinctive, the doorway in the upper left corner takes on individuality and character with any of the three treatments shown, achieved with just a few vertical molding strips.

Plain almost to the point of nonentity, the simple flush door shown in the upper left corner is brightened with simulated "panels" formed by moldings, together with a polished brass knocker. Use any of the three designs shown or dream up one of your own.

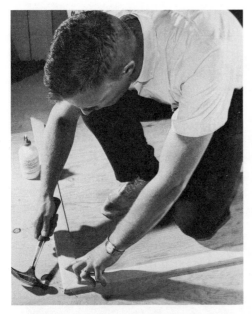

The best way to make accurately fitted corners is with a miter box and backsaw. Once cut, fasten the molding pieces together at each corner with waterproof wood glue and small finishing nails. Wipe away all excess glue, then set the frame aside to give the glue time to dry.

You'll find this project even easier when the door is removed from the hinges and placed on a couple of horizontal supports. Apply glue to the back of each frame, spread it, then place the frame on the door face.

Position the frames carefully to assure proper spacing. Use a rule or try-square to get the frame sides parallel to the edges of the door. If the frame is square, its top and bottom will then be parallel to the top and bottom of the door.

Tack molding frames to the door. When the glue is dry, the nails may be countersunk, and the nail holes filled with putty. For an eye-catching scheme, the moldings can be painted in a color which contrasts with the main shade.

show the treatment of exterior entrance doors, the identical scheme can be used throughout the house just as well.

Bold designs can be achieved with wide molding, painting it in colors which contrast strongly with the door face. Various degrees of prominence can be assigned to the design by choosing brighter or more subdued shades—or even using the same color as the rest of the door, letting the 3-D effect come through subtly.

All you need is a supply of molding, some glue and finishing nails, a hack saw and miter box, paint and brush, and a carpenter's square.

Draw some designs on paper until you find one that pleases you. Then cut the molding. Place it on the door temporarily and see how it looks. At this point, you can easily change the design. Once settled, nail and glue the moldings.

LIGHT THE WAY TO YOUR HOUSE

Front lawn lamps have more than just a function. They can also add an extra touch of good taste to the appearance of any home, for there are so many varieties of lamps that one can be matched to any style of architecture.

At nominal additional cost, a light-sensitive control can be installed in the post. It will turn the light on at dusk and off again in the morning. The post is also convenient for installing an electrical outlet—the weatherproof type should be used here, as in all exposed locations—for connecting electric power mowers, hedge clippers, or Christmas lights. And, to top it all off, a small signboard can be hung from the post to identify your residence. It can carry either your name or the house number, or both, if you choose.

Several precautions must be taken to ensure a safe, long-lasting installation. The wire that connects the lamp to the power line inside the house must be a type suitable for underground service. If the distance from the house exceeds 50', use no. 12 wire; if less, no. 14 wire should do the job. In some areas, building codes may call for specific types of wiring materials. Some allow plastic-jacketed cable; others require the use of conduit. Check with your building authorities to be sure you adopt the approved method. In the absence of any code, be sure to use a type of wire suitable for below-ground installation. Your hardware store or electrical supply dealer will give you the correct kind.

How better to welcome your guests than with a front lawn post lantern that lights their way to your door.

Cover Underground Wire

Both wire and conduit placed underground must be protected against damage from digging, although wire is, of course, the more vulnerable. If the possibility exists of disturbing the line later, protect with flat redwood boards—rot and decay resistant—placed over the line. Bury the line 6" or more below grade in a slit trench which may be cut with a spade. If boards are to be used, the trench will have to be widened accordingly.

For safety, all outdoor electrical fixtures should be grounded to eliminate shock hazard. An adequate ground is provided by a 6' copper-plated steel rod or solid copper rod, hammered into the ground adjacent to the post. Connect the fixture to the ground rod with a length of no. 6 solid copper wire, attaching the wire to the rod with a tight clamp. Do not rely on simply wrapping the wire

A hole drilled in the foundation below grade will completely conceal the power line where it passes out of the house and into the ground. Use a carbide-tipped bit or a masonry drill.

Calk the hole in the foundation so that ground moisture cannot seep in and cause damage. Ask your local building bureau which type of cable is approved for underground service.

A junction box on the inside of the wall, placed over the wire exit, provides a convenient place to terminate the indoor wiring. Calk inside also. Attach the box with expansion bolts.

Dig a hole for the post as deep as it requires, but be sure to go below the frostline. Drive a length of steel angle into the ground and plumb it carefully with a level. Set angle securely.

Set post in hole and tie it to the angle with two or three loops of baling wire. This will provide a temporary support, until the concrete you pour later has time to harden, hold firm.

With post in position, drive ground rod at least 6 feet deep. Rod should then reach moist earth. Rod and fixture are connected by #6 wire for protection against electrical failures.

Mix the required quantity of concrete and pour into hole, to within three inches of surface. Allow it to begin to set; then trowel a slope into the top so that rainwater will drain away.

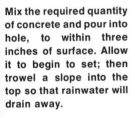

Wire the lighting fixture according to the manufacturer's instructions, which will vary from unit to unit. Use solderless connectors on all joints after twisting splices securely.

365

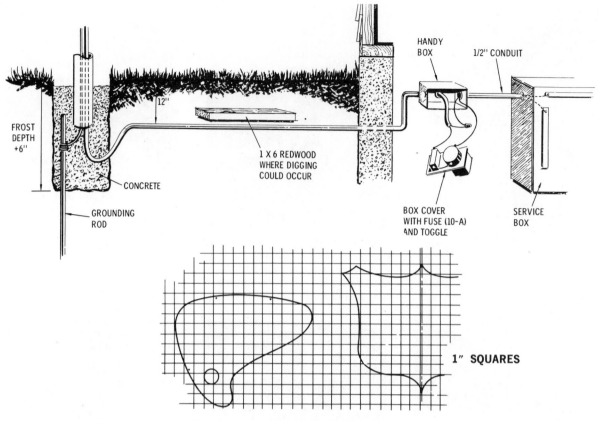

FROST DEPTH +6"

CONCRETE

GROUNDING ROD

1 X 6 REDWOOD WHERE DIGGING COULD OCCUR

HANDY BOX

1/2" CONDUIT

BOX COVER WITH FUSE (10-A) AND TOGGLE

SERVICE BOX

1" SQUARES

Plan of typical post installation and wiring.

around the rod a few times. Don't use aluminum grounding wire with a copper ground rod, for the contact of the two dissimilar metals in the presence of ground moisture will start the process of electrolysis, corroding one of the metals and eventually making the ground contact ineffectual.

Power for the lantern may be picked up at any convenient junction box in the basement. Pull the fuse to be sure the line is inoperative before attempting any work. Connect the new line with a fuse wired into the circuit as shown in the photos and diagram. An indoor toggle switch to override or take the place of the light-sensing control is also a good idea. Provide an exit from the basement for the new line by drilling through the concrete foundation below grade, and calk well after drawing the wire through.

Be sure to position the light-sensitive cell carefully. It should not be affected by such misleading influences as auto headlights or indoor lights that

may shine on it, fooling the cell into "thinking" the sun is up and turning off the lantern.

MAKING A DRAMATIC ENTRANCE

Few modern homes boast a gracious entry hall. Usually, the entrance door opens directly into the living room, so that there's no feeling of a reception area, and conversational groupings are difficult to maintain. While these may not be regarded by many as serious problems, the illustration here shows how an interesting open-work divider adds character and spaciousness to the entryway.

The plain, lattice-style entry divider consists of a floor-to-ceiling framework made of 2-by-2 uprights, connected by 1-by-2 dado-recessed horizontal members, with a paneled kickboard at the bottom.

Use selected lumber, either clear pine, which can be painted or used in its light natural color with a coat of shellac, or one of the more expensive hardwoods such as white oak or walnut in cabinet-grade

Lattice-type divider makes an entranceway, providing a separation for the living room, but leaving an open view that preserves the maximum feeling of spaciousness.

Sketches show all necessary details for construction of entryway divider. Vertical members, toenailed to top and bottom plates, are dadoed to support the crossmembers, while the panel kickboard at bottom is held with quarter-round molding nailed all around on both sides. Dimensions and spacings of the crossmembers are left to your individual situation and preference.

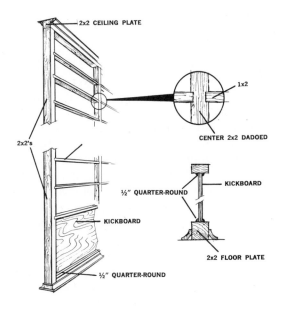

stock for a really rich-looking installation. Floor and ceiling plates of 2-by-2 stock are nailed directly to the flooring and ceiling joists respectively. The uprights are dadoed for mortise joints to hold the cross members—the inside verticals have shallow dado mortises on both sides, the end uprights are dadoed only on the inside surface. Space the dadoes uniformly, at the desired distance for separation of the cross members. The latter may be spaced 8″ apart as in the photograph, making a suitable proportion, or the separations can be varied to suit your preference.

The uprights are toenailed to the top and bottom plates, then the horizontal cross members are glued in place, using pipe clamp pressure. The kickboards, which may be of ½″ or ¾″ plywood, are secured with ¼-round molding tacked all around on both sides of the divider, as shown in the sketch, followed by trim moldings. This completes the basic construction, leaving only the finishing, although that might be done even better on the separate parts before the unit is assembled. Careful sanding is the essential step in a good finishing job. The rest may be simple coating with shellac to retain the original color, or staining as desired with a final protective coat of shellac or brushed lacquer.

Some hints about the wood supply may be useful. Dimensions of the materials stated above require adjustment according to the actual stock sizes obtainable. For example, you may be able to purchase oak boards that are only ¾″ thick, rather than the 1″ cited, and that would be suitable.

Also, suppose you can purchase the ¾″-thick stock in 7½″ width, which could be ripped into four pieces, each approximately 1¾″ wide, instead of the 2″ shown in the sketch. The adjustments are easily made, and will not affect the overall plan or method of construction. For the 2-by-2 stock, you might use boards 1⁵⁄₁₆″ or 1¾″ thick, ripping five lengths from a 9½″ wide board. Thus you might end up with uprights that are 1⁵⁄₁₆″ x 1¾″. The only requirement for this project is that the cross-section widths of the verticals be uniform with that of the cross members. The problem is considerably simplified with standard white pine or ponderosa pine stock sizes, either in shelving boards or construction lumber sold at nominal 1″ and 2″ thicknesses.

Filigree Entrance Wall

As an eye-catching entryway divider and backdrop for a planter, this project is uniquely suitable. And because it is both decorative and functional, you'll want to treat it with all the care of a fine furniture project.

A study of the sketch will explain the assembling process. The entire unit is made of 2-by-2 stock, neatly constructed with half-lapped and mitered joints. Though delicate looking, it is nevertheless sturdy and handsome. The joinery is itself interesting and instructive, and completion of this project will win kudos from every visitor to your home.

First step is to determine the most desirable dimensions for the divider, based on its location and a suitable proportion of length to width of the entry corridor, so that it is neither overwhelming in size nor so small as to lose its significance. You would then be able to compute the relative sizes of the inside frames and their connection bars. When you've made this decision, install the four outer frame members, at top, bottom, and sides.

There are three full-length internal uprights, and four full-length horizontals, as seen in the photograph. These are cut to the required lengths laid out on the floor, and marked for half-laps where parts intersect. These laps are cut and the internal members are temporarily assembled.

The horizontals are lapped again midway between the vertical posts to accommodate the short frame connectors, which will be joined in later. In making these half-lap cuts, it's far better to clamp a group of equal parts together and make the cuts on all at one time, with a saw or router, than to do them individually.

Cutting the Parts

Next make the 20 small interior frames, all with mitered corners, glued solidly together into compact individual units. You will now need 16 lapped vertical connectors to fit vertically between two frames, with a lap joint at the center where they intersect a horizontal bar.

Also, you will need 15 horizontal connectors, of a length to fit between two frames and lapped at the intersection with the uprights, and 10 half-length horizontal connectors. The assembly procedure consists of installing one small frame at a time, gluing and clamping the connector bars, and butt-nailing at the four points where these connectors meet each frame.

The procedure is not as complex as it sounds, primarily because each of the components is repeated many times and is uniform throughout.

Ornamental divider in filigree design forms an entrance corridor. The unit, built entirely of wood in uniform cross-section, makes an interesting and instructive project for the home handyman who has developed some workshop skills.

AROUND THE HOUSE

The main effort is devoted to producing the necessary parts in bulk—the parts for all 20 frames (80 pieces) are all precisely uniform, as are the assembled frames. The lap mortises are identical throughout as to width and depth, so by clamping together a half-dozen or so of the connectors or uprights or horizontals you can do them all with the same dado blade setting and a single pass of the saw.

And as all material is uniform, a power sander will do a batch all at one time, when the parts are clamped together. Finishing, including the staining and waxing, can be done before the parts are assembled, but in that case be careful to clean up immediately any squeeze-out glue from the joints.

SLIDING WALL MAGIC

The traditional Shoji wall, mainstay of Japanese home arrangements, can have an important role in American family life, too. The sliding wall is so very useful, permitting manipulation of the family living space so that the maximum benefit is obtained by all. Among its countless practical applications, one example is its use in large recreation rooms or playrooms that are fine for entertaining many guests but would be more pleasant and conversationally comfortable for everyday use when reduced to a more intimate size by closing off a section with the sliding wall.

In another circumstance, a Shoji wall can temporarily partition off a segment of the room to form a separate guest room, providing complete privacy. Or, perhaps, such a sliding wall would be perfect in apartments where children sharing a bedroom have reached the age where they are keen about having "their own place," but separate rooms aren't available for them.

While highly effective for solving these and similar space problems, there's no denying that the translucent Shoji wall has considerable merit by itself, in the handsome appearance resulting from a design that has been almost unaltered through many centuries. The design appeals not only to aficionados of oriental furnishings, but has also the amazing capacity to blend well with every kind of room decorations, particularly modern Scandinavian furniture, with its sleek lines and bland natural colors.

The lightweight and sturdy wall is built in sectional panels, faced with translucent fiberglass substituting for the original rice paper. Suspended

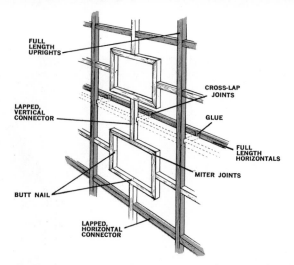

All dimensions of divider unit are optional with the homeowner, but the basic design is classic following well-defined principles. The wall has unusual strength despite the lightness of its structure, as all intersecting parts are half-lapped and glued.

on an overhead track, the sections move smoothly and effortlessly on single-wheel nylon rollers that never need lubricating.

The frames are made of any wood that has the quality of retaining its shape and resisting warpage —in the wall illustrated, redwood was used in stock 1-by-4 and 1-by-6 sizes, ripped to required widths.

The sides of the frames are made of 1-by-4's, ripped in half, while the frame tops are made of full-width strips set flat on their edges, and the 1-by-6's are used similarly for the bottom rails. The frames are all uniform in size, and so arranged that when the wall is closed, each panel overlaps the side rail of the adjacent panel, thus avoiding the irregularity and excessively heavy appearance that would result when double rails are visible.

Making the Panels

The divider strips are glued into notches in the frame rails on both sides of the fiberglass, thus holding the plastic sheeting flat and firm. The easiest way to join the sides to the top and bottom rails is by the spline method—cutting ¼" wide grooves exactly at the center of the members to be joined, locking them together with ¼" plywood strips tapped tightly into the grooves with white resorcinol glue. Use pipe clamps to apply pressure for about four hours at each clamped joint.

The wall panels may ride on two or three separate tracks, depending on their planned movement. One track will run the entire length, the others will possibly be in sections as short as 4'. The tracks are fastened to a length of 2-by-4, which is put up ei-

Sliding Shoji wall, with translucent fiberglass panels, contributes to the appearance of any home, blends well with almost every furniture period. The wall can help solve many space problems, partitioning a room for overnight guests, as an example, or dividing a bedroom shared by two children.

Sliding panels are rolled back, allowing full use of the room. Some homeowners have found the Shoji wall excellent for use in front of large picture windows, instead of draperies or blinds, providing more complete privacy while permitting ample daylight in room.

AROUND THE HOUSE

Sides for all frames are cut at same time by ripping 1x4 stock in half, then are clamped together. Notches for the dividers are made uniformly with a router.

End of the rails are deeply grooved for the ¼" splines to joint them to the side pieces. Inside surfaces of the rails and side pieces are grooved along the center of their entire length.

The sheeting can be cut with shears, but a stacked batch of sheets can be cut at one time with a metal-cutting blade in a sabre saw. Clamp the sheets together so they won't shift.

After plastic is inserted into kerf grooves, tap in plywood splines and lock corner joints together.

Resorcinol glue is brushed into the spline grooves and the panel frame joints clamped together.

With sheeting inserted into grooves, divider retainer strips are cut and fitted into frame notches.

Tracks are fastened to length of 2x4, which is put up to the ceiling. One track runs full length, others may extend only at sides to required length for door movement.

If top of Shoji wall is to be kept some distance below ceiling height, use spacer blocks to which the track support can be attached.

Overhead support is boxed in neatly with ¼" plywood, forming an attractive ceiling beam that is finished to match sliding wall frame.

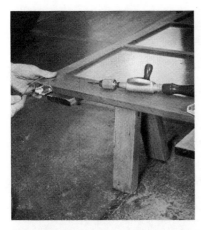

Single-wheel nylon hangers are fastened to top of the frames, set 1" inward from each corner, to ride in hanger track.

Panels are tested to see that they slide freely and have sufficient clearance to avoid interference from adjoining panel.

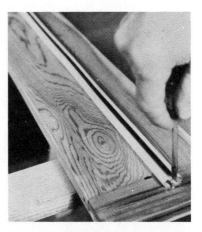

Panels are cleverly coordinated with lengths of standard drapery traverse rod, using nylon hangers that ride horizontally in the rod. Attach rod with a screw at each end.

Clip off the hook eyes in the nylon hangers and drill screw holes; attach to the panels on sides opposite the rod sections.

The hanger engages the rod and slides along it when panels are banked. When door is closed, panels move until hangers meet stop screw at end of rod.

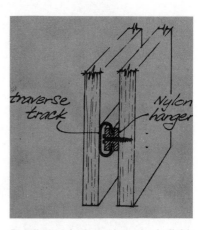

Detail sketch shows how the individual panels are held together at the bottom by nylon clips in traverse rods.

ther directly on the ceiling, or attached to spacer blocks at the desired level. The supports for these tracks are boxed in with ¼" plywood to form the shape of a ceiling beam.

Panels are guided at the bottom by drapery traverse tracks on the inside surface of the rail panels. Nylon hanger blocks from the traverse rod are attached with screws to the rail on the opposing panel, and these blocks ride inside the traverse rod as the panels are moved back and forth, as shown in the sketch.

AMAZING INDOOR/OUTDOOR CARPETING

This carpeting, woven of industrial fibers that resist moisture damage and retain their color, can be used anywhere inside or outside your home. Once upon a time, as they used to say, carpet was something that covered the parlor floor. Period. Now, with the development of new materials and manufacturing processes, varieties of carpeting are made for us that were unimaginable just a few years ago.

No longer are you restricted to fake "grass" outdoor carpets—now they come in a wide range of colors and patterns, some even with tufted construction as shown on this porch deck which could be an extension of your living-room carpet.

This proliferation has brought with it a certain amount of confusion. There are "outdoor" carpets that can be used indoors. There are "indoor" carpets that are actually well suited for kitchen areas and "outdoor" carpets that are recommended for basement and on-grade floors.

Said another way—most indoor/outdoor carpets can be used in kitchens but "kitchen" carpets cannot necessarily be used outdoors. If a carpet contains any natural fiber, such as jute, it cannot withstand the elements. Carpeting *al fresco* must consist entirely of man-made fibers, which are moisture-resistant, can take rain, snow, or sleet. They won't rot or mildew and don't shrink. Summer heat has no harmful effect. Solution dyed, the colors are *in* the fiber, do not fade under normal conditions. Maintenance is not much of a problem. Outdoor carpet can be kept clean by vacuuming up loose dirt or by hosing it down.

If you'll provide a smooth, flat surface for it, carpet can be laid loose wherever you want it outdoors. On porches, decks, steps, and patios you can use double-faced tape to hold it in place. On concrete the manufacturer will suggest the proper adhesive for a more permanent installation, particularly for safety around your swimming pool.

Originally, the clue to outdoor suitability was what is called needlebond construction. This is still the least expensive type of outdoor carpet. But you are no longer limited to fake grass—there is a wide range of colors, some printed designs and now even multicolored patterns. Recently, acrylic has been utilized and now there are also carpets of tufted construction.

Ideal for Playrooms

For indoor use, there is an even greater variety with the addition of more acrylic, polyester, and nylon fibers. In addition to needlebond, you will find low level, tight-loop construction offered for greatest durability and easiest care, both types available with backings of latex or foam. The moisture-resistant qualities of most indoor/outdoor carpets make them ideal for basement and playroom or laundry installations, too. While no carpet will cure a wet basement, outdoor carpets make a hard, concrete floor comfortable, insulate it a bit, and make it a lot warmer.

Carpet can be a real asset in your kitchen. It is warm and comfortable for small kids to creep and crawl on, and will lessen a housewife's fatigue.

New indoor-outdoor carpeting used around swimming pool patios is a lot warmer than cold concrete—it's safer too. You'll have to use carpets of man-made fiber which won't rot, mildew, or shrink.

No carpet will cure a wet basement, but installations such as shown sure go far toward making such hard surfaces a lot more comfortable, insulating them a bit as well as making your basement more inviting than a bare one.

Where comfort underfoot, style, quiet, less china and glass breakage are the major points to consider, where the occasional spill is the rule and loose, dry soil the problem, carpet is the easy choice. Maintenance is pretty simple: a bit of daily vacuuming, a thorough weekly going-over with a vacuum cleaner equipped with a revolving agitator brush, and an annual shampoo is the general schedule suggested. Kitchen carpet is not as easy to clean as a smooth resilient floor, but if you're willing to live with that fact, it will be your choice for its other advantages.

If your kids are still in the food-slinging-and-spilling stage, you should take note that all manufacturer's maintenance notes read "attend to spills immediately!" Two types of spotting mixes are suggested: one, a solution of neutral detergent and white vinegar mixed with warm water, and second, a household dry cleaning fluid. Remove excess material with a blunt knife or spoon. Classify the stain and then check your handy list of which solution to use and follow those directions.

The new carpets won't flame but there's going to be a burn mark where a careless cigarette lands. One manufacturer supplies you with a cookie-cutter that cuts out the damaged carpet area as well as a replacement patch to match.

It's not as easy to clean as a smooth, resilient floor but it can be a real asset to your kitchen. The carpeting shown below is comfortable for kids to crawl on, lessens mother's fatigue as well and helps minimize your chinaware and glass breakage.

Three Installation Methods

As for installation, while a few companies recommend that skilled installers do the job (particularly on large areas where seams could be a problem) most manufacturers consider installation well within the skill of the homeowner. For most areas, indoors and out, carpet can be loose-laid over any solid, flat, smooth surface, and trimmed to fit. Kitchen shears, a razor, or knife will do the job, even on the foam- or latex-backed materials. Laying the carpet loose is actually preferred, even indoors. You can roll it up, take it out and hose it off. Outdoors, on wood decks and porches, loose-laid carpet can be lifted after a heavy rain, permitting the wood beneath to dry out.

There are minor variations in installation instruction details so read those supplied by the manufacturer. Double-faced tape usually is suggested at seams and for much-trafficked areas, but as some carpeting is available in 15′ widths (most are 12′ wide) seams can often be avoided. Where molding is used at the perimeter, you need tape only intermittently, but always at doorways. For carpet tiles, secure one row across the room with the tape, a second row at right angles to that. Lay the rest of the tiles loose. Once the whole area is covered, it can be vacuumed and of course walked on without disturbance. Individual tiles can still be picked up should the time come when spot removing has to be done at the sink.

Because man-made fibers are dimensionally stable, it is important not to stretch the carpet as you lay it. Pull it tight, no more. With installation easy and maintenance requirements minimal, there remains only one problem—burns. These carpets will scorch and scar but will not burst into flame. Repairs are pretty simple—just cut out the damaged area, cut a patch to match. One company even has a gadget to take the guesswork out of the cutting.

With all the plus factors for the new carpets, you'll find them useful in many more places—children's rooms and on your boat, bathrooms, and at your sauna suite, upstairs decks, and vacation cottages.

BRICK PATH FOR CHARM

An excellent way to add a touch of charm to your grounds is by installing a brick path. The job can be done with either new or used bricks held together with a dry cement-sand mixture.

The area of the path should be excavated, a 2″ base laid, then the bricks laid on edge—not flat—on the base and the joints filled. The finished path should be slightly higher than the ground, so make the excavation deep enough to accomplish this. For instance, if you were using bricks 4″ deep (height when laid on edge), you'd dig down about 5½″. The 4″ brick plus the 2″ base would bring the surface of the path above the ground, marking the path clearly.

If your soil is water-logged, clay, or extremely light, there are advantages in providing a wet concrete base. Installation is the same as with the dry mix except the bricks are worked into the wet concrete to half their depth. Joints are also filled with wet concrete, then pointed.

Whether you use a wet or dry mix, the curbing or edging must be laid wet. (Incidentally, the curbing is installed first.) Just set the bricks on edge—end to end in a two-inch base of wet cement. Fill the joints between bricks and draw a fillet of ce-

Lay the curbs first. Set the bricks on edge in a 2-inch bed of cement and add a fillet of cement on the outside for support. Then continue as shown at right.

Path bricks are installed after the dry base is laid. They also should be stood on edge. Space them about ⅜-inch apart.

A dry mix in the same proportions as for the base is used to fill the joints. Just shovel it on, about a yard at a time.

Next, use a brush or broom to sweep the mix into the joints. A long-handled one will save wear and tear on your back.

Wash the mix well down into the joints, sweep in more mix and spray again. Repeat this until the joints are filled.

You can lay bricks in many different patterns, such as this herringbone. Brick dealers have many free patterns.

If pattern calls for cutting bricks to size, score brick all around with a trowel or chisel, then sharply rap the waste side.

Determine the area of your new stoop and dig up earth around and a little outward, to frost depth.

When a stoop is too small for comfort and safety, the way to get a bigger one is to stretch the slab size.

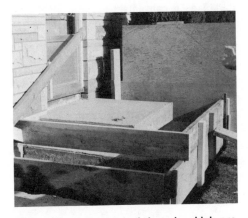

Build your form of 2-inch boards which are strong enough to withstand pressure of freshly poured mix.

With everything braced firmly, the concrete can be poured; be sure to protect shrubs and the door from splatter.

ment up against the outside of the curbing for additional support.

A BIGGER STOOP IS BETTER

Chances are your front stoop has proved to be too small, too narrow, or just plain skimpy, even if your home is of recent vintage. The thing to do is to make it larger for appearance's sake as well as function. You can expand the original simply by pouring a new stoop right over it.

The photographs show how a small stoop which measured 3'-by-4' (with a narrow, 10" wide step on

Using a crossboard as a convenient support, level and trowel everything to a smooth surface.

Cover the slab and keep it moistened for at least 72 hours. If slab dries too quickly, it could shell off sometime later.

two sides) was enlarged to a more practical 5'-by-6'. The improved version, with a 15" step on one side only, was begun by digging to a point just below the frost line, all along the outer perimeter.

Heavy 2"-thick boards were used for the forms, retained by stakes driven into the ground. Note how one board was secured to the framework at step height (in this case, 8"), forming the riser for the one step at the side.

Pouring the Concrete

In essence, the old stoop was simply capped. The new mix adhered well to the old, because the original surfaces were first thoroughly cleaned, then treated with a bonding agent.

One cubic yard of ready-mix concrete filled the form, with particular attention paid to the edges—care was taken to tightly pack the cement against the frame, puddling the mix with a stick in an up-and-down motion, preventing air pockets from forming. A minimum of 2½" of concrete caps the old slab, resisting weathering and cracking. But before you go ahead and pour, double-check the clearance to the door saddle. You should have more than enough space, but if not, cap the top surface with less cement.

Proper curing is the secret for getting tough concrete, for the tensile strength of concrete increases when the newly poured mix is kept moist and covered for periods of seventy-two hours and longer. If a job is allowed to dry out too readily, concrete will

begin to shell off prematurely, but kept adequately moistened for the curing process, the job will last many years.

After completion, ground fill around the stoop is packed in and freshly seeded, perhaps a small shrub added. If your version is similar, you may want to add a wrought-iron railing.

WROUGHT-IRON RAILINGS

Until quite recently, anyone who wanted something made of wrought iron had to go to a skilled ironworker, who was perhaps as much an artist as a craftsman. Mass-production methods have brought costs down so that many wrought-iron items are available at modest prices in prefabricated kit form. Installation of even an extensive stoop railing has been greatly simplified by predrilling and special fastener fittings so that any handyman can do a professional quality job.

After you've purchased the various parts you need, apply paint over the priming with which the parts are prepared at the factory.

The installation procedure is about the same whether you're working indoors on a wood stairway, or outdoors on masonry. The big difference is in the type of fastenings used.

Drill holes in the bottom step with a carbide bit or star drill for anchor bolts to fasten the base of the newel post. Install base, then insert posts, cutting, if need be, to the desired height. Tighten the

Wrought iron railings and columns make dramatic improvements in the home's appearance while serving utilitarian purposes, as seen in the three examples shown. Pre-fabricated products reduce cost and make possible professional quality homeowner installations.

Fencing comes in sections, primed and ready to install. First, spray or brush a finish coat of paint on it.

Drill holes in concrete that align with holes in base, then fasten the base to the floor with anchor bolts.

Insert post into base and plumb. Make sure it is true, or it can throw the whole fence out of allignment.

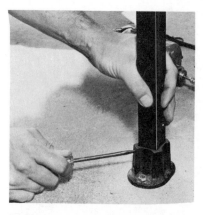

Tighten the post in the base with screws that are inserted in pre-drilled holes. Be sure post is plumb.

Position the fence section as shown and mark it at the points where it will fasten to the house wall and the post.

Cut off excess, then fit the fence section between wall and post, and fasten with special fittings provided.

Sections can be bent to the shape desired. To bend a section to pitch of steps, press down and across as shown.

Special fitting slips into grooves in rails and is screwed to posts. It can be bent for fastening pitched fence.

set screw in the base to hold the post, making sure the post is perfectly plumb.

Fit railings between the posts and cut to length, then bend to the desired angle by placing the bottom on a flat firm support and applying sidewise pressure. Attach rail to newel posts by aligning the holes in the fittings with the predrilled holes in the posts, tightening the screws firmly.

The end of the railing may be attached to a wall also, again using the type of fastener to suit the material—a lag screw into wood or an anchor bolt into masonry. The angle of the fitting may be easily adjusted by tapping with a hammer, as shown.

Ornaments of various types can be added when everything else is installed.

UPDATING YOUR WINDOWS

If any of your windows do not please you for one reason or another—they may be troublesome, or drafty, or just downright ugly to the extent of downgrading your home's appearance—the right step is to replace them. There's no need to feel locked in with whatever windows the builder happened to stick in. In fact, there's nothing permanent about windows, period!

Changing to a type that you prefer is neither a major construction project, nor a big financial operation. You can switch to any style you like: bow, bay, double-hung, casement, sliding panel, awning, jalousie, or any other of the dozens of different styles and types. You can also select the features you prefer from variations galore, such as removable sash for safe and easy cleaning, fixed sash (or any combination of fixed and movable sash), or the outswinging and inswinging awning types.

Options include rotary openers and latches, concealed draft-proof vents, extension hinges that permit washing from the inside, double glazing and even triple glazing for thermal insulation, and many more products of advanced technology.

This is the opportunity to make some basic physical changes that you've had in mind, perhaps setting the new windows higher to shut out some part of the view or expanding the opening to install a large bow window, or a single-pane picture window to bring the outdoors indoors. Not every wish can be fulfilled, since there may be some structural limitations, but this is the time to see what changes can be made.

The actual changeover is not a very complicated process, and can be tackled by any home owner

When a window has seen better days, and begins to give you some bad ones, the best move may be to replace it.

A pair of double-hung wood windows, in tandem, may be just the kind you've always wanted. Replacement procedure is shown in photographic sequence.

Here are examples
of window types.

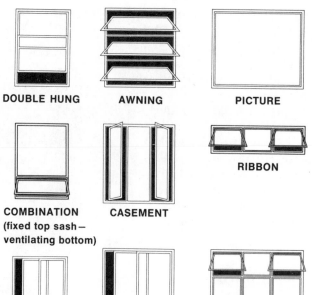

DOUBLE HUNG   AWNING   PICTURE

COMBINATION
(fixed top sash—
ventilating bottom)   CASEMENT

RIBBON

SLIDING   SLIDING DOOR   WINDOW WALL

Make sure you have the correct replacement before starting removal of the old window. Surrounding siding usually is damaged in the process, but is easily repaired. Continue as shown at right.

Steel casements of this size are quite heavy, so adequate support must be provided. In this case, a ramp of 2x4s was built.

A crowbar is used to pry the window loose from its frame. Try to locate the retainer screws at the sides, and remove them first.

With the ramp taking the bulk of the window's weight, all you do is ease it down the incline to the ground.

The opening must be prepared for the new window. First, clean it out to the basic wood framework.

Check the opening for plumb and level, shimming the new filler boards to correct any deviations.

Only the sides and bottom need filler in this installation. The new boards should be the same width as the original framing.

Heavy grade builder's paper is stapled to the sheathing to provide a fully sealed weather and moisture barrier.

With the preparations completed, the project is ready for the next step, putting in the new windows which have been selected.

Up she goes! The window is light, but its size made the services of a helper advisable for easier and safer manipulation.

The window is wedged in place, then checked to be sure that it is sitting level so that it will operate smoothly.

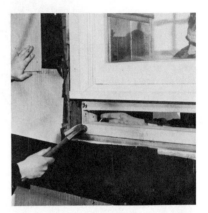

Because the new window is somewhat shorter than the original one, by intention, the bottom is raised on parallel 2x4s, separated by a wedge block to obtain tight fitting.

Bottom opening is enclosed with sheathing nailed to the supports. indow also is securely nailed in place.

Drip cap is metal extrusion, comes in stock lengths and is cut to fit with shears, then nailed in place.

All open spaces on the inside are packed with insulation material, pressed tightly into the openings with a broad blade knife.

Moldings are fitted and nailed in to provide the surface trim and assure a neat finish. Inside woodwork is fully painted later.

Area under window and above the radiator must be fully insulated and provided with a vapor barrier facing the inside of the room.

The inside sill is a standard item, available in stock lengths which must be cut down to size and accurately shaped to fit.

Wall area around the new window may need retouching or replacement, same as with the shingles or siding on the outside.

with general home maintenance experience and a modest collection of tools.

The photographic sequence included here shows the removal of a steel casement that had outlived its usefulness, and its replacement with a pair of attractive double-hung wood windows. The new window comes complete, all parts intact and assembled, so installation consists of framing the new windows, squaring them up, insulating, then repairing the walls and attaching the finish trim.

Prime windows are available in a variety of stock sizes, and in a wide price range. Your best first step is to write to the major window manufacturers requesting the current catalogs of styles, stock sizes, and prices. There may be window types you haven't thought of, which may be just right for your home. Then careful examination of the present window structure will give you the needed clues for planning the replacement installation.

DRESS UP YOUR DRIVEWAY

A gravel driveway is quite attractive; a brick driveway is undoubtedly much more handsome and

serviceable. Converting to a mortarless brick driveway is an interesting and rewarding project, and a money-saving one as well. The one shown, providing full-width access to a double garage 50' from the curb, was put down for less than a third the cost quoted for a concrete job, and half the cost of a blacktop asphalt driveway.

Selecting the Brick

Use a hard, uncored brick for the job. There are paving bricks at higher prices, but a solid red brick will do very well for this purpose. To determine how many bricks are needed, first figure the square footage of the driveway, and multiply by the number of bricks in a square foot. In the standard $2\frac{1}{4}''$ x $3\frac{3}{4}''$ x 8" size, there are $4\frac{1}{2}$ bricks per square foot of surface. Thus a driveway 20' wide by 50' long would cover 1,000 square feet and require 4,500 bricks. But a one-car garage may have a driveway 12' wide, and extend back only 30', thus covering 360 square feet and requiring only 1,350 bricks.

Paving Procedure

The gravel should be well settled and have good drainage. If it's been there a couple of years, the settling should be sufficient. Any surface depressions that result in water pooling should be corrected by scraping away the gravel and leveling the base with well-tamped soil, then replacing and smoothing the gravel.

The first installation step is to provide an edging along the sides of the driveway to contain the gravel and keep the bricks from moving. An inexpensive material for this is white pine 2-by-4's, carefully treated with Penta compound or other preser-

Most homemakers agree that bricks make the most attractive driveway surface, adding color and design to the home environment. Even grease drippings from parked cars do not spoil the appearance, as is the case with concrete and gravel.

Herringbone pattern, one of more than a dozen possibilities, is particularly suitable for the mortarless installation because the bricks are interlocked.

Before laying each brick, make sure the spot it will rest upon is smooth and level. Wear heavy gloves to protect the hands.

After each brick is set in place, tap it gently with a medium weight hammer to level it and bring it close to the others for tight joints.

In every installation, some brick must be broken to fit. Here a hammer is used to break off a corner. This can be done also by scoring with a chisel, then tapping the hand-held brick with a hammer on the scored line.

vative and coated with tar. These 2-by-4's are secured in position with 1-by-2 stakes driven into the ground and nailed to the 2-by-4's. More serviceable, but somewhat more expensive, are redwood boards, while the most attractive and permanent driveway border can be obtained with a "soldier course" of brick—placed on end, close together and set in concrete.

After the edging is installed, use a rake to level the gravel, that is, level with the slope of the driveway so that drainage is retained. If the gravel is fine, raking will provide a sufficiently smooth base for the brick. If the gravel is coarse, add a 1″ base of moist sand, tamped or rolled to prevent it from shifting later. Without the sand, leveling of the coarse gravel is difficult. If you want to prevent grass and weed growth between the brick, spread a layer of tarpaper or polyethylene plastic film over the sand. Neither of these coverings is recommended directly over gravel; a chemical weed killer may be used instead.

Laying the Brick

Work out your own design if you wish, for the brick. Dozens of arrangements are possible—placing the bricks end-to-end, or in checkerboard squares. The herringbone pattern shown is recommended as it provides a good interlock to hold the bricks in place. Start by laying in a single course, wide side down and end to end, all along the edging on both sides of the driveway. Then start at either end, filling in according to the design. At some points you will need half bricks to fill in. The professional bricklayer can do this with a single sharp blow of his trowel, but you're not likely to duplicate that trick by casual attempts. A dependable method is to score the brick lightly with a chisel, then rap sharply with a hammer on the scored line while holding the brick in your hand. It should cleave neatly on the line.

The main concentration should be to see that the bricks all lie in flat and level. Any bumps or other unevenness will surely show up after every rain as pools of water, and also will detract from the general appearance of what should be a very attractive, colorful driveway, one that will add greatly to the overall appearance of your home.

OPEN GARAGE DOOR
WITH ONE FINGER

It's after midnight. Cold rain is running down your neck while you mutter nasty things and try to unlock your garage door. After you've tried every key, the door finally opens and you dash back to your car and drive inside the garage. You go in the house hoping for hot coffee, a dry shirt, and some sympathy from your wife. Instead she looks at you accusingly and tells you you're raining on the rug.

You start muttering again. But you're also doing some thinking. . . . How difficult would it be to install an automatic garage door operator?

Remote-control motorized door openers now are more compact and installation has been simplified. You can save the installation charge by doing the work yourself, and if you're able to handle a soldering gun, you will save even more by buying the unit in kit form, such as the Heathkit, which is shown being assembled in the photographs. The kit comes complete with everything you need to do the entire job.

It can operate overhead track, jamb, and pivot doors up to 8' high. At least 2½" of clearance are needed above the highest point of door travel. This is no problem in the average garage, but where the ceiling is too low, a recess will have to be cut to allow space for the trolley mechanism.

Ordinary Tools Used

The Heathkit assembly manual is easy to understand and is thoroughly illustrated. Installation takes about four hours. The entire job—assembly and installation—can certainly be completed in a weekend. You can work on the assembly of the unit whenever you have a few spare minutes. It's a simple matter to complete as many steps as you have time for, checking off each one in turn as it is completed. In fact, it's probably a good idea to take a break or two during assembly to help avoid fatigue and lessen the chances of making mistakes. Though it may seem obvious, it's absolutely essential to read the assembly manual carefully and to follow the assembly sequence recommended.

Practice in Soldering

If you've never soldered before, it's a good idea to practice before going to work on the kit. You'll find it easy to recognize a well-soldered connection—it will look smooth and shiny.

The operator unit is thoughtfully engineered. For example, a safety release disengages the drive mechanism if anything gets in the way of the door. If the power fails, the door can be operated manually. However, in the case of a folding door, the mechanism will prevent manual operation from outside the garage. One-piece garage doors can be opened by hand if necessary, but considerable force will be needed.

The mechanism can be actuated by either a radio transmitter or a doorbell pushbutton. One such switch is included in the kit, but others may be purchased if needed. For example, you may prefer a key-type switch on the outside of the garage. Installation of the opener unit is best done by two persons working together.

Radio transmitter in car signals receiver inside garage to open or close door. Pushbutton also can control the door.

Automatic garage door opener is installed on the ceiling, actuated by the radio receiver which controls the motor. Motor action pulls bracket on door.

Garage opener here is in kit form, for cost savings. Check parts list to be certain nothing is missing, then study the instruction booklet.

Electronic work consists of assembling the parts in this chassis and soldering the connections. Do only what the manual says should be done.

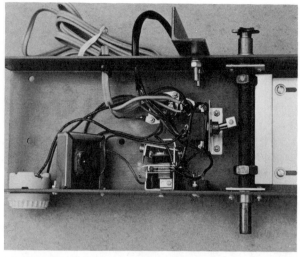

Large threaded rod at right turns as door moves up or down. The switch is disconnected when the door is completely open.

When assembling the chain drive and beam, rest it at comfortable working height on bench.

Connections to the motor must be carefully insulated. The kit includes a supply of plastic "spaghetti" for this purpose.

Mechanism is equipped with safety latch to stop the door if it meets an obstruction on the way down.

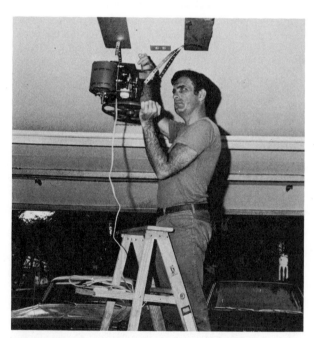

Ceiling mounting can be done by various methods. Steel strapping is used here.

Arm exerts pull on bracket attached to the door. This system has built-in flexibility to meet every requirement.

Final step is installing the radio receiver which triggers the mechanism, so door opens or closes on signal.

NEW GARAGE DOOR PERKS UP HOUSE

When it comes to garage doors, swingers are as out of date as the Model T. If you have vintage doors that make driving into or out of your garage a test of skill and fortitude, the time has surely come to spare yourself and the car fenders further abuse. The simplest answer is substitution with a sectional overhead door that you can raise effortlessly, and which rolls up completely out of your way, giving added clearance at the sides—so important in any tightly dimensioned garage. The doors are handsome in appearance, and have at least one row of glass panels to allow light into the garage.

You can save quite a lot by installing the door yourself. Order it from your local lumber-dealer or a mail-order house. It comes in a compact package, weighing 150 to 200 lbs. for a single-car garage door. When ordering, specify the width and height and number of sections. Everything you need for assembly is included, the screw holes for hinges and other hardware are predrilled, and there's always an instruction sketch showing the mechanism details. Actual installation should take less than five hours, but you may have to spend some additional time on preparatory work, such as correcting any misalignment of the garage framework and perhaps reinforcing the supporting vertical members at the garage entryway.

The first step, then, is to plumb and secure the garage framework with a 2-by-4 or 2-by-6 upright on each side, and a header across the top if one is needed. Then the door is assembled, starting with the vertical and horizontal track parts. Put them aside for the moment and attach the hinges to the bottom section of the door, placing this section into the garage opening, propped up in place with paint cans or whatever is available for this purpose.

Add the second door section by joining the hinge leaves, then build up with the third section, and finally the top section, all now connected by their hinges, but do not yet attach the top roller carriers.

Insert the rollers in the hinge joints, roughly position the track (it is provided with slotted holes) with lag screws driven into the vertical frame members, jockey the rollers into the tracks, and align the tracks accordingly. Now roughly aligned, attach the top roller carriers and roller, inserting the latter into the tracks; realign the tracks if necessary, and tighten their carriage bolts firmly.

At this point, the horizontal tracks, being unattached, are wobbly. Nevertheless, cautiously test the

New-style sectional overhead door is a good investment that pays off in convenience, good appearance for house, and greater ease in using the garage.

Old-style swinging doors are not very attractive at best, have tendency to sag, and require hinge posts that take up part of the narrow space.

door's action and alignment by raising it to about half-opening (don't forget to remove the temporary braces). Alignment corrections should be made at this time.

This stage consists of sounding out ceiling joists and attaching the angle iron base, followed by the angle iron connector, between each track's end and the base. When the horizontal tracks' alignment is set, a third, cross brace can be installed. The final stages consist of assembling the cables, cable rollers, and springs—anchoring the springs to the metal connectors and securing the cables (one end attaching to the corner bracket of the bottom door section, the other to a cable anchor at the corner of the track.) Just remember though, the door must be blocked in the open position before you will be able to start making the necessary adjustments on the cables.

At this point, the door will open fully on its own, and it will close to within about 4″ to 6″ of the floor. Have someone hold the door fully closed, then attach the vertical stop strips, snug them against the door and nail them to the side panels. The stops in effect become friction strips at the bot-

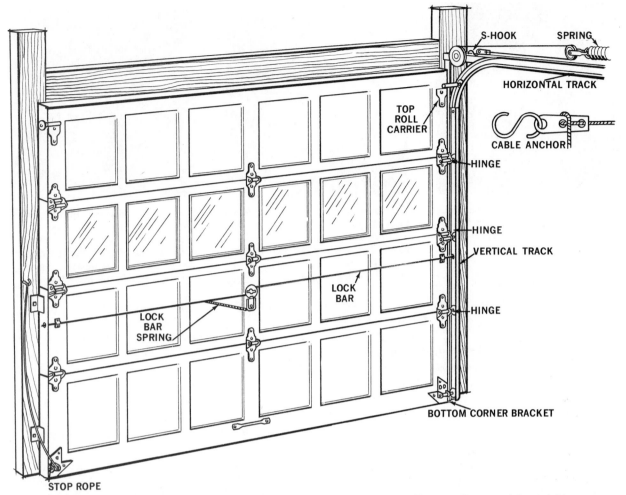

Assembly and installation details of the overhead door are shown in sketch. Door sections are joined right in the garage opening so no shifting of the heavy assembled door will be necessary.

Before starting installation, check that both door jambs are parallel and in solid condition. If needed, add lengths of 2x4 or 2x6, and shim out so they are plumb.

Hinges are quickly attached because the screw holes are predrilled. The carriage bolts used for the hinges are tapped partway in with hammer.

Most doors come from factory complete with glass panes installed in one of the sections. Rest of section panels are hardboard or plywood.

AROUND THE HOUSE

The lock is secured to its section from the rear. When the complete lock is installed, a portion of it will engage the locking bars on the left.

The perforated angle iron being fastened to the ceiling joist will later anchor one of the two horizontal tracks, one of which is shown at lower right. The same angle iron also will anchor the door's springs.

Finished installation shows cable and pulley in place. One end of the cable is attached to the bottom section of the door, the other end looped around a wheel secured to the spring and anchored in the track frame.

tom, as well as serving as closures. A third horizontal stop strip is secured to the top of the door frame.

If the floor of the garage is not level at the opening, the new door will not close flush. This difficulty can be overcome simply by attaching a strip of rubber skirting along the bottom edge that will seal the uneven space. Special rubber gaskets also are available which provide a perfect seal.

New doors should be treated with a wood preservative before priming. Use an oil-base exterior primer on all the edges, as well as inside and out. Allow this coat to dry about forty-eight hours before applying the finish coat.

ALUMINUM STORM DOORS MATCH HOME'S DECOR

The value of a storm door in terms of fuel savings and comfort is unquestionable. Despite these benefits, many home owners have refrained from putting on storm doors because of certain objections. Wood storm doors are subject to warping and require frequent painting. The main complaint about aluminum doors was their metallic color, to which some people have an aversion.

Technology finally has solved the problem of coating aluminum by an electrostatic process. The new aluminum storm and screen doors (and storm sash as well) are beautifully finished with smooth, baked-on enamel, available in a choice of popular colors. Another feature that will be welcomed is the built-in hinge that extends the full height of the

door, providing a more enduring trouble-free support.

You can save considerably on the cost by purchasing your storm doors over the counter at a lumberyard or by mail order, and doing the installation yourself. This will take about three hours if the door frame is in good condition; any additional time spent repairing and squaring a rotted door frame will be an essential maintenance chore, in any event.

The door itself comes completely assembled but must be of the correct size to fit the door opening, with about 1/4" clearance at sides and top.

The installation requires attaching three metal framing strips that come with the door. The prime detail here is that these strips must be set absolutely plumb and square to assure a weathertight fit and finger-touch operation of the door.

One strip consists of the full-length hinge; the second is the adjustable top closure flange; the third is on the latch side of the doorway. In addition, a weatherstrip is attached later into the bottom door channel.

First put up the hinge, temporarily attaching it with screws through the predrilled holes, and placing wood shims or wedges where necessary to align it plumb in both directions—outward and toward the doorway opening. Use a carpenter's level for plumbing the hinge.

Attach the top closure strip temporarily and place the door into the opening atop a wood strip 1/4" thick for bottom clearance, and with a few screws from the hinge side into the door to hold it. Shift the top strip so that it just clears the door

Hinge is full length of door. Start by attaching it to the offset of the doorway.

Use level to plumb the hinge, shimming where necessary. Hinge must be plumb in both directions.

If there is a gap of more than ¼ inch in the doorway dimensions, add a wood filler strip at top or side, securely nailed.

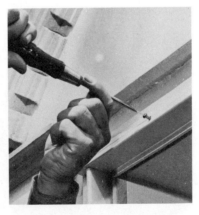

The top and latch side strips, or bars, go up next. They are attached only temporarily until door adjustment is made for permanent use.

and is level with it along its entire length, then tighten the attaching screws and put in several additional screws to secure it.

Now place the strip on the latch side, also adjusting it so that the door closes square against the flange for its entire length, and tighten its screws. If the door is short and the strip would have to move too far, nail a wood filler strip into the door frame to narrow the gap. Test the door swing now, making sure that it moves freely.

Now drill the holes for the latch, the closure check, which is best placed at the center rail, and the wind return spring. Also, insert the neoprene weatherstrip into the bottom channel, adjusting it to just touch the door sill when the door is closed. Replace the door and make a final check to be sure the door operates properly, then put in all the additional screws into the hinge and adjusting strips. Screws used with the aluminum storm door should be chrome-plated on brass.

Door is set into the opening, placed on ¼" wood strip for bottom clearance, and holes marked for screws.

Drill holes of proper size for self-threading screws into the door frame. Drill only three holes now, rest when door is installed.

Bottom channel of door is adjustable, has groove for inserting a neoprene weatherseal strip.

The channel is replaced with the weatherstrip, but adjustment is left until door is hung.

Holes are drilled and reamed for the handle and latch, leaving ample clearance for the hand between knob and wall.

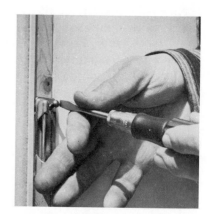

Last steps are attaching the windbreak spring, closure check, and the latch strike plate.

Chapter 13
HANDY TECHNIQUES

Every effort has been made to plan the home improvement projects of this book so that, as far as possible, they can be done by the home owner. Even so, many of the projects call for a considerable range of skills. Some require experience in cabinetmaking or carpentry, others may need ability in masonry, ceramic tile work, electrical installations, painting and wallpapering, plumbing, bricklaying, concrete work, ironwork, and others.

Which parts can the individual home owner tackle on his own? How much experience is needed before he can do a particular phase of the work? Is it possible for one person to develop such a wide range of skills that he can do the complete projects on his own?

These questions are not as difficult as they seem —they properly answer themselves. Anyone who has done a little work of any kind is more than ready to take on the next, and more complicated, step in that field.

A person who has put a dimmer switch in a wall panel would feel no qualms about installing a ceiling fixture. Anyone who has done some carpentry can do a bigger and more complicated woodworking job. Experience brings capability, and that in turn adds confidence.

What about the person who never has done any work of this sort? He must start somewhere, or remain always reliant on the skills of others. But let him make the first effort, then another, and he soon relishes the product of newly learned ability.

There are, of course, any number of home owners who bemoan the tasks that are needed around the house, and prefer to seek outside professional services, often at excessive cost. But there are a great many others, including some astute observers of our society, who regard the varied manual skills that can be developed by the householder as truly his salvation, a balance wheel in an otherwise confined and highly specialized life-style. The early American settler not only cared for his farm single-handedly, but made almost everything he needed, including his own home, all the furniture, and even the implements that it contained.

We certainly can manage without the backbreaking sunup-to-sundown labor of those days, but we really do benefit when we sharpen our manual capabilities by creating and improving the home we live in and the things we use. At the least, such activity widens our working skills, broadens our knowledge of tools and materials, and brings us closer to the hearthstone.

In several chapters in this book there are sections devoted to detailed instructions on the techniques or procedures involved in relevant subjects. In the chapter on basement finishing, for example, there was information on framing the walls and erecting partitions, together with instructions on fitting pipe and sweat soldering copper tubing to make branch water line connections for a wet bar or laundry washer.

Specific directions are given, when their value is indicated, for other installations or applications, such as the one-arm faucet in the chapter on kitchens.

Considerable coverage is given in other sections of this book to concrete work, framing doorways, and similar subjects. Additional techniques are explained in this chapter. It was not the authors' intention to cover every technique involved in home improvement work, nor was it possible to do so in one book. However, the selection includes those areas of the projects that will likely appeal to the home owner or provide basic guidance in proceeding with the work.

FINISHING WALLS WITH GYPSUM PANELS

Gypsum wallboard, known also as drywall and plasterboard, is being used today in more new homes and for additions than is any other similar building material—a distinction it has earned because of what it offers: low cost, durability, and installation ease.

Few other building materials are equally well suited for home improvement projects. Using wallboard, the do-it-yourself home owner can cover walls and ceilings, tape the joints, bead corners and spackle the nailheads, and then paint or paper the surface for a most attractive result.

The wallboard can last indefinitely if not abused. However, if you miss when hammering a picture hook, or your offspring ever chops a hole in it, the patching job is fast and neat.

The professional mechanics who handle and install wallboard daily have made an art of the installation techniques. These are the same basic procedures that are outlined here, and which should be followed by the home handyman as well to the extent to which they specifically apply to his project situations.

The tricks of the trade, revealed here, will see you through from start to finish for a successful job, and help you escape some of the hangups that occasionally are involved in an extensive project such as this one.

First, though, some facts about availability and costs. Wallboard is delivered to most dealers in four basic sizes, 4'-by-8', 4'-by-10', 4'-by-12', 4'-by-14'—all of which are available in either ⅜" or ½" thicknesses, the most commonly used sizes. The cost, regionally, is about 5 to 6 cents a square foot if you take it with you, and about 6 to 7 cents a square foot delivered. Some dealers may require a special order for 4'-by-14' panels—perhaps even for 4'-by-12' panels, and the cost increases about 1 cent a square foot accordingly.

Size and Thickness Factors

Always order the largest size panel you can use: the difference in price, if any, is worth it. It covers larger areas with less total effort and greater speed, and reduces the number of joints to be taped. The smaller boards *are* easier for one man to handle, but this should never be a consideration.

If, for example, the new room is 13'-by-21', you should plan on one 4'-by-14' panel and one 4'-by-8' panel to cover one full length, trimming the extra foot from one of the panels. This saves on labor and the small additional expense you would have had with, say, three 4'-by-8' panels and the extra joint.

If you are planning what is called a heavy-use room, such as a child's playroom or a rumpus room, it is best to order panels with ½" thicknesses. This extra stability stands up well against abuse, and will in the long run keep maintenance at a minimum. The ⅜" panel is considered standard and, in every other specification, is equal to the ½" board.

Preparations and Installation

The first routine to establish when installing wallboard is to work from the top of the room down; i.e., the ceiling and/or top half of the walls, in that order. On walls, this approach provides a better joint, and panels already installed are less likely to be marred by other panels being handled.

For the ceiling, first set several planks on horses or other supports so that your head just touches the ceiling when you stand on the planks; the idea is to brace the panel against the ceiling with your head while nailing, in lieu of using a separate supporting T-brace which could slip and throw the panel off line. The maneuver sounds tricky, but is actually very workable once you get the gist of it.

When hammering nails into the ceiling, use a backhand motion and hit the head with the crown of the hammer. The pros say it enables you to keep a sharp eye on the nailhead.

Paneling Top to Bottom

For an orderly wall installation, there are two preparatory steps, one of which you should use, depending on the system chosen. If you are going to follow the nailing pattern, first nail a level starter strip (drive the nails only halfway in so that you can easily remove the strip) of 1-by-2 stock across the wall studs, at a height that will support the top panel flush with the ceiling joint. You will then have a base for the panel to rest on, and you can easily manage the nailing pattern of center-to-left and center-to-right. Remove the strip and reuse it for other top panel installations.

To simplify nailing, lightly rule guidelines on the face of the panel, equal to the stud spacing.

Following the adhesive system, simply drive a few nails partway into the top edge of the upper panel. Apply adhesive to the studding, lift the panel up into place (butted against the ceiling) and drive the anchor nails home. Press firmly against the studs beneath, and nail the four edges.

Before installing the bottom panels, make a lever using a short length of 1-by-4 stock, beveling one side to form a wedge that can be used to jockey the wallboard up against the top panel. Foot-operated, it permits you to use both hands, and works equally well for nailing or cementing bottom panels. Professionals have also developed a knack for using the tips of their shoes for the same purpose.

Leverage control for shifting the panel is important because a ⅛" space is required between panels for the bonding/taping of the joints. Plaster seeps into the space, strengthening joints.

Two Ways to Install Panel

Two basic methods are practiced today for installation of wallboard panels—overall nailing according to a set pattern (the approved method of wallboard manufacturers, although most professional mechanics are assumed to have modified the method by using fewer nails without sacrificing reliability), and a method of adhesive in combination with nailed edges only. Of the two, full nailing, as noted, is the preferred system, and an explanation of the process follows below. The adhesive system, however, being faster in application, is a practical shortcut in keeping with our theme. The illustrations printed here show this system in operation, but the general procedure still applies if you choose to use the overall nailing method.

Overall nailing of panels, following a definite pattern, applies to both ceilings and walls. The sketch shows the tacking plan for a full panel, and for odd cuts and panels which will have cutouts, follow the same formula as closely as possible.

Always nail panels in the center first, and work outward to the left and right. Nailing 8" on center, in this manner, prevents bows from developing over the panel's surface. After you have nailed the edges, return to the center and drive a second set of nails approximately 2" below each nail of the first set—omitting, however, the double-nail treatment around the edges.

When nailing, drive the head slightly below the panel's surface, no more than $\frac{1}{32}$" deep, causing a dimple or slight depression. The trick is to seat the nailhead without breaking the panel's paper surface. Later, the dimples are plastered flush with the surface, concealing any evidence of nailheads.

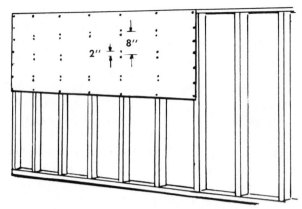

Panels are installed horizontally on wall, first panels go at top of wall, then bottom space filled in. For nailed installation, follow pattern shown having single nails all around the edge, then double nailing every 8" on all studs. All studs and plates must be in perfect alignment so that panels will not bulge and pop away from the nails.

Panel is pressed tightly against the ceiling joists while nails are driven home. Two men are needed to put up ceiling.

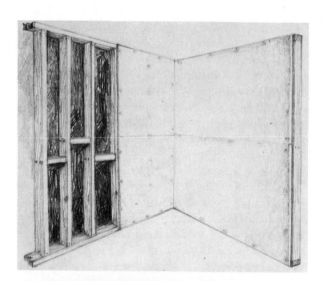

Before installing ceiling panels against end wall, positions of joists are indicated with pencil marks on plates.

Mechanic standing on a platform of the right height, uses his head to raise and support gypsum panel for ceiling installation.

A final word on nailing. Always apply pressure with your free hand against the panel, near the nail being driven. It is extra assurance for a secure fastening to the stud beneath.

Adhesive method of panel installation provides additional strength. Adhesive is applied along the stud faces or furring with caulking gun.

Panel in horizontal postion is lifted to upper section of wall, and the anchor nails along the top edge are driven at once to secure it.

When adhesive method is used, row of nails is driven partway along top edge of panel to provide a quick means of support.

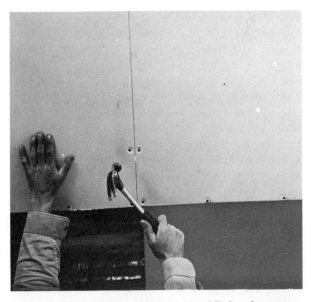

Nails are placed all around the edges, while hand pressure keeps panel close against studding so panels are tight.

The use of adhesive in wall board paneling is relatively new, having been test-marketed and proven as reliable, primarily in the Midwestern states. Builders in the East have begun to use it, and it's expected to be widely available in a short time, although at this printing, there is only one type of adhesive now available, Sheet Rock Brand DWA 14 Adhesive.

The technique of using wallboard adhesive is practically a duplication of other adhesive applications now in practice with prefinished hardboards and wood panels. The compound is squirted onto studs with a gun and the panels nailed in place around their edges. But it is not a contact type and therefore permits you to shift the panel if a placement requires correction.

Cutting Openings, Fitting Odd Pieces

Cut your odd pieces of wallboard with a linoleum knife, guided by a straightedge held firmly along the cut line. Run the knife along the board so that it scores the panel covering and cuts into the gypsum; then, bend the board back along the sliced line. A crease will show on the opposite side of the board, and this is used as a guide for a second (back) cut. Finally, snap the board again in the direction of the first cut, using your knee or elbow as a brace.

When small cutouts are needed for electrical fixtures and heating or air-conditioning ducts, place the panel against the wall (in the exact position it will be installed) and press firmly against the object. The pressure will dent the panel's back, outlining the exact shape; then all you have to do is make a pilot hole in the center of the workspace for a keyhole saw. Cut along the outside line of the imprint to allow free pass-through of the fixture.

A true, professional shortcut is used for doors and windows—paneling is applied directly over the opening and cutouts made with a saw (using the door or window frame as a guide). The scraps or cuttings from openings are saved for use in small areas and for wall ends, around corner windows and doors.

Always use metal corner beads on outside corners of any kind, as they protect the edges of open ends of panels against chipping.

TAPING JOINTS AND PLASTERING NAILHEADS

The last stages consist of taping and cementing joints, filling dimples, and smoothing over any surface irregularities. You may even have a dent or two to patch if you inadvertently bumped the wall while moving equipment around. A broadblade, flexible putty knife is going to be your best friend on this job. Also a trowel.

The consistency of the joint cement is one of the most important preparations. It should be well mixed, to a buttery-smooth texture, and in amounts that are easy to handle. One of the tests is to scoop

To cut gypsum board, score one side of panel with wallboard knife. Use T-square as guide and cut through paper.

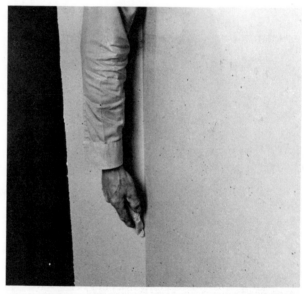

After scoring, snap the panel to break it on the scored line, then run knife along crease to cut second paper coat.

up some on a knife and turn the knife upside down; if it sticks for a few seconds before dropping off, it is properly mixed. Too tacky and too thin mixes either adhere or run.

Begin by filling the joints with a heavy application of compound, overlapping the sides so as to create a "bed" for the tape to be set into. Then, using perforated tape (which permits compound to

Opening for electric fixture can be made by hammering hole in panel, then cutting opening with a keyhole saw.

For electric boxes, wallboard can cover the edges of the installed box, as the box plate will go over the wallboard.

Opening can be trimmed neatly with the wallboard knife after initial sawing. Fixtures wiring must be roughed in.

Panels for doors and window frames are not pre-cut but instead are nailed completely over the openings.

seep through and bond more strongly) and your knife, cover the joint, passing the knife along behind the roll in an even, steady pressure. Remove excess compound, but leave a thin, even coating over the tape. Allow it to remain as is until throughly dry.

Then, apply the second, third, and fourth layers, overlapping each previous layer, allowing thorough drying time between treatments. It's a good idea to buy a special topping compound for the third and fourth layers, as it helps to produce a fine, unblemished surface. Make it a practice also to lightly sand each layer before going to the next.

Cover nailheads with the same compound used for the joints, where at least three separate layers will be needed. Follow a gradual building-up pro-

Window cutouts are made with short hand saw, following the edge of the window frame. Use an old worn-out saw for cutting gypsum.

Same window cutout technique is used on lower portion of the window, this time using penciled lines as cutting guide.

First step in removing a window cutout is to break the top edge by pulling outward, then cut through inside paper covering.

Panel scraps should not be discarded as they are excellent for filling small areas, cutting down on both waste and expense.

Panel joints are treated with special perforated tape. Start by spreading a heavy application of topping compound.

After first coats of compound are dried, sand thoroughly and apply a surface coating of compound with a broad trowel.

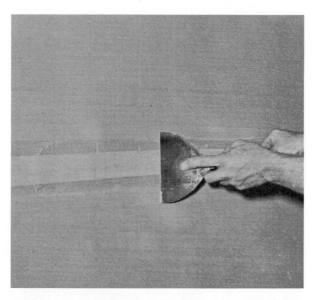

Perforated tape is applied to the joint, pressed firmly into the bed of topping compound with a steady pressure of the blade.

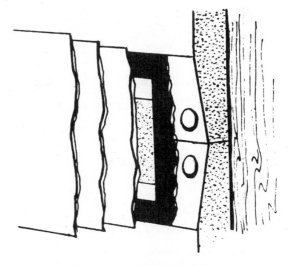

Cross section of taped joint shows first "bed" of compound covering also the nails, then the perforated tape, and three additional coats of topping compound, each coat sanded smooth.

Metal corner beads are installed on outside corners of doors and around recessed windows to prevent chipping of edges.

All nailheads, driven just deeply enough so the heads slightly dimple the wallboard surface, are covered with two layers of compound.

Center-creased non-perforated tape is used to cover inside corners, using same technique as with taped joints.

cess (the compound will contract as it dries), lightly sanding after each drying, and troweling the final coat glass-smooth.

For inside corners, professionals use an unperforated tape which is easier to smooth flat—a trick when working in cramped space. You simply measure the length you'll need and crease it carefully to form a right angle. Fill the corner joint thoroughly with compound, as before, and place the tape into

it. Then apply more compound, this time over the tape, and smooth it out.

Wherever you detect small surface irregularities, spackle lightly with your putty knife. Let dry and sand smooth.

GUIDE TO WALL FASTENERS

There are special kinds of fasteners suitable for every type of wall, and for every job you are ever likely to have to do.

Fasteners for hollow walls pass through the surface covering into the interior void, where they spread out to anchor themselves against the back face of the wall. Fasteners for solid and masonry walls are placed in a hole into which they lock when the sides of the fastener expand. Some fasteners usually associated with solid wall installations can also do double duty in hollow construction.

In addition to the type of wall, two factors affect the choice of a fastener: the weight it will have to support and the type of pull to be exerted against it.

With rare exceptions, two kinds of forces are encountered in the home. *Shear* is the downward force exerted by a load. For example, the pull of a mirror hanging from a nail driven horizontally into a wall is shear. You need only consider whether the weight of the mirror will bend the nail—assuming the wall material doesn't crumble. *Combination*

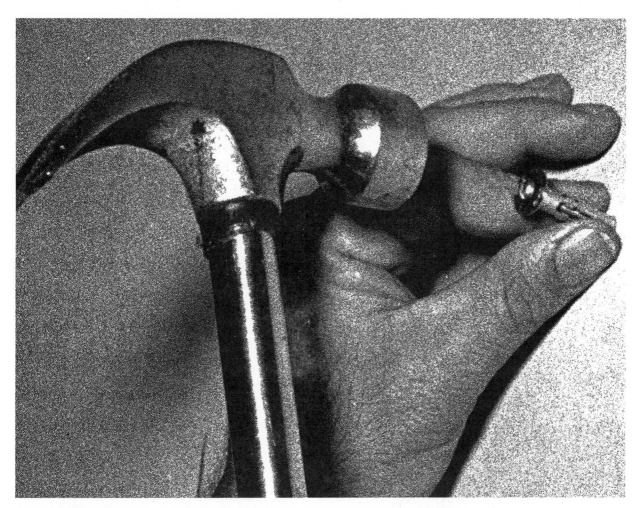

You can hang anything on any wall in your house—if you know how to select and install the correct fasteners.

force describes outward and downward pull, exerted by a wide bookshelf supported by a bracket. The bracket must carry the weight of the load and has to keep it from toppling forward as well. It's easy to see that a load of this sort requires a different fastener, or at the very least, one that is stronger than if you were concerned only with shear.

There's still another force to consider—vibration. It's really more of a condition than a force. If you want to support an air conditioner, for instance, you must remember that it will vibrate when it is turned on. If it were held in place by nails, the vibration would tend to loosen their grip. A screw-type fastener of some sort is better.

Proper choice of a fastener for a hollow wall sometimes depends on the thickness of the wall, often unknown but easy to measure. Bend a short,

sharp, hooklike U in the end of a piece of stiff wire. Insert it in a hole drilled in an inconspicuous place. Catch the point of the hook against the wall's back, then mark the protruding wire where it is level with the face of the wall. Measure the distance between the mark you made and the point of the hook; that's the thickness of the wall, and it is also the distance the fastener must penetrate before its anchoring device functions.

In general, loads of less than 10 lbs. are considered light and those of 10 to 25 lbs. medium; anything in excess of that amount is heavy. The fastener must, of course, be capable of supporting the heaviest load for which it will ever be called on—plus a margin of safety.

The accompanying charts were prepared to help you select the fastener that best fits both the job and the wall.

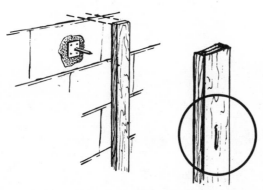
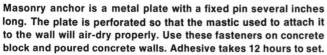

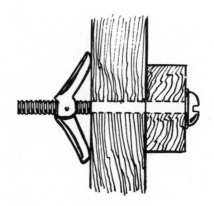

Masonry anchor is a metal plate with a fixed pin several inches long. The plate is perforated so that the mastic used to attach it to the wall will air-dry properly. Use these fasteners on concrete block and poured concrete walls. Adhesive takes 12 hours to set.

Toggle bolt, used in hollow walls, has two spring-loaded wings which spread apart after they pass through hole into open space. Hole must be drilled large enough to allow toggle wings to enter. Shown here is cross section of furring strip on gypsum panel wall.

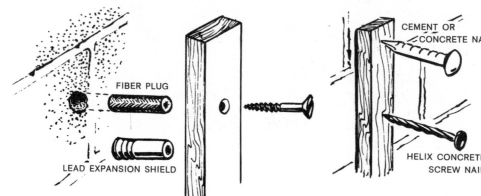

FIBER PLUG

LEAD EXPANSION SHIELD

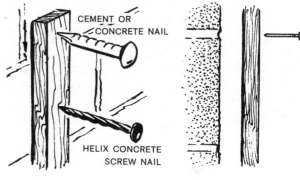

CEMENT OR CONCRETE NAIL

HELIX CONCRETE SCREW NAIL

Fiber plugs and lead expansion shields are very effective when used properly in the right locations. They should be used on masonry walls, or on materials such as ceramic tile, brick, plaster. A perfectly round hole, of precise size, is essential.

Specially hardened nails can be driven into concrete walls or floor. Use serrated or screw-type nails for better grip. Hardened cut nails are brittle, tend to snap when driven out of line.

FASTENERS FOR HOLLOW WALLS ONLY

Name	Recommended Uses	Installation Methods	Size and Load Capacity		
			Length (inches)	Diameter (inches)	Load (pounds)
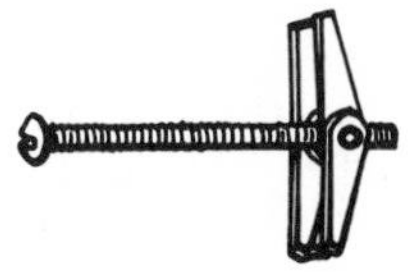 Toggle Bolt Wings are folded back to push bolt through hole. They then spread back against the backside of the wall.	Excellent for combination pressures exerted by mass loads, such as hanging cabinets, wide shelves, wall radiators and bathroom grip bars. Can also be used for vibration loads. Bolt can be retightened if it loosens.	Insert bolt through fixture and spin toggle onto bolt a few turns. Fold wings of toggle and push through hole in wall. Wings spread against back of wall. Tighten bolt to draw wings up snugly.	2,3,4	⅛	200
			2,3,4,5,6	3/16	450
			3,4,5,6	¼	925
			3,4,5,6	5/16	1150
			3,4,5,6	⅜	1500
			4,6,8	½	1800

Name	Recommended Uses	Installation Methods	Size	Overall Length (inches)	For Wall Thickness (inches)
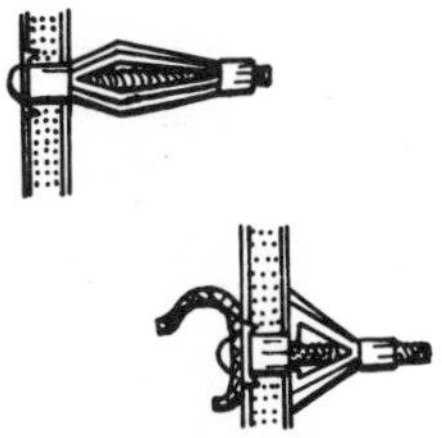 Expansion Bolt The expansion bolt utilizes a split sleeve. As the screw is tightened, the sleeve expands and anchors itself in back of the wall.	Will accommodate weights of from 200 to 500 lbs., depending on overall bolt length. Bolt is selected according to wall thickness. Used for hanging mirrors, shallow wall cabinets, clocks, coat hooks, wall lamps and other close-to-wall items. Generally for lighter duty than toggle bolts.	Insert entire unit into drilled hole. Tap pronged cap into wall and turn screw until it tightens. As screw is tightened, split sleeve behind wall expands and anchors itself. Remove screw from sleeve, insert into mounting hole of fixture and screw back into sleeve. New type eliminates need for drilling hole. Drive unit into wall. It has pointed tip to facilitate installation.	XS	¾-⅞	¼
			MS	1-1½	1/16-½
			S	1½-2¼	⅛-¾
			L	2-2¾	⅝-1¼
			XL	2½-3½	1¼-1¾

FASTENERS FOR USE IN MASONRY WALLS

Name	Recommended Uses	Installation Methods	Size and Load Capacity		
			Screw Size	Anchor Length (inches)	Load (pounds)
 Fiber Anchor (lead core) Anchor is positioned in a drilled hole. Screw is mounted in fixture and screwed into anchor.	For mounting anything you would normally attach with wood or sheet metal screws such as outlet and fuse boxes, mirrors, awnings, vent covers, etc. Do not use in masonry which is in poor condition and crumbling. Holding power depends on strength of wall material.	Use a drill, plug and screw of same size. Drill hole, clean out loose material and insert plug just below surface. Drive screw through fixture and into lead core. Only the threaded section of the screw should enter the plug, so use correct length plug or recess deeper in hole, if necessary.	5-6	⅝,¾,1	550
			7-8	⅝,¾,1	885
			9-10	¾,1,1¼,1½,2	1150
			11-12	¾,1,1¼,1½,2	1525
			14	1,1¼,1½,2	1590
			16	1,1½,2	2150
			20	1,1½,2	2830
			22	2	3500

Name	Recommended Uses	Installation Methods	Size and Load Capacity

Lead Screw Anchor

Anchor is set flush with wall. Screw is driven through fixture into anchor.

Recommended Uses: Same as fiber anchor. Size for size, though, it has less holding power than fiber anchor.

Installation Methods: Select a screw length that equals thickness of any mounting plate plus length of anchor plus 1/4". Drill hole 1/4" deeper than anchor, set flush with wall surface, and drive screw through fixture into anchor.

Screw Size	Anchor Length (inches)	Load (pounds)
6-8		
10-12	3/4, 1, 1 1/2	to 400
14	1, 1 1/2	to 900
16-18	1, 1 1/2	to 1300
20		
22-24	1 3/4, 2	1600 up

Lag Screw Shield

As screw is tightened with a wrench, shield expands and anchors itself to solid wall.

Recommended Uses: When load is too great for ordinary screws, especially on brick wall where hole can be drilled in mortar joint without marring brick.

Installation Methods: Drill hole same size as outside diameter of shield. Set shield flush with or slightly below surface, insert screw through fixture and into shield. Shield expands as screw enters. Screw is driven with wrench.

Screw Size	Shield Length (inches)	Load (pounds)
1/4	1, 1 1/2	450, 600
5/16	1 1/4, 1 3/4	800, 1200
3/8	1 3/4, 2 1/2	1200, 2000
7/16	2 1/4	1650
5/8	2, 3 1/2	2500, 3500
3/4	2, 3 1/2	3000, 4000

Machine Bolt Shield

As bolt is tightened with wrench, a nut is drawn up and expands split sleeve into anchor with wall.

Recommended Uses: For heavy fixtures that can be bolted to solid masonry, such as cabinets, hanging shelves, ducts, hand rails.

Installation Methods: Insert shield in snug, press-fit hole with top flush with surface. Insert bolt in fixture and turn into shield. As bolt tightens, it draws nut forward, expanding split sleeve.

Bolt Size	Shield Length (inches)	Hole Diameter (inches)	Load (pounds)
1/4	1 1/2	1/2	500
5/16	1 1/2-2	5/8	800
3/8	1 1/2-2 3/8	3/4	1000
7/16	2-2 1/2	7/8	1000
1/2	2-2 7/8	7/8	1500
5/8	2 1/2-3 1/4	1-1 1/8	2000
3/4	3 1/2-4	1 1/4-1 3/8	2000
7/8	4-4 1/4	1 3/8-1 1/2	2300
1	4 1/4-4 1/2	1 3/8-1 3/4	2400
1 1/4	5 1/2-6	2 1/8	2500

Nail Anchor

The anchor is inserted through fixture mounting hole, into hole in wall and is driven home with hammer. As it is, the shield expands and anchors against wall.

Recommended Uses: For installing light dead loads in concrete block, brick, mortar and stone, including furring strips, pipe, metal window frame, downspouts, outlet boxes.

Installation Methods: Drill hole the same diameter as shield. Insert through fixture and into wall. With flange seated firmly against fixture, drive nail with hammer.

Shield Diameter	Shield Length (inches)	Load (pounds)
3/16	7/8	375
	1 1/4	110
1/4	1	200
	1 1/4	240
	1 1/2	325
5/16	1 1/4	300
	1 3/4	350
	2 1/4	375
	2 3/4	375
3/8	2	450
	3 1/4	485
1/2	2 1/4	450
	3 1/2	485

Name	Recommended Uses	Installation Methods	Size and Load Capacity		

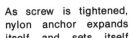

Plastic Anchor

As screw is driven into anchor, it expands and sets itself.

For mounting any fixture normally held by wood screws in hollow plaster walls, concrete, tile and brick, including large pictures, shelf brackets, drapery hardware, kitchen and bath accessories, awnings, Peg-Board panels.

Force anchor into hole, which must be drilled to exact size. Insert screw through fixture and drive into anchor.

Screw Size	Anchor No. & Length	Load (pounds)
4,6,8	no. 1($\frac{7}{8}$″)	650
10,12	no. 2(1″)	850
14,16	no. 3(1$\frac{1}{2}$″)	1075

Nylon Expansion Anchor

As screw is tightened, nylon anchor expands itself and sets itself firmly into both hollow and solid walls.

For mounting any lightweight item to any type of wall-plaster, drywall, brick, wood, concrete, cinder block.

Drill hole at least 1½″ deep. Pinch anchor between fingers and tap in place with hammer. Insert screw through fixture into anchor and tighten.

One size, 1″ long, which requires ⅜″ hole, serves all purposes. Comes with 1⅛″ self-tapping screw and is able to withstand shear loads of 280 lbs. in concrete and 50 lbs. in ⅜″ thick wallboard.

Nylon Drive Anchor

The shank of the nylon drive anchor bulges as screw is tightened to form a rivethead in a hollow wall and a pressure fit in a solid wall.

To mount lightweight items on drywall, tile, plaster, masonry, wood. Hollow walls cannot be more than $\frac{9}{16}$″ thick.

Drill hole same diameter as sleeve. In solid walls, drill slightly deeper than the length of the screw. Push sleeve in up to flange, hold fixture against it while tightening screw through mounting hole. The shank of the sleeve bulges as the nut is drawn tight and forms a rivethead against the back of a hollow wall or a pressure fit in a solid wall.

One standard size with ¼″ shank diameter, $\frac{15}{16}$″ long. Load capacity is 370 lbs. in concrete, 440 lbs. in brick and 470 lbs. in cinder block.

CHOOSING THE RIGHT GLUE

There are so many adhesives on the market that it is often difficult to know which to use. Here's how to select the type that is best for your project.

The average home owner who has a gluing job to perform is often bewildered when he walks into a hardware or building supply store and is confronted by the tremendous array of containers and blister packages of adhesives. After reading the directions on these adhesives, he is further confused by the numerous manufacturers who claim their glue can seemingly do almost everything imaginable.

To help the handyman select the right adhesive for the job he has in mind, a variety of adhesives,

HANDY TECHNIQUES

their properties, and the jobs for which they have proved *best* suited, are described.

Specialized glues have not been included, since they usually go with the material on which the glue is used.

Casein Glue

A powdered wood adhesive which you mix with water just before you use it, casein glue is ideal where strong joints are required. It works very well on loose-fitted joints because it fills voids and gaps by supplying the needed bulk. This glue requires firm clamping while the glue sets.

It is the only glue which permits you to glue wood at low temperatures in an unheated garage or basement. On the other hand, a casein joint is not waterproof and may stain some dark woods. It is highly recommended however, for oily, hard-to-glue woods such as teak.

Contact Cement

Because it bonds instantly—on contact—and without clamping, contact cement is perfect for many awkward gluing jobs around the house. It is used for bonding broad surfaces where strength is not important, such as laminating plastic sheeting to counter tops, tables, and other flat surfaces. In addition, it may be used for light jobs such as adhering leather, linoleum, thin gauge metal, and many other dissimilar materials in situations where clamping is impossible or difficult, as well as for installation of stair treads and wall paneling.

Both a highly flammable, solvent-thinned cement and a newer, water-thinned kind are available. The latter type is nonflammable, quick-drying, and gives off no toxic odors as do the solvent-thinned cements. Although the newer type generally costs more, it does cover a bit more area.

All contact cements are used in a similar manner; the adhesive is applied to both surfaces to be bonded, then allowed to dry from five to forty minutes, according to the manufacturer's directions. The parts are then pressed together, bonding instantly. Once the surfaces come into contact, they can't be shifted around. Therefore, when bonding large surfaces such as plastic laminate to counter tops, a slip-sheet of wrapping paper should be used while aligning the two parts; after they are lined up, the sheet can be slid out of the way and the surfaces pressed together.

Hot Melt Plastic Glue

This material is not actually a glue but a thermoplastic that acts like a glue when it is melted, and then hardens. Sticks of solid plastic (ethyl vinyl acetate) are inserted into the magazine of an electric glue gun. The gun is pointed directly at the joint between the parts to be bonded, and as the trigger of the gun is squeezed, the plastic is melted at the front of the gun. As the gun is moved along the joint, the plastic is automatically distributed.

This plastic will securely bond any combination of wood, tile, leather, plastics, metal, and masonry. No clamping is necessary, and the plastic hardens in one minute. Although it is not meant for major jobs, it is ideal for light bonding tasks because it provides a quick, very strong, waterproof bond.

Resorcinol Adhesives

For any job that requires completely waterproof wood joints, the best adhesive is resorcinol. This is a two-part adhesive and comes in twin cans, one of

which contains a tan powder and the other a thick cherry-colored liquid that looks like syrup. The two components must be mixed in precise proportions—4 parts powder and 3 parts liquid. The result is a loose paste of a dark chocolate color.

Resorcinol adhesives must be used at room temperature and the wood parts kept in clamps over night at room temperature. Glues of this type tend to shrink as they dry so joints must be smooth and fit closely.

Plastic Resin Glue

Excellent for cabinetwork and veneering, plastic resin glue is very strong and water-resistant. Used correctly, it will produce joints stronger than the wood itself. Another good quality is that it will not stain such hardwoods as mahogany and oak. It is extremely resistant to mold and rot.

Plastic resin glue comes as a powder and is mixed with water. Wood parts must be held in clamps for about ten hours at a temperature not less than 70 degrees.

Epoxy Resin Glue

Epoxy adhesives are the strongest adhesives available to the handyman. They are waterproof and highly resistant to heat and cold, most solvents and household chemicals, and will withstand tremendous pressures. They are ideal for bonding glass, metal, plastics, and concrete.

They harden by chemical action instead of the evaporation of solvents and will therefore work satisfactorily even where there is no air. Because they are heat-resistant, they are excellent for such jobs as gluing metal hooks and other objects to tile or masonry walls. They do not have any "grab" and on a vertical surface the object being glued should be taped in place until the adhesive hardens.

Epoxies are usually packaged in two tubes, a plastic resin and a hardener. Both of these must be mixed in equal amounts. Once mixed, the compound will harden in about an hour although some will set in about five minutes, so mix only as much as you can use within the time allowed for setting. Epoxies are also available in thick pastes and in the form of two sticks of clay which you knead together and use for patching and filling.

White Glue

One of the most widely used glues available to the general public, polyvinyl white glue is inexpensive, nontoxic and nonflammable. Although milky white in color, it dries clear and is usually sold in a plastic squeeze bottle with a nozzle which makes it very convenient to apply.

Primarily a wood glue, it is excellent for woodwork when used with nails or screws. It is nonstaining and can be used with most porous materials.

It requires a moderate amount of pressure while setting and will harden in about thirty minutes but requires about twenty-four hours to attain full strength. Not meant for joints that have to withstand great pressure.

Mastic Cement

Mastic cement is a rubber-based, thick, usually black (but also tan or white) cement frequently used to bond wood to concrete. For example, wood supports or sleepers are often laid in mastic which has been applied to a concrete floor; wood flooring can then be put over the wooden supports. It can also be used to adhere furring strips to concrete walls, and is generally the basic adhesive used for putting down vinyl asbestos floor tile and other resilient flooring. This cement is usually applied with a notched trowel.

It is also used for applying metal, plastic and ceramic tile to walls, and in various formulations is used in cartridges as a paneling adhesive. Mastics take hold quickly but require several hours to set.

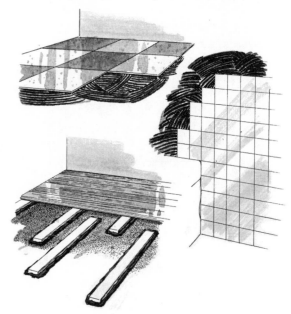

INSTALLING A NEW CHANDELIER

Replacing an old light fixture with a new one is quite a simple job. Before you start, of course, be sure to turn off the switch that controls the fixture so that there will be no danger of electric shock.

To remove the old ceiling fixture, unscrew the canopy support nut—a large plastic or metal nut that holds the canopy against the ceiling. The canopy is the decorative metal plate that covers the hole in the ceiling for the outlet box. Let the nut and the canopy slide down the cord of the old fixture. This will expose the mounting bar from which the old fixture hangs. The mounting bar may be a flat strip with a threaded hole in the middle and smaller holes or slots on the ends for the screws that fasten the bar to the outlet box. Instead of being flat, some mounting bars have a square U-shaped bend in the middle.

Remove the old mounting bar by loosening the screws at the ends and at the same time hold onto the cord or chain since only the mounting bar supports the fixture. Let the mounting bar and the threaded nipple in its center hole slide down the cord. Now disconnect the wires and the old fixture can be removed.

First step in installing your fixture is to fasten the new mounting bar into place. This particular bar has a square bend in the middle and is fastened by a single screw at each end. The bend should face toward the floor. Next, screw the threaded nipple (a short piece of tubing with threads on the outside) into the hole in the center of the bend.

The nipple and mounting bar are among the hardware that comes with your new fixture. Don't rely on the old nipple that you removed as it may not fit the new bar. Screw a hex nut (from the hardware envelope) on the nipple and bring it

First step, after turning off the switch, is to unscrew canopy support and let canopy slide down wire.

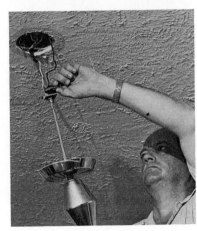

Old mounting bar is removed, wires disconnected, while the fixture is supported by one hand.

Pull-down dining room fixture is quite modern, but is being changed for a larger chandelier.

New mounting bar supplied with chandelier is fastened into the metal ceiling box with screws.

Threaded nipple is turned into the mounting bar and hex nut loosely turned onto this nipple.

Chain link spread open so that it can be slipped over the chandelier ring.

Chain is measured for desired height of fixture and excess links are removed.

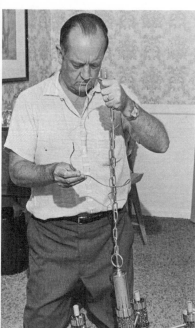

Fixture wires are threaded through the chain, interwoven at every third link.

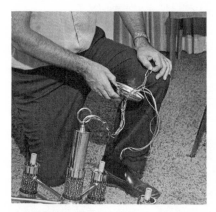

The end of the chain is brought through the opening in the new canopy.

The top hander loop is slipped over the end chain link, and the link closed with pliers.

close to the underside of the bar but do not tighten it yet.

Take the chandelier out of the carton and the chain from which it will hang. Open one link (they are slotted) with a pair of pliers, put it on the ring at the top of the fixture and close the link. You may have to use two pairs of heavy-duty pliers for this job.

The fixture should be about 30″ to 36″ above the table. Hold the fixture up with a chain link touching the threaded nipple. Mark the link at the height you want, take the fixture down and open that link, removing the rest of the chain. But don't close the link yet.

Thread the wires through the chain. Holding the chain with one hand and working with one wire, weave it into every third link. The other wire and the ground wire go up the opposite side of the chain in the same manner. Be sure they cross at the same link so that the wires are concealed as much as possible.

The chandelier hangs from a little device called a hanger loop which you will find in the hardware envelope. The loop has a knurled nut around the outside. Unscrew this nut and slip it over the free end of the chain. Put the loop aside for the moment.

The new canopy should then be slipped over the end of the chain. Be sure that it faces downward. Slip the open link into the hole in the hanger loop and close the link. Run the wires through the small holes in the top of this piece.

You are now ready to secure the chandelier chain to the mounting bar. Screw the nipple that you have placed in the mounting bar into the threaded hole you will find in the top of the hanger loop which you have just put on the end of the chain. Unless there is a hole in the center of this piece the wires from the fixture *do not* go up through the nipple.

With the fixture securely attached, and before you start wiring, push the canopy up against the ceiling. Check to see whether the bottom of the hanger loop sticks out enough from the canopy to catch the threads of the canopy support nut. If not, rotate the hanger loop until it has backed out sufficiently. Then tighten the hex nut on the nipple against the bottom of the mounting bar to prevent the nipple from turning.

Make the wiring connections now, white to white, black to black or green to black, using plastic wire nuts to insulate the wires you have twisted together. Then gently stuff the wires into the outlet box above the bar.

The hanger loop is turned onto the nipple which had been placed into the mounting bar.

Next, the fixture is suspended, and the wires are connected with wire nuts.

As the new canopy is smaller than previous one, exposed area of ceiling is painted.

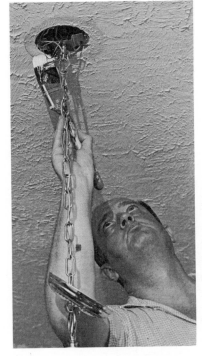

Canopy is pressed up against ceiling and supporting nut turned into place.

New chandelier installation completed.

If the canopy of the old fixture was larger than the new one, it will be necessary to paint a small area of the ceiling around the outlet box. Of course, if the canopy of your new fixture is larger, or the same size, you won't need to do any painting.

Once the paint has dried, press the canopy up against the ceiling. Bring the canopy support nut up the chain and screw it on the part of the hanger loop that projects below the canopy, locking the canopy in place.

HOW TO MAKE A DRAWER

Drawers are essentially alike. The differences are mostly in the type of joint—whether the sides are joined to the front by dadoing or dovetailing, for example—and in the shape of the front—whether it is flush with the cabinet face, or partly recessed and has rounded edges that help to conceal the bulky appearance of the material.

Drawer construction is not really difficult, but it can be very complex; that's because so many different cuts are required. A drawer could be made by nailing four pieces of wood together at the corners, then tacking on a panel at the bottom. But such a drawer would not be very serviceable, since it would soon twist out of shape, the bottom panel would fall off, and the corner joints would pull apart.

A properly made drawer, on the other hand, can give many years of service. Some have lasted for a century or more in perfect condition. That is not because the materials are so solid. On the contrary, a good drawer should be as light as possible, made of the thinnest possible stock, or at least made to look light and delicate.

The reason these drawers function so well and stand up under constant use is the jointing: the sides are closely fitted to the front and back in rabbet or dado grooves, which provide both mechanical grip and offer multiple gluing surfaces; the bottom panel slides into a full-length groove in each

418

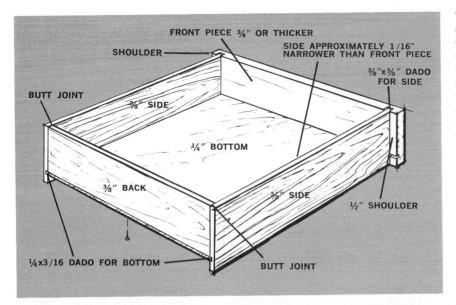

FRONT PIECE ¾" OR THICKER

SHOULDER

SIDE APPROXIMATELY 1/16"
NARROWER THAN FRONT PIECE

⅜"x⅜" DADO
FOR SIDE

BUTT JOINT

⅜" SIDE

¼" BOTTOM

⅜" BACK

⅜" SIDE

½" SHOULDER

¼x3/16 DADO FOR BOTTOM

BUTT JOINT

Typical drawer construction has dado joint locking sides to the front, the back piece held with nails through sides in butt joints. Grooves in sides and front receive the ¼" plywood bottom, which is locked with nails into bottom edge of the back. Front fits flush in cabinet, has ½" shoulders at side to allow for the thickness of the drawer guides inside cabinet.

Drawer sides and front are grooved ³/₁₆" from the bottom to accept the bottom panel of ¼" plywood.

Side fits snug into dado groove, cut ⅜" deep, in the front. Use only glue for this type of joint, under clamped pressure.

Assembled parts have the grooves in perfect alignement so that the bottom panel will slip in, be fully supported.

side, again providing ample support. These joints are fully described later.

Power Tools Needed

Good drawers can be made only with the right power tools. The essential tool is a bench saw, which permits precise cutting of the drawer parts, and also turns out the required number of duplicate pieces, all identical. The same saw will cut the various joints, such as the rabbet and dado. For the

fancier cuts like dovetail joints, and for dressing up the drawer front with rounded edges or decorative designs, the portable router is perfect. The latter tool should be used more widely by home handymen, who would finds its versatility of great value around the home and shop.

Materials Used

The choice of materials generally will depend on the purpose for which the drawer will be used, as often it will have to match cabinets into which it will be placed. But there are basic requirements: the sides and back of the drawer may be ⅜" or ½" stock, preferably solid lumber, but plywood also is suitable. For the bottom, ¼" plywood or hardboard are nearly always used. The front is usually of ¾" plywood.

Useful Hints

If you are building a number of drawers at the same time, it is desirable that they all be of uniform size, if possible, since each drawer requires many steps for cutting the parts and making the joints. Cutting all the needed pieces of each part at a time, and making the required dado or other grooves before going on to the next part, will save considerable effort. This will also eliminate the need for trying to recapture the exact setting later to duplicate a needed part. By having all the parts precisely uniform, the drawers also will be the same, and thus can be interchanged.

One important caution, though, is that any minor mistake will ruin the whole batch. An error that is made frequently, even by experienced shopworkers, is to cut the joint groove on the wrong side of the stock. For instance, the pieces are identical for both sides of the drawer, but when rabbet cuts are made in the sides for jointing with the back, then the groove for the bottom panel must be made for half the sides one way, but the rest of the sides must be reversed and the bottom groove cut into the opposite edge. Thus when the rabbeted ends of two sides are facing each other, the bottom groove will also be on the inside surface.

Typical Construction

A typical construction design is shown in the sketch. In this drawer, the front has a square face to fit flush into the cabinet, and a ½" shoulder at each side. The end shoulders compensate for the depth taken inside the cabinet by the drawer guide or slide.

The side pieces are joined to the front inside dado grooves. The front, and both sides, have a ¼" groove located 3/16" from the bottom edge. The ¼" bottom panel slides into this groove, is tapped to seat tightly into the three-drawer parts, then the back is put on, butt jointed to the sides with nails. One or two thin nails are driven up through the bottom panel into the back piece, completing the basic drawer assembly.

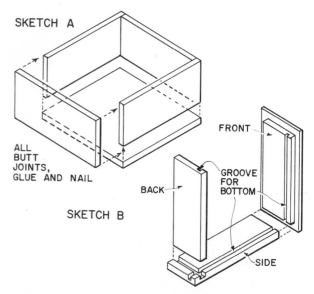

(Sketch A) Tray-type drawer is simplest to make, requires heavy stock for all parts, which are simply butted together, or if thin plywood is used for bottom, reinforced with glue blocks, which are triangular wood strips.
(Sketch B) The front is built up of two pieces, an inside ½" plywood block to which the sides are glued, and a panel of ¼" plywood. The back is held in a full dado groove.

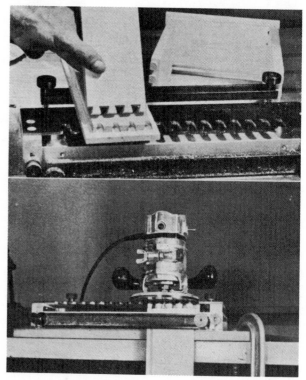

Two component pieces are shown, dovetailed and ready for assembling. Dovetails interlock as strongest joint.

Dovetails are cut with router, using a special template jig. The action is quite automatic, as router bit follows the template fingers.

Metal sliding bars for drawers provide smoothest, most carefree action. Sample of partly open slide is shown.

by simply joining the sides to the recessed part of the front panel. Dovetail joints are perhaps strongest of all, made with a drill press or router, but require a special dovetail template.

Exposed plywood edges of drawers should be sanded smooth, then the grain packed with sealer and shellacked.

PUTTING UP BIFOLD DOORS

Quite a few of the home improvement projects presented in this book call for installation of bifold louver doors on closets, kitchen pantries, built-in wall units, and other cabinets. These doors are recommended because they are functional and attractive—easy to open, providing access to the entire inside area of a closet or cabinet instead of just the immediate front part, and also permitting constant ventilation of the closets to keep them and their contents fresh and pleasant.

Folding doors, either louvered or solid panel, are available at all lumberyards in a wide range of widths and lengths, so you are sure to get the ones close to the size needed, and it's a simple matter to

There are modifications of this design, of course. One that is quite important calls for dado grooves for the back piece, giving support to an essential point of stress. The front, on the other hand, often is attached by means of a rabbet joint, or even just

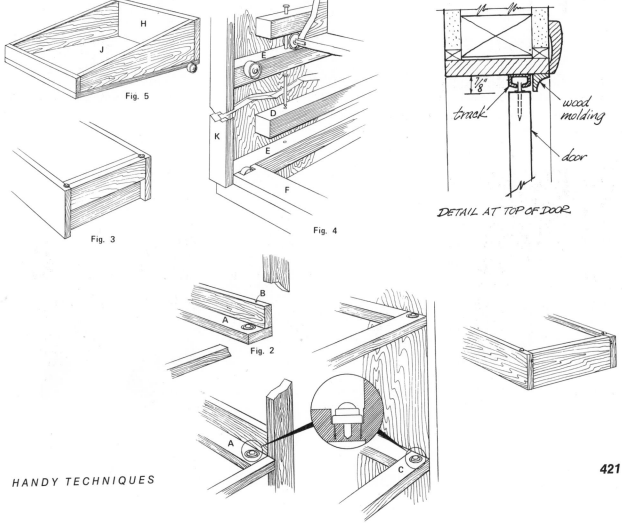

Fig. 5

Fig. 3

Fig. 4

DETAIL AT TOP OF DOOR

track

wood molding

door

Fig. 2

Fig. 1

HANDY TECHNIQUES

421

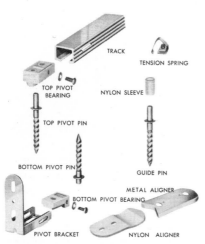

TRACK

TENSION SPRING

TOP PIVOT BEARING

NYLON SLEEVE

TOP PIVOT PIN

BOTTOM PIVOT PIN

GUIDE PIN

METAL ALIGNER

BOTTOM PIVOT BEARING

PIVOT BRACKET

NYLON ALIGNER

Folding doors come complete with all hardware items necessary for their installation, including the track.

Nail pivot and guide pins into the top of doors and pivot pin into bottom of the door.

Slide the nylon sleeves over the guide pins located at top of the hinged doors.

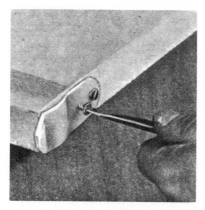

Install the nylon aligner on the bottom of one of the inner doors with screws.

Install metal aligner on the bottom of the other inner door with screws.

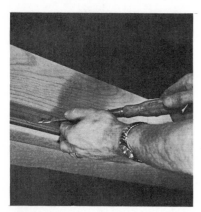

Locate track on center line drawn across top jamb and fasten it into place.

Extend the center line down side jambs and fasten the pivot brackets at bottom of jambs.

Insert doors in track. Adjust the bottom bracket heights if doors do not clear them.

Loosen screw on bracket and move pivot point so that the door clears the jamb by 3/8".

Loosen the top screw and align the door tops to make them parallel with the track.

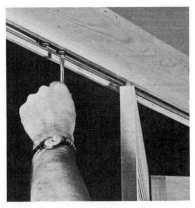

Adjust tension springs so that the guide pin contact will hold the doors when closed.

After adjustments are made, retighten all adjustment screws, and the job is done.

trim the stiles or rails slightly to fit where necessary. For installation, follow the step-by-step procedure illustrated.

To determine the correct size of doors required, measure the distance between jambs and subtract 1" clearance. The doors should be 1½" shorter than the height of the opening. First, install the pivot pins at the top of the doors and the pivot brackets and aligners at the bottom of the doors. Then mount the track across the top of the jamb as shown in the sketch. The doors are hung in place by inserting the pivot pins into the track and raising the doors until they slide into place over the

bottom brackets. The height of the bottom brackets should be adjusted if there is insufficient clearance for slipping the doors into place.

A wood molding strip may be nailed at the top of the opening, after the doors are installed, to hide the door track from sight, if desired. After all adjustments are made to the doors, as shown in the photos, carefully retighten all the adjustment screws to assure permanent alignment and smooth action.

SMOOTH ROLLING
FOR CABINET DRAWERS

Here is a simple and inexpensive way to make drawers glide smoothly and easily, and to make shelves that bring hard-to-reach items in the back out to the front with little more than a flick of the wrist. Especially in kitchen cabinets, which are usually fairly deep, these "rolling shelves" are real wife-pleasers.

It's all done with ¾" furniture ball casters and 1" rollers. The casters can be bought at hardware or variety stores. One set of four is needed for each drawer, two set into the rear of the drawer itself and two in the cabinet front crosspiece. This way the drawer actually rolls in and out on four ball bearings; the two in the drawer ride on the cabinet drawer glides, while the bottom of the drawer sides ride over the two front casters in the cabinet. The rollers for the shelves can be made quite easily of whatever you have available: steel, aluminum, nylon, or even wood. Four are needed for each shelf.

Rollers on bottom rear of shelf (left) and ball casters on bottom rear of drawers (right) provide smooth, easy operation.

Note the ball casters, shown installed in the drawer glides, not on the front crosspiece which is also possible. The dark lines on the L-shaped drawer glides are made by the oiled bearings in the drawer.

The shelf rollers and roller supports look like this when installed in the cabinet. Cabinet door must be wide open as shown to roll shelves out.

Here's how to get things in back of cabinet easily: just pull them to the front on these "rolling shelves." Ball casters for three drawers opposite the shelves can also be seen here.

These ball-bearing drawers are constructed just like any other drawer. When the drawer is completed, turn it upside down and bore a ¾" hole 1" from the back in each side piece. The hole should be deep enough so the ball bearing protrudes ⅛" above the wood surface. Fig. 1 detail shows how the installed casters should look in the holes. If using ½" stock for the drawers, add an extra piece across the back and center the hole at the joints as shown in Fig. 3. Incidentally, the three-pronged type of casters are better than those with a single prong in the center, especially in the cabinet drawer glides where the longer single prong would protrude through and have to be cut off.

When building the cabinet, make all drawer openings ¼" higher than the drawer height to allow room for the casters. Fig. 2 shows an L-shaped drawer glide designed especially for ball caster use. After gluing and nailing the two pieces [A and B] together, the casters are installed as shown. Piece B acts as the side guide for the drawer. The photos also show this method.

The casters may also be installed in a 3" wide front crosspiece (C). Whatever method used, be sure the drawer glides [A] are wide enough to allow the casters in the drawers to ride on them freely. And be very sure to install the casters in the drawer glides or crosspieces *before* they are fastened into the cabinet. Otherwise, unless it is a very deep drawer, you won't be able to get a drill in to bore the holes. When everything is finished, put a drop of oil on each ball bearing and roll the drawers into the cabinet. You'll find you have some of the easiest working drawers you've ever seen.

The shelves, which operate on the same principle as the drawers, use rollers instead of ball casters. Make the rollers 1" in diameter and 5/16" thick. Drill and countersink the center hole for a no. 9 flat head screw. If you can't make them of metal or nylon, buy a length of 1" hardwood dowel and make wooden rollers. A little oil in the bearing holes should make them last a long time. In fact, if you have any discarded wheel type furniture casters lying around your shop you can use the wheels from them for the rollers. Simply space the roller supports in the cabinet to match the wheel diameter.

The shelf roller supports [D and E, Fig. 4] are ripped from 1" stock and fastened into the cabinet.

The front rollers should be fastened to the lower support [E] with no. 9 x 1¼″ flat head screws, keeping the top edge ⅛″ higher than the support. Lubricate the roller-bearing holes and screws at assembly and occasionally afterward to keep them rolling smoothly. Note also how the lower cabinet crosspiece [F, Fig. 4] is notched to clear the bottom shelf roller.

The 12d nail, which goes all the way through D and halfway through E, acts as a stop so the shelf cannot be accidentally pulled all the way out, dumping everything on the floor. Drill the holes for this stop large enough so the nail can be lifted out easily when installing or removing the shelf. Fig. 4 also shows how the shelf roller (fastened to the rear of the shelf) rides between the supports D and E.

The shelves are made in the shape of trays, higher in the back than the front (Fig. 5). The sides and back prevent things from sliding off when the shelf is moved. You can make the back (H),

front (G) and bottom (J) from ¾″ plywood and the sides of ½″ plywood. Glue and nail everything together, then install the rollers on the bottom, 1¼″ from the back, using no. 9 x 1½″ flat head screws. The width dimension will, of course, be made to fit between the shelf supports. All other dimensions will be governed by the size of the cabinet you are building.

If there is a facing board on your cabinet (K, Fig. 4) here's how to install or remove the completed shelf. First, tilt it enough to clear everything and put it all the way in. Then straighten it so the rollers are resting on the top of roller support D and pull it out in the level position until the rollers drop down on E. Push it back in, drop in the 12d stop pin and it is ready to go. To remove, reverse the procedure.

You probably won't want to make all the shelves in your cabinet this way, but several of them, combined with the ball caster drawers, will make any cabinet not only more useful but easier to use.

Chapter 14
WORKSHOPS

Home improvement projects get started more quickly, and are brought to a satisfactory result, when there's a handy workshop all set up and waiting to go. Planned storage for tools and supplies eliminates wasteful clutter, speeds the job. Shown here is a workbench and storage unit built along an entire wall of a double garage.

Take a giant step toward all those improvements you want for your home by building a workshop. Once you have the setup with a good bench and an array of at least the basic tools, you'll be rarin' to go, maybe with small projects at first like window cornices and bookshelves, then advancing to some of the practical home improvements described throughout this book.

Where to set up the workshop? Any place where it will fit into the scheme of things at your house. The basement is fine, and that's where most work-shops are located. But where there is no access to a basement, ingenuity will provide the alternatives such as the hideaway workshop described on page 434. The garage often makes an excellent choice, particularly for those fortunate enough to have a large double garage, or a one and-a-half car garage. Even where there's a tight one-car space, a workshop may be fitted in so that it can be used by ousting the car temporarily during the working sessions.

The garage workshop shown here will no doubt

Walls of garage are paneled in knotty pine. The tongue-and-groove boards are tapped together lightly at the joints, nailed directly to the furring strips placed over the garage wall studs.

Pine boards are nailed alongside the tongues, not on the face. Here a nail is driven into the baseboard.

excite the envy of many a family handyman. Set up in half of a spacious two-car garage, it includes a wall-to-wall workbench complex, with plenty of storage space for tools, materials, and other needed supplies.

There are, of course, certain difficulties and problems in connection with using the garage as a workshop, but many advantages, too. The most difficult problem is that of heating. The simplest solution is to weatherseal the door and windows so that the workshop may be used on all but the rawest winter days. A practical solution that is widely used for a garage set back from the property line is to install an oil-fired space heater, or potbelly coal stove, vented through the wall. Where the garage is attached to the house, and there is a forced air heating system, a duct can be run into the garage.

Electricity for light and power tools also is necessary. While the garage may have a connection for lighting, an additional 20-amp or 30-amp circuit will be required if stationary power tools are to be used.

GARAGE ADVANTAGES

Countering the difficulties are the many decided advantages that make the conversion of a garage worthwhile. Noise transmission is minimized, a fac-

tor particularly important when power tools are used. Moreover, no sawdust is blown around the house. The grade-level garage makes it much easier to bring in large panels and lumber and to carry out the finished projects, and usually there is a clear open space in the garage for maneuvering the lumber.

Novel and effective tool hangers are shown: the pegs take hammers, hacksaw, and similar tools, while the notched rack accepts screwdrivers, awls, pliers, and many other items.

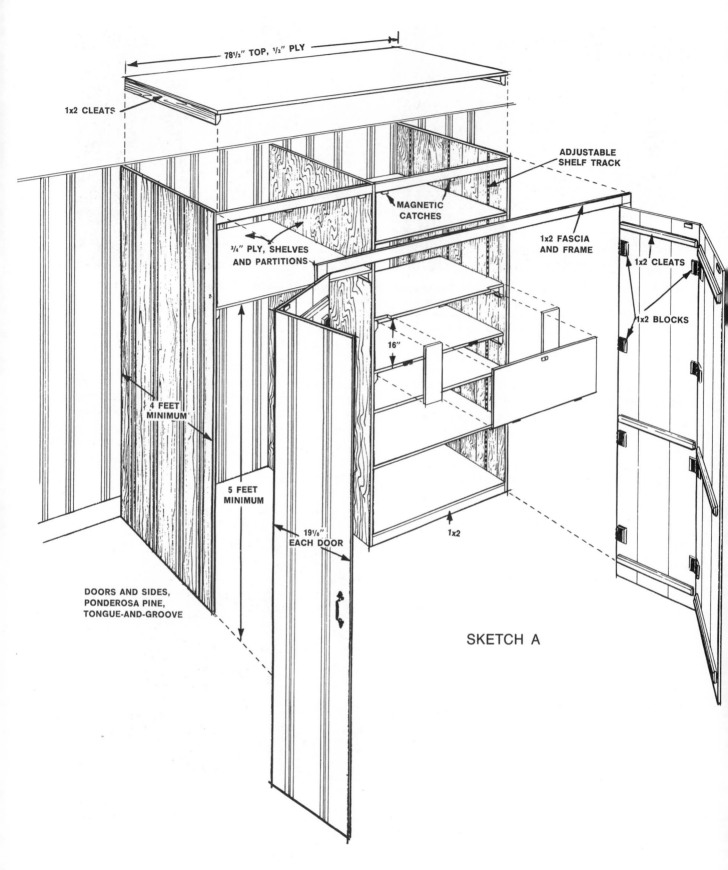

78½" TOP, ½" PLY

1x2 CLEATS

ADJUSTABLE
SHELF TRACK

MAGNETIC
CATCHES

1x2 FASCIA
AND FRAME

1x2 CLEATS

¾" PLY, SHELVES
AND PARTITIONS

1x2 BLOCKS

16"

4 FEET
MINIMUM

5 FEET
MINIMUM

19⅛"
EACH DOOR

1x2

DOORS AND SIDES,
PONDEROSA PINE,
TONGUE-AND-GROOVE

SKETCH A

428

SKETCH B-C

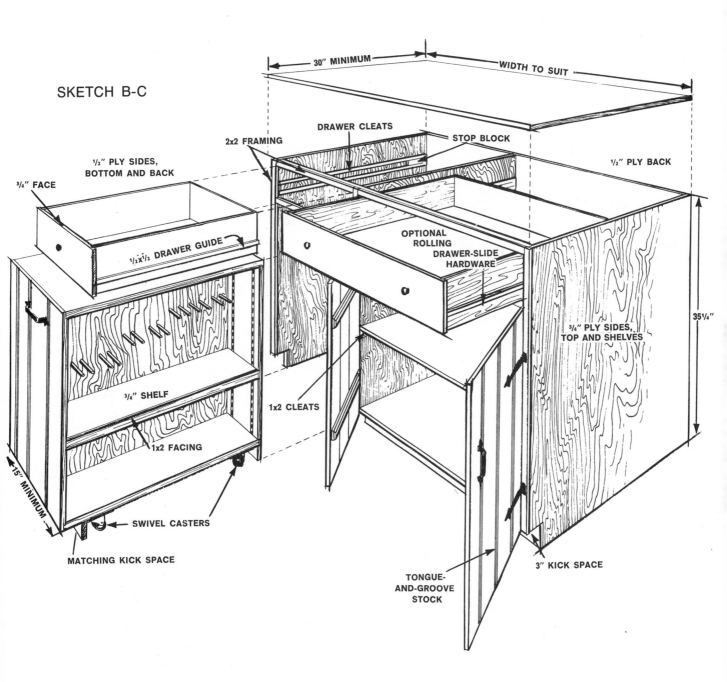

30" MINIMUM

WIDTH TO SUIT

DRAWER CLEATS

STOP BLOCK

2x2 FRAMING

½" PLY SIDES,
BOTTOM AND BACK

¾" FACE

½" PLY BACK

OPTIONAL
ROLLING
DRAWER-SLIDE
HARDWARE

½"x½" DRAWER GUIDE

35¼"

¾" PLY SIDES,
TOP AND SHELVES

¾" SHELF

1x2 CLEATS

15" MINIMUM

1x2 FACING

SWIVEL CASTERS

3" KICK SPACE

MATCHING KICK SPACE

TONGUE-
AND-GROOVE
STOCK

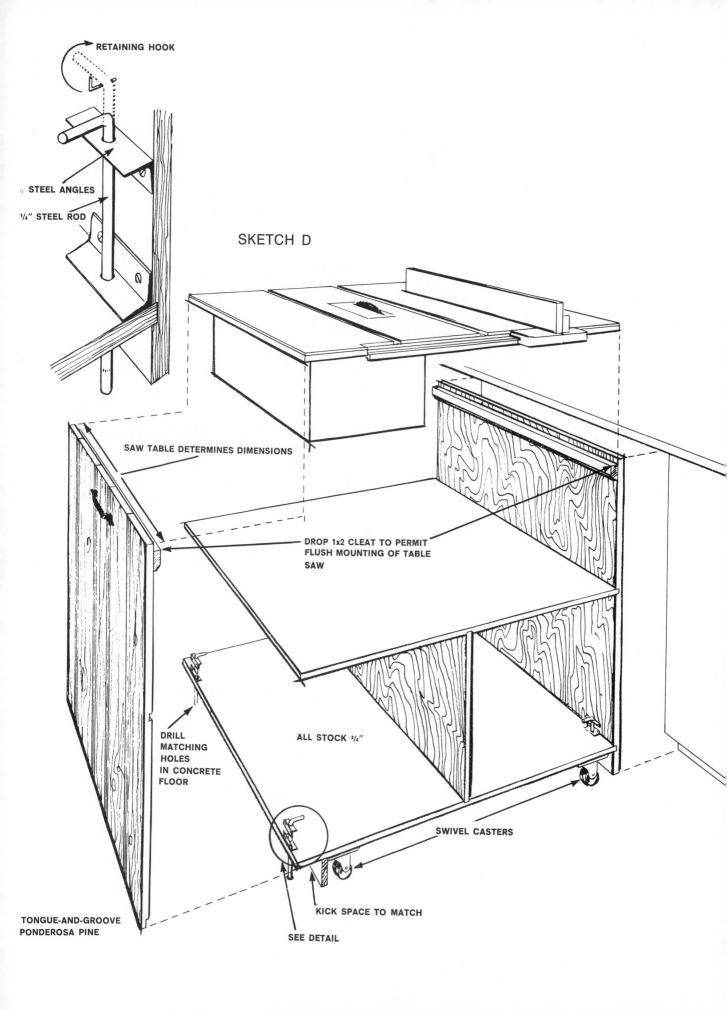

RETAINING HOOK

STEEL ANGLES

¼" STEEL ROD

SKETCH D

SAW TABLE DETERMINES DIMENSIONS

DROP 1x2 CLEAT TO PERMIT
FLUSH MOUNTING OF TABLE
SAW

DRILL
MATCHING
HOLES
IN CONCRETE
FLOOR

ALL STOCK ¾"

SWIVEL CASTERS

TONGUE-AND-GROOVE
PONDEROSA PINE

KICK SPACE TO MATCH

SEE DETAIL

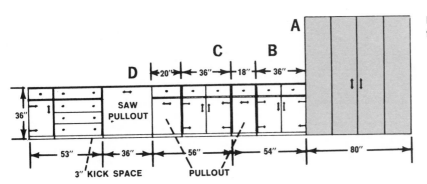

The garage workshop illustrated has wood paneled walls, making the environment not only more attractive but also warmer. Most garages have unfinished walls—usually of unadorned concrete blocks, or wood sheathing with exposed 2-by-4 studs. The effort and expense to panel the walls are not very great, and the benefits of a warmer and more pleasant shop atmosphere are considerable.

Building the Cabinets

The row of cabinets in the illustrations occupies a garage wall 24′ long, an exceptional size. Very likely you don't have that much space, but the units, individually described in the detail sketches, can be modified in width or arranged differently to make the best use of your particular space.

The ceiling-height storage cabinet is detailed in sketch A as 80″ wide, and that may pose your first big question if your garage dimensions are not so generous. Is it better to have this huge storage cabinet at the sacrifice of some working counter length? There's so much to be said for both sides that a compromise is the best answer: either reduce the width to about half (for a 3′ wide cabinet) or plan on adding a separate tool storage shed outside the garage. Another option that is more reasonable, is to eliminate one of the B-C cabinets (which are practically duplicates) thus saving about 4½′ in the wall length and still giving you an adequate work counter of about 12′.

An important feature of the storage unit, as shown, is the security compartment, where dangerous poisons like weed killers and insecticides can be kept under lock and key. Thus, even though the cabinet door may be left open while you're working on some home project, the toxic substances will be safe from prying hands and always under your control. This compartment is fitted with a drop-leaf

Spacious cabinet at one end of wall has dual sections for storing large garden tools such as the lawnmower shown and for bulky objects such as sports equipment. Drop-door security section at center is for toxic garden chemicals and similar hazardous items.

Drop-hinged panel in security section, shown open and supported with chains on inside, has cabinet-type lock so chemicals are under control even when the cabinet doors are left open.

Table saw mounted in a mobile cabinet rolls out on casters from under counter, can be turned in any direction for maximum work clearance. Cabinet has latch arrangement to lock it in place during use.

Roll-out cabinet is fitted with metal tracks for adjustable shelf supports. This pull-out unit is used for paint and supplies.

Pegs are placed at convenient height, glued into holes drilled in the side. Shelf of ¾" plywood has a facing strip.

door, hinged at the bottom, and supported by chains at the sides when open. One or more additional locked sections may be included if you need safe storage for portable power tools such as hedge trimmers, circular saws, and chain saw.

Planning the Bench

The workbench and associated storage units are integral and must be planned as a combination unit, since the individual parts not only must fit the whole, but will determine the overall height. The bench consists of at least two storage sections, one or more pull-out carts to hold tools and supplies, and a roll-out saw cabinet on casters. The saw cabinet must be wide enough to receive the saw table, while the work counter height must allow the saw table to roll underneath (when the saw blade is retracted). There should be no problem about the latter requirement, since an acceptable workbench height is usually 34" to 36" while a 32" height is usually preferred for the table saw.

The saw cabinet rolls on swivel casters, and thus can be swung in either direction for maximum rip-ping or cross-cutting clearance, and for handling large panels. Various means are available for locking the cabinet in position; in the sketch, an arrangement of steel rods is shown that permits latching the cabinet by dropping two or more rods into shallow holes drilled into the concrete floor. Other methods include retractable or locking casters, and wheel blocks.

The undercounter cabinets are constructed of ¾" fir plywood for the sides and shelves, ½" plywood backs, and 1" jointed tongue-and-groove stock for the fronts or doors, assembled on a frame of 2-by-2 stock. Shelves may be fitted into dado grooves in the sides, or supported on 1-by-2 cleats. Drawers of

Door hinges are mounted on blocks so that the door cleats won't bind when the door opens.

Hinges are shimmed so the door hangs plumb. Mortised butt hinges are used for storage cabinet, surface H-hinges for the base cabinets.

Saw table must be fitted into frame of cart and secured in place. Set shelf height to allow for sawdust collection bin.

Workshop drawers often contain heavy loads of tools and metal supplies. The drawer guides shown provide the needed support.

½" and ¾" plywood should be well made with fitted dado and rabbet joints, as they will hold heavy workshop tools and supplies.

In the saw table cabinet, provision should be made for sawdust collection, either through a cutout in the shelf directly under the saw, or with a removable drawer. This is not shown in the sketch as the clearance required for various makes of saws varies, and the shelf may be located to allow placing a sawdust container under the saw.

The counter top, with a recommended 30" depth, covers the entire length of the cabinet arrangement along one wall. Choice of counter mate-

rial may be based on the kind of shop work you intend to do. If it will involve some metal-working, or you are concerned about "bounce," the top may be built of 2-by-6 lumber, tightly joined with cleats and covered with a panel of tempered hardboard which is glued down or fastened with screws. For general shop work, however, a counter top of ¾" plywood, or better still, particle board, will be quite satisfactory. The counter panel should be fastened down securely with screws driven into the supporting cabinets below and covered with a panel of ¼" tempered hardboard laminated directly to the underlying counter-top material.

You'd have to have a sharp eye indeed to discover that there's a well-equipped workshop hiding here. The wall unit normally is used as a serving buffet.

But when the guests leave, the panel with the photographs drops down and becomes a workbench surface, with an array of tools handy at the back.

HIDEAWAY WORKSHOP

Here's a way to have a workshop without taking up any extra space or leaving tools around where they can be handled by children or unauthorized persons. The idea is practical for the do-it-yourselfer who does only occasional repairs around the house or small improvement projects. Although designed for a basement playroom, it will be of particular interest also to apartment dwellers who do not have access to a regular basement workshop.

The unit, which includes a work table, a handy rack for tools, and plenty of storage space for supplies, is part built-in and part built-on. Thus it can serve as a wall unit in a recreation room, and is so planned that it presents an attractive appearance to the room without a hint of its primary purpose.

The floor-to-ceiling built-in section contains an enclosed storage cabinet at the top, a recess for tools in the middle, and shelving at the bottom. The built-on part consists of two storage cabinets that are attached at right angles to the bottom shelving section.

The heart of the unit is a panel that swings up or down to cover or uncover the tool recess. When closed, the face of the panel reveals only whatever decorative items are displayed on it, perhaps family photographs as in the illustration. When the panel is lowered, it forms the workbench counter, while clearing access to the tool rack mounted on the rear wall. The workbench surface is securely supported on the two sturdy storage cabinets at the sides of the unit, which are so attractive in their hardwood veneer plywood construction that they serve as furniture pieces.

Building the Unit

The built-in section is constructed first. The framing consists of a pair of floor-to-ceiling 2-by-6's, 8' apart, with a 2-by-4 vertical member at the center. As shown in the sketch, lengths of 2-by-4 are fastened to the inside faces of the end uprights to support the 2-by-6 horizontal member on which the overhead storage section will be built.

If you're in the process of framing out the basement room, just substitute the pair of 2-by-6's at the necessary points in place of the wall studs—but these 2-by-6's are notched at top and bottom corners to fit over your floor and ceiling plates. If the basement is already finished, remove the paneling at this location and cut in the 2-by-6 uprights as above without disturbing the existing 2-by-4's.

Next, build the storage cabinet at the top, slotting each shelf to fit neatly around the studs and flush against the back wall.

The height of this storage section will depend on the ceiling clearance of your room; you should leave about 6' of free space underneath. Thus, an 8' ceiling height will leave 2' for the storage section. Fluorescent lighting strips will be placed underneath this storage section, with a plywood strip along the front to serve as a baffle. The upper cabinet section has ¼" thick hardboard doors that slide in wood tracks, and which are a standard item available at lumberyards and hardware dealers.

Floor Cabinet Details

The two floor cabinets are built of ¾" plywood as separate units, dimensioned to fit your space and workshop requirements, then attached to the main uprights. These cabinets can be surfaced with white Formica laminate to do double duty as refreshment buffets or bars for social gatherings.

The front panel, mounted on a piano hinge at the bottom to swing down to the level of the side cabinets, should be installed after the rest of the construction is completed. The panel, 30" high, and wide enough to just fit the space, is ripped from a 3'-by-8' plywood panel, the cut made at a

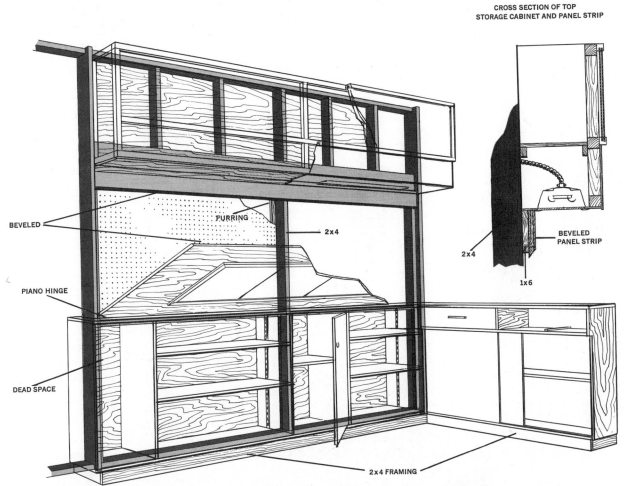

CROSS SECTION OF TOP
STORAGE CABINET AND PANEL STRIP

BEVELED

PURRING

2x4

BEVELED
PANEL STRIP

2x4

PIANO HINGE

1x6

DEAD SPACE

2x4 FRAMING

Hideaway workshop unit is supported mainly by two 2×6 uprights, cut into the wall framing plate. Storage is provided by cabinets along the top, the shelf spaces under the worktable drop-panel, and the two side cabinets. Back wall has perforated hardboard for tool-holding clips. Front panel has bevel along the top edge to match the angle-cut of the strip that is fastened over a 1×6 cross-member.

bevel. The narrower strip is attached under the light so that when the workshop unit is closed, the drop panel fits neatly into the bevel cut along the bottom of the strip.

The back wall is paneled with ⅛″ perforated hardboard, which can be supplied with the various fittings needed to hold all your hand tools, handy to your workshop counter.

When closed, the unit has a decorative appearance that can be a conversation piece, your guests little knowing that its real purpose is to serve as a modest workshop.

THE ELECTRIC DRILL

Always the most useful power tool in the shop, today's portable electric drill does even more jobs, saves even more work. Its price remains lower than that of any other power tool. If you don't own one, it is the first tool you should get. If you do own one, now may be the time to make it two. With two drills, you have one for normal use. The other can be set up exclusively as a drill press, a grinder, or a power screwdriver—or even as a spare to lend a neighbor.

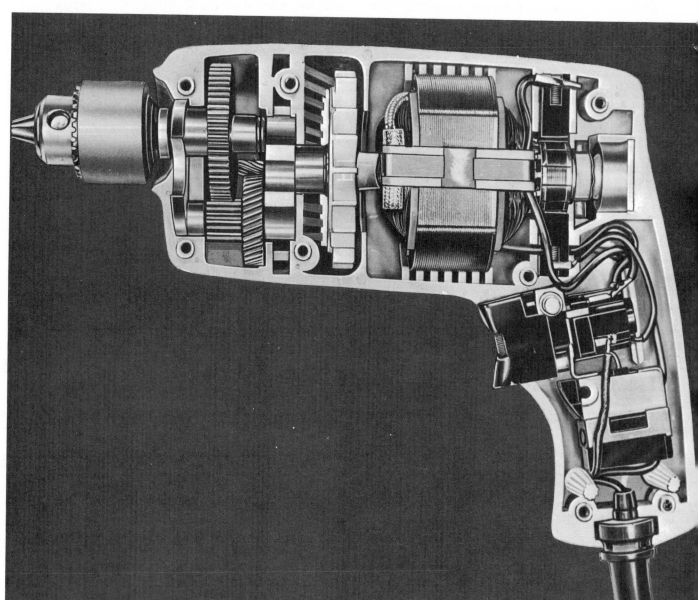

If you were to be restricted to owning a single tool, you'd choose an electric drill—and with good reason, because its versatility is unmatched. Here's a report that tells you how to select the one that suits you best.

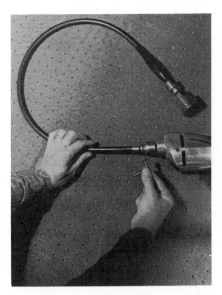

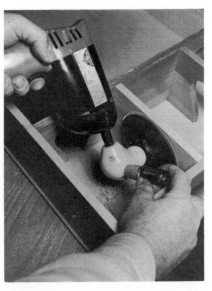

A flexible shaft reaches places a drill can't go. Fasten the shaft by turning the key in all three holes of the chuck.

Right-angle attachment makes working in tight places easy. It allows you to double the speed of your drill.

Polishing with this right-angle device can be done in no time at all. Handle on device makes it easy to guide the pad.

A drill is the power tool you can't do without. You need holes to start screws, insert dowels, snake BX cable, and for installing plumbing. You need holes for starting cutouts which you complete with a saw. You need holes in wood, masonry, plastics, steel, tile, plaster.

But drilling holes is only part of the story. You can use its muscle for sanding, wirebrushing, polishing, buffing, mixing paint, for turning a grindstone, driving a circular saw. You can also use it as a power screwdriver and a power wrench.

Drills come in more varieties and are made by more manufacturers than any other power tool. A drill's size is measured by the largest shaft its chuck will accommodate. For home use, a drill may be ¼″, ⅜″, or ½″. It may weigh a little more than 2 lbs. or almost 10. Its top speed may be 600 rpm or 2500. Its case may be plastic or metal. Its cost may be under $10 or more than $50.

The ¼″ drill is unquestionably your best bet. The free-running speed of a standard drill of this size is 2250 rpm. It will handle most of the jobs you have around the house. A typical manufacturer will offer a "good," "better," and "best" ¼″ model. The soundest advice is to get the best drill your budget allows. Generally, the higher-priced drills will have more power, more durability, and added versatility.

Don't be misled by the Underwriters Laboratories (UL) "Industrial Rating" given a drill. It is the only rating that UL now gives power tools when it

Drilling a hole through the studs of an existing wall with a long bit is simple if you use this handy right-angle drive.

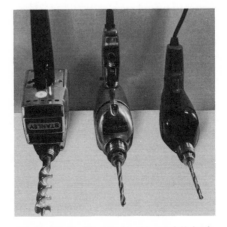

Above, (L to R), are ½-, ⅜- and ¼-inch drills. The larger drills have more power and turn more slowly.

437

approves of their safety. Most companies, however, classify their power tools as consumer or industrial. Unless you have special needs, your concern will be only with the consumer variety.

Variable Speed

One of the features you'll get in a better drill is variable speed. The speed depends upon how far you pull the trigger. It can range right up to 2250 rpm. Slow speed lets you drive screws without use of any special attachment. It lets you tighten bolts and nuts. You know how a drill can jump all over the place when you start drilling in a hard material. Slow speed lets you start drilling tile or steel without first scratching or punching a starting point.

Typically, the multispeed feature will add $7 to $14 to the cost. A reversing feature lets you extract screws or loosen nuts with the same efficiency as driving them. The reversing feature is a good one if you do a lot of work involving screws or thread cutting. You can get a kit for adding a speed trigger to an old drill for under $6.

Some variable speed drills have an arrangement so that you can set maximum speed. A full pull on the trigger then gives you this speed. In addition to infinitely-variable-speed drills, you can get two-speed 1/4″ drills. Usually, they are offered in a choice of 1600 or 2250 rpm.

Shocks Are Out

Some drills are "double-insulated" and "shockproof." No matter what goes wrong inside the drill, you can't get an electrical jolt. Double-insulated drills don't require grounding and have a standard 2-prong plug.

Drills that aren't double-insulated have a 3-prong plug. The third prong—a big round one—is for grounding the metal frame of the drill, so that in case of a short circuit the electricity will go through the grounding plug instead of through you. An adapter makes it possible to plug a 3-pronger into an ordinary socket, but you must attach the adapter's green wire to the screw on the outlet plate. Most people don't do this. Some even go so far as to hack-saw off the third prong, making their drill potentially hazardous.

All or most of the case of a shockproof drill is made of plastic. Besides being a nonconductor, plastic has other advantages. It makes drills more colorful and eye-appealing. Further, the plastic safe-

When shopping for a drill, be sure to read the specification plate—it gives you the size, speed, h.p. or amperage.

Multi-speed controls provide slow speeds needed to drive screws. Drill above has a special Phillips-head screwdriver bit.

Many drills are reversible and can back screws out or loosen nuts. Reversing feature is useful when tapping metal for screws.

Drill point in this variable-speed model won't jump around on the surface of ceramic tile because it can start slowly.

Some drills have 3-pronged plugs and need adapters (L) for ordinary outlets. Shockproof types have 2-prong plugs.

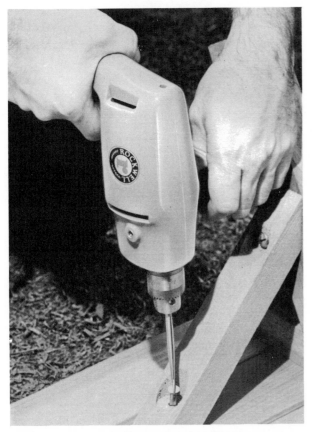

The ⅜-inch drill has the power for tough jobs like drilling big holes with a holesaw as shown in the photo above.

Double-insulated, shockproof drill, such as this new Rockwell model, can be used outdoors with greater safety even where a grounding connection is not accessible.

If you are a "big project man" and drill big holes in concrete, metal and other hard materials, you need a ½-inch drill.

If you have two drills you can keep one in a permanent set-up for special jobs such as sharpening tools and drill bits.

guards the drill against damage if it is dropped. Finally, it's pleasanter to the touch.

More Power, Less Speed

If you frequently drill holes in steel or concrete, you need a ⅜″ drill. Many have the same motor as ¼″ models, but they are geared down. This gives less speed, but more power. They can cut tough materials without stalling. Typically, a ⅜″ drill will have a maximum speed of 1000 to 1250 rpm. A variable-speed control on a ¼″ drill may give you the same low speed, but it won't have the same torque, or turning force.

Some ⅜″ models sell for little more than the ¼″ units. They are not necessarily bigger or heavier. Because they are now in the same price range as quarter-inchers, they have spurted in popularity. They will do everything a ¼″ drill will do, and more besides. They can accommodate the shanks of drills and attachments that won't fit a ¼″ chuck. They may have an extra handle. This extra grip means extra steadiness—important for slow, continuous drilling. Some have cords 10′ long, as against the 6′ size that's almost universal with quarter-inchers. Where outlets are scarce, this added reach can be a decided advantage.

You can get ⅜″ drills that offer variable speed, reversibility, and which are shockproof. Typical multispeed models have ranges from 0 to 1000 rpm. At least one offers dial-controlled speeds from 1000 to 2500 rpm. Other 2-speed varieties may give you a choice of 800 rpm or 1750 rpm. Still another, a 6-speed drill, lets you dial 450, 750, 900, 1050, 1200, or 1350 rpm.

Battery-operated drill is ideal for outdoor work where there is no electricity.

For Big Project Men

If you're the kind who tackles everything from wiring and plumbing to adding a wing on the house, you'll find a ½″ drill almost indispensable. It may be too big and heavy for small jobs—for these you'll want one of the smaller models—

but for drilling big, deep holes in wood, concrete, and steel, this is the rig. They don't cost a fortune either. Countless numbers are in the $30 and $40 brackets.

How About Battery Drills?

If your work takes you up on the roof, into trees, and out in the woods where electricity is not readily available, a battery-operated drill is for you. Their power supply may be a battery pack located in the handle, or in a separate case which you can slip on your belt. The battery-operated drill can be used with absolutely no danger of shock in the rain, on soaked ground, in damp cellars, or on a wet boat dock.

The number of holes that can be drilled on one charge varies. Typically, one may drill 75 one-half inch or 200 quarter-inch holes in ¾" fir plywood. For keeping the drill's power up, there is a compact charger to which the drill can be left connected when not in use. It keeps the drill ready to go, but won't overcharge or damage it. A typical quarter-inch cordless drill recharges in ten hours.

Horsepower and Amps

Because manufacturers differ in the way they rate tools, you can't make a close comparison on the basis of horsepower or amperes between tools from two different companies. But you can use them to compare the various tools in a single manufacturer's line.

It would seem obvious that a ⅓ horsepower drill is more powerful than a ¼ one, a 3 amp. drill more powerful than a 2 amp. But this is not always the case. You will sometimes find that a manufacturer's more expensive and more powerful drill has a slightly lower rating than a cheaper model. This is because tool design, particularly gears and bearings, is important.

Ten Tips On Use

1. Always insert bits into the chuck the full length of the jaws. The bit end should rest on the chuck bottom. For the best grip on a bit, tighten the chuck by turning the key in each of the three holes.

2. Never support the weight of the drill on its bit. If you need added support, extend an index finger along the side of the drill or use both hands.

3. Don't force a drill beyond its capabilities. If it stalls, or overheats, you are forcing it. Running a

drill at low speed or in reverse for an extended time will also overheat it. Run it with no load until it cools off. It will cool off faster by running than if you shut it off.

4. In drilling metal, lubricate the bit with oil. Lubrication is not needed for drilling cast iron or brass. For drilling aluminum, use turpentine or kerosene. If you are drilling a hole ⅜" or larger, drill a small pilot hole first.

5. You can use twist drills for small holes in wood, but clean the flutes frequently. Ease up on pressure when you are about to break through. Better yet, clamp a back-up board to the work. Keep the drill running when backing out of a hole. It prevents jamming.

6. When a twist drill or bit cuts easily into material, it is not likely to overheat. When a drill is turning fast and cutting slow, that's when there's danger of overheating. High speed can ruin an expensive carbide-tip drill in short order.

7. Most drills have locking buttons so that the drill can be kept running without need to pull on the trigger. This is an advantage for such operations as sanding and polishing. On most variable-speed drills, the locking button is on full speed only.

8. The most popular twist drills are 1/16", 3/32", 1/8", 3/16", and 1/4". High-speed twist drills will cut holes in wood, steel, plastics. An advantage of multispeed control is that it makes it possible to drill at low speed and get by with using inexpensive low-carbon twist drills.

9. By using spade-type bits you can drill holes up to 1½" with a ¼" drill. The most popular spade-type bits are ⅜", ½", ⅝", ¾", ⅞", and 1".

10. Avoid using overlong or lightweight extension cords. They don't deliver enough voltage. A 50-foot cord should be at least 18 gauge wire. A 100-footer should be 16 gauge.

Maintenance Is Easy

Follow the manufacturer's directions that come with the drill. Some bearings are lubricated for life. Those that require oiling, typically, may need two drops of machine oil every six months or after sixty hours of use.

Carbon brushes may eventually require replacement. Usually, when either brush is worn to about ¼" in length it is a good idea to get new ones. Always replace both brushes. Be sure that the curvature of the brush matches the curvature of the motor armature. You can get a maintenance kit,

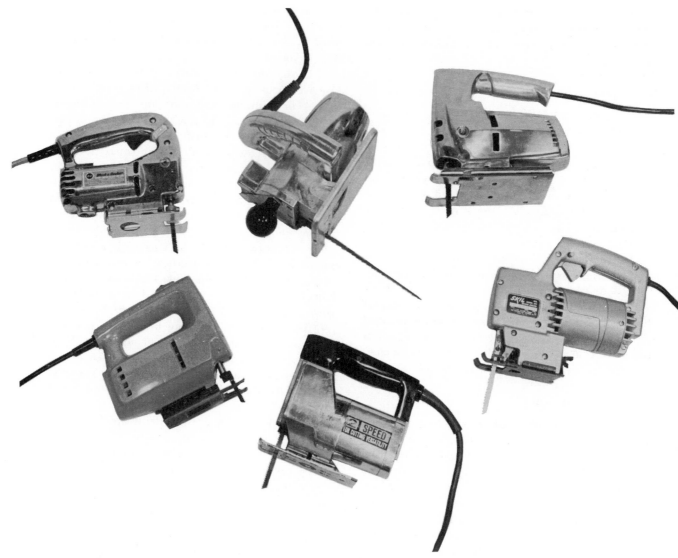

If ever a tool earned its popularity, it's the sabre saw. Versatility is its most prominent trait—there are few cutting jobs it cannot do.

consisting of gear lubricant, a set of brushes, springs, and brush caps for less than $1.50. Before you lubricate, though, read the instruction manual and warranty carefully. Some manufacturers disclaim responsibility if you lubricate their product.

If the motor overheats easily, check for clogging of vent holes and blow dust from them while the motor is running. Be cautious in using your drill on fiberglass. The dust is very abrasive. Clean your tool with an air jet to prevent damage.

If the drill won't run when you press the trigger, first check to see if the outlet is live. Do it by plugging in another tool or lamp. If they don't work ei-

ther, there is likely a blown fuse or tripped circuit breaker. If there is current at the outlet, check the fit of the drill's plug. If it still doesn't work, have it checked by the service shop recommended by the manufacturer. If you attempt any major repair yourself, you may invalidate your guarantee.

THE SABRE SAW

What it lacks in cutting speed, the sabre saw, or portable jigsaw as it is also known, more than makes up by its ability to do so many jobs well. It

Many of the better saws have more than one speed, selected by the operator with a switch. This model has three choices; most have two. Some have continuously variable speeds.

Your saw can cut angles by adjusting the calibrated base as needed. You can expect to set it fairly accurately at 15, 30 and 45 degrees, at which points most saws are calibrated.

There's a blower in every sabre saw to get the sawdust out of the blade's path. This one also has a snap-on plastic deflector through which you can see the guideline on the surface of the work.

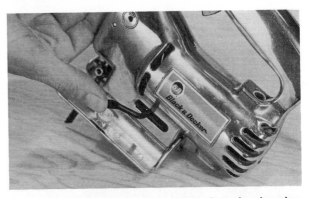

This model has a unique quick release clamp for changing the setting of the base angle. Thumb pressure flips a lever, you set the desired angle, then tighten it just as easily as it was loosened.

can handle almost any operation of which the circular saw is capable, except dadoing and rabbeting. Ripping, crosscutting, mitering, and beveling are its meat—to say nothing of the tool's ability to make "plunge" cuts, large or small arcs and circles, scrollwork, and others.

It is versatile in other ways, too. With the right blade you may cut metal, leather, plastic, and fabric. Many better saws have improved their ability to cut materials other than the wood for which they were primarily designed by allowing you to adjust the blade speed, which really helps in suiting the saw to the work. In most cases, the speed is switch-selected; you merely flip to one of two, or sometimes, three positions. At least one new saw has a dial that you set for a choice of any speed from "blast-off" to a slow crawl. Matching the speed and the blade to the work is the equivalent of having a saw custom made for every job.

In principle, all are the same. Differences appear in their refinements—variable speeds, the assort-

ment of blades that fit, convenience of operation, and so on. An important difference is ease of blade changing, which goes hand in hand with the security of the clamp that holds the blade. When choosing a saw, be sure to examine this feature carefully. A solidly clamped blade is *not* always the easiest to change, but the safety it gives you is to be preferred. Many of the better clamps have two set screws, both of which must be loosened to change blades.

A feature of every saw is a blower that keeps the path of the blade clear, and the cutting line visible. Blower force depends on motor speed; slow a multispeed tool and you also slow the speed of the air stream.

Most, if not all, sabre saws are adjustable to cut miters, usually up to 45 degrees, the angle being easily read (and set) from a scale at the saw's base. Many have a wing nut or screw to clamp the saw at the desired angle.

A rip guide comes with most saws, or is available

The rip guide is adjustable and is clamped by the thumb-screw at the right side of the shoe. This particular guide is offset, and so can make narrower rips than usual.

Each manufacturer tries to get one or two unique features into his tools. The model shown here has a roller guide behind the blade. It tends to stabilize the action and reduce flexing somewhat.

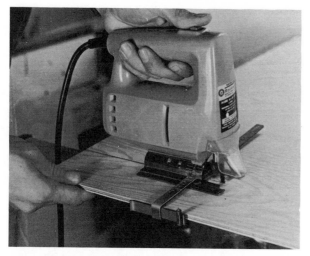

Most models come with an adjustable rip guide that uses the edge of the workpiece as a guide line. Obviously, the guide edge must be straight or your rip won't be. Set the guide and clamp it in place.

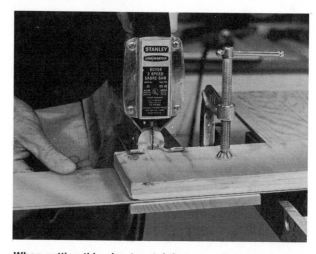

When cutting thin sheet metal that may vibrate and cause you to lose control, clamp it first between two pieces of scrap, then cut through the sandwich in one operation. Use a metal cutting blade.

When ripping so far from the edge of the board that the guide will not reach, a piece of scrap can be tacked to the work instead. Or, if you don't want the tacks to mar the work, use two C-clamps.

This brute of a sabre saw is even capable of cutting heavy pipe. It has extra-length blades that increase the work capacity. Always use a blade to match your job.

as an extra-cost accessory with others. It is handy and useful, but you can get along without it if your hand is steady enough to follow a guideline accurately, or if you take the trouble to clamp a straight-edge to the workpiece.

Other innovations are also worth mentioning. Some are made of high-impact plastic, guaranteed against breakage, which also insulates it electrically so that grounding is unnecessary. The blade of one rides on a roller guide which stabilizes it and reduces flexing. There are 2-speed, 3-speed, and continuously variable speed models. One model takes blades that can handle 4-by-4's and will cut heavy steel pipe.

Using a sabre saw skillfully requires little practice. It's easy to follow guidelines accurately with the saw's rather slow cutting speed (compared with a circular saw). Mistakes can be corrected before they get out of hand if you haven't strayed into the "good" side of the cut. If there is a knack to using this tool, it is in not forcing it. You are working with a fairly light blade, reciprocating on a relatively short stroke. Give it time to cut. If you use excessive force, the blade may snap. Exert firm pressure, but with care. Too heavy a load on the blade will slow the motor; when you hear that happen, ease off. Blades stay sharp longer when used properly, too.

Plunge cutting—making an opening in the center of a board—is one of the sabre saw's most valuable uses. Not even a starting hole is needed, because the saw cuts its own. To make a plunge cut, with the switch off and the blade motionless, place the saw on the workpiece holding it at such an angle that the blade is entirely free of the work and the saw is resting on the forward edge of the base. Switch on the saw and, using the edge of the base as a pivot, slowly but firmly lower it until the blade makes contact with, and cuts into the workpiece. Expect a good deal of vibration and some resistance when the blade makes contact, so grasp the handle firmly. You'll quickly learn the technique with a few practice cuts in scrap.

Although helpful in ripping, as already mentioned, the accessory guide has its limitations, most important of which is the width of the rip it lets you make. When ripping a long board, where the guide's capacity is insufficient, tack or clamp a straightedge to the work instead. For shorter cuts, a steel square provides a handy and accurate line.

Many sabre saws have provision for cutting arcs and circles of various sizes. Most use the rip guide here, too. You'll find a small hole at each end of

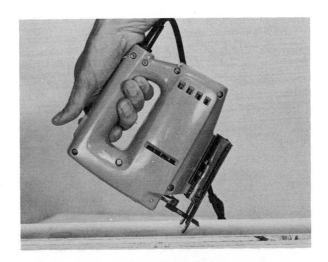

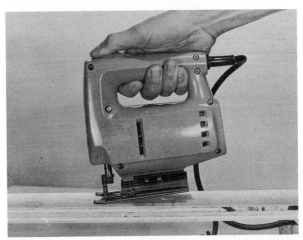

These are the two steps in plunge cutting, another unique ability of the sabre saw. First angle the saw on the work, turn it on. lower slowly as the blade digs in.

Another way to make internal cuts is shown here. Drill holes at the corners of the area to be removed, making them large enough to clear the blade.

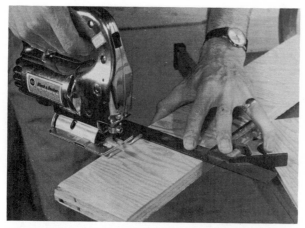

If the size of the workpiece permits and the cut is as short as this one, a steel carpenter's square provides a more than adequate guide for the saw. Hold it firmly against the work, or clamp.

To preserve and protect your saw, follow the recommendations in your instruction booklet. It will tell you how often to remove old grease. Wipe it out; never use a solvent.

Arcs and circles are another of the cuts the sabre saw masters. In this model, a nail is driven through a hole in the rip guide, and the saw pivots around it. Change the curve by resetting the guide.

An occasional check of the motor brushes will tell you when they have worn sufficiently to need replacement. With normal use, one set should last for years, but keep an eye on them.

Some saws require occasional oiling. Your instruction booklet will advise you where, when, and how much. Over-oiling is as harmful as under-oiling; follow the manufacturer's instructions.

the part of the guide that is parallel to the direction of cutting. A small nail driven through one of the holes into the work will provide a pivot point around which the saw will swing as it cuts. The radius of the arc or circle is equal to the distance from the center of the pivot point to the cutting edge of the blade. Set the guide accordingly.

Maintenance and Care

Although any good sabre saw will last for years, one preventive measure and a bit of occasional maintenance will lengthen its life. The preventive measure is easy—don't let the saw overheat. When the body gets hot, not just warm, let it run free for a few minutes. That's the quickest way of cooling it, even better than just shutting it off. Clogged vents also cause overheating. Keep them clear by frequent cleaning with a stiff bristle brush.

Every tool needs lubrication and the sabre saw is no exception. Your instruction booklet will tell you how often it should be greased and oiled. Remove old grease by wiping with a rag; never use solvent. Replace with fresh lubricant of the kind recommended for your tool. Points where oil should be applied vary from one saw to another; follow the instruction booklet's recommendations here also.

Motor brushes will eventually wear, causing rough or erratic operation. An occasional but regular checkup of the condition of the brushes will give you advance notice that they are wearing, and you can replace them before trouble actually occurs.

SANDERS FOR SMOOTH FINISHING

With most materials, beauty is only skin deep. A finishing sander is the power tool that brings out that beauty. It's called a *finishing* sander for good reason.

By hand, you can make 375 strokes a minute. With a sander, you can make 3,450 to 14,400. That's 9 to 41 times faster and a million times better.

You'll use a finishing sander for finishing and refinishing of furniture, wood, metal. You'll use it for leveling dry-wall joints, buffing wax, smoothing edges of glass, polishing marble, removing rust, feathering painted edges, even slicking door and drawer edges so they don't stick. And, most certainly, you'll use it to cut gloss on enamel, and to prepare paint undercoats for a slick finish coat.

But remember, it's a finishing sander. It's not for fast stock removal or taking off layers of stubborn paint. That's a job for a belt sander. You may want one of these later, but you should get a finishing sander first. It costs less, and you need it more.

Three Varieties

You have your choice of three varieties: orbital, straight line, and dual action. Orbital action means your abrasive is moving in a flat, tight oval, rather than straight back and forth. Each orbit, typically, is less than ¼" wide, so it's scarcely as if you were sanding against the grain, but you are doing just that, and enough to make cutting faster. It still produces a fine finish, while at the same time expanding the tool's capability for some rougher jobs.

Straight-line sanders are for extra-fine finishing. There are enough jobs of that kind in the average house to let it earn its keep. The straight-liner doesn't remove much material, or do it quickly, but it does it with ultimate smoothness. And it doesn't cut corners. It gets up into them. It can almost completely eliminate the need for hand sanding. At 9,000 strokes a minute, each ³⁄₁₆" long, how can you compete?

The dual-action sander combines both orbital and straight-line action, and thus gives you the best of both worlds. You can start out with orbital

Pushing a lever shifts this dual sander from straight-line to orbital action.

Orbital to straight-line shift on this sander is done with a plastic wrench.

When sanding close to an obstruction front handle swings up out of the way.

Felt sanding pads (right) are better for flat surfaces, neoprene for contours.

Holding roller turned by a screwdriver is used here to attach paper to sander.

Simple mousetrap arrangement secures the sandpaper to the pad of this model.

action for heavier stock removal, then at the flick of a lever or turn of a key switch to straight-line action for finish and flush sanding.

A dual-action sander does not cost quite as much as a straight-line and orbital sander combined, but it approaches it. It's the old you-get-what-you-pay-for routine.

Look at the Pad

Finishing sanders differ in the size, shape, and kind of pad they have. The bigger the pad area, the more work a sander is likely to do. Standard size of sheet abrasives is 9"-by-11". Some sanders use half a sheet, others use a third, still others a quarter, a fifth, or less.

In tight situations, and on irregular surfaces, a small pad is at its best. On broad flat surfaces, the big pad goes to town. So an in-between size is a compromise that satisfies most of the time. But it may not satisfy you, and you're the one who's going to be using it.

The pad on which the paper goes may be felt or neoprene (synthetic rubber) sponge. The felt may have a little more firmness and bite, good especially for flat surfaces. The neoprene may adapt to uneven contours slightly better, and can be used for either wet or dry sanding. For some sanders, you can get either kind of pad, or both kinds and use them interchangeably.

The way the paper attaches to the pad may be of some significance to you, too. They all add up to the same thing, but some may be slightly different in appeal to different people.

448

What Does It Weigh?

Some sanders feel twice as heavy as others, either because of a difference in balance or because of an actual difference in weight. Weight is important. Pressure should not be applied on a sander. It will slow its speed and cause its paper to clog. The weight of the sander alone, plus the natural weight of your hand, are all the pressure required in normal operation. A heavier sander usually has a more powerful motor, and will be more of a work horse.

But how about on vertical surfaces or overhead?

Here is where a lighter tool has an advantage. On vertical surfaces or overhead, you have to supply your own pressure, and you become aware of the weight of a tool. A lightweight sander will be less tiring. So compromise between the two, or select on the basis of which kind of work you do more.

Well-designed knobs, intelligently located, are intended to improve control and make the application of even pressure simpler. In some cases, you can move the knob from front to sides. In others, you can change its angle. You can remove knobs altogether when sanding into corners, or approaching obstructions.

Many excellent sanders are designed without extra knobs. You may like this arrangement better. For extra control, you can grip the housing if you wish. One type has no knobs and no handle. It's strictly a palm-grip deal, especially good for underside finishing, overhead surfaces, hard-to-reach places and contour sanding.

In selecting a tool, get the heft of it. Try its feel with the handle or handles in different positions. Try its on-off switch. Most sanders have a slide thumb-switch on top of the handle. At least one has a push-on push-off handle switch. Other models have under-handle triggers.

Metal or Plastic?

Most sanders have housings that are all metal, usually polished aluminum alloy. Others are all or partly plastic. The trend seems to be toward plastic. Plastic is comfortable to touch in any weather. It can be colored attractively. It doesn't have the shock hazard of metal.

You may find a tag attached to a plastic sander proclaiming it "shockproof" and "double-insulated." You will find it has a two-prong plug. Sanders that are not double-insulated have three-prong plugs. The round third prong is designed to connect to ground and prevent shock hazard. But grounding can be a nuisance. With a plastic, double-insulated tool, you don't have this problem.

Drop a sander with a metal housing and one with a plastic housing and don't be surprised which takes it better. After all, crash helmets are made of plastic. In any case, you'll probably find the manufacturer guarantees the housing to be unbreakable.

You will, however, find some of the best finishing sanders with metal housings. They're the choice of most professionals who should know what will give good service.

They All Run

There is a difference in motors, but it's not always easy to tell what the differences mean, except in a general way.

Brush type, or universal motors, are used in almost all sanders designed for home-shop use.

Lightweight, inexpensive sanders may have vibration, electromagnetic, or magnetic-impulse drive. It's not powerful, but it doesn't have to be.

The power of a motor is often indicated by its ampere rating. A 3.5 ampere motor is generally more powerful than one with 1.8 amperes. But what kind of bearings a sander has, their number, and the overall tool design may be equally significant. It's not very scientific, but you can make a quick test of a sander's power by turning it on and holding it with increasing pressure against a surface. Can you make the motor stall? Chances are that most will seem to have about equal power, even though one may carry a 2.3 and another a 4 amp. rating. You may try a half-dozen models before you find one that will stand out from all the rest, and it won't necessarily have the highest ampere rating.

The sander you select doesn't necessarily have to have stand-out-power to give good service. There is a difference among sanders, but it's not as great as you might imagine. If you like its looks, the way it feels in your hands, and the price is right, you can't go far wrong.

Sanders kick up a lot of dust. Often, a sander must be used in a living area. Occasionally, you may find it necessary to sand where there are freshly painted surfaces nearby.

To overcome these problems, you can use a dust collector. Many sanders have vacuum attachments available as an extra. Some have their own vacuum bag. Others have a hose which you can attach to almost any tank-type vacuum cleaner.

Shockproof sander (right) with plastic housing requires only a 2-prong plug.

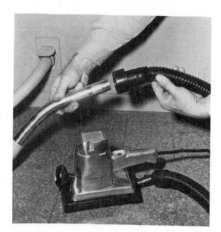

Some sanders can be attached to any standard vacuum dust collection system.

Sander with independent vacuum system does dustless job on plaster joints.

It's not exactly "dustless" sanding, but most of the dust does get picked up. Removing dust as you sand enables you to sand faster. Some say 25 per cent faster. With no layer of dust to obscure your work, it's much easier to see what you're doing and how much more remains to be done.

With a vacuum attachment it is necessary to place an enclosing skirt around the sander's pad. This can be somewhat of a nuisance when you're trying to sand close to vertical surfaces and when you want to change paper. But you'll gain the greater benefit of getting rid of most of the dust.

The tank-type arrangement may offer a stronger vacuum than the integral bag pick-up. But the bag is handier to use. Just remember to empty it when it becomes about a quarter full.

Paper Pointers

Selection of the right kind of paper is important. Don't use ordinary flint sandpaper. It's cheap to buy, but it wears out so fast it's more expensive to use.

The paper most commonly used for finishing sanders is aluminum oxide. You can recognize it by its brownish color. Also used is garnet, a natural abrasive which is slightly softer. It is recognizable by its reddish color, and is used exclusively for wood. Silicon carbide has limited application. It is black, and very hard and is used mostly for very fine finishing of lacquered and varnished surfaces.

Garnet and silicon carbide papers are available waterproof. You can recognize the waterproof type by its oiled-paper look. It can be used with oil, water, or other liquids as lubricants, just as long as they're not flammable.

For best results on a typical sanding job, use only open coat paper with a grit no coarser than ½-60 (some manufacturers say 1½-40). An open coat paper works faster than closed coat, doesn't clog, and produces just as smooth a finish.

The usual run of grit, from very coarse to extra fine, is 40, 50, 60, 80, 100, 120, 150, and 220. These numbers are mesh sizes, the number of openings per square inch in each direction on sieves used in grading the grit. Formerly (and sometimes still) you'll find grit size indicated by old-style arbitrary numbers like 1½, 0, ⅔, etc. They transfer like this: 1½ is 40, 1 is 50, ½ is 60, 0 is 80, 00 is 100, 0000 is 150.

One accessory you can get for a sander is a felt rubbing pad. It can be used with loose abrasives, finer than any that come on paper. Another good

450

accessory is a lamb's wool polishing pad for "hand-finish" polishing of furniture and paneling, also waxing the car.

Flick the Switch

When you start sanding, and when you finish, flick the switch only when the sander is not in contact with the work. If you start up or shut down while the sanding surface is in contact, you may make marks you'll be sorry about.

Keep the sander moving. If you park in one place for long you'll make a rut. With a straight-line sander, if you go across the grain you'll tear the wood fibers. With an orbital sander, grain direction isn't quite so critical.

Follow the manufacturer's directions for care and maintenance. Some sanders never require lubrication, others do.

On most sanders, you can replace worn carbon brushes on your own, but you may invalidate your guarantee rights if you undertake any major repairs.

Keep the tool clean. It is especially important that ventilating holes never become clogged. Overheating can affect the life of the motor. If the motor does overheat, remove the sander from the work and run it at no-load speed to cool it off.

THE CIRCULAR SAW

The portable circular saw is probably the second most popular power tool among home owners after the power drill. Actually, it's a simple tool and with a little care can be used quite well and safely.

Home owners generally prefer a 6" to 8" saw, not too small and not too big; most models can cut a 45 degree angle through a 2-by-4 laid flat—or deep enough for workshop and around-home purposes. All portable saws have spring-loaded guards which cover the bottom or exposed section of blade. Push the saw into the material being cut and the guard moves out of the way; finish the cut or draw the saw from the material and the guard automatically springs back to its protective position. Always be sure this guard is working; if it isn't, you are in danger.

Some new models are shockproof and require no grounding; all others should be equipped with a three-wire cable and always grounded when in use.

It wasn't always the case, but today most blades come with adaptors or knock-out bushings in their

centers to fit most standard makes of saws, new and old.

When you purchase a new saw, a chisel tooth combination blade generally comes with it. This blade is fine for rough-cutting 2-by-4's, hard and soft woods, and some other materials, but don't use it on plywood or painted lumber. You'll get less performance and perhaps a ruined blade and work.

It's easy to get a type of blade designed to do a specific cutting job best. A "plywood" blade, for instance, while doing a clean job on plywood, also works well with chipboard, hardboard, and fiberboard, as well as copper, brass, bronze, and lead. When cutting any of these soft metals, lubricate the blade with tallow.

For construction work, cutting a variety of materials, including painted or dirty lumber, a carbide-tipped blade is advantageous; it holds its edge for a long time. You can get one with 8 or 12 teeth for rough-cutting, or with 24 to 60 teeth, which will cut smooth. Do not use it on hard metals or where nails may be encountered; you will damage the teeth.

For brick, slate, stone, tile, fiberglass, metals, bone, and most hard plastics, you can get a cutoff wheel, which is like a thin grinding wheel reinforced with plastic—if it is not reinforced it is dangerous and should not be used. Wear a face mask and safety glasses, always, when working with this type of blade. And a tip: for faster cutting and longer blade life, let the brick or ceramic soak in a

Plastic laminates and corrugated panels also are quickly sawed, using a carbide-tipped blade, as shown.

Equipped with the proper blade, the circular saw can cut a variety of materials. Here it neatly trims a metal downspout.

Even concrete block, brick, and other masonry materials can be cut to needed dimensions by using a plastic-reinforced cutoff wheel.

bucket of water for ten or fifteen minutes before cutting.

There are numerous other specialty blades—hollow-ground for smooth cutting, grit wheels for slicing through wood and Plexiglas, friction wheels for burning through iron and steel.

As if all this isn't enough there is a brand-new breed of blade that holds great promise. It's covered with Teflon, the coating with nonstick properties. The manufacturer claims it lasts many times longer than uncoated blades, has greatly reduced blade drag, and gives longer life to the motor. There are 19 different blade styles, covering all the cutting jobs the home owner is likely to do.

If you haven't been changing the blades because it seems too difficult, take heart. Here are two ways to turn the trick.

Use a box wrench to turn the arbor nut counterclockwise, first holding the blade stationary by means of a small block of wood wedged between the teeth and the shoe. When the nut is off, you can remove the blade. Or, if the blade teeth are too small to get a bit on the wedge-block, you'll find that the blade has a small hole into which you can insert a nail or rod, then rotate the blade until this metal wedge "locks" the blade against the shoe. Then turn the nut.

Some saws have a slip-clutch—you can turn the nut, but you'll only succeed in rotating it without

The circular saw is particularly useful for such outside jobs as trimming all the boards of a porch deck or roof to uniform length. Use extension cord of adequate wire gauge in relation to distance from power source.

having it loosen. For this type, place the box wrench on the nut, then sharply rap its opposite end with a hammer. One or two shots should free it for further loosening by turning. If the nut is extremely tight (it gets tighter as you saw), don't give up. Keep rapping. It *will* come off.

Using the Saw

There are two ways to cut boards accurately. You can draw a guide line with a straightedge, then follow it with the blade. But don't cut *on* the line or your dimensions will be shorter by at least half the thickness of the blade. Rather, cut as close as you can to the outer (waste) edge of the line. The second way, used when accuracy is required, is to clamp or nail a straightedge to the board, then let the edge of the saw shoe ride against it.

When cutting a board, make sure to support it well on horses or on a table, and allow room for the cutoff to fall free. This way the cutoff piece can't lean in and then pinch the blade.

Before starting, set the blade so that it protrudes at least a quarter-inch below the material; otherwise it has a tendency to bind and, worse, kick back. (For safety always keep your body out of the line of cut in case of a kickback.) Most professionals keep the saw at maximum cutting depth; but it's safer to reset it according to the thickness of the material being cut.

In addition to square cuts, most models let you tilt the blade for beveling. Most have a line marked on the front of the shoe to show where the saw's cutting. But when you tilt the blade this line is no longer correct. Some saws have two such lines, one to indicate square cuts, the other for 45 degrees. And some others have a moving indicator attached to the bevel mechanism which will show you where the cut will be at any angle setting.

When cross-cutting boards (against the grain of the wood) the base shoe provides support when cutting a lefthand piece. Otherwise, approach the work for the base to rest on the left side.

Cutting Plywood

A most important home owner use of the circular saw is cutting plywood. The handling and cutting technique for plywood is the same as for other large paneling materials. Support the left, or main piece of plywood with sawhorses or have someone hold the cutoff piece. The cutoff piece will most likely be heavy, and you don't want it breaking off midway through the cut. For a clean, straight cut place the good, or finished, side of the plywood face down, then clamp or nail on a straightedge guide. Then cut, letting your blade just barely protrude out the bottom. And make sure that the cut line is not over the supports to avoid accidentally cutting them.

Grooves and Dadoes

The portable circular saw was not designed for

Ripping, when you go against grain, is more difficult, but is aided by guide fence that rides along with the work, keeps the blade in line.

When cutting plywood, place the finished side down, away from the blade, with the blade just barely protruding through the bottom. For straight cuts, clamp a guide strip along the plywood so the saw shoe rides against it.

A compound bevel cut, also known as a compound miter, is made. Bevel cuts are easier if the blade used is deep enough to make the cut in one pass.

To make a bevel cut adjust the tilting mechanism and lock it at any angle you want to cut. In the photo, a bevel rip is made with the help of the rip guide.

Cross-cut is made at 45-degree angle. Calibration markings on base show angle of tilt. Blade is locked in position with thumb nut.

Any number of pieces can be ripped to the same width by setting the rip guide so you can make duplicate cuts.

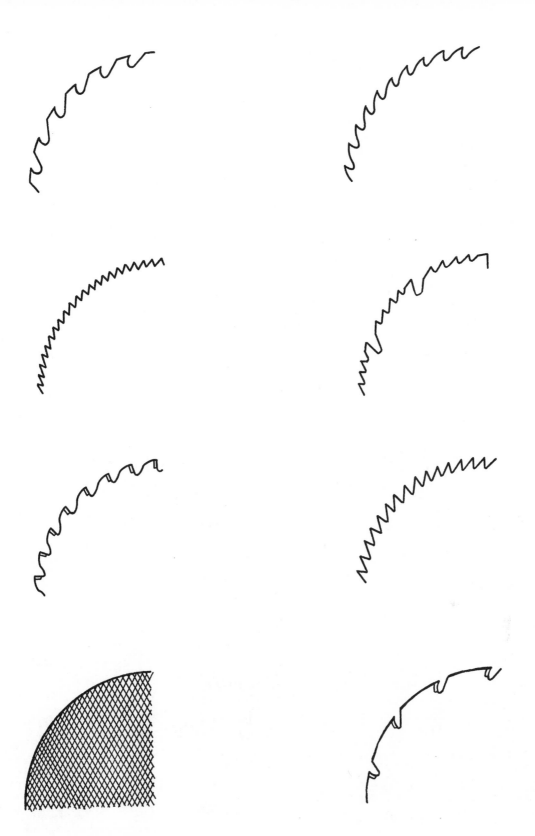

Varieties of Circular Saw Blades: (from left to right) Combination set tooth, rip, cross-cut ply, HG combination, carbide 8-12 teeth, carbide multi-tooth, tool steel HG cross-cut, and cut-off wheel.

cutting grooves or dadoes—you can't fit a dado set on the arbor. A few saws will take two ⅛" thick blades which together make a ¼" groove. Beyond that, blades won't fit under the guard.

But with a little knowledge, it can be done anyway. To make a wide groove, make two separate cuts at the left and right boundaries of the groove-to-be, then a few in the center ¼" or so apart. Then clean out the groove with a chisel.

Care and Maintenance

Most of the popular saw brands have sealed bearings and cannot be lubricated by the owner. The reduction gear drive from motor to blade is packed with grease which should be replenished every seventy-five to a hundred hours of use. Liquid graphite lubricates the spring guard. Oil is bad here because sawdust can cling to it. Periodically tighten all screws and nuts on the saw, as cutting vibration tends to loosen them. The most important maintenance is to keep a sharp blade. It's safer, it cuts faster, and it causes less wear on the motor.

WORKBENCH IMPROVES RADIAL SAW PERFORMANCE

This solidly built custom workbench provides an extra large working surface that supports even large plywood panels securely in position, without tricky juggling, so you are able to do precision jointing and other difficult operations with your radial saw more comfortably and safely. Additional desirable features of the bench design are a positive dust collector, convenient lumber storage, handy drawers for accessories and supplies. Above the saw-bench there's an open shelf cabinet for tools and instruments.

The bench is built by joining front and back H-shaped frames, each consisting of 4-by-4 legs

Custom workbench helps you get the most from your radial saw, with greatest safety and ease of handling stock. The bench includes an effective sawdust collecting arrangement, handy tool drawers, and lumber storage shelf. The wall unit above holds needed accessories.

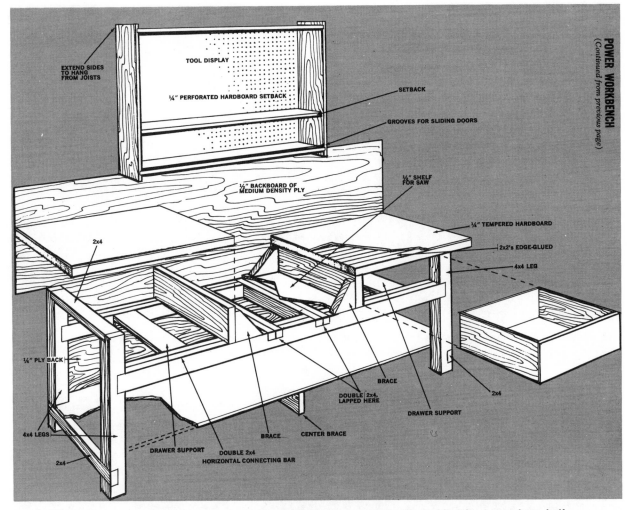

EXTEND SIDES TO HANG FROM JOISTS

TOOL DISPLAY

¼" PERFORATED HARDBOARD SETBACK

SETBACK

GROOVES FOR SLIDING DOORS

¼" BACKBOARD OF MEDIUM DENSITY PLY

¼" SHELF FOR SAW

¼" TEMPERED HARDBOARD

2x4

2x2's EDGE-GLUED

4x4 LEG

¼" PLY BACK

BRACE

DOUBLE 2x4, LAPPED HERE

2x4

DRAWER SUPPORT

4x4 LEGS

BRACE

CENTER BRACE

2x4

DRAWER SUPPORT

DOUBLE 2x4 HORIZONTAL CONNECTING BAR

Powersaw bench is 8 feet long, 36 inches deep. The 4-by-4 legs are joined with double 2-by-4 stretchers, half-lapped cross rails near the bottom and recessed 2-by-4s across the top. The top is of two 32-inch-wide sections, each consisting of edge-glued 2-by-2 strips, with a center space of 32 inches for the saw housing.

joined with double 2-by-4 stretchers. All four legs are notched at the top end and near the bottom to receive 2-by-4 front-to-back cross members. The stretchers are notched at two places for double 2-by-4 braces which are neatly half-lapped near the center saw position. The other framing details, including the drawer supports, center braces, and saw enclosure boards, are all indicated in the sketch.

The bench top of the unit illustrated is 8' long consisting of two 32" sections on each side of the saw housing, which itself is 32" wide. The front-to-back depth is an expansive 36", thus providing ample bench support for whatever material is handled. The saw is positioned flush with the front edge of the bench, leaving a catch space at the back for collecting sawdust. On all crosscuts, the blade will fan sawdust against the backboard, and into the rear opening of the middle section, then onto the board below. Dust from rip cuts cannot be controlled, however.

In this instance, the top is made of 2-by-2 strips, edge bonded into chopping block lamination. These are perfectly square and smooth segments, glued under clamped pressure, then trimmed and squared to the required dimensions. The result obtained is preferable because of dimensional stability to using 2-by-6 or 2-by-8 stock, or ¾" plywood. The top, as shown, is covered with a panel of ¼" hardboard for smoothness so that the work can be shifted easily into blade position.

The sketch also shows details for building the bench drawers and the wall-hung tool shelves.

Top ends of 4×4 legs are notched to recess 2×4 cross-members. The deep mortise close by is for the long double 2×4 stretcher.

The double 2×4s serving as the stretchers are mortised simultaneously to receive the half-lapped center connectors.

This is the space under the saw's top showing ½″ shelf resting on lapped rails, supporting the base of the saw.

Space between the backboard and the rear edge of the saw's cutting surface serves as a trap for the sawdust, which drops below.

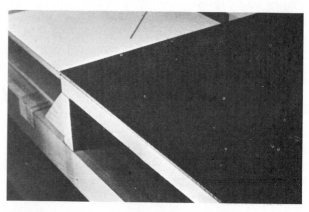

Top of laminated 2×2s is fastened into position, its surface ¼″ below that of the saw's top, seen at far left.

Sawbench top is surfaced with panel of ¼″ tempered hardboard, which is flush with the cutting surface of the radial saw.

Space below the horizontal connecting rails and the work top is used for tool drawer, which has an ample 5-inch depth.

ALL ABOUT PLANES

Ever since some medieval craftsman came up with the idea of mounting a sharp chisel in a block of wood so that it would be held firmly at a constant angle (and thus invented the first wood plane), professional and amateur carpenters alike have found that no other woodworking tool can match the accuracy and the smoothness of finish that can be achieved with a correctly sharpened and properly adjusted plane.

However, there have been many changes since those early days when a plane consisted primarily of a sharp chisel mounted in a block of wood. Many refinements and improvements have been made, and there are now many different sizes and styles—both hand and motor-driven. Some are designed to fill special needs, while others are for general trimming, shaping, and smoothing. Before you

Typical assortment of bench and block planes: 18-inch for plane (top), smoothing plane (middle), block plane (bottom).

Smoothing planes are easy to handle because they measure 8 or 9 inches in length. A properly adjusted smoothing plane should curl shavings off in uniform thickness. It is an all-purpose plane and is generally held in a manner which allows the blade to be at a slight angle to surface, giving shearing action to the cut.

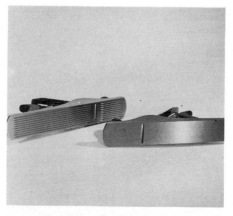

Jack planes are available with either a smooth or a corrugated bottom, as shown here. The smooth bottom is most popular, but the corrugated bottom offers less friction, especially on sappy wood.

can select the models that best meet your requirements for various jobs, you will have to know something about the different types that are available. You should also be familiar with the characteristics of each type of plane.

Hand Planes

The hand planes most commonly used around the home workshop are of two general types: bench planes and block planes. Bench planes are bigger and come in various styles that measure from 8″ to 22″ in length; block planes usually measure 6″ or 7″ in length. Bench planes are held with both hands—they have a large handle at the back for one hand and a knob at the front for the other. Block planes are used with only one hand. You butt the palm of your hand against a contoured rest at the back end and place your forefinger on the small knob at the front end. The other fingers are wrapped around the body of the tool to hold it firmly.

In both styles—bench and block planes—there is a chisel-like blade (called the plane-iron) that is held in place so that it projects down through the base or sole of the tool at a sharp angle. A second piece of metal (called the plane-iron cap) is clamped on top of this blade to reinforce it and to curl the shavings away in a continuous ribbon without splintering the wood and without permitting the shaving to get any thicker than the clearance provided between the bottom of the tool and the projecting edge of the blade.

All modern planes have some means for controlling the depth of cut by adjusting the amount that the plane-iron blade projects down through the base of the tool.

Bench Planes

These are the most versatile of all hand planes and they are the ones that you will use most often. The plane-iron cap assembly is held in place by a heavy cast piece which is called the lever cap. It locks the plane-iron and cap against an angled metal casting (called the frog) which has an adjusting screw which permits raising or lowering the blade for regulating the depth of cut. Also, a lever at the top provides for a slight lateral adjust-

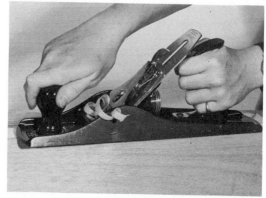

Fore and jointer planes, which are the longest of the bench planes, (a model of an 18-inch fore plane is shown) are best for trimming and truing up doors and other long edges. Their longer base permits them to slide over low spots.

ment—if you move the lever to one side, the whole assembly pivots slightly so that you can tilt the blade to line its cutting edge up exactly parallel across the base of the plane. The easiest way to do this is to turn the plane upside down and sight along the base while you move the adjusting lever to one side or the other, until you can see that the blade projection is equal across the width of the tool. This will ensure a shaving of uniform thickness across the width of the blade and will minimize the possibility of gouging.

Depending on their length, bench planes generally fall into three categories. The smallest and most popular group are the smoothing planes, which may be either 8″ or 9″ in length. Next are the jack planes which vary from 11″ to 15″ in length, and the longest ones of all are the fore and jointer planes which may be anywhere from 18″ to 24″ in length. Actually there is only a slight difference between a fore and a jointer plane (jointer planes are longer—22″ to 24″ in length) so the names are often used interchangeably. Both are used for trimming and truing up the edges of doors and long boards. The long base on these tools makes it much easier to trim to a straight line; shorter planes, like the smoothing planes which are only 8″ or 9″ in length, will tend to follow dips and curves without leveling them out. Longer planes will slide over the low spots and knock off the high spots until a level surface—or a straight edge—is attained.

The smoothing planes are the most popular with home carpenters because their shorter length makes them easier to use on most projects and because they are generally easier to carry around (they also cost less than the longer models). Jack planes are in between the two. Of the various size jack planes, the 14″ size is most popular. Jack planes are excellent for rough work where you have to dress lumber to size, as well as for trimming doors and taking waves out of warped lumber. Jack planes are available with either a smooth or corrugated bottom. The corrugated bottom is preferred by some because it offers less friction, especially on green wood where it minimizes sticking or gumming up.

The plane iron (blade) on all bench planes—regardless of length—has a cutting edge which is beveled on one side only, like a chisel. It is ground to angle of about 25 or 30 degrees and sits in place with its beveled side down. The plane-iron cap is clamped on top so that there is approximately $\frac{1}{16}$″ clearance between the cutting edge of the blade and the lower edge of the cap, and the curved edge

of this cap must fit snugly against the top face of the blade so that shavings cannot get wedged between the two. The assembled unit should be held firmly by the cam-action lever cap so that there is no chance of the blade wobbling or slipping.

Block Planes

These are the little brothers of the hand plane family and, as previously mentioned, are designed to be held with only one hand. There are tiny models only about 3″ in length for light trimming and model making, but the most popular versions are either 6″ or 7″ in length. In addition to compact size, the principal difference between a block plane and a bench plane is that it has the blade mounted at a much lower angle. This makes it much more suitable for trimming end grain, as well as for taking off very thin shavings on fine trimming jobs.

Block planes also have a plane-iron cap to keep the blade from digging in and to curl shavings off in a uniform thickness. Block planes also have controls for adjusting the depth of cut by raising or lowering the blade. On the simplest and cheapest models, the blade is held in place by a wedge, while in the better quality models there are regular adjusting screws and lateral adjusting levers similar to those on the larger bench planes. Unlike bench planes, however, block planes are almost always designed so that the beveled edge on the blade faces upward, instead of downward, because it cuts at a much lower angle. In addition, the beveled edge of

Block plane has blade set at a much lower angle than a bench plane and is ideal for smooth trimming of end grain, as shown. To avoid splintering edges, cuts should be made from end toward middle.

the block plane's blade is usually ground to an angle of about 20 degrees, as compared with the 25 or 30 degree angle on a bench plane's blade.

Since block planes are used primarily on end grain and other trimming jobs where thin shavings are desired, they should be adjusted so that the blade barely projects beyond the base of the tool. Most people allow the blade to project too far and then find that it tends to dig in or gouge the surface. A small projection will actually cut faster because it will enable you to use the block plane the way it was intended—with a series of light, rapid strokes, rather than the way you bear down with long strokes when using a bench plane.

When trimming end grain, however, regardless of the type plane you are using, remember always to work from each edge in toward the center. Running your plane all the way across the end grain of a board will invariably split it at the far end. However, if the piece is too small or located in such a way that it is impractical to work from both sides in toward the middle, then a backup block of scrap wood can be clamped on the far end. If this is clamped tightly against the edge of the board it should help prevent splitting, but to play safe cut with light strokes only.

Special Purpose Hand Planes

If you go in for cabinetmaking, model making or furniture building, then there are several specialized hand planes that you will probably find useful, particularly if your shop is not equipped with power tools such as a router or table saw with dado cutter.

Rabbets, dadoes, and grooves can be cut with a number of different types of rabbet planes. The most versatile is an 8″ model which has a large handle at the back end and two positions for the cutter blade—one in the middle for regular work, and one way up at the front end for bullnose work (for working close into tight corners and up against right angle corners). The 1½″ cutter blade goes across the full width of the frame so that you can cut flush up against either side. The tool also has an adjustable fence that can be used on either side and a removable depth gauge which enables you to control the depth of cut precisely. A special spur cutter is supplied for cutting across the grain (you don't use it when you're cutting parallel to the grain) and with the blade in the bullnose position you can cut stopped or blind rabbets that do not go all the way across the work.

In addition to this combination rabbet plane there are also smaller specialty versions. One is a 5½″ side rabbet plane with cutters only ½″ wide which is handy for side rabbeting jobs when trimming dadoes, moldings, and grooves. You'll find it handy for such jobs as widening the grooves in a tongue-and-groove joint or taking off thin shavings

Combination rabbet plane can be used to cut dadoes and rabbets with cutter in normal position, as shown here, or with blade in forward (bullnose) position for work close to vertical part. Adjustable fence on side regulates width of cut and an adjustable depth guide permits trimming to the precise depth required.

Side rabbet plane can be used on either side of a groove for trimming or widening as shown here.

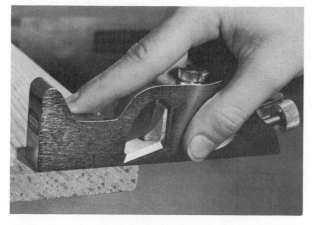

Cabinetmaker's rabbet plane is handy for fitting and trimming narrow shoulders and rabbeted edges. Both sides of this small plane are ground square so that it can be used on either side.

This trimming plane is only three inches long and is ideal for trimming small pieces, shaping curved surfaces or working on models.

from the side of a stopped groove or blind dado.

A small 5½″ regular rabbet plane is also available with a cutter 1″ wide, as is a tiny bullnose rabbet plane which measures only 4″ in length. Both have adjustable blades and both have sides and bottoms ground square to one another for use on either side.

Portable Power Planes

Although most home handymen are quite familiar with the advantages of electric drills, power saws, and motor-driven sanders, many are not aware of the fact that they can also buy electric planes that will do trimming and smoothing jobs in a fraction of the time required for hand planing and with no more effort than that which is required to move the tool along the surface. Professional carpenters have been using these to speed the work of trimming and hanging doors or installing cabinets, but it is only in recent years that home-size models have been introduced by four or five manufacturers.

The cutting action of an electric plane is derived from a high speed rotating cutter head similar to that on a stationary jointer-planer or wood shaper. Usually equipped with two spiral blades, the cutter

Here is a typical assortment of portable power planes for both the professional and non-professional handyman: a power block plane (left); an electric plane with a removable guide fence (middle); and a planing attachment, with an adjustable right-angle fence, connected to a router motor (right).

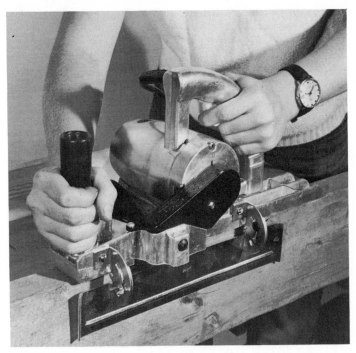

Inexpensive version of power plane being used to trim edge of a long plank. Guide fence, which is removable, is attached to bottom of plane to provide a straight, right-angle guide for the trimming of square edges.

Closeup of spiral cutter blade used in electric block plane, viewed from bottom with side guard swung out of way. Right angle fence is in place on bottom.

head is mounted in the middle of a sole plate or base so that the cutting edges project down slightly below the surface. Although they are relatively compact and light in weight, electric planers must have powerful motors since a very high speed is essential for a smooth and rapid cut. Like shapers, routers and other tools which cut with rotating knives, the higher the speed the smoother the cut.

The most popular type is actually a planing attachment which uses a router motor as the source of power. Consisting of a 16″ long base with a pistol grip handle at the back end, these tools are used with the appropriate router motor by taking off the router's base, then slipping the motor sideways into the plane attachment. A special spiral cutter blade fits on the arbor of the router motor and projects down under the plane's base so that it contacts the wood when the tool is resting on the surface.

The depth of cut is regulated by a micrometer adjustment which moves the cutters up and down. Since router motors operate at 20,000 revolutions per minute or more, and since the ones that are adaptable for use as planes are generally rated at approximately one horsepower, they are ideal power sources for an electric plane. Many carpenters carry complete kits which consist of a router motor, planing attachment, router base, and accessories for both in one metal box.

Planing attachments of this kind usually sell for $45 to $60 while the necessary router motor may cost anywhere from $40 to $80 more. When assembled as an electric plane, it will plane stock slightly wider than 2″ and will cut as deep as $3/32$″ in one pass. Since the base or sole plate of the tool is about 16″ long, it is ideal for rapid planing and trimming of doors and long boards as well as for edge-trimming of long panels. All come equipped with an adjustable fence to help guide the tool accurately along the face of the work, and almost all have bevel adjustments for planing at any angle.

At least one company also makes a complete 16″ long plane with its own motor and with a list price under $50. It has a ½-horsepower motor that gives a cutter speed of 14,500 revolutions per minute, and it will plane boards up to $2\frac{1}{8}$″ thick. The depth of cut is adjustable to a maximum of $1/16$″ in one pass.

As with the hand planes, electric planes also come in a smaller version known as a power block plane. Although its width of cut is almost the same as the larger 16″ planes (it will dress lumber up to $1\frac{3}{4}$″ wide) its maximum depth of cut is only $1/64$″ in one

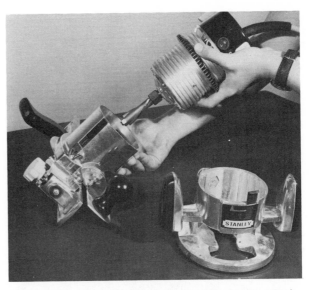

Most popular electric hand plane is really planing attachment for a router. Special spiral cutter blade fits on router motor's arbor. Motor slips out of rotor base and slides into plane attachment. Changeover requires no tools.

This heavy-duty power plane uses a router motor as its source of power (1 h.p.) and is often used by carpenters for rapid planing and trimming of doors and long boards, as well as for the edge-trimming of long panels.

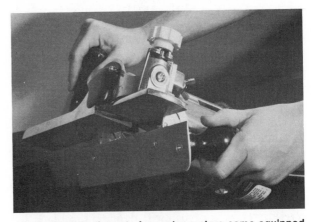

All planing attachments for router motors come equipped with a right-angle adjustable fence to control squareness of cut. Guide fence can be tilted to as much as 45-degree angle for bevel cutting, or can be removed entirely.

Electric block plane being used to trim storm and screen door without taking down door. This kind of power plane is light enough for one-hand use, yet many times faster than hand planing.

pass. However, because it is much smaller and lighter and is designed to be operated with one hand, most home handymen actually find it easier to use on many jobs, including trimming doors, fitting storm sash, or shaving off end grain on lumber. Its high speed gives an extremely smooth cut even on end grains and plastics, and it is designed so that the cutter fits flush on one side to permit cutting into corners. You can also use this handy little electric tool for cutting rabbets and tenons, as well as for planing flat surfaces and edges.

The motor-driven block plane also comes with a removable fence that clamps to the bottom to provide a straight right angle guide when trimming edges. It can be adapted for bevel cutting and chamfering and, like its big brothers, it is available in kit form with a metal carrying case and a special sharpening attachment for the cutter head.

SCREWDRIVERS THAT SERVE YOU BEST

Before discussing the various types of screwdrivers needed in the home workshop, it is desirable to turn the spotlight on two very common practices that involve misuse and subsequent damage to these tools.

The first is to use a screwdriver as a prying tool —to take the lids off paint cans, force open metal housings, and the like. The efficiency of any type of screwdriver depends on its tip being in good shape, literally—which means that it is square, flat, has the right bevel, and the corners are intact. Using a screwdriver as a prybar will damage the blade by

nicking or rounding it, and also will bend the shaft.

The second practice is not so much wrong as incorrect, and therefore, inefficient. This is to use a screwdriver with a tip too large or too small for the screw slot. If the tip is so big it overlaps the slot, you risk marring the work when you run the screw in flush; if it's too small, you can chew up the screwhead, which makes turning difficult so that the screwdriver may slip and gouge your hand or the surface. It isn't always possible, but it is always desirable to have the tip fit the screwhead snugly.

Common Screwdrivers

The screwdriver that is most used around the home is the common type everyone knows. It has a handle with a straight shaft, a tip that is tapered on two sides and a square end. You can use this type on all kinds of screws which have the conventional straight slots.

Common screwdrivers are classified by *shaft* length (not total length) and tip width, with dimensions usually proportionate. Shaft sizes range from 1½″ to 20″ with tips correspondingly smaller or larger. But, if you had to, you could get one with disproportionate dimensions, say a long shaft and narrow tip, such as is needed for some electrical work.

The great majority of common screwdrivers have round shafts, but you can get a square variety, handy for grabbing with a wrench when you need extra torque to loosen a rusted-on screw.

For the many straight slot screws used around the home—and keeping to our dictum of matching screwdriver size to screw size—a minimum assortment would be the following: a $\frac{7}{32}$″ tip with a 3″ shaft; ¼″ with a 4″ shaft; a $\frac{5}{16}$″ with a 6″ shaft and an 8″ and 10″ with ⅜″ wide tips. And, for getting into especially tight places, a stubby 1½″ with a ¼″ tip.

Phillips Screwdrivers

A blood relative of the common screwdriver is the Phillips; it's the same in every way except for the tip. A Phillips screwdriver fits only Phillips screws, which have heads with two slots that cross at the center. You can get this type in many different blade lengths, but the shafts are all round.

Phillips screwdrivers are number 0, 1, 2, 3, and 4 according to tip size, or, as it is technically known, point size. For around the home, a 1 and a 3 with

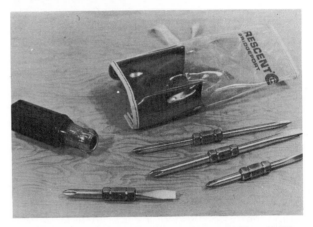

A tip that fits a screw snugly will make it much easier to turn.

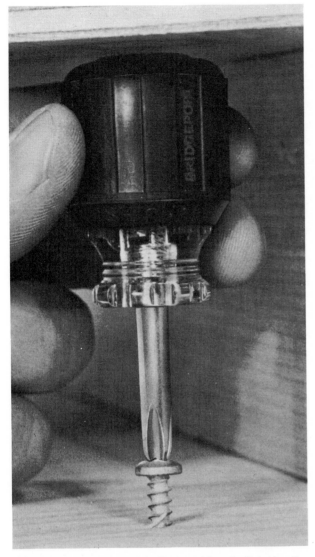

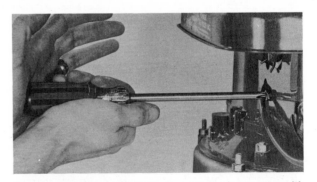

In effect, this pouch carries four common and four Phillips screwdrivers in different sizes. Interchangeable blades snap into handle.

The most common and indispensable of all tools, the screwdriver, comes in a large range of types and sizes, to do specific jobs better. Some homeowners try to carry on with just one screwdriver, at considerable loss in efficiency.

Phillips screwdriver won't slip if you brace it on screw with palm as you turn.

Whatever type screwdriver you're using, match tip to screw size.

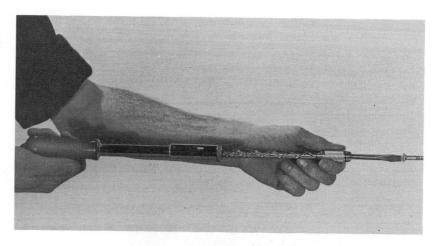

Spiral ratchet screwdriver is semi-automatic, operates much like a push drill. It can drive or draw Phillips or straight-slot screws quickly and easily.

3″ and 6″ blades, respectively, will handle most jobs. You may also want to get a short 1″ or 1½″ with a medium point, because Phillips screws can be in hard-to-get-at places also.

Spiral Ratchet Screwdriver

The two types of screwdrivers discussed above are so important that they should be considered absolute musts for your toolbox. But there are a number of others that make tempting additions.

One is the spiral ratchet, considered indispensable by many handymen. It operates like a push drill. You can snap in a variety of blades with either Phillips or common blade tips, and it makes quick work of either running in or drawing screws, with the action controlled by the flip of a ratchet selector. Some models have a hollow handle, convenient for storing a variety of blades and bits used for making pilot holes.

Spring Jaw Holders

An ingenious design is the screw-holding screwdriver, which cures the headache of starting a screw in an otherwise inaccessible spot. There are two types. One has a split blade which spreads apart as you slide a collar down the shaft. As the blade spreads, it squeezes against the sides of the screw slot, holding it firmly. The second type has two little spring clamps which also slide up and down the shaft. The clamps hold the screw in place until it bites into the hole. The spring clamps work better if you have to make do with an old screw whose slot may be somewhat chewed up.

Spring jaw holder grips screw so you can start it in tight quarters.

Power screwdriver accepts a variety of bits and blades and makes driving a lot of screws easy.

Powered Screwdrivers

If you do a lot of cabinet work, you should consider a power screwdriver, a torpedo-shaped affair with a small motor and chuck for accepting a variety of bits and screwdriver blades, or a screwdriving, reduction-gear attachment for your electric drill. Ziiip! that's all there is to running in a screw. Or, if you have one of the new variable speed drills, you can save by buying a set of screwdriver bits made especially for it.

Special Screwdrivers

Several special-purpose screwdrivers are of interest. Two tiny types, the offset, double-end mechanic's and the offset ratchet, can both sneak into places that are so cramped even a stubby tool can't get in. The mechanic's type is really a straight bar with the ends curved in opposite directions terminating in regular and/or Phillips tips. Its shape yields a large amount of leverage for turning extra-stubborn screws. The offset ratchet does everything its brother can, only faster, because you don't have to change driver ends with every partial turn of the screw.

While not a member of the screwdriver family, a ratchet drive socket wrench is needed for driving lag screws. And, at the other extreme of size, you can get a set of jeweler's screwdrivers, usually a single handle with four or five snap-in blades, the

Nut drivers look like common screwdrivers but have little sockets at the end that fit hex nuts, hex screws and Allen heads.

Profile bit which you chuck into your drill is excellent for preparing pilot holes.

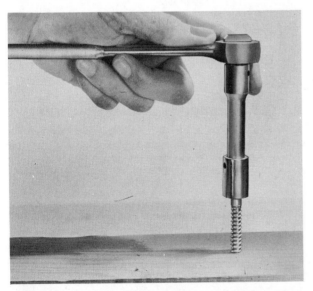

Lag screw, which has head shaped like a hex bolt, must be driven by a wrench. Socket wrench with ratchet drive makes it easy.

A tip that fits a screw snugly will make it much easier to turn.

smallest of which has a tip so tiny you can hardly see it with the naked eye.

Screwdriver Use

There aren't a great many tricks to using a screwdriver properly. On new work, you should always drill pilot holes; it quickens the job and avoids splitting. You can purchase profile bits made specifically for this job that chuck into your electric drill.

For softwoods, you can drill the pilot hole about half the depth of the threaded part of the screw. For hardwoods, drill the hole as deep as the shank of the screw. When joining boards, a pilot hole that goes through both is needed for tightest joining.

While coating screws with soap makes them much easier to drive, you should know that it cements the screw in place, making it very difficult to remove. Of course, you may count this as a plus. Don't use oil to lubricate wood screws because it will stain. Candle wax or graphite are good in place of soap.

If you have difficulty removing a screw, try this method: tighten it a little, then try to loosen it. By working it both ways like this it usually backs up a little at a time until it's out.

Screws are much easier to drive if they are first liberally coated with soap, graphite or candle wax. Don't use oil; it works, but it will stain the wood.

Whatever screwdrivers you buy, make sure they're of good quality. Poor tools are a bad investment. The tips are badly ground and of low-grade steel. They'll soon round off or bend and become practically useless.

Even the finest of screwdrivers eventually wears and becomes rounded. But it's easy to regrind it with an emery wheel or file.

ALL ABOUT PLIERS

With an assortment of five different types of pliers in your workshop toolbox, you'll be equipped for the many odds and ends of chores that can't be done without them. Of all the tools used around the home, none is called upon to do such a variety of tasks as are pliers. They open and close chain links (those on ladies' bracelets as well as chains for auto tires) pull nails, extract cotter

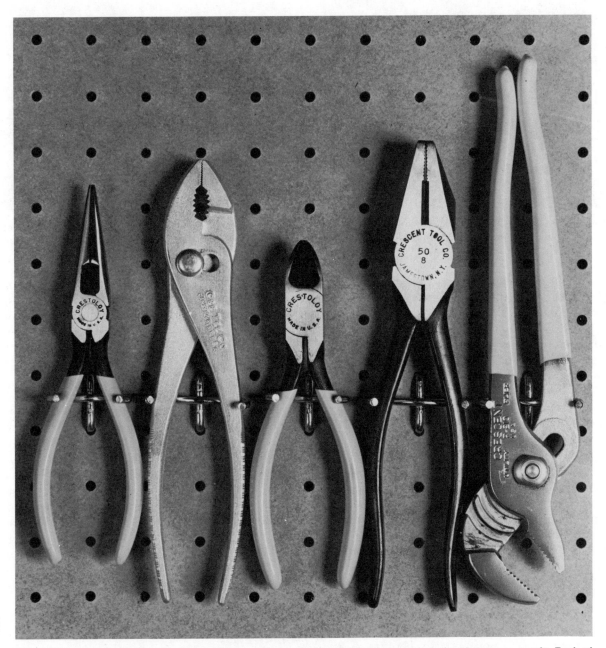

Five different pliers in the workshop toolbox enable you to cope with most repair and maintenance needs. Each of the pliers has a particular purpose—and jobs that it does best—so if you're working with less than the collection shown here, you're at a disadvantage.

Combination slip joint pliers are made so that the pivot bolt will hold until jaw position is purposely changed.

Coarse serrations on back teeth hold round work when slip joint pliers are used in combination with a bench vise.

pins, hold pipe, clip wires, and generally do a job of bending, straightening, twisting, and reaching into confined areas.

Just five different types will serve for nearly all purposes, though there are hundreds of special pliers designed to do particular jobs, and a wide range of sizes in each type. But it would be impossible to have all of them on hand, so a careful selection, as recommended below, will outfit you quite efficiently. Special purpose pliers can be added as the need arises.

Because they are so versatile and adaptable, pliers are particularly subject to abuse. Fortunately, good quality pliers will stand up to almost any kind of service, but using the wrong type of pliers for a job or using pliers as a substitute for another tool can cause such damage as throwing the jaws out of alignment, chipping the teeth so that they no longer have uniform grip, and destroying the cutting edges of certain types.

Pliers need little maintenance attention aside from occasional oiling of the pivot bolts and are not so delicate they must be handled with kid gloves. While it is not especially harmful to keep them piled in a drawer, you'll find it much more convenient to hang them on a Peg-Board wall panel in special brackets made for the purpose.

The five basic pairs of pliers for the home shop are (1) combination slip joint pliers; (2) utility pliers (3) long nosed pliers; (4) diagonal cutting pliers; and (5) heavy duty side cutting pliers, sometimes called linesman's pliers.

Combination Pliers

These are the most frequently used. They can serve on occasion as a pipe vise, and when the jaws are taped can be used to hold all kinds of delicate workpieces. With the handles held together by rubber bands, they provide a viselike grip for holding work to be drilled or soldered. The best combination pliers have fine serrations on the inside tips of the jaws for gripping small objects like wire, and coarser teeth farther back for holding larger objects. The slip joint permits adjusting the jaws so that they are parallel when opened a certain distance. The combination pliers are a modern refined version of the famed old gas pliers.

Utility Pliers

These are a relatively new design, an advance on the combination slip joint pliers, that permits setting the jaws into a series of parallel openings so

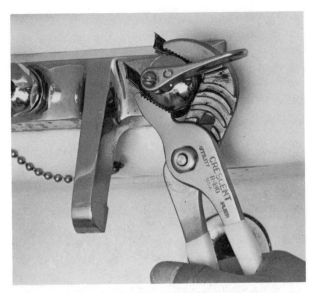

Utility pliers with multiple slip joint feature provide big secure bite when you work on a faucet bonnet.

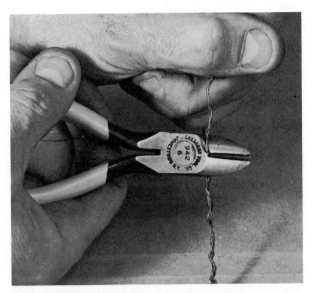

Diagonal cutting pliers slice through very thin to medium grades of wire, electric lines, metal and plastics.

that the pliers really can be used like a wrench on plumbing and electrical work. Unlike the combination pliers, the utility type has teeth of uniform size running the full length of both jaws, giving a firmly distributed grip.

Long-Nosed Pliers

This tool is extremely useful to have on hand for applications such as shaping the wire ends to fit

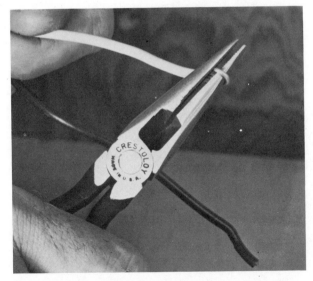

Long-nosed pliers form loop on end of wire for connection to terminal, and also serve to extend reach of fingers.

around terminals in electrical connections, for holding small wires while soldering, for forming small parts and electronic components of all kinds and, probably most important, acting as an extension of the fingers in reaching into inaccessible spots. One common application is that of holding small brads to start them into the work without banging the fingers.

Diagonal Cutting Pliers.

These small pliers excel as cutters, since the jaws are diagonal to the handles at about 15 degrees and thus come closer to the work. The pliers are handy for cutting picture wire, metal and plastic parts of model kits, and many small nails and brads. They are also excellent for clipping off deeply embedded brads, flush with the surface. Some diagonal pliers have notches for controlled stripping of wire insulation without breaking off segments of the wire strands.

Of the heavier duty model, the 6″ size is more suitable for home and auto repair tasks. Diagonal pliers are quite delicate and cannot withstand abuse that can be imposed on other types of pliers. Misuse will chip the hardened cutting edges and also can spring the jaws so that the cutting edges no longer meet evenly.

Side Cutting Pliers.

Larger and huskier than diagonal cutters, side

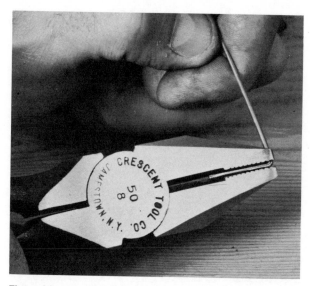

Flat, wide serrated jaws of side cutters are practical for neatly bending and shaping wire and metal.

cutting pliers are designed for bigger jobs and general all-round work. Known as linesman's pliers, they have large square jaws that can solidly grip pieces of flat metal for bending, cutting, and drilling jobs. They can be used on electrical projects requiring the cutting of 12 gauge and heavier wire.

HAND SAWS YOU WILL NEED

In every home there will be occasions when each of the six hand saws described here will be required for an important task—a task that could be done by a substitute tool only at considerable extra effort, loss of working time, possible damage to the substitute tool and, most likely, inaccurate or shoddy results in the job at hand.

The six saws are: the crosscut and rip saws, both similar in appearance but with distinctly different cutting teeth; a hack saw, back saw, coping saw, and a keyhole saw.

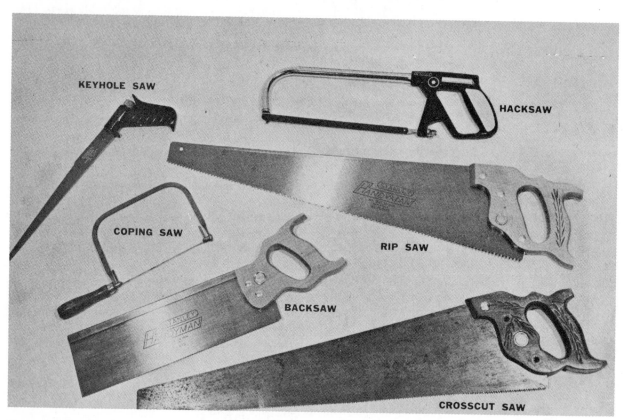

These six basic saws equip the homeowner to handle most cutting jobs. They supplement power saws, which are quicker and more precise.

474

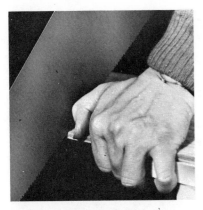

To begin a cut, use your knuckle as a guide, pulling saw backwards only on first or starting stroke.

To assure a square cut with hand saw, place blade of a try square on guide line, flush against saw.

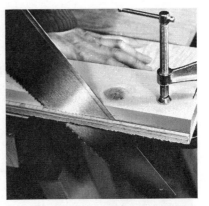

When you must make a long, thin edge cut that could wander, clamp a length of stock as guide.

To make a bevel cut, clamp guide parallel to cut line; start saw on slant, the blade against guide.

Prevent kerf from closing and binding the saw's blade by inserting a nail as a spacer or wedge.

Whipping of cut parts can be prevented by clamping the ends with some small blocks of scrap stock.

Crosscut and Rip Saws

Both saws may have the same number of teeth, per inch, on the blade, but there is a big difference in the way the teeth are cut and ground, and how they do the job. A crosscut saw severs the wood fibers, and because of this each tooth is shaped like a tiny knife. They are set in alternate series so that each succeeding tooth balances the cut of the one before it. In that way, tiny wedge-shaped scraps of wood are sliced out. Cross-cut saws are ground so that there is some cutting action on the up stroke, although most of the work is done as the blade moves forward. The average crosscut saw has 8 to 10 teeth per inch.

Rip saws usually have 5½ teeth per inch, and because the wood is scraped out with the grain, the teeth on these saws are shaped and ground like small chisels. The rip saw cuts only on the down stroke. Each stroke of the saw can deliver a hundred and more blows of tiny chisels, all in a perfect line to cut the wood.

Protect the newly purchased saw against rust with a heavy coating of paste wax on the blade. This will also lubricate the blade to make sawing easier. If rust ever develops, it can be removed by rubbing the blade with lump pumice and water. The most important maintenance detail is always to keep these saws sharp and clean, stored in a special place where they will not be subject to mois-

A backsaw used in combination with a miter box guarantees you quick and accurate miter cuts or crosscuts.

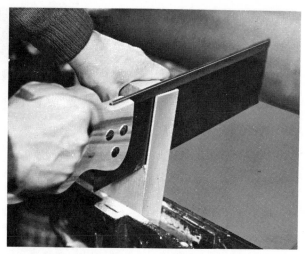

The backsaw also makes an excellent trim saw for notching, lapping, making tenons, but depth of cut is limited.

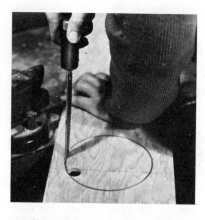

Keyhole saw has narrow, pointed blade which is excellent for starting inboard cuts from small pilot holes like this.

Interchangeable keyhole saws permit switching to alternate metal-cutting blade or a special pruning blade.

ture conditions or mechanical damage by contact with other metal tools.

Back Saw and Keyhole Saw

The back saw is used usually in combination with a miter box to cut moldings for wall trim, to make picture frames, and similar duties. Used freehand, the saw is more easily controlled because of the stiffening bar along the top, and is therefore used for such fine work as cutting tenons and notches. Similar to the back saw, but considerably smaller and with finer teeth, is a dovetail saw which many find perfect for precision work.

The keyhole saw is a tough, versatile tool that accepts interchangeable pointed blades for cutting metals, plastic, plaster, and wallboard. Because one end is entirely open, the saw can be used for interior cuts which are started, where necessary, by drilling.

Coping Saw and Hack Saw

For about a dollar you can buy a coping saw, and for another dollar get a dependable hack saw frame that holds the various hack saw blades. The coping saw will equip you to cut wood in any shape, no matter how intricate, and to "cope" cove moldings at the back so they can fit together into corners. With the hack saw, you will be able to slice right through any metal from steel bars to brass curtain rods.

The coping saw uses very thin blades that permit

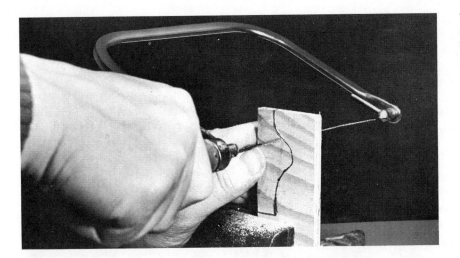

The modest little coping saw will save your projects more than once, because of its ability to make intricate cuts with precision —as long as you are practiced.

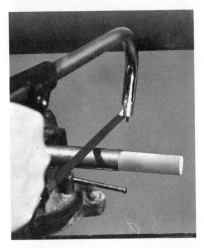

Cutting thin metal tubing with a hacksaw, you'll find that a dowel stiffener in core prevents collapsing and buckling.

If you're going to cut sheets of thin metal, clamp the workpiece between two scraps of wood for a neater job.

This is a little-known technique for cutting wide slots; install two or more blades, using long retaining pins.

making sharply rounded radius turns in the cut. Interior cuts are made by first drilling a small hole, then inserting the blade through the hole and attaching the blade in its frame. The interior cut must be within the "reach" of the saw frame depth.

For the hack saw a range of blades in various hardness is available, with blades having 18 teeth to the inch preferred for general cutting, while blades with 24 or 32 teeth are used for brass, aluminum, and other soft metals.

ALL ABOUT WRENCHES

Having the right wrench on hand when you need it could be considered a godsend, but really it's just the result of a little careful forethought. You couldn't possibly stock your workshop with every type and size of wrench that you might possibly need, since the range is almost infinite. Therefore it comes down to making a selection with care, of those that (1) are essential for emergency repairs; (2) those that are most versatile to take care of the widest range of work, and (3) wrenches for special tasks, that no other tools can do properly or in a reasonable time, and without causing extreme aggravation or damage.

If you could have just one wrench in the house, it should be one of the old-time monkey wrenches, since the homely F-shaped wrench with adjustable smooth jaws can be adapted to so many uses and would come in very handy, time and time again, for various chores. But working with this clumsy wrench could be difficult, often to the point of exasperation, because the jaws may not hold tightly, or fit into a confined area, or for hundreds of other reasons, and in the end you would be spending extra hours on a task that most likely could have been done in minutes, smoothly and neatly, and without rounding off a hex nut or doing other damage.

The vast extent of equipment inside the home today, the plumbing facilities and the number of appliances, together with other installations, not only require more frequent maintenance or adjustment, but also a wider range of fastener types and sizes than even just a few years ago. Some of these can be handled now only with the wrench specifically designed for the purpose.

The Hex Wrench

The Allen wrench is a good example. The little L-shaped bars of hexagonal tool steel, in a range of perhaps twelve common sizes, are designed to fit into the heads of Allen setscrews. Without the Allen wrench of the proper size, it would be almost impossible to release the tiny setscrew to remove, say, the pulley of a garden mower or the deeply set washer seat of a faucet. These wrenches are surprisingly inexpensive, and you can keep a set of all popular sizes, from 1/16" to 3/8", in a little plastic container in the workshop, always available.

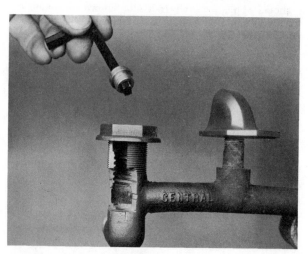

Deeply set washer seats are easily removed with the Allen wrench of correct size. The L-shaped wrench is small but made of powerful tool steel, is often used for releasing set screws on appliances.

Pipe Wrenches

Two other wrenches are essential for any home owner. These are a pipe wrench (often called Stillson wrenches) and an adjustable smooth-jaw wrench. The pipe wrench has toothed jaws, which grip pipe and other rounded surfaces—the greater the torque on the wrench handle, the tighter the jaw grip. Pipe wrenches come in several common sizes based on length of handle. The wrenches are usually used in pairs (to control the torque, or twist, otherwise the water lines could be pulled down). A 6" and an 8" wrench would make an adequate tool acquisition.

Tongue-and-groove slip-joint pliers form square jaw openings, can be used as handy wrench. Long handle provides leverage for tight closure.

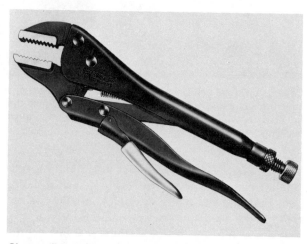

Clamp pliers grip and automatically lock on nut, can be quickly released by squeezing the small lever. The pliers will be handy for loosening nuts which have become rounded by misuse.

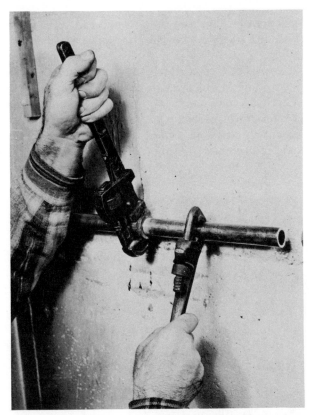

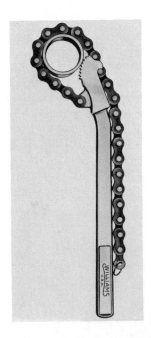

Chain wrench has sprocket chain similar to that on a bicycle. Toothed end of the handle grips pipe when pressure is applied and chain tightens.

Two pipe wrenches are used simultaneously to turn pipe, so that the force does not distort entire water line.

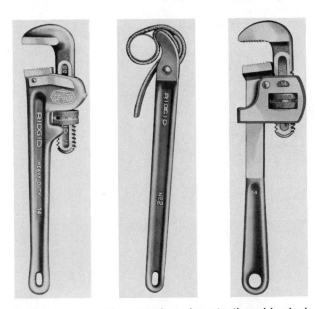

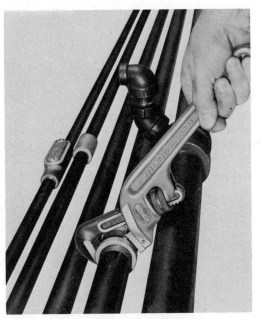

Pipe wrench with offset head can be used on larger diameter pipes and fixtures.

Typical pipe wrenches: one has sharp teeth and hooked head which is movable. Stillson is shown at center. The strap wrench (right) is used in places where it is difficult to obtain adequate grip with other wrenches.

Adjustable Wrenches

For the smooth-jawed adjustable wrench, a choice may be made from several types. The most widely accepted is the kind with jaws slightly offset at the end, that are moved by turning a knurled screw. Even here, there are at least a half-dozen lengths, some with straight shafts, others with curved handles. Similar are the self-adjusting wrenches which tighten their jaws as pressure is applied to the handle. These wrenches, like the mon-key wrench, have smooth jaws and can be used for loosening the nuts on faucets and for similar purposes.

A special wrench which anyone would be thankful to have if it is ever needed, is a basin wrench. This has a long handle and swivel jaws, and is used for reaching up behind a sink and similar close spots on water-line connections. Even if used only once, the saving in time and trouble is worth a great deal more than the cost.

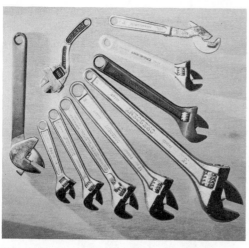

Adjustable wrenches, widely used by home-owners, have a knurled screw at top of handle for adjusting the jaw opening. Jaws are smooth.

Self-adjusting wrenches have jaws which tighten as pressure is applied on the handle. Some have toothed jaws for pipes.

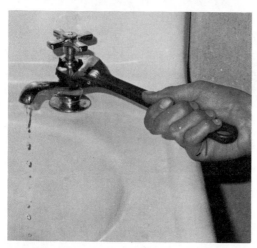

Replacement of faucet washers begins with loosening of hex nut around the faucet stem, an easy job for this type of adjustable wrench.

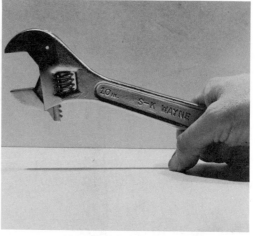

Closeup view of an adjustable wrench showing jaws open to maximum size. Smooth flat jaws can grip large hex nuts used on plumbing fixtures without damaging the polished surface.

Fixed-Size Wrenches

For the standard fixed-size wrenches that meet the widest range of everyday use, there are the open end, the box, and socket wrenches. These come in sets starting as small as $\frac{1}{16}''$. For home needs a set with $\frac{1}{16}''$ gradations will be quite satisfactory.

Socket wrenches also come in sets of sizes from $\frac{1}{4}''$ but may be obtained in quite large sizes, perhaps $1\frac{1}{2}''$. In addition to their regular use as wrenches, they are the only tools that can be used to reach the core of deeply set bathtub and shower faucet stems.

The wrenches described above, selected according to common sizes, will give you a good basic assortment. If you go in for auto repairing, or extensive workshop hobbies, there are many additional types, and extra fittings that will be most helpful, including speed ratchets, turn handles, swivel sockets, and other refinements.

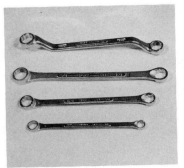

Box wrenches are used similarly with open end type, but provide more dependable grip on hex nuts. They are ideal in tight places where wrench can swing as little as 15 degrees.

Socket wrenches are the same as box wrenches, only with deep walls, come in a full range of sizes, and with 6 or 12 points. In addition to automobile work, they are used for some plumbing repairs.

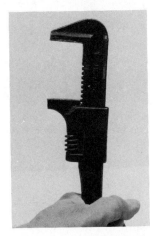

The basin wrench is a freak to look at, but it has saved many a homeowner hours of exasperating effort on water line connections far up behind the sink.

Monkey wrench has a very wide opening and is adjustable to many sizes of nuts. It is treasured by many owners, often performs better than other wrenches on certain jobs.

Open end wrenches are standard equipment for every active workshop, but are used mostly by homeowners who do their own appliance repairs or work on their cars. A good assortment for the average home would be $\frac{1}{4}$ and $\frac{3}{16}$ inch; $\frac{1}{2}$ and $\frac{9}{16}$ inch; $\frac{5}{8}$ and $\frac{11}{16}$ inch; $\frac{3}{4}$ and $\frac{7}{8}$ inch.

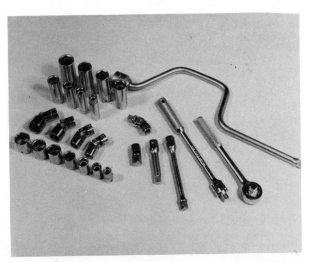

Photograph shows range of equipment available to facilitate use of socket wrenches. Shown are swivel-heads, arms of various lengths, ratchet types, and turn handle, with assortment of both deep and shallow sockets.

481

THE FORGOTTEN RASP

You remember the rasp. That's the tool that looks like a potato grater and is half-brother to the file.

Probably haven't used one since your last high school shop class. It's still around though, still able to trim flat surfaces, cut notches, curves, and other irregular shapes, quickly but with lathe precision.

Today, you not only have what might be called conventional rasps to select for your toolbox, but a whole new breed whose main virtue is jet-speed cutting—you can take a 1-by-8 down to a virtual toothpick in amazingly little time.

We'll talk about both new and old in a moment, but let's first clear up the confusion that exists as to what constitutes a rasp, what a file. Many competent handymen confuse them—and using one where the other is called for can only lead to trouble.

The difference between the two is in their teeth. The teeth of a rasp are individual raised surfaces more or less trangular in shape, arranged in rows. Single cut files have parallel rows of shallow grooves; double cut files have two sets of rows of grooves which crisscross to form a grid.

A rasp cuts rapidly, so it is the tool to use for removing a lot of wood rapidly; a file, however, cuts slowly, and is used on work where you want to make sure you don't shave off too much. So, you'd use a rasp to remove most of the wood from a work piece, but a file to remove the material next to the stop line.

Conventional Rasps

For around the home, you could safely limit yourself to one or two selections within one type— the wood rasp, It's for general woodworking and is available in three forms—flat, half-round or round —and bastard (coarse) or smooth-cut teeth, depending on the form.

Here you can clearly see the difference between fine teeth of a file, left, and the coarse ones of a rasp.

This is a half-round wood rasp with bastard cut teeth. One side is for making curved and irregular cuts, the other is for flat cuts.

As its name implies, the flat wood rasp is for use on flat surfaces, such as the edge of a board. It's only available with bastard cut teeth and is designed for maximum removal of wood in the shortest time. You can get it in 8″, 10″, 12″, and 14″ lengths. As with any rasp, the length to select is the one you find most comfortable.

Half-round wood rasps have one flat side, one round; the flat side is used as just mentioned, the round side for making curved and irregular cuts. It

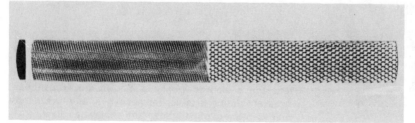

The shoe rasp has both rasp and file sections on it. Unlike other rasps, it has no tang for a handle.

also comes in various lengths and in smooth and bastard cuts.

The round wood rasp is for enlarging holes. It's especially useful on very small holes, where a half-round rasp won't fit. It's available in various lengths, but only with bastard cut teeth.

The shoe rasp, also known as the four-in-hand, is another type worth considering. It is really half-rasp, half-file, with one side half-round, the other flat. It's available in bastard, smooth, or second-cut teeth (between bastard and smooth in coarseness). While it is convenient to have a two-in-one tool, it also has disadvantages—the shoe rasp doesn't have a tang for a handle—which some craftsmen say reduces control—and it's slower than other rasps. The shoe rasp is available in 8″, 9″, and 10″ lengths.

New Breed

Conventional rasps present one problem. Sawdust tends to clog the teeth, impairing cutting efficiency. You have to stop frequently and wirebrush the rasp clean.

To overcome this, and provide even greater cutting speed, two companies have produced another type of rasp. Stanley Works calls theirs the Surform; Arco Tools refers to theirs simply as a rasp.

Available in a number of forms and tooth cuts, the heart of the tool's personality is its razor-sharp teeth. They are different from the teeth of a conventional rasp because they are open instead of solid metal. The openings allow shavings and sawdust to pass through freely.

When using this new rasp on critical work you have to be careful, even if the tool has so-called fine-cut teeth. Each stroke cuts very deeply, unless carefully controlled.

As mentioned, the new rasp comes in various forms, the standard one looking very much like a conventional flat rasp. Another resembles a plane, with front and rear handles. It has a cutting surface 5″ or 10″ long and can be used for planing, beveling, trimming, and rounding corners. Typical jobs would be freeing doors and drawers, and removing paint.

Another one of this new breed is the round plane rasp. It is 5″ long and has a convex shape, good for making concave cuts, shaping contours, and finishing curved cuts.

The three-way plane rasp is an interesting innovation. It's like the plane rasp except its handle can be positioned and locked at different angles for more comfortable handling: at a 90 degree angle

This is the standard kind of new rasp. It cuts wood and other materials very fast and its open teeth prevent clogging.

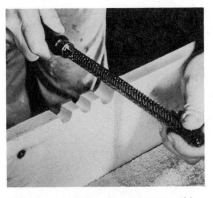

Like its conventional counterpart, this new-breed round rasp is for making irregular and round cuts—only much faster.

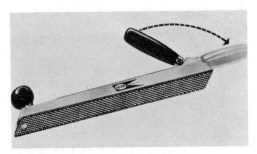

The new 3-way plane rasp has a handle that you can adjust and lock so the tool can be used as a plane, rasp or something in between.

The new rasp has also been made in various shapes for attachment to power tools. One type, the drum rasp, makes round and irregular cuts.

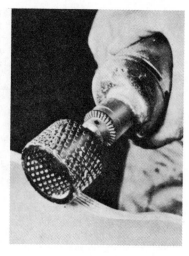

like a plane, flat like a conventional rasp or at a 45 degree angle.

The new rasp has also been adapted for use with power tools. You can get one in the form of a drum for use with a drill, drill press, or lathe for power shaping of irregular and round surfaces. Or, a disk rasp for power shaving of flat surfaces.

Conventional rasps cost less than the new kind. The former, depending on type and length, costs from 80 cents to $2; the new ones from $1 to $4.

How to Use the Rasp

As mentioned, rasp use is simple. Keep in mind, though, that if the tool has a tang you should first fit it with a handle. Otherwise, the tang could take a bite from your hand, if the rasp slips.

Purchase a handle that fits the tang exactly. Just insert the tang into the hole in the handle, then rap the back end of the handle to seat it. Make sure the handle is straight.

Using a rasp, first firmly clamp the work in a vise. Since the tool only cuts on the forward stroke, that's when you apply pressure, but just enough to keep it cutting. Work with smooth and even strokes. There should be no pressure on the back stroke.

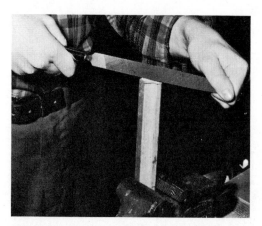

When your rasp has cut off most of the wood, use a file for the clerical cut near the stop line.

Chapter 15

SOME HELPFUL FACTS

The charts and tables presented in this chapter are intended for ready reference when certain data may be required in the course of a project. The chart on new standard lumber dimensions, for example, may help prevent errors in laying out the framework for a project, since actual dimensions are not the same as the stated sizes. The same is true of plumbing pipe, so the external dimensions are given here.

The charts on concrete mixes, designations and quantities of nails, selection of drills for tapping threads, and for calculating quantities of materials for various projects will be helpful. Frequent and proper use of these charts will save time, help prevent costly errors in calculations, and assure a more workmanlike progress in your shop activities.

STANDARD LUMBER DIMENSIONS

New national softwood lumber standards bring board sizes into the more readily computed "even" fractions of ¼″ or ½″, eliminating the odd fractions like ²⁵⁄₃₂″ which were difficult to add up when figuring an assembly.

These sizes are for lumber that has been properly cured and rated as "dry." The old dimensions still are used for "green" lumber to allow for shrinkage.

STANDARD SOFTWOOD LUMBER SIZES

	Unseasoned	Dry
1 x 4	²⁵⁄₃₂ x 3⁹⁄₁₆	¾ x 3½
1 x 6	²⁵⁄₃₂ x 5⅝	¾ x 5½
1 x 8	²³⁄₃₂ x 7½	¾ x 7¼
1 x 10	²⁵⁄₃₂ x 9½	¾ x 9¼
1 x 12	²⁵⁄₃₂ x 11½	¾ x 11¼
2 x 4	1⁹⁄₁₆ x 3⁹⁄₁₆	1½ x 3½
2 x 6	1⁹⁄₁₆ x 5⅝	1½ x 5½
2 x 8	1⁹⁄₁₆ x 7½	1½ x 7¼
2 x 10	1⁹⁄₁₆ x 9½	1½ x 9¼
2 x 12	1⁹⁄₁₆ x 11½	1½ x 11¼

The dry thicknesses of nominal 3″ and 4″ lumber are 2½″ and 3½″. Product Standard 20-70 defines dry lumber as being 19% or less in moisture content and unseasoned lumber as being over 19% moisture content.

WOOD TURNING SPEEDS

Wood lathe speeds are altered by shifting the belt onto the pulleys of differing sizes. A variable speed changer accessory, providing a range from one-fifth to five times the standard motor's 1725 rpm, is more convenient than shifting the belts, and permits starting the work more slowly while building up smoothly to the required full speed without chatter.

WOOD LATHE SPEED GUIDE

Work Diameter	Starting Cuts (roughing)	Ending Cuts (finishing)
2″ and under	800 to 1,500	2,000 to 4,000
2″ to 4″	700 to 1,000	2,000 to 3,000
4″ to 6″	600 to 800	1,500 to 2,500
6″ to 8″	400 to 600	1,000 to 2,000
8″ to 10″	300 to 600	900 to 1,500
more than 10″	300 to 500	600 to 900

BOARD MEASURE
for One Lineal Foot of Timber

Width in Inches	Thickness in Inches												
	1	2	3	4	5	6	7	8	9	10	11	12	13
18	1.5	3.	4.5	6.	7.5	9.	10.5	12.	13.5	15.	16.5	18	19.5
17	1.42	2.83	4.25	5.66	7.08	8.5	9.92	11.33	12.75	14.17	15.58	17	18.42
16	1.33	2.67	4.	5.33	6.67	8.	9.33	10.67	12.	13.33	14.67	16	17.33
15	1.25	2.5	3.75	5.	6.25	7.5	8.75	10.	11.25	12.5	13.75	15	16.25
14	1.17	2.33	3.5	4.67	5.83	7.	8.17	9.33	10.5	11.67	12.83	14	15.17
13	1.09	2.17	3.25	4.33	5.42	6.5	7.58	8.67	9.75	10.83	11.92	13	14.08
12	1.	2.	3.	4.	5.	6.	7.	8.	9.	10.	11.	12	
11	.92	1.83	2.75	3.67	4.58	5.5	6.42	7.33	8.25	9.17	10.08		
10	.84	1.67	2.5	3.33	4.17	5.	5.83	6.67	7.5	8.33			
9	.75	1.5	2.25	3.	3.75	4.5	5.25	6.	6.75				
8	.67	1.33	2.	2.67	3.33	4.	4.67	5.33					
7	.59	1.17	1.75	2.33	2.92	3.5	4.08						
6	.50	1.	1.5	2.	2.5	3.							
5	.42	.83	1.25	1.67	2.08								
4	.34	.67	1.	1.33									
3	.25	.5	.75										
2	.17	.33											

FURNITURE DIMENSIONS

Single Size Bed	3′ 2″ wide
Twin Size Bed	3′ 5″ wide
¾ Size Bed	3′ 8″ wide
Full Size Bed	4′ 8″ wide
Desk	28″ to 30″ high
Typewriter Desk	26″ high
Kitchen and Dining Chairs	18″ high
Doorknobs (locks)	36″ above floor
Kitchen Work Counters	32″ to 34″ high
Workbench	34″ to 36″ high

SANDPAPER SELECTION

Good results in wood finishing start with proper sanding. Progressive changes from rough or coarse sandpapers to the finer grits are made as smoothness is achieved. You'll find the grain size marked on all abrasive sheets, disks, belts, grinding wheels.

COMPARATIVE CHART OF ABRASIVE GRAIN SIZES

Garnet Silicon Carbide Aluminum Oxide	Flint Paper	Emery Cloth	
400			
320 or ¹⁰⁄₀			
240 or ⁷⁄₀	⁵⁄₀		Very Fine
220 or ⁶⁄₀	⁴⁄₀		
	³⁄₀		
180 or ⁵⁄₀		³⁄₀	
150 or ⁴⁄₀		²⁄₀	
	²⁄₀		Fine
120 or ³⁄₀			
	0	0	
100 or ²⁄₀			
	½	½	
80 or 0		1	
	1	1½	
60 or ½			Medium
		2	
50 or 1	1½		
40 or 1½	2	2½	
36 or 2			Coarse
30 or 2½	3	3	
24 or 3	3½		
20 or 3½			Very Coarse
16 or 4			

NAIL SIZES AND QUANTITIES

The terms "4 penny" and "8 penny" and so on, as applied to nails, originated with the English system in which the size was reckoned by the weight (number of pounds) per 1,000 nails. The 4d, or 4-penny nails, weighed 4 pounds per thousand, while the 8d weighed 8 pounds per thousand. Thus, the higher number means larger (and heavier) nails. Today, there are many varieties of nails, and the quantities per pound in each type vary considerably. But you still get just about 1,000 common 6d nails in every 6 pounds.

	Bright Common Nails				Finishing Nails		
Size	Length, In.	Gage No.	No. per Lb.	Size	Length, in.	Gage No.	No. per Lb.
2d	1	15	876	2d	1	16½	1351
3d	1¼	14	568	3d	1¼	15½	807
4d	1½	12½	316	4d	1½	15	584
5d	1¾	12½	271	5d	1¾	15	500
6d	2	11½	174	6d	2	13	309
7d	2¼	11½	161	7d	2¼	13	238
8d	2½	10¼	106	8d	2½	12½	189
10d	3	9	69	10d	3	11½	121
12d	3¼	9	63	12d	3¼	11½	113
16d	3½	8	49	16d	3½	11	90
20d	4	6	31	20d	4	10	62
30d	4½	5	24				
40d	5	4	18				
50d	5½	3	14	**Galvanized Finishing Nails**			
60d	6	2	11	3d	1¼	15½	807
				4d	1½	15	584
Blued Common Nails				6d	2	13	309
2d	1	15	876	8d	2½	12½	189
3d	1¼	14	568	10d	3	11½	121

TABLE OF NAIL QUANTITIES FOR VARIOUS WORK

Material	Size of Nail	Lbs. Required
1000 Shingles	4d	5
1000 Laths	3d	7
1000 Square Feet Beveled Siding	6d	18
1000 ″ ″ Sheathing	8d	20
1000 ″ ″ ″	10d	25
1000 ″ ″ Flooring	8d	30
1000 ″ ″ ″	10d	40
1000 ″ ″ Studding	10d	15
1000 ″ ″ Furring 1 x 2 in.	10d	10
1000 ″ ″ Finished Flooring, ⅞ in.	8d to 10d Fin.	20
1000 ″ ″ ″ 1⅛ in.	10d Fin.	30

Long Measure (Measures of Length)

Ins.	Feet	Yards	Fathoms	Rods	Furlongs	Mile
12 =	1					
36 =	3 =	1				
72 =	6 =	2 =	1			
198 =	16½ =	5½ =	2¾ =	1		
7920 =	660 =	220 =	110 =	40 =	1	
63360 =	5280 =	1760 =	880 =	320 =	8 =	1

6080.26 Feet = 1.15 Statute Miles = 1 Nautical Mile or Knot.

Square Measure (Measures of Surface)

Sq. Ins.	Sq. Feet	Sq. Yards	Sq. Rods	Roods	Acre
144 =	1				
1296 =	9 =	1			
39204 =	272¼ =	30¼ =	1		
1568160 =	10890 =	1210 =	40 =	1	
6272640 =	43560 =	4840 =	160 =	4 =	1

640 Acres = 1 Square Mile.

An Acre = a square whose side is 69.57 Yards or 208.71 Feet.

Cubic Measure (Measures of Volume)

Cu. Ins.	Cu. Feet	Cu. Yards
1728 =	1	
46656 =	27 =	1

A Cord of Wood = 128 Cubic Feet, being 4 feet x 4 feet x 8 feet.

42 Cubic Feet = a Ton of Shipping

1 Perch of Masonry = 24¾ Cubic Feet, being 16½ feet x 1½ feet x 1 foot.

PIPE SIZES

There is considerable confusion in regard to the designation of pipe sizes. The nominal size has no relation to the actual dimension, as seen in the table below. Copper tubing, on the other hand, is identified by its true external diameter.

Nominal Pipe Size	Approx. Actual Inside Diameter	Approx. Actual Outside Diameter
⅛″	¼″	⅜″
¼″	⅜″	17/32″
⅜″	½″	11/16″
½″	⅝″	13/16″
¾″	13/16″	1″
1″	1 1/16″	1 5/16″
1¼″	1⅜″	1⅝″
1½″	1⅝″	1⅞″
2″	2 1/16″	2⅜″

DECIMAL AND METRIC EQUIVALENTS

This reference table can be invaluable for transposing fractions of an inch in computing dimensions, selecting drills and many workshop activities.

Fractions of an Inch	Decimals of an Inch	Millimeters
1/64	0.0156	0.379
1/32	0.0313	0.794
3/64	0.0469	1.191
1/16	0.0625	1.588
5/64	0.0781	1.984
3/32	0.0938	2.381
7/64	0.1094	2.778
1/8	0.1250	3.175
9/64	0.1406	3.572
5/32	0.1563	3.969
11/64	0.1719	4.366
3/16	0.1875	4.763
13/64	0.2031	5.159
7/32	0.2188	5.556
15/64	0.2344	5.933
1/4	0.2500	6.350
17/64	0.2656	6.747
9/32	0.2813	7.144
19/64	0.2969	7.541
5/16	0.3125	7.938
21/64	0.3281	8.334
11/32	0.3438	8.731
23/64	0.3594	9.128
3/8	0.3750	9.525
25/64	0.3906	9.922
13/32	0.4063	10.319
27/64	0.4219	10.716
7/16	0.4375	11.113
29/64	0.4531	11.509
15/32	0.4688	11.906
31/64	0.4844	12.303
1/2	0.5000	12.700
33/64	0.5156	13.097
17/32	0.5313	13.494
35/64	0.5469	13.891
9/16	0.5625	14.288
37/64	0.5781	14.684
19/32	0.5938	15.081
39/64	0.6094	15.478
5/8	0.6250	15.875
41/64	0.6406	16.272
21/32	0.6563	16.669
43/64	0.6719	17.066
11/16	0.6875	17.463
45/64	0.7031	17.859
23/32	0.7188	18.256
47/64	0.7344	18.653
3/4	0.7500	19.050
49/64	0.7656	19.447
25/32	0.7813	19.844
51/64	0.7969	20.241

Fractions of an Inch	Decimals of an Inch	Millimeters
13/16	0.8125	20.638
53/64	0.8281	20.034
27/32	0.8438	21.431
55/64	0.8594	21.828
7/8	0.8750	22.225
57/64	0.8906	22.622
29/32	0.9063	23.019
59/64	0.9219	23.416
15/16	0.9375	23.813
61/64	0.9531	24.209
31/32	0.9688	24.606
63/64	0.9844	25.003
	1.0000	25.400

The mix ratio formulas refer to cement-sand aggregates. Water quantity is stated separately, and is related to the condition of the sand. When in doubt, use less water—adding more if necessary. A bag of cement weighs 94 pounds and equals one cubic foot. Five gallons of water per bag of cement is the general proportion.

GENERAL-PURPOSE MIX:

1 part portland cement	3 parts gravel
2¼ parts sand	(max. size=1″)
	⅔ parts water

TO MAKE UP ONE YARD OF CONCRETE:

6¼ bags cement	19 cubic feet of gravel
14 cubic feet of sand	31½ gals. of water

CONCRETE FACTS AND FIGURES

Concrete mixes vary according to the work that is being done. The critical factors are the proportions of sand, gravel, and water in the mixture with one bag of portland cement. The condition of the sand also is important—it should be screened when used for fine work to eliminate extraneous materials. Also, the degree of moisture will affect the water ratio, as shown in the chart. The size of the aggregates also is a determinant for the different projects.

AMOUNT OF CONCRETE REQUIRED

	Area in Square Feet (width x length)					
	10	25	50	100	200	300
Thickness	cubic yards					
4 In.	0.12	0.31	0.62	1.20	2.47	3.70
5 In.	0.16	0.39	0.77	1.54	3.10	4.64
6 In.	0.18	0.45	0.90	1.80	3.60	5.40

CONCRETE MIXES FOR VARIOUS PURPOSES

		Water (Gallons) Per Sack			
		Sand Condition			
Type of Project	Mix	Dry	Damp	Wet	Excessive Moisture
Heavy-Duty Subject to Extreme Wear and Weather	1–2–2¼ ¾″ max. aggregate	5	4¼	4	3½
Floors-Driveway- Walks Tanks-Slabs-Patios Columns	1–2¼–3 1″ max. aggregate	6	5½	5	4¼
Foundations Footings Walls	1–3–4 1½″ max. aggregate	7	6¼	5½	4¾

QUANTITIES MODULAR BRICK WITHOUT HEADERS

Nominal Brick Size Hgt. Th. Lgth.	Brick Per Sq. Ft. of Wall
2⅔ x 4 x 8	7.4
3⅕ x 4 x 8	6.2
4 x 4 x 8	5.0
5⅓ x 4 x 8	3.7
2 x 4 x 8	6.6
2⅔ x 4 x 12	5.0
3 x 4 x 12	4.4
3⅕ x 4 x 12	4.1
4 x 4 x 12	3.3
5⅓ x 4 x 12	2.5
2⅔ x 6 x 12	5.0
3⅕ x 6 x 12	4.1
4 x 6 x 12	3.3

ESTIMATING WALLPAPER QUANTITY

Most wallpaper is sold by the "single roll" although it usually come in double or triple rolls which offer the advantages of wider latitude in matching patterns and also helps avoid waste. Most paper is 18″ wide, although the "vinyls" vary from 16″ to 24″ wide. A single roll has the standard length of 8 yards or 24 feet. Measure two walls of the room and find the listing on the chart for the room height. Deduct a single roll for each two doors or two large windows. It's a good idea to buy an extra single or double roll for repairs.

Single Rolls for Walls

Size of Room	Height of Ceiling 8 ft.	Height of Ceiling 9 ft.	Height of Ceiling 10 ft.	Single Rolls for Ceiling
6 x 10	8	9	10	2
6 x 12	9	10	11	3
8 x 10	9	10	11	3
8 x 12	10	11	13	3
8 x 14	11	12	14	4
10 x 12	11	12	14	4
10 x 14	12	14	15	5
10 x 16	13	15	16	6
12 x 14	13	15	16	6
12 x 16	14	16	17	7
12 x 20	16	18	20	8
14 x 14	14	16	17	6
14 x 16	15	17	19	7
14 x 18	16	18	20	8
14 x 20	17	19	21	9
14 x 22	18	20	22	10
15 x 16	15	17	19	8
15 x 18	16	18	20	9
15 x 20	17	20	22	10
15 x 23	19	21	23	11
16 x 16	16	18	20	8
16 x 18	17	19	21	10
16 x 20	18	20	22	10
16 x 22	19	21	23	11
16 x 24	20	22	25	12
16 x 26	21	23	26	13
17 x 22	19	22	24	12
17 x 25	21	23	26	13
17 x 28	22	25	28	15
17 x 32	24	27	30	17
17 x 35	26	29	32	18
18 x 18	18	20	22	11
18 x 20	19	21	23	12
18 x 22	20	22	25	12
18 x 24	21	23	26	14
18 x 28	23	26	28	16
20 x 26	23	26	28	17
20 x 28	24	27	30	18
20 x 34	27	30	33	21

CEILING AND FLOOR TILE CALCULATOR

You can quickly learn the number of tiles needed for your floor or ceiling by measuring the length of two adjoining walls and multiplying the numbers to get the square footage of the area. Then find the number of tiles needed in the size you will use shown in the proper column. For an uneven number, like 317, find the quantities in the largest round figure first, then go on to the smaller figures to find the correct total. Allow about 10 per cent excess for waste. Most floor tiles are packed 45 square feet to the carton.

Square Feet	Number of Tiles Needed 9″ x 9″	12″ x 12″	6″ x 6″	9″ x 18″
1	2	1	4	1
2	4	2	8	2
3	6	3	12	3
4	8	4	16	4
5	9	5	20	5
6	11	6	24	6
7	13	7	28	7
8	15	8	32	8
9	16	9	36	8
10	18	10	40	9
20	36	20	80	18
30	54	30	120	27
40	72	40	160	36
50	98	50	200	45
60	107	60	240	54
70	125	70	280	63
80	143	80	320	72
90	160	90	360	80
100	178	100	400	90
200	356	200	800	178
300	534	300	1200	267
400	712	400	1600	356
500	890	500	2000	445
600	1068	600	2400	534
700	1246	700	2800	623
800	1424	800	3200	712
900	1602	900	3600	801
1000	1780	1000	4000	890

WHAT SIZE IS THAT DRILL?

Drills have several designations, all of which make for considerable confusion and complications. You're not likely to have on hand every size in the numbered, lettered, and fractional groups, but you can get a very close approximation if you know the actual dimension of the drill; in other words, the decimal equivalent, as shown in the table below.

Diameter	Decimal equivalent	Diameter	Decimal equivalent
80	0.0135	66	0.033
79	0.0145	65	0.035
1/64	0.0156	64	0.036
78	0.016	63	0.037
77	0.018	62	0.038
76	0.02	61	0.039
75	0.021	60	0.04
74	0.0225	59	0.041
73	0.024	58	0.042
72	0.025	57	0.043
71	0.026	56	0.0465
70	0.028	3/64	0.0469
69	0.0292	55	0.052
68	0.031	54	0.055
1/32	0.0313	53	0.0595
67	0.032	1/16	0.0625
52	0.0635	10	0.1935
51	0.067	9	0.196
50	0.07	8	0.199
49	0.073	7	0.201
48	0.076	13/64	0.203
5/64	0.0781	6	0.204
47	0.0785	5	0.2055
46	0.081	4	0.209
45	0.082	3	0.213
44	0.086	7/32	0.21875
43	0.089	2	0.221
42	0.0935	1	0.228
3/32	0.0938	A	0.234
41	0.096	15/64	0.2344
40	0.098	B	0.238
39	0.0995	C	0.242
38	0.1015	D	0.246
37	0.104	1/4	0.250
36	0.1065	E	0.250
7/64	0.1094	F	0.257
35	0.11	G	0.261
34	0.111	17/64	0.2656
33	0.113	I	0.266
32	0.116	H	0.272
31	0.12	J	0.277
1/8	0.125	9/32	0.2813
30	0.1285	K	0.281
29	0.136	L	0.290
9/64	0.1406	M	0.295
28	0.1405	19/64	0.2969
27	0.144	N	0.302
26	0.147	5/16	0.3125
25	0.1495	O	0.316
24	0.152	P	0.323
23	0.154	21/64	0.328
5/32	0.15625	Q	0.332
22	0.157	R	0.339
21	0.159	11/32	0.34375
20	0.161	S	0.348
19	0.166	T	0.358

Diameter	Decimal equivalent	Diameter	Decimal equivalent
18	0.1695	23/64	0.359
11/64	0.1719	U	0.368
17	0.173	3/8	0.375
16	0.177	V	0.377
15	0.18	W	0.386
14	0.182	25/64	0.3906
13	0.185	X	0.397
3/16	0.1875	Y	0.404
12	0.189	13/32	0.4063
11	0.191	Z	0.413

THREAD AND TAP DRILL SIZES

Nominal Size	Thr'd Series	Major Diameter, Inches	Root Diameter, Inches	Tap Drill to Produce Approx. 75% Full Thread	Decimal Equivalent of Tap Drill
0–80	N. F.	.0600	.0438	3/64	.0469
64	N. C.	.0730	.0527	53	.0595
72	N. F.	.0730	.0550	53	.0595
2–56	N. C.	.0860	.0628	50	.0700
64	N. F.	.0860	.0657	50	.0700
3–48	N. C.	.0990	.0719	47	.0785
56	N. F.	.0990	.0758	45	.0820
4–40	N. C.	.1120	.0795	43	.0890
48	N. F.	.1120	.0849	42	.0935
5–40	N. C.	.1250	.0925	38	.1015
44	N. F.	.1250	.0955	37	.1040
6–32	N. C.	.1380	.0974	36	.1065
40	N. F.	.1380	.1055	33	.1130
8–32	N. C.	.1640	.1234	29	.1360
36	N. F.	.1640	.1279	29	.1360
10–24	N. C.	.1900	.1359	25	.1495
32	N. F.	.1900	.1494	21	.1590
12–24	N. C.	.2160	.1619	16	.1770
28	N. F.	.2160	.1696	14	.1820
1/4–20	N. C.	.2500	.1850	7	.2010
28	N. F.	.2500	.2036	3	.2130
5/16–18	N. C.	.3125	.2403	F	.2570
24	N. F.	.3125	.2584	I	.2720
3/8–16	N. C.	.3750	.2938	5/16	.3125
24	N. F.	.3750	.3209	Q	.3320
7/16–14	N. C.	.4375	.3447	U	.3680
20	N. F.	.4375	.3726	25/64	.3906
1/2–13	N. C.	.5000	.4001	27/64	.4219
20	N. F.	.5000	.4351	29/64	.4531
9/16–12	N. C.	.5625	.4542	31/64	.4844
18	N. F.	.5625	.4903	33/64	.5156
5/8–11	N. C.	.6250	.5069	17/32	.5312
18	N. F.	.6250	.5528	37/64	.5781
3/4–10	N. C.	.7500	.6201	21/32	.6562
16	N. F.	.7500	.6688	11/16	.6875
7/8– 9	N. C.	.8750	.7307	49/64	.7656
14	N. F.	.8750	.7822	13/16	.8125
1–8	N. C.	1.0000	.8376	7/8	.8750
14	N. F.	1.0000	.9072	15/16	.9375

CREDITS

All photographs and diagrams in this book have appeared in *The Family Handyman* magazine. Many of the photographs were provided originally by manufacturers and are credited as follows:

Aluminum Company of America
American Hardboard Association
American Olean Tile Company
American Plywood Association
Armstrong Cork Company
Better Heating-Cooling Council
Black & Decker Mfg. Co.
Building Stone Institute
Samuel Cabot, Inc.
California Redwood Association
Champion International Corporation
Congoleum-Nairn, Inc.
E. I. Dupont Company

Filon Plastics Corporation
Formica Corporation
Georgia-Pacific Corporation
Kentile, Inc.
Masonite Corporation
Millers Falls Company
National Concrete & Masonry Association
National Gypsum Company
Owens Corning Fiberglas Corporation
Portland Cement Association
Rockwell Mfg. Company
Sears, Roebuck & Company
Simpson Timber Company
Skil Corporation
The Stanley Works
Tile Council of America
Wallpaper Council
Western Wood Products Association

INDEX